THE
BOOK

Ford Focus
Service and Repair Manual

R M Jex and Peter T Gill

Models covered

(3759-400-9AL2)

Hatchback, Saloon & Estate models with petrol and diesel engines, including special/limited editions
1.4 litre (1388cc), 1.6 litre (1596cc), 1.8 litre (1796cc) & 2.0 litre (1989cc) petrol
1.8 litre (1753cc) Endura-DI turbo-diesel

Does NOT cover ST or RS models, or 'Duratorq-TDCi' diesel engine introduced Spring 2001

© Haynes Publishing 2007

ABCDE
FG

A book in the **Haynes Service and Repair Manual Series**

ISBN **978 1 85960 759 6**

British Library Cataloguing in Publication Data
A catalogue record for this book is available from the British Library.

Printed in the USA

Haynes Publishing
Sparkford, Yeovil, Somerset BA22 7JJ, England

Haynes North America, Inc
861 Lawrence Drive, Newbury Park, California 91320, USA

Haynes Publishing Nordiska AB
Box 1504, 751 45 UPPSALA, Sverige

Contents

Contents

Advanced driving

Many people see the words 'advanced driving' and believe that it won't interest them or that it is a style of driving beyond their own abilities. Nothing could be further from the truth. Advanced driving is straightforward safe, sensible driving - the sort of driving we should all do every time we get behind the wheel.

An average of 10 people are killed every day on UK roads and 870 more are injured, some seriously. Lives are ruined daily, usually because somebody did something stupid. Something like 95% of all accidents are due to human error, mostly driver failure. Sometimes we make genuine mistakes - everyone does. Sometimes we have lapses of concentration. Sometimes we deliberately take risks.

For many people, the process of 'learning to drive' doesn't go much further than learning how to pass the driving test because of a common belief that good drivers are made by 'experience'.

Learning to drive by 'experience' teaches three driving skills:

☐ Quick reactions. (Whoops, that was close!)
☐ Good handling skills. (Horn, swerve, brake, horn).
☐ Reliance on vehicle technology. (Great stuff this ABS, stop in no distance even in the wet...)

Drivers whose skills are 'experience based' generally have a lot of near misses and the odd accident. The results can be seen every day in our courts and our hospital casualty departments.

Advanced drivers have learnt to control the risks by controlling the position and speed of their vehicle. They avoid accidents and near misses, even if the drivers around them make mistakes.

The key skills of advanced driving are **concentration,** effective all-round **observation, anticipation** and **planning.** When **good vehicle handling** is added to these skills, all driving situations can be approached and negotiated in a safe, methodical way, leaving nothing to chance.

Concentration means applying your mind to safe driving, completely excluding anything that's not relevant. Driving is usually the most dangerous activity that most of us undertake in our daily routines. It deserves our full attention.

Observation means not just looking, but seeing and seeking out the information found in the driving environment.

Anticipation means asking yourself what is happening, what you can reasonably expect to happen and what could happen unexpectedly. (One of the commonest words used in compiling accident reports is 'suddenly'.)

Planning is the link between seeing something and taking the appropriate action. For many drivers, planning is the missing link.

If you want to become a safer and more skilful driver and you want to enjoy your driving more, contact the Institute of Advanced Motorists at www.iam.org.uk, phone 0208 996 9600, or write to IAM House, 510 Chiswick High Road, London W4 5RG for an information pack.

Working on your car can be dangerous. This page shows just some of the potential risks and hazards, with the aim of creating a safety-conscious attitude.

General hazards

Scalding

• Don't remove the radiator or expansion tank cap while the engine is hot.
• Engine oil, automatic transmission fluid or power steering fluid may also be dangerously hot if the engine has recently been running.

Burning

• Beware of burns from the exhaust system and from any part of the engine. Brake discs and drums can also be extremely hot immediately after use.

Crushing

• When working under or near a raised vehicle, always supplement the jack with axle stands, or use drive-on ramps. *Never venture under a car which is only supported by a jack.*
• Take care if loosening or tightening high-torque nuts when the vehicle is on stands. Initial loosening and final tightening should be done with the wheels on the ground.

Fire

• Fuel is highly flammable; fuel vapour is explosive.
• Don't let fuel spill onto a hot engine.
• Do not smoke or allow naked lights (including pilot lights) anywhere near a vehicle being worked on. Also beware of creating sparks (electrically or by use of tools).
• Fuel vapour is heavier than air, so don't work on the fuel system with the vehicle over an inspection pit.
• Another cause of fire is an electrical overload or short-circuit. Take care when repairing or modifying the vehicle wiring.
• Keep a fire extinguisher handy, of a type suitable for use on fuel and electrical fires.

Electric shock

• Ignition HT voltage can be dangerous, especially to people with heart problems or a pacemaker. Don't work on or near the ignition system with the engine running or the ignition switched on.

• Mains voltage is also dangerous. Make sure that any mains-operated equipment is correctly earthed. Mains power points should be protected by a residual current device (RCD) circuit breaker.

Fume or gas intoxication

• Exhaust fumes are poisonous; they often contain carbon monoxide, which is rapidly fatal if inhaled. Never run the engine in a confined space such as a garage with the doors shut.
• Fuel vapour is also poisonous, as are the vapours from some cleaning solvents and paint thinners.

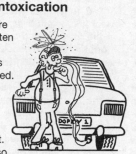

Poisonous or irritant substances

• Avoid skin contact with battery acid and with any fuel, fluid or lubricant, especially antifreeze, brake hydraulic fluid and Diesel fuel. Don't syphon them by mouth. If such a substance is swallowed or gets into the eyes, seek medical advice.
• Prolonged contact with used engine oil can cause skin cancer. Wear gloves or use a barrier cream if necessary. Change out of oil-soaked clothes and do not keep oily rags in your pocket.
• Air conditioning refrigerant forms a poisonous gas if exposed to a naked flame (including a cigarette). It can also cause skin burns on contact.

Asbestos

• Asbestos dust can cause cancer if inhaled or swallowed. Asbestos may be found in gaskets and in brake and clutch linings. When dealing with such components it is safest to assume that they contain asbestos.

Special hazards

Hydrofluoric acid

• This extremely corrosive acid is formed when certain types of synthetic rubber, found in some O-rings, oil seals, fuel hoses etc, are exposed to temperatures above 400°C. The rubber changes into a charred or sticky substance containing the acid. *Once formed, the acid remains dangerous for years. If it gets onto the skin, it may be necessary to amputate the limb concerned.*
• When dealing with a vehicle which has suffered a fire, or with components salvaged from such a vehicle, wear protective gloves and discard them after use.

The battery

• Batteries contain sulphuric acid, which attacks clothing, eyes and skin. Take care when topping-up or carrying the battery.
• The hydrogen gas given off by the battery is highly explosive. Never cause a spark or allow a naked light nearby. Be careful when connecting and disconnecting battery chargers or jump leads.

Air bags

• Air bags can cause injury if they go off accidentally. Take care when removing the steering wheel and/or facia. Special storage instructions may apply.

Diesel injection equipment

• Diesel injection pumps supply fuel at very high pressure. Take care when working on the fuel injectors and fuel pipes.

⚠ *Warning: Never expose the hands, face or any other part of the body to injector spray; the fuel can penetrate the skin with potentially fatal results.*

Remember...

DO

• Do use eye protection when using power tools, and when working under the vehicle.
• Do wear gloves or use barrier cream to protect your hands when necessary.
• Do get someone to check periodically that all is well when working alone on the vehicle.
• Do keep loose clothing and long hair well out of the way of moving mechanical parts.
• Do remove rings, wristwatch etc, before working on the vehicle – especially the electrical system.
• Do ensure that any lifting or jacking equipment has a safe working load rating adequate for the job.

DON'T

• Don't attempt to lift a heavy component which may be beyond your capability – get assistance.
• Don't rush to finish a job, or take unverified short cuts.
• Don't use ill-fitting tools which may slip and cause injury.
• Don't leave tools or parts lying around where someone can trip over them. Mop up oil and fuel spills at once.
• Don't allow children or pets to play in or near a vehicle being worked on.

Introduced to universal acclaim in October 1998, the Ford Focus won the prestigious Car of the Year award in 1999. With its bold 'New Edge' styling and class-leading fully-independent 'Control Blade' rear suspension, the Focus could not have been more different from the Escort range which it replaced.

Models are available in three- and five-door Hatchback, four-door Saloon, and five-door Estate configurations, and all are impressively equipped with safety and security equipment. Safety features include door side impact bars, airbags for the driver and front seat passenger, anti-submarining front seats, and an advanced seat belt system with pre-tensioners and load limiters. Vehicle security is enhanced, with an engine immobiliser, shielded locks, key-operated bonnet release and security-coded audio equipment being fitted as standard, as well as double-locking doors on most models.

The Zetec and Zetec-SE 16-valve four-cylinder petrol engines are derived from units previously used in the Fiesta and Mondeo, available in 1.4, 1.6, 1.8 and 2.0 litre capacities. The engines are controlled by a sophisticated engine management system, which combines multi-point sequential fuel injection and distributorless ignition systems with evaporative emissions control, exhaust gas recirculation and a three-way regulated catalytic converter to ensure compliance with increasingly stringent emissions control standards, while providing the levels of performance and fuel economy expected.

The Endura-DI turbo-diesel engine is also based on an earlier engine used in the Mondeo, but features so great a number of revisions as to almost be called a new engine. Very much a 'state of the art' unit, the direct injection Endura-DI has an electronically-controlled injection pump, and an engine management system very similar to the petrol-engined models, ensuring good performance and economy, with low emissions.

The transversely-mounted engine drives the front roadwheels through either a five-speed manual transmission with a hydraulically-operated clutch, or through an electronically-controlled four-speed automatic transmission (available on 1.6 litre petrol engines only).

The fully-independent suspension is by MacPherson struts and transverse lower arms at the front, with the unique 'Control Blade' independent suspension (derived from that used in the Mondeo Estate) at the rear; anti-roll bars are fitted at front and rear.

The vacuum servo-assisted brakes are disc at the front, with drums at the rear on most models; disc rear brakes and an electronically-controlled Anti-lock Braking System (ABS) are fitted on some models, with a Traction Control System (TCS) available as a further option where ABS is fitted.

The steering is power-assisted, the pump being belt-driven from the engine, and the rack-and-pinion steering gear mounted behind the engine. All models have passive rear wheel steering geometry built into the rear suspension, which helps to steer the car in conditions where the rear suspension is at full load (during heavy cornering or a sudden lane-change manoeuvre). Models with ABS may also be equipped with the Electronic Stability Program (ESP), which senses when the front or rear end of the car is sliding, and can apply the brakes at individual wheels to help steer the car.

Provided that regular servicing is carried out in accordance with the manufacturer's recommendations, the Focus should prove a reliable and economical car. The engine compartment is well-designed, and most of the items needing frequent attention are easily accessible.

Your Ford Focus manual

The aim of this manual is to help you get the best value from your vehicle. It can do so in several ways. It can help you decide what work must be done (even should you choose to get it done by a garage). It will also provide information on routine maintenance and servicing, and give a logical course of action and diagnosis when random faults occur. However, it is hoped that you will use the manual by tackling the work yourself. On simpler jobs it may even be quicker than booking the car into a garage and going there twice, to leave and collect it. Perhaps most important, a lot of money can be saved by avoiding the costs a garage must charge to cover its labour and overheads.

The manual has drawings and descriptions to show the function of the various components so that their layout can be understood. Tasks are described and photographed in a clear step-by-step sequence. The illustrations are numbered by the Section number and paragraph number to which they relate – if there is more than one illustration per paragraph, the sequence is denoted alphabetically.

References to the 'left' or 'right' of the vehicle are in the sense of a person in the driver's seat, facing forwards.

Acknowledgements

Thanks are due to Draper Tools Limited, who provided some of the workshop tools, and to all those people at Sparkford who helped in the production of this manual.

We take great pride in the accuracy of information given in this manual, but vehicle manufacturers make alterations and design changes during the production run of a particular vehicle of which they do not inform us. No liability can be accepted by the authors or publishers for loss, damage or injury caused by any errors in, or omissions from, the information given.

Focus 5-door Hatchback

Focus Saloon and Estate

The following pages are intended to help in dealing with common roadside emergencies and breakdowns. You will find more detailed fault finding information at the back of the manual, and repair information in the main chapters.

If your car won't start and the starter motor doesn't turn

☐ If it's a model with automatic transmission, make sure the selector is in P or N.
☐ Open the bonnet and make sure that the battery terminals are clean and tight (unclip the battery cover for access).
☐ Switch on the headlights and try to start the engine. If the headlights go very dim when you're trying to start, the battery is probably flat. Get out of trouble by jump starting (see next page) using a friend's car.

If your car won't start even though the starter motor turns as normal

☐ Is there fuel in the tank?
☐ Has the engine immobiliser been deactivated? This should happen automatically, on inserting the ignition key. However, if a replacement key has been obtained (other than from a Ford dealer), it may not contain the transponder chip necessary to deactivate the system. Even 'proper' replacement keys have to be coded to work properly – a procedure for this is outlined in the vehicle handbook.
☐ Is there moisture on electrical components under the bonnet? Switch off the ignition, then wipe off any obvious dampness with a dry cloth. Spray a water-repellent aerosol product (WD-40 or equivalent) on ignition and fuel system electrical connectors like those shown in the photos. Pay special attention to the ignition coil wiring connector and HT leads (where applicable).

A Check the security and condition of the battery connections – unclip and remove the battery cover for access.

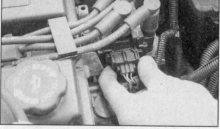

B Check the wiring plug and HT lead connections to the ignition coil (petrol models).

C Check the ECU power supply connector plug.

Check that all electrical connections are secure (with the ignition switched off). Spray the connector plugs with a water-dispersant spray like WD-40 if you suspect a problem due to damp. Diesel models do not usually suffer from damp starting problems, but check all visible connector plugs just in case.

D Check that the HT leads are securely connected to the spark plugs (petrol models).

E Check that none of the engine compartment fuses have blown.

Jump starting

Jump starting will get you out of trouble, but you must correct whatever made the battery go flat in the first place. There are three possibilities:

1 *The battery has been drained by repeated attempts to start, or by leaving the lights on.*

2 *The charging system is not working properly (alternator drivebelt slack or broken, alternator wiring fault or alternator itself faulty).*

3 *The battery itself is at fault (electrolyte low, or battery worn out).*

When jump-starting a car using a booster battery, observe the following precautions:

✔ Before connecting the booster battery, make sure that the ignition is switched off.

✔ Ensure that all electrical equipment (lights, heater, wipers, etc) is switched off.

✔ Take note of any special precautions printed on the battery case.

✔ Make sure that the booster battery is the same voltage as the discharged one in the vehicle.

✔ If the battery is being jump-started from the battery in another vehicle, the two vehicles MUST NOT TOUCH each other.

✔ Make sure that the transmission is in neutral (or PARK, in the case of automatic transmission).

1 Connect one end of the red jump lead to the positive (+) terminal of the flat battery

2 Connect the other end of the red lead to the positive (+) terminal of the booster battery.

3 Connect one end of the black jump lead to the negative (-) terminal of the booster battery

4 Connect the other end of the black jump lead to a bolt or bracket on the engine block, well away from the battery, on the vehicle to be started.

5 Make sure that the jump leads will not come into contact with the fan, drive-belts or other moving parts of the engine.

6 Start the engine using the booster battery and run it at idle speed. Switch on the lights, rear window demister and heater blower motor, then disconnect the jump leads in the reverse order of connection. Turn off the lights etc.

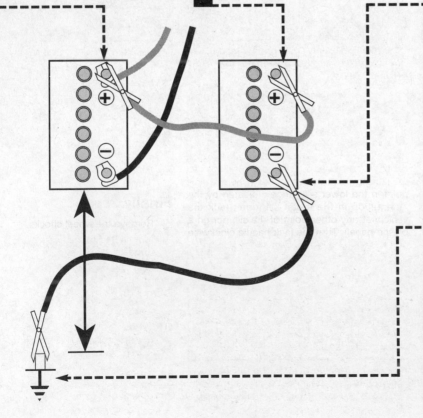

Wheel changing

⚠️ *Warning: Do not change a wheel in a situation where you risk being hit by other traffic. On busy roads, try to stop in a lay-by or a gateway. Be wary of passing traffic while changing the wheel – it is easy to become distracted by the job in hand.*

Preparation

- [ ] When a puncture occurs, stop as soon as it is safe to do so.
- [ ] Park on firm level ground, if possible, and well out of the way of other traffic.
- [ ] Use hazard warning lights if necessary.
- [ ] If you have one, use a warning triangle to alert other drivers of your presence.

- [ ] Apply the handbrake and engage first or reverse gear (or P on models with automatic transmission).
- [ ] Chock the wheels opposite the one being removed – a couple of large stones will do for this. Estate models are supplied with a wheel chock in the car's tool kit –

pull and twist the two halves of the chock to form the triangular shape.
- [ ] If the ground is soft, use a flat piece of wood to spread the load under the foot of the jack.

Changing the wheel

1 The spare wheel and tools are stored in the luggage compartment. Fold back the floor covering and lift up the cover panel. On Estate models, turn the two floor handles to the unlocked position, then raise the cover panel and support it using the strut provided.

2 Unscrew the retaining bolt, and lift the spare wheel out. The jack and wheel brace are located beneath the spare wheel, as is the screw-in towing eye.

3 Where applicable, using the flat end of the wheel brace, prise off the wheel trim or centre cover for access to the wheel nuts. Models with alloy wheels may have special locking nuts – these are removed with a special tool, which should be provided with the wheel brace (or it may be in the glovebox).

4 Slacken each wheel nut by a half turn, using the wheel brace. If the nuts are too tight, DON'T stand on the wheel brace to undo them – call for assistance from one of the motoring organisations.

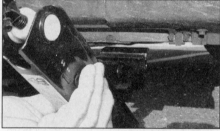

5 Two jacking points are provided on each side – use the one nearest the punctured wheel. Some models have a plastic trim panel which must be pulled off for access to the jacking point. Locate the jack head at the point in the lower sill flange indicated by the indentation in the metal sill (don't jack the vehicle at any other point of the sill, nor on a plastic panel). Turn the jack handle clockwise until the wheel is raised clear of the ground.

6 Unscrew the wheel nuts, noting which way round they fit (tapered side inwards), and remove the wheel.

Finally . . .

- [ ] Remove the wheel chocks.
- [ ] Stow the punctured wheel and tools back in the luggage compartment, and secure them in position.
- [ ] Check the tyre pressure on the tyre just fitted. If it is low, or if you don't have a pressure gauge with you, drive slowly to the next garage and inflate the tyre to the correct pressure. In the case of the narrow 'space-saver' spare wheel this pressure is much higher than for a normal tyre.
- [ ] Have the punctured wheel repaired as soon as possible, or another puncture will leave you stranded.

7 Fit the spare wheel, and screw on the nuts. Lightly tighten the nuts with the wheel brace, then lower the vehicle to the ground. Securely tighten the wheel nuts, then refit the wheel trim or centre cover, as applicable. Note that the wheel nuts should be slackened and re-tightened to the specified torque at the earliest possible opportunity.

Note: *Some models are supplied with a special lightweight 'space-saver' spare wheel, the tyre being narrower than standard. The 'space-saver' spare wheel is intended only for temporary use, and **must** be replaced with a standard wheel as soon as possible. Drive with particular care with this wheel fitted, especially through corners and when braking; do not exceed 50 mph (80 km/h).*

Identifying leaks

Puddles on the garage floor or drive, or obvious wetness under the bonnet or underneath the car, suggest a leak that needs investigating. It can sometimes be difficult to decide where the leak is coming from, especially if the engine bay is very dirty already. Leaking oil or fluid can also be blown rearwards by the passage of air under the car, giving a false impression of where the problem lies.

 Warning: Most automotive oils and fluids are poisonous. Wash them off skin, and change out of contaminated clothing, without delay.

HAYNES HiNT *The smell of a fluid leaking from the car may provide a clue to what's leaking. Some fluids are distinctively coloured. It may help to clean the car carefully and to park it over some clean paper overnight as an aid to locating the source of the leak. Remember that some leaks may only occur while the engine is running.*

Sump oil

Engine oil may leak from the drain plug...

Oil from filter

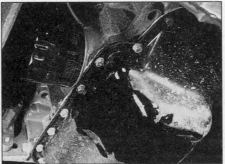

...or from the base of the oil filter.

Gearbox oil

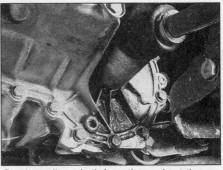

Gearbox oil can leak from the seals at the inboard ends of the driveshafts.

Antifreeze

Leaking antifreeze often leaves a crystalline deposit like this.

Brake fluid

A leak occurring at a wheel is almost certainly brake fluid.

Power steering fluid

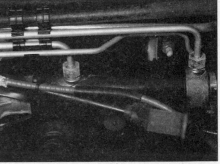

Power steering fluid may leak from the pipe connectors on the steering rack.

Towing

When all else fails, you may find yourself having to get a tow home – or of course you may be helping somebody else. Long-distance recovery should only be done by a garage or breakdown service. For shorter distances, DIY towing using another car is easy enough, but observe the following points:

☐ Use a proper tow-rope – they are not expensive. The vehicle being towed must display an ON TOW sign in its rear window.

☐ Always turn the ignition key to the 'on' position when the vehicle is being towed, so that the steering lock is released, and that the direction indicator and brake lights will work.

☐ The towing eye is of the screw-in type, and is found in the spare wheel well. The towing eye screws into a threaded hole, accessible after prising out a round cover on the right-hand side of the bumper, and has a **left-hand** thread – ie, it screws in **anti-clockwise**.

☐ Before being towed, release the handbrake and make sure the transmission is in neutral.

☐ On models with automatic transmission, special precautions apply – the front wheels should ideally be off the ground when towing. If in doubt, do not tow, or transmission damage may result.

☐ Note that greater-than-usual pedal pressure will be required to operate the brakes, since the vacuum servo unit is only operational with the engine running.

☐ The driver of the car being towed must keep the tow-rope taut at all times to avoid snatching.

☐ Make sure that both drivers know the route before setting off.

☐ Only drive at moderate speeds, and keep the distance towed to a minimum. Drive smoothly, and allow plenty of time for slowing down at junctions.

Introduction

There are some very simple checks which need only take a few minutes to carry out, but which could save you a lot of inconvenience and expense.

These *Weekly checks* require no great skill or special tools, and the small amount of time they take to perform could prove to be very well spent, for example:

☐ Keeping an eye on tyre condition and pressures, will not only help to stop them wearing out prematurely, but could also save your life.

☐ Many breakdowns are caused by electrical problems. Battery-related faults are particularly common, and a quick check on a regular basis will often prevent the majority of these.

☐ If your car develops a brake fluid leak, the first time you might know about it is when your brakes don't work properly. Checking the level regularly will give advance warning of this kind of problem.

☐ If the oil or coolant levels run low, the cost of repairing any engine damage will be far greater than fixing the leak, for example.

Underbonnet check points

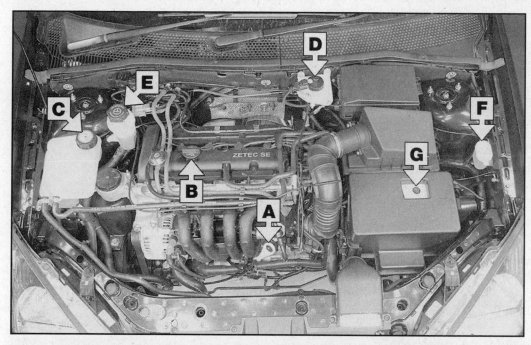

◀ **Petrol engine (1.6 litre shown)**

A *Engine oil level dipstick*

B *Engine oil filler cap*

C *Coolant expansion tank*

D *Brake and clutch fluid reservoir*

E *Power steering fluid reservoir*

F *Screen washer fluid reservoir*

G *Battery*

◀ **Diesel engine**

A *Engine oil level dipstick*

B *Engine oil filler cap*

C *Coolant expansion tank*

D *Brake and clutch fluid reservoir*

E *Power steering fluid reservoir*

F *Screen washer fluid reservoir*

G *Battery*

Engine oil level

Before you start
✔ Make sure that your car is on level ground.
✔ Check the oil level before the car is driven, or at least 5 minutes after the engine has been switched off.

 HAYNES HiNT *If the oil is checked immediately after driving the vehicle, some of the oil will remain in the upper engine components, resulting in an inaccurate reading on the dipstick!*

The correct oil
Modern engines place great demands on their oil. It is very important that the correct oil for your car is used (See "Lubricants and fluids").

Car Care
● If you have to add oil frequently, you should check whether you have any oil leaks. Place some clean paper under the car overnight, and check for stains in the morning. If there are no leaks, the engine may be burning oil (see *Fault finding*), or the oil may only be leaking when the engine is running.

● Always maintain the level between the upper and lower dipstick marks (see photo 3). If the level is too low severe engine damage may occur. Oil seal failure may result if the engine is overfilled by adding too much oil.

1 The dipstick top is yellow for easy identification (see *Underbonnet check points* on page 0•11 for exact location). Withdraw the dipstick. Using a clean rag or paper towel, remove all oil from the dipstick.

3 Oil is added through the filler cap. Unscrew the cap . . .

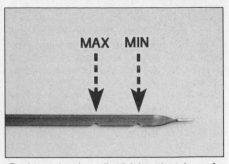

2 Insert the clean dipstick into the tube as far as it will go, then withdraw it again. Note the oil level on the end of the dipstick, which should be between the MAX and MIN marks. If the oil level is only just above, or below, the MIN mark, topping-up is required.

4 . . . and top-up the level; a funnel may be useful in reducing spillage. Add the oil slowly, checking the level on the dipstick often, and allowing time for the oil to fall to the sump. Add oil until the level is just up to the MAX mark on the dipstick – don't overfill (see *Car care*)

Coolant level

 Warning: DO NOT attempt to remove the expansion tank pressure cap when the engine is hot, as there is a very great risk of scalding. Do not leave open containers of coolant about, as it is poisonous.

Car Care
● With a sealed-type cooling system, adding coolant should not be necessary on a regular basis. If frequent topping-up is required, it is likely there is a leak. Check the radiator, all hoses and joint faces for signs of staining or wetness, and rectify as necessary.

● It is important that antifreeze is used in the cooling system all year round, not just during the winter months. Don't top-up with water alone, as the antifreeze will become too diluted.

1 The coolant level varies with the temperature of the engine, and is visible through the expansion tank. When the engine is cold, the coolant level should be between the MAX and MIN marks on the front of the reservoir. When the engine is hot, the level may rise slightly above the MAX mark.

2 If topping-up is necessary, **wait until the engine is cold**. Slowly unscrew the expansion tank cap, to release any pressure present in the cooling system, and remove it.

3 Add a mixture of water and antifreeze to the expansion tank until the coolant level is halfway between the level marks. Use only the specified antifreeze – if using Ford antifreeze, make sure it is the same type and colour as that already in the system. Refit the cap and tighten it securely.

Brake and clutch fluid level

All models have a hydraulically-operated clutch, which uses the same fluid as the braking system

⚠️ **Warning:**

● Brake fluid can harm your eyes and damage painted surfaces, so use extreme caution when handling and pouring it.

● Do not use fluid that has been standing open for some time, as it absorbs moisture from the air, which can cause a dangerous loss of braking effectiveness.

HAYNES HINT
• Make sure that your car is on level ground.
• The fluid level in the reservoir will drop slightly as the brake pads wear down, but the fluid level must never be allowed to drop below the MIN mark.

Safety First!

● If the reservoir requires repeated topping-up this is an indication of a fluid leak somewhere in the system, which should be investigated immediately.

● If a leak is suspected, the car should not be driven until the braking system has been checked. Never take any risks where brakes are concerned.

1 The brake fluid reservoir is located on the left-hand side of the engine compartment.

2 The MAX and MIN marks are indicated on the front of the reservoir. The fluid level must be kept between the marks at all times.

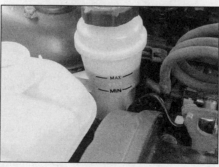

3 If topping-up is necessary, first wipe clean the area around the filler cap to prevent dirt entering the hydraulic system. Unscrew the reservoir cap and carefully lift it out of position, holding the wiring connector plug and taking care not to damage the level sender float. Inspect the reservoir; if the fluid is dirty, the hydraulic system should be drained and refilled (see the relevant part of Chapter 1).

4 Carefully add fluid, taking care not to spill it onto the surrounding components. Use only the specified fluid; mixing different types can cause damage to the system. After topping-up to the correct level, securely refit the cap and wipe off any spilt fluid.

Power steering fluid level

Before you start:

✔ Park the vehicle on level ground.
✔ Set the steering wheel straight-ahead.
✔ The engine should be cold and turned off.

HAYNES HINT For the check to be accurate, the steering must not be turned once the engine has been stopped.

Safety First!

● The need for frequent topping-up indicates a leak, which should be investigated immediately.

1 The reservoir is mounted at the rear of the engine compartment, next to the coolant expansion tank.

2 The fluid level can be viewed through the reservoir body, and should be between the MIN and MAX marks when the engine is cold. If the level is checked when the engine is running or hot, the level may rise slightly above the MAX mark.

3 If topping-up is necessary, use the specified type of fluid – do not overfill the reservoir. Take care not to introduce dirt into the system when topping-up. When the level is correct, securely refit the cap.

Tyre condition and pressure

It is very important that tyres are in good condition, and at the correct pressure - having a tyre failure at any speed is highly dangerous. Tyre wear is influenced by driving style - harsh braking and acceleration, or fast cornering, will all produce more rapid tyre wear. As a general rule, the front tyres wear out faster than the rears. Interchanging the tyres from front to rear ("rotating" the tyres) may result in more even wear. However, if this is completely effective, you may have the expense of replacing all four tyres at once! Remove any nails or stones embedded in the tread before they penetrate the tyre to cause deflation. If removal of a nail does reveal that the tyre has been punctured, refit the nail so that its point of penetration is marked. Then immediately change the wheel, and have the tyre repaired by a tyre dealer.

Regularly check the tyres for damage in the form of cuts or bulges, especially in the sidewalls. Periodically remove the wheels, and clean any dirt or mud from the inside and outside surfaces. Examine the wheel rims for signs of rusting, corrosion or other damage. Light alloy wheels are easily damaged by "kerbing" whilst parking; steel wheels may also become dented or buckled. A new wheel is very often the only way to overcome severe damage.

New tyres should be balanced when they are fitted, but it may become necessary to re-balance them as they wear, or if the balance weights fitted to the wheel rim should fall off. Unbalanced tyres will wear more quickly, as will the steering and suspension components. Wheel imbalance is normally signified by vibration, particularly at a certain speed (typically around 50 mph). If this vibration is felt only through the steering, then it is likely that just the front wheels need balancing. If, however, the vibration is felt through the whole car, the rear wheels could be out of balance. Wheel balancing should be carried out by a tyre dealer or garage.

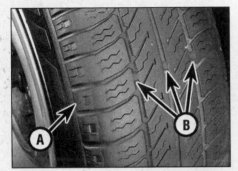

1 Tread Depth - visual check

The original tyres have tread wear safety bands (B), which will appear when the tread depth reaches approximately 1.6 mm. The band positions are indicated by a triangular mark on the tyre sidewall (A).

2 Tread Depth - manual check

Alternatively, tread wear can be monitored with a simple, inexpensive device known as a tread depth indicator gauge.

3 Tyre Pressure Check

Check the tyre pressures regularly with the tyres cold. Do not adjust the tyre pressures immediately after the vehicle has been used, or an inaccurate setting will result.

Tyre tread wear patterns

Shoulder Wear

Underinflation (wear on both sides)
Under-inflation will cause overheating of the tyre, because the tyre will flex too much, and the tread will not sit correctly on the road surface. This will cause a loss of grip and excessive wear, not to mention the danger of sudden tyre failure due to heat build-up.
Check and adjust pressures
Incorrect wheel camber (wear on one side)
Repair or renew suspension parts
Hard cornering
Reduce speed!

Centre Wear

Overinflation
Over-inflation will cause rapid wear of the centre part of the tyre tread, coupled with reduced grip, harsher ride, and the danger of shock damage occurring in the tyre casing.
Check and adjust pressures

If you sometimes have to inflate your car's tyres to the higher pressures specified for maximum load or sustained high speed, don't forget to reduce the pressures to normal afterwards.

Uneven Wear

Front tyres may wear unevenly as a result of wheel misalignment. Most tyre dealers and garages can check and adjust the wheel alignment (or "tracking") for a modest charge.
Incorrect camber or castor
Repair or renew suspension parts
Malfunctioning suspension
Repair or renew suspension parts
Unbalanced wheel
Balance tyres
Incorrect toe setting
Adjust front wheel alignment
Note: *The feathered edge of the tread which typifies toe wear is best checked by feel.*

Washer fluid level

● The windscreen washer reservoir also supplies the tailgate washer jet, where applicable. On models so equipped, the same reservoir also serves the headlight washers.

● Screenwash additives not only keep the windscreen clean during foul weather, they also prevent the washer system freezing in cold weather – which is when you are likely to need it most. Don't top up using plain water as the screenwash will become too diluted, and will freeze during cold weather. *On no account use coolant antifreeze in the washer system – this could discolour or damage paintwork.*

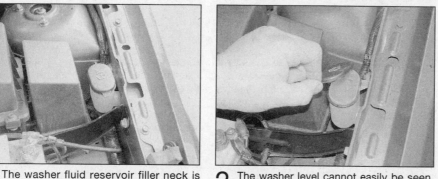

1 The washer fluid reservoir filler neck is located on the right-hand side of the engine compartment, next to the battery.

2 The washer level cannot easily be seen. Remove the filler cap, and look down the filler neck – if fluid is not visible, topping-up may be required.

3 When topping-up the reservoir, add a screenwash additive in the quantities recommended on the additive bottle.

Wiper blades

✔ Only fit good-quality replacement blades.
✔ When removing an old wiper blade, note how it is fitted. Fitting new blades can be a tricky exercise, and noting how the old blade came off can save time.
✔ While the wiper blade is removed, take care not to knock the wiper arm from its locked position, or it could strike the glass.
✔ Offer the new blade into position the same way round as the old one. Ensure that it clicks home securely, otherwise it may come off in use, damaging the glass.

Note: *Fitting details for wiper blades vary according to model, and according to whether genuine Ford wiper blades have been fitted. Use the procedures and illustrations shown as a guide for your car.*

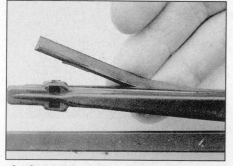

1 Check the condition of the wiper blades; if they are cracked or show any signs of deterioration, or if the glass swept area is smeared, renew them. Wiper blades should be renewed annually, regardless of their apparent condition.

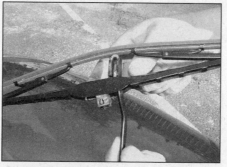

2 To remove a windscreen wiper blade, pull the arm fully away from the glass until it locks. Swivel the blade through 90°, press the locking tab with your fingers and slide the blade out of the arm's hooked end.

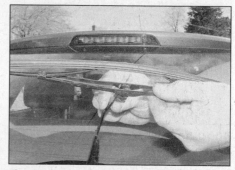

3 Don't forget to check the tailgate wiper blade as well (where applicable). Remove the blade using a similar technique to the windscreen wiper blades.

HAYNES HiNT *If smearing is still a problem despite fitting new wiper blades, try cleaning the glass with neat screenwash additive or methylated spirit.*

Battery

Caution: Before carrying out any work on the vehicle battery, read the precautions given in "Safety first" at the start of this manual.

✔ Make sure that the battery tray is in good condition, and that the clamp is tight. Any 'white' corrosion on the terminals or surrounding area can be removed with a solution of water and baking soda; thoroughly rinse all cleaned areas with water. Any metal parts damaged by corrosion should be covered with a zinc-based primer, then painted.

✔ Periodically check the charge condition of the battery. On the original-equipment battery, the state of charge is shown by an indicator 'eye' in the top of the battery, which should be green – if the indicator is clear, or red, the battery may need charging or even renewal (see Chapter 5A).

✔ If the battery is flat, and you need to jump start your vehicle, see *Roadside Repairs*.

1 The battery is located in the left-hand front corner of the engine compartment – unclip and remove the battery cover to gain access. The exterior of the battery should be inspected periodically for damage such as a cracked case or cover.

2 Check the tightness of battery clamps to ensure good electrical connections. You should not be able to move them. Also check each cable for cracks and frayed conductors.

HAYNES HINT

Battery corrosion can be kept to a minimum by applying a layer of petroleum jelly to the clamps and terminals after they are reconnected.

3 If corrosion (white, fluffy deposits) is evident, remove the cables from the battery terminals, clean them with a small wire brush, then refit them. Automotive stores sell a tool for cleaning the battery post . . .

4 . . . as well as the battery cable clamps

Bulbs and fuses

✔ Check all external lights and the horn. Refer to the appropriate Sections of Chapter 12 for details if any of the circuits are found to be inoperative.

✔ Visually check all accessible wiring connectors, harnesses and retaining clips for security, and for signs of chafing or damage.

 If you need to check your brake lights and indicators unaided, back up to a wall or garage door and operate the lights. The reflected light should show if they are working properly.

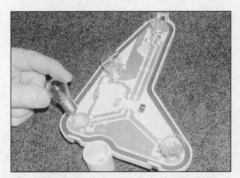

1 If a single indicator light, stop-light or headlight has failed, it is likely that a bulb has blown and will need to be replaced. Refer to Chapter 12 for details. If both stop-lights have failed, it is possible that the switch has failed (see Chapter 9).

2 If more than one indicator light or tail light has failed, it is likely that either a fuse has blown or that there is a fault in the circuit (see Chapter 12). The main fusebox is located below the facia panel on the passenger's side, and is accessed by opening and removing the glovebox (press in the sides of the glovebox, and lower it completely). The auxiliary fusebox is located next to the brake fluid reservoir – unclip and remove the cover for access.

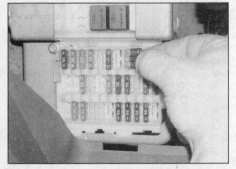

3 To replace a blown fuse, simply pull it out and fit a new fuse of the correct rating (see Chapter 12). Spare fuses, and a fuse removal tool, are provided in the auxiliary fusebox. If the fuse blows again, it is important that you find out why – a complete checking procedure is given in Chapter 12.

Lubricants and fluids

Engine	Multigrade engine oil, viscosity SAE 5W/30, 5W/40, 10W/30 or 10W/40*, to Ford specification WSS-M2C913-A or WSS-M2C912-A1, API SH, ACEA A1/B1 or A3/B3
Cooling system	Motorcraft Super Plus 4 antifreeze (blue/green) to Ford specification ESD-M97 B49-A, or Motorcraft Super Plus 2000 antifreeze (orange) to Ford specification WSS-M97 B44-D**
Manual transmission	SAE 75W/90 gear oil, to Ford specification WSD-M2C 200-C
Automatic transmission	Automatic transmission fluid to Ford specification WSS-M2C 202-B
Brake and clutch hydraulic system	Hydraulic fluid to Ford specification ESD-M6C 57-A, Super DOT 4, paraffin-free
Power steering	Automatic transmission fluid to Ford specification WSA-M2C 195-A

Do not use engine oils of higher viscosity, eg, 15W/40, 15W/50 or 20W/50, as doing so may lead to engine running problems. Certain oil additives may increase effective oil viscosity, and are not recommended in these engines.
**Do not mix the two types of coolant listed with each other, nor top-up with any other type of coolant.*

Choosing your engine oil

Engines need oil, not only to lubricate moving parts and minimise wear, but also to maximise power output and to improve fuel economy.

HOW ENGINE OIL WORKS

• Beating friction

Without oil, the moving surfaces inside your engine will rub together, heat up and melt, quickly causing the engine to seize. Engine oil creates a film which separates these moving parts, preventing wear and heat build-up.

• Cooling hot-spots

Temperatures inside the engine can exceed 1000° C. The engine oil circulates and acts as a coolant, transferring heat from the hot-spots to the sump.

• Cleaning the engine internally

Good quality engine oils clean the inside of your engine, collecting and dispersing combustion deposits and controlling them until they are trapped by the oil filter or flushed out at oil change.

OIL CARE - FOLLOW THE CODE

To handle and dispose of used engine oil safely, always:

OIL CARE — FOLLOW THE CODE
OIL BANK LINE
0800 66 33 66
www.oilbankline.org.uk

  • *Avoid skin contact with used engine oil. Repeated or prolonged contact can be harmful.*
  • *Dispose of used oil and empty packs in a responsible manner in an authorised disposal site. Call 0800 663366 to find the one nearest to you. Never tip oil down drains or onto the ground.*

Tyre pressures (cold)

	Front	Rear
Except 195/55 R15 tyres:		
Normally-laden (up to 3 people)	2.2 bar (32 psi)	2.2 bar (32 psi)
Fully-laden:		
Petrol models	2.2 bar (32 psi)	3.1 bar (45 psi)
Diesel models	2.3 bar (33 psi)	3.1 bar (45 psi)
195/55 R15 tyres:		
Normally-laden (up to 3 people)	2.0 bar (29 psi)	2.0 bar (29 psi)
Fully-laden:		
Petrol models	2.2 bar (32 psi)	3.1 bar (45 psi)
Diesel models	2.4 bar (35 psi)	3.1 bar (45 psi)
Temporary 'space-saver' spare wheel	4.2 bar (61 psi)	4.2 bar (61 psi)

Note 1: *Pressures apply to original-equipment tyres, and may vary if any other make of tyre is fitted; check with the tyre manufacturer or supplier for the correct pressures if necessary.*
Note 2: *For sustained high speeds above 100 mph (160 km/h), increased pressures are necessary. Consult the driver's handbook supplied with the vehicle. The 'space-saver' spare wheel appears not to be designed for use at high speeds, however.*

Chapter 1 Part A:
Routine maintenance & servicing – petrol models

Contents

Degrees of difficulty

Easy, suitable for novice with little experience	**Fairly easy,** suitable for beginner with some experience	**Fairly difficult,** suitable for competent DIY mechanic	**Difficult,** suitable for experienced DIY mechanic	**Very difficult,** suitable for expert DIY or professional

Lubricants and fluids

Refer to end of *Weekly checks*

Capacities

Engine oil (including filter)
1.4 litre engines .... 3.75 litres
All other engines .... 4.25 litres

Cooling system (approximate)
1.4 and 1.6 litre engines .... 5.0 litres
1.8 and 2.0 litre engines .... 5.75 litres

Transmission
Manual transmission:
   1.4, 1.6 and 1.8 litre models .... 2.3 litres
   2.0 litre models .... 2.0 litres
Automatic transmission (total capacity) .... 6.8 litres

Washer fluid reservoir .... 3.6 litres

Fuel tank
All models .... 55.0 litres

Cooling system

Antifreeze mixture:
   50% antifreeze .... Protection down to –37°C
   55% antifreeze .... Protection down to –45°C
Note: *Refer to antifreeze manufacturer for latest recommendations.*

Ignition system

Spark plugs:	Type	Electrode gap
1.4 litre engines	Bosch HR 8 MEV	1.3 mm
1.6 litre engines	Bosch HR 7 MPP 22 U	1.0 mm
1.8 and 2.0 litre engines	Bosch HR 7 MPP+V	1.3 mm

Brakes

Friction material minimum thickness:
   Front or rear brake pads .... 1.5 mm
   Rear brake shoes .... 1.0 mm

Torque wrench settings

	Nm	lbf ft
Auxiliary drivebelt idler pulley bolt:		
1.4 and 1.6 litre engines	25	18
1.8 and 2.0 litre engines	48	35
Auxiliary drivebelt tensioner mounting nuts	25	18
Engine oil drain plug:		
1.4 and 1.6 litre engines	37	27
1.8 and 2.0 litre engines	24	18
Manual transmission drain plug (2.0 litre models only)	45	33
Manual transmission filler/level plug:		
1.4, 1.6 and 1.8 litre models	35	26
2.0 litre models	45	33
Roadwheel nuts	85	63
Spark plugs	15	11

The maintenance intervals in this manual are provided with the assumption that you, not the dealer, will be carrying out the work. These are the minimum maintenance intervals recommended by us for vehicles driven daily. If you wish to keep your vehicle in peak condition at all times, you may wish to perform some of these procedures more often. We encourage frequent maintenance, because it enhances the efficiency, performance and resale value of your vehicle.

If the vehicle is driven in dusty areas, used to tow a trailer, or driven frequently at slow speeds (idling in traffic) or on short journeys, more frequent maintenance intervals are recommended.

When the vehicle is new, it should be serviced by a factory-authorised dealer service department, in order to preserve the factory warranty.

Every 250 miles (400 km) or weekly
☐ Refer to *Weekly checks*

Every 5000 miles or 6 months, whichever comes first
☐ Renew the engine oil and filter (Section 3)
Note: *Ford recommend that the engine oil and filter are changed every 10 000 miles or 12 months. However, oil and filter changes are good for the engine and we recommend that the oil and filter are renewed more frequently, especially if the vehicle is used on a lot of short journeys.*

Every 10 000 miles or 12 months, whichever comes first
☐ Check the automatic transmission fluid level and selector cable adjustment (Section 4)
☐ Check the condition of the auxiliary drivebelt (Section 5)
☐ Check the operation of the lights and electrical equipment (Section 6)
☐ Check under the bonnet for fluid leaks and hose condition (Section 7)
☐ Check the condition of all engine compartment wiring (Section 8)
☐ Check the condition of all air conditioning system components (Section 9)
☐ Check the braking system components (Section 10)
☐ Check the exhaust system (Section 11)
☐ Check the steering and suspension components for condition and security (Section 12)
☐ Check the condition of the driveshaft joints and gaiters (Section 13)
☐ Check the underbody, and all fuel/brake lines (Section 14)
☐ Lubricate all hinges and locks (Section 15)
☐ Check the roadwheel nuts are tightened to the specified torque (Section 16)
☐ Carry out a road test (Section 17)

Every 20 000 miles
☐ Renew the pollen filter (Section 18)
Note: *If the vehicle is used in dusty conditions, the pollen filter should be renewed more frequently.*
☐ Renew the spark plugs, and check the HT leads (Section 19)
Note: *If the recommended (platinum) spark plugs are used, the spark plug renewal interval can be increased to 40 000 miles.*

Every 30 000 miles
☐ Renew the air filter (Section 20)
Note: *If the vehicle is used in dusty conditions, the air filter should be renewed more frequently.*
☐ Check the crankcase ventilation system (Section 21)
☐ Check the manual transmission oil level (Section 22)
☐ Renew the fuel filter (Section 23)

Every 3 years, regardless of mileage
☐ Renew the brake fluid (Section 24)
☐ Renew the coolant and check the condition of the expansion tank pressure cap (Section 25)
Note: *If Ford antifreeze is used, Ford state that the coolant renewal interval can be extended. Refer to Section 24.*

Every 80 000 miles
☐ Renew the timing belt (Section 26)
Note: *The Ford interval for belt renewal is actually at a higher mileage than this. It is strongly recommended, however, that the interval is reduced to 80 000 miles, particularly on vehicles which are subjected to intensive use, ie, mainly short journeys or a lot of stop-start driving. The actual belt renewal interval is therefore very much up to the individual owner, but bear in mind that severe engine damage will result if the belt breaks.*

Every 100 000 miles
☐ Check and if necessary adjust the valve clearances (Section 27)

Underbonnet view of 1.4 litre model (1.6 litre similar)

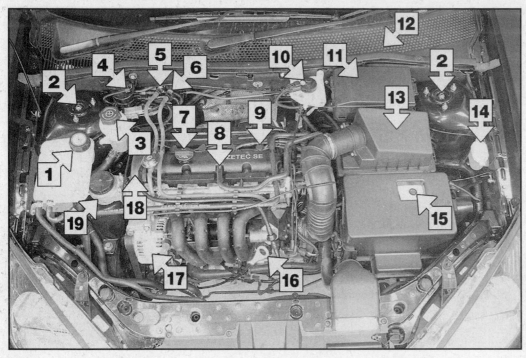

1 Cooling system expansion tank
2 Suspension strut upper mounting
3 Power steering fluid reservoir
4 Charcoal canister purge valve
5 Fuel supply hose (white)
6 Fuel return hose (red)
7 Engine oil filler cap
8 Breather hose
9 No 4 spark plug HT lead
10 Brake/clutch fluid reservoir
11 Auxiliary fusebox
12 Pollen filter access panel
13 Air cleaner
14 Washer reservoir filler
15 Battery (beneath plastic cover)
16 Engine oil dipstick
17 Alternator
18 Timing belt cover
19 Engine right-hand mounting

Underbonnet view of 1.8 litre model (2.0 litre similar)

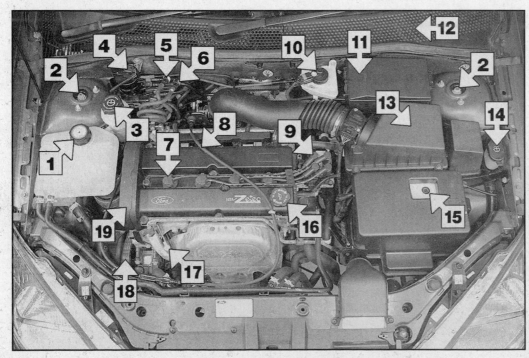

1 Cooling system expansion tank
2 Suspension strut upper mounting
3 Power steering fluid reservoir
4 Charcoal canister purge valve
5 Fuel supply hose (white)
6 Fuel return hose (red)
7 No 1 spark plug HT lead
8 Accelerator cable
9 Ignition coil
10 Brake/clutch fluid reservoir
11 Auxiliary fusebox
12 Pollen filter access panel
13 Air cleaner
14 Washer reservoir filler
15 Battery (beneath plastic cover)
16 Engine oil filler cap
17 Engine oil dipstick
18 Auxiliary drivebelt
19 Timing belt cover

Front underside view of 1.8 litre model

1 Air conditioning receiver/dryer
2 Auxiliary drivebelt lower cover
3 Air conditioning compressor
4 Radiator bottom hose
5 Catalytic converter
6 Cooling fans
7 Radiator top hose
8 Radiator drain plug
9 Horn
10 Front brake caliper
11 Front suspension arm
12 Steering track rod
13 Engine/transmission rear mounting
14 Exhaust pipe
15 Oil filter
16 Engine oil drain plug

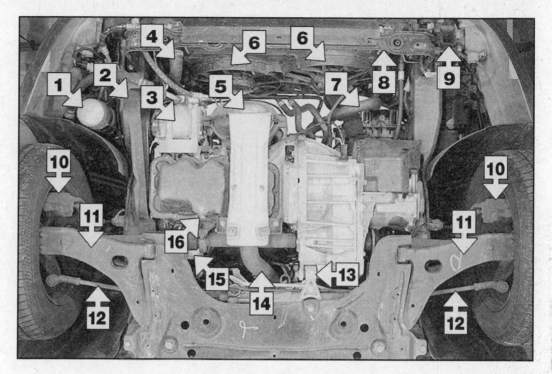

Rear underside view of 1.8 litre Estate model

1 Rear suspension rear lower arm
2 Rear anti-roll bar
3 Rear crossmember
4 Brake load sensing valve
5 Rear shock absorber
6 Rear suspension upper arm
7 Rear suspension front lower arm
8 Tie-bar ('control blade')
9 Handbrake cable
10 Fuel tank
11 Fuel filter
12 Exhaust centre silencer

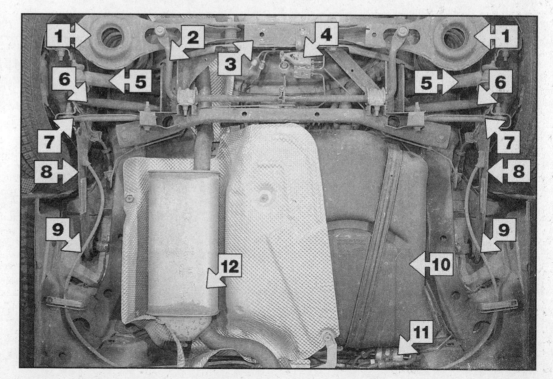

1 General information

1 This Chapter is designed to help the home mechanic maintain his/her vehicle for safety, economy, long life and peak performance.
2 The Chapter contains a master maintenance schedule, followed by Sections dealing specifically with each task in the schedule. Visual checks, adjustments, component renewal and other helpful items are included. Refer to the accompanying illustrations of the engine compartment and the underside of the vehicle for the locations of the various components.
3 Servicing your vehicle in accordance with the mileage/time maintenance schedule and the following Sections will provide a planned maintenance programme, which should result in a long and reliable service life. This is a comprehensive plan, so maintaining some items but not others at the specified service intervals, will not produce the same results.
4 As you service your vehicle, you will discover that many of the procedures can – and should – be grouped together, because of the particular procedure being performed, or because of the proximity of two otherwise-unrelated components to one another. For example, if the vehicle is raised for any reason, the exhaust can be inspected at the same time as the suspension and steering components.
5 The first step in this maintenance programme is to prepare yourself before the actual work begins. Read through all the Sections relevant to the work to be carried out, then make a list and gather all the parts and tools required. If a problem is encountered, seek advice from a parts specialist, or a dealer service department.

2 Regular maintenance

1 If, from the time the vehicle is new, the routine maintenance schedule is followed closely, and frequent checks are made of fluid levels and high-wear items, as suggested throughout this manual, the engine will be kept in relatively good running condition, and the need for additional work will be minimised.
2 It is possible that there will be times when the engine is running poorly due to the lack of regular maintenance. This is even more likely if a used vehicle, which has not received regular and frequent maintenance checks, is purchased. In such cases, additional work may need to be carried out, outside of the regular maintenance intervals.
3 If engine wear is suspected, a compression test (refer to Chapter 2A or 2B, as applicable) will provide valuable information regarding the overall performance of the main internal components. Such a test can be used as a basis to decide on the extent of the work to be carried out. If, for example, a compression test indicates serious internal engine wear, conventional maintenance as described in this Chapter will not greatly improve the performance of the engine, and may prove a waste of time and money, unless extensive overhaul work is carried out first.
4 The following series of operations are those most often required to improve the performance of a generally poor-running engine:

Primary operations

a) Clean, inspect and test the battery (refer to 'Weekly checks').
b) Check all the engine-related fluids (refer to 'Weekly checks').
c) Check the condition and tension of the auxiliary drivebelt (Section 5).
d) Renew the spark plugs (Section 19).
e) Check the condition of the air filter, and renew if necessary (Section 20).
f) Renew the fuel filter (Section 23).
g) Check the condition of all hoses, and check for fluid leaks (Section 7).

5 If the above operations do not prove fully effective, carry out the following secondary operations:

Secondary operations

All items listed under *Primary operations*, plus the following:

a) Check the charging system (refer to Chapter 5A).
b) Check the ignition system (refer to Chapter 5B).
c) Check the fuel system (refer to Chapter 4A).

Every 5000 miles or 6 months

3 Engine oil and filter renewal

1 Frequent oil and filter changes are the most important preventative maintenance procedures which can be undertaken by the DIY owner. As engine oil ages, it becomes diluted and contaminated, which leads to premature engine wear.
2 Before starting this procedure, gather together all the necessary tools and materials. Also make sure that you have plenty of clean rags and newspapers handy, to mop up any spills. Ideally, the engine oil should be warm, as it will drain more easily, and more built-up sludge will be removed with it.
3 Take care not to touch the exhaust (especially the catalytic converter) or any other hot parts of the engine when working under the vehicle. To avoid any possibility of scalding, and to protect yourself from possible skin irritants and other harmful contaminants in used engine oils, it is advisable to wear gloves when carrying out this work.

4 Firmly apply the handbrake, then jack up the front of the vehicle and support it on axle stands (see *Jacking and vehicle support*).
5 Remove the oil filler cap.
6 Using a spanner, or preferably a socket and bar, slacken the drain plug (at the rear of the sump) about half a turn **(see illustration)**. Position the draining container under the drain plug, then remove the plug completely.

3.6 Engine oil drain plug at rear of sump

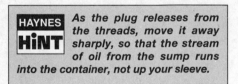
HAYNES HiNT *As the plug releases from the threads, move it away sharply, so that the stream of oil from the sump runs into the container, not up your sleeve.*

7 Allow some time for the oil to drain, noting that it may be necessary to reposition the container as the oil flow slows to a trickle.
8 After all the oil has drained, wipe the drain plug with a clean rag. Examine the condition of the drain plug sealing ring, and renew it if it shows signs of flattening or other damage which may prevent an oil-tight seal (it is generally considered good practice to fit a new seal every time, but on the Focus the seal is not available separately from the drain plug). Clean the area around the drain plug opening, and refit the plug complete with the seal and tighten it to the specified torque.
9 Move the container into position under the oil filter, which is located on the front of the cylinder block on 1.4 and 1.6 litre models, and on the rear of the block on 1.8 and 2.0 litre models **(see illustration)**.

10 Use an oil filter removal tool if necessary to slacken the filter initially, then unscrew it by hand the rest of the way **(see illustration)**. Empty the oil from the old filter into the container, then puncture the top of the filter, and allow the remaining oil to drain from the filter into the container.

11 Use a clean rag to remove all oil, dirt and sludge from the filter sealing area on the engine.

12 Apply a light coating of clean engine oil to the sealing ring on the new filter, then screw the filter into position on the engine. Tighten the filter firmly by hand only – **do not** use any tools.

13 Remove the old oil and all tools from under the car, then lower the car to the ground.

14 With the car on level ground, fill the engine, using the correct grade and type of oil (refer to *Weekly checks* for details of topping-up). An oil can spout or funnel may help to reduce spillage. Pour in half the specified quantity of oil first, then wait a few minutes for the oil to run to the sump.

15 Continue adding oil a small quantity at a time until the level is up to the MIN mark on the dipstick. Adding around 1.0 litre of oil will

3.9 Oil filter location at front of engine – 1.4 and 1.6 litre models

3.10 Using a chain wrench to loosen the oil filter

now bring the level up to the MAX on the dipstick – do not worry if a little too much goes in, as some of the excess will be taken up in filling the oil filter. Refit the dipstick and the filler cap.

16 Start the engine and run it for a few minutes; check for leaks around the oil filter seal and the sump drain plug. Note that there may be a few seconds' delay before the oil pressure warning light goes out when the engine is started, as the oil circulates through the engine oil galleries and the new oil filter

before the pressure builds up.

17 Switch off the engine, and wait a few minutes for the oil to settle in the sump once more. With the new oil circulated and the filter completely full, recheck the level on the dipstick, and add more oil as necessary.

18 Dispose of the used engine oil and the old oil filter safely, with reference to *General repair procedures* in the *Reference* section of this manual. Many local recycling points have containers for waste oil, with oil filter disposal receptacles alongside.

Every 10 000 miles or 12 months

4 Automatic transmission fluid level check and selector cable adjustment

Fluid level check

1 The fluid level **must** be checked with the engine/transmission at operating temperature. This can be achieved by checking the level after a journey of at least 10 miles. If the level is checked when cold, follow this up with a level check when the fluid is hot.

2 Park the car on level ground, and apply the handbrake very firmly. As an added precaution, chock the front and rear wheels, so that the car cannot move.

3 With the engine idling, apply the footbrake, then move the selector lever gently from position P to position 1, and back to P.

4 The fluid level dipstick is located on the rear of the transmission. Before removing the dipstick, thoroughly clean the area around it – no dirt or debris must be allowed to enter the transmission.

5 Extract the dipstick, and wipe it clean using a clean piece of rag or tissue. Re-insert the dipstick completely, then pull it out once more. The fluid level should be between the reference marks on the side of the dipstick **(see illustration)**. Note: *If the level is checked when cold, the reading obtained will appear to be low – recheck the level when hot before topping-up, as the transmission must not be over-filled.*

6 If topping-up is required, this is done via the dipstick tube. It is most important that no dirt or debris enters the transmission as this is done – use a clean funnel (preferably with a filter) and fresh fluid from a clean container.

7 Pour the fresh fluid a little at a time down

the dipstick tube, checking the level frequently. The difference between the MIN and MAX marks is 0.4 litres.

8 When the level is correct, refit the dipstick and switch off the engine.

9 The need for regular topping-up of the transmission fluid indicates a leak, which should be found and rectified without delay.

Selector cable adjustment

10 This procedure is described in Chapter 7B.

5 Auxiliary drivebelt check and renewal

Drivebelt check

1 A single auxiliary drivebelt is fitted at the right-hand side of the engine. The length of the drivebelt varies according to whether air conditioning is fitted. An automatic adjuster is fitted, so checking the drivebelt tension is unnecessary.

2 Due to their function and material make-up, drivebelts are prone to failure after a long period of time, and should therefore be inspected regularly.

3 Since the drivebelt is located very close to the right-hand side of the engine compartment, it is possible to gain better access by raising the front of the vehicle and removing the right-hand wheel, then unbolting the drivebelt lower cover from the underbody **(see illustration)**.

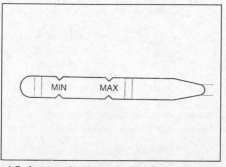

4.5 Automatic transmission fluid dipstick markings

5.3 Removing the drivebelt lower cover

5.4 Twist the drivebelt to check its condition

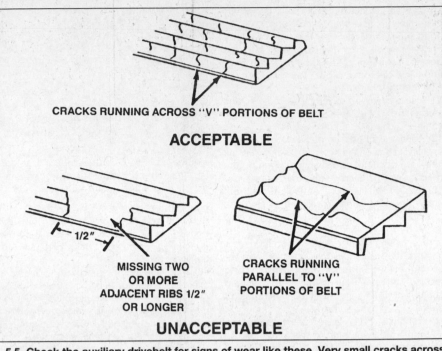

CRACKS RUNNING ACROSS ''V'' PORTIONS OF BELT

ACCEPTABLE

1/2"

MISSING TWO
OR MORE
ADJACENT RIBS 1/2"
OR LONGER

CRACKS RUNNING
PARALLEL TO ''V''
PORTIONS OF BELT

UNACCEPTABLE

5.5 Check the auxiliary drivebelt for signs of wear like these. Very small cracks across the drivebelt ribs are acceptable. If the cracks are deep, or if the drivebelt looks worn or damaged in any other way, renew it

4 With the engine stopped, inspect the full length of the drivebelt for cracks and separation of the belt plies. It will be necessary to turn the engine (using a spanner or socket and bar on the crankshaft pulley bolt) in order to move the belt from the pulleys so that the belt can be inspected thoroughly. Twist the belt between the pulleys so that both sides can be viewed (see illustration). Also check for fraying, and glazing which gives the belt a shiny appearance. Check the pulleys for nicks, cracks, distortion and corrosion.

5 Note that it is not unusual for a ribbed belt to exhibit small cracks in the edges of the belt ribs, and unless these are extensive or very deep, belt renewal is not essential (see illustration).

Drivebelt renewal

6 To remove the drivebelt, first raise the front of the vehicle and support on axle stands (see *Jacking and vehicle support*). Remove the drivebelt lower cover, which is secured by two bolts.

7 Using a spanner on the tensioner centre bolt, turn the tensioner to release the drivebelt tension. Note how the drivebelt is routed, then remove the belt from the pulleys (see illustrations).

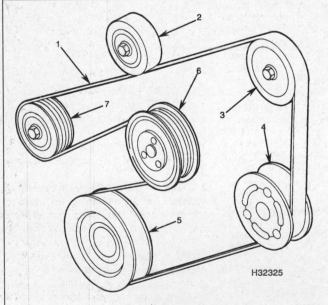

H32325

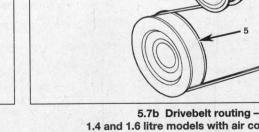

H32324

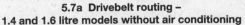
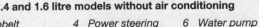

5.7a Drivebelt routing – 1.4 and 1.6 litre models without air conditioning

1	Drivebelt	4	Power steering pump	6	Water pump
2	Idler pulley	5	Crankshaft	7	Belt tensioner
3	Alternator				

5.7b Drivebelt routing – 1.4 and 1.6 litre models with air conditioning

1	Drivebelt	4	Air conditioning compressor	7	Belt tensioner
2	Idler pulley	5	Crankshaft	8	Power steering pump
3	Alternator	6	Water pump		

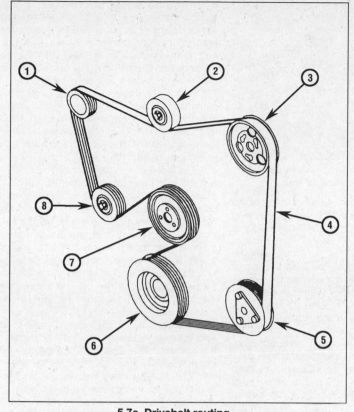

5.7c Drivebelt routing –
1.8 and 2.0 litre models with air conditioning

On models without air conditioning, the belt routing is identical, except that the compressor pulley is deleted

1 Alternator	5 Air conditioning compressor
2 Idler pulley	6 Crankshaft
3 Power steering pump	7 Water pump
4 Drivebelt	8 Belt tensioner

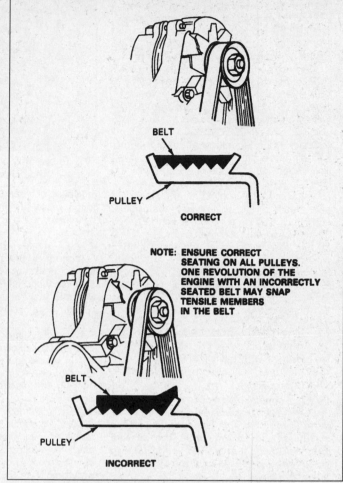

5.8 When installing the auxiliary drivebelt, make sure that it is centred – it must not overlap either edge of the grooved pulleys

8 Fit the new drivebelt onto the crankshaft, alternator, power steering pump, and air conditioning compressor pulleys, as applicable, then turn the tensioner and locate the drivebelt on the pulley. Make sure that the drivebelt is correctly seated in all of the pulley grooves, then release the tensioner **(see illustration)**.
9 Refit the drivebelt lower cover and lower the car to the ground.

Drivebelt tensioner

Removal

10 The drivebelt tensioner is attached to the right-hand rear corner of the engine block (right as seen from the driver's seat). Remove the auxiliary drivebelt as described previously in this Section.
11 Access to the three tensioner mounting nuts is not that easy – it will be a matter of personal preference whether to work from above or below. Unscrew the mounting nuts, and remove the tensioner from the engine.
12 Spin the tensioner pulley, checking it for signs of roughness. The tensioner should be

capable of providing significant tension when tested – rotate the pulley to load the spring, and check for free movement. Also inspect the tensioner pulley for signs of cracking or other deterioration.
13 The tensioner is not a serviceable component – if it has failed, or is not keeping the belt at a satisfactory tension, a new unit must be fitted.

Refitting

14 Refitting is a reversal of removal.

Drivebelt idler pulley

Removal

15 The idler pulley is fitted at the top of the drivebelt 'run'. Remove the auxiliary drivebelt as described previously in this Section.
16 Unscrew the pulley mounting bolt, and remove the pulley from the engine.
17 Spin the idler pulley, checking it for signs of roughness. Also inspect the pulley for signs of cracking or other deterioration.

Refitting

18 Refitting is a reversal of removal.

6 Lights and horn operation check

1 With the ignition switched on where necessary, check the operation of all exterior lights.
2 Check the brake lights with the help of an assistant, or by reversing up close to a reflective door. Make sure that all the rear lights are capable of operating independently, without affecting any of the other lights – for example, switch on as many rear lights as possible, then try the brake lights. If any unusual results are found, this is usually due to an earth fault or other poor connection at that rear light unit.
3 Again with the help of an assistant or using a reflective surface, check as far as possible that the headlights work on both main and dipped beam.
4 Replace any defective bulbs with reference to Chapter 12.

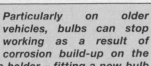

HAYNES HiNT

Particularly on older vehicles, bulbs can stop working as a result of corrosion build-up on the bulb or its holder – fitting a new bulb may not cure the problem in this instance. When replacing any bulb, if you find any green or white-coloured powdery deposits, these should be cleaned off using emery cloth.

5 Check the operation of all interior lights, including the glovebox and luggage area illumination lights. Switch on the ignition, and check that all relevant warning lights come on as expected – the vehicle handbook should give details of these. Now start the engine, and check that the appropriate lights go out. When you are next driving at night, check that all the instrument panel and facia lighting works correctly. If any problems are found, refer to Chapter 12.

6 Finally, choose an appropriate time of day to test the operation of the horn.

7 Underbonnet check for fluid leaks and hose condition

⚠ *Warning: Renewal of air conditioning hoses must be left to a dealer service department or air conditioning specialist who has the equipment to depressurise the system safely. Never remove air conditioning components or hoses until the system has been depressurised.*

General

1 Visually inspect the engine joint faces, gaskets and seals for any signs of water or oil leaks. Pay particular attention to the areas around the cylinder head cover, cylinder head, oil filter and sump joint faces. Bear in mind that, over a period of time, some very slight seepage from these areas is to be expected – what you are really looking for is any

HAYNES HiNT

A leak in the cooling system will usually show up as white- or rust-coloured deposits on the areas adjoining the leak.

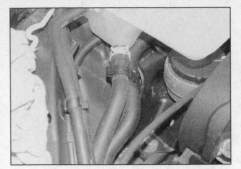

7.3 Ensure that all hoses are retained by their clips or cable-ties

indication of a serious leak. Should a leak be found, renew the offending gasket or oil seal by referring to the appropriate Chapters in this manual.

2 High temperatures in the engine compartment can cause the deterioration of the rubber and plastic hoses used for engine, accessory and emission systems operation. Periodic inspection should be made for cracks, loose clamps, material hardening and leaks.

3 When checking the hoses, ensure that all the cable-ties or clips used to retain the hoses are in place, and in good condition **(see illustration)**. Clips which are broken or missing can lead to chafing of the hoses, pipes or wiring, which could cause more serious problems in the future.

4 Carefully check the large top and bottom radiator hoses, along with the other smaller-diameter cooling system hoses and metal pipes; do not forget the heater hoses/pipes which run from the engine to the bulkhead. Inspect each hose along its entire length, replacing any that is cracked, swollen or shows signs of deterioration **(see Haynes Hint)**. Cracks may become more apparent if the hose is squeezed, and may often be apparent at the hose ends.

5 Make sure that all hose connections are tight. If the large-diameter air hoses from the air cleaner are loose, they will leak air, and upset the engine idle quality **(see illustration)**. If the spring clamps that are used to secure some of the hoses appear to be slackening, they should be replaced with worm-drive clips to prevent the possibility of leaks.

7.5 Ensure that the air hose clips are tight

6 Some other hoses are secured to their fittings with clamps. Where clamps are used, check to be sure they haven't lost their tension, allowing the hose to leak. If clamps aren't used, make sure the hose has not expanded and/or hardened where it slips over the fitting, allowing it to leak.

7 Check all fluid reservoirs, filler caps, drain plugs and fittings, etc, looking for any signs of leakage of oil, transmission and/or brake hydraulic fluid, coolant and power steering fluid. Also check the clutch hydraulic fluid lines which lead from the fluid reservoir and slave cylinder (on the transmission).

8 If the vehicle is regularly parked in the same place, close inspection of the ground underneath it will soon show any leaks; ignore the puddle of water which will be left if the air conditioning system is in use. Place a clean piece of cardboard below the engine, and examine it for signs of contamination after the vehicle has been parked over it overnight – be aware, however, of the fire risk inherent in placing combustible material below the catalytic converter.

9 Remember that some leaks will only occur with the engine running, or when the engine is hot or cold. With the handbrake firmly applied, start the engine from cold, and let the engine idle while you examine the underside of the engine compartment for signs of leakage.

10 If an unusual smell is noticed inside or around the car, especially when the engine is thoroughly hot, this may point to the presence of a leak.

11 As soon as a leak is detected, its source must be traced and rectified. Where oil has been leaking for some time, it is usually necessary to use a steam cleaner, pressure washer or similar, to clean away the accumulated dirt, so that the exact source of the leak can be identified.

Vacuum hoses

12 It's quite common for vacuum hoses, especially those in the emissions system, to be colour-coded, or to be identified by coloured stripes moulded into them. Various systems require hoses with different wall thicknesses, collapse resistance and temperature resistance. When renewing hoses, be sure the new ones are made of the same material.

13 Often the only effective way to check a hose is to remove it completely from the vehicle. If more than one hose is removed, be sure to label the hoses and fittings to ensure correct installation.

14 When checking vacuum hoses, be sure to include any plastic T-fittings in the check. Inspect the fittings for cracks, and check the hose where it fits over the fitting for distortion, which could cause leakage.

15 A small piece of vacuum hose (quarter-inch inside diameter) can be used as a stethoscope to detect vacuum leaks. Hold one end of the hose to your ear, and probe around vacuum hoses and fittings, listening for the 'hissing' sound characteristic of a vacuum leak.

⚠ *Warning: When probing with the vacuum hose stethoscope, be very careful not to come into contact with moving engine components such as the auxiliary drivebelt, radiator electric cooling fan, etc.*

Fuel hoses

⚠ *Warning: There are certain precautions which must be taken when inspecting or servicing fuel system components. Work in a well-ventilated area, and do not allow open flames (cigarettes, appliance pilot lights, etc) or bare light bulbs near the work area. Mop up any spills immediately, and do not store fuel-soaked rags where they could ignite.*

16 Check all fuel hoses for deterioration and chafing. Check especially for cracks in areas where the hose bends, and also just before fittings, such as where a hose attaches to the fuel rail (see illustration).

17 High-quality fuel line, usually identified by the word 'Fluoroelastomer' printed on the hose, should be used for fuel line renewal. Never, under any circumstances, use unreinforced vacuum line, clear plastic tubing or water hose as a substitute for fuel lines.

18 Spring-type clamps may be used on fuel lines. These clamps often lose their tension over a period of time, and can be 'sprung' during removal. Replace all spring-type clamps with proper petrol pipe clips whenever a hose is replaced.

Metal lines

19 Sections of metal piping are often used for fuel line between the fuel filter and the engine, and for some power steering and air conditioning applications. Check carefully to be sure the piping has not been bent or crimped, and that cracks have not started in the line; also check for signs of excessive corrosion.

20 If a section of metal fuel line must be renewed, only seamless steel piping should be used, since copper and aluminium piping don't have the strength necessary to withstand normal engine vibration.

21 Check the metal lines where they enter the brake master cylinder, ABS hydraulic unit or clutch master/slave cylinders (as applicable) for cracks in the lines or loose fittings. Any sign of brake fluid leakage calls for an immediate and thorough inspection.

8 Engine compartment wiring check

1 With the vehicle parked on level ground, apply the handbrake firmly and open the bonnet. Using an inspection light or a small electric torch, check all visible wiring within and beneath the engine compartment.

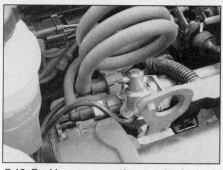

7.16 Fuel hose connections at the fuel rail

2 What you are looking for is wiring that is obviously damaged by chafing against sharp edges, or against moving suspension/transmission components and/or the auxiliary drivebelt, by being trapped or crushed between carelessly-refitted components, or melted by being forced into contact with the hot engine castings, coolant pipes, etc. In almost all cases, damage of this sort is caused in the first instance by incorrect routing on reassembly after previous work has been carried out.

3 Depending on the extent of the problem, damaged wiring may be repaired by rejoining the break or splicing-in a new length of wire, using solder to ensure a good connection, and remaking the insulation with adhesive insulating tape or heat-shrink tubing, as appropriate. If the damage is extensive, given the implications for the vehicle's future reliability, the best long-term answer may well be to renew that entire section of the loom, however expensive this may appear.

4 When the damage has been repaired, ensure that the wiring loom is re-routed correctly, so that it is clear of other components, and not stretched or kinked, and is secured out of harm's way using the plastic clips, guides and ties provided.

5 Check all electrical connectors, ensuring that they are clean, securely fastened, and that each is locked by its plastic tabs or wire clip, as appropriate (see illustration). If any connector shows external signs of corrosion (accumulations of white or green deposits, or streaks of 'rust'), or if any is thought to be

8.5 Check that all wiring plugs are securely connected

dirty, it must be unplugged and cleaned using electrical contact cleaner. If the connector pins are severely corroded, the connector must be renewed; note that this may mean the renewal of that entire section of the loom – see your local Ford dealer for details.

6 If the cleaner completely removes the corrosion to leave the connector in a satisfactory condition, it would be wise to pack the connector with a suitable material which will exclude dirt and moisture, preventing the corrosion from occurring again; a Ford dealer may be able to recommend a suitable product.

7 Check the condition of the battery connections – remake the connections or renew the leads if a fault is found (see Chapter 5A). Use the same techniques to ensure that all earth points in the engine compartment provide good electrical contact through clean, metal-to-metal joints, and that all are securely fastened.

8 Refer to Section 19 for details of spark plug (HT) lead checks.

9 Air conditioning system check

⚠ *Warning: The air conditioning system is under high pressure. Do not loosen any fittings or remove any components until after the system has been discharged. Air conditioning refrigerant must be properly discharged at a dealer service department or an automotive air conditioning repair facility capable of handling R134a refrigerant. Always wear eye protection when disconnecting air conditioning system fittings.*

1 The following maintenance checks should be performed on a regular basis, to ensure that the air conditioner continues to operate at peak efficiency:

a) *Check the auxiliary drivebelt. If it's worn or deteriorated, renew it (see Section 5).*
b) *Check the system hoses. Look for cracks, bubbles, hard spots and deterioration. Inspect the hoses and all fittings for oil bubbles and seepage. If there's any evidence of wear, damage or leaks, renew the hose(s).*
c) *Inspect the condenser fins (in front of the radiator) for leaves, insects and other debris. Use a 'fin comb' or compressed air to clean the condenser.*

⚠ *Warning: Wear eye protection when using compressed air.*

d) *Check that the drain tube from the front of the evaporator (under the right-hand front wing) is clear – note that it is normal to have clear fluid (water) dripping from this while the system is in operation, to the extent that quite a large puddle can be left under the vehicle when it is parked (see illustration).*

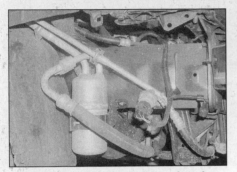

9.1 Air conditioning pipework and evaporator – seen with front bumper removed

2 It's a good idea to operate the system for about 30 minutes at least once a month, particularly during the winter. Long-term non-use can cause hardening, and subsequent failure, of the seals.

3 Because of the complexity of the air conditioning system and the special equipment necessary to service it, in-depth fault diagnosis and repairs are not included in this manual.

4 The most common cause of poor cooling is simply a low system refrigerant charge. If a noticeable drop in cool air output occurs, the following quick check will help you determine if the refrigerant level is low.

5 Warm the engine up to normal operating temperature.

6 Place the air conditioning temperature selector at the coldest setting, and put the blower at the highest setting. Open the doors – to make sure the air conditioning system doesn't cycle off as soon as it cools the passenger compartment.

7 With the compressor engaged – the compressor clutch will make an audible click, and the centre of the clutch will rotate – feel the inlet and outlet pipes at the compressor. One side should be cold, and one hot. If there's no perceptible difference between the two pipes, there's something wrong with the compressor or the system. It might be a low charge – it might be something else. Take the vehicle to a dealer service department or an automotive air conditioning specialist.

10.12 Check the flexible hoses at the brake calipers

10 Braking system check

1 The work described in this Section should be carried out at the specified intervals, or whenever a defect is suspected in the braking system. Any of the following symptoms could indicate a potential brake system defect:
  a) *The vehicle pulls to one side when the brake pedal is depressed.*
  b) *The brakes make squealing, scraping or dragging noises when applied.*
  c) *Brake pedal travel is excessive, or pedal feel is poor.*
  d) *The brake fluid requires repeated topping-up. Note that, because the hydraulic clutch shares the same fluid as the braking system (see Chapter 6), this problem could be due to a leak in the clutch system.*

Front disc brakes

2 Apply the handbrake, then loosen the front wheel nuts. Jack up the front of the vehicle, and support it on axle stands.

3 For better access to the brake calipers, remove the wheels.

4 Look through the inspection window in the caliper, and check that the thickness of the friction lining material on each of the pads is not less than the recommended minimum thickness given in the Specifications.

> **HAYNES HINT** *Bear in mind that the lining material is normally bonded to a metal backing plate. To differentiate between the metal and the lining material, it is helpful to turn the disc slowly at first – the edge of the disc can then be identified, with the lining material on each pad either side of it, and the backing plates behind.*

5 If it is difficult to determine the exact thickness of the pad linings, or if you are at all concerned about the condition of the pads, then remove them from the calipers for further inspection (refer to Chapter 9).

6 Check the other caliper in the same way.

7 If any one of the brake pads has worn down to, or below, the specified limit, *all four* pads at that end of the car must be renewed as a set. If the pads on one side are significantly more worn than the other, this may indicate that the caliper pistons have partially seized – refer to the brake pad renewal procedure in Chapter 9, and push the pistons back into the caliper to free them.

8 Measure the thickness of the discs with a micrometer, if available, to make sure that they still have service life remaining. Do not be fooled by the lip of rust which often forms on the outer edge of the disc, which may make the disc appear thicker than it really is – scrape off the loose rust if necessary, without scoring the disc friction (shiny) surface.

9 If any disc is thinner than the specified minimum thickness, renew it (refer to Chapter 9).

10 Check the general condition of the discs. Look for excessive scoring and discolouration caused by overheating. If these conditions exist, remove the relevant disc and have it resurfaced or renewed (refer to Chapter 9).

11 Make sure that the handbrake is firmly applied, then check that the transmission is in neutral. Spin the wheel, and check that the brake is not binding. Some drag is normal with a disc brake, but it should not require any great effort to turn the wheel – also, do not confuse brake drag with resistance from the transmission.

12 Before refitting the wheels, check all brake lines and hoses (refer to Chapter 9). In particular, check the flexible hoses in the vicinity of the calipers, where they are subjected to most movement **(see illustration)**. Bend them between the fingers (but do not actually bend them double, or the casing may be damaged) and check that this does not reveal previously-hidden cracks, cuts or splits.

13 On completion, refit the wheels and lower the car to the ground. Tighten the wheel nuts to the specified torque.

Rear disc brakes

14 Loosen the rear wheel nuts, then chock the front wheels. Jack up the rear of the car, and support it on axle stands. Release the handbrake and remove the rear wheels.

15 The procedure for checking the rear brakes is much the same as described in paragraphs 2 to 13 above. Check that the rear brakes are not binding, noting that transmission resistance is not a factor on the rear wheels. Abnormal effort may indicate that the handbrake needs adjusting – see Chapter 9.

Rear drum brakes

16 Loosen the rear wheel nuts, then chock the front wheels. Jack up the rear of the car, and support on axle stands. Release the handbrake and remove the rear wheels.

17 Spin the wheel to check that the brake is not binding. A small amount of resistance from the brake is acceptable, but no great effort should be required to turn the wheel hub. Abnormal effort may indicate that the handbrake needs adjusting – see Chapter 9.

18 To check the brake shoe lining thickness without removing the brake drums, prise the rubber plugs from the backplates, and use an electric torch to inspect the linings of the leading brake shoes. Check that the thickness of the lining material on the brake shoes is not less than the recommendation given in the Specifications.

19 If it is difficult to determine the exact thickness of the brake shoe linings, or if you are at all concerned about the condition of the shoes, then remove the rear drums for a more comprehensive inspection (refer to Chapter 9).

20 With the drum removed, check the shoe return and hold-down springs for correct installation, and check the wheel cylinders for leakage of brake fluid. Apart from fluid being visible, a leaking wheel cylinder may be characterised by an excessive build-up of brake dust (stuck to the fluid which has leaked) at the cylinder seals.

21 Check the friction surface of the brake drums for scoring and discoloration. If excessive, the drum should be resurfaced or renewed.

22 Before refitting the wheels, check all brake lines and hoses (refer to Chapter 9). On completion, apply the handbrake and check that the rear wheels are locked. The handbrake can be adjusted as described in Chapter 9.

23 On completion, refit the wheels and lower the car to the ground. Tighten the wheel nuts to the specified torque.

11 Exhaust system check

1 With the engine cold (at least three hours after the vehicle has been driven), check the complete exhaust system, from its starting point at the engine to the end of the tailpipe. Ideally, this should be done on a hoist, where unrestricted access is available; if a hoist is not available, raise and support the vehicle on axle stands.

2 Make sure that all brackets and rubber mountings are in good condition, and tight; if any of the mountings are to be renewed, ensure that the replacements are of the correct type – in the case of the rubber mountings, their colour is a good guide. Those nearest to the catalytic converter are more heat-resistant than the others **(see illustration)**.

3 Check the pipes and connections for evidence of leaks, severe corrosion, or damage. One of the most common points for a leak to develop is around the welded joints between the pipes and silencers **(see illustration)**. Leakage at any of the joints or in other parts of the system will usually show up as a black sooty stain in the vicinity of the leak. **Note:** *Exhaust sealants should not be used on any part of the exhaust system upstream of the catalytic converter (between the converter and engine) – even if the sealant does not contain additives harmful to the converter, pieces of it may break off and foul the element, causing local overheating.*

4 At the same time, inspect the underside of the body for holes, corrosion, open seams, etc. which may allow exhaust gases to enter the passenger compartment. Seal all body openings with silicone or body putty.

5 Rattles and other noises can often be traced to the exhaust system, especially the rubber mountings. Try to move the system, silencer(s), heat shields and catalytic converter. If any components can touch the

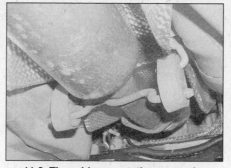

11.2 The rubber mountings near the catalytic converter are colour-coded red, indicating greater heat resistance

body or suspension parts, secure the exhaust system with new mountings.

6 Check the running condition of the engine by inspecting inside the end of the tailpipe; the exhaust deposits here are an indication of the engine's state of tune. The inside of the tailpipe should be dry, and should vary in colour from dark grey to light grey/brown; if it is black and sooty, or coated with white deposits, this may indicate the need for a full fuel system inspection.

12 Steering, suspension and roadwheel check

Front suspension and steering check

1 Apply the handbrake, then raise the front of the vehicle and support it on axle stands.

2 Visually inspect the balljoint dust covers and the steering gear gaiters for splits, chafing or deterioration **(see illustration)**. Any wear of these components will cause loss of lubricant, together with dirt and water entry, resulting in rapid deterioration of the balljoints or steering gear.

3 Check the power-assisted steering fluid hoses for chafing or deterioration, and the pipe and hose unions for fluid leaks. Also check for signs of fluid leakage under pressure from the steering gear rubber gaiters, which would indicate failed fluid seals within the steering gear.

12.2 Check the balljoint dust covers either side (arrowed)

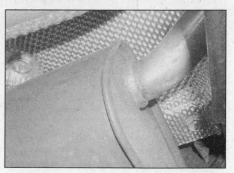

11.3 The area around a welded exhaust joint is a common place for leakage

4 Grasp the roadwheel at the 12 o'clock and 6 o'clock positions, and try to rock it **(see illustration)**. Very slight free play may be felt, but if the movement is appreciable, further investigation is necessary to determine the source. Continue rocking the wheel while an assistant depresses the footbrake. If the movement is now eliminated or significantly reduced, it is likely that the hub bearings are at fault. If the free play is still evident with the footbrake depressed, then there is wear in the suspension joints or mountings.

5 Now grasp the wheel at the 9 o'clock and 3 o'clock positions, and try to rock it as before. Any movement felt now may again be caused by wear in the hub bearings or the steering track rod balljoints. If the outer track rod balljoint is worn, the visual movement will be obvious. If the inner joint is suspect, it can be felt by placing a hand over the rack-and-pinion rubber gaiter, and gripping the track rod. If the wheel is now rocked, movement will be felt at the inner joint if wear has taken place.

6 Using a large screwdriver or flat bar, check for wear in the suspension mounting and subframe bushes by levering between the relevant suspension component and its attachment point. Some movement is to be expected as the mountings are made of rubber, but excessive wear should be obvious. Also check the condition of any visible rubber bushes, looking for splits, cracks or contamination of the rubber.

7 With the vehicle standing on its wheels, have an assistant turn the steering wheel back-and-forth, about an eighth of a turn each

12.4 Checking for wear in the front suspension and hub bearings

13.2a Check the outer constant velocity (CV) joint gaiters . . .

13.2b . . . and, though less prone to wear, check the inner tripod joint gaiters also

way. There should be very little, if any, lost movement between the steering wheel and roadwheels. If this is not the case, closely observe the joints and mountings previously described, but in addition, check the steering column joints for wear, and also check the rack-and-pinion steering gear itself.

Rear suspension check

8 Chock the front wheels, then raise the rear of the vehicle and support it on axle stands.
9 Check the rear hub bearings for wear, using the method described for the front hub bearings (paragraph 4).
10 Using a large screwdriver or flat bar, check for wear in the suspension mounting bushes by levering between the relevant suspension component and its attachment point. Some movement is to be expected as the mountings are made of rubber, but excessive wear should be obvious.

Roadwheel check and balancing

11 Periodically remove the roadwheels, and clean any dirt or mud from the inside and outside surfaces. Examine the wheel rims for signs of rusting, corrosion or other damage. Light alloy wheels are easily damaged by 'kerbing' whilst parking, and similarly, steel wheels may become dented or buckled. Renewal of the wheel is very often the only course of remedial action possible.
12 The balance of each wheel and tyre assembly should be maintained, not only to avoid excessive tyre wear, but also to avoid

wear in the steering and suspension components. Wheel imbalance is normally signified by vibration through the vehicle's bodyshell, although in many cases it is particularly noticeable through the steering wheel. Conversely, it should be noted that wear or damage in suspension or steering components may cause excessive tyre wear. Out-of-round or out-of-true tyres, damaged wheels and wheel bearing wear/maladjustment also fall into this category. Balancing will not usually cure vibration caused by such wear.
13 Wheel balancing may be carried out with the wheel either on or off the vehicle. If balanced on the vehicle, ensure that the wheel-to-hub relationship is marked in some way prior to subsequent wheel removal, so that it may be refitted in its original position.

13 Driveshaft rubber gaiter and joint check

1 The driveshaft rubber gaiters are very important, because they prevent dirt, water and foreign material from entering and damaging the joints. External contamination can cause the gaiter material to deteriorate prematurely, so it's a good idea to wash the gaiters with soap and water occasionally.
2 With the vehicle raised and securely supported on axle stands, turn the steering onto full-lock, then slowly rotate each front wheel in turn. Inspect the condition of the

outer constant velocity (CV) joint rubber gaiters, squeezing the gaiters to open out the folds. Check for signs of cracking, splits, or deterioration of the rubber, which may allow the escape of grease, and lead to the ingress of water and grit into the joint. Also check the security and condition of the retaining clips. Repeat these checks on the inner tripod joints **(see illustrations)**. If any damage or deterioration is found, the gaiters should be renewed as described in Chapter 8.
3 At the same time, check the general condition of the outer CV joints themselves, by first holding the driveshaft and attempting to rotate the wheels. Repeat this check on the inner joints, by holding the inner joint yoke and attempting to rotate the driveshaft.
4 Any appreciable movement in the joint indicates wear in the joint, wear in the driveshaft splines, or a loose driveshaft retaining nut.

14 Underbody and fuel/brake line check

1 With the vehicle raised and supported on axle stands or over an inspection pit, thoroughly inspect the underbody and wheelarches for signs of damage and corrosion. In particular, examine the bottom of the side sills, and any concealed areas where mud can collect.
2 Where corrosion and rust is evident, press and tap firmly on the panel with a screwdriver, and check for any serious corrosion which would necessitate repairs.
3 If the panel is not seriously corroded, clean away the rust, and apply a new coating of underseal. Refer to Chapter 11 for more details of body repairs.
4 At the same time, inspect the lower body panels for stone damage and general condition.
5 Inspect all of the fuel and brake lines on the underbody for damage, rust, corrosion and leakage. Also make sure that they are correctly supported in their clips **(see illustration)**. Where applicable, check the PVC coating on the lines for damage.

15 Hinge and lock lubrication

1 Work around the vehicle and lubricate the hinges of the bonnet, doors and tailgate with a light machine oil **(see illustration)**.
2 Check carefully the security and operation of all hinges, latches and locks, adjusting them where required. Check the operation of the central locking system (if fitted).
3 Where applicable, check the condition and operation of the tailgate struts, renewing them if either is leaking or no longer able to support the tailgate securely when raised.

14.5 Check the pipes attached to the underbody for damage

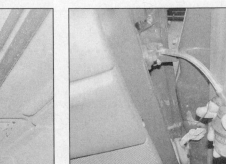

15.1 Lubricate the hinges regularly

16 Roadwheel nut tightness check

1 Checking the tightness of the wheel nuts is more relevant than you might think. Apart from the obvious safety aspect of ensuring they are sufficiently tight, this check will reveal whether they have been over-tightened, as may have happened the last time new tyres were fitted, for example. If the car suffers a puncture, you may find that the wheel nuts cannot be loosened with the wheelbrace.

2 Apply the handbrake, chock the wheels, and engage 1st gear (or P).

3 Remove the wheel cover (or wheel centre cover), using the flat end of the wheelbrace supplied in the tool kit.

4 Loosen the first wheel nut, using the wheelbrace if possible. If the nut proves stubborn, use a close-fitting socket and a long extension bar.

⚠️ **Warning: Do not use makeshift means to loosen the wheel nuts if the proper tools are not available. If extra force is required, make sure that the tools fit properly, and are of good quality. Even so, consider the consequences of the tool slipping or breaking, and take precautions – wearing stout gloves is advisable to protect your hands. Do not be tempted to stand on the tools used – they are not designed for this, and there is a high risk of personal injury if the tool slips or breaks. If the wheel nuts are simply too tight, take the car to a garage equipped with suitable power tools.**

5 Once the nut has been loosened, remove it and check that the wheel stud threads are clean. Use a small wire brush to clean any rust or dirt from the threads, if necessary.

6 Refit the nut, with the tapered side facing inwards. Tighten it fully, using the wheelbrace alone – no other tools. This will ensure that the wheel nuts can be loosened using the wheelbrace if a puncture occurs. However, if a torque wrench is available, tighten the nut to the specified torque wrench setting.

7 Repeat the procedure for the remaining three nuts, then refit the wheel cover or centre cover, as applicable.

8 Work around the car, checking and re-tightening the nuts for all four wheels.

17 Road test

Braking system

1 Make sure that the vehicle does not pull to one side when braking, and that the wheels do not lock prematurely when braking hard.

2 Check that there is no vibration through the steering when braking. On models equipped with ABS brakes, if vibration is felt through the pedal under heavy braking, this is a normal characteristic of the system operation, and is not a cause for concern.

3 Check that the handbrake operates correctly, without excessive movement of the lever, and that it holds the vehicle stationary on a slope, in both directions (facing up and down a slope).

4 With the engine switched off, test the operation of the brake servo unit as follows. Depress the footbrake four or five times to exhaust the vacuum, then start the engine. As the engine starts, there should be a noticeable 'give' in the brake pedal as vacuum builds up. Allow the engine to run for at least two minutes, and then switch it off. If the brake pedal is now depressed again, it should be possible to detect a hiss from the servo as the pedal is depressed. After about four or five applications, no further hissing should be heard, and the pedal should feel considerably harder.

Steering and suspension

5 Check for any abnormalities in the steering, suspension, handling or road 'feel'.

6 Drive the vehicle, and check that there are no unusual vibrations or noises.

7 Check that the steering feels positive, with no excessive sloppiness or roughness, and check for any suspension noises when cornering and driving over bumps.

Drivetrain

8 Check the performance of the engine, transmission and driveshafts.

9 Check that the engine starts correctly, both when cold and when hot.

10 Listen for any unusual noises from the engine and transmission.

11 Make sure that the engine runs smoothly when idling, and that there is no hesitation when accelerating.

12 On manual transmission models, check that all gears can be engaged smoothly without noise, and that the gear lever action is smooth and not abnormally vague or 'notchy'.

13 On automatic transmission models, make sure that all gearchanges occur smoothly without snatching, and without an increase in engine speed between changes. Check that all the gear positions can be selected with the vehicle at rest. If any problems are found, they should be referred to a Ford dealer.

14 Listen for a metallic clicking sound from the front of the vehicle as the vehicle is driven slowly in a circle with the steering on full-lock. Carry out this check in both directions. If a clicking noise is heard, this indicates wear in a driveshaft joint, in which case renew the joint if necessary.

Clutch

15 Check that the clutch pedal moves smoothly and easily through its full travel, and that the clutch itself functions correctly, with no trace of slip or drag.

16 If the clutch is slow to release, it is possible that the system requires bleeding (see Chapter 6). Also check the fluid pipes under the bonnet for signs of leakage.

17 Check the clutch as described in Chapter 6, Section 2.

Instruments and electrical equipment

18 Check the operation of all instruments and electrical equipment.

19 Make sure that all instruments read correctly, and switch on all electrical equipment in turn, to check that it functions properly.

Every 20 000 miles

18 Pollen filter renewal

1 Pull the windscreen wiper arms away from the windscreen until they lock in their vertical position, then open the bonnet.

2 The pollen filter housing is located at the left-hand corner of the grille panel at the rear of the engine compartment (left as seen from the driver's seat). On left-hand-drive models, the housing is on the right-hand side of the grille panel.

3 On early models (up to 1999) prise out the covers and remove the three retaining screws. On later models only one screw is used.

4 Using a small screwdriver if necessary, release the three retaining catches at the front of the access panel (see illustration). Access to the centre catch can be improved by opening the fusebox lid.

5 Lift out the filter access panel (see illustration).

6 Release the clip at either side, and lift up the pollen filter. Pull the filter element from the housing, and discard it (see illustration).

7 Fit the new filter using a reversal of the removal procedure, noting the following points:

18.4 Release the clips at the front of the pollen filter panel

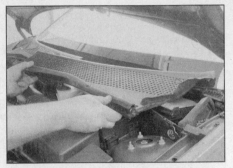

18.5 Removing the filter panel

18.6 Lift out the filter, noting the direction-of-fitting arrow

a) Make sure that the filter is fitted with the TOP/OBEN arrow marking facing upwards.
b) Clean the rubber seals on the filter access cover; renew if damaged or distorted.
c) Ensure that the filter access cover is properly seated, otherwise the cover seals will leak, allowing water into the car interior.

19 Spark plug renewal and HT lead check

Note: The spark plugs fitted as original equipment are of platinum type, but non-platinum (cheaper) replacements are available. If platinum plugs are used, the renewal interval can be doubled to 40 000 miles. Because of their importance to efficient and reliable operation, the DIY user may prefer to renew

the spark plugs at 20 000 miles, regardless of their type.

Spark plug renewal

1 The correct functioning of the spark plugs is vital for the correct running and efficiency of the engine. It is essential that the plugs fitted are appropriate for the engine; suitable types are specified at the beginning of this Chapter, on the Vehicle Emissions Control Information (VECI) label located on the underside of the bonnet (only on models sold in some areas) or in the vehicle handbook.

2 If the correct type is used and the engine is in good condition, the spark plugs should not need attention between scheduled replacement intervals. Spark plug cleaning is rarely necessary, and should not be attempted unless specialised equipment is available, as damage can easily be caused to the firing ends.

19.4 Lift off the centre panel for access to the spark plugs

19.6 Pull off the HT leads

19.8a Unscrew the plugs . . .

19.8b . . . and remove them from the engine – 1.4 litre engine

3 Spark plug removal and refitting requires a spark plug socket, with an extension which can be turned by a ratchet handle or similar. This socket is lined with a rubber sleeve, to protect the porcelain insulator of the spark plug, and to hold the plug while you insert it into the spark plug hole. You will also need feeler blades, to check and adjust the spark plug electrode gap, and (ideally) a torque wrench to tighten the new plugs to the specified torque.

4 To remove the spark plugs, first open the bonnet; the plugs are easily reached at the top of the engine. On 1.6 litre engines, first unclip the hoses from the top of the engine (noting how they are routed), then unscrew and remove the six bolts securing the plastic centre panel fitted over the spark plug HT leads, and lift the panel away **(see illustration)**.

5 Note how the spark plug (HT) leads are routed and secured by the clips on the cylinder head cover; unclip the leads as necessary, to provide enough slack in the lead. To prevent the possibility of mixing up spark plug (HT) leads, it is a good idea to try to work on one spark plug at a time.

6 If the marks on the original-equipment spark plug (HT) leads cannot be seen, mark the leads 1 to 4, to correspond to the cylinder the lead serves (No 1 cylinder is at the timing belt end of the engine). Pull the leads from the plugs by gripping the rubber boot sealing the cylinder head cover opening, not the lead, otherwise the lead connection may be fractured **(see illustration)**.

7 It is advisable to soak up any water in the spark plug recesses with a rag, and to remove any dirt from them using a clean brush, vacuum cleaner or compressed air before removing the plugs, to prevent any dirt or water from dropping into the cylinders.

⚠ *Warning: Wear eye protection when using compressed air.*

8 Unscrew the spark plugs, ensuring that the socket is kept in alignment with each plug – if the socket is forcibly moved to either side, the porcelain top of the plug may be broken off. Remove the plug from the engine **(see illustrations)**.

9 If any undue difficulty is encountered when unscrewing any of the spark plugs, carefully check the cylinder head threads and sealing surfaces for signs of wear, excessive corrosion or damage; if any of these conditions is found, seek the advice of a Ford dealer as to the best method of repair.

10 As each plug is removed, examine it as follows – this will give a good indication of the condition of the engine:
a) If the insulator nose of the spark plug is clean and white, with no deposits, this is indicative of a weak mixture.
b) If the tip and insulator nose are covered with hard black-looking deposits, then this is indicative that the mixture is too rich.

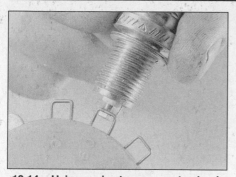

19.14a Using a wire-type gauge to check the spark plug electrode gap

19.14b Checking the spark plug gap using a feeler blade

19.14c To set the gap, bend the plug outer electrode only

c) *Should the plug be black and oily, then it is likely that the engine is fairly worn, as well as the mixture being too rich.*

d) *If the insulator nose is covered with light tan to greyish-brown deposits, then the mixture is correct, and it is likely that the engine is in good condition.*

11 If you are renewing the spark plugs, purchase the new plugs, then check each of them first for faults such as cracked insulators or damaged threads. Note also that, whenever the spark plugs are renewed as a routine service operation, the spark plug (HT) leads should be checked as described below.

12 The spark plug electrode gap is of considerable importance as, if it is too large or too small, the size of the spark and its efficiency will be seriously impaired. The gap should be set to the value given in the Specifications Section of this Chapter. New plugs will not necessarily be set to the correct gap, so they should always be checked before fitting.

13 Special spark plug electrode gap adjusting tools are available from most motor accessory shops, and may also be available from the spark plug manufacturers themselves.

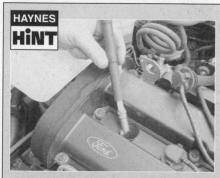

HAYNES HINT

It is very often difficult to insert spark plugs into their holes without cross-threading them. To avoid this possibility, fit a short length of 5/16 inch internal diameter rubber hose over the end of the spark plug. The flexible hose acts as a universal joint to help align the plug with the plug hole. Should the plug begin to cross-thread, the hose will slip on the spark plug, preventing thread damage to the aluminium cylinder head.

14 To set the electrode gap, measure the gap with a feeler gauge, and then bend open, or closed, the outer plug electrode until the correct gap is achieved **(see illustrations)**. The centre electrode should never be bent, as this may crack the insulation and cause plug failure, if nothing worse. If the outer electrode is not exactly over the centre electrode, bend it gently to align them.

15 Before fitting the spark plugs, check that the threaded connector sleeves at the top of the plugs are tight, and that the plug exterior surfaces and threads are clean. Brown staining on the porcelain, immediately above the metal body, is quite normal, and does not necessarily indicate a leak between the body and insulator.

16 On installing the spark plugs, first check that the cylinder head thread and sealing surface are as clean as possible; use a clean rag wrapped around a paintbrush to wipe clean the sealing surface. Apply a smear of copper-based grease or anti-seize compound to the threads of each plug, and screw them in by hand where possible. Take extra care to enter the plug threads correctly, as the cylinder head is made of aluminium alloy – it's often difficult to insert spark plugs into their holes without cross-threading them **(see Haynes Hint)**.

17 When each spark plug is started correctly on its threads, screw it down until it just seats lightly, then tighten it to the specified torque wrench setting. If a torque wrench is not available – and this is one case where the use of a torque wrench is strongly recommended – tighten each spark plug through *no more than* 1/16th of a turn. *Do not* exceed the specified torque setting, and *NEVER* overtighten these spark plugs – their tapered seats mean they are almost impossible to remove if abused.

18 Reconnect the spark plug (HT) leads in their correct order, using a twisting motion on the boot until it is firmly seated on the end of the spark plug and on the cylinder head cover.

Spark plug (HT) lead check

19 The spark plug (HT) leads should be checked whenever the plugs themselves are renewed. Start by making a visual check of the leads while the engine is running. In a darkened garage (make sure there is ventilation) start the engine and observe each lead. Be careful not to come into contact with any moving engine parts. If there is a break in the lead, you will see arcing or a small spark at the damaged area.

20 The spark plug (HT) leads should be inspected one at a time, to prevent mixing up the firing order, which is essential for proper engine operation. Each original lead should be numbered to identify its cylinder. If the number is illegible, a piece of tape can be marked with the correct number, and wrapped around the lead (the leads should be numbered 1 to 4, with No 1 lead nearest the timing belt end of the engine). The lead can then be disconnected.

21 Check inside the boot for corrosion, which will look like a white crusty powder. Clean this off as much as possible; if it is excessive, or if cleaning leaves the metal connector too badly corroded to be fit for further use, the lead must be renewed. Push the lead and boot back onto the end of the spark plug. The boot should fit tightly onto the end of the plug – if it doesn't, remove the lead and use pliers carefully to crimp the metal connector inside the boot until the fit is snug.

22 Using a clean rag, wipe the entire length of the lead to remove built-up dirt and grease. Once the lead is clean, check for burns, cracks and other damage. Do not bend the lead sharply, because the conductor might break.

23 Disconnect the lead from the ignition coil by pulling the end fitting off the coil terminal. Check for corrosion and for a tight fit **(see illustration)**.

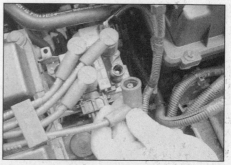

19.23 Check the HT lead end fittings for 'white' corrosion

24 If a meter with the correct measuring range is available, measure the resistance of the disconnected lead from its coil connector to its spark plug connector. If the resistance recorded for any of the leads greatly exceeds 30 000 ohms per metre length, all the leads should be renewed as a set.

25 Refit the lead to the coil, noting that each coil terminal is marked with its respective cylinder number, so that there is no risk of mixing up the leads and upsetting the firing order.

26 Inspect the remaining spark plug (HT) leads, ensuring that each is securely fastened at the ignition coil and spark plug when the check is complete. If any sign of arcing, severe connector corrosion, burns, cracks or other damage is noticed, obtain new spark plug (HT) leads, renewing them as a set. If new spark plug leads are to be fitted, remove and refit them one at a time, to avoid mix-ups in the firing order.

27 If new spark plug (HT) leads are required, purchase a set for your specific car and engine.

28 Even with the ignition system in first-class condition, some engines may still occasionally experience poor starting attributable to damp ignition components. To disperse moisture, a water-dispersant aerosol can be very effective.

Every 30 000 miles

20 Air filter element renewal

Caution: Never drive the vehicle with the air cleaner filter element removed. Excessive engine wear could result, and backfiring could even cause a fire under the bonnet.

1 The air filter element is located in the air cleaner assembly on the left-hand side of the engine compartment.

2 Remove the four screws securing the cover to the air cleaner housing **(see illustration)**.

3 The cover can now be lifted, and the filter element removed **(see illustration)**. If preferred, the cover can be removed completely – this will allow a more thorough cleaning of the filter housing.

4 Loosen the clip and disconnect the air inlet duct from the mass airflow sensor on the air cleaner.

5 Disconnect the wiring from the airflow sensor.

6 Disconnect the breather hose leading to the cylinder head cover.

7 Withdraw the cover and remove the filter element, noting its direction of fitting.

8 If carrying out a routine service, the element must be renewed regardless of its apparent condition.

9 If you are checking the element for any other reason, inspect its lower surface; if it is oily or very dirty, renew the element. If it is only moderately dusty, it can be re-used by blowing it clean from the upper to the lower surface with compressed air. Because it is a pleated-paper type filter, it cannot be washed or re-oiled. If it cannot be cleaned satisfactorily with compressed air, discard and renew it.

 Warning: Wear eye protection when using compressed air.

10 Where the air cleaner cover was removed, wipe out the inside of the housing. Check that no foreign matter is visible, either in the air intake or in the air mass meter.

11 Where applicable, before fitting the new filter, check and if necessary renew the PCV filter located in the base of the air cleaner (see Section 21).

12 Refitting is the reverse of the removal procedure, noting the following points:
a) Make sure that the filter is fitted the correct way up (observe any direction-of-fitting markings).
b) Ensure that the element and cover are securely seated, so that unfiltered air cannot enter the engine.
c) Where removed, secure the cover with the screws, and ensure that the air inlet duct securing clip is fully tightened.

21 Positive Crankcase Ventilation (PCV) system check

1 The Positive Crankcase Ventilation (PCV) valve is located at the front of the engine (refer to Chapter 4C, Section 3, for further information).

2 Check that all components of the system are securely fastened, correctly routed (with no kinks or sharp bends to restrict flow) and in sound condition; renew any worn or damaged components.

3 The PCV valve is designed to allow gases to flow out of the crankcase only, so that a depression is created in the crankcase under most operating conditions, particularly at idle. Therefore, if either the oil separator or the PCV valve are thought to be blocked, they must be renewed (see Chapter 4C). In such a case, however, there is nothing to be lost by attempting to flush out the blockage using a suitable solvent. The PCV valve should rattle when shaken.

4 If oil leakage is noted, disconnect the various hoses and pipes, and check that all are clear and unblocked.

5 A PCV filter is located at the base of the air cleaner on some models. With the air filter element removed as described in the previous Section, the foam filter can be prised out and inspected. The foam could be washed in a suitable solvent, dried and refitted, but if heavily contaminated, a new filter should be fitted **(see illustrations)**. Note that a new PCV filter is supplied with a genuine Ford air filter, and is intended to be renewed at the same time.

20.2 Air filter cover screws (arrowed)

20.3 Lift the cover and remove the element, noting how it is installed

21.5a Crankcase ventilation filter (arrowed) at the base of the air cleaner

21.5b The filter can be cleaned, but it is preferable to fit a new one

6 On completion, ensure that all connections which were disturbed are securely re-made, so that there are no air (or oil) leaks.

22 Manual transmission oil level check

1 The manual transmission does not have a dipstick. To check the oil level, raise the vehicle and support it securely on axle stands, making sure that the vehicle is level.
2 Except on 2.0 litre models, to gain access to the filler/level plug, it is first necessary to unclip the plastic cover from the gear selector cables at the front of the transmission.
3 On the lower front side of the transmission housing, you will see the filler/level plug, which has a large Allen key fitting. Note it is the plug furthest from the engine; where applicable, do not confuse it with the blanking plug near the bellhousing.
4 Remove all traces of dirt, then unscrew the filler/level plug from the front face of the transmission. Access to the plug is not that easy; use a suitable Allen key or socket, and take care, as the plug will probably be very tight.

Except 2.0 litre models

5 The oil level must be between 10 mm and 15 mm below the bottom edge of the filler/level plug hole (use a cranked tool such as an Allen key, or a piece of bent wire, to check the level).
6 If necessary, top up the level with the specified grade of oil (see *Lubricants and fluids*). Add the oil in very small amounts, and allow time for the oil level to stabilise before re-checking the level.
7 When the level is correct, clean and refit the filler level plug and tighten it to the specified torque.
8 Refit the plastic cover over the transmission cables.

2.0 litre models

9 If the lubricant level is correct, the oil should be up to the lower edge of the hole.
10 If the transmission needs more lubricant (if the level is not up to the hole), use a syringe, or a plastic bottle and tube, to add more.
11 Stop filling the transmission when the oil begins to run out of the hole, then wait until the flow of oil ceases – do not refit the plug immediately, or the transmission may end up being overfilled.
12 When the level is correct, clean and refit the filler level plug and tighten it to the specified torque.

All models

13 Drive the vehicle a short distance, then check for leaks.
14 A need for regular topping-up can only be due to a leak, which should be found and rectified without delay.

23.1 Fuel filter location in front of the fuel tank

23 Fuel filter renewal

> **Warning: Petrol is extremely flammable, so extra precautions must be taken when working on any part of the fuel system. Do not smoke, or allow open flames or bare light bulbs, near the work area. Also, do not work in a garage if a natural gas-type appliance with a pilot light is present. While performing any work on the fuel system, wear safety glasses, and have a suitable (Class B) fire extinguisher on hand. If you spill any fuel on your skin, rinse it off immediately with soap and water.**

1 The fuel filter is located at the front right-hand corner of the fuel tank, just forward of the vehicle's right-hand rear jacking point **(see illustration)**. The filter performs a vital role in keeping dirt and other foreign matter out of the fuel system, and so must be renewed at regular intervals, or whenever you have reason to suspect that it may be clogged.
2 It is always unpleasant working under a vehicle – pressure-washing or hosing clean the underbody in the filter's vicinity will make working conditions more tolerable, and will reduce the risk of getting dirt into the fuel system.
3 Before disturbing any fuel lines, which may contain fuel under pressure, any residual pressure in the system must be relieved as follows.
4 With the ignition switched off, open the

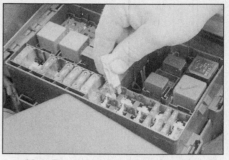

23.4 Removing the fuel pump fuse

engine compartment fusebox and remove the fuel pump fuse (No 12) **(see illustration)**.
5 Start the engine, if possible – if the engine will not start, turn it over on the starter for a few seconds.
6 If the engine starts, allow it to idle until it dies. Turn the engine over once or twice on the starter, to ensure that all pressure is released, then switch off the ignition.

> **Warning: This procedure will merely relieve the increased pressure necessary for the engine to run – remember that fuel will still be present in the system components, and take precautions accordingly before disconnecting any of them.**

7 Disconnect the battery negative lead, and position the lead away from the battery (also see *Disconnecting the battery*).
8 Jack up the rear right-hand side of the vehicle, and support it securely on an axle stand.
9 The fuel filter is removed complete with its mounting bracket, which is secured to the underbody by a single bolt (this bolt is extremely difficult to reach). Unscrew the bolt, and lower the filter and bracket for access to the pipe fittings **(see illustration)**.
10 To improve access, disconnect the connector (blue) on the evaporative emission pipe in front of the filter, and move the pipes aside.
11 Prise out the coloured locking clips with a small screwdriver, then separate the fuel pipe fittings at either end of the filter by pulling apart – be prepared for fuel spillage **(see illustration)**. Note the positions of the pipes for refitting.

23.9 Unscrewing the filter mounting bracket bolt

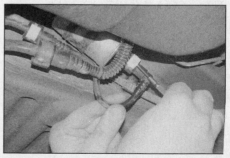

23.11 Prise the fuel pipe locking clip out with a small screwdriver

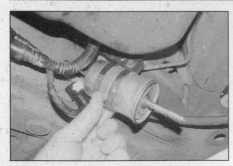

23.12 Lower the filter and mounting bracket

23.13a Loosen the filter clamp screw . . .

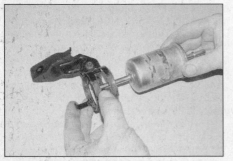

23.13b . . . and slide out the old filter

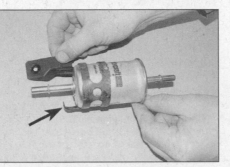

23.14 Slide the new filter into the bracket, until it touches the stop (arrowed)

12 Lower the filter and bracket out from under the car – note that the filter will still contain fuel; care should be taken, to avoid spillage and to minimise the risk of fire **(see illustration)**.

13 Loosen the filter retaining clamp screw, and slide the filter out of the mounting, noting the arrows and/or other markings on the filter showing the direction of fuel flow (towards the engine) **(see illustrations)**.

14 Slide the new filter fully into its clamp so that the arrow marked on it faces the same direction as noted when removing the old filter **(see illustration)**. Tighten the clamp screw so that the filter is held firm, but without crushing the filter body.

15 Offer the filter and mounting bracket into position under the car, and secure with the retaining bolt.

16 Slide each pipe union onto its (correct) respective filter stub, and press it down until the locking lugs click into their groove.

17 Refit the fuel pump fuse and reconnect the battery earth terminal, then switch the ignition on and off five times, to pressurise the system. Check for any sign of fuel leakage around the filter unions before lowering the vehicle to the ground and starting the engine.

Every 3 years, regardless of mileage

24 Brake fluid renewal

> **Warning: Brake hydraulic fluid can harm your eyes and damage painted surfaces, so use extreme caution when handling and pouring it. Do not use fluid that has been standing open for some time, as it absorbs moisture from the air. Excess moisture can cause a dangerous loss of braking effectiveness. Brake fluid is also highly flammable – treat it with the same respect as petrol.**

1 The procedure is similar to that for the bleeding of the hydraulic system as described in Chapter 9 except that, on models with a conventional braking system, the brake fluid reservoir should be emptied by syphoning, using a clean poultry baster or similar before starting, and allowance should be made for the old fluid to be expelled when bleeding a section of the circuit.

> **Warning: Do not syphon the fluid by mouth; it is poisonous.**

2 On models fitted with ABS, reduce the fluid level in the reservoir (by syphoning or using a poultry baster), but do not allow the fluid level to drop far enough to allow air into the system – if air enters the ABS hydraulic unit, the unit must be bled using special Ford test equipment (see Chapter 9).

3 Working as described in Chapter 9, open the first bleed screw in the sequence, and pump the brake pedal gently until nearly all the old fluid has been emptied from the master cylinder reservoir. Top-up to the MAX level with new fluid, and continue pumping until only the new fluid remains in the reservoir, and new fluid can be seen emerging from the bleed screw. Tighten the screw, and top the reservoir level up to the MAX level line.

HAYNES HiNT *Old hydraulic fluid is invariably much darker in colour than the new, making it easy to distinguish the two.*

4 Work through all the remaining bleed screws in the sequence until new fluid can be seen at all of them. Be careful to keep the master cylinder reservoir topped-up to above the MIN level at all times, or air may enter the system and greatly increase the length of the task.

5 When the operation is complete, check that all bleed screws are securely tightened, and that their dust caps are refitted. Wash off all traces of spilt fluid, and recheck the master cylinder reservoir fluid level.

6 Check the operation of the brakes before taking the car on the road.

7 Finally, check the operation of the clutch. Since the clutch shares the same fluid reservoir as the braking system, it may also be necessary to bleed the clutch as described in Chapter 6.

25 Coolant renewal and expansion tank cap check

Note: *If the antifreeze used is Ford's own, or of similar quality, Ford state that the coolant need not be renewed for 6 years (blue/green coolant) or for 10 years (orange coolant). If the vehicle's history is unknown, if antifreeze of lesser quality is known to be in the system, or simply if you prefer to follow conventional servicing intervals, the coolant should be changed periodically (typically, every 3 years) as described here.*

> **Warning: Do not allow antifreeze to come in contact with your skin or painted surfaces of the vehicle. Flush contaminated areas immediately with plenty of water. Don't store new coolant, or leave old coolant lying around, where it's accessible to children or pets – they're attracted by its sweet smell. Ingestion of even a small amount of coolant can be fatal. Wipe up garage-floor and drip-pan spills immediately. Keep antifreeze containers covered, and repair cooling system leaks as soon as they're noticed.**

> **Warning: Never remove the expansion tank filler cap when the engine is running, or has just been switched off, as the cooling system will be hot, and the consequent escaping steam and scalding coolant could cause serious injury.**

Coolant draining

Warning: Wait until the engine is cold before starting this procedure.

1 To drain the system, first remove the expansion tank filler cap.

2 If the additional working clearance is required, raise the front of the vehicle and support it securely on axle stands.

3 Place a large drain tray underneath, and unscrew the radiator drain plug **(see illustration)**; direct as much of the escaping coolant as possible into the tray.

System flushing

4 With time, the cooling system may gradually lose its efficiency, as the radiator core becomes choked with rust, scale deposits from the water, and other sediment. To minimise this, as well as using only good-quality antifreeze and clean soft water, the system should be flushed as follows whenever any part of it is disturbed, and/or when the coolant is renewed.

5 With the coolant drained, refit the drain plug and refill the system with fresh water. Refit the expansion tank filler cap, start the engine and warm it up to normal operating temperature, then stop it and (after allowing it to cool down completely) drain the system again. Repeat as necessary until only clean water can be seen to emerge, then refill finally with the specified coolant mixture.

6 If only clean, soft water and good-quality antifreeze (even if not to Ford's specification) has been used, and the coolant has been renewed at the suggested intervals, the above procedure will be sufficient to keep clean the system for a considerable length of time. If, however, the system has been neglected, a more thorough operation will be required, as follows.

7 First drain the coolant, then disconnect the radiator top and bottom hoses **(see illustration)**. Insert a garden hose into the radiator top hose connection, and allow water to circulate through the radiator until it runs clean from the bottom outlet.

8 To flush the engine, insert the garden hose into the radiator bottom hose, wrap a piece of rag around the garden hose to seal the connection, and allow water to circulate until it runs clear.

9 Try the effect of repeating this procedure in the top hose, although this may not be effective, since the thermostat will probably close and prevent the flow of water.

10 In severe cases of contamination, reverse-flushing of the radiator may be necessary. This may be achieved by inserting the garden hose into the bottom outlet, wrapping a piece of rag around the hose to seal the connection, then flushing the radiator until clear water emerges from the top hose outlet.

11 If the radiator is suspected of being severely choked, remove the radiator (Chapter 3), turn it upside-down, and repeat the procedure described in paragraph 10.

25.3 Radiator drain plug (arrowed)

12 Flushing the heater matrix can be achieved using a similar procedure to that described in paragraph 10, once the heater inlet and outlet hoses have been identified. These two hoses will be of the same diameter, and pass through the engine compartment bulkhead (refer to the heater matrix removal procedure in Chapter 3, Section 9, for more details).

13 The use of chemical cleaners is not recommended, and should be necessary only as a last resort; the scouring action of some chemical cleaners may lead to other cooling system problems. Normally, regular renewal of the coolant will prevent excessive contamination of the system.

Coolant filling

14 With the cooling system drained and flushed, ensure that all disturbed hose unions are correctly secured, and that the radiator drain plug is securely tightened. If it was raised, lower the vehicle to the ground.

15 Prepare a sufficient quantity of the specified coolant mixture (see below); allow for a surplus, so as to have a reserve supply for topping-up.

1.4 and 1.6 litre models

16 Disconnect the heater supply hose, located at the rear of the engine, below the ignition coil.

17 Using a funnel, slowly fill the cooling system via the disconnected supply hose, until coolant emerges from the engine, then reconnect the hose.

25.7 Radiator bottom hose connection (arrowed)

All models

18 Slowly fill the system through the expansion tank. Since the tank is the highest point in the system, all the air in the system should be displaced into the tank by the rising liquid. Slow pouring reduces the possibility of air being trapped and forming airlocks.

19 Continue filling until the coolant level reaches the expansion tank MAX level line (see *Weekly checks*), then cover the filler opening to prevent coolant splashing out.

20 Start the engine and run it at idle speed, until it has warmed-up to normal operating temperature and the radiator electric cooling fan has cut in; watch the temperature gauge to check for signs of overheating. If the level in the expansion tank drops significantly, top-up to the MAX level line, to minimise the amount of air circulating in the system.

21 Stop the engine, wash off any spilt coolant from the engine compartment and bodywork, then leave the car to cool down *completely* (overnight, if possible).

22 With the system cool, uncover the expansion tank filler opening, and top-up the tank to the MAX level line. Refit the filler cap, tightening it securely, and clean up any further spillage.

23 After refilling, always check carefully all components of the system (but especially any unions disturbed during draining and flushing) for signs of coolant leaks. Fresh antifreeze has a searching action, which will rapidly expose any weak points in the system.

Antifreeze type and mixture

Note: *Do not use engine antifreeze in the windscreen/tailgate washer system, as it will damage the vehicle's paintwork. A screenwash additive should be added to the washer system in its maker's recommended quantities.*

24 When new, the cooling system in the Focus will have been filled with Super Plus 4 antifreeze (which is blue/green), to specification ESD-M97B-49-A. More recently, the system will have Super Plus 2000 antifreeze (which is orange) to specification WSS-M97 B44-D. The two types of coolant must not be mixed with each other, and should also not be mixed with any other type of coolant.

25 If the vehicle's history (and therefore the quality of the antifreeze in it) is unknown, owners are advised to drain and thoroughly reverse-flush the system, before refilling with fresh coolant mixture. If the Ford antifreeze is used, the coolant can then be left for 6 years (Super Plus 4, blue/green coolant type) or 10 years (Super Plus 2000, orange coolant type).

26 If any antifreeze other than Ford's is to be used, the coolant must be renewed at regular intervals to provide an equivalent degree of protection; the conventional recommendation is to renew the coolant every three years.

27 If the antifreeze used is to Ford's specification, the levels of protection it affords are indicated in the Specifications Section of this Chapter. To give the recommended *standard* mixture ratio for antifreeze, 50% (by volume) of antifreeze must be mixed with 50% of clean, soft water; if you are using any other type of antifreeze, follow its manufacturer's instructions to achieve the correct ratio.

28 You are unlikely to fully drain the system at any one time (unless the engine is being completely stripped), and the capacities quoted in Specifications are therefore slightly academic for routine coolant renewal. As a guide, only two-thirds of the system's total capacity is likely to be needed for coolant renewal.

29 As the drained system will be partially filled with flushing water, in order to establish the recommended mixture ratio, measure out 50% of the system capacity in antifreeze and pour it into the hose/expansion tank as described above, then top-up with water. Any topping-up while refilling the system should be done with water - for *Weekly checks* use a suitable mixture.

30 Before adding antifreeze, the cooling system should be completely drained, preferably flushed, and all hoses checked for condition and security. As noted earlier, fresh antifreeze will rapidly find any weaknesses in the system.

31 After filling with antifreeze, a label should be attached to the expansion tank, stating the type and concentration of antifreeze used, and the date installed. Any subsequent topping-up should be made with the same type and concentration of antifreeze.

General cooling system checks

32 The engine should be cold for the cooling system checks, so perform the following procedure before driving the vehicle, or after it has been shut off for at least three hours.

33 Remove the expansion tank filler cap, and clean it thoroughly inside and out with a rag. Also clean the filler neck on the expansion tank. The presence of rust or corrosion in the filler neck indicates that the coolant should be changed. The coolant inside the expansion tank should be relatively clean and transparent. If it is rust-coloured, drain and flush the system, and refill with a fresh coolant mixture.

34 Carefully check the radiator hoses and heater hoses along their entire length; renew any hose which is cracked, swollen or deteriorated (see Section 7).

35 Inspect all other cooling system components (joint faces, etc.) for leaks. A leak in the cooling system will usually show up as white- or rust-coloured deposits on the area adjoining the leak. Where any problems of this nature are found on system components, renew the component or gasket with reference to Chapter 3.

36 Clean the front of the radiator with a soft brush to remove all insects, leaves, etc, embedded in the radiator fins. Be careful not to damage the radiator fins, or cut your fingers on them. To do a more thorough job, remove the radiator grille as described in Chapter 11.

Airlocks

37 If, after draining and refilling the system, symptoms of overheating are found which did not occur previously, then the fault is almost certainly due to trapped air at some point in the system, causing an airlock and restricting the flow of coolant; usually, the air is trapped because the system was refilled too quickly.

38 If an airlock is suspected, first try gently squeezing all visible coolant hoses. A coolant hose which is full of air feels quite different to one full of coolant, when squeezed. After refilling the system, most airlocks will clear once the system has cooled, and been topped-up.

39 While the engine is running at operating temperature, switch on the heater and heater fan, and check for heat output. Provided there is sufficient coolant in the system, lack of heat output could be due to an airlock in the system.

40 Airlocks can have more serious effects than simply reducing heater output – a severe airlock could reduce coolant flow around the engine. Check that the radiator top hose is hot when the engine is at operating temperature – a top hose which stays cold could be the result of an airlock (or a non-opening thermostat).

41 If the problem persists, stop the engine and allow it to cool down **completely**, before unscrewing the expansion tank filler cap or loosening the hose clips and squeezing the hoses to bleed out the trapped air. In the worst case, the system will have to be at least partially drained (this time, the coolant can be saved for re-use) and flushed to clear the problem.

Expansion tank pressure cap check

42 Wait until the engine is completely cold – perform this check before the engine is started for the first time in the day.

43 Place a wad of cloth over the expansion tank cap, then unscrew it slowly and remove it

44 Examine the condition of the rubber seal on the underside of the cap. If the rubber appears to have hardened, or cracks are visible in the seal edges, a new cap should be fitted.

45 If the car is several years old, or has covered a large mileage, consider renewing the cap regardless of its apparent condition – they are not expensive. If the pressure relief valve built into the cap fails, excess pressure in the system will lead to puzzling failures of hoses and other cooling system components.

Every 80 000 miles

26 Timing belt renewal

The procedure is described in Chapter 2A or Chapter 2B, as applicable.

Every 100 000 miles

27 Valve clearance check and adjustment

The procedure is described in Chapter 2A or Chapter 2B, as applicable.

Chapter 1 Part B:
Routine maintenance & servicing – diesel models

Contents

Degrees of difficulty

Easy, suitable for novice with little experience	Fairly easy, suitable for beginner with some experience	Fairly difficult, suitable for competent DIY mechanic	Difficult, suitable for experienced DIY mechanic	Very difficult, suitable for expert DIY or professional

Lubricants and fluids
Refer to end of *Weekly checks*

Capacities
Engine oil (including filter) .... 5.6 litres

Cooling system (approximate) .... 6.5 litres

Transmission (approximate) .... 2.0 litres

Washer fluid reservoir .... 3.6 litres

Fuel tank .... 52.7 litres

Engine
Valve clearances (cold):
   Inlet .... 0.30 to 0.40 mm
   Exhaust .... 0.45 to 0.55 mm
Tappet shim thicknesses available .... 3.00 to 4.75 mm in varying increments

Cooling system
Antifreeze mixture:
   50% antifreeze .... Protection down to –37°C
   55% antifreeze .... Protection down to –45°C
Note: *Refer to antifreeze manufacturer for latest recommendations.*

Brakes
Friction material minimum thickness:
   Front brake pads .... 1.5 mm
   Rear brake shoes .... 1.0 mm

Torque wrench settings

	Nm	lbf ft
Auxiliary drivebelt idler pulley bolt	48	35
Auxiliary drivebelt tensioner mounting nuts	48	35
Engine oil drain plug	25	18
Manual transmission drain and filler/level plugs	45	33
Roadwheel nuts	85	63

The maintenance intervals in this manual are provided with the assumption that you, not the dealer, will be carrying out the work. These are the minimum maintenance intervals recommended by us for vehicles driven daily. If you wish to keep your vehicle in peak condition at all times, you may wish to perform some of these procedures more often. We encourage frequent maintenance, because it enhances the efficiency, performance and resale value of your vehicle.

If the vehicle is driven in dusty areas, used to tow a trailer, or driven frequently at slow speeds (idling in traffic) or on short journeys, more frequent maintenance intervals are recommended.

When the vehicle is new, it should be serviced by a factory-authorised dealer service department, in order to preserve the factory warranty.

Every 250 miles (400 km) or weekly

☐ Refer to *Weekly checks*

Every 5000 miles or 6 months, whichever comes first

☐ Renew the engine oil and filter (Section 3)

Note: *Ford recommend that the engine oil and filter are changed every 10 000 miles or 12 months. However, oil and filter changes are good for the engine and we recommend that the oil and filter are renewed more frequently, especially if the vehicle is used on a lot of short journeys.*

Every 10 000 miles or 12 months, whichever comes first

☐ Check the condition of the auxiliary drivebelt (Section 4)
☐ Check the operation of the lights and electrical equipment (Section 5)
☐ Check under the bonnet for fluid leaks and hose condition (Section 6)
☐ Check the condition of all engine compartment wiring (Section 7)
☐ Check the condition of all air conditioning system components (Section 8)
☐ Check the braking system components (Section 9)
☐ Check the exhaust system (Section 10)
☐ Check the steering and suspension components for condition and security (Section 11)
☐ Check the condition of the driveshaft joints and gaiters (Section 12)
☐ Check the underbody, and all fuel/brake lines (Section 13)
☐ Lubricate all hinges and locks (Section 14)
☐ Check the roadwheel nuts are tightened to the specified torque (Section 15)
☐ Carry out a road test (Section 16)

Every 20 000 miles

☐ Renew the fuel filter (Section 17)
☐ Renew the pollen filter (Section 18)

Note: *If the vehicle is used in dusty conditions, the pollen filter should be renewed more frequently.*

Every 30 000 miles

☐ Renew the air filter (Section 19)

Note: *If the vehicle is used in dusty conditions, the air filter should be renewed more frequently.*

☐ Check the crankcase ventilation system (Section 20)
☐ Check the manual transmission oil level (Section 21)
☐ Check the valve clearances (Section 22)

Every 3 years, regardless of mileage

☐ Renew the brake fluid (Section 23)
☐ Renew the coolant and check the condition of the expansion tank pressure cap (Section 24)

Note: *If Ford antifreeze is used, Ford state that the coolant renewal interval can be extended. Refer to Section 24.*

Every 80 000 miles

☐ Renew the timing belt (Section 25)

Note: *The Ford interval for belt renewal is actually at a higher mileage than this. It is strongly recommended, however, that the interval is reduced to 80 000 miles, particularly on vehicles which are subjected to intensive use, ie, mainly short journeys or a lot of stop-start driving. The actual belt renewal interval is therefore very much up to the individual owner, but bear in mind that severe engine damage will result if the belt breaks.*

Underbonnet view of diesel model

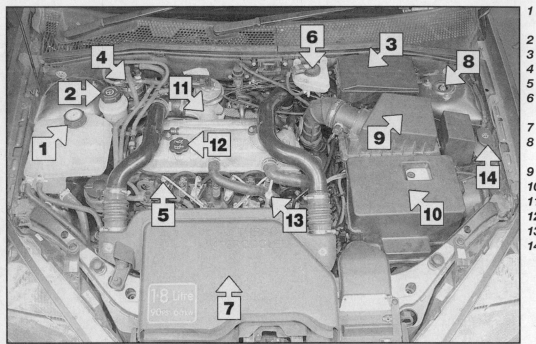

1 Cooling system expansion tank
2 Power steering reservoir
3 Main fusebox
4 Fuel filter
5 Injectors
6 Brake master cylinder reservoir
7 Intercooler
8 Suspension strut upper mounting
9 Air cleaner
10 Battery
11 Inlet manifold
12 Oil filler cap
13 Engine oil dipstick
14 Washer reservoir filler

Front underside view of diesel model

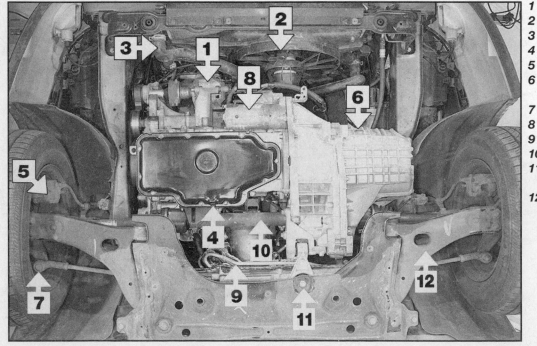

1 Alternator
2 Radiator fan/shroud
3 Radiator bottom hose
4 Engine oil drain plug
5 Front brake caliper
6 Manual transmission level plug
7 Track rod end
8 Starter motor
9 Power steering fluid pipes
10 Right-hand driveshaft
11 Rear engine/gearbox mounting
12 Suspension control arm

Rear underside view of diesel model

1   Exhaust rear silencer
2   Exhaust centre silencer
3   Rear anti-roll bar
4   Rear suspension rear lower arm
5   Handbrake cable
6   Shock absorber lower mounting
7   Heat shield
8   Fuel tank
9   Fuel filler neck
10 Rear coil spring
12 Rear suspension tie-bar (control blade)
13 Rear suspension front lower arm

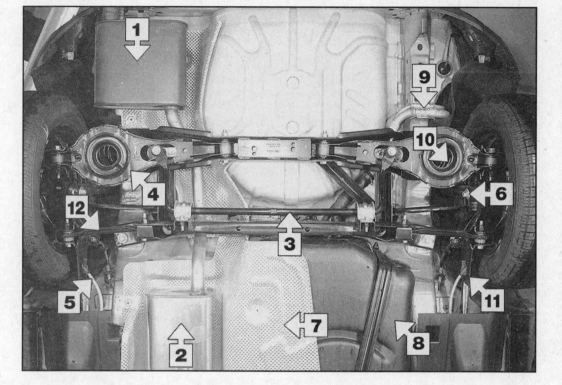

Maintenance procedures

1   General information

1 This Chapter is designed to help the home mechanic maintain his/her vehicle for safety, economy, long life and peak performance.

2 The Chapter contains a master maintenance schedule, followed by Sections dealing specifically with each task in the schedule. Visual checks, adjustments, component renewal and other helpful items are included. Refer to the accompanying illustrations of the engine compartment and the underside of the vehicle for the locations of the various components.

3 Servicing your vehicle in accordance with the mileage/time maintenance schedule and the following Sections will provide a planned maintenance programme, which should result in a long and reliable service life. This is a comprehensive plan, so maintaining some items but not others at the specified service intervals will not produce the same results.

4 As you service your vehicle, you will discover that many of the procedures can – and should – be grouped together, because of the particular procedure being performed, or because of the proximity of two otherwise-unrelated components to one another. For example, if the vehicle is raised for any reason, the exhaust can be inspected at the same time as the suspension and steering components.

5 The first step in this maintenance programme is to prepare yourself before the actual work begins. Read through all the Sections relevant to the work to be carried out, then make a list and gather all the parts and tools required. If a problem is encountered, seek advice from a parts specialist, or a dealer service department.

2   Regular maintenance

1 If, from the time the vehicle is new, the routine maintenance schedule is followed closely, and frequent checks are made of fluid levels and high-wear items, as suggested throughout this manual, the engine will be kept in relatively good running condition, and the need for additional work will be minimised.

2 It is possible that there will be times when the engine is running poorly due to the lack of regular maintenance. This is even more likely if a used vehicle, which has not received regular and frequent maintenance checks, is purchased. In such cases, additional work may need to be carried out, outside of the regular maintenance intervals.

3 If engine wear is suspected, a compression test or leakdown test (refer to Chapter 2C) will provide valuable information regarding the overall performance of the main internal components. Such a test can be used as a basis to decide on the extent of the work to be carried out. If, for example, a compression or leakdown test indicates serious internal engine wear, conventional maintenance as described in this Chapter will not greatly improve the performance of the engine, and may prove a waste of time and money, unless extensive overhaul work is carried out first.

4 The following series of operations are those most often required to improve the performance of a generally poor-running engine:

Primary operations

a) Clean, inspect and test the battery (refer to 'Weekly checks').
b) Check all the engine-related fluids (refer to 'Weekly checks').
c) Check the condition and tension of the auxiliary drivebelt (Section 4).
d) Check the condition of the air filter, and renew if necessary (Section 19).
e) Renew the fuel filter (Section 17).
f) Check the condition of all hoses, and check for fluid leaks (Section 6).

5 If the above operations do not prove fully effective, carry out the following secondary operations:

Secondary operations

All items listed under *Primary operations*, plus the following:

a) Check the charging system (refer to Chapter 5A).
b) Check the pre-heating system (refer to Chapter 4B, Section 16).
c) Check the fuel system (refer to Chapter 4B).

Every 5000 miles or 6 months

3 Engine oil and filter renewal

1 Frequent oil and filter changes are the most important preventative maintenance procedures which can be undertaken by the DIY owner. As engine oil ages, it becomes diluted and contaminated, which leads to premature engine wear.

2 Before starting this procedure, gather together all the necessary tools and materials. Also make sure that you have plenty of clean rags and newspapers handy, to mop up any spills. Ideally, the engine oil should be warm, as it will drain more easily, and more built-up sludge will be removed with it. Take care not to touch the exhaust or any other hot parts of the engine when working under the vehicle. To avoid any possibility of scalding, and to protect yourself from possible skin irritants and other harmful contaminants in used engine oils, it is advisable to wear gloves when carrying out this work.

3.9 Removing the oil filter, at the rear of the engine above the driveshaft

3 Firmly apply the handbrake, then jack up the front of the vehicle and support it on axle stands (see *Jacking and vehicle support*).

4 Remove the oil filler cap.

5 To improve access, unscrew the fasteners and remove the plastic undershield below the engine.

6 Using a spanner, or preferably a suitable socket and bar, slacken the drain plug (at the rear of the sump) about half a turn. Position the draining container under the drain plug, then remove the plug completely.

7 Allow some time for the oil to drain, noting that it may be necessary to reposition the container as the oil flow slows to a trickle.

8 After all the oil has drained, wipe the drain plug and the sealing washer with a clean rag. Examine the condition of the sealing washer, and renew it if it shows signs of scoring or other damage which may prevent an oil-tight seal (it is generally considered good practice to fit a new washer every time). Clean the area around the drain plug opening, and refit the plug complete with the washer and tighten it securely.

9 Move the container into position under the oil filter which is located on the rear of the cylinder block **(see illustration)**.

10 Use an oil filter removal tool if necessary to slacken the filter initially, then unscrew it by hand the rest of the way. Empty the oil from the old filter into the container, then puncture the top of the filter, and allow the remaining oil to drain from the filter into the container.

11 Use a clean rag to remove all oil, dirt and sludge from the filter sealing area on the engine.

12 Apply a light coating of clean engine oil to the sealing ring on the new filter, then screw the filter into position on the engine. Tighten the filter firmly by hand only – **do not** use any tools.

13 Remove the old oil and all tools from under the vehicle, refit the undershield, then lower the vehicle to the ground.

14 With the car on level ground, fill the engine, using the correct grade and type of oil (refer to *Weekly checks* for details of topping-up). An oil can spout or funnel may help to reduce spillage. Pour in half the specified quantity of oil first, then wait a few minutes for the oil to run to the sump.

15 Continue adding oil a small quantity at a time until the level is up to the MIN mark on the dipstick. Adding around 1.0 litre of oil will now bring the level up to the MAX on the dipstick – do not worry if a little too much goes in, as some of the excess will be taken up in filling the oil filter. Refit the dipstick and the filler cap.

16 Start the engine and run it for a few minutes, while checking for leaks around the oil filter seal and the sump drain plug. Note that there may be a delay of a few seconds before the low oil pressure warning light goes out when the engine is first started, as the oil circulates through the new oil filter and the engine oil galleries before the pressure builds up.

17 Stop the engine, and wait a few minutes for the oil to settle in the sump once more. With the new oil circulated and the filter now completely full, recheck the level on the dipstick, and add more oil as necessary.

18 Dispose of the used engine oil and the old oil filter safely, with reference to *General repair procedures* in the *Reference* section of this manual. Many local recycling points have containers for waste oil, with oil filter disposal receptacles alongside.

Every 10 000 miles or 12 months

| 4 | Auxiliary drivebelt check and renewal | |

Drivebelt check

1 A single auxiliary drivebelt is fitted at the right-hand side of the engine. The length of the drivebelt varies according to whether air conditioning is fitted. An automatic adjuster is fitted, so checking the drivebelt tension is unnecessary.

2 Due to their function and material make-up, drivebelts are prone to failure after a long period of time, and should therefore be inspected regularly.

3 Since the drivebelt is located very close to the right-hand side of the engine compartment, it is possible to gain better access by raising the front of the vehicle and removing the right-hand wheel, then unbolting the drivebelt lower cover from the underbody.

4 With the engine stopped, inspect the full length of the drivebelt for cracks and separation of the belt plies. It will be necessary to turn the engine (using a spanner or socket and bar on the crankshaft pulley bolt) in order to move the belt from the pulleys so that the belt can be inspected thoroughly. Twist the belt between the pulleys so that both sides can be viewed. Also check for fraying, and glazing which gives the belt a shiny appearance. Check the pulleys for nicks, cracks, distortion and corrosion.

5 Note that it is not unusual for a ribbed belt to exhibit small cracks in the edges of the belt ribs, and unless these are extensive or very deep, belt renewal is not essential (see illustration).

Drivebelt renewal

6 To remove the drivebelt, first raise the front of the vehicle and support on axle stands (see *Jacking and vehicle support*). Remove the drivebelt lower cover, which is secured by two bolts.

7 Using a spanner on the tensioner centre bolt, turn the tensioner clockwise to release the drivebelt tension. Note how the drivebelt is routed, then remove the belt from the pulleys (see illustrations).

8 Fit the new drivebelt onto the crankshaft, alternator, power steering pump, and air conditioning compressor pulleys, as applicable, then turn the tensioner anti-clockwise and locate the drivebelt on the

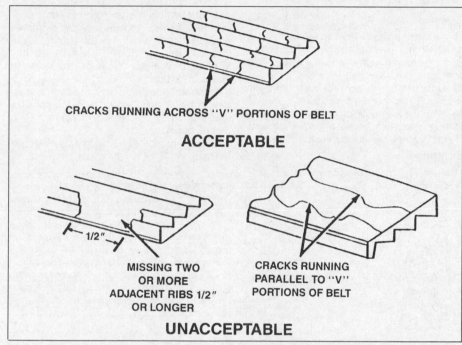

CRACKS RUNNING ACROSS "V" PORTIONS OF BELT

ACCEPTABLE

1/2"

MISSING TWO OR MORE ADJACENT RIBS 1/2" OR LONGER

CRACKS RUNNING PARALLEL TO "V" PORTIONS OF BELT

UNACCEPTABLE

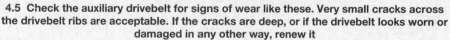

4.5 Check the auxiliary drivebelt for signs of wear like these. Very small cracks across the drivebelt ribs are acceptable. If the cracks are deep, or if the drivebelt looks worn or damaged in any other way, renew it

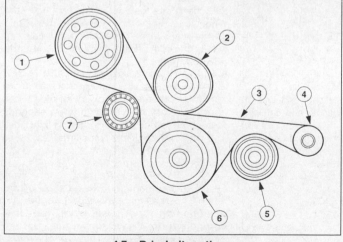

4.7a Drivebelt routing – models without air conditioning

1	Power steering pump	5	Idler pulley
2	Water pump	6	Crankshaft
3	Drivebelt	7	Belt tensioner
4	Alternator		

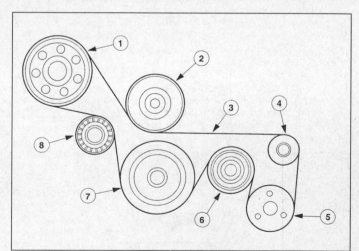

4.7b Drivebelt routing – models with air conditioning

1	Power steering pump	5	Air conditioning compressor
2	Water pump	6	Idler pulley
3	Drivebelt	7	Crankshaft
4	Alternator	8	Belt tensioner

pulley. Make sure that the drivebelt is correctly seated in all of the pulley grooves, then release the tensioner **(see illustration)**.
9 Refit the drivebelt lower cover and lower the car to the ground.

Drivebelt tensioner

Removal

10 The drivebelt tensioner is attached to the right-hand rear corner of the engine block (right as seen from the driver's seat). Remove the auxiliary drivebelt as described previously in this Section.
11 Lift the power steering fluid reservoir upwards, and unclip it from its mounting on the inner wing. Move the reservoir to one side, without disconnecting the fluid hoses, and keeping it as upright as possible.
12 Unscrew the three tensioner mounting nuts, and remove the tensioner from the engine.
13 Spin the tensioner pulley, checking it for signs of roughness. The tensioner should be capable of providing significant tension when tested – rotate the pulley to load the spring, and check for free movement. Also inspect the tensioner pulley for signs of cracking or other deterioration.
14 The tensioner is not a serviceable component – if it has failed, or is not keeping the belt at a satisfactory tension, a new unit must be fitted.

Refitting

15 Refitting is a reversal of removal.

Drivebelt idler pulley

Removal

16 The idler pulley is fitted at the front of the drivebelt 'run', next to the crankshaft pulley. Remove the auxiliary drivebelt as described previously in this Section.
17 Unscrew the pulley mounting bolt, and remove the pulley from the engine.
18 Spin the idler pulley, checking it for signs of roughness. Also inspect the pulley for signs of cracking or other deterioration.

Refitting

19 Refitting is a reversal of removal.

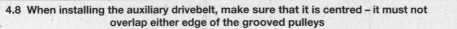

4.8 When installing the auxiliary drivebelt, make sure that it is centred – it must not overlap either edge of the grooved pulleys

5 Lights and horn operation check

1 With the ignition switched on, where necessary, check the operation of all exterior lights.
2 Check the brake lights with the help of an assistant, or by reversing up close to a reflective door. Make sure that all the rear lights are capable of operating independently, without affecting any of the other lights – for example, switch on as many rear lights as possible, then try the brake lights. If any unusual results are found, this is usually due to an earth fault or other poor connection at that rear light unit.
3 Again with the help of an assistant or using a reflective surface, check as far as possible that the headlights work on both main and dipped beam.
4 Replace any defective bulbs with reference to Chapter 12.

> **HAYNES HiNT**
>
> *Particularly on older vehicles, bulbs can stop working as a result of corrosion build-up on the bulb or its holder – fitting a new bulb may not cure the problem in this instance. When replacing any bulb, if you find any green or white-coloured powdery deposits, these should be cleaned off using emery cloth.*

5 Check the operation of all interior lights, including the glovebox and luggage area illumination lights. Switch on the ignition, and check that all relevant warning lights come on as expected – the vehicle handbook should give details of these. Now start the engine, and check that the appropriate lights go out. When you are next driving at night, check that all the instrument panel and facia lighting works correctly. If any problems are found, refer to Chapter 12.
6 Finally, choose an appropriate time of day to test the operation of the horn.

6 Underbonnet check for fluid leaks and hose condition

> ⚠ *Warning: Renewal of air conditioning hoses must be left to a dealer service department or air conditioning specialist who has the equipment to depressurise the system safely. Never remove air conditioning components or hoses until the system has been depressurised.*

1 Visually inspect the engine joint faces, gaskets and seals for any signs of water or oil leaks. Pay particular attention to the areas around the cylinder head cover, cylinder head,

oil filter and sump joint faces. Bear in mind that, over a period of time, some very slight seepage from these areas is to be expected – what you are really looking for is any indication of a serious leak. Should a leak be found, renew the offending gasket or oil seal by referring to the appropriate Chapters in this manual.

2 High temperatures in the engine compartment can cause the deterioration of the rubber and plastic hoses used for engine, accessory and emission systems operation. Periodic inspection should be made for cracks, loose clamps, material hardening and leaks.

3 When checking the hoses, ensure that all the cable-ties or clips used to retain the hoses are in place, and in good condition. Clips which are broken or missing can lead to chafing of the hoses, pipes or wiring, which could cause more serious problems in the future.

4 Carefully check the large top and bottom radiator hoses, along with the other smaller-diameter cooling system hoses and metal pipes; do not forget the heater hoses/pipes which run from the engine to the bulkhead. Inspect each hose along its entire length, replacing any that is cracked, swollen or shows signs of deterioration (see Haynes Hint). Cracks may become more apparent if the hose is squeezed, and may often be apparent at the hose ends.

5 Make sure that all hose connections are tight. If the large-diameter air hoses from the air cleaner are loose, they will leak air, and upset the engine idle quality. If the spring clamps that are used to secure many of the hoses appear to be slackening, they should be replaced with worm-drive clips to prevent the possibility of leaks.

6 Some other hoses are secured to their fittings with clamps. Where clamps are used, check to be sure they haven't lost their tension, allowing the hose to leak. If clamps aren't used, make sure the hose has not expanded and/or hardened where it slips over the fitting, allowing it to leak.

7 Check all fluid reservoirs, filler caps, drain plugs and fittings, etc, looking for any signs of leakage of oil, transmission and/or brake hydraulic fluid, coolant and power steering fluid. Also check the clutch hydraulic fluid lines which lead from the fluid reservoir and slave cylinder (on the transmission).

8 If the vehicle is regularly parked in the same place, close inspection of the ground underneath it will soon show any leaks; ignore the puddle of water which will be left if the air conditioning system is in use. Place a clean piece of cardboard below the engine, and examine it for signs of contamination after the vehicle has been parked over it overnight – be aware, however, of the fire risk inherent in placing combustible material below the catalytic converter.

9 Remember that some leaks will only occur with the engine running, or when the engine is hot or cold. With the handbrake firmly applied, start the engine from cold, and let the engine idle while you examine the underside of the engine compartment for signs of leakage.

10 If an unusual smell is noticed inside or around the car, especially when the engine is thoroughly hot, this may point to the presence of a leak.

11 As soon as a leak is detected, its source must be traced and rectified. Where oil has been leaking for some time, it is usually necessary to use a steam cleaner, pressure washer or similar, to clean away the accumulated dirt, so that the exact source of the leak can be identified.

Vacuum hoses

12 It's quite common for vacuum hoses, especially those in the emissions system, to be colour-coded, or to be identified by coloured stripes moulded into them. Various systems require hoses with different wall thicknesses, collapse resistance and temperature resistance. When renewing hoses, be sure the new ones are made of the same material.

13 Often the only effective way to check a hose is to remove it completely from the vehicle. If more than one hose is removed, be sure to label the hoses and fittings to ensure correct installation.

14 When checking vacuum hoses, be sure to include any plastic T-fittings in the check. Inspect the fittings for cracks, and check the hose where it fits over the fitting for distortion, which could cause leakage.

15 A small piece of vacuum hose (quarter-inch inside diameter) can be used as a stethoscope to detect vacuum leaks. Hold one end of the hose to your ear, and probe around vacuum hoses and fittings, listening for the 'hissing' sound characteristic of a vacuum leak.

⚠ **Warning: When probing with the vacuum hose stethoscope, be very careful not to come into contact with moving engine components such as the auxiliary drivebelt, radiator electric cooling fan, etc.**

Fuel hoses

⚠ **Warning: There are certain precautions which must be taken when inspecting or servicing fuel system components. Work in a well-ventilated area, and do not allow open flames (cigarettes, appliance pilot lights, etc) or bare light bulbs near the work area. Mop up any spills immediately, and do not store fuel-soaked rags where they could ignite.**

16 Check all fuel hoses for deterioration and chafing. Check especially for cracks in areas where the hose bends, and also just before fittings, such as where a hose attaches to the fuel filter.

17 It is not unusual for a high-mileage diesel engine to exhibit a 'film' of diesel fuel around

A leak in the cooling system will usually show up as white- or rust-coloured deposits on the areas adjoining the leak.

the injectors, resulting in an oily appearance. Unless there is clear evidence of a significant fuel leak, this is not normally a matter for concern. The best course of action would be to first clean the engine thoroughly; then, after several more miles have been covered, the source of the leak can be identified and its severity assessed.

18 High-quality fuel line, usually identified by the word 'Fluoroelastomer' printed on the hose, should be used for fuel line renewal. Never, under any circumstances, use unreinforced vacuum line, clear plastic tubing or water hose as a substitute for fuel lines.

19 Spring-type clamps are commonly used on fuel lines. These clamps often lose their tension over a period of time, and can be 'sprung' during removal. Replace all spring-type clamps with proper petrol pipe clips whenever a hose is replaced.

Metal lines

20 Sections of metal piping are often used for fuel line between the fuel filter and the engine. Check carefully to be sure the piping has not been bent or crimped, and that cracks have not started in the line.

21 If a section of metal fuel line must be renewed, only seamless steel piping should be used, since copper and aluminium piping don't have the strength necessary to withstand normal engine vibration.

22 Check the metal lines where they enter the brake master cylinder, ABS hydraulic unit or clutch master/slave cylinders (as applicable) for cracks in the lines or loose fittings. Any sign of brake fluid leakage calls for an immediate and thorough inspection.

7 Engine compartment wiring check

1 With the vehicle parked on level ground, apply the handbrake firmly and open the bonnet. Using an inspection light or a small electric torch, check all visible wiring within and beneath the engine compartment. Make

sure that the ignition is switched off – take out the key.

2 What you are looking for is wiring that is obviously damaged by chafing against sharp edges, or against moving suspension/transmission components and/or the auxiliary drivebelt, by being trapped or crushed between carelessly-refitted components, or melted by being forced into contact with the hot engine castings, coolant pipes, etc. In almost all cases, damage of this sort is caused in the first instance by incorrect routing on reassembly after previous work has been carried out.

3 Depending on the extent of the problem, damaged wiring may be repaired by rejoining the break or splicing-in a new length of wire, using solder to ensure a good connection, and remaking the insulation with adhesive insulating tape or heat-shrink tubing, as appropriate. If the damage is extensive, given the implications for the vehicle's future reliability, the best long-term answer may well be to renew that entire section of the loom, however expensive this may appear.

4 When the actual damage has been repaired, ensure that the wiring loom is re-routed correctly, so that it is clear of other components, and not stretched or kinked, and is secured out of harm's way using the plastic clips, guides and ties provided.

5 Check all electrical connectors, ensuring that they are clean, securely fastened, and that each is locked by its plastic tabs or wire clip, as appropriate. If any connector shows external signs of corrosion (accumulations of white or green deposits, or streaks of 'rust'), or if any is thought to be dirty, it must be unplugged and cleaned using electrical contact cleaner. If the connector pins are severely corroded, the connector must be renewed; note that this may mean the renewal of that entire section of the loom – see your local Ford dealer for details.

6 If the cleaner completely removes the corrosion to leave the connector in a satisfactory condition, it would be wise to pack the connector with a suitable material which will exclude dirt and moisture, preventing the corrosion from occurring again; a Ford dealer may be able to recommend a suitable product.

7 Check the condition of the battery connections – remake the connections or renew the leads if a fault is found (see Chapter 5A). Use the same techniques to ensure that all earth points in the engine compartment provide good electrical contact through clean, metal-to-metal joints, and that all are securely fastened.

8 Check the wiring to the glow plugs, referring to Chapter 4B if necessary. The wiring is in the form of a metal strip (or busbar), secured by a nut at each plug terminal. Also check the connection to the busbar, at No 4 glow plug (at the transmission end of the engine).

8 Air conditioning system check

⚠️ **Warning: The air conditioning system is under high pressure. Do not loosen any fittings or remove any components until after the system has been discharged. Air conditioning refrigerant must be properly discharged at a dealer service department or an automotive air conditioning repair facility capable of handling R134a refrigerant. Always wear eye protection when disconnecting air conditioning system fittings.**

1 The following maintenance checks should be performed on a regular basis, to ensure that the air conditioner continues to operate at peak efficiency:

a) Check the auxiliary drivebelt. If it's worn or deteriorated, renew it (see Section 4).

b) Check the system hoses. Look for cracks, bubbles, hard spots and deterioration. Inspect the hoses and all fittings for oil bubbles and seepage. If there's any evidence of wear, damage or leaks, renew the hose(s).

c) Inspect the condenser fins for leaves, insects and other debris. Use a 'fin comb' or compressed air to clean the condenser.

⚠️ **Warning: Wear eye protection when using compressed air.**

d) Check that the drain tube from the front of the evaporator is clear – note that it is normal to have clear fluid (water) dripping from this while the system is in operation, to the extent that quite a large puddle can be left under the vehicle when it is parked.

2 It's a good idea to operate the system for about 30 minutes at least once a month, particularly during the winter. Long-term non-use can cause hardening, and subsequent failure, of the seals.

3 Because of the complexity of the air conditioning system and the special equipment necessary to service it, in-depth fault diagnosis and repairs are not included in this manual.

4 The most common cause of poor cooling is simply a low system refrigerant charge. If a noticeable drop in cool air output occurs, the following quick check will help you determine if the refrigerant level is low.

5 Warm the engine up to normal operating temperature.

6 Place the air conditioning temperature selector at the coldest setting, and put the blower at the highest setting. Open the doors – to make sure the air conditioning system doesn't cycle off as soon as it cools the passenger compartment.

7 With the compressor engaged – the compressor clutch will make an audible click, and the centre of the clutch will rotate – feel

the inlet and outlet pipes at the compressor. One side should be cold, and one hot. If there's no perceptible difference between the two pipes, there's something wrong with the compressor or the system. It might be a low charge – it might be something else. Take the vehicle to a dealer service department or an automotive air conditioning specialist.

9 Braking system check

1 The work described in this Section should be carried out at the specified intervals, or whenever a defect is suspected in the braking system. Any of the following symptoms could indicate a potential brake system defect:

a) The vehicle pulls to one side when the brake pedal is depressed.

b) The brakes make squealing, scraping or dragging noises when applied.

c) Brake pedal travel is excessive, or pedal feel is poor.

d) The brake fluid requires repeated topping-up. Note that, because the hydraulic clutch shares the same fluid as the braking system (see Chapter 6), this problem could be due to a leak in the clutch system.

Front disc brakes

2 Apply the handbrake, then loosen the front wheel nuts. Jack up the front of the vehicle, and support it on axle stands.

3 For better access to the brake calipers, remove the wheels.

4 Look through the inspection window in the caliper, and check that the thickness of the friction lining material on each of the pads is not less than the recommended minimum thickness given in the Specifications.

> **HAYNES HiNT** *Bear in mind that the lining material is normally bonded to a metal backing plate. To differentiate between the metal and the lining material, it is helpful to turn the disc slowly at first – the edge of the disc can then be identified, with the lining material on each pad either side of it, and the backing plates behind.*

5 If it is difficult to determine the exact thickness of the pad linings, or if you are at all concerned about the condition of the pads, then remove them from the calipers for further inspection (refer to Chapter 9).

6 Check the other caliper in the same way.

7 If any one of the brake pads has worn down to, or below, the specified limit, *all four* pads at that end of the car must be renewed as a set. If the pads on one side are significantly more worn than the other, this may indicate that the caliper pistons have partially seized – refer to the brake pad renewal procedure in

Chapter 9, and push the pistons back into the caliper to free them.

8 Measure the thickness of the discs with a micrometer, if available, to make sure that they still have service life remaining. Do not be fooled by the lip of rust which often forms on the outer edge of the disc, which may make the disc appear thicker than it really is – scrape off the loose rust if necessary, without scoring the disc friction (shiny) surface.

9 If any disc is thinner than the specified minimum thickness, renew it (refer to Chapter 9).

10 Check the general condition of the discs. Look for excessive scoring and discolouration caused by overheating. If these conditions exist, remove the relevant disc and have it resurfaced or renewed (refer to Chapter 9).

11 Make sure that the handbrake is firmly applied, then check that the transmission is in neutral. Spin the wheel, and check that the brake is not binding. Some drag is normal with a disc brake, but it should not require any great effort to turn the wheel – also, do not confuse brake drag with resistance from the transmission.

12 Before refitting the wheels, check all brake lines and hoses (refer to Chapter 9). In particular, check the flexible hoses in the vicinity of the calipers, where they are subjected to most movement **(see illustration)**. Bend them between the fingers (but do not actually bend them double, or the casing may be damaged) and check that this does not reveal previously-hidden cracks, cuts or splits.

13 On completion, refit the wheels and lower the car to the ground. Tighten the wheel nuts to the specified torque.

Rear drum brakes

14 Loosen the rear wheel nuts, then chock the front wheels. Jack up the rear of the car, and support on axle stands. Release the handbrake and remove the rear wheels.

15 Spin the wheel to check that the brake is not binding. A small amount of resistance from the brake is acceptable, but no great effort should be required to turn the wheel hub. Abnormal effort may indicate that the handbrake needs adjusting – see Chapter 9.

16 To check the brake shoe lining thickness without removing the brake drums, prise the rubber plugs from the backplates, and use an electric torch to inspect the linings of the leading brake shoes. Check that the thickness of the lining material on the brake shoes is not less than the recommendation given in the Specifications.

17 If it is difficult to determine the exact thickness of the brake shoe linings, or if you are at all concerned about the condition of the shoes, then remove the rear drums for a more comprehensive inspection (refer to Chapter 9).

18 With the drum removed, check the shoe return and hold-down springs for correct installation, and check the wheel cylinders for leakage of brake fluid. Apart from fluid being

9.12 Check the flexible hoses at the brake calipers

visible, a leaking wheel cylinder may be characterised by an excessive build-up of brake dust (stuck to the fluid which has leaked) at the cylinder seals.

19 Check the friction surface of the brake drums for scoring and discoloration. If excessive, the drum should be resurfaced or renewed.

20 Before refitting the wheels, check all brake lines and hoses (refer to Chapter 9). On completion, apply the handbrake and check that the rear wheels are locked. The handbrake can be adjusted as described in Chapter 9.

21 On completion, refit the wheels and lower the car to the ground. Tighten the wheel nuts to the specified torque.

10 Exhaust system check

1 With the engine cold (at least three hours after the vehicle has been driven), check the complete exhaust system, from its starting point at the engine to the end of the tailpipe. Ideally, this should be done on a hoist, where unrestricted access is available; if a hoist is not available, raise and support the vehicle on axle stands.

2 Make sure that all brackets and rubber mountings are in good condition, and tight; if any of the mountings are to be renewed, ensure that the replacements are of the correct type – in the case of the rubber mountings, their colour is a good guide.

10.3 The area around a welded exhaust joint is a common place for leakage

Those nearest to the catalytic converter are more heat-resistant than the others.

3 Check the pipes and connections for evidence of leaks, severe corrosion, or damage. Leakage at any of the joints or in other parts of the system will usually show up as a black sooty stain in the vicinity of the leak **(see illustration)**. **Note:** *Exhaust sealants should not be used on any part of the exhaust system upstream of the catalytic converter (between the engine and the converter) – even if the sealant does not contain additives harmful to the converter, pieces of it may break off and foul the element, causing local overheating.*

4 At the same time, inspect the underside of the body for holes, corrosion, open seams, etc, which may allow exhaust gases to enter the passenger compartment. Seal all body openings with silicone or body putty.

5 Rattles and other noises can often be traced to the exhaust system, especially the rubber mountings. Try to move the system, silencer(s) and catalytic converter. If any components can touch the body or suspension parts, secure the exhaust system with new mountings.

11 Steering, suspension and roadwheel check

Front suspension and steering check

1 Apply the handbrake, then raise the front of the vehicle and support it on axle stands.

2 Visually inspect the balljoint dust covers and the steering gear gaiters for splits, chafing or deterioration **(see illustration)**. Any wear of these components will cause loss of lubricant, together with dirt and water entry, resulting in rapid deterioration of the balljoints or steering gear.

3 Check the power-assisted steering fluid hoses for chafing or deterioration, and the pipe and hose unions for fluid leaks. Also check for signs of fluid leakage under pressure from the steering gear rubber gaiters, which would indicate failed fluid seals within the steering gear.

11.2 Check the balljoint dust covers either side (arrowed)

11.4 Checking for wear in the front suspension and hub bearings

4 Grasp the roadwheel at the 12 o'clock and 6 o'clock positions, and try to rock it **(see illustration)**. Very slight free play may be felt, but if the movement is appreciable, further investigation is necessary to determine the source. Continue rocking the wheel while an assistant depresses the footbrake. If the movement is now eliminated or significantly reduced, it is likely that the hub bearings are at fault. If the free play is still evident with the footbrake depressed, then there is wear in the suspension joints or mountings.

5 Now grasp the wheel at the 9 o'clock and 3 o'clock positions, and try to rock it as before. Any movement felt now may again be caused by wear in the hub bearings or the steering track rod balljoints. If the outer track rod balljoint is worn, the visual movement will be obvious. If the inner joint is suspect, it can be felt by placing a hand over the rack-and-pinion rubber gaiter, and gripping the track rod. If the wheel is now rocked, movement will be felt at the inner joint if wear has taken place.

6 Using a large screwdriver or flat bar, check for wear in the suspension mounting and subframe bushes by levering between the relevant suspension component and its attachment point. Some movement is to be expected as the mountings are made of rubber, but excessive wear should be obvious. Also check the condition of any visible rubber bushes, looking for splits, cracks or contamination of the rubber.

7 With the vehicle standing on its wheels,

have an assistant turn the steering wheel back-and-forth, about an eighth of a turn each way. There should be very little, if any, lost movement between the steering wheel and roadwheels. If this is not the case, closely observe the joints and mountings previously described, but in addition, check the steering column joints for wear, and also check the rack-and-pinion steering gear itself.

Rear suspension check

8 Chock the front wheels, then raise the rear of the vehicle and support it on axle stands.
9 Check the rear hub bearings for wear, using the method described for the front hub bearings (paragraph 4).
10 Using a large screwdriver or flat bar, check for wear in the suspension mounting bushes by levering between the relevant suspension component and its attachment point. Some movement is to be expected as the mountings are made of rubber, but excessive wear should be obvious.

Roadwheel check and balancing

11 Periodically remove the roadwheels, and clean any dirt or mud from the inside and outside surfaces. Examine the wheel rims for signs of rusting, corrosion or other damage. Light alloy wheels are easily damaged by 'kerbing' whilst parking, and similarly, steel wheels may become dented or buckled. Renewal of the wheel is very often the only course of remedial action possible.
12 The balance of each wheel and tyre assembly should be maintained, not only to avoid excessive tyre wear, but also to avoid wear in the steering and suspension components. Wheel imbalance is normally signified by vibration through the vehicle's bodyshell, although in many cases it is particularly noticeable through the steering wheel. Conversely, it should be noted that wear or damage in suspension or steering components may cause excessive tyre wear. Out-of-round or out-of-true tyres, damaged wheels and wheel bearing wear/maladjustment also fall into this category. Balancing will not usually cure vibration caused by such wear.

13 Wheel balancing may be carried out with the wheel either on or off the vehicle. If balanced on the vehicle, ensure that the wheel-to-hub relationship is marked in some way prior to subsequent wheel removal, so that it may be refitted in its original position.

12 Driveshaft rubber gaiter and joint check

1 The driveshaft rubber gaiters are very important, because they prevent dirt, water and foreign material from entering and damaging the joints. External contamination can cause the gaiter material to deteriorate prematurely, so it's a good idea to wash the gaiters with soap and water occasionally.
2 With the vehicle raised and securely supported on axle stands, turn the steering onto full-lock, then slowly rotate each front wheel in turn. Inspect the condition of the outer constant velocity (CV) joint rubber gaiters, squeezing the gaiters to open out the folds. Check for signs of cracking, splits, or deterioration of the rubber, which may allow the escape of grease, and lead to the ingress of water and grit into the joint. Also check the security and condition of the retaining clips. Repeat these checks on the inner tripod joints **(see illustrations)**. If any damage or deterioration is found, the gaiters should be renewed as described in Chapter 8.
3 At the same time, check the general condition of the outer CV joints themselves, by first holding the driveshaft and attempting to rotate the wheels. Repeat this check on the inner joints, by holding the inner joint yoke and attempting to rotate the driveshaft.
4 Any appreciable movement in the joint indicates wear in the joint, wear in the driveshaft splines, or a loose driveshaft retaining nut.

13 Underbody and fuel/brake line check

1 With the vehicle raised and supported on axle stands or over an inspection pit, thoroughly inspect the underbody and wheelarches for signs of damage and corrosion. In particular, examine the bottom of the side sills, and any concealed areas where mud can collect.
2 Where corrosion and rust is evident, press and tap firmly on the panel with a screwdriver, and check for any serious corrosion which would necessitate repairs.
3 If the panel is not seriously corroded, clean away the rust, and apply a new coating of underseal. Refer to Chapter 11 for more details of body repairs.
4 At the same time, inspect the lower body panels for stone damage and general condition.

12.2a Check the outer constant velocity (CV) joint gaiters . . .

12.2b . . . and, though less prone to wear, check the inner joint gaiters also

5 Inspect all of the fuel and brake lines on the underbody for damage, rust, corrosion and leakage. Also make sure that they are correctly supported in their clips **(see illustration)**. Where applicable, check the PVC coating on the lines for damage.

14 Hinge and lock lubrication

1 Work around the vehicle and lubricate the hinges of the bonnet, doors and tailgate with a light machine oil.
2 Check carefully the security and operation of all hinges, latches and locks, adjusting them where required. Check the operation of the central locking system (if fitted).
3 Where applicable, check the condition and operation of the tailgate struts, renewing them if either is leaking or no longer able to support the tailgate securely when raised.

15 Roadwheel nut tightness check

1 Checking the tightness of the wheel nuts is more relevant than you might think. Apart from the obvious safety aspect of ensuring they are sufficiently tight, this check will reveal whether they have been over-tightened, as may have happened the last time new tyres were fitted, for example. If the car suffers a puncture, you may find that the wheel nuts cannot be loosened with the wheelbrace.
2 Apply the handbrake, chock the wheels, and engage 1st gear.
3 Remove the wheel cover (or wheel centre cover), using the flat end of the wheelbrace supplied in the tool kit.
4 Loosen the first wheel nut, using the wheelbrace if possible. If the nut proves stubborn, use a close-fitting socket and a long extension bar.

⚠️ *Warning: Do not use makeshift means to loosen the wheel nuts if the proper tools are not available. If extra force is required, make sure that the tools fit properly, and are of good quality. Even so, consider the consequences of the tool slipping or breaking, and take precautions – wearing stout gloves is advisable to protect your hands. Do not be tempted to stand on the tools used – they are not designed for this, and there is a high risk of personal injury if the tool slips or breaks. If the wheel nuts are simply too tight, take the car to a garage equipped with suitable power tools.*

5 Once the nut has been loosened, remove it and check that the wheel stud threads are clean. Use a small wire brush to clean any rust or dirt from the threads, if necessary.
6 Refit the nut, with the tapered side facing inwards. Tighten it fully, using the wheelbrace alone – no other tools. This will ensure that the wheel nuts can be loosened using the wheelbrace if a puncture occurs. However, if a torque wrench is available, tighten the nut to the specified torque wrench setting.
7 Repeat the procedure for the remaining three nuts, then refit the wheel cover or centre cover, as applicable.
8 Work around the car, checking and re-tightening the nuts for all four wheels.

16 Road test

Braking system

1 Make sure that the vehicle does not pull to one side when braking, and that the wheels do not lock prematurely when braking hard.
2 Check that there is no vibration through the steering when braking. On models equipped with ABS brakes, if vibration is felt through the pedal under heavy braking, this is a normal characteristic of the system operation, and is not a cause for concern.
3 Check that the handbrake operates correctly, without excessive movement of the lever, and that it holds the vehicle stationary on a slope, in both directions (facing up and down a slope).
4 With the engine switched off, test the operation of the brake servo unit as follows. Depress the footbrake four or five times to exhaust the vacuum, then start the engine. As the engine starts, there should be a noticeable 'give' in the brake pedal as vacuum builds up. Allow the engine to run for at least two minutes, and then switch it off. If the brake pedal is now depressed again, it should be possible to detect a hiss from the servo as the pedal is depressed. After about four or five applications, no further hissing should be heard, and the pedal should feel considerably harder.

Steering and suspension

5 Check for any abnormalities in the steering, suspension, handling or road 'feel'.
6 Drive the vehicle, and check that there are no unusual vibrations or noises.
7 Check that the steering feels positive, with no excessive sloppiness or roughness, and check for any suspension noises when cornering and driving over bumps.

13.5 Check the pipes attached to the underbody for damage

Drivetrain

8 Check the performance of the engine, transmission and driveshafts.
9 Check that the engine starts correctly, both when cold and when hot. Observe the glow plug warning light, and check that it comes on and goes off correctly.
10 Listen for any unusual noises from the engine and transmission.
11 Make sure that the engine runs smoothly when idling, and that there is no hesitation when accelerating.
12 Check that all gears can be engaged smoothly without noise, and that the gear lever action is smooth and not abnormally vague or 'notchy'.
13 Listen for a metallic clicking sound from the front of the vehicle as the vehicle is driven slowly in a circle with the steering on full-lock. Carry out this check in both directions. If a clicking noise is heard, this indicates wear in a driveshaft joint, in which case renew the joint if necessary.

Clutch

14 Check that the clutch pedal moves smoothly and easily through its full travel, and that the clutch itself functions correctly, with no trace of slip or drag.
15 If the clutch is slow to release, it is possible that the system requires bleeding (see Chapter 6). Also check the fluid pipes under the bonnet for signs of leakage.
16 Check the clutch as described in Chapter 6, Section 2.

Instruments and electrical equipment

17 Check the operation of all instruments and electrical equipment.
18 Make sure that all instruments read correctly, and switch on all electrical equipment in turn, to check that it functions properly.

17.2 Lift the power steering reservoir to one side

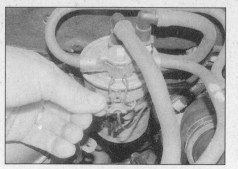

17.4 Remove the control valve retaining clip from the top of the filter

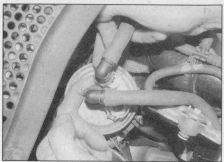

17.5a Release the fuel pipe securing clips . . .

Every 20 000 miles

17 Fuel filter renewal

1 The fuel filter is located at the rear of the engine compartment, behind the power steering fluid reservoir on the right-hand side (right as seen from the driver's seat).
2 To improve access to the filter, lift the power steering fluid reservoir upwards and unclip it from its mounting on the inner wing. Move the reservoir to one side, without disconnecting the fluid hoses, and keeping it as upright as possible **(see illustration)**.
3 Note the positions of the fuel pipes on top of the filter carefully, so that they can be refitted correctly. The filter supply pipe and the outlet pipe (to the injection pump) have a white band, while the return pipe has a red band. Have some clean rags ready, to soak up any fuel spillage.
4 Pull out the spring clip retaining the return pipes and control valve to the top of the filter, and lift the assembly off without disconnecting the pipes **(see illustration)**.
5 Squeeze together the lugs on the quick-release pipe fittings, and disconnect the fuel supply and filter outlet pipes from the top of the filter – be prepared for some fuel spillage **(see illustrations)**. It is most important not to introduce any dirt into the fuel pipes while they are disconnected, and as little fuel as possible should be lost from the pipes, to make starting the engine easier on completion. If the pipes are to be left disconnected for long, they should be capped or plugged.
6 To remove the filter, loosen the clamp screw, and remove the filter from its holder, noting the alignment arrows on the holder and filter **(see illustration)**.
7 Refitting is a reversal of removal, noting the following points:
  a) Line up the arrows on the filter and its holder **(see illustrations)**.
  b) Tighten the filter clamp screw securely, but without crushing the filter body.
  c) Before fitting the pipes, the filter should be filled with clean fuel – use a small, clean funnel **(see illustration)**, and have plenty of clean rags available, to soak up any spillage.
  d) Make sure that the pipe connections are correctly and securely remade.
  e) Start the engine, noting that it may be necessary to crank the engine for longer than normal. With the engine running, check for fuel leaks from the disturbed pipes.

18 Pollen filter renewal

1 Pull the windscreen wiper arms away from the windscreen until they lock in their vertical position, then open the bonnet.

17.5b . . . and disconnect the fuel pipes

17.6 Lift out the filter from its holder

17.7a Line up the arrow on the holder with the mark on the new filter (arrowed)

17.7b Diagrams on the side of the filter to show the procedure for fitting

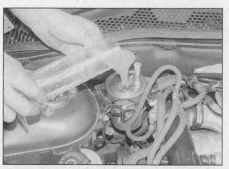

17.7c Fill the new filter with clean fuel, approx 0.25 litre

2 The pollen filter housing is located at the left-hand corner of the grille panel at the rear of the engine compartment (left as seen from the driver's seat). On left-hand-drive models, the housing is on the right-hand side of the grille panel.

3 On early models (up to 1999) prise out the covers and remove the three retaining screws. On later models only one screw is used.

4 Using a small screwdriver, release the three retaining catches at the front of the access panel. Access to the centre catch can be improved by opening the fusebox lid.

5 Lift out the filter access panel.

6 Release the clip at either side, and lift up the pollen filter. Pull the filter element from the housing, and discard it.

7 Fit the new filter using a reversal of the removal procedure, noting the following points:

a) Make sure that the filter is fitted with the TOP/OBEN arrow marking facing upwards.

b) Clean the rubber seals on the filter access cover; renew if damaged or distorted.

c) Ensure that the filter access cover is properly seated, otherwise the cover seals will leak, allowing water into the car interior.

Every 30 000 miles

19 Air filter element renewal

Caution: Never drive the vehicle with the air cleaner filter element removed. Excessive engine wear could result, and backfiring could even cause a fire under the bonnet.

1 The air filter element is located in the air cleaner assembly on the left-hand side of the engine compartment.

2 Remove the four screws securing the cover to the air cleaner housing.

3 The cover can now be lifted, and the filter element removed. If preferred, the cover can be removed completely – this will allow a more thorough cleaning of the filter housing.

4 Loosen the clip and disconnect the air inlet duct from the air cleaner.

5 Disconnect the wiring from the inlet air temperature sensor.

6 Withdraw the cover and remove the filter element, noting its direction of fitting.

7 If carrying out a routine service, the element must be renewed regardless of its apparent condition.

8 If you are checking the element for any other reason, inspect its lower surface; if it is oily or very dirty, renew the element. If it is only moderately dusty, it can be re-used by blowing it clean from the upper to the lower surface with compressed air. Because it is a pleated-paper type filter, it cannot be washed or re-oiled. If it cannot be cleaned satisfactorily with compressed air, discard and renew it.

⚠️ **Warning: Wear eye protection when using compressed air.**

9 Where the air cleaner cover was removed, wipe out the inside of the housing. Check that no foreign matter is visible, either in the air intake or in the air mass meter.

10 Refitting is the reverse of the removal procedure, noting the following points:

a) Make sure that the filter is fitted the correct way up (observe any direction-of-fitting markings).

b) Ensure that the element and cover are securely seated, so that unfiltered air cannot enter the engine.

c) Where removed, secure the cover with the screws, and ensure that the air inlet duct securing clip is fully tightened.

20 Positive Crankcase Ventilation (PCV) system check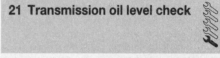

1 The Positive Crankcase Ventilation (PCV) valve is located in the camshaft cover, with an oil separator fitted to the left-hand end of the engine (refer to Chapter 4C, Section 3, for further information).

2 Check that all components of the system are securely fastened, correctly routed (with no kinks or sharp bends to restrict flow) and in sound condition; renew any worn or damaged components.

3 The PCV valve is designed to allow gases to flow out of the crankcase only, so that a depression is created in the crankcase under most operating conditions, particularly at idle. Therefore, if either the oil separator or the PCV valve are thought to be blocked, they must be renewed (see Chapter 4C). In such a case, however, there is nothing to be lost by attempting to flush out the blockage using a suitable solvent. The PCV valve should rattle when shaken.

4 If oil leakage is noted, disconnect the various hoses and pipes, and check that all are clear and unblocked.

5 On completion, ensure that all connections which were disturbed are securely re-made, so that there are no air (or oil) leaks.

21.3 Filler/level plug on the front of the manual gearbox

21 Transmission oil level check

1 The transmission does not have a dipstick. To check the oil level, raise the vehicle and support it securely on axle stands, making sure that the vehicle is level.

2 Remove the engine undershields as necessary for access to the front of the transmission.

3 On the lower front side of the transmission housing, you will see the filler/level plug. Using a suitable Allen key or socket, unscrew and remove it – take care, as it will probably be very tight **(see illustration)**.

4 If the lubricant level is correct, the oil should be up to the lower edge of the hole.

5 If the transmission needs more lubricant (if the level is not up to the hole), use a syringe, or a plastic bottle and tube, to add more.

6 Stop filling the transmission when the oil begins to run out of the hole, then wait until the flow of oil ceases – do not refit the plug immediately, or the transmission may end up being overfilled.

7 Refit the filler/level plug, and tighten it to the specified torque wrench setting. Drive the vehicle a short distance, then check for leaks.

8 A need for regular topping-up can only be due to a leak, which should be found and rectified without delay.

22 Valve clearance check and adjustment

The procedure is described in Chapter 2C.

Every 3 years, regardless of mileage

23 Brake fluid renewal

Warning: Brake hydraulic fluid can harm your eyes and damage painted surfaces, so use extreme caution when handling and pouring it. Do not use fluid that has been standing open for some time, as it absorbs moisture from the air. Excess moisture can cause a dangerous loss of braking effectiveness. Brake fluid is also highly flammable – treat it with the same respect as petrol.

1 The procedure is similar to that for the bleeding of the hydraulic system as described in Chapter 9 except that, on models with a conventional braking system, the brake fluid reservoir should be emptied by syphoning, using a clean poultry baster or similar before starting, and allowance should be made for the old fluid to be expelled when bleeding a section of the circuit.

2 On models fitted with ABS, reduce the fluid level in the reservoir (by syphoning or using a poultry baster), but do not allow the fluid level to drop far enough to allow air into the system – if air enters the ABS hydraulic unit, the unit must be bled using special Ford test equipment (see Chapter 9).

Warning: Do not syphon the fluid by mouth; it is poisonous.

3 Working as described in Chapter 9, open the first bleed screw in the sequence, and pump the brake pedal gently until nearly all the old fluid has been emptied from the master cylinder reservoir. Top-up to the MAX level with new fluid, and continue pumping until only the new fluid remains in the reservoir, and new fluid can be seen emerging from the bleed screw. Tighten the screw, and top the reservoir level up to the MAX level line.

 HAYNES HINT *Old hydraulic fluid is invariably much darker in colour than the new, making it easy to distinguish the two.*

4 Work through all the remaining bleed screws in the sequence until new fluid can be seen at all of them. Be careful to keep the master cylinder reservoir topped-up to above the MIN level at all times, or air may enter the system and greatly increase the length of the task.

5 When the operation is complete, check that all bleed screws are securely tightened, and that their dust caps are refitted. Wash off all traces of spilt fluid, and recheck the master cylinder reservoir fluid level.

6 Check the operation of the brakes before taking the car on the road.

7 Finally, check the operation of the clutch. Since the clutch shares the same fluid reservoir as the braking system, it may also be necessary to bleed the clutch as described in Chapter 6.

24 Coolant renewal and expansion tank cap check

Note: *If the antifreeze used is Ford's own, or of similar quality, Ford state that the coolant need not be renewed for 6 years (blue/green coolant) or for 10 years (orange coolant). If the vehicle's history is unknown, if antifreeze of lesser quality is known to be in the system, or simply if you prefer to follow conventional servicing intervals, the coolant should be changed periodically (typically, every 3 years) as described here.*

Warning: Do not allow antifreeze to come in contact with your skin or painted surfaces of the vehicle. Flush contaminated areas immediately with plenty of water. Don't store new coolant, or leave old coolant lying around, where it's accessible to children or pets – they're attracted by its sweet smell. Ingestion of even a small amount of coolant can be fatal. Wipe up garage-floor and drip-pan spills immediately. Keep antifreeze containers covered, and repair cooling system leaks as soon as they're noticed.

24.3 Radiator drain plug (arrowed)

Warning: Never remove the expansion tank filler cap when the engine is running, or has just been switched off, as the cooling system will be hot, and the consequent escaping steam and scalding coolant could cause serious injury.

Coolant draining

Warning: Wait until the engine is cold before starting this procedure.

1 To drain the system, first remove the expansion tank filler cap.

2 If the additional working clearance is required, raise the front of the vehicle and support it securely on axle stands. Unscrew a total of nine fasteners, and remove the large plastic undershield from below the engine.

3 Place a large drain tray underneath, and unscrew the radiator drain plug; direct as much of the escaping coolant as possible into the tray **(see illustration)**.

System flushing

4 With time, the cooling system may gradually lose its efficiency, as the radiator core becomes choked with rust, scale deposits from the water, and other sediment. To minimise this, as well as using only good-quality antifreeze and clean soft water, the system should be flushed as follows whenever any part of it is disturbed, and/or when the coolant is renewed.

5 With the coolant drained, refit the drain plug and refill the system with fresh water. Refit the expansion tank filler cap, start the engine and warm it up to normal operating temperature, then stop it and (after allowing it to cool down completely) drain the system again. Repeat as necessary until only clean water can be seen to emerge, then refill finally with the specified coolant mixture.

6 If only clean, soft water and good-quality antifreeze (even if not to Ford's specification) has been used, and the coolant has been renewed at the suggested intervals, the above procedure will be sufficient to keep clean the system for a considerable length of time. If, however, the system has been neglected, a more thorough operation will be required, as follows.

7 First drain the coolant, then disconnect the radiator top and bottom hoses **(see illustration)**. Insert a garden hose into the radiator top hose connection, and allow water to circulate through the radiator until it runs clean from the bottom outlet.

8 To flush the engine, insert the garden hose into the radiator bottom hose, wrap a piece of rag around the garden hose to seal the connection, and allow water to circulate until it runs clear.

9 Try the effect of repeating this procedure in the top hose, although this may not be effective, since the thermostat will probably close and prevent the flow of water.

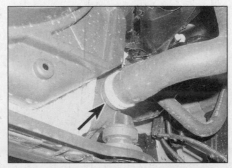
24.7 Radiator bottom hose connection (arrowed)

10 In severe cases of contamination, reverse-flushing of the radiator may be necessary. This may be achieved by inserting the garden hose into the bottom outlet, wrapping a piece of rag around the hose to seal the connection, then flushing the radiator until clear water emerges from the top hose outlet.

11 If the radiator is suspected of being severely choked, remove the radiator (Chapter 3), turn it upside-down, and repeat the procedure described in paragraph 10.

12 Flushing the heater matrix can be achieved using a similar procedure to that described in paragraph 10, once the heater inlet and outlet hoses have been identified. These two hoses will be of the same diameter, and pass through the engine compartment bulkhead (refer to the heater matrix removal procedure in Chapter 3, Section 9, for more details).

13 The use of chemical cleaners is not recommended, and should be necessary only as a last resort; the scouring action of some chemical cleaners may lead to other cooling system problems. Normally, regular renewal of the coolant will prevent excessive contamination of the system.

Coolant filling

14 With the cooling system drained and flushed, ensure that all disturbed hose unions are correctly secured, and that the radiator drain plug is securely tightened. Refit the radiator undershield, noting that it is located by three clips at its front edge; tighten the retaining screws securely. If it was raised, lower the vehicle to the ground.

15 Prepare a sufficient quantity of the specified coolant mixture (see below); allow for a surplus, so as to have a reserve supply for topping-up.

16 Slowly fill the system through the expansion tank. Since the tank is the highest point in the system, all the air in the system should be displaced into the tank by the rising liquid. Slow pouring reduces the possibility of air being trapped and forming air-locks.

17 Continue filling until the coolant level reaches the expansion tank MAX level line, then cover the filler opening to prevent coolant splashing out.

18 Start the engine and run it at idle speed, until it has warmed-up to normal operating temperature and the radiator electric cooling fan has cut in; watch the temperature gauge to check for signs of overheating. If the level in the expansion tank drops significantly, top-up to the MAX level line, to minimise the amount of air circulating in the system.

19 Stop the engine, wash off any spilt coolant from the engine compartment and bodywork, then leave the car to cool down *completely* (overnight, if possible).

20 With the system cool, uncover the expansion tank filler opening, and top-up the tank to the MAX level line. Refit the filler cap, tightening it securely, and clean up any further spillage.

21 After refilling, always check carefully all components of the system (but especially any unions disturbed during draining and flushing) for signs of coolant leaks. Fresh antifreeze has a searching action, which will rapidly expose any weak points in the system.

Antifreeze type and mixture

Note: *Do not use engine antifreeze in the windscreen/tailgate washer system, as it will damage the vehicle's paintwork. A screenwash additive should be added to the washer system in its maker's recommended quantities.*

22 When new, the cooling system in the Focus will have been filled with Super Plus 4 antifreeze (which is blue/green), to specification ESD-M97B-49-A. More recently, the system will have Super Plus 2000 antifreeze (which is orange) to specification WSS-M97 B44-D. The two types of coolant must not be mixed with each other, and should also not be mixed with any other type of coolant.

23 If the vehicle's history (and therefore the quality of the antifreeze in it) is unknown, owners are advised to drain and thoroughly reverse-flush the system, before refilling with fresh coolant mixture. If the Ford antifreeze is used, the coolant can then be left for 6 years (Super Plus 4, blue/green coolant type) or 10 years (Super Plus 2000, orange coolant type).

24 If any antifreeze other than Ford's is to be used, the coolant must be renewed at regular intervals to provide an equivalent degree of protection; the conventional recommendation is to renew the coolant every three years.

25 If the antifreeze used is to Ford's specification, the levels of protection it affords are indicated in the Specifications Section of this Chapter. To give the recommended *standard* mixture ratio for antifreeze, 50% (by volume) of antifreeze must be mixed with 50% of clean, soft water; if you are using any other type of antifreeze, follow its manufacturer's instructions to achieve the correct ratio.

26 You are unlikely to fully drain the system at any one time (unless the engine is being completely stripped), and the capacities quoted in Specifications are therefore slightly academic for routine coolant renewal. As a guide, only two-thirds of the system's total capacity is likely to be needed for coolant renewal.

27 As the drained system will be partially filled with flushing water, in order to establish the recommended mixture ratio, measure out 50% of the system capacity in antifreeze and pour it into the hose/expansion tank as described above, then top-up with water. Any topping-up while refilling the system should be done with water - for *Weekly checks* use a suitable mixture.

28 Before adding antifreeze, the cooling system should be completely drained, preferably flushed, and all hoses checked for condition and security. As noted earlier, fresh antifreeze will rapidly find any weaknesses in the system.

29 After filling with antifreeze, a label should be attached to the expansion tank, stating the type and concentration of antifreeze used, and the date installed. Any subsequent topping-up should be made with the same type and concentration of antifreeze.

General cooling system checks

30 The engine should be cold for the cooling system checks, so perform the following procedure before driving the vehicle, or after it has been shut off for at least three hours.

31 Remove the expansion tank filler cap, and clean it thoroughly inside and out with a rag. Also clean the filler neck on the expansion tank. The presence of rust or corrosion in the filler neck indicates that the coolant should be changed. The coolant inside the expansion tank should be relatively clean and transparent. If it is rust-coloured, drain and flush the system, and refill with a fresh coolant mixture.

32 Carefully check the radiator hoses and heater hoses along their entire length; renew any hose which is cracked, swollen or deteriorated (see Section 6).

33 Inspect all other cooling system components (joint faces, etc) for leaks. A leak in the cooling system will usually show up as white- or rust-coloured deposits on the area adjoining the leak. Where any problems of this nature are found on system components, renew the component or gasket with reference to Chapter 3.

34 Clean the front of the radiator with a soft brush to remove all insects, leaves, etc, embedded in the radiator fins. Be careful not to damage the radiator fins, or cut your fingers on them. To do a more thorough job, remove the radiator grille as described in Chapter 11.

Airlocks

35 If, after draining and refilling the system, symptoms of overheating are found which did not occur previously, then the fault is almost certainly due to trapped air at some point in the system, causing an airlock and restricting the flow of coolant; usually, the air is trapped because the system was refilled too quickly.

36 If an airlock is suspected, first try gently squeezing all visible coolant hoses. A coolant hose which is full of air feels quite different to one full of coolant, when squeezed. After refilling the system, most airlocks will clear once the system has cooled, and been topped-up.

37 While the engine is running at operating temperature, switch on the heater and heater fan, and check for heat output. Provided there is sufficient coolant in the system, lack of heat output could be due to an airlock in the system.

38 Airlocks can have more serious effects than simply reducing heater output – a severe airlock could reduce coolant flow around the engine. Check that the radiator top hose is hot when the engine is at operating temperature – a top hose which stays cold could be the result of an airlock (or a non-opening thermostat).

39 If the problem persists, stop the engine and allow it to cool down **completely**, before unscrewing the expansion tank filler cap or loosening the hose clips and squeezing the hoses to bleed out the trapped air. In the worst case, the system will have to be at least partially drained (this time, the coolant can be saved for re-use) and flushed to clear the problem.

Expansion tank pressure cap check

40 Wait until the engine is completely cold – perform this check before the engine is started for the first time in the day.

41 Place a wad of cloth over the expansion tank cap, then unscrew it slowly and remove it

42 Examine the condition of the rubber seal on the underside of the cap. If the rubber

appears to have hardened, or cracks are visible in the seal edges, a new cap should be fitted.

43 If the car is several years old, or has covered a large mileage, consider renewing the cap regardless of its apparent condition – they are not expensive. If the pressure relief valve built into the cap fails, excess pressure in the system will lead to puzzling failures of hoses and other cooling system components.

Every 40 000 miles

25 Timing belt renewal

The procedure is described in Chapter 2C.

Chapter 2 Part A:
1.4 & 1.6 litre engine in-car repair procedures

Contents

Degrees of difficulty

Easy, suitable for novice with little experience	Fairly easy, suitable for beginner with some experience	Fairly difficult, suitable for competent DIY mechanic	Difficult, suitable for experienced DIY mechanic	Very difficult, suitable for expert DIY or professional

Specifications

General

Engine type	Four-cylinder, in-line, double overhead camshafts, aluminium alloy cylinder head and engine block
Designation	Zetec-SE

Engine code:
1.4 litre	FXDA (or FXDC – German market)
1.6 litre	FYDA or FYDG (or FYDC – German market)

Capacity:
1.4 litre	1388 cc
1.6 litre	1596 cc

Bore:
1.4 litre	76.0 mm
1.6 litre	79.0 mm

Stroke:
1.4 litre	76.5 mm
1.6 litre	81.4 mm
Compression ratio	11.0:1
Firing order	1-3-4-2 (No 1 cylinder at timing belt end)
Direction of crankshaft rotation	Clockwise (seen from right-hand side of vehicle)

Valves

Valve clearances (cold):	Inlet	Exhaust
Checking:		
1.4 litre	0.17 to 0.23 mm	0.27 to 0.33 mm
1.6 litre	0.17 to 0.23 mm	0.31 to 0.37 mm
Setting:		
1.4 litre	0.20 mm	0.30 mm
1.6 litre	0.20 mm	0.34 mm

Cylinder head
Maximum permissible gasket surface distortion . . . . 0.05 mm

Camshafts
Camshaft bearing journal diameter . . . . Unavailable at time of writing
Camshaft bearing journal-to-cylinder head running clearance . . . . Unavailable at time of writing
Camshaft endfloat (typical) . . . . 0.05 to 0.13 mm

Lubrication
Engine oil type/specification . . . . See *Lubricants and fluids*
Engine oil capacity . . . . See Chapter 1A
Oil pressure (warm engine):
   Idling (800 rpm) . . . . 1.0 bar
   At 2000 rpm . . . . 2.5 bars
Pressure relief valve opens at . . . . 4.0 bars
Oil pump clearances . . . . Not specified

Torque wrench settings

	Nm	lbf ft
Air conditioning compressor mountings	25	18
Alternator mounting bracket to engine	48	35
Auxiliary drivebelt idler pulley	25	18
Big-end bearing cap:		
Stage 1	8	6
Stage 2	Angle-tighten a further 90°	
Camshaft bearing cap:		
Stage 1	7	5
Stage 2	16	12
Camshaft sprocket bolt	60	44
Coolant outlet to cylinder head	20	15
Coolant pump mounting bolts	9	7
Coolant pump pulley bolt	25	18
Crankshaft pulley/vibration damper:		
Stage 1	40	30
Stage 2	Angle-tighten a further 90°	
Crankshaft oil seal housing (flywheel/driveplate end)	9	7
Cylinder head:		
Stage 1	15	11
Stage 2	30	22
Stage 3	Angle-tighten a further 90°	
Cylinder head cover	10	7
Engine mountings:		
Left-hand mounting (transmission):		
Lower section	80	59
Upper section:		
Centre nut	133	98
Four outer nuts	48	35
Rear mounting to subframe (roll restrictor)	48	35
Right-hand mounting lower bracket	55	41
Right-hand mounting upper section:		
To body	48	35
To engine	80	59
Exhaust manifold to cylinder head	53	39
Flywheel/driveplate:		
Stage 1	30	22
Stage 2	Angle-tighten a further 80°	
Oil baffle to cylinder block	9	7
Oil drain plug	37	27
Oil pressure switch	15	11
Oil pump to cylinder block	9	7
Power steering pump to engine	25	18
Roadwheel nuts	85	63
Sump:		
To engine (see text)	20	15
To transmission	44	32
Thermostat housing to cylinder block	9	7
Timing belt covers	9	7
Timing belt tensioner	20	15

1 General information

How to use this Chapter

This Part of Chapter 2 is devoted to in-car repair procedures on the 1.4 and 1.6 litre Zetec-SE petrol engine. All procedures concerning engine removal and refitting, and engine block/cylinder head overhaul can be found in Chapter 2D.

Refer to *Vehicle identification numbers* in the Reference Section at the end of this manual for details of engine code locations.

Most of the operations included in this Chapter are based on the assumption that the engine is still installed in the car. Therefore, if this information is being used during a complete engine overhaul, with the engine already removed, many of the steps included here will not apply.

Engine description

The Zetec-SE engine is of sixteen-valve, double overhead camshaft (DOHC), four-cylinder, in-line type, mounted transversely at the front of the vehicle, with the transmission on its left-hand end. It is available in the Focus in 1.4 and 1.6 litre versions.

Apart from the plastic timing belt covers and inlet manifold, and the cast-iron cylinder liners, the engine (including the sump) is manufactured entirely of aluminium alloy.

Caution: When tightening bolts into aluminium castings, it is important to adhere to the specified torque wrench settings to avoid stripping threads and the resultant time-consuming consequences.

The crankshaft runs in five main bearings, the centre main bearing's upper half incorporating thrustwashers to control crankshaft endfloat. Due to the very fine bearing clearances and bearing shell tolerances incorporated during manufacture, it is not possible to renew the crankshaft separately to the cylinder block; in fact it is not possible to remove and refit the crankshaft accurately using conventional tooling. This means that if the crankshaft is worn excessively, it must be renewed together with the cylinder block.

Caution: Do not unbolt the main bearing cap/ladder from the cylinder block, as it is not possible to refit it accurately using conventional tooling. Additionally, the manufacturers do not supply torque settings for the main bearing cap/ladder retaining bolts.

The connecting rods rotate on horizontally-split bearing shells at their big-ends, however the big-ends are of unusual design in that the caps are sheared from the rods during manufacture, thus making each cap individually matched to its own connecting rod. The big-end bearing shells are also unusual in that they do not have any locating tabs, and they must be accurately positioned during refitting. The pistons are attached to the connecting rods by gudgeon pins which are an interference fit in the connecting rod small-end eyes. The aluminium alloy pistons are fitted with three piston rings: two compression rings and an oil control ring. After manufacture, the cylinder bores and pistons are measured and classified into three grades, which must be carefully matched together to ensure the correct piston/cylinder clearance; no oversizes are available to permit reboring.

The inlet and exhaust valves are each closed by coil springs; they operate in guides which are shrink-fitted into the cylinder head, as are the valve seat inserts.

Both camshafts are driven by the same toothed timing belt, each operating eight valves via cam followers and shims. Each camshaft rotates in five bearings that are line-bored directly in the cylinder head and the (bolted-on) bearing caps; this means that the bearing caps are not available separately from the cylinder head, and must not be interchanged with caps from another engine.

The water pump is bolted to the right-hand end of the cylinder block, beneath the front run of the timing belt, and is driven by the auxiliary drivebelt from the crankshaft pulley.

Lubrication is by means of an eccentric-rotor trochoidal pump, which is mounted on the crankshaft right-hand end, and draws oil through a strainer located in the sump. The pump forces oil through an externally-mounted full-flow cartridge-type filter.

Repair operations possible with the engine in the car

The following work can be carried out with the engine in the car:

a) Cylinder head cover – removal and refitting.
b) Timing belt – renewal.
c) Timing belt tensioner and sprockets – removal and refitting.
d) Camshaft oil seals – renewal.
e) Camshafts, cam followers and shims – removal and refitting.
f) Cylinder head – removal and refitting.
g) Sump – removal and refitting.
h) Crankshaft oil seals – renewal.
i) Oil pump – removal and refitting.
j) Flywheel/driveplate – removal and refitting.
k) Engine/transmission mountings – removal and refitting.

Note: *It is possible to remove the pistons and connecting rods (after removing the cylinder head and sump) without removing the engine. However, this is not recommended; work of this nature is more easily and thoroughly completed with the engine on the bench, as described in Chapter 2D.*

Clean the engine compartment and the exterior of the engine with some type of degreaser before any work is done (and/or clean the engine using a steam cleaner). It will make the job easier and will help to keep dirt out of the internal areas of the engine.

Depending on the components involved, it may be helpful to remove the bonnet, to improve access to the engine as repairs are performed (refer to Chapter 11 if necessary). Cover the wings to prevent damage to the paint; special covers are available, but an old bedspread or blanket will also work.

2 Compression test – description and interpretation

1 When engine performance is down, or if misfiring occurs which cannot be attributed to the ignition or fuel systems, a compression test can provide diagnostic clues as to the engine's condition. If the test is performed regularly, it can give warning of trouble before any other symptoms become apparent.

2 The engine must be fully warmed-up to operating temperature, the oil level must be correct and the battery must be fully charged. The help of an assistant will also be required.

3 Referring to Chapter 12, identify and remove the fuel pump fuse from the engine compartment fusebox. Now start the engine and allow it to run until it stalls. If the engine will not start, at least keep it cranking for about 10 seconds.

4 Unscrew and remove the oil filler cap, then unbolt the plastic cover for access to the spark plugs. Refit the oil filler cap.

5 Disable the ignition system by disconnecting the multi-plug from the DIS ignition coil. Remove all the spark plugs with reference to Chapter 1A.

6 Fit a compression tester to the No 1 cylinder spark plug hole – the type of tester which screws into the spark plug thread is to be preferred.

7 Arrange for an assistant to hold the accelerator pedal fully depressed to the floor, while at the same time cranking the engine over for several seconds on the starter motor. Observe the compression gauge reading.

8 The compression will build up fairly quickly in a healthy engine. Low compression on the first stroke, followed by gradually-increasing pressure on successive strokes, indicates worn piston rings. A low compression on the first stroke which does not rise on successive strokes, indicates leaking valves or a blown head gasket (a cracked cylinder head could also be the cause). Deposits on the underside of the valve heads can also cause low compression. Record the highest gauge reading obtained, then repeat the procedure for the remaining cylinders.

9 Due to the variety of testers available, and the fluctuation in starter motor speed when cranking the engine, different readings are often obtained when carrying out the compression test. For this reason, actual compression pressure figures are not quoted by Ford. However, the most important factor is that the compression pressures are uniform in all cylinders, and that is what this test is mainly concerned with.

10 Add some engine oil (about three squirts from a plunger type oil can) to each cylinder through the spark plug holes, and then repeat the test.

11 If the compression increases after the oil is added, the piston rings are probably worn. If the compression does not increase significantly, the leakage is occurring at the valves or the head gasket. Leakage past the valves may be caused by burned valve seats and/or faces, or warped, cracked or bent valves.

12 If two adjacent cylinders have equally low compressions, it is most likely that the head gasket has blown between them. The appearance of coolant in the combustion chambers or on the engine oil dipstick would verify this condition.

13 If one cylinder is about 20 percent lower than the other, and the engine has a slightly rough idle, a worn lobe on the camshaft could be the cause.

14 On completion of the checks, refit the spark plugs and reconnect the HT leads and the DIS ignition coil plug. Refit the plastic cover and oil filler cap. Refit the fuel pump fuse to the fusebox.

3 Top Dead Centre (TDC) for No 1 piston – locating

Note: *A timing pin and camshaft setting bar are required for this procedure (see text).*

1 Top dead centre (TDC) is the highest point of the cylinder that each piston reaches as the crankshaft turns. Each piston reaches its TDC position at the end of its compression stroke, and then again at the end of its exhaust stroke. For the purpose of engine timing, TDC on the compression stroke for No 1 piston is used. No 1 cylinder is at the timing belt end of the engine. Proceed as follows.

2 Disconnect the battery negative (earth) lead (refer to *Disconnecting the battery*).

3.7a Unscrew the blanking plug from the right-hand rear side of the cylinder block . . .

3 Apply the handbrake, then jack up the front of the vehicle and support it on axle stands (see *Jacking and vehicle support*). If the engine is to be turned using the right-hand front roadwheel with 4th gear engaged, it is only necessary to raise the right-hand front roadwheel off the ground.

4 Remove the auxiliary drivebelt lower cover for access to the crankshaft pulley and bolt.

5 Remove the cylinder head cover as described in Section 4.

6 The piston of No 1 cylinder must now be positioned just before top dead centre (TDC). To do this, have an assistant turn the crankshaft until the slots in the left-hand ends of the camshafts are parallel with the upper surface of the cylinder head. Note that the slots are slightly offset, so make sure that the lower edges of the slots are aligned with the cylinder head. Turn the crankshaft slightly anti-clockwise (viewed from the right-hand end of the engine).

7 Unscrew the blanking plug from the right-hand rear side of the engine cylinder block. A timing pin must now be inserted and tightened into the hole. If the special Ford timing pin (303-507) is unavailable, a home-made tool can be fabricated out of a bolt having the same thread as the blanking plug. The length of the pin must be 38.24 mm, and

this measurement can be accurately adjusted using a self-locking nut screwed onto the bolt as shown **(see illustrations)**. Use vernier calipers to set the position of the nut on the bolt.

8 With the timing pin in position, turn the crankshaft clockwise until the specially machined surface on the crank web just touches the timing pin. No 1 piston is now at TDC on its compression stroke. To confirm this, check that the camshaft lobes for No 4 cylinder are 'rocking' (ie, exhaust valves closing and inlet valves opening).

9 It should now be possible to insert the camshaft setting bar into the slots in the left-hand ends of the camshafts. If the Ford setting tool (303-376) is unavailable, a home-made tool can be fabricated out of a length of flat metal bar 5.00 mm thick. The bar must be a good fit in the slots, and should be approximately 180 to 230 mm long by 20 to 30 mm wide **(see illustration)**.

10 If the bar cannot be inserted in the slots with the crankshaft at TDC, the valve timing must be adjusted as described in Section 8 of this Chapter.

11 Once the work requiring the TDC setting has been completed, remove the metal bar from the camshaft slots, then unscrew the timing pin and refit the blanking plug. Refit the cylinder head cover (Section 4), auxiliary drivebelt lower cover, and where necessary the engine undershield. Lower the vehicle to the ground and reconnect the battery negative lead.

4 Cylinder head cover – removal and refitting

Removal

1 Disconnect the battery negative (earth) lead (see *Disconnecting the battery*).

3.7b . . . then insert the timing pin

3.9 Home-made camshaft setting bar located in the camshaft slots

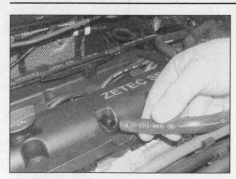

4.2 Disconnecting the breather hose at the front . . .

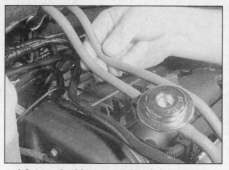

4.3a . . . fuel hoses at the right side . . .

4.3b . . . and coolant hose at the left side of the cover – 1.4 litre engine

2 Disconnect the crankcase breather hose at the front of the cylinder head cover **(see illustration)**.
3 Unclip the fuel, vacuum, and coolant pipes from the front and sides of the cover, and move them aside without disconnecting them **(see illustrations)**. Note how they are fitted into the clips, to preserve the routing when refitting.
4 Similarly, unclip the charcoal canister hose from the rear of the cover, and move it back out of the way **(see illustration)**.
5 Disconnect the camshaft position sensor wiring at the rear of the cylinder head **(see illustration)**.
6 On 1.6 litre models, undo the six screws and lift away the plastic centre cover for access to the spark plug HT leads **(see illustration)**.
7 Disconnect the HT leads from the spark plugs and ignition coil, and position them to the left-hand side of the engine compartment **(see illustration)**.
8 Where applicable, prise out the rubber bung for the cylinder head temperature sensor, fitted between Nos 2 and 3 spark plugs. The wiring plug for the sensor is a little inaccessible on 1.4 litre engines, but can be released with a finger. Pull out the wiring, and lay it aside **(see illustration)**.
9 At the timing belt cover end, prise up and release the clips securing the wiring harness to the cylinder head cover. Move the wiring harness to one side as far as possible.
10 Loosen the three top bolts securing the timing belt cover **(see illustration)** – the bolts need not be removed completely, though

4.4 Unclip the charcoal canister hose at the rear of the cover

there is no harm in doing so (the bolts are, however, of different lengths). The timing belt cover has to be free so that it can be prised back slightly, to release the cylinder head cover.

4.6 Removing the centre cover for access to the HT leads – 1.6 litre engine

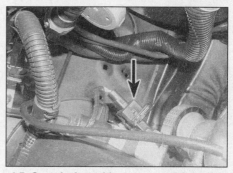

4.5 Camshaft position sensor wiring plug (arrowed)

11 On 1.4 litre models, unscrew the twelve bolts securing the cylinder head cover to the top of the cylinder head **(see illustration)**. The bolts are of captive type, and cannot be removed completely.

4.7 Disconnecting the HT leads from the spark plugs

4.8 Disconnect the cylinder head temperature sensor wiring plug, and remove it

4.10 Two of the three timing cover bolts to be loosened/removed (arrowed) – one more to the rear

4.11 On 1.4 litre engines, there are twelve cover bolts . . .

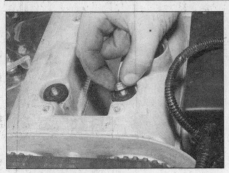

4.12 . . . there are four cover nuts on 1.6 litre engines

4.13a Removing the cylinder head cover – 1.4 litre engine . . .

4.13b . . . and 1.6 litre engine

4.14 Check the condition of the cover gasket

4.15a Locate the plastic installer on the rubber plug . . .

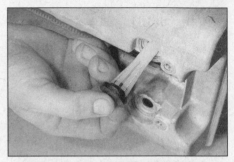

4.15b . . . then press the plug into the cylinder head cover, and remove the installer

12 On 1.6 litre models, unscrew the four nuts which secure the cylinder head cover. The rubber plugs beneath are a push-fit in the cover, and do not have to be removed **(see illustration)**.

13 Prise back the timing belt cover slightly, and have an assistant hold all the pipework aside as required. Carefully lift the cover straight upwards from the top of the cylinder head, and remove it **(see illustrations)**.

14 On 1.4 litre models, check the condition of the rubber gasket, and if necessary, renew it **(see illustration)**.

15 On 1.6 litre models, check the cover gasket and the rubber plugs. The cover gasket is vulcanised to the metal cover, and cannot be renewed separately. If the rubber plugs need renewing, these come together with a special plastic installer which is located on the lower lip of the plug. After pressing the plug into the cover, remove the installer **(see illustrations)**.

5.5 Checking a valve clearance with a feeler blade

Refitting

16 Clean the surface of the cylinder head and the cover gasket.

17 Lower the cover onto the cylinder head, making sure that none of the surrounding pipework becomes trapped. Tighten the cover bolts/nuts to the specified torque.

18 Further refitting is a reversal of removal. Ensure that all hoses and wiring are routed as before, and securely clipped into place.

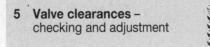

5 Valve clearances – checking and adjustment

Checking

1 Remove the cylinder head cover as described in Section 4.

2 Remove the spark plugs (Chapter 1A) in order to make turning the engine easier. The engine may be turned using a spanner on the crankshaft pulley bolt or by raising the front right-hand roadwheel clear of the ground, engaging 4th gear (manual transmission models only) and turning the wheel. If the former method is used, jack up and support the front of the vehicle (see *Jacking and vehicle support*) then unbolt the lower cover for access to the pulley bolt; if the latter method is used, apply the handbrake then jack up the front right-hand side of the vehicle until the roadwheel is clear of the ground and support with an axle stand.

3 Draw the valve positions on a piece of paper, numbering them 1 to 8 inlet and exhaust, from the timing belt (right-hand) end of the engine (ie, 1E, 1I, 2E, 2I and so on). As there are two inlet and two exhaust valves for each cylinder, draw the cylinders as large circles and the four valves as smaller circles. The inlet valves are at the front of the cylinder head, and the exhaust valves are at the rear.

4 Turn the engine in a clockwise direction until both inlet valves of No 1 cylinder are fully shut and the apex of the camshaft lobes are pointing upwards away from the valve positions.

5 Use feeler blade(s) to measure the exact clearance between the heel of the camshaft lobe and the shim on the cam follower **(see illustration)**; the feeler blades should be a firm sliding fit. Record the measured clearance on the drawing. From this clearance it will be possible to calculate the thickness of the new shim to be fitted, where necessary.

6 Measure the clearance of the second inlet valve for No 1 cylinder, and record it on the drawing.

7 Now turn the engine until the inlet valves of No 2 cylinder are fully shut and the camshaft lobes pointing away from the valve positions. Measure the clearances as described previously. After measuring all of the inlet valve clearances, measure the exhaust valve clearances in the same way.

8 Compare the measured clearances with the values give in the Specifications – any which fall within the range do not require adjustment. Note that the clearances for inlet and exhaust valves are different.

Adjustment

9 Where adjustment is required, the procedure is to remove the shim from the top of the cam follower and fit a new shim to provide the correct clearance. Ford technicians use a special tool (303-361) consisting of a bar bolted to the camshaft bearing caps. A sliding lever on the bar is used, together with a pushrod, to depress the relevant cam follower in order to remove the old shim and fit the new one. Use of this tool (or a similar tool) will save a considerable amount of time, as the alternative is to remove the camshafts with the additional time of disconnecting the timing belt and resetting the valve timing. However, if TDC setting tools are available (see Section 3) removal of the camshafts is to be preferred to using an ill-fitting tool to depress the cam followers.

10 If the recorded clearance was too small, a thinner shim must be fitted, and conversely if the clearance was too large, a thicker shim must be fitted. To calculate the thickness of the new shim, first use a micrometer to measure the thickness of the existing shim (C) and add this to the measured clearance (B). Deduct the desired clearance (A) to provide the thickness (D) of the new shim. The thickness of the shim should be etched on the downward facing surface, but use the micrometer to verify this. The formula is as follows.

$$D = C + B - A$$

Where:

A = *Required clearance*
B = *Measured clearance*
C = *Existing shim thickness*
D = *New shim thickness*
All measurements in mm

Sample calculation – clearance too small

Required clearance (A)	= 0.20
Measured clearance (B)	= 0.15
Existing shim thickness (C)	= 2.725
Shim thickness required (D)	= C+B–A
	= 2.675

Sample calculation – clearance too large

Required clearance (A)	= 0.30
Measured clearance (B)	= 0.40
Existing shim thickness (C)	= 2.550
Shim thickness required (D)	= C+B–A
	= 2.650

11 The shims are available in thicknesses from 2.000 mm to 3.300 mm in increments of 0.025 mm. If the Ford tool (or similar) is being used to remove the shims without removing the camshafts, turn the cam followers so that the slot is facing towards the centre of the engine. It will then be possible to use a small screwdriver to lift out the old shim. Fit the new shim then release the tool.

12 When fitting the new shim, make sure that the etched thickness is facing downwards onto the cam follower.

13 It will be helpful for future adjustment if a record is kept of the thickness of shim fitted at each position. The shims required can be purchased in advance once the clearances

and the existing shim thicknesses are known. It is permissible to interchange shims between cam followers to achieve the correct clearances, but it is not advisable to turn the camshaft with any shims removed, since there is a risk that the cam lobe will jam in the empty cam follower.

14 When all the clearances have been checked and adjusted, refit the lower cover (where removed), lower the vehicle to the ground and refit the cylinder head cover as described in Section 4.

---

6 Crankshaft pulley/ vibration damper – removal and refitting

Caution: Removal of the crankshaft pulley effectively loses the valve timing setting, and it will be necessary to reset the timing using the procedure and tools described in Section 3.

Note: *The vibration damper retaining bolt may only be used once. Obtain a new bolt for the refitting procedure.*

Removal

1 Disconnect the battery negative (earth) lead (see *Disconnecting the battery*).

2 Apply the handbrake, then jack up the front of the vehicle and support it on axle stands (see *Jacking and vehicle support*). Remove the engine undershield if fitted.

3 Remove the right-hand front roadwheel, then undo the retaining screws/fasteners and remove the wheelarch liner.

4 Unbolt and remove the auxiliary drivebelt lower cover for access to the crankshaft pulley.

5 Remove the auxiliary drivebelt as described in Chapter 1A.

6 Set the engine to the top dead centre (TDC) position as described in Section 3, then remove the camshaft position bar and the crankshaft timing pin. Do not leave the tools in position while the crankshaft pulley bolt is being loosened.

7 Hold the crankshaft pulley stationary using a home-made tool like the one shown **(see illustration)**. The bolt ends locate in the pulley

6.7 Loosening the crankshaft pulley bolt while holding the pulley with a home-made tool

holes and an extension bar and socket can then be used to loosen the bolt. Do not allow the crankshaft to turn, otherwise it will be more difficult to reset the valve timing; also, with the bolt loose, the crankshaft sprocket may not turn with the crankshaft, and the pistons may touch the valves.

8 With the bolt loosened several turns, use a suitable puller to free the pulley from the taper on the end of the crankshaft. Fully unscrew the bolt and withdraw the pulley **(see illustrations)**.

9 Clean the end of the crankshaft and the pulley.

Refitting

10 The procedure in this paragraph is necessary in order to be able to set the valve timing after the crankshaft/vibration pulley has been refitted. Unbolt and remove the timing belt upper cover (see Section 7). While holding each of the camshaft sprockets stationary in turn using the home-made tool described in paragraph 7, loosen the sprocket retaining bolts until they are just finger-tight to enable the sprockets to turn on the camshafts. Alternatively, the camshafts can be held stationary using a spanner on the special hexagon flats. If necessary, use a soft-metal drift to release the sprockets from the taper on the camshafts.

11 Locate the pulley on the end of the crankshaft, and press it onto the taper as far as it will go. This procedure must always be carried out before inserting and tightening the new bolt.

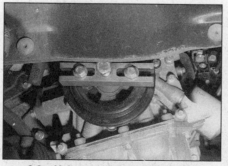

6.8a Using a puller to remove the crankshaft pulley

6.8b Remove the retaining bolt, and withdraw the pulley from the end of the crankshaft

6.11 Use a long bolt threaded into the crankshaft to draw the pulley onto the taper

Do not simply insert and tighten the new bolt, as in certain circumstances, the torque will not be sufficient to press the pulley fully onto the end of the taper on the crankshaft. Ford technicians use a special installer which consists of a threaded rod screwed into the crankshaft, together with a spacer which locates on the pulley. In the absence of this tool, use a long bolt or threaded rod together with washers and a nut **(see illustration)**. As a last resort use the removed (old) bolt, however, this is not recommended as the threads may be stretched (see Note at the beginning of this Section).

12 Remove the tool, then insert the new bolt **(see illustration)** and tighten it to the specified Stage 1 torque setting while holding the pulley stationary with the special tool.

13 Now angle-tighten the bolt through the specified Stage 2 angle.

14 The valve timing must now be set and the camshaft sprocket bolts tightened as described in Section 8.

15 Refit the timing belt upper cover.

16 Refit and tension the auxiliary drivebelt as described in Chapter 1A.

17 Refit the auxiliary drivebelt lower cover and tighten the retaining bolts.

18 Refit the wheelarch liner and where fitted the engine undershield, then lower the vehicle to the ground.

19 Reconnect the battery negative lead.

7 Timing belt covers – removal and refitting

Upper cover

Removal

1 Remove the auxiliary drivebelt as described in Chapter 1A.

2 To improve access, lift the power steering fluid reservoir from its location, and move it aside without disconnecting the hoses **(see illustration)**. The reservoir locates on three rubber mountings – note how they are fitted.

3 Unbolt and remove the upper idler pulley **(see illustration)**.

4 Unscrew the timing belt securing screws – there are three near the top, two halfway down and two at the bottom **(refer to illustration 4.10)**.

5 Manoeuvre the timing cover rearwards from behind the engine right-hand mounting

6.12 Inserting the new crankshaft pulley retaining bolt

brackets, and withdraw it from the engine compartment **(see illustration)**.

Refitting

6 Refitting is a reversal of removal, but tighten the retaining bolts to the specified torque.

Lower cover

Removal

7 The timing belt lower cover is located around the crankshaft. First remove the crankshaft pulley/vibration damper as described in Section 6.

8 Working beneath the right-hand wheelarch, unscrew the retaining bolts and withdraw the timing cover **(see illustrations)**.

Refitting

9 Refitting is a reversal of removal, but tighten the retaining bolts to the specified torque.

8 Timing belt – removal and refitting

Removal

1 Disconnect the battery negative lead, and position the lead away from the battery (also see *Disconnecting the battery*).

2 Loosen the four bolts securing the coolant pump pulley.

3 Remove the crankshaft pulley/vibration damper as described in Section 6. This work includes removing the cylinder head cover, and setting the engine at top dead centre (TDC).

7.2 Lift the power steering reservoir out of its mounting bracket

7.3 Removing the upper idler pulley

7.5 Removing the upper timing cover

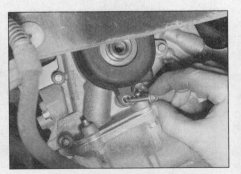

7.8a Undo the bolts . . .

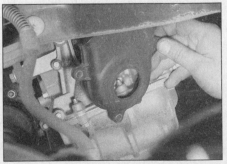

7.8b . . . and remove the lower timing cover

8.4 Idler and coolant pump pulley bolts (arrowed)

8.9 Support the engine with a trolley jack and block of wood

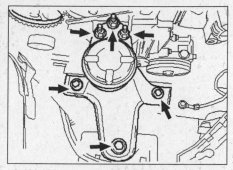

8.10a Engine right-hand mounting upper bracket nuts and bolts (arrowed)

8.10b Removing the engine right-hand mounting upper bracket

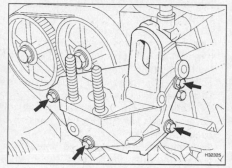

8.11 Engine right-hand mounting lower bracket bolts (arrowed)

8.13 Showing the manufacturer's markings on the timing belt

4 Unbolt and remove the auxiliary drivebelt idler pulley, and the coolant pump pulley **(see illustration)**.

5 Remove the timing belt upper and lower covers as described in Section 7.

6 With the camshaft timing bar removed, loosen the camshaft sprocket bolts several turns while holding the sprockets with a suitable tool. Alternatively, the camshafts can be held stationary using a 21 mm open-ended spanner on the special hexagon flats. Using a soft-metal drift from behind the sprockets, release the sprockets from the tapers on the ends of the camshafts so that they are free to rotate.

7 Remove the bolt securing the coolant expansion tank to the inner wing, and move the tank as far as possible out of the way, without disconnecting any of the hoses.

8 Remove the alternator as described in Chapter 5A.

9 Using a trolley jack and large wooden block to spread the load, support the weight of the engine beneath the right-hand side of the sump **(see illustration)**.

10 Progressively unscrew the nuts and bolts, and remove the upper bracket from the engine right-hand mounting **(see illustrations)**.

11 Unbolt and remove the right-hand mounting lower bracket from the cylinder head **(see illustration)**.

12 One of two different types of timing belt tensioner may be fitted; on the first type, the tensioner roller is mounted on an eccentric, while the second type has a fixed roller, with

the belt being tensioned by pivoting the tensioner mounting bracket. Loosen the timing belt tensioner centre bolt, or the two tensioner mounting bolts. Move the tensioner away from the belt, then tighten the bolt (or bolts) to hold the tensioner temporarily in this position.

13 If the timing belt is to be re-used (and this is **not** recommended), use white paint or similar to mark its direction of rotation, and note from the manufacturer's markings which way round it is fitted **(see illustration)**.

14 Withdraw the belt from the sprockets and from over the tensioner **(see illustrations)**. *Do not* attempt to turn the crankshaft or camshafts until the timing belt is refitted.

15 If the belt is likely to be refitted, check it carefully for any signs of uneven wear, splitting, cracks (especially at the roots of the belt teeth).

16 Even if a new belt is to be fitted, check the

old one for signs of oil or coolant. If evident, trace the source of the leak and rectify it, then wash down the engine timing belt area and related components to remove all traces of oil or coolant. Do not simply fit a new belt in this instance, or its service life will be greatly reduced, increasing the risk of engine damage if it fails in service.

17 Always renew the belt if there is the slightest doubt about its condition. As a precaution against engine damage, the belt must be renewed as a matter of course at the intervals given in Chapter 1A; if the car's history is unknown, the belt should be renewed irrespective of its apparent condition whenever the engine is overhauled.

18 Similarly check the belt tensioner, renewing it if there is any doubt about its condition. Check also the toothed sprockets for signs of wear or damage (and particularly cracking), and ensure that the tensioner pulley

8.14a Removing the timing belt from the camshaft sprockets . . .

8.14b . . . and crankshaft sprocket

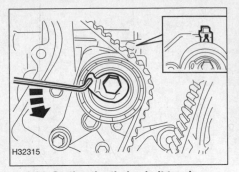

8.21 Setting the timing belt tension – eccentric type tensioner

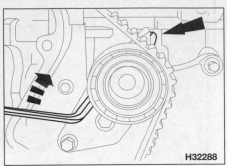

8.22 Setting the timing belt tension – mounting bracket type tensioner

rotates smoothly on its bearings; renew any worn or damaged components. **Note:** *It is considered good practice by many professional mechanics to renew tensioner assemblies as a matter of course, whenever the timing belt is renewed.*

Refitting

19 Check that the engine is still at TDC, with the timing pin and camshaft setting bar in position.
20 Locate the timing belt on the crankshaft sprocket, then feed it over the tensioner pulley and finally over the two camshaft sprockets. If the original belt is being refitted, make sure that it is the correct way round as noted during removal. Any slack in the belt should be on the tensioner side of the belt.
21 On models with the eccentric type tensioner, loosen the centre bolt, then using a 6 mm Allen key in the hole provided, turn the tensioner roller anti-clockwise to tension the belt. The correct tension is indicated by the pointer being exactly central in the rectangular window above and behind the tensioner roller **(see illustration)**. Hold the tensioner in this position, and tighten the centre bolt to the specified torque.
22 On models where the tensioner moves with its mounting bracket, loosen the two bolts so that the tensioner is free to pivot. Using an 8 mm Allen key in the hole provided, turn the tensioner and bracket clockwise to tension the belt. The correct tension is indicated by the pointer being exactly central between the two marks behind the tensioner roller **(see illustration)**. Hold the tensioner in

this position, and tighten the two bolts to the specified torque.
23 Moderately tighten the bolts retaining the camshaft sprockets to the camshafts, then remove the setting bar and timing pin and fully tighten the bolts while holding the sprockets using the tool described in Section 6 **(see illustration)**.
24 Refit the engine right-hand mounting lower bracket, and tighten the bolts to the specified torque.
25 Refit the upper mounting bracket, and tighten the nuts and bolts to the specified torque. Withdraw the trolley jack from under the vehicle.
26 Refit the timing belt lower cover, and tighten the bolts.
27 Locate the crankshaft pulley/vibration damper on the end of the crankshaft, and press it onto the taper as far as it will go. This procedure must always be carried out before inserting and tightening the new bolt – it is not sufficient to press on the pulley by hand only. Ford technicians use a special installer which consists of a threaded rod screwed into the crankshaft, together with a metal ring which locates on the pulley. In the absence of this tool, use the old pulley bolt together with a suitable metal ring to press the pulley squarely onto the crankshaft as far as it will go. Do not use the new bolt for this initial operation.
28 Insert the new bolt and tighten it to the specified Stage 1 torque setting while holding the pulley stationary with the special tool (see Section 6).
29 Now angle-tighten the bolt further through the specified Stage 2 angle. The crankshaft sprocket is now effectively clamped to the crankshaft.
30 Check the accuracy of the valve timing by first turning the crankshaft two complete turns. Refit the TDC timing pin and position the crankshaft at TDC, then insert the setting bar in the camshaft slots (see Section 3).
31 If the bar does not fit, a small error can be corrected by loosening the sprocket bolt of the camshaft affected, and turning the camshaft until the bar will fit; retighten the sprocket bolt to the specified torque to complete.
32 On completion, remove the timing pin and bar, and refit the blanking plug.
33 Further refitting is a reversal of removal.

8.23 Tightening the camshaft sprocket retaining bolts

9 Timing belt tensioner and sprockets – removal, inspection and refitting

Tensioner

Removal

1 Disconnect the battery negative (earth) lead (see *Disconnecting the battery*).
2 Apply the handbrake, then jack up the front of the vehicle and support it on axle stands (see *Jacking and vehicle support*). Remove the engine undershield, if fitted.
3 Remove the right-hand front roadwheel, then undo the retaining screws/fasteners and remove the wheelarch liner.
4 Unbolt and remove the auxiliary drivebelt lower cover for access to the crankshaft pulley.
5 Remove the auxiliary drivebelt as described in Chapter 1A.
6 Remove the timing belt upper cover as described in Section 7.
7 As a precaution against losing the valve timing, use string to tie the front and rear runs of the timing belt together. This will ensure that the belt remains engaged with the camshaft sprockets while the tensioner and pulley are removed.
8 One of two different types of timing belt tensioner may be fitted; on the first type, the tensioner roller is mounted on an eccentric, while the second type has a fixed roller, with the belt being tensioned by pivoting the tensioner mounting bracket. Loosen the timing belt tensioner centre bolt, or the two tensioner mounting bolts. Move the tensioner away from the belt; on the eccentric-type tensioner, tighten the centre bolt to hold it in the retracted position.
9 Loosen and/or completely remove the two tensioner mounting bracket bolts, and withdraw the tensioner from the engine.
10 While the tensioner is removed, make sure that the timing belt remains fully engaged with the camshaft and crankshaft sprockets.

Inspection

11 Spin the tensioner pulley and check that it turns freely without any roughness or tightness. Do not attempt to clean the pulley by immersing in any cleaning fluid. Check the pulley itself for signs of damage, and in particular, signs of cracking. If there is any doubt as to the condition of the tensioner, renew it, particularly if the engine has completed a high mileage.

Refitting

12 Clean the cylinder block in the area of the tensioner.
13 Locate the tensioner pulley on the block, and insert the two mounting bolts.
14 On models with the eccentric-type tensioner, tighten the two mounting bolts to the specified torque.
15 Tension the timing belt using the information in Section 8.

16 Provided that the timing belt has remained fully engaged with the camshaft and crankshaft sprockets, it should not be necessary to check the valve timing. However, if there is any doubt, check the valve timing as described in Sections 3 and 8.
17 Refit the timing belt upper cover as described in Section 7.
18 Refit the auxiliary drivebelt as described in Chapter 1A.
19 Refit the auxiliary drivebelt lower cover and tighten the bolts.
20 Refit the wheelarch liner and the right-hand front roadwheel.
21 Refit the engine undershield (where applicable) and lower the vehicle to the ground.
22 Reconnect the battery negative lead.

Camshaft sprockets

Removal

23 Disconnect the battery negative (earth) lead (see *Disconnecting the battery*).
24 Apply the handbrake, then jack up the front of the vehicle and support it on axle stands (see *Jacking and vehicle support*).
25 Remove the right-hand front roadwheel, then undo the retaining screws/fasteners and remove the wheelarch liner.
26 Unbolt and remove the auxiliary drivebelt lower cover.
27 Remove the auxiliary drivebelt as described in Chapter 1A.
28 Remove the timing belt upper cover as described in Section 7.
29 Set the No 1 piston and camshafts to top dead centre (TDC) as described in Section 3. This procedure includes removal of the cylinder head cover.
30 One of two different types of timing belt tensioner may be fitted; on the first type, the tensioner roller is mounted on an eccentric, while the second type has a fixed roller, with the belt being tensioned by pivoting the tensioner mounting bracket.
31 Loosen the timing belt tensioner centre bolt, or the two tensioner mounting bolts. Move the tensioner away from the belt, then tighten the bolt (or bolts) to hold the tensioner temporarily in this position.
32 Using a trolley jack and large wooden block to spread the load, support the weight of the engine beneath the right-hand side of the sump.
33 Progressively unscrew the nuts and bolts, and remove the upper bracket from the engine right-hand mounting.
34 Unbolt and remove the right-hand mounting lower bracket from the cylinder head.
35 Disengage the timing belt from the camshaft sprockets and position it to one side, taking care not to bend it sharply. The belt will remain engaged with the crankshaft sprocket, but as a precaution, keep a little upward pressure on the belt by tying it to the side of the engine compartment.

36 Hold each of the camshaft sprockets stationary in turn using a home-made tool (see Section 6), then loosen the sprocket retaining bolts. Alternatively, the camshafts can be held stationary using a spanner on the special hexagon flats **(see illustration)**. The TDC setting bar must not be used to hold the camshafts stationary.
37 Unscrew the bolts and remove the sprockets from the camshafts **(see illustrations)**. If necessary, use a soft-metal drift to release the sprockets from the taper on the camshafts.

Inspection

38 Examine the teeth of the sprockets for wear and damage, and renew them if necessary.

Refitting

39 Check that the engine is still at TDC, with the timing pin and camshaft setting bar in position.
40 Locate the sprockets on the camshafts, and screw in the retaining bolts by hand only at this stage.
41 Engage the timing belt with the camshaft sprockets.
42 On models with the eccentric type tensioner, loosen the centre bolt, then using a 6 mm Allen key in the hole provided, turn the tensioner roller anti-clockwise to tension the belt. The correct tension is indicated by the pointer being exactly central in the rectangular window above and behind the tensioner roller. Hold the tensioner in this position, and tighten the centre bolt to the specified torque.
43 On models where the tensioner moves with its mounting bracket, loosen the two bolts so that the tensioner is free to pivot. Using an 8 mm Allen key in the hole provided, turn the tensioner and bracket clockwise to tension the belt. The correct tension is indicated by the pointer being exactly central in the rectangular window above and behind the tensioner roller. Hold the tensioner in this position, and tighten the two bolts to the specified torque.
44 Moderately tighten the bolts retaining the camshaft sprockets to the camshafts, then remove the setting bar and timing pin and fully tighten the bolts while holding the sprockets using the tool described in Section 6.
45 Refit the engine right-hand mounting

9.36 Using a spanner to hold the camshafts stationary

lower bracket, and tighten the bolts to the specified torque.
46 Refit the upper mounting bracket, and tighten the nuts and bolts to the specified torque. Withdraw the trolley jack from under the vehicle.
47 Check the accuracy of the valve timing by first turning the crankshaft two complete turns. Refit the TDC timing pin and position the crankshaft at TDC, then insert the setting bar in the camshaft slots.
48 If the bar does not fit, a small error can be corrected by loosening the sprocket bolt of the camshaft affected, and turning the camshaft until the bar will fit; retighten the sprocket bolt to the specified torque to complete. An error larger than this would mean that the belt has been incorrectly fitted; in this case, the belt would have to be removed and the procedure repeated.
49 On completion, remove the timing pin and bar, and refit the blanking plug.
50 Refit the timing belt upper cover as described in Section 7.
51 Refit and tension the auxiliary drivebelt as described in Chapter 1A.
52 Refit the auxiliary drivebelt lower cover and tighten the retaining bolts.
53 Refit the wheelarch liner, then lower the vehicle to the ground.
54 Reconnect the battery negative lead.

Crankshaft sprocket

Removal

55 Remove the timing belt as described in Section 8.

9.37a Unscrew the bolt . . .

9.37b . . . and remove the camshaft sprocket

9.56 Slide the sprocket from the end of the crankshaft

10.3a Drill a small hole and insert a self-tapping screw . . .

10.3b . . . then pull out the oil seal using a pair of pliers

56 Slide the sprocket off the end of the crankshaft, noting how it fits **(see illustration)**.

Inspection

57 Examine the teeth of the sprocket for wear and damage, and renew if necessary.

Refitting

58 Wipe clean the end of the crankshaft, then slide on the sprocket.

59 Refit the timing belt as described in Section 8.

10 Camshaft oil seals – renewal

1 Remove the camshaft sprockets as described in Section 9.

2 Note the fitted depths of the oil seals as a guide for fitting the new ones.

3 Using a screwdriver or similar tool, carefully prise the oil seals from the cylinder head/camshaft bearing caps. Take care not to damage the oil seal contact surfaces on the ends of the camshafts or the oil seal seatings. An alternative method of removing the seals is to drill a small hole, then insert a self-tapping screw and use pliers to pull out the seal **(see illustrations)**.

4 Wipe clean the oil seal seatings and also the ends of the camshafts.

5 Working on the first camshaft, dip the new oil seal in fresh oil, then locate it over the camshaft and into the cylinder head/camshaft bearing cap **(see illustration)**. Make sure that the oil seal lips face inwards.

10.5 Locating the new oil seal into the cylinder head/camshaft bearing cap

6 Using a socket or length of metal tubing, drive the oil seals squarely into position to the previously-noted depths **(see illustration)**. Wipe away any excess oil.

7 Refit the camshaft sprockets as described in Section 9.

11 Camshafts and cam followers – removal, inspection and refitting

Removal

1 Before removing the camshafts, it may be useful to check and record the valve clearances as described in Section 5. If any clearance is not within limits, new shims can be obtained and fitted.

2 Remove the camshaft sprockets as described in Section 9.

10.6 Driving the new oil seal into position with a socket

3 The camshaft bearing caps are marked for position – the inlet caps have the letter I and exhaust caps have the letter E. On the project vehicle these were not very clear, and if this is the case, mark them using paint or a marker pen **(see illustrations)**. Make sure the caps are identified for inlet and exhaust camshafts, numbered from the timing belt end.

4 Position the crankshaft so that No 1 piston is approximately 25 mm before TDC.

5 Position the camshafts so that none of the valves are at full lift. To do this, turn each camshaft using a 21 mm open-ended spanner on the hexagon flats provided.

6 Progressively loosen the camshaft bearing cap retaining bolts in the sequence shown, noting the location of the extended bolts which secure the cylinder head cover **(see illustration)**. Work only as described, to release gradually and evenly the pressure of the valve springs on the caps.

11.3a No 3 Inlet camshaft bearing cap marking

11.3b No 3 Exhaust camshaft bearing cap marking

11.3c Number the camshaft bearing caps with paint if they are not marked

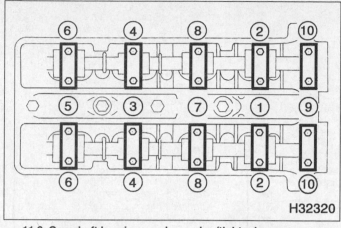

11.6 Camshaft bearing cap loosening/tightening sequence

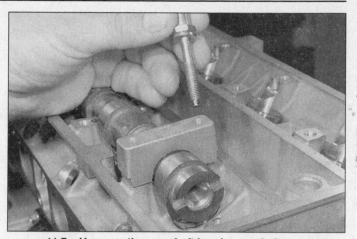

11.7a Unscrew the camshaft bearing cap bolts . . .

7 Withdraw the caps, keeping them in order to aid refitting, then lift the camshafts from the cylinder head and withdraw their oil seals **(see illustrations)**. The exhaust camshaft can be identified by the reference lobe for the camshaft position sensor; therefore, there is no need to mark the camshafts.

8 Obtain sixteen small, clean containers, and number them 1 to 8 for both the inlet and exhaust camshafts. Lift the cam followers one by one from the cylinder head, keeping the shims with the respective cam followers **(see illustration)**.

Inspection

9 With the camshafts and cam followers removed, check each for signs of obvious wear (scoring, pitting, etc) and for ovality, and renew if necessary.

10 If possible, use a micrometer to measure the outside diameter of each cam follower – take measurements at the top and bottom of each cam follower, then a second set at right-angles to the first; if any measurement is significantly different from the others, the cam follower is tapered or oval (as applicable) and must be renewed. If the cam followers or the cylinder head bores are excessively worn, new cam followers and/or a new cylinder head will be required.

11 Visually examine the camshaft lobes for score marks, pitting, and evidence of overheating (blue, discoloured areas). Look for flaking away of the hardened surface layer of each lobe. If any such signs are evident, renew the component concerned.

12 Examine the camshaft bearing journals and the cylinder head bearing surfaces for signs of obvious wear or pitting. If any such signs are evident, renew the component concerned.

13 To check camshaft endfloat, remove the cam followers, clean the bearing surfaces carefully, and refit the camshafts and bearing caps. Tighten the bearing cap bolts to the specified torque wrench setting, then measure the endfloat using a dial gauge mounted on the cylinder head so that its tip bears on the camshaft right-hand end.

14 Tap the camshaft fully towards the gauge, zero the gauge, then tap the camshaft fully away from the gauge, and note the gauge reading. If the endfloat measured is found to be more than the typical value given, fit a new camshaft and repeat the check; if the clearance is still excessive, the cylinder head must be renewed.

Refitting

15 Commence reassembly by lubricating the cylinder head cam follower bores and the cam followers with engine oil. Carefully refit the cam followers (together with their respective shims) to the cylinder head, ensuring that each cam follower is refitted to its original bore. Some care will be required to enter the cam followers squarely into their bores.

16 Liberally oil the camshaft bearings and lobes. Ensuring that each camshaft is in its original location, refit the camshafts, locating each so that the slot in its left-hand end is approximately parallel to, and just above, the cylinder head mating surface **(see illustration)**. At this stage, position the camshafts so that none of the valves are at full lift.

17 Clean the mating faces of the cylinder head and camshaft bearing caps, and ensure that the locating dowels are firmly in place.

18 Apply a thin coating of suitable sealant (Ford recommend WSK-M2G348-A5) to the No 1 camshaft bearing caps at the oil seal ends only, as shown **(see illustrations)**, and to the corresponding surface on the cylinder head.

19 Oil the bearing surfaces, then locate the camshaft bearing caps on the camshafts and insert the retaining bolts loosely **(see illustrations)**. Make sure that each cap is located in its previously noted position.

20 Ensuring that each cap is kept square to the cylinder head as it is tightened down, and working in the same sequence as for

11.7b . . . and withdraw the caps

11.8 Removing the cam followers

11.16 Locating the camshafts in the cylinder head

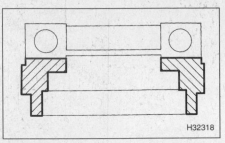

11.18a Sealant should be applied to the shaded area on the No 1 bearing caps, and to the corresponding surfaces of the cylinder head

11.18b Applying sealant to the No 1 camshaft bearing caps

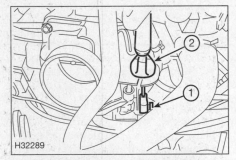

11.19a Oil the bearing surfaces . . .

11.19b . . . then refit the camshaft bearing caps

loosening (refer to illustration 11.6), tighten the camshaft bearing cap bolts slowly and by one turn at a time, until each cap touches the cylinder head. Next, go round again in the same sequence, tightening the bolts to the

specified Stage 1 torque wrench setting, then once more, tightening them to the Stage 2 setting. Work only in the sequence shown, so that pressure is gradually applied to the valve springs.

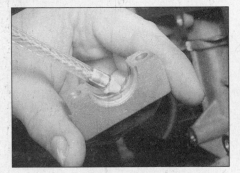

12.8a Accelerator cable end fitting securing clip (1) and outer cable attachment at the throttle housing (2)

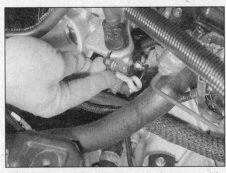

12.8b Disconnecting the accelerator cable end fitting from the throttle body

12.10 Disconnect the large multi-plug next to the power steering reservoir bracket

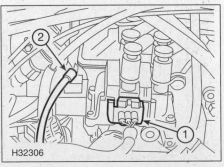

12.11a Ignition coil main wiring plug (1) and condenser wire (2)

21 Wipe off any surplus sealant, then check the valve clearances as described in Section 5.
22 Fit new oil seals with reference to Section 10.
23 Refit the camshaft sprockets (Section 9).

12 Cylinder head – removal, inspection and refitting

Removal

Note: The following paragraphs assume that the cylinder head will be removed together with the inlet manifold attached. This simplifies the procedure, but makes it a bulky and heavy assembly to handle – ideally an engine hoist will be required, to prevent the risk of injury, and to prevent damage to any delicate components as the assembly is removed and refitted. If it is wished first to remove the inlet manifold, refer to Chapter 4A, then amend the following procedure accordingly.

1 Depressurise the fuel system as described in Chapter 4A.
2 Set the engine to TDC compression on piston No 1 as described in Section 3. This procedure includes disconnecting the battery and removing the cylinder head cover, then setting the engine to TDC using a timing pin and camshaft setting bar.
3 Remove the right-hand front roadwheel, then undo the retaining screws/fasteners and remove the wheelarch liner.
4 Remove the auxiliary drivebelt as described in Chapter 1A.
5 Disconnect the engine earth cable at the rear, then unscrew and remove the bolts securing the heatshield assembly to the catalytic converter and exhaust manifold at the rear of the engine. Access to the lower bolt is best from under the vehicle.
6 Drain the cooling system (see Chapter 1A).
7 Remove the air cleaner and inlet duct completely as described in Chapter 4A.
8 Detach the accelerator cable end fitting from the throttle body by pulling off the securing clip. Withdraw the cable outer from the mounting bracket (see illustrations).
9 Trace the crankcase breather hose down to its connection on the engine, and disconnect it.
10 Disconnect the engine wiring harness multi-plug near the power steering reservoir bracket (see illustration).
11 Disconnect the main wiring plug from the ignition coil assembly, and the smaller wire on the condenser (see illustrations).
12 Disconnect the knock sensor wiring plug next to the engine oil dipstick, and unclip the connector halves (see illustration).
13 Loosen and remove the three inlet manifold lower bolts, and withdraw the oil dipstick tube.
14 Detach the charcoal canister hose and brake servo vacuum hose from the inlet

12.11b Disconnecting the ignition coil main wiring plug

12.12 Disconnect the knock sensor wiring plug

12.14 Disconnecting the servo hose from the manifold – also note charcoal canister and pressure regulator hoses (arrowed)

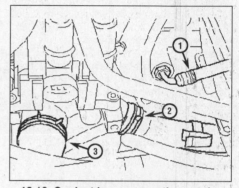

12.16 Coolant hose connections at the thermostat housing

1 Expansion tank hose	*2 Heater hose*
	3 Radiator hose

manifold/throttle body **(see illustration)**. Also disconnect the wiring plug from the throttle position sensor.

15 Where necessary, unscrew the two flange bolts from the EGR pipe, and separate the EGR pipe (recover the O-ring seal); if preferred, the EGR pipe can be removed completely, as described in Chapter 4C, Section 4.

16 Release the hose clips (where applicable) and disconnect the expansion tank hose, heater hose and radiator top hose from the thermostat housing **(see illustration)**.

17 Unclip the fuel feed and return hoses from their supports, then squeeze together the quick-release fittings and disconnect the hoses from the fuel rail. Alternatively, the fuel hoses can be disconnected at the connections near the engine compartment bulkhead **(see illustration)**. The feed hose connection is white, while the return connection is colour-coded red.

18 Remove the camshafts as described in Section 11.

19 Unscrew the bolts securing the rear timing cover to the cylinder head **(see illustrations)**.

20 Working under the car, unscrew the nuts securing the exhaust pipe front joint, but do not attempt to separate the joint at this stage.

21 Progressively unscrew and remove the nuts securing the exhaust manifold **(see illustration)**. Use plenty of penetrating oil if the studs are rusty. If a nut appears to be sticking, do not try to force it; turn the nut back half a turn, apply some more penetrating oil to the stud threads, wait several seconds for it to soak in, then gradually unscrew the nut by one turn. Repeat this process until the nut is free.

22 In some cases, the manifold studs will come out with the nuts – this poses no great problem, and the studs can be refitted if they are in good condition. For preference, however, a complete set of manifold and downpipe studs and nuts should be obtained, as the old ones are likely to be in less-than-perfect condition.

23 Taking care that the flexible section of the exhaust front pipe is not bent or strained excessively, slide the manifold off its cylinder head studs, separate the front pipe joint, and remove the manifold from under the car.

Recover the gaskets – new ones must be obtained for refitting.

24 Check around the head, to make sure that there is nothing still attached to it which would prevent or hinder its removal.

25 Working in the reverse sequence to that shown for tightening **(refer to illustration 12.41)**, loosen the cylinder head bolts a little at a time until they are all loose. Lift out the bolts – Ford state that they can be re-used, but check them for signs of damage as described below. It is probably not advisable to re-use the bolts more than once, however.

26 Lift the cylinder head away; use assistance if possible, as it is a heavy assembly.

27 If the head is stuck (as is possible), be careful how you choose to free it. Remember that the cylinder head and block are made of aluminium alloy, which is easily damaged. Striking the head with tools carries the risk of

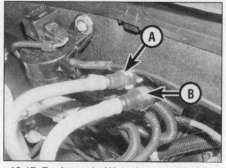

12.17 Fuel supply (A) and return (B) hose connections

12.19a Unscrew the upper bolt securing the rear timing cover to the cylinder head . . .

12.19b . . . and the lower bolt

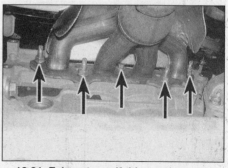

12.21 Exhaust manifold securing nuts (arrowed) – seen from below

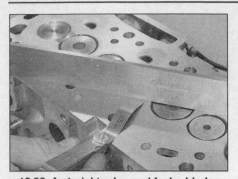

12.32 A straight-edge and feeler blades can be used to check for cylinder head distortion

12.37 Locating the new cylinder head gasket on the cylinder block dowels

damage, and the head is located on two dowels, so its movement will be limited. Do not, under any circumstances, lever the head between the mating surfaces, as this will certainly damage the sealing surfaces for the gasket, leading to leaks. Try inserting two lengths of wood into the exhaust ports, and using them as levers to break the seal.

28 Once the head has been removed, recover the gasket from the two dowels, and discard it. The gasket is manufactured from laminated steel, and cannot be re-used.

Inspection

Note: *For dismantling the cylinder head, and other procedures relating to the valves, refer to Chapter 2D.*

29 The mating faces of the cylinder head and cylinder block must be perfectly clean before refitting the head. Use a hard plastic or wood scraper to remove all traces of gasket and carbon; also clean the piston crowns.

30 Take particular care during the cleaning operations, as aluminium alloy is easily damaged. Also, make sure that the carbon is not allowed to enter the oil and water passages – this is particularly important for the lubrication system, as carbon could block the oil supply to the engine's components. Using adhesive tape and paper, seal the

water, oil and bolt holes in the cylinder block. To prevent carbon entering the gap between the pistons and bores, smear a little grease in the gap. After cleaning each piston, use a small brush to remove all traces of grease and carbon from the gap, then wipe away the remainder with a clean rag.

31 Check the mating surfaces of the cylinder block and the cylinder head for nicks, deep scratches and other damage. If slight, they may be removed carefully with a file, but if excessive, renewal is necessary as it is not permissible to machine the surfaces.

32 If warpage of the cylinder head gasket surface is suspected, use a straight-edge to check it for distortion **(see illustration)**. If feeler blades are used, the degree of distortion can be assessed more accurately, and compared with the value specified. Check for distortion along the length and across the width of the head, and along both diagonals. If the head is warped, it may be possible to have it machined flat ('skimmed') at an engineering works – check with an engine specialist before dismantling the head as described in Chapter 2D.

33 Ford state that the cylinder head bolts can be re-used, but they should be checked carefully before doing so. Examine the threads in particular for any signs of damage.

If any of the thread inside the cylinder head holes has been removed with the bolts, seek expert advice before proceeding. Lay the bolts out next to each other, and compare their length – if any one has stretched, so that it is longer than the rest, it should not be re-used, and it is probably advisable to renew all the bolts as a set. If there is any doubt as to the condition of the bolts, fit new ones – the cost of a set of bolts is nothing compared to the problems which may be caused if a bolt shears or strips when being tightened.

Refitting

34 Wipe clean the mating surfaces of the cylinder head and cylinder block. Check that the two locating dowels are in position in the cylinder block.

35 The cylinder head bolt holes must be free from oil or water. This is most important, as a hydraulic lock in a cylinder head bolt hole as the bolt is tightened can cause a fracture of the block casting.

36 Turn the crankshaft anti-clockwise so that pistons 1 and 4 are approximately 25 mm before TDC, in order to avoid the risk of valve/piston contact. Turn the crankshaft using a spanner on the pulley bolt.

37 Position a new gasket over the dowels on the cylinder block surface – it can only be fitted one way round **(see illustration)**.

38 To make aligning the cylinder head easier, it is helpful to make up a pair of guide studs from two 10 mm (thread size) studs approximately 90 mm long, with a screwdriver slot cut in one end – two old cylinder head bolts with their heads cut off would make a good starting point. Screw these guide studs, screwdriver slot upwards to permit removal, into the bolt holes at diagonally-opposite corners of the cylinder block surface (or into those where the locating dowels are fitted); ensure that approximately 70 mm of stud protrudes above the gasket.

39 Refit the cylinder head, sliding it down the guide studs (if used) and locating it on the dowels. Unscrew the guide studs (if used) when the head is in place.

40 Ford do not state whether or not the cylinder head bolts should be oiled when refitting, but experience suggests that coating the threads with a little light oil is useful – do not apply more than a light film of oil, however. Fit the cylinder head bolts carefully, and screw them in by hand only until finger-tight.

41 Working progressively and in the sequence shown **(see illustration)**, first tighten all the bolts to the specified Stage 1 torque setting.

42 With all the bolts tightened to Stage 1, tighten them further in sequence to the Stage 2 torque setting **(see illustration)**.

43 Stage 3 involves tightening the bolts though an angle, rather than to a torque. Each bolt in sequence must be rotated through the specified angle – special angle gauges are available from tool outlets, but a 90° angle is

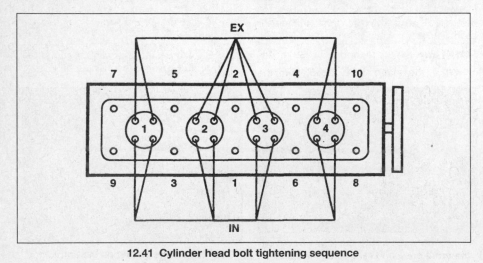

12.41 Cylinder head bolt tightening sequence

equivalent to a quarter-turn, and this is easily judged by assessing the start and end positions of the socket handle or torque wrench **(see illustration)**.

44 Once all the bolts have been tightened to Stage 3, no subsequent tightening is necessary.

45 Before proceeding with refitting, turn the crankshaft forwards to TDC, and check that the setting tools described in Section 3 can be inserted. Do not turn the engine more than necessary while the timing belt is removed, or the valves may hit the pistons – for instance, if the engine is accidentally turned past the TDC position, turn it back slightly and try again – do not bring the engine round a full turn.

46 Refitting of the other components removed is a reversal of removal, noting the following points:

a) *Refit the camshafts as described in Section 11, and the timing belt as described in Section 8.*

b) *Refit the exhaust manifold with reference to Chapter 4C if necessary.*

c) *Tighten all fasteners to the specified torque, where given.*

d) *Ensure that all hoses and wiring are correctly routed, and that hose clips and wiring connectors are securely refitted.*

e) *Refill the cooling system as described in Chapter 1A.*

f) *Check all disturbed joints for signs of oil or coolant leakage once the engine has been restarted and warmed-up to normal operating temperature.*

13 Sump –
removal and refitting

Removal

1 Apply the handbrake, then jack up the front of the vehicle and support it on axle stands (see *Jacking and vehicle support*).

2 Drain the engine oil, then check the drain plug sealing washer and renew if necessary. Clean and refit the engine oil drain plug, together with the washer, and tighten it to the specified torque wrench setting. Although not strictly necessary as part of the dismantling

12.42 Tighten the bolts to the specified torques . . .

procedure, owners are advised to remove and discard the oil filter, so that it can be renewed with the oil (see Chapter 1A).

3 Unscrew and remove the bolts securing the sump to the transmission, and place them to one side, as they should not be mixed up with the sump-to-engine bolts.

4 Progressively unscrew and remove the sump retaining bolts **(see illustration)**.

Models up to November 1999

5 Lower the sump from the crankcase, and withdraw it from under the vehicle.

6 Recover the sump gasket. Due to its laminated steel and vulcanised rubber construction, this gasket is expensive, therefore if it is in good condition it is possible to re-use it. Unlike more conventional gaskets, this gasket should release from the crankcase and sump surfaces easily.

Models from December 1999

7 On later models, a sump gasket is not used, and sealant is used instead.

8 Unfortunately, the use of sealant makes removal of the sump more difficult. If care is taken not to damage the surfaces, the sealant can be cut around using a sharp knife.

9 On no account lever between the mating faces, as this will almost certainly damage them, resulting in leaks when finished. Ford technicians have a tool comprising a metal rod which is inserted through the sump drain hole, and a handle to pull the sump downwards.

Refitting

10 While the sump is removed, take the

12.43 . . . then angle-tighten them – note the use of an angle gauge

opportunity to remove the oil pump pick-up/strainer pipe and clean it with reference to Section 14.

11 Thoroughly clean the contact surfaces of the sump and crankcase. If necessary, use a cloth rag to clean the interior of the sump and crankcase. If the oil pump pick-up/strainer pipe was removed, fit a new gasket and refit the pipe with reference to Section 14.

Models up to November 1999

12 Apply a smear of sealant (Ford recommend WSE M4G323-A4, or equivalent) to the bottom face of the crankshaft rear oil seal housing. Also apply the sealant over the joints between the crankshaft rear oil seal and crankcase, and oil pump housing and crankcase **(see illustration)**. The sump bolts must be fitted and tightened within 10 minutes of applying the sealant.

13 Locate the gasket on the sump or crankcase **(see illustration)**, then offer the sump onto the crankcase and insert the retaining bolts finger-tight.

14 Before tightening the bolts, the sump must be accurately aligned with the end face of the cylinder block. If the transmission is still attached to the engine, this presents no problem, provided that the sump-to-transmission bolts are tightened before the sump bolts. However, if the engine is detached from the transmission (eg, for overhaul), a straight-edge must be used for alignment.

15 Where possible, insert the sump-to-transmission bolts and tighten them to the specified torque.

13.4 Sump seen from below, showing the engine and transmission bolts

13.12 Apply sealant to the joints between the crankcase and rear oil seal/oil pump housing

13.13 Locate the gasket on the crankcase or sump

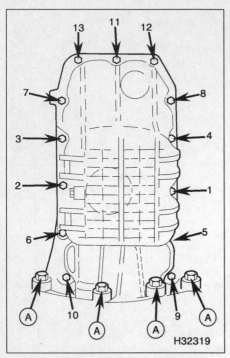

13.16 Sump bolt-to-engine tightening sequence – also note sump-to-transmission bolts (A)

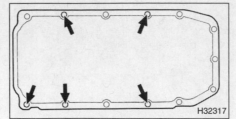

13.17 Sump alignment stud positions (arrowed)

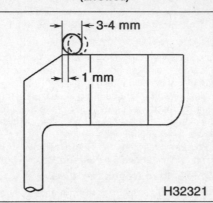

13.18 Showing how the bead of sealant is to be applied to the sump mating surface

16 Once the sump is correctly aligned, progressively tighten the sump-to-crankcase bolts to the specified torque using the sequence shown **(see illustration)**.

Models from December 1999

17 Ford state that, to refit the sump, five M8x20 studs must be screwed into the base of the engine, in the positions shown **(see illustration)**. This not only helps to align the sump, ensuring that the bead of sealant is not displaced as the sump is fitted, but also ensures that the sealant does not enter the blind holes. Cut a slot across the end of each stud, to make removal easier when the sump is in place.

18 Apply a 3 to 4 mm diameter bead of sealant (Ford recommend WSE M4G323-A4, or equivalent) to the sump pan, to the inside of the bolt holes, as shown **(see illustration)**. The sump bolts must be fitted and tightened within 10 minutes of applying the sealant.

19 Offer the sump up into position over the studs, and fully refit the remaining bolts by hand. Unscrew the studs, and refit the sump bolts in their place.

20 Insert the sump-to-transmission bolts and tighten them to the specified torque.

21 The sump-to-engine bolts are tightened in the same sequence as for earlier models **(refer to illustration 13.16)**, but in two stages. First, following the sequence, tighten all the sump bolts to half the specified torque, then go around again in sequence, and tighten them fully to the specified torque.

All models

22 Lower the car to the ground, and where necessary, fit a new oil filter. To be on the safe side, wait a further 30 minutes for the sealant to cure before filling the sump with fresh oil, as described in Chapter 1A.

23 Finally start the engine and check for signs of oil leaks.

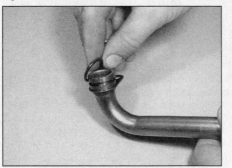

14.6 Removing the O-ring from the oil pump pick-up/strainer pipe

14.8 Removing the oil pump gasket

14 Oil pump – removal, inspection and refitting

Removal

1 Remove the timing belt as described in Section 8.

2 Remove the crankshaft sprocket as described in Section 9.

3 Refit the engine right-hand mounting lower and upper brackets and tighten the mounting bolts/nuts to their specified torques. Remove the trolley jack from under the sump.

4 Remove the sump as described in Section 13.

5 Unscrew the bolts securing the oil pump pick-up/strainer pipe to the baffle plate/main bearing cap.

6 Unscrew the bolt securing the oil pump pick-up/strainer pipe to the oil pump, then withdraw the pipe and recover the sealing O-ring **(see illustration)**. Discard the O-ring.

7 Unscrew the bolts securing the oil pump to the cylinder block/crankcase **(see illustration)**. Withdraw the pump over the nose of the crankshaft.

8 Recover then discard the gasket **(see illustration)**.

9 Support the oil pump on wooden blocks, then use a screwdriver to hook or drive out the crankshaft front oil seal.

10 If necessary, unbolt and remove the baffle plate from the main bearing cap/ladder **(see illustration)**. Thoroughly clean all components, particularly the mating surfaces of the pump, the sump, and the cylinder block/crankcase.

14.7 Removing the oil pump mounting bolts

14.10 Unbolting the baffle plate from the main bearing cap/ladder

15.7 Locating the new front oil seal over the crankshaft

Inspection

11 It is not possible to obtain individual components of the oil pump, furthermore, there are no torque settings available for tightening the pump cover plate bolts. However, the following procedure is provided for owners wishing to dismantle the oil pump for examination.

12 Unscrew the screws, and remove the pump cover plate; noting any identification marks on the rotors, withdraw the rotors.

13 Inspect the rotors for obvious signs of wear or damage, and renew if necessary; if either rotor, the pump body, or its cover plate are scored or damaged, the complete oil pump assembly must be renewed.

14 The oil pressure relief valve can be dismantled as follows.

15 Unscrew the threaded plug, and recover the valve spring and plunger. If the plug's sealing O-ring is worn or damaged, a new one must be obtained, to be fitted on reassembly.

16 Reassembly is the reverse of the dismantling procedure; ensure the spring and valve are refitted the correct way round, and tighten the threaded plug securely.

Refitting

17 If removed, refit the oil baffle plate to the crankcase and tighten the bolts.

18 The oil pump must be primed on installation, by pouring clean engine oil into it, and rotating its inner rotor a few turns.

19 Use a little grease to stick the new gasket in place on the cylinder block/crankcase.

20 Offer the oil pump over the nose of the crankshaft, and turn the inner rotor as necessary to align its flats with the flats on the crankshaft. Locate the pump on the dowels, then insert the retaining bolts and progressively tighten them to the specified torque.

21 Fit a new crankshaft front oil seal (see Section 15).

22 Locate a new O-ring (dipped in oil) on the pick-up/strainer pipe, then locate the pipe in the oil pump and insert the retaining bolts. Insert the bolts retaining the pipe on the baffle plate/main bearing cap. Tighten the bolts to the specified torque.

23 Refit the sump as described in Section 13.

24 Support the weight of the engine with a

trolley jack and wood block beneath the sump, then unscrew the nuts and bolts and remove the engine right-hand mounting upper and lower brackets.

25 Refit the crankshaft sprocket with reference to Section 9.

26 Refit the timing belt with reference to Section 8.

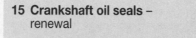

15 Crankshaft oil seals – renewal

Oil pump housing oil seal

1 Remove the timing belt as described in Section 8.

2 Remove the crankshaft sprocket as described in Section 9.

3 As a safety precaution, refit the engine right-hand mounting lower and upper brackets and tighten the mounting bolts/nuts.

4 Note the fitted depth of the oil seal as a guide for fitting the new one.

5 Using a screwdriver, prise the old oil seal from the oil pump housing. Take care not to damage the seal contact surface on the nose of the crankshaft or the seating in the housing.

6 Wipe clean the seating and the nose of the crankshaft.

7 Dip the new oil seal in fresh oil, then locate it over the crankshaft and into the oil pump housing **(see illustration)**. Make sure that the closed end of the oil seal faces outwards.

8 Using a socket or length of metal tubing, drive the oil seal squarely into position to the previously noted depth. The Ford installation tool (303-395) is used together with an old crankshaft pulley bolt to press the oil seal into position. The same effect may be achieved with metal tubing and a large washer – do not use a new crankshaft pulley bolt, as it is only permissible to use the bolt once. With the oil seal in position, wipe away any excess oil.

9 Support the weight of the engine with a trolley jack and wood block beneath the sump, then unscrew the nuts and bolts and remove the engine right-hand mounting upper and lower brackets.

10 Refit the crankshaft sprocket with reference to Section 9.

15.20 With the oil seal housing bolted in position, remove the fitting ring

15.18 Locating the new rear oil seal housing (complete with fitting ring) over the rear of the crankshaft

11 Refit the timing belt with reference to Section 8.

Flywheel end oil seal

12 Remove the transmission (see the relevant Part of Chapter 7).

13 On manual transmission models, remove the clutch as described in Chapter 6.

14 Remove the flywheel/driveplate as described in Section 16.

15 Unscrew the retaining bolts and withdraw the rear oil seal housing over the end of the crankshaft. Note that the seal and housing are manufactured as one unit, incorporating a vulcanised gasket. It is not possible to obtain the seal separately.

16 Clean the housing contact surface on the cylinder block and the end of the crankshaft.

17 The new oil seal housing is supplied complete with a fitting ring which ensures that the oil seal lips are correctly located on the crankshaft.

18 Smear the end of the crankshaft with fresh engine oil, then locate the oil seal housing with fitting ring over the end of the crankshaft **(see illustration)**. Press the housing into position, noting that the centre bolt holes are formed into locating dowels.

19 Insert the retaining bolts and progressively tighten them to the specified torque. Wipe away any surplus oil.

20 Remove the fitting ring, and check that the oil seal lips are correctly located **(see illustration)**.

21 Refit the flywheel/driveplate as described in Section 16.

22 On manual transmission models refit the clutch as described in Chapter 6.

23 Refit the transmission (see the relevant Part of Chapter 7).

16 Flywheel/driveplate – removal, inspection and refitting

Removal

1 Remove the transmission (see the relevant Part of Chapter 7).

2 On manual transmission models, remove the clutch as described in Chapter 6.

16.3 Home-made tool for holding the flywheel stationary while loosening the bolts

16.4 Removing the flywheel retaining bolts (note the location dowel in the crankshaft)

3 Hold the flywheel/driveplate stationary using one of the following methods:

a) If an assistant is available, insert one of the transmission mounting bolts into the cylinder block, and have the assistant engage a wide-bladed screwdriver with the starter ring gear teeth while the bolts are loosened.

b) Alternatively, a piece of angle-iron can be engaged with the ring gear, and located against the transmission mounting bolt.

c) A further method is to fabricate a piece of flat metal bar with a pointed end to engage the ring gear – fit the tool to the transmission bolt, and use washers and packing to align it with the ring gear, then tighten the bolt to hold it in position **(see illustration).**

4 Unscrew and remove the retaining bolts, then lift the flywheel/driveplate off the locating dowel on the crankshaft **(see illustration).**

Inspection

5 Clean the flywheel/driveplate to remove grease and oil. Inspect the surface for cracks, rivet grooves, burned areas and score marks. Light scoring can be removed with emery cloth. Check for cracked and broken ring gear teeth. Lay the flywheel/driveplate on a flat surface, and use a straight-edge to check for warpage.

6 Clean and inspect the mating surfaces of the flywheel/driveplate and the crankshaft. If the crankshaft oil seal is leaking, renew it (see Section 15) before refitting the flywheel/driveplate.

7 While the flywheel/driveplate is removed, carefully clean its inner face, particularly the recesses which serve as the reference points for the crankshaft speed/position sensor. Clean the sensor's tip, and check that the sensor is securely fastened. The sensor mounting may be removed if necessary by first removing the sensor, then unscrewing the bolt and withdrawing the mounting from the cylinder block.

Refitting

8 Make sure that the mating faces of the flywheel/driveplate and crankshaft are clean, then locate the flywheel/driveplate on the crankshaft and engage it with the locating dowel.

9 Insert the retaining bolts finger-tight.

10 Lock the flywheel/driveplate (see paragraph 3), then tighten the bolts in two stages to the specified torque using a diagonal sequence; first tighten all six bolts to the Stage 1 torque, then further tighten all six through the specified Stage 2 angle. Special angle-measuring gauges are available from tool suppliers, but (for example) a 90° angle is equivalent to a quarter-turn, and this is easily judged by assessing the start and end positions of the socket handle or torque wrench.

11 On manual transmission models, refit the clutch with reference to Chapter 6.

12 Refit the transmission (see the relevant Part of Chapter 7).

---

17 Engine/transmission mountings – inspection and renewal

Inspection

1 The engine/transmission mountings seldom require attention, but broken or deteriorated mountings should be renewed immediately, as the added strain placed on the driveline components may cause damage or wear.

2 During the check, the engine/transmission must be raised slightly, to remove its weight from the mountings.

3 Apply the handbrake, then jack up the front of the vehicle and support it on axle stands (see *Jacking and vehicle support*). Remove

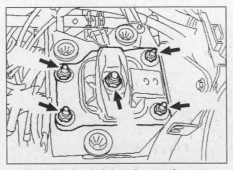

17.10 Engine left-hand mounting nuts (arrowed) – note larger centre nut

the engine undershield where fitted. Position a jack under the sump, with a large block of wood between the jack head and the sump, then carefully raise the engine/transmission just enough to take the weight off the mountings.

4 Check the mountings to see if the rubber is cracked, hardened or separated from the metal components. Sometimes, the rubber will split right down the centre.

5 Check for relative movement between each mounting's brackets and the engine/transmission or body (use a large screwdriver or lever to attempt to move the mountings). If movement is noted, lower the engine and check the mounting nuts and bolts for tightness.

Renewal

6 The engine mountings can be removed if the weight of the engine/transmission is supported by one of the following alternative methods.

7 Either support the weight of the assembly from underneath using a jack and a suitable piece of wood between the jack and the sump (to prevent damage), or from above by attaching a hoist to the engine. A third method is to use a suitable support bar with end pieces which will engage in the water channel each side of the bonnet lid aperture. Using an adjustable hook and chain connected to the engine, the weight of the engine and transmission can then be taken from the mountings.

8 Once the weight of the engine and transmission is suitably supported, any of the mountings can be unbolted and removed.

9 To remove the engine right-hand mounting, first mark the positions of the three bolts relative to the mounting plate. Unscrew the three bolts securing the mounting to the inner wing, and the three nuts securing it to the engine **(refer to illustration 8.10a)**. Lift off the mounting complete.

10 To remove the left-hand mounting, first remove the battery and battery tray as described in Chapter 5A, then loosen the clips and remove the air inlet duct. Unscrew the five mounting nuts (noting that the centre one is larger than the rest) from the engine left-hand mounting, then lift off the upper bracket **(see illustration)**. Unscrew the three nuts and remove the lower half of the mounting from the transmission.

11 To remove the engine rear mounting/link, apply the handbrake, then jack up the front of the vehicle and support it on axle stands (see *Jacking and vehicle support*). Unscrew the through-bolts and remove the engine rear mounting link from the bracket on the transmission and from the bracket on the underbody **(see illustration)**. Hold the engine stationary while the bolts are being removed, since the link will be under tension. **Note:** *The two through-bolts are of different lengths – if the bolts are refitted in the wrong positions, the rearmost bolt will foul the steering rack.*

17.11 Engine rear mounting/link

12 Refitting of all mountings is a reversal of the removal procedure. Do not fully tighten the mounting nuts/bolts until all of the mountings are in position. Check that the mounting rubbers do not twist or distort as the mounting bolts and nuts are tightened to their specified torques.

18 Oil pressure warning light switch – removal and refitting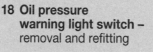

Removal

1 The switch is screwed into the cylinder block, next to the oil filter.
2 With the vehicle parked on firm level ground, open the bonnet and disconnect the battery negative (earth) lead – see *Disconnecting the battery*.
3 Raise the front of the vehicle and support it securely on axle stands.
4 Unplug the wiring from the switch and unscrew it; be prepared for some oil loss.

Refitting

5 Refitting is the reverse of the removal procedure; apply a thin smear of suitable sealant to the switch threads, and tighten it to the specified torque wrench setting. Check the engine oil level and top-up as necessary (see *Weekly checks*). Check for correct warning light operation, and for signs of oil leaks once the engine has been restarted and warmed-up to normal operating temperature.

Notes

Chapter 2 Part B:
1.8 & 2.0 litre engine in-car repair procedures

Contents

Degrees of difficulty

Easy, suitable for novice with little experience	**Fairly easy,** suitable for beginner with some experience	**Fairly difficult,** suitable for competent DIY mechanic	**Difficult,** suitable for experienced DIY mechanic	**Very difficult,** suitable for expert DIY or professional

Specifications

General

Engine type	Four-cylinder, in-line, double overhead camshafts, aluminium alloy cylinder head, cast-iron engine block
Designation	Zetec-E
Engine code:	
1.8 litre	EYDA (or EYDC – German market)
2.0 litre	EDDA (or EDDC – German market)
Capacity:	
1.8 litre	1796 cc
2.0 litre	1989 cc
Bore:	
1.8 litre	80.6 mm
2.0 litre	84.8 mm
Stroke	88.0 mm
Compression ratio	10.0:1
Firing order	1-3-4-2 (No 1 cylinder at timing belt end)
Direction of crankshaft rotation	Clockwise (seen from right-hand side of vehicle)

Camshafts

Camshaft bearing journal diameter	25.96 to 25.98 mm
Camshaft bearing journal-to-cylinder head running clearance	0.02 to 0.07 mm
Camshaft endfloat	0.08 to 0.22 mm

Valves

	Inlet	**Exhaust**
Valve clearances (cold):		
Checking	0.11 to 0.18 mm	0.27 to 0.34 mm
Setting	0.15 mm	0.30 mm
Shim thicknesses available	1.8 to 3.3 mm in varying increments	

Cylinder head

Maximum permissible gasket surface distortion . . . . 0.1 mm

Lubrication

Engine oil type/specification . . . . See end of *Weekly checks*
Engine oil capacity . . . . See Chapter 1A
Oil pressure (engine at operating temperature):
   At idle (800 to 850 rpm) . . . . 1.3 to 2.5 bars
   At 4000 rpm . . . . 3.7 to 5.5 bars
Note: *On 2.0 litre engines, the piston-cooling oil jets are fully open at 4000 rpm, resulting in a pressure drop of approximately 0.3 to 0.8 bar. This should be borne in mind if a pressure reading is recorded close to the lower end of the tolerance range.*
Oil pump clearances . . . . No information available at time of writing

Torque wrench settings

	Nm	lbf ft
Air conditioning compressor mounting bracket:		
Lower bolts	25	18
Upper nuts	48	35
Alternator bracket:		
Lower bolts/nut	65	48
Upper bolts	25	18
Auxiliary drivebelt idler pulley	40	30
Big-end bearing cap bolts:		
Stage 1	15	11
Stage 2	Angle-tighten a further 90°	
Camshaft bearing cap bolts:		
Stage 1	10	7
Stage 2	19	14
Camshaft sprocket bolts	68	50
Catalytic converter nuts/bolts	48	35
Coolant pump housing-to-engine bolts	18	13
Coolant pump pulley bolts	24	18
Coolant pump-to-housing bolts	9	7
Crankshaft pulley bolt	115	85
Crankshaft rear oil seal carrier bolts	20	15
Cylinder head bolts:		
Stage 1	15	11
Stage 2	40	30
Stage 3	Angle-tighten a further 90°	
Cylinder head cover bolts:	7	5
Engine mountings:		
Left-hand mounting (transmission):		
Lower section	80	59
Upper section:		
Centre nut	133	98
Four outer nuts	48	35
Rear mounting to subframe (roll restrictor)	48	35
Right-hand mounting lower bracket	55	41
Right-hand mounting upper section:		
To body	48	35
To engine	80	59
Exhaust manifold heat shield bolts	10	7
Exhaust manifold nuts and bolts	16	12
Flywheel bolts	112	83
Inlet manifold nuts and bolts	18	13
Lower crankcase to cylinder block	30	22
Main bearing cap bolts	85	63
Oil pick-up pipe bolts	10	7
Oil pressure switch	27	20
Oil pump-to-cylinder block bolts	11	8
Power steering pump bracket nuts	48	35
Roadwheel nuts	85	63
Spark plugs	15	11
Starter motor mounting bolts	35	26
Sump drain plug	24	18
Sump pan to lower crankcase:		
Stage 1	6	4
Stage 2	10	7
Thermostat housing	20	15

Torque wrench settings (continued)

	Nm	lbf ft
Timing belt covers:		
Lower cover bolts	7	5
Middle cover bolts	50	37
Upper cover bolts	10	7
Timing belt guide pulley bolt:		
Up to January 1999 (upper and lower pulleys)	38	28
January 1999 onwards	23	17
Timing belt tensioner bolt	25	18
Transmission-to-engine bolts	48	35

1   General information

How to use this Chapter

This Part of Chapter 2 is devoted to repair procedures possible while the engine is still installed in the vehicle. Since these procedures are based on the assumption that the engine is installed in the vehicle, if the engine has been removed from the vehicle and mounted on a stand, some of the preliminary dismantling steps outlined will not apply.

Information concerning engine/transmission removal and refitting and engine overhaul, can be found in Part D of this Chapter.

Engine description

The Zetec-E engine is of sixteen-valve, double overhead camshaft (DOHC), four-cylinder, in-line type, mounted transversely at the front of the vehicle, with the transmission on its left-hand end. It is available in the Focus in 1.8 and 2.0 litre versions.

Apart from the plastic timing belt covers and the cast-iron cylinder block/crankcase, all major engine castings are of aluminium alloy. The engines differ from previous generations of the Zetec (fitted to the Mondeo, and others) in that it has a cast aluminium alloy lower crankcase which is bolted to the underside of the cylinder block/crankcase, with a pressed-steel sump bolted under that. This arrangement offers greater rigidity than the normal sump arrangement, and helps to reduce engine vibration.

The crankshaft runs in five main bearings, the centre main bearing's upper half incorporating thrustwashers to control crankshaft endfloat. The connecting rods rotate on horizontally-split bearing shells at their big-ends. The pistons are attached to the connecting rods by gudgeon pins which are an interference fit in the connecting rod small-end eyes. The aluminium alloy pistons are fitted with three piston rings: two compression rings and an oil control ring. After manufacture, the cylinder bores and piston skirts are measured and classified into three grades, which must be carefully matched together to ensure the correct piston/cylinder clearance; no oversizes are available to permit reboring.

The inlet and exhaust valves are each closed by coil springs; they operate in guides which are shrink-fitted into the cylinder head, as are the valve seat inserts.

The two camshafts are driven by the same toothed timing belt, each operating eight valves via conventional cam followers with shims. Each camshaft rotates in five bearings that are line-bored directly in the cylinder head and the (bolted-on) bearing caps; this means that the bearing caps are not available separately from the cylinder head, and must not be interchanged with caps from another engine.

The coolant pump is bolted to the right-hand end of the cylinder block, inboard of the timing belt, and is driven with the steering pump and alternator by a multi-ribbed auxiliary drivebelt from the crankshaft pulley.

When working on this engine, note that Torx-type (both male and female heads) and hexagon socket (Allen head) fasteners are widely used; a good selection of bits, with the necessary adapters, will be required, so that these can be unscrewed without damage and, on reassembly, tightened to the torque wrench settings specified.

Lubrication system

Lubrication is by means of an eccentric-rotor trochoidal pump, which is mounted on the crankshaft right-hand end, and draws oil through a strainer located in the sump. The pump forces oil through an externally-mounted full-flow cartridge-type filter. From the filter, the oil is pumped into a main gallery in the cylinder block/crankcase, from where it is distributed to the crankshaft (main bearings) and cylinder head.

The big-end bearings are supplied with oil via internal drillings in the crankshaft. On 2.0 litre engines, each piston crown is cooled by a spray of oil directed at its underside by a jet. These jets are fed by passages off the crankshaft oil supply galleries, with spring-loaded valves to ensure that the jets open only when there is sufficient pressure to guarantee a good oil supply to the rest of the engine components; where the jets are not fitted, separate blanking plugs are provided so that the passages are sealed, but can be cleaned at overhaul. The cylinder head is provided with two oil galleries, one on the inlet side and one on the exhaust, to ensure constant oil supply to the camshaft bearings and cam followers. A

retaining valve (inserted into the cylinder head's top surface, in the middle, on the inlet side) prevents these galleries from being drained when the engine is switched off. The valve incorporates a ventilation hole in its upper end, to allow air bubbles to escape from the system when the engine is restarted.

While the crankshaft and camshaft bearings receive a pressurised supply, the camshaft lobes and valves are lubricated by splash, as are all other engine components.

Repair operations possible with the engine in the car

The following major repair operations can be accomplished without removing the engine from the vehicle. However, owners should note that any operation involving the removal of the sump requires careful forethought, depending on the level of skill and the tools and facilities available; refer to the relevant text for details.

a) Compression pressure – testing.
b) Cylinder head cover – removal and refitting.
c) Timing belt covers – removal and refitting.
d) Timing belt – renewal.
e) Timing belt tensioner and sprockets – removal and refitting.
f) Camshaft oil seals – renewal.
g) Camshafts and cam followers – removal and refitting.
h) Cylinder head – removal, overhaul and refitting.
i) Cylinder head and pistons – decarbonising.
j) Sump – removal and refitting.
k) Crankshaft oil seals – renewal.
l) Oil pump – removal and refitting.
m) Piston/connecting rod assemblies – removal and refitting (but see note below).
n) Flywheel – removal and refitting.
o) Engine/transmission mountings – removal and refitting.

Note: It is possible to remove the pistons and connecting rods (after removing the cylinder head and sump) without removing the engine. However, this is not recommended; work of this nature is more easily and thoroughly completed with the engine on the bench, as described in Chapter 2D.

Clean the engine compartment and the exterior of the engine with some type of degreaser before any work is done (and/or clean the engine using a steam cleaner). It will make the job easier and will help to keep dirt out of the internal areas of the engine.

3.5a Turn the engine so that the camshaft end slots are aligned . . .

3.5b . . . then fit the metal strip to locate and set the shafts to TDC

Depending on the components involved, it may be helpful to remove the bonnet, to improve access to the engine as repairs are performed (refer to Chapter 11 if necessary). Cover the wings to prevent damage to the paint; special covers are available, but an old bedspread or blanket will also work.

2 Compression test – description and interpretation

1 When engine performance is down, or if misfiring occurs which cannot be attributed to the ignition or fuel systems, a compression test can provide diagnostic clues as to the engine's condition. If the test is performed regularly, it can give warning of trouble before any other symptoms become apparent.
2 The engine must be fully warmed-up to normal operating temperature, the oil level must be correct, the battery must be fully charged. The aid of an assistant will also be required.
3 Referring to Chapter 12, identify and remove the fuel pump fuse from the fusebox. Now start the engine and allow it to run until it stalls. If the engine will not start, at least keep it cranking for about 10 seconds. The fuel system should now be depressurised, preventing unburnt fuel from soaking the catalytic converter as the engine is turned over during the test.
4 Disable the ignition system by unplugging the ignition coil's electrical connector. Remove the spark plugs.
5 Fit a compression tester to the No 1 cylinder spark plug hole – the type of tester which screws into the plug thread is to be preferred.
6 Have the assistant hold the throttle wide open and crank the engine on the starter motor; after one or two revolutions, the compression pressure should build up to a maximum figure and then stabilise. Record the highest reading obtained.
7 The compression will build up fairly quickly in a healthy engine. Low compression on the first stroke, followed by gradually-increasing pressure on successive strokes, indicates worn piston rings. A low compression on the

first stroke which does not rise on successive strokes, indicates leaking valves or a blown head gasket (a cracked cylinder head could also be the cause). Deposits on the underside of the valve heads can also cause low compression. Record the highest gauge reading obtained, then repeat the procedure for the remaining cylinders.
8 Due to the variety of testers available, and the fluctuation in starter motor speed when cranking the engine, different readings are often obtained when carrying out the compression test. For this reason, specific compression pressure figures are not quoted by Ford. However, the most important factor is that the compression pressures are uniform in all cylinders, and that is what this test is mainly concerned with.
9 If the pressure in any cylinder is considerably lower than the others, introduce a teaspoonful of clean oil into that cylinder through its spark plug hole and repeat the test.
10 If the addition of oil temporarily improves the compression pressure, this indicates that bore or piston wear is responsible for the pressure loss. No improvement suggests that leaking or burnt valves, or a blown head gasket, may be to blame.
11 A low reading from two adjacent cylinders is almost certainly due to the head gasket having blown between them; the presence of coolant in the engine oil will confirm this.
12 If one cylinder is about 20 percent lower than the others and the engine has a slightly rough idle, a worn camshaft lobe or faulty cam follower/shim could be the cause.

3.6 Removing the timing hole blanking plug – catalytic converter removed for clarity

13 If the compression is unusually high, the combustion chambers are probably coated with carbon deposits. If this is the case, the cylinder head should be removed and decarbonised.
14 On completion of the test, refit the spark plugs, then reconnect the ignition system coil and refit the fuel pump fuse.

3 Top Dead Centre (TDC) for No 1 piston – locating

1 Top dead centre (TDC) is the highest point of the cylinder that each piston reaches as the crankshaft turns. Each piston reaches its TDC position at the end of its compression stroke, and then again at the end of its exhaust stroke. For the purpose of engine timing, TDC on the compression stroke for No 1 piston is used. No 1 cylinder is at the timing belt end of the engine. Proceed as follows.
2 Disconnect the battery negative (earth) lead (refer to *Disconnecting the battery*).
3 Remove all the spark plugs as described in Chapter 1A, then remove the cylinder head cover as described in Section 4.
4 Using a spanner or socket on the crankshaft pulley bolt (remove the panel in the wheelarch liner for access), rotate the crankshaft clockwise until the inlet valves for No 1 cylinder have opened and just closed again.
5 The camshafts each have a machined slot at the transmission end of the engine; both slots will be completely horizontal, and at the same height as the cylinder head machined surface, when the engine is at TDC on No 1 cylinder. Ford service tool 303-376 is used to check this position, and to positively locate the camshafts in position. Fortunately, a substitute tool can be made from a strip of metal 5 mm thick (while the strip's thickness is critical, its length and width are not, but should be approximately 180 to 230 mm long by 20 to 30 mm wide) **(see illustrations)**.
6 A TDC timing hole is provided on the front of the cylinder block to permit the crankshaft to be located more accurately at TDC. The blanking plug is located behind the catalytic converter, and access is not easy – also, take care against burning if the engine is still warm **(see illustration)**.
7 Unscrew the timing pin blanking plug and screw in the timing pin (Ford service tool 303-620); this tool is obtainable from Ford dealers or a tool supplier. An alternative pin can be made from an M10 diameter bolt, cut down so that the length from the underside of the bolt head to the tip is exactly 63.4 mm **(see illustrations)**. It may be necessary to slightly turn the crankshaft either way (remove the tool from the camshafts first) to be able to fully insert the timing pin.
8 Turn the engine forwards slowly until the

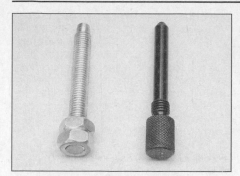

3.7a Home-made (left) and genuine (right) timing pins

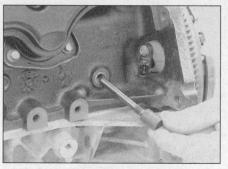

3.7b Insert the timing pin in the hole . . .

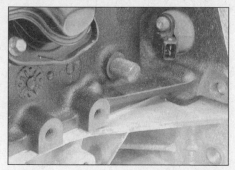

3.7c . . . and screw it fully into position

crankshaft comes into contact with the timing pin – in this position, the engine is set to TDC on No 1 cylinder.

9 Before rotating the crankshaft again, make sure that the timing pin is removed. When operations are complete, do not forget to refit the blanking plug.

10 If the timing pin is not available, insert a length of wooden dowel (about 150 mm/ 6 in long) or similar into the No 1 spark plug hole until it rests on the piston crown. Turn the engine back from its TDC position, then forward (taking care not to allow the dowel to be trapped in the cylinder) until the dowel stops rising – the piston is now at the top of its compression stroke and the dowel can be removed.

11 There is a 'dead' area around TDC (as the piston stops rising, pauses and then begins to descend) which makes difficult the exact location of TDC by this method; if accuracy is

required, either carefully establish the exact mid-point of the dead area (perhaps by using a dial gauge and probe), or refer to paragraph 5.

12 Once No 1 cylinder has been positioned at TDC on the compression stroke, TDC for any of the other cylinders can then be located by rotating the crankshaft clockwise 180° at a time and following the firing order (see Specifications).

---

4 Cylinder head cover –
removal and refitting

Removal

1 Disconnect the battery negative (earth) lead (refer to *Disconnecting the battery*).

2 Where applicable, disconnect the earth cable and power steering pipe support

bracket from the cylinder head rear support plate/engine lifting eye. Move the pipe to one side.

3 Unscrew the four bolts securing the plastic timing belt upper cover to the cylinder head **(see illustration)**. It will not be possible to completely remove the cover, as the engine/transmission right-hand mounting restricts this; however, once unbolted, the cover can be moved to one side to permit the removal of the cylinder head cover.

4 Disconnect the crankcase breather hose from the cylinder head cover union **(see illustration)**.

5 Unplug the HT leads from the spark plugs and withdraw them, unclipping the leads from the cover **(see illustration)**.

6 Working progressively, unscrew the cylinder head cover retaining bolts, noting the (captive) spacer sleeve and rubber seal at each, then withdraw the cover **(see illustrations)**.

7 Discard the cover gasket; this must be renewed whenever it is disturbed. Check that the sealing faces are undamaged and that the rubber seal at each bolt hole is serviceable; renew any worn or damaged seals.

Refitting

8 On refitting, clean the cover and cylinder head gasket faces carefully, then fit a new gasket to the cover, ensuring that it is located correctly by the rubber seals and spacer sleeves.

9 Refit the cover to the cylinder head, ensuring as the cover is tightened that the gasket remains seated.

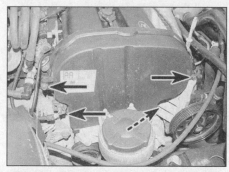

4.3 Unscrew the timing belt upper cover bolts (arrowed)

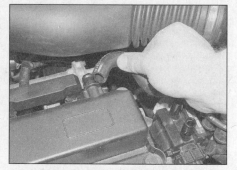

4.4 Disconnect the crankcase breather hose from the cover

4.5 Removing the HT leads

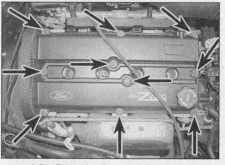

4.6a Remove the retaining bolts (arrowed) . . .

4.6b . . . and lift off the cylinder head cover

10 Working in a diagonal sequence from the centre outwards, first tighten the cover bolts by hand only. Once all the bolts are hand-tight, go around once more in sequence, and tighten the bolts to the specified torque wrench setting.

11 Refit the HT leads, clipping them into place so that they are correctly routed; each is numbered and can also be identified by the numbering on its respective coil terminal.

12 Reconnect the crankcase breather hose and refit the timing belt upper cover bolts.

13 Reconnect the earth cable and power steering pipe to the engine lifting eye, and reconnect the battery. On completion, run the engine and check for signs of oil leakage.

5 Valve clearances – checking and adjustment

Note: *For DIY purposes, note that while checking the valve clearances is an easy operation, changing the shims requires the use of a Ford special tool – owners may prefer to have this work carried out by a Ford dealer.*

Checking

1 Remove the cylinder head cover as described in Section 4.

2 Set No 1 cylinder to TDC on the compression stroke as described in Section 3. The inlet and exhaust cam lobes of No 1 cylinder will be pointing upwards (though not vertical) and the valve clearances can be checked.

3 Working on each valve in turn, measure the clearance between the base of the cam lobe and the shim using feeler blades **(see illustration)**. Record the thickness of the blade required to give a firm sliding fit on all four valves of No 1 cylinder.

4 Now turn the crankshaft clockwise through 180° so that the valves of cylinder No 3 are pointing upwards. Measure and record the valve clearances for cylinder No 3. The clearances for cylinders 4 and 2 can be measured after turning the crankshaft through 180° each time. Any measured valve clearances which do not fall in the specified range (see Specifications) must be adjusted.

Adjustment

Note: *Use of the Ford special tool is highly recommended, as the design of the camshafts and cylinder head and the lack of space mean that it would not be possible to use a screwdriver or similar tool to depress the cam follower without serious risk of damage to the cylinder head. The only alternative for the DIY mechanic is to measure the clearances very carefully indeed (measure each several times, record the clearances measured, and take the average as determining the true value. Access can then be gained to the shims by removing the camshafts (see Section 11) so that all relevant shims can be changed without the need for special tools. This approach requires*

very careful, methodical work if the camshafts are not to be removed and refitted several times.

5 If adjustment is required, the shim thicknesses must be changed by depressing the cam follower and removing the old shim, then fitting a new one.

6 Before changing a shim, the piston for the relevant cylinder needs to be lowered from its TDC position by turning the crankshaft approximately 90° clockwise. If this is not done, the piston will be too close to the valve to allow the cam follower to be depressed, and there is a risk of the valve being bent.

7 Ford technicians use service tool 303-563A, which is bolted onto the cylinder head above each camshaft in turn using two of the camshaft bearing cap bolt locations – a spacer 8 x 12 mm (or equivalent thickness of 8 mm washers) may be required to allow the tool to be bolted onto the head. Locate the operating end of the tool onto the cam follower and operate the handle to depress the cam follower.

8 Take great care not to scratch or otherwise damage the cam follower and its housing. Remove the shim with a small screwdriver or magnetic probe, taking care not to scratch or damage the cam follower, then slowly release the pressure applied to the tool. **Do not** rotate the camshaft while a shim is removed – the risk of damage to the cam lobe and/or cam follower is too great.

9 Record the thickness of the shim (in mm) which is engraved on the side facing away from the camshaft. If the marking is missing or illegible, a micrometer will be needed to establish shim thickness.

10 If the valve clearance was too small, a thinner shim must be fitted. If the clearance was too large, a thicker shim must be fitted. When the shim thickness and the valve clearance are known, the required thickness of the new shim can be calculated as follows:

Sample calculation – clearance too small

Desired clearance (A)	*= 0.15 mm*
Measured clearance (B)	*= 0.09 mm*
Shim thickness found (C)	*= 2.55 mm*
Thickness required (D)	*= C + B – A*
	= 2.49 mm

Sample calculation – clearance too large

Desired clearance (A)	*= 0.30 mm*
Measured clearance (B)	*= 0.36 mm*

5.3 Checking the valve clearances

Shim thickness found (C)	*= 2.19 mm*
Thickness required (D)	*= C + B – A*
	= 2.25 mm

11 Depress the cam follower again, and press the correct shim into the recess in the cam follower with the thickness marking facing downwards. Ensure that the shim is properly located in the cam follower, and apply a smear of clean oil to it.

12 When all the clearances of the first cylinder's valves have been set, rotate the crankshaft through two full turns clockwise to settle the shims. Return the cylinder to TDC on the compression stroke and recheck the valve clearances. Repeat the procedure from step 10 onwards if any are still incorrect.

13 Repeat the process for the remaining cylinders, turning the crankshaft to bring each in turn first to the TDC position and then 90° after TDC, as described above.

14 It will be helpful for future adjustment if a record is kept of the thickness of shim fitted at each position. The shims required can be purchased in advance once the clearances and the existing shim thicknesses are known. It is permissible to interchange shims between cam followers to achieve the correct clearances, but it is not advisable to turn the camshaft with any shims removed, since there is a risk that the cam lobe will jam in the empty cam follower.

15 When all the clearances are correct, remove the tool, then refit the cylinder head cover as described in Section 4.

6 Crankshaft pulley – removal and refitting

Removal

1 Remove the auxiliary drivebelt – either remove the drivebelt completely, or just secure it clear of the crankshaft pulley, depending on the work to be carried out (see Chapter 1A).

2 If the pulley is being removed as part of another procedure (such as timing belt renewal) it will be easier to set the engine to TDC now (as described in Section 3) before removing the crankshaft pulley bolt.

3 The crankshaft must now be held or locked to prevent its rotation while the pulley bolt is unscrewed. Two holes are provided in the front face of the pulley, for use with a forked holding tool (with a bolt at each end of the forks, to locate in the holes). Such a tool can easily be fabricated from metal strips **(see Tool Tip)**, but if preferred, proceed as follows:

a) If the engine/transmission is still installed in the vehicle, select top gear and have an assistant apply the brakes hard.

b) If the engine/transmission has been removed but not yet separated, remove the starter motor (see Chapter 5A) and lock the flywheel ring gear by jamming it with a screwdriver against the bellhousing.

A forked holding tool for removing the crankshaft pulley can be made from two strips of thick steel – one long, one short, bolted together but still able to pivot. If bolts of appropriate diameter (to fit the holes in the pulley) are fitted to each 'fork', the pulley can be held and the pulley bolt unscrewed.

c) If the engine/transmission has been removed and separated, use the method shown in Section 17, for removing the flywheel.

Note: *NEVER use the timing pin as a means of locking the crankshaft – it is not strong enough for this, and will shear off. Always ensure that the timing pin is removed before the crankshaft pulley bolt (or similar fasteners) is slackened or tightened.*

4 Unscrew the pulley bolt and remove the pulley, noting which way round it is fitted (**see illustrations**).

Refitting

5 Ford do not require that a new pulley bolt be fitted; however, note that it is tightened to a very high torque (probably greater than that of the cylinder head bolts). Given its important role, it would be worth renewing the bolt when refitting the pulley, especially if it is known to have been loosened previously.

6 Refitting is the reverse of the removal procedure; ensure that the pulley's keyway is aligned with the crankshaft's locating key. Tighten the pulley bolt to the specified torque wrench setting, locking the crankshaft using the same method as for loosening.

7 Timing belt covers – removal and refitting

Upper cover

Removal

1 To improve access to the cover, remove the coolant expansion tank mounting bolt, unclip it at the rear, and move the tank to one side without disconnecting the hoses (**see illustrations**).

2 Unclip the power steering fluid reservoir from its location, and move it aside, again without disturbing the hoses (**see illustration**).

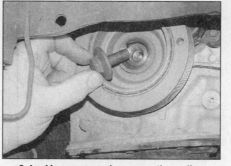

6.4a Unscrew and remove the pulley bolt . . .

3 Unscrew the four bolts and withdraw the upper cover as far as possible (**see illustrations**). To remove the upper cover completely, the engine must be supported, as the right-hand engine mounting must be removed.

7.1a Unscrew the expansion tank mounting bolt (arrowed) . . .

7.2 Lift out the power steering fluid reservoir

7.3b . . . and at the rear (arrowed)

6.4b . . . and remove the crankshaft pulley

4 Position a jack at the timing belt end of the sump, with a large block of wood between the sump and the jack head, and raise the jack so that the weight of the engine is supported (**see illustration**).

7.1b . . . and unclip the tank at the rear

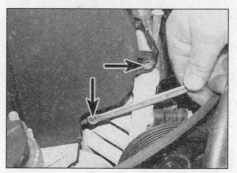

7.3a Unscrew the timing belt upper cover bolts at the front . . .

7.4 Jack and block of wood supporting the engine

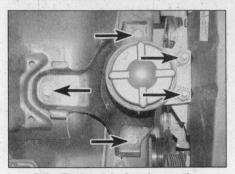

7.5a Engine right-hand mounting nuts/bolts (arrowed)

7.5b Loosen the nuts and bolts . . .

7.5c . . . and take off the engine mounting

5 Mark the fitted position of the engine mounting on the inner wing before removing it. Progressively loosen and remove the nuts/bolts, then lift off the right-hand mounting **(see illustrations)**.

6 To completely remove the cover, the engine right-hand mounting studs must be unscrewed – these have Torx end fittings, so can be unscrewed using a suitable socket **(see illustration)**.

7 Unclip the cylinder head temperature sensor wiring plug attached to the rear of the cover, then lift off the upper cover and remove it **(see illustrations)**.

Refitting

8 Refitting is the reverse of the removal procedure. Tighten the mounting studs securely, align the engine mounting with the marks made before removal, and tighten all bolts to the specified torque wrench setting.

Middle cover

Removal

9 Unbolt the coolant expansion tank, unclip it from the wing, and position it to one side without disconnecting the hoses.

10 Unclip the power steering fluid reservoir from its location, and move it aside, again without disturbing the hoses.

11 Support the engine using a trolley jack and large block of wood beneath the sump. Unbolt the engine right-hand mounting.

12 Slacken the coolant pump pulley bolts.

13 Remove the auxiliary drivebelt (see Chapter 1A).

14 Remove the timing belt upper cover as described previously in this Section.

15 Unbolt the coolant pump pulley, and also the auxiliary drivebelt idler pulley **(see illustrations)**.

16 Unscrew the four middle cover bolts (one of which is a Torx type – note its location) and withdraw the alloy cover **(see illustration)**.

Refitting

17 Refitting is the reverse of the removal procedure. Ensure the cover edges engage correctly with each other, and note the torque wrench settings specified for the various fasteners.

Lower cover

Removal

18 Remove the crankshaft pulley (see Section 6).

7.6 Unscrew and remove the engine mounting studs

7.7a Unclip the wiring plug at the rear of the cover . . .

7.7b . . . then lift off the cover

7.15a Unbolt and remove the coolant pump pulley . . .

7.15b . . . and the auxiliary drivebelt idler pulley

7.16 Removing the timing belt middle cover

7.19a Unscrew the bolts (arrowed) . . .

7.19b . . . and remove the timing belt lower cover

7.22 Removing the inner shield (seen with the cylinder head removed)

19 Unscrew the cover's securing bolts and withdraw it **(see illustrations)**.

Refitting

20 Refitting is the reverse of the removal procedure. Ensure the cover edges engage correctly with each other, and note the torque wrench settings specified for the various fasteners.

Inner shield/cover

Removal

21 Remove the timing belt, its tensioner components and the camshaft sprockets (see Sections 8 and 9).

22 The shield is secured to the cylinder head by two bolts at the top; unscrew these and withdraw the shield **(see illustration)**.

Refitting

23 Refitting is the reverse of the removal procedure; note the torque wrench settings specified for the various fasteners.

---

8 Timing belt – removal, refitting and tensioning

Note: *To carry out this operation, a new timing belt (where applicable), a new cylinder head cover gasket and some special tools (see text) will be required.*

Removal

1 Disconnect the battery negative (earth) lead (refer to *Disconnecting the battery*).

2 Apply the handbrake, then jack up the right-hand front wheel, and support the vehicle on an axle stand (see *Jacking and vehicle support*).

3 Remove the fasteners securing the right-hand front wheelarch liner in position, and withdraw the liner for access to the auxiliary drivebelt and crankshaft pulley **(see illustration)**. Also unbolt and remove the auxiliary drivebelt lower cover.

4 Slacken the three coolant pump pulley bolts while the drivebelt is still fitted.

5 Remove the crankshaft pulley as described in Section 6, then unbolt and remove the timing belt lower cover, referring to Section 7

if necessary. Also unbolt and remove the coolant pump pulley. Once this has been done, the car can be lowered if preferred.

6 Remove the timing belt upper and middle covers as described in Section 7.

7 Remove the cylinder head cover as described in Section 4.

8 Set the engine to TDC on No 1 cylinder, as described in Section 3 – for this operation, the timing pin described **must** be used, to ensure accuracy. Once the spark plugs have been removed, cover their holes with clean rag, to prevent dirt or other foreign bodies from dropping in.

9 Before removing the timing belt, note that Ford service tool 303-376 will be needed, to set the camshafts to their TDC position. Fortunately, a substitute tool can be made from a strip of metal 5 mm thick (while the strip's thickness is critical, its length and width are not, but should be approximately

180 to 230 mm long by 20 to 30 mm wide) (refer to illustration 3.5b).

10 If the timing belt is to be re-used (and this is **not** recommended), mark it with paint to indicate its direction of rotation (clockwise, viewed from the timing belt end of the engine).

11 Slacken the timing belt tensioner bolt, and turn the tensioner clockwise, using an Allen key in the hole provided. Now unscrew the bolt a further four turns, and unhook the tensioner from the inner shield **(see illustrations)**.

12 Ensuring that the sprockets are turned as little as possible, slide the timing belt off the sprockets and pulleys, and remove it **(see illustration)**.

13 If the timing belt is not being fitted straight away (or if the belt is being removed as part of another procedure, such as cylinder head removal), temporarily refit the engine right-hand mounting and tighten the bolts securely.

8.3 Removing the right-hand front wheelarch liner

8.11a Unscrew the bolt . . .

8.11b . . . then unhook and remove the timing belt tensioner

8.12 When removing the timing belt, ensure the sprockets do not turn

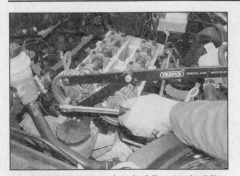

8.19 Using a sprocket-holding tool while loosening the camshaft sprocket bolts

14 If the old belt is likely to be refitted, check it carefully for any signs of uneven wear, splitting, cracks (especially at the roots of the belt teeth).

15 Even if a new belt is to be fitted, check the old one for signs of oil or coolant. If evident, trace the source of the leak and rectify it, then wash down the engine timing belt area and related components, to remove all traces of oil or coolant. Do not simply fit a new belt in this instance, or its service life will be greatly reduced, increasing the risk of engine damage if it fails in service.

16 Always renew the belt if there is the slightest doubt about its condition. As a precaution against engine damage, the belt must be renewed as a matter of course at the intervals given in Chapter 1A; if the car's history is unknown, the belt should be renewed irrespective of its apparent condition whenever the engine is overhauled.

17 Similarly check the belt tensioner, renewing it if there is any doubt about its condition. Check also the sprockets and pulleys for signs of wear or damage (and particularly cracking), and ensure that the tensioner and guide pulleys rotate smoothly on their bearings; renew any worn or damaged components. **Note:** *It is considered good practice by many professional mechanics to renew tensioner and guide pulley assemblies as a matter of course, whenever the timing belt is renewed.*

Refitting

18 Without turning the crankshaft more than a few degrees, check that the engine is still set to TDC on No 1 cylinder – ie, that the timing pin is still inserted.

19 The TDC position of the camshafts must now be set, and for this, the camshaft sprocket bolts must be loosened. A holding tool will be required to prevent the camshaft sprockets from rotating while their bolts are slackened and retightened; either obtain Ford service tool 205-072, or fabricate a substitute as follows. Find two lengths of steel strip, one approximately 600 mm long and the other about 200 mm, and three bolts with nuts and washers; one nut and bolt forming the pivot of a forked tool, with the remaining nuts and bolts at the tips of the 'forks', to engage with the sprocket spokes **(see illustration). Note:** *Do not use the camshaft setting tool (whether genuine Ford or not) to prevent rotation while the camshaft sprocket bolts are slackened or tightened; the risk of damage to the camshaft concerned and to the cylinder head is far too great. Use only a forked holding tool applied directly to the sprockets, as described.*

20 Loosen the camshaft sprocket bolts, ensuring that the camshafts are turned as little as possible as this is done. The bolts should be loose enough that the sprockets are free to turn on the shafts. It is essential that the bolts are left loose until the timing belt has been fitted and tensioned, otherwise the valve timing will not be accurate.

21 The tool described in paragraph 9 is now required. Rest the tool on the cylinder head mating surface, and slide it into the slot in the left-hand end of both camshafts. The tool should slip snugly into both slots while resting on the cylinder head mating surface. If one camshaft is only slightly out of alignment, rotate the camshaft gently and carefully until the tool will fit. Once the camshafts are set at TDC, the positions of the sprockets are less important – they can move independently of the camshafts, to allow the timing belt to be accurately fitted and tensioned.

22 When fitting the belt, note that the tensioner must not be fitted until after the belt is fully positioned around the sprockets and pulley(s). At this point, it is worth pointing out that models up to January 1999 have an extra timing belt guide pulley, fitted next to the crankshaft sprocket – after this date, the extra guide pulley has been deleted (procedures are not affected, in either case).

23 Fit the timing belt; if the original is being refitted, ensure that the marks and notes made on removal are followed, so that the belt is refitted to run in the same direction. Starting at the crankshaft sprocket, work anti-clockwise around the guide pulley(s) and camshaft sprockets. Ensure that the belt teeth engage correctly with those on the sprockets.

24 Any slack in the belt should be kept on the tensioner side – the 'front' run must be kept taut, without altering the position either of the crankshaft or of the camshafts. If necessary, the camshaft sprockets can be turned slightly in relation to the camshafts (which remain fixed by the aligning tool).

25 When the belt is a good fit on the sprockets and guide pulley(s), the belt tensioner can be fitted. Hook the tensioner into the timing belt inner shield, and insert the bolt loosely. Using the Allen key, turn the tensioner anti-clockwise until the arrow is aligned with the mark or square hole on the bracket, then tighten the tensioner bolt to its specified torque **(see illustrations). Note:** *The timing belt tensioner automatically adjusts the tension by internal spring forces – checking the tension once set, for instance by depressing or twisting the timing belt, will not give a meaningful result.*

26 Tighten both camshaft sprocket bolts to the specified torque, holding the sprockets stationary using the tool described in paragraph 19 **(see illustration)**.

27 Remove the camshaft aligning tool and the timing pin. Temporarily refit the crankshaft pulley, and rotate the crankshaft through two full turns clockwise to settle and tension the timing belt, returning to the position described in Section 3. Check that the timing pin can be fully fitted, then fit the camshaft aligning tool; it should slip into place as described in paragraph 21. If all is well, proceed to paragraph 30 below.

28 If one camshaft is only just out of line, fit the forked holding tool to its sprocket, adjust its position as required, and check that any slack created in the belt has been taken up by the tensioner; rotate the crankshaft through two further turns clockwise and refit the cam-

8.25a Use an Allen key to set the tensioner pointer in the centre of the square window . . .

8.25b . . . then hold it while the tensioner bolt is tightened to the specified torque

8.26 Tightening the camshaft sprocket bolts to the specified torque

shaft aligning tool to check that it now fits as it should. If all is well, proceed to paragraph 29 below.

29 If either camshaft is significantly out of line, use the holding tool described in paragraph 19 above to prevent its sprocket from rotating while its retaining bolt is slackened – the camshaft can then be rotated carefully until the camshaft aligning tool will slip into place; take care not to disturb the relationship of the sprocket to the timing belt. Without disturbing the sprocket's new position on the camshaft, tighten the sprocket bolt to its specified torque wrench setting. Remove the camshaft aligning tool and timing pin, and rotate the crankshaft through two further turns clockwise, and refit the tool to check that it now fits as it should.

30 The remainder of the reassembly procedure is the reverse of removal, noting the following points:

   a) *Make sure that the timing pin and camshaft aligning tool are removed.*
   b) *When refitting the engine right-hand mounting, remember to refit the timing belt upper cover.*
   c) *Tighten all fasteners to the specified torque wrench settings.*

9 Timing belt tensioner and sprockets – removal and refitting

Tensioner

1 Removing the tensioner should only be attempted as part of the timing belt renewal procedure, described in Section 8. While it is possible to reach the tensioner once the timing belt upper and middle covers only have been removed (see Section 7), the whole timing belt procedure must be followed, to ensure that the valve timing is correctly reset once the belt's tension has been disturbed.

2 Remove and check the tensioner as described in Section 8. **Note:** *It is considered good practice by many professional mechanics to renew tensioner assemblies as a matter of course, whenever the timing belt is renewed.*

3 Once the old tensioner has been removed as described, the new tensioner can be fitted in its place during the belt refitting procedure – there are no special procedures involved in setting the new tensioner.

Camshaft and crankshaft sprockets

4 As with the tensioner, removing any of the sprockets involves releasing the timing belt tension, so the whole timing belt procedure (Section 8) must be followed. While it may be possible to remove the sprockets once their respective covers have been removed (Section 7), the complete timing belt removal/refitting procedure must be followed, to ensure that the valve timing is correctly reset once the belt's tension has been disturbed.

9.5a Unscrew and remove the retaining bolt from each . . .

5 With the timing belt removed, the camshaft sprockets can be detached once their retaining bolts have been loosened as described in Section 8; although not essential, it is good working practice to mark the sprockets for position **(see illustrations)**.

6 The crankshaft sprocket can be pulled off the end of the crankshaft once the crankshaft (grooved) pulley and the timing belt have been removed. Note the FRONT marking identifying the sprocket's outboard face and the thrustwasher behind it; note which way round the thrustwasher is fitted **(see illustrations)**. Note the sprocket-locating Woodruff key; if this is loose, it should be removed for safe storage with the sprocket.

7 Check the sprockets as described in Section 8.

Refitting

8 Refitting is the reverse of the removal

9.6a Crankshaft sprocket FRONT marking

9.6c Remove the thrustwasher if necessary

9.5b . . . and remove the camshaft sprockets

procedure. Fit and tension the timing belt as described in Section 8.

Timing belt guide pulley(s)

Removal

9 Models up to January 1999 have two guide pulleys – one next to the crankshaft sprocket, and one opposite the belt tensioner. Models after this date have only one guide pulley, the one next to the crankshaft sprocket having been deleted.

10 To remove the upper guide pulley, remove the timing belt upper and middle covers as described in Section 7.

11 To remove the lower guide pulley (early models only), remove the timing belt lower cover as described in Section 7.

12 Loosen the guide pulley bolt, and withdraw the pulley from the belt **(see illustration)**. Care must be taken as the pulley is removed, so that

9.6b The sprocket simply slides off the crankshaft

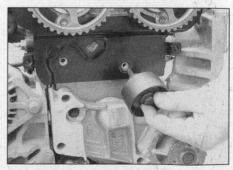

9.12 Removing the timing belt guide pulley (timing belt already removed)

the timing belt does not come off the sprockets. On early models, if both pulleys are to be changed, it may be advisable to only remove one at a time, if possible.

13 Check the condition of the pulley(s) as described in Section 8. **Note:** *It is considered good practice by many professional mechanics to renew guide pulley assemblies as a matter of course, whenever the timing belt is renewed.*

Refitting

14 Refitting is the reverse of the removal procedure; tighten the pulley bolts to the specified torque wrench setting.

10 Camshaft oil seals – renewal

Note: *While it is possible to reach either oil seal, once the respective sprocket has been removed (see Section 9) to allow the seal to be prised out, this procedure is not recommended. Not only are the seals very soft, making this difficult to do without risk of damage to the seal housing, but it would be very difficult to ensure that the valve timing and the timing belt's tension, once disturbed, are correctly reset. Owners are advised to follow the whole procedure outlined below.*

1 Remove the timing belt as described in Section 8, and take off the camshaft sprocket(s) as required, as described in Section 9. Even if only one seal is leaking, it is prudent to renew both at the same time.

11.3 No 2 camshaft bearing marking (central bearing on exhaust camshaft)

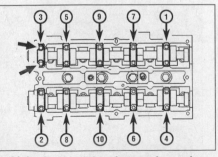

11.4a Camshaft bearing cap loosening sequence – loosen each pair of bolts (arrowed) in the sequence

10.6a Fit the seal, lips inwards, using your fingers . . .

2 Try prising the seal out first, but take care not to damage the head, bearing cap, or camshaft, as this will result in further leaks, even with a new seal. An alternative is to drill a small hole in the seal, thread in a small self-tapping screw, and use pliers on the screw head to pull the seal out.

3 If the seal proves difficult to remove, unbolt the camshaft right-hand bearing cap and withdraw the defective oil seal; note that the cap is fitted using sealant, which must be cleaned off, and fresh sealant applied when refitting.

4 Clean the seal housing and polish off any burrs or raised edges, which may have caused the seal to fail in the first place. Where applicable, refit the bearing cap, using sealant and tightening the cap bolts as described in Section 11.

5 To fit a new seal, Ford recommend the use of their service tool 303-039, with a bolt (10 mm thread size, 70 mm long) and a washer, to draw the seal into place when the camshaft bearing cap is bolted down; a substitute is to use a suitable socket.

6 Grease the seal lips to ease installation, then fit it over the end of the camshaft using your fingers. Draw or tap the seal into place until it is flush with the housing/bearing cap outer edge **(see illustrations)**.

7 Refit the sprocket to the camshaft, tightening the retaining bolt loosely.

8 The remainder of the reassembly procedure, including checking the camshaft alignment (valve timing) and setting the timing belt tension, is as described in Section 8.

11.4b Loosening the camshaft bearing caps

10.6b . . . then tap it home using a large socket

11 Camshafts and cam followers – removal, inspection and refitting

Removal

1 Remove the timing belt as described in Section 8.

2 Remove the camshaft sprockets as described in Section 9; while both are the same and could be interchanged, it is good working practice to mark them so that each is refitted only to its original location.

3 All the camshaft bearing caps have a single-digit identifying number etched on them. The exhaust camshaft's bearing caps are numbered in sequence 0 (right-hand cap) to 4 (left-hand cap), the inlet's 5 (right-hand cap) to 9 (left-hand cap). Each cap is to be fitted so that its numbered side faces outwards, to the front (exhaust) or to the rear (inlet) **(see illustration)**. If no marks are present, or they are hard to see, make your own – the bearing caps must be refitted to their original positions.

4 Working in the sequence shown, slacken the camshaft bearing cap bolts progressively by half a turn at a time **(see illustrations)**. Work only as described, to release gradually and evenly the pressure of the valve springs on the caps.

5 Withdraw the caps, noting their markings and the presence of the locating dowels, then remove the camshafts and withdraw their oil seals **(see illustrations)**. The inlet camshaft

11.5a Remove the bearing caps . . .

11.5b . . . then lift out the camshafts

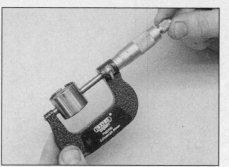

11.8 Measure the cam follower outside diameter at several points

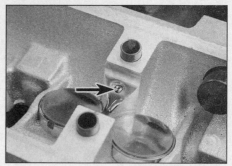

11.11 Check that the camshaft bearing oilways are not blocked with swarf like this one (arrowed)

can be identified by the reference lobe for the camshaft position sensor; therefore, there is no need to mark the camshafts.

6 Obtain sixteen small, clean containers, and number them 1 to 16. Using a rubber sucker, withdraw each cam follower in turn and place them in the containers. Do not interchange the cam followers, or the rate of wear will be much increased. Make sure the shims remain with their corresponding cam followers, to ensure correct refitting. **Note:** *If the camshafts are being removed as part of the cylinder head removal procedure, the cam followers and shims can be left in place if preferred.*

Inspection

7 With the camshafts and cam followers removed, check each for signs of obvious wear (scoring, pitting, etc) and for ovality and renew if necessary.

8 Measure the outside diameter of each cam follower – take measurements at the top and bottom of each cam follower, then a second set at right-angles to the first; if any measurement is significantly different from the others, the cam follower is tapered or oval (as applicable) and must be renewed **(see illustration)**. If the necessary equipment is available, measure the inside diameter of the corresponding cylinder head bore. No manufacturer's specifications were available at time of writing; if the cam followers or the cylinder head bores are excessively worn, new cam followers and/or a new cylinder head may be required.

9 If the engine's valve components have sounded noisy, it may be just that the valve clearances need adjusting. Although this is part of the routine maintenance schedule in Chapter 1A, the extended checking interval and the need for dismantling or special tools may result in the task being overlooked.

10 Visually examine the camshaft lobes for score marks, pitting, galling (wear due to rubbing) and evidence of overheating (blue, discoloured areas). Look for flaking away of the hardened surface layer of each lobe. If any such signs are evident, renew the component concerned.

11 Examine the camshaft bearing journals and the cylinder head bearing surfaces for signs of

obvious wear or pitting. If any such signs are evident, consult an engineering works for advice. Also check that the bearing oilways in the cylinder head are clear **(see illustration)**.

12 Using a micrometer, measure the diameter of each journal at several points. If the diameter of any one journal is less than the specified value, renew the camshaft.

13 To check the bearing journal running clearance, remove the cam followers, use a suitable solvent and a clean lint-free rag to clean carefully all bearing surfaces, then refit the camshafts and bearing caps with a strand of Plastigauge across each journal. Tighten the bearing cap bolts in the given sequence (see *Refitting*) to the specified torque wrench setting (do not rotate the camshafts), then remove the bearing caps and use the scale provided to measure the width of the compressed strands. Scrape off the Plastigauge with your fingernail or the edge of a credit card – don't scratch or nick the journals or bearing caps.

14 If the running clearance of any bearing is found to be worn to beyond the specified service limits, fit a new camshaft and repeat the check; if the clearance is still excessive, the cylinder head must be renewed.

15 To check camshaft endfloat, remove the cam followers, clean the bearing surfaces carefully and refit the camshafts and bearing caps. Tighten the bearing cap bolts to the specified torque wrench setting, then measure the endfloat using a DTI (Dial Test Indicator, or dial gauge) mounted on the cylinder head so that its tip bears on the camshaft right-hand end.

16 Tap the camshaft fully towards the gauge, zero the gauge, then tap the camshaft fully away from the gauge and note the gauge reading. If the endfloat measured is found to be at or beyond the specified service limit, fit a new camshaft and repeat the check; if the clearance is still excessive, the cylinder head must be renewed.

Refitting

17 As a precaution against the valves hitting the pistons when the camshafts are refitted, remove the timing pin and turn the engine approximately 90° back from the TDC position

– this should move all the pistons an equal distance down the bores. This is only a precaution – if the engine is known to be at TDC on No 1 cylinder, and the camshafts are refitted as described below, valve-to-piston contact should not occur.

18 On reassembly, liberally oil the cylinder head cam follower bores and the cam followers. Carefully refit the cam followers to the cylinder head, ensuring that each cam follower is refitted to its original bore, and is the correct way up. Some care will be required to enter the cam followers squarely into their bores. Make sure that the shims are fitted in their previously-noted positions.

19 It is highly recommended that new camshaft oil seals are fitted, as a precaution against later failure – it would seem a false economy to refit old seals, especially since they may not seal, having been disturbed. The new seals are fitted after the caps are tightened – see Section 10.

20 Liberally oil the camshaft bearings (not the caps) and lobes. Ensuring that each camshaft is in its original location, refit the camshafts, locating each so that the slot in its left-hand end is approximately parallel to, and just above, the cylinder head mating surface **(see illustrations)**. Check that, as each camshaft is laid in position, the metal strip TDC setting tool will (broadly speaking) fit into the slot.

21 Ensure that the locating dowels are pressed firmly into their recesses and check that all mating surfaces are completely clean, unmarked and free from oil. Apply a thin film of suitable sealant (Ford recommend a sealant

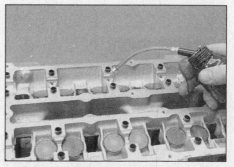

11.20a Lubricate the camshaft bearing surfaces . . .

11.20b . . . then refit the camshafts . . .

11.20c . . . ensuring that the slot at the transmission end is approximately horizontal

11.21 Apply sealant to each of the bearing caps at the timing belt end

to specification WSK-M4G348-A5) to the mating surfaces of each camshaft's right-hand bearing cap **(see illustration)**.

22 Apply a little oil to the camshaft as shown, then refit each of the camshaft bearing caps to its previously-noted position, so that its numbered side faces outwards, to the front (exhaust) or to the rear (inlet) **(see illustrations)**.

23 Ensuring that each cap is kept square to the cylinder head as it is tightened down and working in the sequence shown, tighten the camshaft bearing cap bolts slowly and by one turn at a time, until each cap touches the cylinder head **(see illustration)**.

24 Next, go round again in the same sequence, tightening the bolts to the specified Stage 1 torque setting.

25 With all the bolts tightened to the Stage 1

setting, go round in sequence once more, tightening them to the Stage 2 setting **(see illustration)**. Work only as described, to impose gradually and evenly the pressure of the valve springs on the caps.

26 Wipe off all surplus sealant, so that none is left to find its way into any oilways. Follow the sealant manufacturer's instructions as to the time needed for curing; usually, at least an hour must be allowed between application of the sealant and starting the engine (including turning the engine for further reassembly work).

27 Once the caps are fully tightened, it makes sense to check the valve clearances before proceeding – assuming that the Ford tool described in Section 5 is not available, the camshafts have to be removed to allow any of the shims to be changed. Turning the

camshafts with the timing belt removed carries a risk of the valves hitting the pistons, so (if not already done) remove the timing pin and turn the crankshaft 90° anti-clockwise first. Set the camshafts to TDC on No 1 cylinder using the setting tool (see Section 8) to establish a starting point, then proceed as described in Section 5 **(see illustration)**. When all the clearances have been checked, bring the crankshaft back to TDC, and refit the timing pin.

28 Fit new camshaft oil seals as described in Section 10.

29 Using the marks and notes made on dismantling to ensure that each is refitted to its original camshaft, refit the sprockets to the camshafts, tightening the retaining bolts loosely **(see illustrations)**.

30 The remainder of the reassembly

11.22a Apply a little oil to the camshaft surface . . .

11.22b . . . then refit the camshaft bearing caps

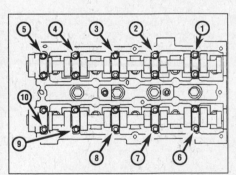

11.23 Camshaft bearing cap tightening sequence

11.25 Tighten the camshaft bearing cap bolts to the specified torque

11.27 Set the camshafts to TDC using the metal strip in the slotted ends

11.29a Refit the camshaft sprockets . . .

11.29b . . . and secure with the retaining bolts, tightened only loosely at this stage

12.7 Disconnect the camshaft position sensor wiring plug

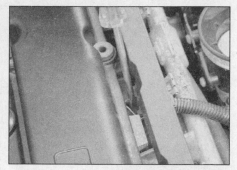

12.8a Use a screwdriver to prise out the wire clips . . .

procedure, including refitting the timing belt and setting the valve timing, is as described in Section 8. On completion (if not already done), check and adjust the valve clearances as described in Section 5.

12 Cylinder head – removal and refitting

Note: *The procedure below describes removing the cylinder head without the inlet manifold, which was found to be the easiest option in practice – the inlet manifold can be unbolted from the head, and moved rearwards to allow the head to be withdrawn. If preferred, however, the inlet manifold may be removed completely as described in Chapter 4A.*

Removal

1 Referring to Chapter 12, identify and remove the fuel pump fuse from the fusebox. Now start the engine and allow it to run until it stalls. If the engine will not start, at least keep it cranking for about 10 seconds. The fuel system should now be depressurised.
2 Disconnect the battery negative (earth) lead (see *Disconnecting the battery*) and position the lead away from the terminal.
3 Drain the cooling system as described in Chapter 1A. It is preferable when removing the cylinder head for the front wheels to remain on the ground as far as possible, as this makes working on the top of the engine easier. Also, once the engine right-hand

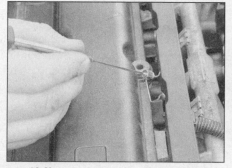

12.8b . . . recover the clips using a magnetic tool . . .

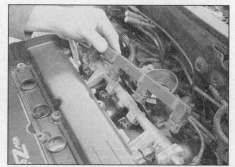

12.8c . . . then lift off the injector wiring busbar

mounting has been removed (for removing the timing belt), the engine must be further supported if the front of the car is raised.
4 Remove the timing belt as described in Section 8, and the camshafts as described in Section 11.
5 Temporarily refit the engine right-hand mounting, tightening the bolts securely. Also refit the cylinder head cover, to protect the top of the engine until the cylinder head bolts are removed.
6 Remove the air cleaner inlet duct, and disconnect the accelerator cable, using the information in Chapter 4A.
7 Disconnect the wiring plug from the camshaft position sensor, located at the rear of the head, at the transmission end **(see illustration)**.
8 Using a small screwdriver, prise up and remove the four wire clips (one on each injector) securing the injector wiring busbar –

use a magnetic holding tool to prevent the wire clips falling down the back of the engine as they are removed. Lift off the wiring busbar, and move it to the rear **(see illustrations)**.
9 The inlet manifold is secured by seven bolts, and a stud and nut at either end. Note that the right-hand nut also secures a wiring support bracket – unclip the wiring before removing the bracket. Loosen and remove the manifold nuts and bolts.
10 The manifold cannot easily be removed from the end studs, so the studs themselves must be unscrewed from the cylinder head – Torx end fittings are provided to make unscrewing the studs easier. Remove the studs, and move the manifold fully to the rear, clear of the head **(see illustrations)**. Note that a set of four new inlet manifold gaskets should be obtained for refitting.
11 Remove the alternator as described in

12.10a The inlet manifold is located on studs (one arrowed) . . .

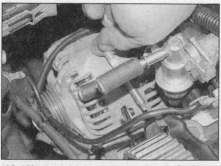

12.10b . . . which must be unscrewed and removed . . .

12.10c . . . before moving the manifold assembly rearwards away from the head

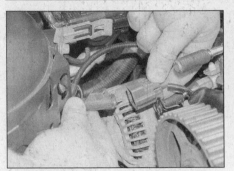

12.11a Disconnect the cylinder head temperature wiring plug . . .

12.11b . . . then unclip and separate the injection harness multi-plug

Chapter 5A. This is necessary, since the alternator mounting bracket is attached to the head, and one of the bracket bolts can only be taken out with the alternator removed. To improve access, disconnect the large

injection harness multi-plug and the cylinder head temperature wiring plug above the alternator **(see illustrations)**.

12 Disconnect the earth wire attached to the engine rear lifting eye. To avoid damaging it,

unscrew and remove the cylinder head temperature sensor **(see illustrations)**.

13 Unbolt and remove the alternator mounting bracket, which is secured by three bolts and one nut. Alternatively, remove just the single bolt securing the bracket to the head, leaving the bracket in place.

14 Remove the ignition coil as described in Chapter 5B.

15 There are two options regarding the thermostat housing – either disconnect the hoses from it (noting their positions), or unscrew the three bolts and detach the housing from the head **(see illustrations)**. If the latter option is chosen, the hoses can remain in place, but a new housing O-ring seal must be obtained for refitting.

16 At the front of the head, unbolt and separate the power steering fluid pipe support brackets at either end **(see illustration)**. Move the pipe forwards, clear of the head, but do not strain the pipe too much.

17 Remove the nut securing the upper end of the dipstick tube, and move the tube away from the head **(see illustration)**.

18 Remove the power steering pump as described in Chapter 10 (the fluid pipes need not be disconnected, providing the pump is supported, clear of the engine). Unbolt the power steering pump mounting bracket, which is secured by three bolts and one nut, and remove the bracket from the head **(see illustration)**.

19 Unscrew the four bolts securing the exhaust manifold heat shield, and lift the shield off **(see illustrations)**. It is quite likely

12.12a Unbolt the earth wire from the engine lifting eye

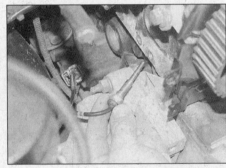

12.12b Unscrew and remove the cylinder head temperature sensor

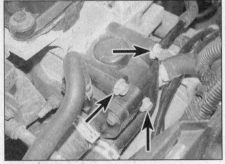

12.15a Unscrew the three bolts (arrowed) . . .

12.15b . . . and remove the thermostat housing from the head

12.16 Unbolting one of the power steering fluid pipe brackets

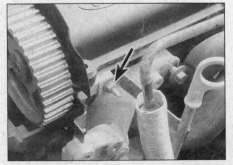

12.17 Dipstick tube securing nut (arrowed)

12.18 Unbolting the power steering pump bracket

12.19a Unscrew the four bolts (arrowed) . . .

that difficulty will be experienced removing the bolts, as corrosion may have effectively rounded-off the bolt heads – be sure to use a close-fitting socket or ring spanner from the outset. If the bolts cannot be removed, as a last resort, the heat shield will have to be destroyed to remove it – take care, however, that the wiring for the oxygen sensor (fitted just below the heat shield) is not damaged during this operation.

20 The front section of the exhaust (which includes the catalytic converter) must now be removed as described in Chapter 4A, leaving the exhaust manifold attached to the head.

21 Before loosening the cylinder head bolts, check around the head to ensure that there is nothing still attached to it, nor anything else which would interfere with the head being lifted off. Move any wiring or hoses aside as necessary.

22 Although it is unlikely to be relevant in the case of the DIY mechanic, it should be noted that, according to Ford, the cylinder head should not be removed until it has cooled to ambient temperature.

23 Using a Torx key or socket (TX 55 size), slacken the ten cylinder head bolts progressively and by half a turn at a time, working in the **reverse** order of the sequence shown for tightening (refer to illustration 12.42). Remove the bolts, and store them carefully if they are to be re-used **(see illustration)**. Ford state that the bolts may be re-used twice only – if there is any doubt about this, it is preferable to obtain a complete set of new bolts for refitting.

24 Lift the cylinder head away; use assistance if possible, as it is a heavy assembly **(see illustration)**.

25 If the head is stuck (as is possible), be careful how you choose to free it. Remember that the cylinder head is made of aluminium alloy, which is easily damaged. Striking the head with tools carries the risk of damage, and the head is located on two dowels, so its movement will be limited. Do not, under any circumstances, lever the head between the mating surfaces, as this will certainly damage the sealing surfaces for the gasket, leading to leaks. Try rocking the head free, to break the seal, taking care not to damage any of the surrounding components.

26 Once the head has been removed, recover the gasket from the two dowels, and discard it.

Inspection

Note: *For dismantling the cylinder head, and other procedures relating to the valves, refer to Chapter 2D.*

27 The mating faces of the cylinder head and cylinder block must be perfectly clean before refitting the head. Use a hard plastic or wood scraper to remove all traces of gasket and carbon; also clean the piston crowns.

28 Take particular care during the cleaning operations, as aluminium alloy is easily damaged. Also, make sure that the carbon is not allowed to enter the oil and water

12.19b . . . and remove the heat shield

passages – this is particularly important for the lubrication system, as carbon could block the oil supply to the engine's components. Using adhesive tape and paper, seal the water, oil and bolt holes in the cylinder block.

29 To prevent carbon entering the gap between the pistons and bores, smear a little grease in the gap. After cleaning each piston, use a small brush to remove all traces of grease and carbon from the gap, then wipe away the remainder with a clean rag.

30 Check the mating surfaces of the cylinder block and the cylinder head for nicks, deep scratches and other damage. If slight, they may be removed carefully with a file, but if excessive, renewal is necessary as it is not permissible to machine the surfaces.

31 If warpage of the cylinder head gasket surface is suspected, use a straight-edge to check it for distortion. Refer to Part D of this Chapter if necessary.

32 Ford state that the cylinder head bolts can be re-used twice, but they should be checked carefully before doing so. Examine the threads in particular for any signs of damage. If any of the thread inside the cylinder head holes has been removed with the bolts, seek expert advice before proceeding. Lay the bolts out next to each other, and compare their length – if any one has stretched, so that it is longer than the rest, it should not be re-used, and it is probably advisable to renew all the bolts as a set. If there is any doubt as to the condition of the bolts, fit new ones – the cost of a set of bolts is nothing compared to the problems which may be caused if a bolt shears or strips when being tightened.

12.24 Lifting off the cylinder head

12.23 Removing one of the cylinder head bolts

33 If the cylinder head bolts are re-used, paint or scribe the top of each bolt with a single dot or line, as a reminder if the head has to be removed at a later date.

Refitting

34 Wipe clean the mating surfaces of the cylinder head and cylinder block. Check that the two locating dowels are in position in the cylinder block.

35 The cylinder head bolt holes must be free from oil or water. This is most important, as a hydraulic lock in a cylinder head bolt hole as the bolt is tightened can cause a fracture of the block casting.

36 The new head gasket is selected according to a number cast on the front face of the cylinder block, in front of No 1 cylinder. Consult a Ford dealer or your parts supplier for details – if in doubt, compare the new gasket with the old one.

37 Position a new gasket over the dowels on the cylinder block surface, so that the TOP/OBEN mark is uppermost; where applicable, the 'tooth' (or teeth, according to engine size) should protrude towards the front of the vehicle **(see illustrations)**.

38 Temporarily refit the crankshaft pulley and rotate the crankshaft anti-clockwise so that No 1 cylinder's piston is lowered to approximately 20 mm before TDC, thus avoiding any risk of valve/piston contact and damage during reassembly.

39 As the cylinder head is such a heavy and awkward assembly to refit, it is helpful to make up a pair of guide studs from two 10 mm (thread size) studs approximately 90 mm long,

12.37a Lay the new head gasket in position over the dowels . . .

12.37b . . . head gasket 'teeth' should be at the front of the block

12.40 Cylinder head locating dowels (arrowed)

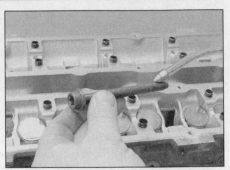

12.41 Apply a light coating of oil to the cylinder head bolt threads

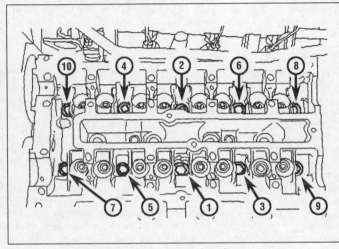

12.42 Cylinder head bolt tightening sequence

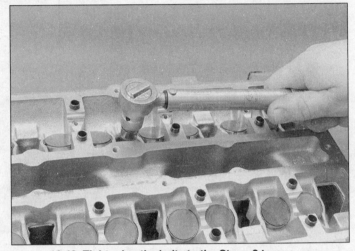

12.43 Tightening the bolts to the Stage 2 torque . . .

with a screwdriver slot cut in one end – two old cylinder head bolts (if available) with their heads cut off would make a good starting point. Screw these guide studs, screwdriver slot upwards to permit removal, into the bolt holes at diagonally-opposite corners of the cylinder block surface (or into those where the locating dowels are fitted); ensure that approximately 70 mm of stud protrudes above the gasket.

40 Refit the cylinder head, sliding it down the guide studs (if used) and locating it on the dowels **(see illustration)**. Unscrew the guide

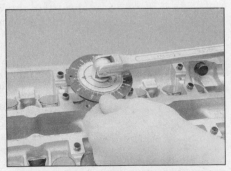

12.44 . . . then through the Stage 3 angle, here using an angle gauge

studs (if used) when the head is in place.

41 Ford do not state whether or not the cylinder head bolts should be oiled when refitting, but experience suggests that coating the threads with a little light oil is useful – do not apply more than a light film of oil, however **(see illustration)**. Fit the cylinder head bolts carefully, and screw them in by hand only until finger-tight.

42 Working progressively and in the sequence shown, first tighten all the bolts to the specified Stage 1 torque setting **(see illustration)**.

43 With all the bolts tightened to Stage 1, tighten them further in sequence to the Stage 2 torque setting **(see illustration)**.

44 Stage 3 involves tightening the bolts though an angle, rather than to a torque. Each bolt in sequence must be rotated through the specified angle – special angle gauges are available from tool outlets, but a 90° angle is equivalent to a quarter-turn, and this is easily judged by assessing the start and end positions of the socket handle or torque wrench **(see illustration)**.

45 Once all the bolts have been tightened to Stage 3, no subsequent tightening is necessary.

46 Before proceeding with refitting, turn the

crankshaft forwards to TDC, and check that the setting tools described in Section 3 can be inserted. Do not turn the engine more than necessary while the timing belt is removed, or the valves may hit the pistons – for instance, if the engine is accidentally turned past the TDC position, turn it back slightly and try again – do not bring the engine round a full turn.

47 Refitting of the other components removed is a reversal of removal, noting the following points:

a) *Refit the catalytic converter with reference to Chapter 4A if necessary, using new gaskets.*

b) *Refit the camshafts as described in Section 11, and the timing belt as described in Section 8.*

c) *Tighten all fasteners to the specified torque, where given, and use new gaskets.*

d) *Ensure that all hoses and wiring are correctly routed, and that hose clips and wiring connectors are securely refitted.*

e) *Refill the cooling system as described in Chapter 1A.*

f) *Check all disturbed joints for signs of oil or coolant leakage once the engine has been restarted and warmed-up to normal operating temperature.*

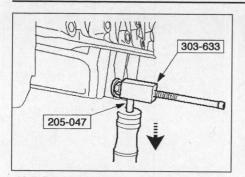

13.5 Ford tools used to break the sealant joint – pull straight down, as indicated

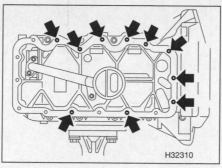

13.7a Stud locations (arrowed) for aligning the sump

13.7b Studs fitted, ready for fitting sump (seen with engine removed)

13 Sump – removal and refitting

Removal

Note: *The full procedure outlined below must be followed so that the mating surfaces can be cleaned and prepared to achieve an oil-tight joint on reassembly.*

1 Apply the handbrake, then jack up the front of the vehicle and support it on axle stands (see *Jacking and vehicle support*).

2 Referring to Chapter 1A if necessary, drain the engine oil, then clean and refit the engine oil drain plug, tightening it to the specified torque wrench setting. Although not strictly necessary as part of the dismantling procedure, owners are advised to remove and discard the oil filter, so that it can be renewed with the oil.

3 A conventional sump gasket is not used, and sealant is used instead.

4 Progressively unscrew the sump retaining bolts. Break the joint by striking the sump with the palm of the hand, then lower the sump away, turning it as necessary to clear the exhaust system.

5 Unfortunately, the use of sealant can make removal of the sump more difficult. Take care when levering between the mating faces, otherwise they will be damaged, resulting in leaks when finished. With care, a knife can be used to cut through the sealant. Ford technicians have a tool comprising a metal rod which is inserted through the sump drain hole, and a handle to pull the sump downwards **(see illustration)**. If using this tool (or a substitute), only use it to pull straight downwards, and **NOT** as a lever – the oil pump pickup tube is directly above the drain hole, and will be damaged if the end of the tool inside the sump is angled upwards.

Refitting

6 On reassembly, thoroughly clean and degrease the mating surfaces of the cylinder block/crankcase and sump, removing all traces of sealant, then use a clean rag to wipe out the sump and the engine's interior.

7 Ford recommend that ten M6x20 mm studs are used when refitting the sump, to ensure that it is aligned correctly. If this is not done, some of the sealant may enter the blind holes for the sump bolts, preventing the bolts from being fully fitted. Obtain ten suitable studs, and cut a slot across the end of each, so that they can be unscrewed; fit them to the locations indicated **(see illustrations)**.

8 Apply a 3.0 mm bead of sealant (Ford specification WSS M4G 323-A7) to the sump flange so that the bead is approximately 5.0 mm from the outside edge of the flange. Make sure the bead is around the inside edge of the bolt holes **(see illustration)**. **Note:** *The sump must be refitted within 10 minutes of applying the sealant.*

9 Fit the sump over the studs, and insert six of the sump bolts into the available holes, tightening them by hand only at this stage **(see illustration)**.

10 Unscrew the studs, then fit the rest of the sump bolts.

11 Tighten all the bolts to the specified Stage 1 torque, in the sequence shown **(see illustration)**.

12 When all the sump bolts have been tightened to Stage 1, go round again in sequence, and tighten the bolts to the Stage 2 setting **(see illustration)**.

13 Lower the car to the ground. Wait at least 1 hour for the sealant to cure (or whatever time is indicated by the sealant manufacturer) before refilling the engine with oil. Trim off the excess sealant with a sharp knife. If removed, fit a new oil filter with reference to Chapter 1A.

13.8 Applying the bead of sealant

13.9 Fit the sump over the studs

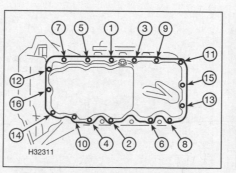

13.11 Sump bolt tightening sequence

13.12 Tightening the sump bolts to the Stage 2 torque

14.7a Remove the oil pump cover . . .

14.7b . . . and withdraw the rotors, noting which way round they are fitted

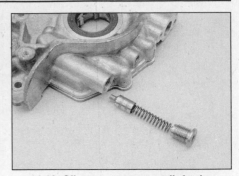

14.10 Oil pump pressure relief valve components (seen with oil pump removed)

14 Oil pump – removal, inspection and refitting

Removal

Note: *While this task is theoretically possible when the engine is in place in the vehicle, in practice, it requires so much preliminary dismantling and is so difficult to carry out due to the restricted access, that owners are advised to remove the engine from the vehicle first. Note, however, that the oil pump pressure relief valve can be removed with the engine in situ – see paragraph 9.*

1 Remove the timing belt (see Section 8).
2 Withdraw the crankshaft sprocket and the thrustwasher behind it, noting which way round the thrustwasher is fitted (see Section 9).
3 Remove the sump (see Section 13).

14.11 Tighten the relief valve cover plug securely

4 Undo the two bolts securing the oil pump pick-up/strainer pipe to the base of the lower crankcase, and withdraw it. Discard the gasket.
5 Progressively unscrew and remove the ten bolts securing the lower crankcase to the base of the engine. Remove the lower crankcase, and recover any spacer washers, noting where they are fitted, as these must be used on refitting. Recover the gasket, and remove any traces of sealant at the joint with the oil pump.
6 Unbolt the pump from the cylinder block/crankcase. Withdraw and discard the gasket, then remove the crankshaft right-hand oil seal. Thoroughly clean and degrease all components, particularly the mating surfaces of the pump, the sump and the cylinder block/crankcase.

Inspection

7 Unscrew the Torx screws and remove the

14.12a Oil the housing and rotors as they are fitted

pump cover plate; noting any identification marks on the rotors, withdraw the rotors **(see illustrations)**.
8 Inspect the rotors for obvious signs of wear or damage, and renew if necessary; if either rotor, the pump body, or its cover plate are scored or damaged, the complete oil pump assembly must be renewed.
9 The oil pressure relief valve can be dismantled, if required, without disturbing the pump. With the vehicle parked on firm level ground, apply the handbrake securely and raise its front end, supporting it securely on axle stands. Remove the front right-hand roadwheel and auxiliary drivebelt cover (see Chapter 1A) to provide access to the valve.
10 Unscrew the threaded plug and recover the valve spring and plunger **(see illustration)**.
11 Reassembly is the reverse of the dismantling procedure; ensure the spring and valve are refitted the correct way round and tighten the threaded plug securely **(see illustration)**.
12 When reassembling the oil pump, oil the housing and components as they are fitted; tighten the oil pump cover bolts securely **(see illustrations)**.

Refitting

13 The oil pump must be primed on installation, by pouring clean engine oil into it and rotating its inner rotor a few turns.
14 Rotate the pump's inner rotor to align with the flats on the crankshaft, then refit the pump (and new gasket) and insert the bolts, tightening them lightly at first **(see illustrations)**.

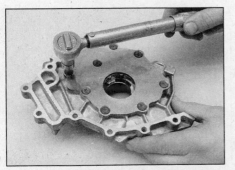

14.12b Tighten the oil pump cover bolts securely

14.14a Offer the new gasket into position . . .

14.14b . . . then refit the oil pump, and tighten the bolts loosely

14.15 Checking the alignment of the oil pump with the crankcase

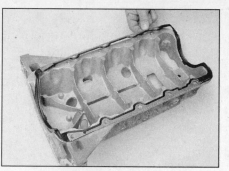

14.19a Fit the new gasket . . .

14.19b . . . then refit the lower crankcase

15 Using a suitable straight-edge and feeler gauges, check that the pump is both centred exactly around the crankshaft and aligned squarely so that its (sump) mating surface is exactly the same amount – between 0.3 and 0.8 mm – below that of the cylinder block/crankcase on each side of the crankshaft (see illustration). Being careful not to disturb the gasket, move the pump into the correct position and tighten its bolts to the specified torque wrench setting.

16 Check that the pump is correctly located; if necessary, unbolt it again and repeat the full procedure to ensure that the pump is correctly aligned.

17 Fit a new crankshaft right-hand oil seal (see Section 16).

18 Apply a little sealant (Ford specification WSK-M4G 320-A) to the joints between the oil pump and cylinder block. Note: Once this

sealant has been applied, the lower crankcase must be fitted and the bolts fully tightened within 10 minutes.

19 Fit the new gasket in place, then offer the lower crankcase into position and loosely secure with the bolts (see illustrations).

20 The lower crankcase must now be aligned with the cylinder block before the bolts are tightened. Using a straight-edge and feeler blades, check the alignment of the end faces (see illustration).

21 Tighten the lower crankcase bolts to the specified torque, ensuring that the alignment with the cylinder block is not lost (see illustration).

22 Using grease to stick the gasket in place on the pump, refit the pick-up/strainer pipe, tightening the retaining bolts to the specified torque (see illustrations).

23 The remainder of reassembly is the

reverse of the removal procedure, referring to the relevant text for details where required.

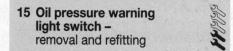

15 Oil pressure warning light switch – removal and refitting

Removal

1 The switch is screwed into the rear of the cylinder block, next to the oil filter.

2 With the vehicle parked on firm level ground, open the bonnet and disconnect the battery negative (earth) lead – see Disconnecting the battery.

3 Raise the front of the vehicle and support it securely on axle stands.

4 Unplug the wiring from the switch and unscrew it; be prepared for some oil loss (see illustrations).

14.20 Checking the alignment of the lower crankcase and engine block

14.21 Tighten the lower crankcase bolts to the specified torque

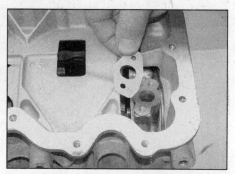

14.22a Using a new gasket . . .

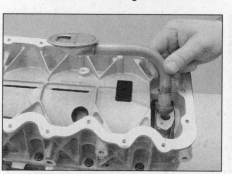

14.22b . . . refit the oil pump pick-up/strainer pipe . . .

14.22c . . . and tighten the bolts to the specified torque

15.4a Disconnect the wiring plug . . .

15.4b . . . then unscrew and remove the oil pressure warning light switch

Refitting

5 Refitting is the reverse of the removal procedure; apply a thin smear of suitable sealant to the switch threads, and tighten it to the specified torque wrench setting. Check the engine oil level and top-up as necessary (see *Weekly checks*). Check for correct warning light operation, and for signs of oil leaks once the engine has been restarted and warmed-up to normal operating temperature.

---

16 Crankshaft oil seals – renewal

Note: *Don't try to prise these seals out without removing the oil pump or seal carrier – the seals are too soft, and the amount of space available is too small, for this to be*

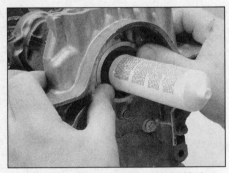

16.7 The oil seal can be pressed in by hand

16.2 Prising out the oil seal from the oil pump housing

possible without considerable risk of damage to the seal housing and/or the crankshaft journal. Follow exactly the procedure given below.

Oil pump housing oil seal

1 Remove the oil pump (see Section 14).
2 Drive the oil seal out of the pump from behind; if care is taken, the seal can be prised out with a screwdriver **(see illustration)**.
3 Clean the seal housing and crankshaft, polishing off any burrs or raised edges, which may have caused the seal to fail in the first place.
4 Refit the oil pump (see Section 14). Grease the lips and periphery of the new seal to ease installation.
5 To fit a new seal, Ford recommend the use of their service tool 21-093A, with the crankshaft pulley bolt, to draw the seal into place.
6 One of the problems with fitting the new seal is that the seal lips may catch on the edge of the crankshaft, which will ruin the seal. A plastic tube or bottle of the right size can be used to overcome this problem **(see Tool Tip)**.
7 As long as the seal is kept square, it can be seated using hand pressure only, but if preferred, a socket of suitable size could be used to tap the seal home **(see illustration)**.
8 The remainder of reassembly is the reverse of the removal procedure, referring to the relevant text for details where required. Check for signs of oil leakage when the engine is restarted.

In the workshop, we cut the end off an old tube of sealant, of the same inside diameter as the seal, and fitted it over the crankshaft to slide the new seal on.

Flywheel end oil seal

9 Remove the transmission as described in Chapter 7A, and the clutch assembly as described in Chapter 6.
10 Unbolt the flywheel (see Section 17).
11 Remove the sump (see Section 13).
12 Unbolt the oil seal carrier; remove and discard its gasket.
13 Supporting the carrier evenly on wooden blocks, drive the oil seal out of the carrier from behind; if care is taken, the seal can be prised out with a screwdriver **(see illustration)**.
14 Clean the seal housing and crankshaft, polishing off any burrs or raised edges, which may have caused the seal to fail in the first place. Clean also the mating surfaces of the cylinder block/crankcase and carrier, using a scraper to remove all traces of the old gasket – be careful not to scratch or damage the material of either – then use a suitable solvent to degrease them.
15 Offer up the carrier, complete with the new gasket **(see illustrations)**.
16 Using a suitable straight-edge and feeler gauges, check that the carrier is both centred exactly around the crankshaft and aligned squarely so that its (sump) mating surface is exactly the same amount – between 0.3 and 0.8 mm – below that of the cylinder block/crankcase on each side of the crankshaft. Being careful not to disturb the gasket, move the carrier into the correct

---

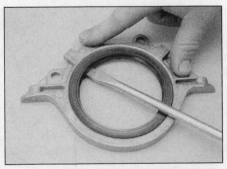

16.13 Prising out the crankshaft rear oil seal

16.15a Using a new gasket . . .

16.15b . . . fit the oil seal carrier, and tighten the bolts loosely

position and tighten its bolts to the specified torque wrench setting **(see illustrations)**.

17 Check that the carrier is correctly located; if necessary, unbolt it again and repeat the full procedure to ensure that the carrier is correctly aligned.

18 Ford's recommended method of seal fitting is to use service tool 303-291, with two flywheel bolts to draw the seal into place. If this is not available, make up a guide from a thin sheet of plastic (perhaps cut from a plastic bottle) **(see illustrations)**. Lubricate the lips of the new seal and the crankshaft shoulder with grease, then offer up the seal, with the guide feeding the seal's lips over the crankshaft shoulder. Press the seal evenly into its housing by hand only and use a soft-faced mallet gently to tap it into place until it is flush with the surrounding housing.

19 Wipe off any surplus oil or grease; the remainder of the reassembly procedure is the reverse of dismantling, referring to the relevant text for details where required. Check for signs of oil leakage when the engine is restarted.

16.16a Check the alignment of the oil seal carrier using feeler blades . . .

16.16b . . . then tighten the bolts to the specified torque

16.18a Slide the oil seal on using a plastic bottle . . .

16.18b . . . or a plastic strip wrapped around the crankshaft

17 Flywheel – removal, inspection and refitting

Removal

1 Remove the transmission as described in Chapter 7A. Now is a good time to check components such as oil seals and renew them if necessary.

2 Remove the clutch as described in Chapter 6. Now is a good time to check or renew the clutch components and release bearing.

3 Use a centre-punch or paint to make alignment marks on the flywheel and crankshaft to make refitting easier – the bolt holes are slightly offset, and will only line up one way, but making a mark eliminates the guesswork (and the flywheel is heavy).

4 Hold the flywheel stationary using one of the following methods:

a) *If an assistant is available, insert one of the transmission mounting bolts into the cylinder block, and have the assistant engage a wide-bladed screwdriver with the starter ring gear teeth while the bolts are loosened.*

b) *Alternatively, a piece of angle-iron can be engaged with the ring gear, and located against the transmission mounting bolt.*

c) *A further method is to fabricate a piece of flat metal bar with a pointed end to engage the ring gear – fit the tool to the transmission bolt, and use washers and packing to align it with the ring gear, then tighten the bolt to hold it in position (see illustration).*

5 Slacken and remove each bolt in turn and ensure that new replacements are obtained for reassembly; these bolts are subjected to

severe stresses and so must be renewed, regardless of their apparent condition, whenever they are disturbed.

6 Withdraw the flywheel, remembering that it is very heavy – do not drop it.

Inspection

7 Clean the flywheel to remove grease and oil. Inspect the surface for cracks, rivet grooves, burned areas and score marks. Light scoring can be removed with emery cloth. Check for cracked and broken ring gear teeth. Lay the flywheel on a flat surface and use a straight-edge to check for warpage.

8 Clean and inspect the mating surfaces of the flywheel and the crankshaft. If the oil seal is leaking, renew it (see Section 16) before refitting the flywheel. If the engine has covered a high mileage, it may be worth fitting a new seal as a matter if course, given the

amount of work needed to access it.

9 While the flywheel is removed, carefully clean its inboard (right-hand) face, particularly the recesses which serve as the reference points for the crankshaft speed/position sensor. Clean the sensor's tip and check that the sensor is securely fastened.

Refitting

10 On refitting, ensure that the engine/transmission adapter plate is in place (where necessary), then fit the flywheel to the crankshaft so that all bolt holes align – it will fit only one way – check this using the marks made on removal. Fit the new bolts, tightening them by hand **(see illustrations)**.

11 Lock the flywheel by the method used on dismantling. Working in a diagonal sequence to tighten them evenly and increasing to the final amount in two or three stages, tighten

17.4 One method of jamming the flywheel ring gear to prevent rotation

17.10a Fit the flywheel into position . . .

17.10b . . . and secure with the new bolts

17.11 Tighten the flywheel bolts to the specified torque

the new bolts to the specified torque wrench setting **(see illustration)**.

12 The remainder of reassembly is the reverse of the removal procedure, referring to the relevant text for details where required.

18 Engine/transmission mountings – inspection and renewal

Inspection

1 The engine/transmission mountings seldom require attention, but broken or deteriorated mountings should be renewed immediately, or the added strain placed on the driveline components may cause damage or wear.

2 During the check, the engine/transmission must be raised slightly, to remove its weight from the mountings.

3 Apply the handbrake, then jack up the front of the vehicle and support it on axle stands (see *Jacking and vehicle support*). Remove the engine undershield where fitted. Position a jack under the sump, with a large block of wood between the jack head and the sump, then carefully raise the engine/transmission just enough to take the weight off the mountings.

4 Check the mountings to see if the rubber is cracked, hardened or separated from the metal components. Sometimes, the rubber will split right down the centre.

5 Check for relative movement between each mounting's brackets and the engine/transmission or body (use a large screwdriver or lever to attempt to move the mountings). If movement is noted, lower the engine and check the mounting nuts and bolts for tightness.

Renewal

6 The engine mountings can be removed if the weight of the engine/transmission is supported by one of the following alternative methods.

7 Either support the weight of the assembly from underneath using a jack and a suitable piece of wood between the jack and the sump (to prevent damage), or from above by attaching a hoist to the engine. A third method is to use a suitable support bar with end pieces which will engage in the water channel each side of the bonnet lid aperture. Using an adjustable hook and chain connected to the engine, the weight of the engine and transmission can then be taken from the mountings.

8 Once the weight of the engine and transmission is suitably supported, any of the mountings can be unbolted and removed.

9 To remove the engine right-hand mounting, first mark the positions of the three bolts relative to the mounting plate. Unscrew the three bolts securing the mounting to the inner wing, and the two nuts securing it to the engine. Lift off the mounting complete **(see illustrations)**.

10 To remove the left-hand mounting, first remove the battery and battery tray as described in Chapter 5A, then loosen the clips and remove the air inlet duct. Unscrew the five mounting nuts (noting that the centre one is larger than the rest) from the engine left-hand mounting, then lift off the upper bracket **(see illustrations)**. Unscrew the three nuts and remove the lower half of the mounting from the transmission **(see illustrations)**.

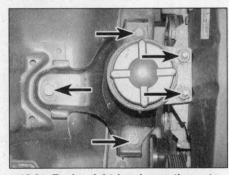

18.9a Engine right-hand mounting nuts and bolts (arrowed)

18.9b Unscrew the nuts and bolts, and remove them . . .

18.9c . . . then take off the mounting complete

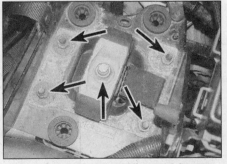

18.10a Engine left-hand mounting nuts (arrowed)

18.10b Unscrew the nuts and lift off the upper section . . .

18.10c . . . then unscrew a further three nuts (arrowed) . . .

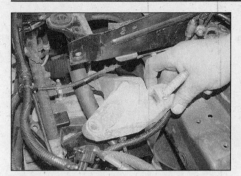

18.10d . . . and remove the lower section from the transmission

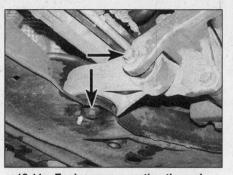

18.11a Engine rear mounting through-bolts (arrowed)

18.11b Removing the engine rear mounting

11 To remove the engine rear mounting/link, apply the handbrake, then jack up the front of the vehicle and support it on axle stands (see *Jacking and vehicle support*). Unscrew the through-bolts and remove the engine rear mounting link from the bracket on the transmission and from the bracket on the underbody **(see illustrations)**. Hold the engine stationary while the bolts are being removed, since the link will be under tension. **Note:** *The two through-bolts are of different lengths – if the bolts are refitted in the wrong positions, the rearmost bolt will foul the steering rack.*

12 Refitting of all mountings is a reversal of the removal procedure. Do not fully tighten the mounting nuts/bolts until all of the mountings are in position. Check that the mounting rubbers do not twist or distort as the mounting bolts and nuts are tightened to their specified torques.

Notes

Chapter 2 Part C:
Diesel engine in-car repair procedures

Contents

Degrees of difficulty

Easy, suitable for novice with little experience | **Fairly easy,** suitable for beginner with some experience | **Fairly difficult,** suitable for competent DIY mechanic | **Difficult,** suitable for experienced DIY mechanic | **Very difficult,** suitable for expert DIY or professional

Specifications

General
Engine type . . . . Four-cylinder, in-line, single overhead camshaft, cast-iron cylinder head and engine block
Designation . . . . Endura-DI
Engine code C9DC
Capacity . . . . 1753 cc
Bore . . . . 82.5 mm
Stroke . . . . 82.0 mm
Compression ratio 19.4:1
Firing order . . . . 1-3-4-2 (No 1 cylinder at timing belt end)
Direction of crankshaft rotation . . . . Clockwise (seen from right-hand side of vehicle)
Timing belt tension frequency (measured using a Clavis gauge):
　Initial setting . . . . 145 to 160 Hz
　Final setting (after turning the engine):
　　Setting . . . . 98 Hz
　　Checking (acceptable range) . . . . 85 to 110 Hz

Camshaft
Camshaft bearing journal diameter . . . . 27.96 to 27.98 mm
Camshaft bearing journal-to-cylinder head running clearance . . . . 0.010 to 0.045 mm
Camshaft endfloat . . . . 0.100 to 0.240 mm

Valves
Valve clearances (cold):
　Inlet . . . . 0.30 to 0.40 mm
　Exhaust . . . . 0.45 to 0.55 mm
Cam follower/shim thicknesses available . . . . 3.00 to 4.75 mm in varying increments

Cylinder head
Camshaft bearing diameter:
　Standard . . . . 30.500 to 30.525 mm
　Oversize . . . . 30.575 to 30.600 mm
Maximum permissible gasket surface distortion . . . . 0.6 mm

Lubrication

Engine oil type/specification	See end of *Weekly checks*
Engine oil capacity	See Chapter 1B
Oil pressure – minimum (engine at operating temperature):	
At idle	0.75 bars
At 2000 rpm	1.50 bars
Oil pump clearance (inner-to-outer rotors)	0.23 mm

Torque wrench settings

	Nm	lbf ft
Air cleaner mounting bracket	23	17
Air conditioning compressor	25	18
Alternator bracket to block	42	31
Alternator mountings:		
M8 bolts	24	18
M10 bolts	50	37
Auxiliary drivebelt idler pulley bolt	48	35
Auxiliary drivebelt tensioner mounting nuts	48	35
Auxiliary shaft oil seal carrier	23	17
Big-end bearing cap bolts:		
Stage 1	25	18
Stage 2	Angle-tighten a further 60°	
Stage 3	Angle-tighten a further 20°	
Camshaft bearing cap	23	17
Camshaft oil baffle	20	15
Camshaft sprocket bolt	50	37
Catalytic converter to bracket	24	18
Coolant pipe bracket	25	18
Coolant pump	12	9
Coolant temperature sensor	20	15
Crankcase ventilation oil separator	25	18
Crankshaft oil seal carrier	20	15
Crankshaft position sensor bracket	20	15
Crankshaft pulley bolt:		
Stage 1	100	74
Stage 2	Angle-tighten a further 180°	
Crankshaft rear oil seal carrier	20	15
Cylinder head bolts:		
Stage 1	20	15
Stage 2	54	40
Stage 3	Angle-tighten a further 90°	
Stage 4:		
Short bolts	Angle-tighten a further 70°	
Long bolts	Angle-tighten a further 90°	
Driveshaft centre bearing to block	48	35
Driveshaft nuts	316	233
EGR pipe union	15	11
Engine mountings:		
Left-hand mounting:		
Centre bolt	120	89
To subframe	48	35
To transmission	84	62
Rear mounting:		
Centre bolt	120	89
To subframe	48	35
Right-hand mounting:		
Bolts to body	50	37
Lower half to engine	83	61
Upper-to-lower half nuts	83	61
Engine oil drain plug	25	18
Exhaust manifold bracket to block	51	38
Exhaust manifold to catalytic converter	40	30
Exhaust manifold to cylinder head	23	17
Flywheel bolts:		
Stage 1	20	15
Stage 2	Angle-tighten a further 45°	
Stage 3	Angle-tighten a further 45°	
Front plate to cylinder block	24	18
Fuel filter to bracket	23	17

Torque wrench settings (continued)

	Nm	lbf ft
Fuel injection pump mountings	23	17
Fuel injection pump pulley bolt	25	18
Fuel injection pump timing belt sprocket	33	24
Fuel injector retaining bolts	24	18
Fuel line unions	25	18
Glow plugs	15	11
Inlet manifold	23	17
Intercooler mounting bolts	18	13
Lower crankcase to cylinder block	11	8
Main bearing cap bolts:		
Stage 1	45	33
Stage 2	70	52
Stage 3	Angle-tighten a further 60°	
Oil baffle plate nuts	23	17
Oil intake pipe bracket to block	22	16
Oil pressure switch	20	15
Oil pump bolts/studs:		
Stage 1	10	7
Stage 2	18	13
Power steering pump bracket to block	47	35
Power steering pump	24	18
Roadwheel nuts	85	63
Starter motor	20	15
Sump bolts	11	8
TDC setting plug cover	24	18
Thermostat housing to cylinder head	23	17
Thermostat cover	9	7
Timing belt adjuster cam to cylinder head	45	33
Timing belt inner cover bolts	24	18
Timing belt outer covers	8	6
Timing belt tensioner bolt	50	37
Timing chain guide retaining bolts	23	17
Timing chain tensioner	63	46
Transmission-to-engine bolts	40	30
Turbocharger bracket to block	24	18
Turbocharger oil feed pipe union	18	13
Turbocharger oil pipe bracket to block	48	35
Vacuum pump to cylinder head	22	16
Vacuum pump union	16	12

1 General information

How to use this Chapter

This Part of Chapter 2 is devoted to repair procedures possible while the engine is still installed in the vehicle. Since these procedures are based on the assumption that the engine is installed in the vehicle, if the engine has been removed from the vehicle and mounted on a stand, some of the preliminary dismantling steps outlined will not apply.

Information concerning engine/transmission removal and refitting and engine overhaul, can be found in Part D of this Chapter.

Engine description

The Endura-DI diesel engine is derived from the previous Endura-DE engine used in the Mondeo range; modified in line with the switch from indirect to direct fuel injection. The engine is an eight-valve, single overhead camshaft (SOHC), four-cylinder, in-line type, mounted transversely at the front of the vehicle, with the transmission on its left-hand end. It is only available in 1.8 litre form.

All major engine castings are of cast-iron; as with the Zetec-E petrol engines fitted to the Focus, the Endura-DI has a lower crankcase which is bolted to the underside of the cylinder block/crankcase, with a pressed-steel sump bolted under that. This arrangement offers greater rigidity than the normal sump arrangement, and helps to reduce engine vibration.

The crankshaft runs in five main bearings, the centre main bearing's upper half incorporating thrustwashers to control crankshaft endfloat. The connecting rods rotate on horizontally-split bearing shells at their big-ends. The pistons are attached to the connecting rods by gudgeon pins which are a floating fit in the connecting rod small-end eyes, secured by circlips. The aluminium alloy pistons are fitted with three piston rings: two compression rings and an oil control ring. After manufacture, the cylinder bores and piston skirts are measured and classified into two grades, which must be carefully matched together to ensure the correct piston/cylinder clearance; no oversizes are available to permit reboring.

The inlet and exhaust valves are each closed by coil springs; they operate in guides which are shrink-fitted into the cylinder head, as are the valve seat inserts.

The Endura-DI engine is unusual in that the fuel injection pump is driven by an offset double-row ('gemini') chain from a sprocket on the crankshaft, with the camshaft being driven from the injection pump sprocket by a conventional toothed timing belt.

The camshaft operates the eight valves via conventional cam followers with shims. The camshaft rotates in five bearings that are line-bored directly in the cylinder head and the (bolted-on) bearing caps; this means that the bearing caps are not available separately from the cylinder head, and must not be interchanged with caps from another engine.

The vacuum pump (used for the brake servo and other vacuum actuators) is driven by a pushrod operated directly by a special lobe on the camshaft.

The coolant pump is bolted to the right-hand end of the cylinder block, and is driven with the steering pump and alternator by a multi-ribbed auxiliary drivebelt from the crankshaft pulley.

When working on this engine, note that Torx-type (both male and female heads) and hexagon socket (Allen head) fasteners are widely used; a good selection of bits, with the necessary adapters, will be required so that these can be unscrewed without damage and, on reassembly, tightened to the torque wrench settings specified.

Lubrication system

Lubrication is by means of a G-rotor pump, which is mounted on the crankshaft right-hand end, and draws oil through a strainer located in the sump. The pump forces oil through an externally-mounted full-flow cartridge-type filter. From the filter, the oil is pumped into a main gallery in the cylinder block/crankcase, from where it is distributed to the crankshaft (main bearings) and cylinder head. An oil cooler is fitted next to the oil filter, at the rear of the block. The cooler is supplied with coolant from the engine cooling system.

While the crankshaft and camshaft bearings receive a pressurised supply, the camshaft lobes and valves are lubricated by splash, as are all other engine components. The undersides of the pistons are cooled by oil, sprayed from nozzles fitted above the upper main bearing shells. The turbocharger receives its own pressurised oil supply.

Repair operations possible with the engine in the car

The following major repair operations can be accomplished without removing the engine from the vehicle. However, owners should note that any operation involving the removal of the sump requires careful forethought, depending on the level of skill and the tools and facilities available; refer to the relevant text for details.

a) Compression pressure – testing.
b) Cylinder head cover – removal and refitting.
c) Timing belt cover – removal and refitting.
d) Timing belt – renewal.
e) Timing belt tensioner and sprockets – removal and refitting.
f) Camshaft oil seals – renewal.
g) Camshaft and cam followers – removal and refitting.
h) Cylinder head – removal, overhaul and refitting.
i) Cylinder head and pistons – decarbonising.
j) Sump – removal and refitting.
k) Crankshaft oil seals – renewal.
l) Oil pump – removal and refitting.
m) Piston/connecting rod assemblies – removal and refitting (but see note below).
n) Flywheel – removal and refitting.
o) Engine/transmission mountings – removal and refitting.

Note: It is possible to remove the pistons and connecting rods (after removing the cylinder head and sump) without removing the engine, however, this is not recommended. Work of this nature is more easily and thoroughly completed with the engine on the bench, as described in Chapter 2D.

Clean the engine compartment and the exterior of the engine with some type of degreaser before any work is done (and/or clean the engine using a steam cleaner). It will make the job easier and will help to keep dirt out of the internal areas of the engine.

Depending on the components involved, it may be helpful to remove the bonnet, to improve access to the engine as repairs are performed (refer to Chapter 11 if necessary). Cover the wings to prevent damage to the paint; special covers are available, but an old bedspread or blanket will also work.

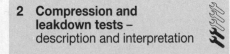

2 Compression and leakdown tests – description and interpretation

Compression test

Note: A compression tester suitable for use with diesel engines will be required for this test.

1 When engine performance is down, or if misfiring occurs which cannot be attributed to the fuel or emissions systems, a compression test can provide diagnostic clues as to the engine's condition. If the test is performed regularly, it can give warning of trouble before any other symptoms become apparent.

2 The engine must be fully warmed-up to normal operating temperature, the battery must be fully charged and the glow plugs must be removed. The aid of an assistant will be required.

3 Make sure that the ignition is switched off (take out the key). Disconnect the wiring plug at the top of the fuel injection pump, and place the wiring to one side. While the plug is disconnected, cover each half of the plug to keep the pins clean, and to prevent any static discharge, which may damage the pump electronic control unit.

4 Remove the glow plugs as described in Chapter 4B.

5 Fit a compression tester to the No 1 cylinder glow plug hole. The type of tester which screws into the plug thread is preferred.

6 Crank the engine for several seconds on the starter motor. After one or two revolutions, the compression pressure should build up to a maximum figure and then stabilise. Record the highest reading obtained.

7 Repeat the test on the remaining cylinders, recording the pressure in each.

8 The cause of poor compression is less easy to establish on a diesel engine than on a petrol engine. The effect of introducing oil into the cylinders (wet testing) is not conclusive, because there is a risk that the oil will sit in the

recess on the piston crown, instead of passing to the rings. However, the following can be used as a rough guide to diagnosis.

9 All cylinders should produce very similar pressures. Any difference greater than that specified indicates the existence of a fault. Note that the compression should build up quickly in a healthy engine. Low compression on the first stroke, followed by gradually increasing pressure on successive strokes, indicates worn piston rings. A low compression reading on the first stroke, which does not build up during successive strokes, indicates leaking valves or a blown head gasket (a cracked head could also be the cause).

10 A low reading from two adjacent cylinders is almost certainly due to the head gasket having blown between them and the presence of coolant in the engine oil will confirm this.

11 On completion, remove the compression tester, and refit the glow plugs, with reference to Chapter 4B.

12 Take out the ignition key, then reconnect the injection pump wiring connector.

Leakdown test

13 A leakdown test measures the rate at which compressed air fed into the cylinder is lost. It is an alternative to a compression test, and in many ways it is better, since the escaping air provides easy identification of where pressure loss is occurring (piston rings, valves or head gasket).

14 The equipment required for leakdown testing is unlikely to be available to the home mechanic. If poor compression is suspected, have the test performed by a suitably-equipped garage.

3 Setting the engine to Top Dead Centre (TDC) on No 1 cylinder

General information

1 TDC is the highest point in the cylinder that each piston reaches as it travels up and down when the crankshaft turns. Each piston reaches TDC at the end of the compression stroke and again at the end of the exhaust stroke, but TDC generally refers to piston position on the compression stroke. No 1 piston is at the timing belt end of the engine.

2 Positioning No 1 piston at TDC is an essential part of many procedures, such as timing belt removal and camshaft removal.

3 The design of the engines covered in this Chapter is such that piston-to-valve contact may occur if the camshaft or crankshaft is turned with the timing belt removed. For this reason, it is important to ensure that the camshaft and crankshaft do not move in relation to each other once the timing belt has been removed from the engine.

Setting TDC on No 1 cylinder

Note: Suitable tools will be required to lock

the camshaft and the fuel injection pump sprocket in position during this procedure – see text.

4 Disconnect the battery negative (earth) lead (refer to *Disconnecting the battery*).

5 Remove the cylinder head cover as described in Section 4.

6 Loosen the right-hand front wheel nuts, then firmly apply the handbrake. Jack up the front of the car, and support on axle stands (see *Jacking and vehicle support*). Remove the right-hand front wheel.

7 Loosen and remove a total of nine screws securing the engine undershield. This is a substantial cover, spanning the length and width of the underside of the engine compartment. Lower the shield, and remove it.

8 When No 1 cylinder is set to TDC on compression, an offset slot in the left-hand end of the camshaft (left as seen from the driver's seat) should align with the top surface of the cylinder head, to allow a special tool (Ford No 303-376) to be fitted. This tool can be substituted by a suitable piece of flat bar **(see illustrations)**. There is no need to fit this tool at this stage, but check that the slot comes into the required alignment while setting TDC – if the slot is above the level of the head, No 1 cylinder could be on the exhaust stroke.

9 If required, further confirmation that No 1 cylinder is on the compression stroke can be inferred from the positions of the camshaft lobes for No 1 cylinder. When the cylinder is on compression, the inlet and exhaust lobes should be pointing upwards (ie, not depressing the cam followers). The camshaft lobes are only visible once the oil baffle plate is removed, and the securing nuts also retain two of the camshaft bearing caps – for more information, refer to Section 9.

10 A TDC timing hole is provided on the front of the cylinder block, to permit the crankshaft to be located more accurately at TDC. A timing pin (Ford service tool 303-193, obtainable from Ford dealers or a tool supplier) screws into the hole, and the crankshaft is then turned so that it contacts the end of the tool. A tool can be fabricated to set the timing at TDC, using a piece of threaded rod **(see illustrations)**.

3.8a Offset slot in camshaft aligned with cylinder head

3.8b Flat bar engaged in camshaft slot

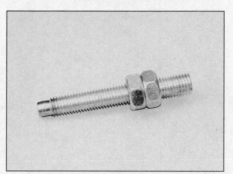

3.10a Tool fabricated to locate crankshaft at TDC . . .

3.10b . . . screw the tool into the cylinder block to locate with the crankshaft

11 To gain access to the blanking plug fitted over the timing pin hole, remove the auxiliary drivebelt as described in Chapter 1B, then unbolt and remove the alternator coupling, as described in the alternator removal procedure in Chapter 5A.

12 Remove the camshaft setting tool from the slot, and turn the engine back slightly from the TDC position. Unscrew the timing pin blanking plug (which is located in a deeply-recessed hole), and screw in the timing pin **(see illustrations)**. Now carefully turn the crankshaft forwards until it contacts the timing pin (it should be possible to feel this point – the crankshaft cannot then be turned any further forward).

13 If the engine is being set to TDC as part of the timing belt removal/renewal procedure, further confirmation of the TDC position can be gained once the timing belt outer cover has

been removed. At TDC, a punched dot on the injection pump sprocket will be in the 12 o'clock position **(see illustration)**. However, removing the timing belt outer cover involves unbolting the engine right-hand mounting, so this is not included as part of this procedure. It is recommended at this point that the right-hand front wheel is refitted, and the car lowered to the ground before proceeding.

14 Once No 1 cylinder has been positioned at TDC on the compression stroke, TDC for any of the other cylinders can then be located by rotating the crankshaft clockwise 180° at a time and following the firing order (see Specifications).

15 Before rotating the crankshaft again, make sure that the timing pin and camshaft setting bar are removed. When operations are complete, do not forget to refit the timing pin blanking plug.

3.12a Unscrew the blanking plug . . .

3.12b . . . and insert the timing pin

3.13 Timing dot (arrowed) on injection pump sprocket at 12 o'clock position

4.2a Two crankcase ventilation hoses at the front (rear hose not visible here)

4.2b Release the hose clips and pull the hoses off their stubs

4.3 Unclip the fuel pipes from the cylinder head cover

4.4a Unscrew the securing bolts . . .

4.4b . . . and lift off the cylinder head cover

4 Cylinder head cover – removal and refitting

Removal

1 Slacken the hose clips and disconnect the two air hoses leading to the intercooler at the front of the engine. Detach the hose brackets from the cylinder head cover, and move the hoses aside. If preferred, also disconnect the hoses at their connections at the rear of the engine, and remove the hoses completely.

2 Noting their positions carefully for refitting, release the hose clips and detach the crankcase ventilation hoses from the cylinder head cover **(see illustrations)**. There are two hoses at the front, and one at the rear. Move the hoses aside as far as possible.

3 Noting how they are located, unclip the fuel pipes from the cylinder head cover, without disconnecting them **(see illustration)**. Unbolt the power steering pipe bracket from the rear of the cover, and move it clear. Make sure, in moving all the pipes aside, that they are not put under undue strain.

4 Unscrew the three securing bolts, and lift the cylinder head cover off the engine **(see illustrations)**. Recover the gasket carefully – it can be re-used several times, but check its condition before doing so.

5 If required, the baffle plate fitted below the cover can be removed by unscrewing the nuts and taking off the spacer plates and sleeves – note, however, that these nuts also secure Nos 2 and 4 camshaft bearing caps. Note the positions of all components carefully for refitting **(see illustration)**.

Refitting

6 Clean the sealing surfaces of the cover and the head, and check the condition of the rubber seals fitted to the cover bolts.

7 Before refitting the cover, check that the crankcase ventilation holes are clear. The connection at the rear of the cover leads to the ventilation valve – if this appears to be blocked, use a suitable degreaser to wash out the valve (it is not advisable to use petrol, as this may damage the valve itself).

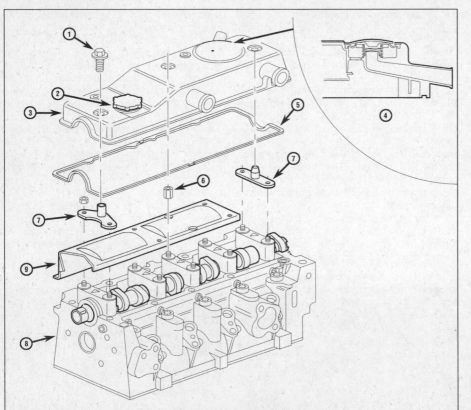

4.5 Cylinder head cover and related components

1 Cover bolt	4 Crankcase ventilation valve	7 Spacer plate
2 Engine oil filler cap	5 Gasket	8 Cylinder head
3 Cylinder head cover	6 Spacer sleeve	9 Baffle plate

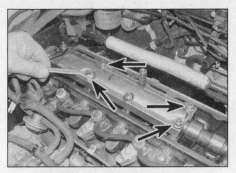
5.2a Unscrew the four nuts . . .

5.2b . . . and lift off the baffle plate . . .

5.2c . . . refit the camshaft bearing cap nuts temporarily

8 Lightly lubricate the surfaces of the gasket with fresh oil, then fit the gasket to the cover, making sure it is correctly located.
9 Lower the cover into position, ensuring that the gasket is not disturbed, then fit the three bolts and tighten them a little at a time, so that the cover is drawn down evenly to make a good seal.
10 Further refitting is a reversal of removal. Ensure that the pipes are routed as noted on removal, and that the ventilation hoses are correctly and securely reconnected.
11 When the engine has been run for some time, check for signs of oil leakage from the gasket joint.

5 Valve clearances – checking and adjustment

Checking

1 Remove the cylinder head cover as described in Section 4.
2 Remove the baffle plate fitted below the cover by unscrewing the four nuts and taking off the spacer plates and sleeves. Note, however, that these nuts also secure Nos 2 and 4 camshaft bearing caps – it is advisable to refit the nuts temporarily, once the baffle plate has been removed **(see illustrations)**. Note the positions of all components carefully for refitting.
3 During the following procedure, the crankshaft must be turned in order to position the peaks of the camshaft lobes away from the valves. To do this, either turn the crankshaft on the pulley bolt or alternatively raise the front right-hand corner of the vehicle, engage 4th gear, and turn the front roadwheel. Access to the pulley bolt is gained by jacking up the front of the vehicle and supporting on axle stands, then removing the auxiliary drivebelt lower cover.
4 If desired, to enable the crankshaft to be turned more easily, remove the glow plugs as described in Chapter 4B.
5 Draw the valve positions on a piece of paper, numbering them 1 to 8 from the timing belt end of the engine. Identify them as inlet or exhaust (ie, 1I, 2E, 3I, 4E, 5I, 6E, 7I, 8E).

6 Turn the crankshaft until the valves of No 4 cylinder (flywheel end) are 'rocking' – the exhaust valve will be closing and the inlet valve will be opening. The piston of No 1 cylinder will be at the top of its compression stroke, with both valves fully closed. The clearances for both valves of No 1 cylinder may be checked at the same time.
7 Use feeler blade(s) to measure the exact clearance between the heel of the camshaft lobe and the shim on the cam follower; the feeler blades should be a firm sliding fit. Record the measured clearance on the drawing. From this clearance it will be possible to calculate the thickness of the new shim to be fitted, where necessary. Note that the inlet and exhaust valve clearances are different, so it is important that you know which valve clearance you are checking.
8 With No 1 cylinder valve clearances checked, turn the engine through half a turn so that No 2 valves are 'rocking', then measure the valve clearances of No 3 cylinder in the same way. Similarly check the valve clearances of No 4 cylinder with No 1 valves 'rocking' and No 2 cylinder with No 3 valves 'rocking'. Compare the measured clearances with the values give in the Specifications – any which fall within the range do not require adjustment.

Adjustment

9 If adjustment is required, turn the engine in the normal direction of rotation through approximately 90°, to bring the pistons to mid-stroke. If this is not done, the pistons at TDC will prevent the cam followers being depressed, and damage may result. Depress the cam followers and then either shim can be withdrawn if the peak of the cam does not prevent access. The Ford tools for this operation are Nos 21-106 and 21-107, but with care and patience a C-spanner or screwdriver can be used to depress the cam follower and the shim can be flicked out with a small screwdriver.
10 If the valve clearance was too small, a thinner shim must be fitted. If the clearance was too large, a thicker shim must be fitted. The thickness of the shim (in mm) is engraved on the side facing away from the camshaft. If the marking is missing or illegible, a micrometer will be needed to establish shim thickness.

11 When the shim thickness and the valve clearance are known, the required thickness of the new shim can be calculated as follows (all measurements in mm):

Sample calculation – clearance too small
Desired clearance (A) = 0.50
Measured clearance (B) = 0.35
Shim thickness found (C) = 3.95
Shim thickness required (D) = C+B–A
= 3.80

Sample calculation – clearance too large
Desired clearance (A) = 0.35
Measured clearance (B) = 0.40
Shim thickness found (C) = 4.05
Shim thickness required (D) = C+B–A
= 4.10

12 With the correct shim fitted, release the cam follower depressing tool. Turn the engine back so that the cam lobes are again pointing upwards and check that the clearance is now correct.
13 Repeat the process for the remaining valves, turning the engine each time to bring a pair of cam lobes upwards.
14 It will be helpful for future adjustment if a record is kept of the thickness of shim fitted at each position. The shims required can be purchased in advance once the clearances and the existing shim thicknesses are known.
15 It is permissible to interchange shims between cam followers to achieve the correct clearances but it is not advisable to turn the camshaft with any shims removed, since there is a risk that the cam lobe will jam in the empty cam follower.
16 When all the clearances are correct, refit the glow plugs (Chapter 4B), then refit the oil baffle plate and tighten the nuts to the specified torque. Refit the cylinder head cover as described in Section 4.

6 Crankshaft pulley – removal and refitting

Removal

1 Disconnect the battery negative lead. **Note:** *Before disconnecting the battery, refer to 'Disconnecting the battery' at the rear of this manual.*

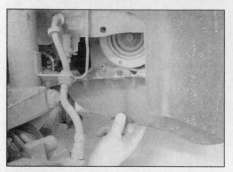

6.4 Remove the lower auxiliary belt cover

6.7 Special tool used to stop the crankshaft from turning

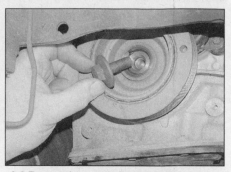

6.8 Renew the crankshaft pulley securing bolt when reassembling

2 Loosen the right-hand front roadwheel nuts, then raise the front of the vehicle, and support securely on axle stands (see *Jacking and vehicle support*). Remove the roadwheel.

3 Remove a total of nine securing screws and withdraw the engine undershield from under the car.

4 Remove the two fasteners securing the auxiliary drivebelt lower cover, and remove the cover from under the car **(see illustration)**.

5 Remove the auxiliary drivebelt, as described in Chapter 1B.

6 The centre bolt which secures the crankshaft pulley must now be slackened. This bolt is tightened to a very high torque, and it is first of all essential to ensure that the car is adequately supported, as considerable effort will be needed.

7 Ford technicians use a special holding tool (205-072) which locates in the outer holes of the pulley and prevents it from turning **(see illustration)**. If this is not available, select a gear, and have an assistant firmly apply the handbrake and footbrake as the bolt is loosened. If this method is unsuccessful, remove the starter motor as described in Chapter 5A, and jam the flywheel ring gear, using a suitable tool, to prevent the crankshaft from rotating.

8 Unscrew the bolt securing the pulley to the crankshaft, and remove the pulley. It is advisable to obtain a new bolt for reassembly **(see illustration)**.

9 With the pulley removed, it is advisable to check the crankshaft front oil seal for signs of oil leakage. If necessary, fit a new seal as described in Section 16.

Refitting

10 Refit the pulley to the crankshaft sprocket, then fit the new pulley securing bolt and tighten it as far as possible before the crankshaft starts to rotate..

11 Holding the pulley against rotation as for removal, first tighten the bolt to the specified Stage 1 torque.

12 Stage 2 involves tightening the bolt though an angle, rather than to a torque. The bolt must be rotated through the specified angle – special angle gauges are available from tool outlets. As a guide, a 90° angle is equivalent to a quarter-turn, and this is easily judged by assessing the start and end positions of the socket handle or torque wrench.

13 Refit and tension the auxiliary drivebelt as described in Chapter 1B.

14 Refit the auxiliary drivebelt lower cover, and where removed, the engine undershield(s) and wheelarch liner panels.

15 Refit the roadwheel, lower the vehicle to the ground, and reconnect the battery negative lead. Tighten the wheel nuts to the specified torque.

---

7 Timing belt –
removal and refitting

Note: *The timing belt tension must be set using a special tool known as a Clavis gauge, which measures the frequency produced when the correctly-tensioned belt is tapped*

with a finger. This gauge will not be available to the DIY mechanic and no alternative 'ballpark' setting is given by Ford. Also unfortunately, if the tension setting is to be checked once refitting is complete, removing the timing belt cover again involves dismantling the engine right-hand mounting. To avoid this inconvenience, try to borrow or hire the required tool before starting work. Besides a Ford dealer, other non-franchised garages may have a belt tension checking tool of the required type – these tools are becoming more widely available from several different suppliers, including Haynes Garage Equipment.

Removal

1 Disconnect the battery negative lead; refer to *Disconnecting the battery* at the rear of this manual.

2 Remove the intercooler (and the air inlet/outlet pipes running over the engine) as described in Chapter 4B.

3 Remove the coolant expansion tank mounting bolt at the front, unclip it at the rear, and move the tank to one side without disconnecting the hoses **(see illustrations)**.

4 Referring to the information in Section 3, set the engine to TDC on No 1 cylinder. The timing pin described must be used, to ensure accuracy.

5 Ford recommend that the engine is further prevented from turning by fitting another special tool, to lock the flywheel ring gear (this prevents the injection pump sprocket from moving). This tool (Ford No 303-393) is also available from Ford dealers, and is quite simple. With the starter motor removed as described in Chapter 5A, the tool bolts across the starter motor aperture in the bellhousing, and a peg on the back of the tool engages and locks the flywheel ring gear. A substitute for this tool could be made, or the ring gear jammed using another suitable tool. Alternatively, if the handbrake is firmly applied with the transmission in gear, the engine will not be able to turn significantly.

6 Before unbolting the engine mounting, it is recommended that the right-hand wheel is refitted, and the car lowered to the ground (assuming the car has been raised as part of setting the engine to TDC).

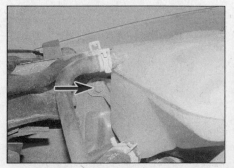

7.3a Remove the mounting bolt (arrowed) at the front . . .

7.3b . . . then unclip the expansion tank at the rear, and remove it

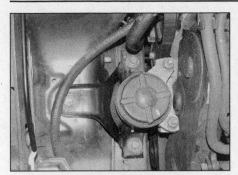

7.8a Engine right-hand mounting nuts and bolts (arrowed)

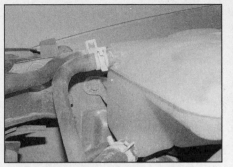

7.8b Unscrew the mounting nuts/bolts . . .

7.8c . . . and lift off the engine mounting

7.9a Using a suitable socket on the Torx end fitting . . .

7.9b . . . unscrew and remove the engine mounting front stud

7 The engine must now be supported before the right-hand mounting is removed. Ford technicians use an engine support bar, which locates in the channels at the top of each inner wing, and a further beam attached to this, which rests on the front crossmember. If such an arrangement is not available, use an engine crane; either way, use a suitable length of chain and hooks to attach the lifting gear to the engine lifting eye. If the engine must be supported from below (and this is not recommended), use a large piece of wood on a trolley jack to spread the load and reduce the chance of damage to the sump.

8 With the weight of the engine supported, unscrew the two nuts and three bolts securing the top half of the engine right-hand mounting, and lift the mounting off the two studs (see illustrations).

9 Before the timing belt outer cover can be removed, the stud fitted to the front of the engine mounting must be unscrewed and removed. This can be achieved using a socket on the Torx end fitting provided (see illustrations).

10 At the rear of the timing belt cover, unbolt the support bracket for the power steering fluid pipe. Unscrew the three bolts (and one stud/bolt at the top), and remove the timing belt outer cover (see illustrations).

11 If the timing belt is not being fitted straight away (or if the belt is being removed as part of another procedure, such as cylinder head removal), temporarily refit the engine right-hand mounting and tighten the bolts securely.

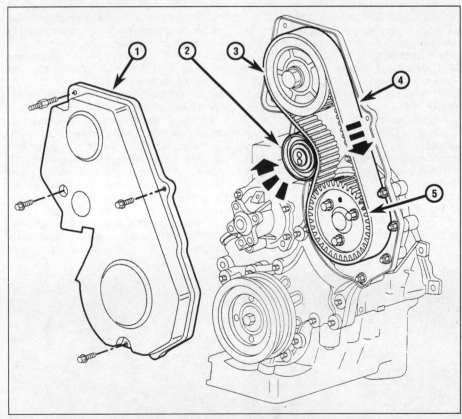

7.10a Timing belt and cover details

1 Timing belt cover	3 Camshaft pulley	5 Fuel injection pump pulley
2 Timing belt tensioner	4 Timing belt	

7.10b Unbolt the power steering pipe bracket . . .

7.10c . . . then unscrew the bolts . . .

7.10d . . . and lift off the timing belt cover

7.13a Slacken the tensioner bolt . . .

7.13b . . . and remove the tensioner completely

7.13c Slip the timing belt from its sprockets

7.15 Using a forked holding tool, unscrew the camshaft sprocket bolt

12 Before proceeding further, check once more that the engine is positioned at TDC on No 1 cylinder, as described in Section 3. The position of the injection pump sprocket can now be confirmed – a dot marking on the sprocket should be at the 12 o'clock position.
13 Slacken the timing belt tensioner bolt, and remove the tensioner completely. Slip the timing belt from the sprockets, and remove it **(see illustrations)**.
14 The camshaft sprocket must be removed – this is necessary as part of setting up the new timing belt, to ensure that the correct valve timing is preserved. Not only will a method for holding the sprocket stationary be required, but the sprocket itself is mounted on a taper, so a puller will be needed to free it from the camshaft. Due to its design, the sprocket cannot readily be removed using an ordinary puller, so either the Ford tool (303-651) must be obtained, or a suitable alternative fabricated.
15 Holding the camshaft sprocket using a suitable tool, loosen the sprocket bolt **(see illustration)**. **Note:** *Do not rely on the TDC*

setting bar engaged in the slot at the opposite end of the camshaft to hold it stationary – not only is this dangerous, it could well result in damage to the camshaft.
16 Using a suitable puller, release the camshaft sprocket from the taper, and remove it **(see illustrations)**.
17 Do **not** be tempted to re-use the old timing belt under any circumstances – even if it is known to have covered less mileage than the renewal interval indicated in Chapter 1B. Ford state that, once a new timing belt has been run on the engine, it is considered worn, and should be discarded. In any case, given the potential expense involved should the belt fail in service, re-using an old belt would be a false economy.
18 Before disposing of the old belt, however, examine it for evidence of contamination by coolant or lubricant. If there are any signs of

7.16a Fitting Ford tool 303-651 to the camshaft sprocket

7.16b Using the special Ford puller, free the sprocket from its taper . . .

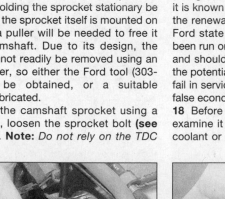
7.16c . . . then remove the sprocket bolt and washer . . .

7.16d . . . and finally remove the camshaft sprocket

7.21 Refit the camshaft sprocket bolt, hand tight at first

7.22 Note the position of the plate on the belt tensioner

7.23 Tool fitted to slot in the end of the camshaft

contamination, find the source of the contamination before progressing any further. If an oil leak is evident, this will most likely be from the camshaft seal. Cure the problem, then wash down the whole area (including the sprockets) with degreaser and allow to dry before fitting the new belt.

19 Check the condition of the timing belt tensioner before refitting it. In particular, spin the tensioner pulley, and check for signs of sticking or roughness, indicating bearing wear. Many professional mechanics will fit a new tensioner as a matter of course when fitting a new timing belt, and this should be considered a good idea, especially if the engine has completed a large mileage.

Refitting

20 Ensure that the crankshaft and camshaft are still set to TDC on No 1 cylinder, as described in Section 3.

21 Refit the camshaft sprocket to the camshaft, tightening the bolt by hand only (see illustration).

22 Fit the timing belt tensioner into position, noting that the plate must be set pointing to the 3 o'clock position (see illustration). Fit the retaining bolt, tightening it finger-tight only at this stage.

23 Fit the timing belt over the sprockets and above the tensioner pulley, ensuring that the injection pump sprocket does not move (the camshaft sprocket must be free to turn – remember that the camshaft itself is locked by the tool fitted to its slotted end) (see illustration).

Initial tensioning

24 Tension the timing belt by turning the tensioner plate anti-clockwise. Ford's information quotes the desired belt tension as a frequency, obtained and measured using a special belt tensioning tool (refer to the Specifications for the acceptable frequency range).

25 In the absence of this tool, set the belt tension to the maximum possible, using reasonable force only (no tools); note that this is NOT the final setting, and is intended for use only to settle the belt.

26 When the belt tension has been correctly set, hold the tensioner and plate against

rotation, and tighten the tensioner bolt securely (to approximately one third of its final torque at this stage). Similarly, hold the camshaft sprocket against rotation, and tighten it to around one third of the final torque value.

27 Remove the locking tools from the engine, so that it can be turned; these may include the timing pin, the plate fitted into the camshaft slot, and the tool used to lock the flywheel.

28 Mark the TDC position of the crankshaft pulley, using paint or typist's correction fluid, to give a rough indication of TDC, and so that the number of turns can be counted.

29 Using a spanner or socket on the crankshaft pulley centre bolt, turn the engine forwards (clockwise, viewed from the timing belt end) through six full turns, bringing the engine almost up to the TDC position on completion.

30 Using the information in Section 3, set the engine to TDC on No 1 cylinder. Make sure that the timing pin and camshaft locking tools are refitted – also lock the flywheel against rotation, using the same method used previously (see paragraph 5).

Final tensioning

31 Slacken (but do not remove) the camshaft sprocket bolt, holding the sprocket using the home-made tool (see paragraph 15), and release the sprocket from its taper, so that it is free to turn relative to the camshaft.

32 Slacken the timing belt tensioner bolt, then re-tighten it finger-tight. Similarly, tighten the camshaft sprocket bolt finger-tight.

33 The belt tension must now be set to its final value, which is as specified at the start of this Chapter, if the special tool is available. If not, as a guide, the final tension is approximately half the value to which the belt was set initially. Given the importance of the setting for its effect on belt life and correct operation, guesswork is not desirable. The old practice of twisting the belt to assess its tension is not recommended, as this can lead to internal fracturing of the belt plies. Set the belt tension as best you can, then on completion of refitting, have the tension checked using the special tool (refer to the Note at the start of this Section).

34 With the belt tension correctly set (or as near as possible), hold the tensioner and its plate against rotation, and tighten the tensioner bolt to the specified torque.

35 Hold the camshaft sprocket using the home-made tool, and tighten the sprocket bolt to the specified torque.

36 If the special belt tension measuring tool is available, re-check the tension once the tensioner and camshaft sprocket bolts have been tightened. If the belt tension is now outside the range quoted in the Specifications, repeat paragraphs 31 to 35.

37 Remove the locking tools from the engine; these may include the timing pin, the plate fitted into the camshaft slot, and the tool used to lock the flywheel.

38 If the engine right-hand mounting had been temporarily refitted as described in paragraph 11, support the engine once more, and remove the mounting.

39 Refit the timing belt outer cover, and tighten the retaining bolts securely. Note: *It is not advisable to drive the car with the belt cover removed, even if the belt tension is to be checked later (see paragraph 33).*

40 Refit the front stud to the engine mounting, and tighten it securely, using a similar method to that used for the stud's removal.

41 Refit the top half of the engine right-hand mounting, and tighten the nuts and bolts to the specified torque's.

42 With the engine securely supported by its mounting once more, the engine supporting tools can be carefully removed.

43 Refit the cylinder head cover as described in Section 4.

44 Refit the coolant expansion tank to the inner wing.

45 Refit the intercooler as described in Chapter 4B.

46 Reconnect the battery negative lead, referring to the precautions in *Disconnecting the battery* at the end of this Manual.

47 If the belt tension has been set without the benefit of the Ford special tool, have the tension checked by a Ford dealer or suitably-equipped garage at the earliest opportunity.

8 Timing belt tensioner and sprockets – removal, inspection and refitting

Timing belt tensioner

1 The timing belt tensioner is removed as part of the timing belt renewal procedure, in Section 7.

Camshaft sprocket

2 The camshaft sprocket is removed as part of the timing belt renewal procedure, in Section 7.

Fuel injection pump sprocket

3 Removal of the injection pump sprocket is described as part of the injection pump removal procedure, in Chapter 4B. Note that the sprocket is sealed to the pump using two types of sealant/locking compound.

9 Camshaft and cam followers – removal, inspection and refitting

Note: *A new camshaft oil seal will be required on refitting.*

Removal

1 Remove the timing belt and camshaft sprocket as described in Section 7.
2 Remove the camshaft oil seal. The seal is quite deeply recessed – Ford dealers have a special seal extractor for this (tool No 303-293). In the absence of this tool, do not use any removal method which might damage the sealing surfaces, or a leak will result when the new seal is fitted **(see Haynes Hint)**.

 One of the best ways to remove an oil seal is to carefully drill or punch two holes through the seal, opposite each other (taking care not to damage the surface behind the seal as this is done). Two self-tapping screws are then screwed into the holes; by pulling on the screw heads alternately with a pair of pliers, the seal can be extracted.

3 Unscrew and remove the nuts securing the oil baffle plate to the top of the engine, noting that these nuts also secure Nos 2 and 4 camshaft bearing caps. Lift off the baffle plate, and recover the bearing caps – if no identification numbers are evident on the caps, mark them for position, as they must be refitted to the correct locations.
4 Progressively unscrew (by half a turn at a time) the nuts securing the remaining (Nos 1, 3 and 5) bearing caps until the camshaft is free.
5 Lift off each bearing cap and bearing shell in turn, and mark it for position if necessary –

all the caps must be refitted in their original positions.
6 Carefully lift out the camshaft, and place it somewhere safe – the lobes must not be scratched. Remove the lower part of the bearing shells in turn, and mark them for position **(see illustration)**.
7 Before lifting out the cam followers and shims, give some thought to how they will be stored while they are removed. Unless new components are being fitted, the cam followers and shims must be identified for position. The best way to do this is to take a box, and divide it into eight compartments, each with a clearly-marked number; taking No 1 cam follower and shim as being that nearest the timing belt end of the engine, lift out each cam follower and shim, and place it in the box. Alternatively, keep the cam follower/shim assemblies in line, in fitted order, as they are removed – mark No 1 to avoid confusion.

Inspection

8 With the camshaft removed, examine the bearing caps and the bearing locations in the cylinder head for signs of obvious wear or pitting. If evident, a new cylinder head will probably be required. Also check that the oil supply holes in the cylinder head are free from obstructions. (New bearing shells should be used on reassembly.)
9 Visually inspect the camshaft for evidence of wear on the surfaces of the lobes and journals. Normally their surfaces should be smooth and have a dull shine; look for scoring, erosion or pitting and areas that appear highly polished, indicating excessive wear. Accelerated wear will occur once the hardened exterior of the camshaft has been damaged, so always renew worn items. **Note:** *If these symptoms are visible on the tips of the camshaft lobes, check the corresponding cam follower/shim, as it will probably be worn as well.*
10 If suitable precision measuring equipment (such as a micrometer) is available, the camshaft bearing journals can be checked for wear, by comparing the values measured with those specified.
11 If the machined surfaces of the camshaft appear discoloured or blued, it is likely that it

9.6 Remove the camshaft bearing shells

has been overheated at some point, probably due to inadequate lubrication. This may have distorted the shaft, in which case the runout should be checked; Ford do not quote a runout tolerance, so if this kind of damage is suspected, an engine reconditioning specialist should be consulted. In the case of inadequate lubrication, distortion is unlikely to be the only damage which has occurred, and a new camshaft will probably be needed.
12 To measure the camshaft endfloat, temporarily refit the camshaft to the cylinder head, then fit Nos 1 and 5 bearing caps and tighten the retaining nuts to the specified torque setting. Anchor a DTI gauge to the timing belt end of the cylinder head. Push the camshaft to one end of the cylinder head as far as it will travel, then rest the DTI gauge probe on the end face of the camshaft, and zero the gauge. Push the camshaft as far as it will go to the other end of the cylinder head, and record the gauge reading. Verify the reading by pushing the camshaft back to its original position and checking that the gauge indicates zero again. **Note:** *The cam followers must **not** be fitted whilst this measurement is being taken.*
13 Check that the camshaft endfloat measurement is within the limit listed in the Specifications. If the measurement is outside the specified limit, wear is unlikely to be confined to any one component, so renewal of the camshaft, cylinder head and bearing caps must be considered.
14 The camshaft bearing running clearance should now be measured. One method (which will be difficult to achieve without a range of micrometers or internal/external expanding calipers) is to measure the outside diameters of the camshaft bearing surfaces and the internal diameters formed by the bearing caps and the bearing locations in the cylinder head. The difference between these two measurements is the running clearance.
15 Another, more accurate, method of measuring the running clearance involves the use of Plastigauge. This consists of a fine thread of perfectly-round plastic which is compressed between the bearing cap and the journal. When the cap is removed, the plastic is deformed, and can be measured with a special card gauge supplied with the kit. The running clearance is determined from this gauge. Plastigauge is sometimes difficult to obtain, but enquiries at one of the larger specialist quality motor factors should produce the name of a stockist in your area. The procedure for using Plastigauge is as follows.
16 Ensure that the cylinder head, bearing cap, bearing shell and camshaft bearing surfaces are completely clean and dry. Lay the lower bearing shells and camshaft in position in the cylinder head.
17 Lay a length of Plastigauge on top of each of the camshaft bearing journals.
18 Place the bearing caps/shells in position over the camshaft, and progressively tighten the retaining nuts to the specified torque.

Note: *Do not rotate the camshaft whilst the bearing caps are in place, as the measurements will be affected.*

19 Unscrew the nuts and carefully remove the bearing caps again, lifting them vertically away from the camshaft to avoid disturbing the Plastigauge. The Plastigauge should remain on the camshaft bearing surface.
20 Hold the scale card supplied with the kit against each bearing journal, and measure the width of the crushed Plastigauge, using the graduated markings on the card. The width of the crushed Plastigauge corresponds to the bearing running clearance.
21 Compare the camshaft running clearance measurements with the figure given in the Specifications; if any are outside the specified tolerance, then check with Ford for new bearing shells. If no other size of shells are available, the camshaft, cylinder head and bearing caps should be renewed.
22 On completion, remove the bearing caps/shells and camshaft, and clean off all remaining traces of Plastigauge.
23 Inspect the cam followers and shims for obvious signs of wear or damage, and renew if necessary.

Refitting

24 Make sure that the top surfaces of the cylinder head, and in particular the camshaft bearings and the mating surfaces for the camshaft bearing caps, are completely clean.
25 Smear some clean engine oil onto the sides of the cam followers, and offer each one into position in their original bores in the cylinder head, together with its respective shim **(see illustration)**. Push them down until they contact the valves, then lubricate the top surface of each shim.
26 Lubricate the camshaft and cylinder head bearing journals with clean engine oil. If the pushrod which operates the brake vacuum pump has been removed from the cylinder head **(see illustration)**, refit it now – once the camshaft is in position, the pushrod cannot be refitted.
27 Carefully lower the camshaft into position in the cylinder head, making sure that the cam lobes for No 1 cylinder are pointing upwards. Also use the position of the locking tool slot at the end of the camshaft as a guide to correct alignment when refitting – the slot should be flush to the top surface of the cylinder head (the larger 'semi-circle' created by the offset slot should be uppermost).
28 Prior to refitting the No 1 camshaft bearing cap, the front halves of the flat sealing surface must be coated with a smear of suitable sealant, as shown **(see illustration)**.
29 Lubricate Nos 1, 3 and 5 bearing caps and shells with clean oil (taking care not to get any on the sealant-coated surfaces of No 1 cap), then place them into their correct positions. Refit the bearing cap nuts, and tighten them progressively to the specified torque wrench setting.

9.25 Lubricate the cam followers before refitting

9.26 Refit the brake vacuum pump pushrod before refitting the camshaft

30 The outer edges of No 1 bearing cap must now be sealed to the cylinder head surface with a thin bead of suitable sealant.
31 Clean out the oil seal housing and the sealing surface of the camshaft by wiping it with a lint-free cloth. Remove any swarf or burrs that may cause the seal to leak.
32 Apply a little oil to the new camshaft oil seal, and fit it over the end of the camshaft, lips facing inwards. To avoid damaging the seal lips, wrap a little tape over the end of the camshaft. Ford dealers have a special tool (No 303-199) for fitting the seal, but if this is not available, a deep socket of suitable size can be used. It is important that the seal is fitted square to the shaft, and is fully seated.
33 Refit the camshaft sprocket and timing belt as described in Section 7.
34 Check the valve clearances as described in Section 5.
35 Oil the bearing surfaces of Nos 2 and 4 bearing caps, then refit them and the oil baffle plate to the engine. Tighten the bearing cap nuts to the specified torque.
36 Refit the cylinder head cover as described in Section 4.
37 Further refitting is a reversal of removal.

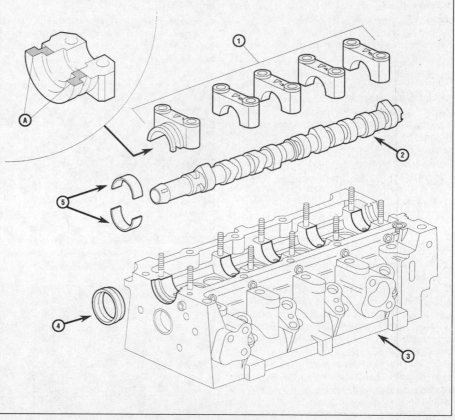

9.28 Camshaft refitting details

1 *Bearing caps (1 to 5)*
2 *Camshaft*
3 *Cylinder head*
4 *Camshaft oil seal*
5 *Bearing shells*
A *Sealant application areas on No 1 bearing cap*

10.4a Lubricate the oil seal before fitting over the camshaft . . .

10.4b . . . and use a suitable socket to tap seal in squarely

10 Camshaft oil seal – renewal

1 Remove the timing belt and camshaft sprocket as described in Section 7. Access to the seal is hampered by the presence of the timing belt backplate, but this can only be removed after taking off the injection pump sprocket; it should not prove necessary to remove the backplate in practice.

2 Remove the camshaft oil seal. The seal is quite deeply recessed – Ford dealers have a special seal extractor for this (tool No 303-293). In the absence of this tool, do not use any removal method which might damage the sealing surfaces, or a leak will result when the new seal is fitted **(see Haynes Hint)**.

HAYNES HINT *One of the best ways to remove an oil seal is to carefully drill or punch two holes through the seal, opposite each other (taking care not to damage the surface behind the seal as this is done). Two self-tapping screws are then screwed into the holes; by pulling on the screw heads alternately with a pair of pliers, the seal can be extracted.*

3 Clean out the seal housing and the sealing surface of the camshaft by wiping it with a lint-free cloth. Remove any swarf or burrs that may cause the seal to leak.

4 Apply a little oil to the new camshaft oil seal, and fit it over the end of the camshaft, lips facing inwards. To avoid damaging the seal lips, wrap a little tape over the end of the camshaft. Ford dealers have a special tool (No 303-199) for fitting the seal, but if this is not available, a deep socket of suitable size can be used. **Note:** *Select a socket that bears only on the hard outer surface of the seal, not the inner lip which can easily be damaged.* It is important that the seal is fitted square to the shaft, and is fully seated **(see illustrations)**.

5 Refit the camshaft sprocket and timing belt as described in Section 7.

11 Cylinder head – removal, inspection and refitting

Note: *Ford technicians remove the cylinder head complete with the inlet and exhaust manifolds. Whilst this may reduce the overall time spent, it makes the cylinder head assembly incredibly heavy and awkward to lift clear (the head is of cast iron, and is quite heavy enough on its own). We felt that, for the DIY mechanic at least, removing the manifolds would be the more sensible option.*

Removal

1 Remove the battery as described in Chapter 5A, then unscrew the three bolts securing the battery tray, and remove the tray from the engine compartment.

11.9a Remove the timing belt backplate bolt from the cylinder head . . .

11.10 Unscrew the nut securing the glow plug supply lead

2 Remove the air cleaner housing and the intercooler, as described in Chapter 4B.

3 Remove the cylinder head cover as described in Section 4.

4 Using the information in Section 3, bring the engine round to just before the TDC position on No 1 cylinder. Do not insert any of the locking tools at this stage.

5 Apply the handbrake, then jack up the front of the car and support it on axle stands (see *Jacking and vehicle support*).

6 Drain the cooling system as described in Chapter 1B.

7 Remove the turbocharger/exhaust manifold and the inlet manifold as described in Chapter 4B.

8 Remove the timing belt as described in Section 7.

9 Remove the bolt securing the timing belt backplate to the cylinder head, and the seven nuts around the injection pump sprocket **(see illustrations)**. While this does not allow the backplate to be removed, it makes it possible to bend the plate enough for the camshaft's tapered end to pass as the head is lifted. If the backplate is to be removed completely, this requires that the injection pump sprocket and its oil seal housing are also removed, as described in Chapter 4B.

10 Disconnect the glow plug supply lead in front of the dipstick tube, and move the wiring harness to one side **(see illustration)**.

11 Release the clips from the crankcase ventilation hoses as necessary, and disconnect the wiring plug from the oil pressure switch, then unbolt and remove the

11.9b . . . and the seven nuts around the injection pump sprocket

11.11a Disconnect the breather hoses . . .

11.11b . . . unscrew the mounting bolt . . .

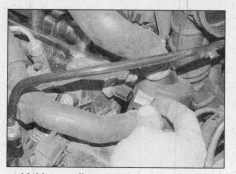

11.11c . . . disconnect the oil pressure warning light switch . . .

11.11d . . . and remove the oil separator from the end of the cylinder head

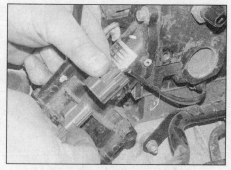

11.12 Disconnecting the cylinder head temperature sensor wiring plug

11.13a Unscrew the vacuum hose union . . .

11.13b . . . release the hose clip and disconnect the oil return pipe . . .

oil separator from the left-hand end of the cylinder head **(see illustrations)**.

12 Unclip and disconnect the large wiring plug for the cylinder head temperature sensor,

next to the brake vacuum pump **(see illustration)**.

13 Disconnect the vacuum hose and the oil return pipe from the vacuum pump at the left-

hand end of the cylinder head (left as seen from the driver's seat). Unscrew the top mounting bolt, and loosen the lower bolt – the lower mounting is slotted, to make removal easier – and lift off the pump. Recover the large O-ring seal – a new one must be used on reassembly **(see illustrations)**.

14 Remove the screw securing the glow plug supply lead to the thermostat housing. Remove the two bolts securing the thermostat housing to the front of the head, then pull the housing forwards and rest it clear of the head without disconnecting any further pipework **(see illustrations)**. Note that a new thermostat housing gasket will be needed for reassembly.

15 Disconnect the injection pump wiring connector, by pulling the securing clip towards the front, then pulling the wiring plug out to the side **(see illustrations)**.

11.13c . . . then unbolt the vacuum pump . . .

11.13d . . . and remove the vacuum pump – recover the O-ring

11.14a Remove the glow plug supply lead securing screw

11.14b Unscrew the thermostat housing bolts

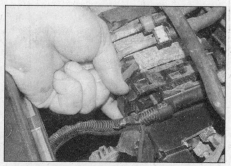

11.15a Pull the locking clip out towards the front . . .

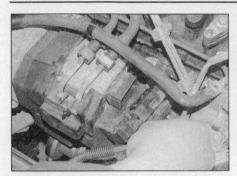

11.15b . . . then separate the wiring plug from the injection pump

11.16 Removing the injection pump insulation cover

11.17a Unscrew the union nuts . . .

11.17b . . . then remove each pair of injection pipes

11.17c Plastic bag taped over the injector pipe unions

11.17d Fingers cut from rubber gloves, secured over the injector unions

16 Cut the cable-ties securing the insulation cover fitted over the pump, and remove the cover (see illustration). Clean around the pipe unions at the injectors and at the pump.

17 Unscrew the union nuts and disconnect

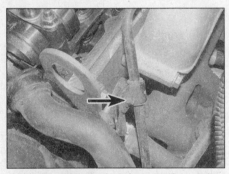

11.18 Remove the bolt (arrowed) securing the power steering pipe support bracket

the leak-off pipes, and remove each pair of fuel injection pipes. When unscrewing the unions at the pump end, counter-hold the pump adapters with one spanner, and loosen the unions with another. Cover over the end fittings on the injection pump and on the injectors, to keep the dirt out (see illustrations).

18 Unbolt the power steering pipe bracket from the left-hand side of the cylinder head (see illustration).

19 If not already done, it is recommended before removing the cylinder head that the engine right-hand mounting is refitted, and the engine supporting tools removed. This will improve working room if a hoist or engine support bar was used, and avoids the risk of the engine slipping if it was supported from below.

20 Remove the four nuts securing the oil baffle plate, and carefully lift the plate off the

engine. Note that these nuts are also used to secure Nos 2 and 4 camshaft bearing caps, which will then be loose. Once the plate is removed, refit the nuts by hand, to keep the caps in place.

21 Loosen the top nut on the power steering pump mounting bracket, then unscrew the stud from the cylinder head, using the stud's Torx end fitting (see illustrations).

22 Check around the head and the engine bay that there is nothing still attached to the cylinder head, nor anything which would prevent it from being lifted away.

23 Working in the reverse order of the tightening sequence (refer to illustration 11.48), loosen the cylinder head bolts by half a turn at a time, until they are all loose. Remove the head bolts, and discard them – Ford state that they must not be re-used, even if they appear to be serviceable (see illustrations). Note the fitted positions of the

11.21a Loosen the nut, then unscrew . . .

11.21b . . . and remove the stud from the power steering pump bracket

11.23a Working in the reverse of the tightening sequence, unscrew . . .

11.23b . . . and remove the cylinder head bolts

11.24 Removing the cylinder head

11.31 Measuring piston protrusion with a dial test indicator (DTI)

two shorter bolts, which should be the two nearest the timing belt end of the engine.

24 Bend the timing belt backplate gently away from the head sufficiently for the camshaft stub to clear it. Lift the cylinder head away; use assistance if possible, as it is a very heavy assembly **(see illustration)**.

25 If the head is stuck (as is possible), be careful how you choose to free it. Striking the head with tools carries the risk of damage, and the head is located on two dowels, so its movement will be limited. Do not, under any circumstances, lever the head between the mating surfaces, as this will certainly damage the sealing surfaces for the gasket, leading to leaks.

26 Once the head has been removed, recover the gasket from the two dowels. The gasket is manufactured from laminated steel, and cannot be re-used, but see paragraph 28.

Inspection

27 If required, dismantling and inspection of the cylinder head is covered in Part D of this Chapter.

Cylinder head gasket selection

28 Examine the old cylinder head gasket for manufacturer's identification markings. These will be in the form of notches (two to seven) on the front edge of the gasket, which indicate the gasket's thickness (refer to illustration 11.44).

29 Unless new components have been fitted, or the cylinder head has been machined (skimmed), the new cylinder head gasket must be of the same type as the old one. Purchase the required gasket, and proceed to paragraph 35.

30 If the head has been machined, or if new pistons have been fitted, it is likely that a head gasket of different thickness to the original will be needed. Gasket selection is made on the basis of the measured piston protrusion above the cylinder head gasket surface (the protrusion must fall within the range specified at the start of Chapter 2D).

31 To measure the piston protrusion, anchor a dial test indicator (DTI) to the top face (cylinder head gasket mating face) of the cylinder block, and zero the gauge on the gasket mating face **(see illustration)**.

32 Rest the gauge probe above No 1 piston crown, and turn the crankshaft slowly by hand until the piston reaches TDC (its maximum height). Measure and record the maximum piston projection at TDC.

33 Repeat the measurement for the remaining pistons, and record the results.

34 If the measurements differ from piston to piston, take the highest figure, and use this to determine the thickness of the head gasket required. At the time of writing, details of the gasket selection (ie, which gasket to use for amount of protrusion) were not published by Ford; however, if the measured protrusion is taken to a Ford dealer, it should be possible for them to suggest the required gasket.

Preparation for refitting

35 The mating faces of the cylinder head and cylinder block must be perfectly clean before refitting the head. Use a hard plastic or wooden scraper to remove all traces of gasket and carbon; also clean the piston crowns. **Note:** *The new head gasket has rubber-coated surfaces, which could be damaged from sharp edges or debris left by a metal scraper.*

36 Take particular care when cleaning the piston crowns, as the soft aluminium alloy is easily damaged.

37 Make sure that the carbon is not allowed to enter the oil and water passages – this is particularly important for the lubrication system, as carbon could block the oil supply to the engine's components. Using adhesive tape and paper, seal the water, oil and bolt holes in the cylinder block.

38 To prevent carbon entering the gap between the pistons and bores, smear a little grease in the gap. After cleaning each piston, use a small brush to remove all traces of grease and carbon from the gap, then wipe away the remainder with a clean rag. Clean all the pistons in the same way.

39 Check the mating surfaces of the cylinder block and the cylinder head for nicks, deep scratches and other damage (refer to the Note in paragraph 35). If slight, they may be removed carefully with a file, but if excessive, machining may be the only alternative to renewal.

40 If warpage of the cylinder head gasket

surface is suspected, use a straight-edge to check it for distortion. Refer to Part D of this Chapter if necessary.

41 Ensure that the cylinder head bolt holes in the crankcase are clean and free of oil. Syringe or soak up any oil left in the bolt holes. This is most important in order that the correct bolt tightening torque can be applied, and to prevent the possibility of the block being cracked by hydraulic pressure when the bolts are tightened.

Refitting

42 Turn the crankshaft anti-clockwise all the pistons at an equal height, approximately halfway down their bores from the TDC position (see Section 3). This will eliminate any risk of piston-to-valve contact as the cylinder head is refitted.

43 To guide the cylinder head into position, screw two long studs (or old cylinder head bolts with the heads cut off, and slots cut in the ends to enable the bolts to be unscrewed) into the end cylinder head bolt locations on the manifold side of the cylinder block.

44 Ensure that the cylinder head locating dowels are in place at the front corners of the cylinder block, then fit the new cylinder head gasket over the dowels, ensuring that the OBEN/TOP marking is uppermost, and the notches are at the front (there is a further cut-out at the timing belt end of the gasket) **(see illustration overleaf)**. Take care to avoid damaging the gasket's rubber coating.

45 Lower the cylinder head into position on the gasket, ensuring that it engages correctly over the guide studs and dowels.

46 Fit the new cylinder head bolts to the eight remaining bolt locations, (remember that the two shorter bolts are fitted at the timing belt end of the engine) and screw them in as far as possible by hand.

47 Unscrew the two guide studs from the exhaust side of the cylinder block, then screw in the two remaining new cylinder head bolts as far as possible by hand.

48 Working in the sequence shown **(see illustration overleaf)**, tighten all the cylinder head bolts to the specified Stage 1 torque.

49 Again working in the sequence shown, tighten all the cylinder head bolts to the specified Stage 2 torque.

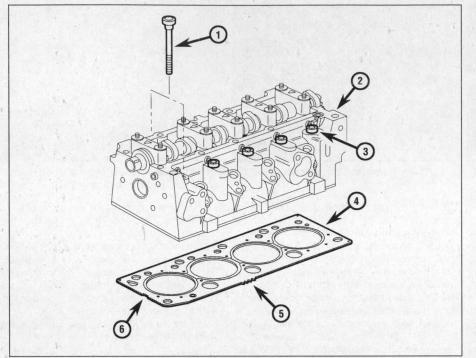

11.44 Cylinder head bolt positions and gasket details

1	Shorter bolts (two, 137 mm long)	3 Longer bolts (eight, 177 mm long)
2	Cylinder head	4 Cylinder head gasket

5 Thickness marking (notches)

6 Position marking (cut-out)

50 When all the bolts have been tightened to the Stage 2 torque, go around again in the tightening sequence, and tighten all the cylinder head bolts to the specified Stage 3 torque.

51 Stage 4 involves tightening the bolts though an angle, rather than to a torque **(see illustration)**. Each bolt in sequence must be rotated through the specified angle – special angle gauges are available from tool outlets. As a guide, a 90° angle is equivalent to a quarter-turn, and this is easily judged by assessing the start and end positions of the

socket handle or torque wrench. **Note:** *The two shorter bolts at the timing belt end of the engine are tightened through a smaller angle than the remaining eight bolts – do not get confused when following the tightening sequence.*

52 After finally tightening the cylinder head bolts, turn the crankshaft forwards to bring No 1 piston up to TDC, so that the crankshaft contacts the timing pin (see Section 3).

53 The remainder of the refitting procedure is a reversal of the removal procedure, bearing in mind the following points:

a) Refit the timing belt with reference to Section 7.
b) Reconnect the exhaust front section to the exhaust manifold with reference to Chapter 4B.
c) Refit the cylinder head cover with reference to Section 4.
d) Refit the air cleaner and intercooler as described in Chapter 4B.
e) Refill the cooling system as described in Chapter 1B.
f) Check and if necessary top up the engine oil level and power steering fluid level as described in 'Weekly checks'.
g) Before starting the engine, read through the section on engine restarting after overhaul, at the end of Chapter 2D.

12 Sump – removal and refitting

Removal

Note: *The full procedure outlined below must be followed so that the mating surfaces can be cleaned and prepared to achieve an oil-tight joint on reassembly.*

1 Apply the handbrake, then jack up the front of the vehicle and support it on axle stands (see *Jacking and vehicle support*).

2 Referring to Chapter 1B if necessary, drain the engine oil, then clean and refit the engine oil drain plug, tightening it to the specified torque wrench setting. Although not strictly necessary as part of the dismantling procedure, owners are advised to remove and discard the oil filter, so that it can be renewed with the oil.

3 A conventional sump gasket is not used, and sealant is used instead.

4 Progressively unscrew the twelve sump retaining bolts, and the two retaining nuts (the bolts are of different lengths, but it will be obvious where they fit on reassembly). Break

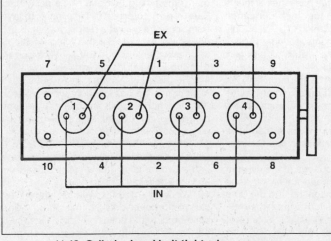

11.48 Cylinder head bolt tightening sequence

11.51 The two shorter bolts are tightened through less of an angle than the longer bolts

the joint by striking the sump with the palm of the hand, then lower the sump away, turning it as necessary.

5 Unfortunately, the use of sealant can make removal of the sump more difficult. If care is taken not to damage the surfaces, the sealant can be cut around using a sharp knife. On no account lever between the mating faces, as this will almost certainly damage them, resulting in leaks when finished. Ford technicians have a tool comprising a metal rod which is inserted through the sump drain hole, and a handle to pull the sump downwards.

> **HAYNES HiNT** *If the sump is particularly difficult to remove, extracting the two studs may prove useful – thread two nuts onto the stud, tightening them against each other, then use a spanner on the inner nut to unscrew the stud. Note the locations of the studs for refitting.*

Refitting

6 On reassembly, thoroughly clean and degrease the mating surfaces of the cylinder block/crankcase and sump, removing all traces of sealant, then use a clean rag to wipe out the sump and the engine's interior.

7 If the two studs have been removed, they must be refitted before the sump is offered up, to ensure that it is aligned correctly. If this is not done, some of the sealant may enter the blind holes for the sump bolts, preventing the bolts from being fully fitted.

8 Referring to the accompanying illustration, apply sealant to the sump flange, making sure the bead is around the inside edge of the bolt holes. Ford specify that the sealant must be applied in two different thicknesses, but this may be difficult to achieve in practice **(see illustrations)**. **Note:** *The sump must be refitted within 10 minutes of applying the sealant.*

9 Fit the sump over the studs, and insert the sump bolts and two nuts, tightening them by hand only at this stage.

10 Tighten all the bolts and nuts in the sequence shown (refer to illustration 12.8b).

12.8a Apply the sealant to the crankcase

11 Lower the car to the ground. Wait at least 1 hour for the sealant to cure (or whatever time is indicated by the sealant manufacturer) before refilling the engine with oil. If removed, fit a new oil filter with reference to Chapter 1B.

13 Oil pump –
removal, inspection and refitting

Removal

1 Remove the crankshaft pulley as described in Section 6.

2 Unbolt the auxiliary drivebelt idler pulley in front of the crank pulley location.

3 Remove the timing belt and camshaft sprocket as described in Section 7.

4 Remove the injection pump sprocket and oil seal housing as described in Chapter 4B.

5 Unbolt and remove the timing belt backplate from the engine.

6 The oil pump is secured by seven studs and twelve bolts – note their positions carefully for refitting. The studs can be unscrewed using a spanner on the hex provided.

7 Once all the fasteners have been removed, carefully lift the pump from its location. Recover the main gasket, and the smaller spacer ring from below the injection pump. Neither gasket may be re-used – obtain new ones for reassembly.

Inspection

8 Undo the retaining screws and remove the cover from the oil pump **(see illustration)**.

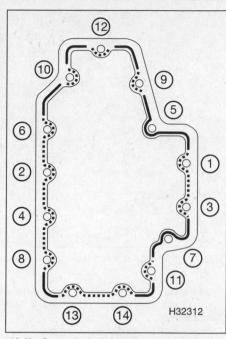

12.8b Sump bolt tightening sequence and sealant application details

Solid line – 3.5 mm diameter bead of sealant
Dotted line – 2.5 mm diameter bead of sealant

Note the location of the identification marks on the inner and outer rotors for refitting.

9 Unscrew the plug and remove the pressure relief valve, spring and plunger, clean out and check condition of components **(see illustration)**.

10 The clearance between the inner and outer rotors can be checked using feeler blades, and compared with the value given in the Specifications **(see illustration)**.

11 Check the general condition of the oil pump, and in particular, its mating face to the cylinder block. If the mating face is damaged significantly, this may lead to oil loss (and a resulting drop in available oil pressure).

12 Inspect the rotors for obvious signs of wear or damage; it is not clear at the time of writing whether individual components are available separately. Lubricate the rotors with fresh engine oil and refit them into the body,

13.8 Undo the retaining screws and remove the rotor cover

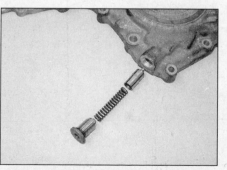

13.9 Check the condition of the pressure relief valve and clean out the oilways

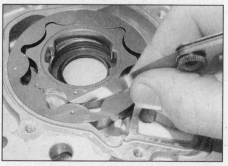

13.10 Checking the clearance between the inner and outer rotor

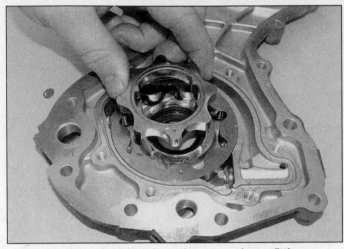

13.12 Check and lubricate the rotors when refitting

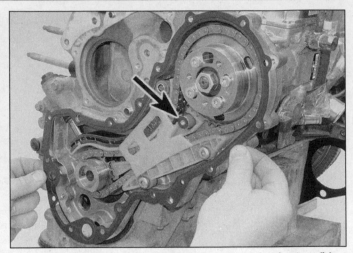

13.15 Fitting the new metal gasket and spacer ring (arrowed) in position

making sure that the identification marks are positioned as noted on removal **(see illustration)**.

13 If the oil pump has been removed as part of a major engine overhaul, it is assumed that the engine will have completed a substantial mileage. In this case, it is often considered good practice to fit a new (or reconditioned) pump as a matter of course. In other words, if the rest of the engine is being rebuilt, the engine has completed a large mileage, or there is any question as to the old pump's condition, it is preferable to fit a new oil pump.

Refitting

14 Before fitting the oil pump, ensure that the mating faces on the pump and the engine block are completely clean.

15 Lay the main metal gasket and a new spacer ring in position on the engine – in the case of the spacer ring, 'stick' it in position with a little oil or grease if required **(see illustration)**.

16 Offer the pump into position, and secure it with the studs and bolts, tightened only loosely at this stage **(see illustration)**.

17 Ford technicians use a special tool (303-652) to align the oil pump as it is being fitted and tightened **(see illustration)**. The tool is basically a circular socket, which fits over the end of the crankshaft, and ensures that the corresponding hole in the oil pump is centrally located over the end of the crankshaft. In the absence of the tool, this alignment could be confirmed visually, or a large socket/piece of tubing (perhaps wrapped with tape) could be used instead.

18 Ensuring that the correct alignment of the pump is maintained, tighten the pump securing studs and bolts to the specified Stage 1 torque, in the sequence shown (refer to illustration 13.16).

19 When all the fasteners have been tightened to the Stage 1 torque, go around again in the sequence, and tighten them all to the specified Stage 2 torque.

20 Refit the timing belt backplate to the engine.

21 Refit the injection pump sprocket and oil seal housing as described in Chapter 4B.

22 Refit the timing belt and camshaft sprocket as described in Section 7.

23 Refit the auxiliary drivebelt idler pulley, and tighten the bolt to the specified torque.

24 Refit the crankshaft pulley as described in Section 6.

25 When the engine is next started, check for correct oil pump operation (at least, as indicated by the oil pressure warning light going out).

14 Oil pressure warning light switch – removal and refitting

Removal

1 The switch is screwed into the left-hand (flywheel) end of the cylinder head, behind the vacuum pump.

2 Open the bonnet and disconnect the battery negative (earth) lead – see *Disconnecting the battery*.

3 To improve access to the switch, it will be necessary to remove (or partially remove) the air cleaner inlet duct and the intercooler right-hand air duct, using the information in Chapter 4B. It will also be helpful to release the hoses and remove the crankcase

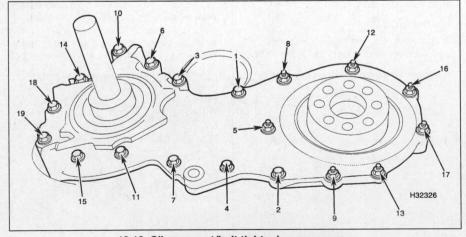

13.16 Oil pump nut/bolt tightening sequence – note special tool 303-652 used to align pump

13.17 Tool used to align the oil pump, before tightening the retaining bolts fully

ventilation system oil separator from the left-hand end of the cylinder head.
4 Unplug the wiring from the switch and unscrew it; be prepared for some oil loss (see illustration).

Refitting

5 Refitting is the reverse of the removal procedure; apply a thin smear of suitable sealant to the switch threads, and tighten it to the specified torque wrench setting.
6 Refit all components removed for access to the switch.
7 Check the engine oil level and top-up as necessary (see *Weekly checks*).
8 Check for correct warning light operation, and for signs of oil leaks, once the engine has been restarted and warmed-up to normal operating temperature.

15 Oil cooler – removal and refitting

Removal

Note: *New sealing rings will be required on refitting.*
1 The oil cooler is mounted next to the oil filter on the rear of the cylinder block. Access to the oil cooler is best obtained from below – apply the handbrake, then jack up the front of the car and support it on axle stands.
2 Position a container beneath the oil filter to catch escaping oil and coolant. To improve access to the coolant hoses, unscrew and remove the oil filter, making sure that the filter sealing ring is removed with the filter cartridge – anticipate a small loss of engine oil as the filter is removed. Provided the filter is not due for renewal, it can be refitted on completion.

14.4 Disconnect the wiring from the oil pressure switch

3 Clamp the oil cooler coolant hoses to minimise spillage, then remove the clips, and disconnect the hoses from the oil cooler. Be prepared for coolant spillage.
4 Loosen the turbocharger oil supply union bolt at the top of the cooler (see illustration), and separate the pipe (be prepared for oil spillage). Recover the copper washers from the union – new ones must be used on reassembly.
5 Unscrew the four bolts securing the oil cooler, noting their positions, as they are of different lengths. Remove the oil cooler from the engine, and recover the gasket (a new gasket must be used on refitting) (see illustration).

Refitting

6 Refitting is a reversal of removal, bearing in mind the following points:
a) Use a new gasket (see illustration).
b) Fit the oil cooler mounting bolts to the positions noted on removal, and tighten them securely. Refit the oil filter if removed – apply a little oil to the filter sealing ring, and tighten the filter securely by hand (do not use any tools).

15.4 Disconnect the turbocharger oil supply union bolt (arrowed)

c) Use new copper washers when reconnecting the oil supply union at the top of the cooler, and tighten the union bolt securely.
d) On completion, lower the car to the ground. Check and if necessary top up the oil and coolant levels, then start the engine and check for signs of oil or coolant leakage.

16 Crankshaft oil seals – renewal

Timing belt end seal

1 Remove the crankshaft pulley (see Section 6).
2 Note the fitted depth of the oil seal as a guide for fitting the new one.
3 Using a screwdriver or similar tool, carefully prise the oil seal from its location. Take care not to damage the oil seal contact surfaces or the oil seal seating. An alternative method of removing the seals is to drill a small hole in the seal (taking care not to drill any deeper than necessary), then insert a self-tapping screw and use pliers to pull out the seal.
4 Wipe clean the oil seal contact surfaces and seating, and clean up any sharp edges or burrs which might damage the new seal as it is fitted, or which might cause the seal to leak once in place.
5 The new oil seal may be supplied fitted with a locating sleeve, which must **not** be removed

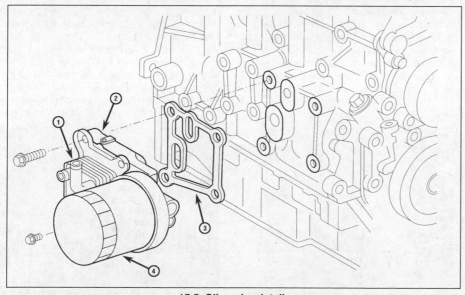

15.5 Oil cooler details

1 Oil cooler   2 Adapter plate   3 Metal gasket   4 Oil filter

15.6 Fit new gasket for oil cooler

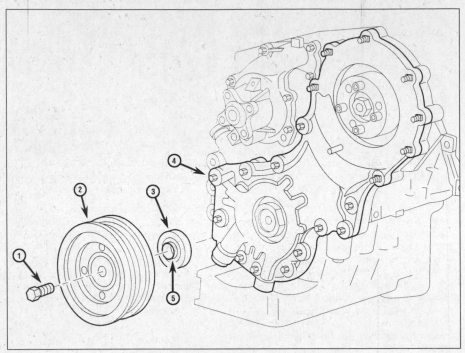

16.5 Crankshaft front oil seal details

| 1 | Crankshaft pulley bolt | 2 | Crankshaft pulley | 4 | Oil pump housing |
| | | 3 | Oil seal | 5 | Seal locating sleeve |

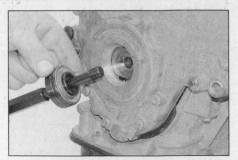

16.7 Using locating tool to press the seal in squarely (locating sleeve not required when using tool)

16.11 The new oil seal is renewed complete with carrier

prior to fitting **(see illustration)**. No oil should be applied to the oil seal, which is made of PTFE.

6 Ford technicians use a special seal-fitting tool (303-652), but an adequate substitute can be achieved using a large socket or piece of tubing of sufficient size to bear on the outer edge of the new seal.

7 Locate the new seal (lips facing inwards) over the end of the crankshaft, using the tool **(see illustration)**, socket, or tubing to press the seal squarely and fully into position, to the previously-noted depth. Once the seal is fully fitted, remove the locating sleeve, if necessary.

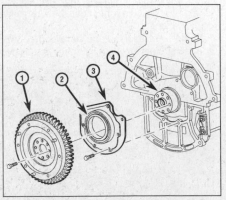

16.13 Crankshaft rear oil seal details

| 1 | Flywheel | 3 | Oil seal housing |
| 2 | Seal locating sleeve | 4 | Crankshaft |

8 The remainder of reassembly is the reverse of the removal procedure, referring to the relevant text for details where required. Check for signs of oil leakage when the engine is restarted.

Flywheel end seal

9 Remove the transmission as described in Chapter 7A, and the clutch assembly as described in Chapter 6.

10 Unbolt the flywheel (see Section 17).

11 Unbolt and remove the oil seal carrier; the seal is renewed complete with the carrier, and is not available separately. A complete set of new carrier retaining bolts should also be obtained for reassembly **(see illustration)**.

12 Clean the end of the crankshaft, polishing off any burrs or raised edges, which may have caused the seal to fail in the first place. Clean

16.14a Fit new seal assembly, complete with locating sleeve over the end of the crankshaft . . .

also the seal carrier mating face on the engine block, using a suitable solvent for degreasing if necessary.

13 The new oil seal is supplied fitted with a locating sleeve, which must **not** be removed prior to fitting (it will drop out on its own when the carrier is bolted into position) **(see illustration)**. No oil should be applied to the oil seal, which is made of PTFE.

14 Offer up the carrier into position, feeding the locating sleeve over the end of the crankshaft. Insert the new seal carrier retaining bolts, and tighten them all by hand **(see illustrations)**.

15 Ford technicians use a special tool (308-204) to centre the oil seal carrier around the end of the crankshaft. In the absence of the tool, this alignment could be confirmed visually, or a large socket/piece of tubing (perhaps

16.14b . . . then remove locating sleeve

17.11 Align the bolt holes in the crankshaft – they will only line up one way

17.12 Tool made to lock the flywheel (arrowed) for slackening and tightening the bolts

17.13 Using an angle gauge to carry out the final tightening stages

wrapped with tape) could be used instead.

16 Ensuring that the correct alignment of the carrier is maintained, tighten the retaining bolts to the specified torque. If the seal locating sleeve is still in position, remove it now.

17 The remainder of the reassembly procedure is the reverse of dismantling, referring to the relevant text for details where required. Check for signs of oil leakage when the engine is restarted.

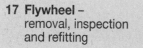

17 Flywheel –
removal, inspection and refitting

Removal

1 Remove the transmission as described in Chapter 7A. Now is a good time to check components such as oil seals and renew them if necessary.

2 Remove the clutch as described in Chapter 6. Now is a good time to check or renew the clutch components and release bearing.

3 Use a centre-punch or paint to make alignment marks on the flywheel and crankshaft, to ensure correct alignment during refitting.

4 Prevent the flywheel from turning by locking the ring gear teeth, or by bolting a strap between the flywheel and the cylinder block/crankcase. Slacken the bolts evenly until all are free.

5 Remove each bolt in turn and ensure that

new replacements are obtained for reassembly; these bolts are subjected to severe stresses and so must be renewed, regardless of their apparent condition, whenever they are disturbed.

6 Withdraw the flywheel, remembering that it is very heavy – do not drop it.

Inspection

7 Clean the flywheel to remove grease and oil. Inspect the surface for cracks, rivet grooves, burned areas and score marks. Light scoring can be removed with emery cloth. Check for cracked and broken ring gear teeth. Lay the flywheel on a flat surface and use a straight-edge to check for warpage.

8 Clean and inspect the mating surfaces of the flywheel and the crankshaft. If the crankshaft seal is leaking, renew it (see Section 16) before refitting the flywheel. If the engine has covered a high mileage, it may be worth fitting a new seal as a matter if course, given the amount of work needed to access it.

9 While the flywheel is removed, clean carefully its inboard (right-hand) face, particularly the recesses which serve as the reference points for the crankshaft speed/position sensor. Clean the sensor's tip and check that the sensor is securely fastened.

10 Thoroughly clean the threaded bolt holes in the crankshaft, removing all traces of locking compound.

Refitting

11 Fit the flywheel to the crankshaft so that all bolt holes align – it will fit only one way – check this using the marks made on removal **(see illustration)**. Apply suitable locking compound to the threads of the new bolts, then insert them.

12 Lock the flywheel by the method used on dismantling **(see illustration)**. Working in a diagonal sequence, tighten the bolts to the specified Stage 1 torque wrench setting.

13 Stages 2 and 3 involve tightening the bolts though an angle, rather than to a torque. Each bolt must be rotated through the specified angle – special angle gauges are available from tool outlets. As a guide, a 90° angle is equivalent to a quarter-turn, and this is easily judged by assessing the start and end positions of the socket handle or torque wrench **(see illustration)**.

14 Go around all the bolts, again working in a diagonal sequence, and tighten the bolts through the Stage 2 angle. Once all the bolts have been tightened to Stage 2, go around again, and tighten them all to Stage 3.

15 The remainder of reassembly is the reverse of the removal procedure, referring to the relevant text for details where required.

18 Engine/transmission mountings –
inspection and renewal

Refer to Chapter 2A, Section 17.

Notes

Chapter 2 Part D:
Engine removal and overhaul procedures

Contents

Degrees of difficulty

Easy, suitable for novice with little experience 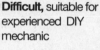	**Fairly easy,** suitable for beginner with some experience	**Fairly difficult,** suitable for competent DIY mechanic	**Difficult,** suitable for experienced DIY mechanic	**Very difficult,** suitable for expert DIY or professional

Specifications

Valves
1.4 and 1.6 litre engines:
  Valve length:
    Inlet – 1.4 litre . . . . 97.35 mm
    Inlet – 1.6 litre . . . . 96.95 mm
    Exhaust . . . . 99.40 mm
  Valve spring free length . . . . 53.2 mm
1.8 and 2.0 litre petrol engines:
  Valve play in guide . . . . 0.017 to 0.064 mm
Diesel engine:
  Valve cam follower bore:
    Standard . . . . 35.000 to 35.030 mm
    Oversize . . . . 35.500 to 35.530 mm
  Valve guide bore:
    Standard . . . . 8.000 to 8.025 mm
    1st oversize . . . . 8.263 to 8.288 mm
    2nd oversize . . . . 8.463 to 8.488 mm

Cylinder head
Maximum permissible gasket surface distortion . . . . 0.1 mm

Cylinder block
Cylinder bore diameter:
  1.4 litre engine:
    Class 1 . . . . 76.000 to 76.010 mm
    Class 2 . . . . 76.010 to 76.020 mm
    Class 3 . . . . 76.020 to 76.030 mm
  1.6 litre engine:
    Class 1 . . . . 79.000 to 79.010 mm
    Class 2 . . . . 79.010 to 79.020 mm
    Class 3 . . . . 79.020 to 79.030 mm
  1.8 litre petrol engine:
    Class 1 . . . . 80.600 to 80.610 mm
    Class 2 . . . . 80.610 to 80.620 mm
    Class 3 . . . . 80.620 to 80.630 mm

Cylinder block (continued)

Cylinder bore diameter (continued):
  2.0 litre engine:

Class 1	84.800 to 84.810 mm
Class 2	84.810 to 84.820 mm
Class 3	84.820 to 84.830 mm
Diesel engine:	
Class A	82.500 to 82.515 mm
Class B	82.515 to 82.530 mm

Pistons and piston rings

Piston diameter:

1.4 litre engine:	
Class 1	75.960 to 75.970 mm
Class 2	75.970 to 75.980 mm
Class 3	75.980 to 75.990 mm
1.6 litre engine:	
Class 1	78.975 to 79.005 mm
Class 2	78.985 to 79.015 mm
Class 3	78.995 to 79.025 mm
1.8 litre petrol engine:	
Class 1	80.570 to 80.580 mm
Class 2	80.580 to 80.590 mm
Class 3	80.590 to 80.600 mm
2.0 litre engine:	
Class 1	84.770 to 84.780 mm
Class 2	84.780 to 84.790 mm
Class 3	84.790 to 84.800 mm
Diesel engine:	
Class A	82.410 to 82.425 mm
Class B	82.425 to 82.440 mm
Oversizes – all engines	None available
Piston-to-cylinder bore clearance:	
1.4 and 1.6 litre engines	Not specified
1.8 litre petrol engine	0.040 to 0.060 mm
2.0 litre engine	0.010 to 0.030 mm
Diesel engine	0.105 to 0.075 mm
Piston ring end gaps – installed:	
Top compression ring:	
1.4 litre engine	0.17 to 0.27 mm
1.6 litre engine	0.18 to 0.28 mm
1.8 and 2.0 litre petrol engines	0.30 to 0.50 mm
Diesel engine	0.31 to 0.50 mm
Second compression ring:	
1.4 and 1.6 litre engines	0.7 to 0.9 mm
1.8 and 2.0 litre petrol engines	0.30 to 0.50 mm
Diesel engine	0.31 to 0.50 mm
Oil control ring:	
1.4 and 1.6 litre engines	0.15 to 0.65 mm
1.8 litre petrol engine	0.38 to 1.14 mm
2.0 litre engine	0.40 to 1.40 mm
Diesel engine	0.25 to 0.58 mm
Ring gap spacing	120°
Piston ring clearance in groove (diesel engine only):	
Top compression ring	0.090 to 0.122 mm
Second compression ring	0.070 to 0.102 mm
Oil control ring	0.050 to 0.082 mm
Piston protrusion at TDC (diesel engine only)	0.500 to 0.840 mm
Gudgeon pin diameter (diesel engine only)	28.004 to 28.010 mm

Crankshaft

Note: *On 1.4 and 1.6 litre engines, the crankshaft should not be removed from the cylinder block (see text).*

Crankshaft endfloat:

1.4 litre engine	0.105 to 0.325 mm
1.6 litre engine	0.220 to 0.430 mm
1.8 and 2.0 litre petrol engines	0.09 to 0.26 mm
Diesel engine	0.11 to 0.37 mm

Crankshaft (continued)

Main bearing journal diameter:
1.8 and 2.0 litre petrol engines . . . .   57.98 to 58 mm
Diesel engine:
    Standard . . . .   53.970 to 53.990 mm
    1st undersize . . . .   53.720 to 53.740 mm
    2nd undersize . . . .   53.470 to 53.490 mm
Main bearing running clearance:
1.8 and 2.0 litre petrol engines . . . .   0.011 to 0.058 mm
Diesel engine . . . .   0.015 to 0.062 mm
Big-end bearings:
1.8 and 2.0 litre petrol engines:
    Big-end bearing journal diameter . . . .   46.89 to 46.91
Diesel engines:
    Big-end bearing journal diameter:
        Standard . . . .   48.970 to 48.990 mm
        1st undersize . . . .   48.720 to 48.740 mm
        2nd undersize . . . .   48.470 to 48.490 mm
    Big-end bearing running clearance . . . .   0.025 to 0.085 mm

Torque wrench settings

Refer to Chapter 2A, 2B or 2C Specifications, as appropriate

1 General information and precautions

How to use this Chapter

This Part of Chapter 2 is devoted to engine/transmission removal and refitting, to those repair procedures requiring the removal of the engine/transmission from the vehicle, and to the overhaul of engine components. It includes only the Specifications relevant to those procedures. Refer to Parts A, B or C for additional Specifications, and for all torque wrench settings.

General information

The information ranges from advice concerning preparation for an overhaul and the purchase of replacement parts, to detailed step-by-step procedures covering removal and installation of internal engine components and the inspection of parts.

The following Sections have been written based on the assumption that the engine has been removed from the vehicle. For information concerning in-vehicle engine repair, as well as removal and installation of the external components necessary for the overhaul, see Parts A, B or C of this Chapter.

When overhauling the engine, it is essential to establish first exactly what replacement parts are available. At the time of writing, very few under- or over-sized components are available for engine reconditioning (the exception being for the diesel engine). In many cases, it would appear that the easiest and most economically-sensible course of action is to replace a worn or damaged engine with an exchange unit.

2 Engine overhaul – general information

It's not always easy to determine when, or if, an engine should be completely overhauled, as a number of factors must be considered.

High mileage is not necessarily an indication that an overhaul is needed, while low mileage doesn't preclude the need for an overhaul. Frequency of servicing is probably the most important consideration. An engine that's had regular and frequent oil and filter changes, as well as other required maintenance, will most likely give many thousands of miles of reliable service. Conversely, a neglected engine may require an overhaul very early in its life.

Excessive oil consumption is an indication that piston rings, valve seals and/or valve guides are in need of attention. Make sure that oil leaks aren't responsible before deciding that the rings and/or guides are worn. Perform a cylinder compression or leakdown check (Part A, B or C of this Chapter) to determine the extent of the work required.

Loss of power, rough running, knocking or metallic engine noises, excessive valve train noise and high fuel consumption rates may also point to the need for an overhaul, especially if they're all present at the same time. If a full service doesn't remedy the situation, major mechanical work is the only solution.

An engine overhaul involves restoring all internal parts to the specification of a new engine. **Note:** *Always check first what replacement parts are available before planning any overhaul operation – refer to Section 1. Ford dealers, or a good engine reconditioning specialist/automotive parts supplier, may be able to suggest alternatives which will enable you to overcome the lack of replacement parts.*

During an overhaul, it is usual to renew the piston rings, and to rebore and/or hone the cylinder bores; where the rebore is done by an automotive machine shop, new oversize pistons and rings will also be installed – all these operations, of course, assume the availability of suitable replacement parts. The main and big-end bearings are generally renewed and, if necessary, the crankshaft may be reground to restore the journals. *Caution: DO NOT attempt to remove the crankshaft or main bearing cap/ladder on the 1.4 or 1.6 litre engines, as it is not possible to refit it accurately using conventional tooling. The manufacturers do not supply torque settings for the main bearing cap/ladder retaining bolts. If the crankshaft is worn excessively, it will be necessary to obtain a new short motor comprising the cylinder block together with the pistons and crankshaft.*

Generally, the valves are serviced as well during an overhaul, since they're usually in less-than-perfect condition at this point. While the engine is being overhauled, other components, such as the starter and alternator, can be renewed as well, or rebuilt, if the necessary parts can be found. The end result should be an as-new engine that will give many trouble-free miles. **Note:** *Critical cooling system components such as the hoses, drivebelt, thermostat and coolant pump MUST be replaced with new parts when an engine is overhauled. The radiator should be checked carefully, to ensure that it isn't*

3.4a Make sure the lifting chains are secure . . .

clogged or leaking (see Chapter 3). Also, as a general rule, the oil pump should be renewed when an engine is rebuilt.

Before beginning the engine overhaul, read through the entire procedure to familiarise yourself with the scope and requirements of the job. Overhauling an engine isn't difficult, but it is time-consuming. Plan on the vehicle being off the road for a minimum of two weeks, especially if parts must be taken to an automotive machine shop for repair or reconditioning. Check on availability of parts, and make sure that any necessary special tools and equipment are obtained in advance. Most work can be done with typical hand tools, although a number of precision measuring tools are required for inspecting parts to determine if they must be replaced. Often, an automotive machine shop will handle the inspection of parts, and will offer advice concerning reconditioning and replacement. **Note:** *Always wait until the engine has been completely dismantled, and all components, especially the cylinder block/crankcase, have been inspected, before deciding what service and repair operations must be performed by an automotive machine shop. Since the block's condition will be the major factor to consider when determining whether to overhaul the original engine or buy a rebuilt one, never purchase parts or have machine work done on other components until the cylinder block/crankcase has been thoroughly inspected.* As a general rule, time is the primary cost of an overhaul, so it doesn't pay to install worn or sub-standard parts.

3.4b . . . and lower the engine/gearbox to the ground

As a final note, to ensure maximum life and minimum trouble from a rebuilt engine, everything must be assembled with care, in a spotlessly-clean environment.

3 Engine/transmission removal – methods and precautions

If you've decided that an engine must be removed for overhaul or major repair work, several preliminary steps should be taken.

Locating a suitable place to work is extremely important. Adequate work space, along with storage space for the vehicle, will be needed. If a workshop or garage isn't available, at the very least, a flat, level, clean work surface made of concrete or asphalt is required.

Cleaning the engine compartment and engine/transmission before beginning the removal procedure will help keep tools clean and organised.

The engine can only be withdrawn by removing it complete with the transmission; the vehicle's body must be raised and supported securely, sufficiently high that the engine/transmission can be unbolted as a single unit and lowered to the ground; the engine/transmission unit can then be withdrawn from under the vehicle and separated. An engine hoist or A-frame will therefore be necessary. Make sure the equipment is rated in excess of the combined weight of the engine and transmission. Safety is of primary importance, considering the potential hazards involved in removing the engine/transmission from the vehicle **(see illustrations)**.

If this is the first time you have removed an engine, a helper should ideally be available. Advice and aid from someone more experienced would also be useful. There are many instances when one person cannot simultaneously perform all of the operations required when removing the engine/transmission from the vehicle.

Plan the operation ahead of time. Arrange for, or obtain, all of the tools and equipment you'll need prior to beginning the job. Some of the equipment necessary to perform engine/transmission removal and installation safely and with relative ease, and which may have to be hired or borrowed, includes (in addition to the engine hoist) a heavy-duty trolley jack, a strong pair of axle stands, some wooden blocks, and an engine dolly (a low, wheeled platform capable of taking the weight of the engine/transmission, so that it can be moved easily when on the ground). A complete set of spanners and sockets (as described in the Reference section of this manual) will obviously be needed, together with plenty of rags and cleaning solvent for mopping-up spilled oil, coolant and fuel. If the hoist is to be hired, make sure that you

arrange for it in advance, and perform all of the operations possible without it beforehand. This will save you money and time.

Plan for the vehicle to be out of use for quite a while. A machine shop will be required to perform some of the work which the do-it-yourselfer can't accomplish without special equipment. These establishments often have a busy schedule, so it would be a good idea to consult them before removing the engine, to accurately estimate the amount of time required to rebuild or repair components that may need work.

Always be extremely careful when removing and installing the engine/transmission. Serious injury can result from careless actions. By planning ahead and taking your time, the job (although a major task) can be accomplished successfully.

4 Engine/transmission (petrol) – removal, separation and refitting

Note: *Read through the entire Section, as well as reading the advice in the preceding Section, before beginning this procedure. In this procedure, the engine and transmission are removed as a unit, lowered to the ground and removed from underneath, then separated outside the vehicle. However, if preferred, the transmission can be removed from the engine first (as described in Chapter 7A or 7B) – this leaves the engine free to be lifted out from above.*

Removal

1 Park the vehicle on firm, level ground, apply the handbrake firmly, and slacken the nuts securing both front roadwheels.
2 Depressurise the fuel system as described in Chapter 4A.
3 Drain the cooling system as described in Chapter 1A.
4 Working on each side in turn, unscrew the front suspension strut centre nuts exactly five turns each while holding the shock absorber centre rods with an Allen key. **Note:** *It is important not to over-loosen the nuts – make sure there is still sufficient thread engaged with the nut.*
5 Remove the battery and battery tray as described in Chapter 5A.
6 Remove the air cleaner and inlet ducting as described in Chapter 4A. Unbolt and remove the air inlet duct fitted below the air cleaner, leading to the engine compartment front panel. Where applicable, also disconnect the earth cable located below the air cleaner.
7 Disconnect the accelerator cable from the throttle body, using the information in Chapter 4A.
8 Disconnect the camshaft position sensor wiring plug at the rear of the cylinder head, then unclip and disconnect the injection wiring harness connector behind the power steering fluid reservoir **(see illustrations)**.

4.8a Disconnect the camshaft position sensor – 1.8 litre (1.4 & 1.6 litre models have the sensor at the timing belt end)

4.8b Unclip the injection wiring connector . . .

4.8c . . . then disconnect it

4.9a Disconnect the condenser wiring plug . . .

4.9b . . . and the coil main wiring plug

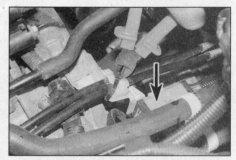

4.10 Cutting the cable-tie securing the gearchange cables to the transmission – disconnect wiring plug (arrowed)

9 Disconnect the wiring plugs at the ignition coil (see illustrations).
10 On manual transmission models, unclip the gearchange cables from the location on top of the transmission, and disconnect the wiring plug next to it (see illustration).
11 At the inlet manifold, disconnect the vacuum hoses from the fuel pressure regulator and for the brake servo. Also disconnect the charcoal canister hoses (see illustrations).
12 On 1.4 and 1.6 litre models, disconnect the knock sensor wiring plug next to the engine oil dipstick tube (see illustration).
13 Referring to Chapter 5A if necessary, disconnect the wiring from the alternator.
14 On models without air conditioning, disconnect the small wiring connector from the power steering pump.
15 Unscrew the bolt securing the coolant expansion tank to the inner wing, unclip the tank at the rear, and move the tank aside without disconnecting the hoses (see illustration).
16 Unclip the power steering fluid reservoir from its location, and lay it to one side without disconnecting the hoses – try to ensure that it stays upright (see illustration).

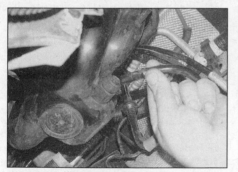

4.11a Disconnect the inlet manifold vacuum hoses

4.11b Note the location of the two charcoal canister hoses

4.12 Knock sensor wiring plug – 1.4 & 1.6 litre models

4.15 Unclip the coolant expansion tank at the rear, and move it aside

4.16 Lift the power steering fluid reservoir out of its location

4.31a Disconnect the oxygen sensor . . .

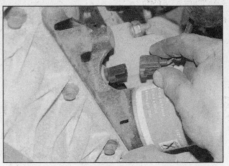

4.31b . . . oil pressure warning light switch . . .

4.31c . . . and the reversing light switch

17 Disconnect the radiator, heater and expansion tank hoses from the thermostat housing. On automatic transmission models, separate the heater hose at the connection above the transmission.

18 Disconnect the radiator bottom hose and heater hose from the connections at the coolant pump.

19 On 1.8 and 2.0 litre models, remove the radiator fan assembly using the information in Chapter 3.

20 Referring to Chapter 6, disconnect the fluid supply pipe for the clutch master cylinder at the connection on the transmission. Be prepared for some fluid spillage, and plug the end of the pipe to prevent further fluid loss. Tie the pipe up out of the way, and wash off any spilt fluid.

> ⚠ **Warning: Hydraulic fluid is poisonous, flammable, and will attack paintwork and plastics.**

21 If not already done, jack up the front of the car and support it on axle stands.

22 Remove the auxiliary drivebelt as described in Chapter 1A.

23 Trace the fluid pipes from the power steering pump under the car, and detach the pipe retaining bracket from the engine/transmission or subframe.

24 Unbolt the power steering pump using the information in Chapter 10, and tie it up without disturbing the pipe connections.

25 On models with air conditioning, unbolt the air conditioning compressor using the information in Chapter 3, and tie it up out of the way.

> ⚠ **Warning: Do not disconnect the refrigerant hoses.**

26 On manual transmission models, referring to Chapter 7A if necessary, disconnect the gearchange cables from the transmission levers. On models with the MTX 75 transmission, disconnect the gearchange cables from the brackets on top of the transmission.

27 On automatic transmission models, unbolt the support bracket for the transmission fluid dipstick, and release the dipstick from its location.

28 Referring to Chapter 5A, unbolt and remove the starter motor – note that, if wished, the electrical connections to the motor need not be removed – simply unbolt and remove the motor, leaving it to one side with the wiring attached.

29 Remove both driveshafts from the transmission, as described in Chapter 8.

30 Support the engine from below, close to the engine rear mounting. Loosen the engine rear mounting bolts, and remove the mounting. Note that it is only necessary to support the engine as the bolts are loosened and removed – once the mounting has been taken off, the support can be carefully removed.

31 Disconnect the wiring plugs from the following:

a) Exhaust gas oxygen sensor (trace the wiring back from the sensor to the plug) **(see illustration)**.

b) Oil pressure warning light switch **(see illustration)**.

c) Crankshaft position sensor (on the front of the engine, at the transmission end).

d) Vehicle speed sensor (on top of the transmission).

e) Reversing light switch (at the front of the transmission) **(see illustration)**.

32 On 1.4 and 1.6 litre models, remove the exhaust manifold heat shield, noting the engine earth cable which is also secured by one of the heat shield bolts. Remove the exhaust manifold as described in Chapter 4A. Ensure that the flexible section of the exhaust front pipe is not bent excessively as the manifold is removed.

33 On 1.8 and 2.0 litre models, remove the exhaust front section as described in Chapter 4A.

34 Taking precautions against fuel spillage, disconnect the fuel lines at the connections into the engine compartment, prising out the coloured locking clip with a small screwdriver. Note that the fuel supply pipe connection is coloured white, with the return connection being red **(see illustrations)**. Where applicable, disconnect the earth cable below the fuel line connections.

> ⚠ **Warning: Refer to 'Safety first!' and the warnings in Chapter 4A when disconnecting fuel lines – extreme fire risk.**

35 Disconnect the hoses from the charcoal canister, located behind the power steering fluid reservoir; note the positions of the hoses, for use when refitting **(see illustration)**.

36 At this stage, the front of the car must be raised sufficiently to allow the engine/

4.34a Prise out the coloured locking clip . . .

4.34b . . . and disconnect the fuel lines at the bulkhead

4.35 Disconnecting the hoses from the charcoal canister

transmission assembly to be lowered and removed from under the front of the car. This will entail raising the car much higher than it would normally be for most servicing work. Do not, however, be tempted to use makeshift means of support – before proceeding further, make sure the car is stable.

37 Connect a hoist and raise it so that the weight of the engine and transmission are just supported. Arrange the hoist and sling so that the engine and transmission are kept level when they are being withdrawn from the vehicle.

38 Unscrew and remove the right- and left-hand engine/transmission mountings, referring to the relevant Part of Chapter 2 as necessary.

39 Check around the engine and transmission assembly from above and below, to ensure that all associated attachments are disconnected and positioned out of the way. Engage the services of an assistant to help in guiding the assembly clear of surrounding components.

40 Consider how the engine will be removed from under the car, before lowering it. If a wheeled trolley is available, this makes the task of moving the engine much easier. If the engine is dropped onto its sump, the sump may be damaged; a piece of old foam or carpet will offer some protection. If the engine is lowered onto a piece of carpet or a sheet of wood, this can be used to drag the engine out from under the car, without damage.

41 Carefully lower the engine/transmission assembly clear of the mountings, guiding the assembly past any obstructions, and taking care that surrounding components are not damaged **(see illustrations)**. Remove the assembly from the front of the vehicle.

42 Once the engine/transmission assembly is clear of the vehicle, move it to an area where it can be cleaned and worked on.

Separation

43 Rest the engine and transmission assembly on a firm, flat surface, and use wooden blocks as wedges to keep the unit steady.

44 Note the routing and location of any wiring on the engine/transmission assembly, then methodically disconnect it.

Manual transmission models

45 Refer to the information in Chapter 7A, Section 8.

Automatic transmission models

46 Refer to the information in Chapter 7B, Section 9.

Reconnection

47 To reconnect the transmission and engine, reverse the operations used to separate them. Above all, do not use excessive force during these operations – if the two will not marry together easily, forcing them will only lead to damage. *Do not tighten the bellhousing bolts to force the engine and transmission together.* Ensure that the bellhousing and cylinder block mating faces

4.41a Lower the engine clear of the mountings . . .

will butt together evenly without obstruction, before tightening the bolts fully. Reconnect any wiring on the engine/transmission assembly, routing it as noted on removal.

Refitting

48 Manoeuvre the engine/transmission under the car, attach the hoist, and lift the unit into position until the right- and left-hand mountings can be reassembled. Initially, tighten the mounting nuts and bolts only lightly.

49 Refit the engine rear mounting, and tighten the bolts by hand.

50 Rock the engine/transmission gently to settle it on its mountings, then tighten all the mounting nuts and bolts to the specified torques. Once the engine/transmission is fully supported by its mountings, the hoist can be removed.

51 The remainder of the refitting procedure is the direct reverse of the removal procedure, noting the following points:

a) *Tighten all fasteners to the specified torque wrench settings, where applicable.*

b) *Ensure that all sections of the wiring harness follow their original routing; use new cable-ties to secure the harness in position, keeping it away from sources of heat and abrasion.*

c) *Ensure that all hoses are correctly routed and are secured with the correct hose clips, where applicable. If the hose clips cannot be used again; proprietary worm-drive clips should be fitted in their place.*

d) *On vehicles with manual transmission, check and if necessary adjust the gearchange cables with reference to Chapter 7A.*

e) *Refill the cooling system as described in Chapter 1A.*

f) *Refill the engine with appropriate grade and quantity of oil, where necessary (Chapter 1A).*

g) *Refill or top-up the transmission oil or fluid (see Chapter 1A).*

h) *Check and if necessary adjust the accelerator cable with reference to Chapter 4A.*

i) *When the engine is started for the first time, check for air, coolant, lubricant and fuel leaks from manifolds, hoses, etc. If the engine has been overhauled, read the notes in Section 21 before attempting to start it.*

4.41b . . . and down so that it can be removed under the front

5 Engine/transmission (diesel) – removal, separation and refitting

Note: *Read through the entire Section, as well as reading the advice in Section 3, before beginning this procedure. The engine and transmission are removed as a unit, lowered to the ground and removed from underneath, then separated outside the vehicle.*

Removal

1 Park the vehicle on firm, level ground, apply the handbrake firmly, and slacken the nuts securing both front roadwheels.

2 Remove the intercooler as described in Chapter 4B.

3 Drain the cooling system as described in Chapter 1B.

4 Remove the battery and battery tray as described in Chapter 5A.

5 Remove the air cleaner and inlet ducting as described in Chapter 4B. Unbolt and remove the air inlet duct fitted below the air cleaner, leading to the engine compartment front panel.

6 At the front of the engine, above the top hose connection, disconnect the wiring for the alternator, injection pump and glow plugs.

7 Disconnect the vehicle speed sensor connector from the top of the transmission, and the large wiring harness connector to the rear of it. Unclip the wiring harness from the transmission **(see illustration)**.

5.7 Disconnect the wiring connectors from the top of the transmission

5.8 Disconnect the connections from the EGR valve

5.10 Undo the expansion tank retaining bolt and move it to one side

5.14 Removing the power steering pump bracket

8 Disconnect the vacuum hoses and wiring from the EGR valve, which is fitted to the top of the inlet manifold **(see illustration)**.
9 Disconnect the coolant hoses from the thermostat housing, and from the radiator itself.
10 Unscrew the bolt securing the coolant expansion tank to the inner wing, unclip the tank from the inner wing and move to one side without disconnecting the hoses **(see illustration)**.
11 If not already done, jack up the front of the car and support it on axle stands.
12 Remove the auxiliary drivebelt as described in Chapter 1B.
13 Taking precautions against oil spillage, unscrew and remove the oil filter.
14 Unbolt the power steering pump using the information in Chapter 10, and tie it up without disturbing the pipe connections. Unbolt and remove the power steering pump mounting bracket **(see illustration)**.

15 Trace the fluid pipes from the power steering pump in the engine compartment, and detach the pipe retaining bracket from the engine/transmission.
16 Taking precautions against fuel spillage, disconnect the fuel lines at the connections into the engine compartment or the connections to the injector pump **(see illustration)**. Note the fitted positions of the pipes for use when refitting.

 Warning: Refer to 'Safety first!' and the warnings in Chapter 4B when disconnecting fuel lines – extreme fire risk.

17 Referring to Chapter 5A, unbolt and remove the starter motor – note that, if wished, the electrical connections to the motor need not be removed – simply unbolt and remove the motor, leaving it to one side with the wiring attached.
18 Remove the radiator as described in

Chapter 3. As this is done, disconnect the horn wiring connector.
19 Disconnect the coolant hose from the oil cooler at the rear of the engine **(see illustration)**.
20 Disconnect the radiator bottom hose and heater hose from the connections at the coolant pump metal feed pipe **(see illustration)**.
21 Working on each side in turn, unscrew the front suspension strut centre nuts exactly five turns each while holding the shock absorber centre rods with an Allen key. **Note:** *It is important not to over-loosen the nuts – make sure there is still sufficient thread engaged with the nut.*
22 Referring to Chapter 7A if necessary, disconnect the gearchange cables from the transmission levers. Disconnect the gearchange cables from the brackets on top of the transmission **(see illustration)**. Also unbolt and remove the wiring support bracket from the top of the transmission.
23 Remove both driveshafts from the transmission, as described in Chapter 8.
24 Referring to Chapter 4C if necessary, remove the catalytic converter.
25 Ensure that both the engine upper mountings are still securely fitted, so that the weight of the engine is fully supported. Under the car, loosen the engine rear mounting bolts, and remove the mounting **(see illustration)**. Note that it will be necessary to swing the engine forwards to remove the mounting.
26 Referring to Chapter 6, disconnect the fluid supply pipe for the clutch master cylinder

5.16 Note the colour of the connectors on the fuel pipes for refitting

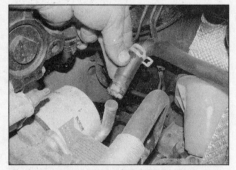

5.19 Disconnecting the coolant hose from the oil cooler

5.20 Bottom hose disconnected, remove heater hose (arrowed)

5.22 Release the gearchange cables from the bracket on the transmission

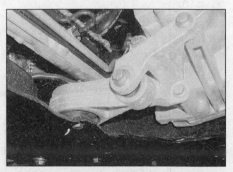

5.25 Undo the rear engine/transmission mounting bolts

5.28 Disconnect the multi-plug from the injector pump

5.30a Disconnect the alternator . . .

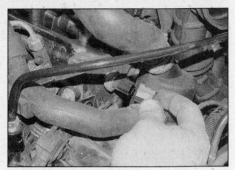

5.30b . . . the oil pressure switch . . .

at the connection on the transmission. Be prepared for some fluid spillage, and plug the end of the pipe to prevent further fluid loss. Tie the pipe up out of the way, and wash off any spilt fluid.

⚠️ **Warning: Hydraulic fluid is poisonous, flammable, and will attack paintwork and plastics.**

27 Noting their fitted positions for use when refitting, disconnect the two wiring harness connectors in front of the left-hand suspension strut mounting (left as seen from the driver's seat).

28 Disconnect the main wiring connector from the top of the injection pump (**see illustration**).

29 On models with air conditioning, unbolt the air conditioning compressor using the information in Chapter 3, and tie it up out of the way.

⚠️ **Warning: Do not disconnect the refrigerant hoses.**

30 Disconnect the wiring from the following (**see illustrations**):
 a) Alternator (if not already done).
 b) Oil pressure warning light switch (in the end of the cylinder head, at the transmission end).
 c) Crankshaft position sensor (on the rear of the engine, at the transmission end).
 d) Reversing light switch (on the top of the transmission).

31 At this stage, the front of the car must be raised sufficiently to allow the engine/transmission assembly to be lowered and removed from under the front of the car. This will entail raising the car much higher than it would normally be for most servicing work. Do not, however, be tempted to use makeshift means of support – before proceeding further, make sure the car is stable.

32 Connect a hoist to the engine and transmission and raise it so that the weight of the engine and transmission are just supported. Arrange the hoist and sling so that the engine and transmission are kept level when they are being withdrawn from the vehicle.

33 Unscrew and remove the right- and left-hand engine/transmission mountings, referring to the relevant Part of Chapter 2 as necessary.

34 Check around the engine and transmission assembly from above and below, to ensure that all associated attachments are disconnected and positioned out of the way. Engage the services of an assistant to help in guiding the assembly clear of surrounding components.

35 Consider how the engine will be removed from under the car, before lowering it. If a wheeled trolley is available, this makes the task of moving the engine much easier. If the engine is dropped onto its sump, the sump may be damaged; a piece of old foam or carpet will offer some protection. If the engine is lowered onto a piece of carpet or a sheet of wood, this can be used to drag the engine out from under the car, without damage.

36 Carefully lower the engine/transmission assembly clear of the mountings, guiding the assembly past any obstructions, and taking care that surrounding components are not damaged. Remove the assembly from under the front of the vehicle.

37 Once the engine/transmission assembly is clear of the vehicle, move it to an area where it can be cleaned and worked on.

Separation

38 Rest the engine and transmission assembly on a firm, flat surface, and use wooden blocks as wedges to keep the unit steady.

39 Note the routing and location of any wiring on the engine/transmission assembly, then methodically disconnect it.

40 Refer to the information in Chapter 7A, Section 8. Diesel models use the MTX 75 transmission.

Reconnection

41 To reconnect the transmission and engine, reverse the operations used to separate them. Above all, do not use excessive force during these operations – if the two will not marry together easily, forcing them will only lead to damage. *Do not tighten the bellhousing bolts to force the engine and transmission together.* Ensure that the bellhousing and cylinder block mating faces will butt together evenly without obstruction, before tightening the bolts fully. Reconnect any wiring on the engine/transmission assembly, routing it as noted on removal.

Refitting

42 Manoeuvre the engine/transmission under the car, attach the hoist, and lift the unit into position until the right- and left-hand mountings can be reassembled. Initially, tighten the mounting nuts and bolts only lightly.

43 Refit the engine rear mounting, and tighten the bolts by hand.

44 Rock the engine/transmission gently to settle it on its mountings, then tighten all the mounting nuts and bolts to the specified torques. Once the engine/transmission is fully supported by its mountings, the hoist can be removed.

45 The remainder of the refitting procedure is the direct reverse of the removal procedure, noting the following points:
 a) Tighten all fasteners to the specified torque wrench settings, where applicable.
 b) Ensure that all sections of the wiring harness follow their original routing; use

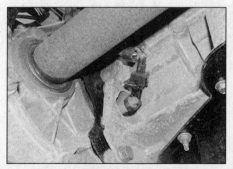

5.30c . . . the crankshaft position sensor . . .

5.30d . . . and the reversing light wiring connectors

new cable-ties to secure the harness in position, keeping it away from sources of heat and abrasion.

c) Ensure that all hoses are correctly routed and are secured with the correct hose clips, where applicable. If the hose clips cannot be used again; proprietary worm-drive clips should be fitted in their place.

d) Check and if necessary adjust the gearchange cables with reference to Chapter 7A.

e) Refill the cooling system as described in Chapter 1B.

f) Refill the engine with appropriate grade and quantity of oil, where necessary (Chapter 1B).

g) Refill or top-up the transmission oil or fluid (see Chapter 1B).

h) When the engine is started for the first time, check for air, coolant, lubricant and fuel leaks from manifolds, hoses etc. If the engine has been overhauled, read the notes in Section 21 before attempting to start it.

6 Engine overhaul – dismantling sequence

1 It is much easier to dismantle and work on the engine if it is mounted on a portable engine stand. These stands can often be hired from a tool hire shop. Before the engine is mounted on a stand, the flywheel/driveplate should be removed (Part A, B or C of this Chapter) so that the stand bolts can be tightened into the end of the cylinder block/crankcase.

2 If a stand is not available, it is possible to dismantle the engine with it mounted on blocks, on a sturdy workbench or on the floor. Be extra-careful not to tip or drop the engine when working without a stand.

3 If you are going to obtain a reconditioned engine, all external components must be removed first, to be transferred to the replacement engine (just as they will if you are doing a complete engine overhaul yourself).

Note: When removing the external components from the engine, pay close attention to details that may be helpful or important during refitting. Note the fitted position of gaskets, seals, spacers, pins, washers, bolts and other small items. These external components include the following:

a) Alternator and mounting bracket (Chapter 5A).

b) Power steering pump and air conditioning compressor mounting brackets.

c) HT leads and spark plugs – petrol models (Chapters 1A and 5B).

d) Fuel injection system components (Chapter 4A or 4B).

e) Brake vacuum pump – diesel models (Chapter 9).

f) Thermostat and housing (Chapter 3).

g) Dipstick tube.

h) All electrical switches and sensors.

i) Inlet and exhaust manifolds (Chapter 4A or 4B).

j) Oil filter (Chapter 1A or 1B).

k) Engine/transmission mounting brackets (Chapter 2A, 2B or 2C).

l) Flywheel/driveplate (Chapter 2A, 2B or 2C).

4 If you are obtaining a 'short' engine (which consists of the engine cylinder block/crank-case, crankshaft, pistons and connecting rods all assembled), then the cylinder head, sump, lower crankcase (where applicable), oil pump and timing belt will have to be removed also.

5 If you are planning a complete overhaul, the engine can be dismantled and the internal components removed in the following order.

a) Alternator and mounting bracket (Chapter 5A).

b) Inlet and exhaust manifolds (Chapter 4A or 4B).

c) Timing belt and toothed pulleys (Chapter 2A, 2B or 2C).

d) Cylinder head (Chapter 2A, 2B or 2C).

e) Power steering pump and air conditioning compressor mounting brackets.

f) Flywheel/driveplate (Chapter 2A, 2B or 2C).

g) Sump (Chapter 2A, 2B or 2C).

h) Oil pump – and, where applicable, lower crankcase (Chapter 2A, 2B or 2C).

i) Piston/connecting rod assemblies (Section 11).

j) Crankshaft – except 1.4 and 1.6 litre engines (Section 12).

Caution: DO NOT attempt to remove the crankshaft or main bearing cap/ladder on the 1.4 or 1.6 litre engines, as it is not possible to refit it accurately using conventional tooling. The manufacturers do not supply torque settings for the main bearing cap/ladder retaining bolts. If the crankshaft is worn excessively, it will be necessary to obtain a new short motor comprising the cylinder block together with the pistons and crankshaft.

6 Before beginning the dismantling and overhaul procedures, make sure that you have all of the correct tools necessary. Refer to the Reference section at the end of this manual for further information.

7 Cylinder head – dismantling

Note: New and reconditioned cylinder heads are available from the manufacturers, and from engine overhaul specialists. Due to the fact that some specialist tools are required for the dismantling and inspection procedures, and new components may not be readily available (refer to Section 1), it may be more practical and economical for the home mechanic to purchase a reconditioned head, rather than to dismantle, inspect and recondition the original head.

1 Remove the camshaft(s) and cam followers (Chapter 2A, 2B or 2C).

2 Remove the cylinder head (Chapter 2A, 2B or 2C).

3 Using a valve spring compressor, compress each valve spring in turn until the split collets can be removed. A special valve spring compressor will be required, to reach into the deep wells in the cylinder head without risk of damaging the cam follower bores; such compressors are now widely available from most good motor accessory shops. Release the compressor, and lift off the spring upper seat and spring **(see illustration)**.

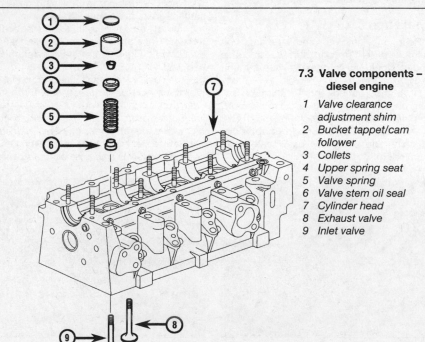

7.3 Valve components – diesel engine

1 Valve clearance adjustment shim
2 Bucket tappet/cam follower
3 Collets
4 Upper spring seat
5 Valve spring
6 Valve stem oil seal
7 Cylinder head
8 Exhaust valve
9 Inlet valve

7.6 Remove the valve stem oil seal from the cylinder head – diesel engine

4 If, when the valve spring compressor is screwed down, the spring upper seat refuses to free and expose the split collets, gently tap the top of the tool, directly over the upper seat, with a light hammer. This will free the seat.

5 Withdraw the valve through the combustion chamber. If it binds in the guide (won't pull through), push it back in, and de-burr the area around the collet groove with a fine file or whetstone; take care not to mark the cam follower bores.

6 Recover the valve stem oil seals from their locations in the cylinder head **(see illustration)**. As the seals are removed, note whether they are of different colours for the inlet and exhaust valves – compare with the new parts, and note this for refitting. As a guide, the inlet valve seals are green, and the exhaust seals are red.

7 On 1.8 and 2.0 litre petrol engines, the valve stem seals are integral with the valve spring lower seat, and are thus an unusual design; removing the seals can be extremely tricky, due to limited access and the shape of the seal 'assembly'. Ford recommend the use of their service tool 303-374 to extract the seals; while this is almost indispensable if the seals are to be removed without risk of (extremely expensive) damage to the cylinder head, we found that a serviceable substitute can be made using a nut of suitable size, a bar and a rollpin **(see Tool Tip)**. Screw on the tool so that it bites into the seal, then draw the seal off the valve guide **(see illustration)**.

8 It is essential that the valves are kept

First find a large nut whose threads will bite firmly into the top of the seal 'assembly', then drill a hole across the top of the nut, to accept a rollpin (or thin nail). As much of the threaded section of the nut as possible must be available in the finished tool. Similarly drill across a section of bar (or another bolt). Assemble the nut and bar using the rollpin, so that the bar will turn the nut – a tee-piece handle can be added to the bar, to make turning easier.

together with their collets, spring seats and springs, and in their correct sequence (unless they are so badly worn that they are to be renewed). If they are going to be kept and used again, place them in a labelled polythene bag or similar small container **(see illustrations)**. Note that No 1 valve is nearest to the timing belt end of the engine; the inlet and exhaust valve positions can be deduced from the fitted positions of the inlet and exhaust manifolds.

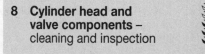

8 Cylinder head and valve components – cleaning and inspection

1 Thorough cleaning of the cylinder head and valve components, followed by a detailed inspection, will enable you to decide how much valve service work must be carried out during the engine overhaul. **Note:** *If the engine has been severely overheated, it is best to assume that the cylinder head is warped, and to check carefully for signs of this.*

7.7 Using home-made tool to remove the valve stem oil seals – 1.8 litre engine

Cleaning

2 Scrape away all traces of old gasket material and sealing compound from the cylinder head.

3 Scrape away the carbon from the combustion chambers and ports, then wash the cylinder head thoroughly with paraffin or a suitable solvent.

4 Scrape off any heavy carbon deposits that may have formed on the valves, then use a power-operated wire brush to remove deposits from the valve heads and stems.

Inspection

Note: *Be sure to perform all the following inspection procedures before concluding that the services of a machine shop or engine overhaul specialist are required. Make a list of all items that require attention.*

Cylinder head

5 Inspect the head very carefully for cracks, evidence of coolant leakage, and other damage. If cracks are found, a new cylinder head should be obtained.

6 If warpage of the cylinder head gasket surface is suspected, use a straight-edge to check it for distortion **(see illustration)**. If feeler blades are used, the degree of distortion can be assessed more accurately, and compared with the value specified. Check for distortion along the length and across the width of the head, and along both diagonals. If the head is warped, it may be possible to have it machined flat ('skimmed') at an engineering works – check with an engine specialist.

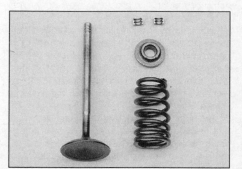

7.8a Valve, collets, upper spring seat and valve spring

7.8b Use a labelled plastic bag to store and identify valve components

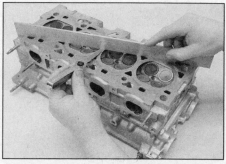

8.6 Check the cylinder head for warpage using a straight edge and feeler blades

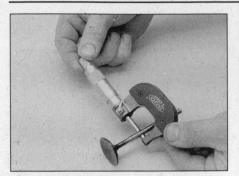

8.12 Measuring the diameter of a valve stem

8.15 Grinding-in a valve seat

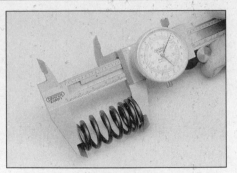

8.18 Measuring the valve spring free length

7 Examine the valve seats in each of the combustion chambers. If they are severely pitted, cracked or burned, then they will need to be renewed or re-cut by an engine overhaul specialist. If they are only slightly pitted, this can be removed by grinding-in the valve heads and seats with fine valve-grinding compound, as described below.

8 If the valve guides are worn, indicated by a side-to-side motion of the valve, new guides must be fitted. On 2.0 litre engines, measure the diameter of the existing valve stems (see below) and the bore of the guides, then calculate the clearance, and compare the result with the specified value; if the clearance is excessive, renew the valves or guides as necessary.

9 The renewal of valve guides is best carried out by an engine overhaul specialist.

10 If the valve seats are to be re-cut, this must be done only after the guides have been renewed.

Valves

11 Examine the head of each valve for pitting, burning, cracks and general wear, and check the valve stem for scoring and wear ridges. Rotate the valve, and check for any obvious indication that it is bent. Look for pits and excessive wear on the tip of each valve stem. Renew any valve that shows any such signs of wear or damage.

12 If the valve appears satisfactory at this stage, measure the valve stem diameter at several points, using a micrometer **(see illustration)**. Any significant difference in the readings obtained indicates wear of the valve stem. Should any of these conditions be

apparent, the valve(s) must be renewed.

13 If the valves are in satisfactory condition, they should be ground (lapped) into their respective seats, to ensure a smooth gas-tight seal. If the seat is only lightly pitted, or if it has been re-cut, fine grinding compound only should be used to produce the required finish. Coarse valve-grinding compound should not be used unless a seat is badly burned or deeply pitted; if this is the case, the cylinder head and valves should be inspected by an expert, to decide whether seat re-cutting, or even the renewal of the valve or seat insert, is required.

14 Valve grinding is carried out as follows. Place the cylinder head upside-down on a bench, with a block of wood at each end to give clearance for the valve stems.

15 Smear a trace of (the appropriate grade of) valve-grinding compound on the seat face, and press a suction grinding tool onto the valve head. With a semi-rotary action, grind the valve head to its seat, lifting the valve occasionally to redistribute the grinding compound **(see illustration)**. A light spring placed under the valve head will greatly ease this operation. If coarse grinding compound is being used, work only until a dull, matt even surface is produced on both the valve seat and the valve, then wipe off the used compound, and repeat the process with fine compound.

16 When a smooth unbroken ring of light grey matt finish is produced on both the valve and seat, the grinding operation is complete. Do not grind in the valves any further than absolutely necessary, or the seat will be prematurely sunk into the cylinder head.

17 When all the valves have been ground-in, carefully wash off all traces of grinding compound, using paraffin or a suitable solvent, before reassembly of the cylinder head.

Valve components

18 Examine the valve springs for signs of damage and discolouration, and also measure their free length (where no length is specified, compare each of the existing springs with new components) **(see illustration)**.

19 Stand each spring on a flat surface, and check it for squareness. If any of the springs are damaged, distorted, or have lost their tension, obtain a complete set of new springs.

20 Check the spring upper seats and collets for obvious wear and cracks. Any questionable parts should be renewed, as extensive damage will occur if they fail during engine operation. Any damaged or excessively-worn parts must be renewed; the valve spring lower seat/stem oil seals must be renewed as a matter of course whenever they are disturbed.

21 Check the cam followers as described in Chapter 2A, 2B or 2C.

9 Cylinder head – reassembly

1 Regardless of whether or not the head was sent away for repair work of any sort, make sure that it is clean before beginning reassembly. Be sure to remove any metal particles and abrasive grit that may still be present from operations such as valve grinding or head resurfacing. Use compressed air, if available, to blow out all the oil holes and passages.

2 Lubricate the new valve stem oil seals, then fit them to the cylinder head, pressing them in squarely using a deep socket of suitable diameter **(see illustration)**. Note that the inlet and exhaust seals are usually different colours – green for the inlet valves, red for the exhaust valves.

3 Beginning at one end of the head, lubricate and install the first valve. Apply molybdenum disulphide-based grease or clean engine oil to the valve stem, and refit the valve **(see illustration)**. Where the original valves are being re-used, ensure that each is refitted in its original guide. If new valves are being

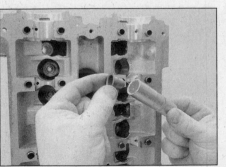

9.2 Fit the valve stem seals using a deep socket

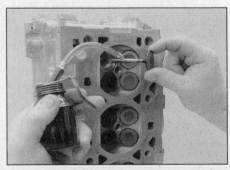

9.3 Lubricate the valve stem, and refit it to the cylinder head

9.4a Refit the valve spring . . .

9.4b . . . and the upper spring seat

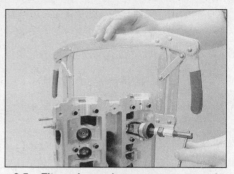

9.5a Fit a valve spring compressor, and compress the valve spring . . .

fitted, insert them into the locations to which they have been ground.

4 Refit the valve spring and upper seat **(see illustrations)**.

5 Compress the spring with a valve spring compressor, and carefully install the collets in the stem groove. Apply a small dab of grease to each collet to hold it in place if necessary; grease is also useful for sticking each half of the collets to a screwdriver, or similar tool, for installation **(see illustrations)**. Slowly release the compressor, and make sure the collets seat properly.

6 When the valve is installed, place the cylinder head flat on the bench and, using a hammer and interposed block of wood, tap the end of the valve stem gently, to settle the components.

7 Repeat the procedure for the remaining valves. Be sure to return the components to their original locations – don't mix them up!

8 Refit the cam followers and camshaft(s) (Chapter 2A, 2B or 2C).

10 Fuel injection pump drive chain (diesel) – removal, inspection and refitting

Removal

1 With the engine removed from the vehicle, proceed as follows.

2 Remove the oil pump as described in Chapter 2C.

3 At the rear of the engine block, locate the drive chain hydraulic tensioner (below and behind the coolant pump). Using the hex in the top of the tensioner body, unscrew and extract the tensioner from the block **(see illustration)**. Be prepared for a small amount of oil spillage as this is done.

4 Temporarily refit the crankshaft pulley if necessary, and turn the engine so that the timing hole in the injection pump sprocket is at the top and aligned – this can be checked by inserting a 6 mm twist drill into the hole in the sprocket and into the injection pump.

5 Unscrew the two bolts securing the chain guides, then carefully slide the two sprockets simultaneously from their locations, and remove

9.5b . . . then fit the collets to the groove, holding them on a screwdriver with grease

the complete chain, guide and sprocket assembly from the engine **(see illustration)**.

Inspection

6 Examine the guides for scoring or wear ridges, and for chipping or wear of the sprocket teeth **(see illustration)**.

7 Check the chains for wear, which will be evident in the form of excess play between the links. If the chains can be lifted at either 'end' of their run so that the sprocket teeth are visible, they have stretched excessively.

8 Check the chain tensioner for signs of wear, and renew if required.

9 At the time of writing, only the chain tensioner is available separately; if the chains or sprockets are worn, the complete assembly, comprising, sprockets, guides and chains must be purchased **(see illustration)**. If possible, compare the old items with new components, or seek the advice of an engineering works, before concluding that renewal is necessary.

10.3 Unscrew the chain tensioner from the housing

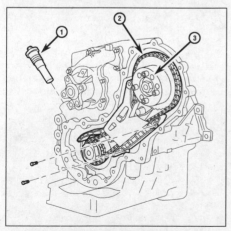

10.5 Fuel injection pump drive chain assembly

1 Hydraulic chain tensioner
2 Chain assembly
3 Injection pump timing hole

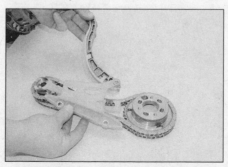

10.6 Examine the chain guides for wear

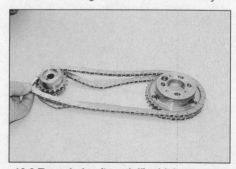

10.9 Two chains ('gemini') which run next to one another, offset by half a link

Refitting

10 Refitting is a reversal of removal, noting the following points:

a) *Align the timing holes in the injection pump sprockets when offering the chain and sprocket assembly into position.*

b) *Tighten the chain guide retaining bolts securely to the specified torque (see illustration).*

c) *Especially if a new chain and sprocket assembly has been fitted, lubricate it thoroughly with fresh engine oil.*

d) *Refit the chain tensioner, and tighten it to the specified torque.*

e) *Refit the oil pump as described in Chapter 2C.*

11 Piston/connecting rod assemblies – removal

Note: *While this task is theoretically possible when the engine is in place in the vehicle, in practice, it requires so much preliminary dismantling, and is so difficult to carry out due to the restricted access, that owners are advised to remove the engine from the vehicle first. The following paragraphs assume the engine is removed from the car.*

1 Remove the cylinder head and sump with reference to Chapter 2A, 2B or 2C.

2 Unbolt the oil pump pick-up tube/filter and return pipe, from the lower crankcase. On 1.8 and 2.0 litre petrol engines, and diesel engines, unbolt and remove the lower

10.10 Tightening the chain guide retaining bolts

crankcase; recover the rubber gasket – a new one must be used when reassembling **(see illustrations)**.

3 On engines except the 1.4 and 1.6 litre, the connecting rods and caps are of 'cracked' design. During production, the connecting rod and cap are forged as one piece, then the cap is broken apart from the rod using a special technique. Because of this design, the mating surfaces of each cap and rod are unique and, therefore, nearly impossible to mix up.

4 There should be markings on the big-end caps, with corresponding marks on the connecting rods **(see illustration)**. Make sure these marks are visible before dismantling, and if not, make your own using paint or a centre-punch. So that you can be certain of refitting each piston/connecting rod assembly the right way round, to its correct (original) bore, with the cap also the right way round.

5 Each piston has an arrow stamped into its

crown, pointing towards the timing belt end of the engine **(see illustration)**.

6 Use your fingernail to feel if a ridge has formed at the upper limit of ring travel (about 6 mm down from the top of each cylinder). If carbon deposits or cylinder wear have produced ridges, they must be completely removed with a special tool called a ridge reamer. Follow the manufacturer's instructions provided with the tool.

Caution: Failure to remove the ridges before attempting to remove the piston/connecting rod assemblies may result in piston ring breakage.

7 Slacken each of the big-end bearing cap bolts half a turn at a time, until they can be removed by hand. Remove the No 1 cap and bearing shell **(see illustrations)**. Don't drop the shell out of the cap.

8 Remove the upper bearing shell, and push the connecting rod/piston assembly out through the top of the engine. Use a wooden hammer handle to push on the connecting rod's bearing recess. If resistance is felt, double-check that all of the ridge was removed from the cylinder (see paragraph 6).

9 Repeat the procedure for the remaining cylinders.

10 After removal, reassemble the big-end bearing caps and shells on their respective connecting rods, and refit the bolts finger-tight. Leaving the old shells in place until reassembly will help prevent the bearing recesses from being accidentally nicked or gouged. New shells should be used on reassembly.

11.2a Unbolt the oil pick-up pipe/filter and return pipe . . .

11.2b . . . then unbolt the lower crankcase and remove

11.4 Each connecting rod and cap can be marked on the flat-machined surface

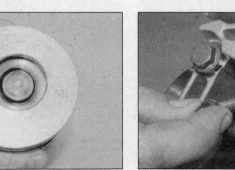

11.5 Arrow stamped on top of piston points to the timing belt end of the engine

11.7a Slacken and remove the bolts . . .

11.7b . . . then take off the big-end cap – 1.4 litre engine

11 On diesel engines only, the gudgeon pins are a floating fit in the pistons, and can be removed after releasing the circlips. On petrol engines, don't attempt to separate the pistons from the connecting rods.

12 Crankshaft (except 1.4 & 1.6 litre engines) – removal

Caution: DO NOT attempt to remove the crankshaft or main bearing cap/ladder on the 1.4 or 1.6 litre engines, as it is not possible to refit it accurately using conventional tooling. The manufacturers do not supply torque settings for the main bearing cap/ladder retaining bolts. If the crankshaft is worn excessively, it will be necessary to obtain a new short motor comprising the cylinder block together with the pistons and crankshaft.

Note: *The crankshaft can be removed only after the engine/transmission has been removed from the vehicle. It is assumed that the transmission and flywheel/driveplate, timing belt, lower crankcase, cylinder head, sump, oil pump pick-up/strainer pipe and oil baffle, oil pump, and piston/connecting rod assemblies, have already been removed. The crankshaft left-hand oil seal carrier must be unbolted from the cylinder block/crankcase before proceeding with crankshaft removal.*

1 Before the crankshaft is removed, check the endfloat. Mount a DTI (Dial Test Indicator, or dial gauge) with the probe in line with the crankshaft and just touching the crankshaft.

2 Push the crankshaft fully away from the gauge, and zero it. Next, lever the crankshaft towards the gauge as far as possible, and check the reading obtained **(see illustration)**. The distance that the crankshaft moved is its endfloat; if it is greater than specified, check the crankshaft thrust surfaces for wear. If no wear is evident, new thrustwashers should correct the endfloat. On some engines, the thrustwasher/thrust control bearing is part of the No 3 (centre) main bearing.

3 If a dial gauge is not available, feeler gauges can be used. Gently lever or push the crankshaft all the way towards the right-hand end of the engine. Slip feeler gauges between

12.2 Checking the crankshaft endfloat with a dial gauge

the crankshaft and the right-hand face of the No 3 (centre) main bearing to determine the clearance.

4 Check the main bearing caps, to see if they are marked to indicate their locations. They should be numbered consecutively from the timing belt end of the engine – if not, mark them with number-stamping dies or a centre-punch. The caps will also have an embossed arrow pointing to the timing belt end of the engine **(see illustration)**. Noting, where applicable, the different fasteners (for the oil baffle nuts) used on caps 2 and 4, slacken the cap bolts a quarter-turn at a time each, starting with the left- and right-hand end caps and working toward the centre, until they can be removed by hand.

5 Gently tap the caps with a soft-faced hammer, then separate them from the cylinder block/crankcase. If necessary, use the bolts as levers to remove the caps. Try not to drop the bearing shells if they come out with the caps.

6 Carefully lift the crankshaft out of the engine. It may be a good idea to have an assistant available, since the crankshaft is quite heavy. With the bearing shells in place in the cylinder block/crankcase and main bearing caps, return the caps to their respective locations on the block, or refit the lower crankcase, and tighten the bolts finger-tight. Leaving the old shells in place until reassembly will help prevent the bearing recesses from being accidentally nicked or gouged. New shells should be used on reassembly.

12.4 Main bearing caps are marked with cylinder number and arrowhead

13 Cylinder block/crankcase – cleaning and inspection

Caution: If cleaning the cylinder block (with fitted crankshaft) on the 1.4 or 1.6 litre engines, it is recommended that only the external surfaces are cleaned, as otherwise the internal oilways and channels may become contaminated, leading to premature wear of the crankshaft and main bearings.

Cleaning

1 For complete cleaning, remove the water pump, all external components, and all electrical switches/sensors **(see illustrations)**. Unbolt the piston-cooling oil jets or blanking plugs (as applicable). Note that Ford states that the piston-cooling oil jets (where fitted) must be renewed whenever the engine is dismantled for full overhaul.

2 Remove the main bearing caps or lower crankcase, and separate the bearing shells from the caps/lower crankcase and the cylinder block. Mark or label the shells, indicating which bearing they were removed from, and whether they were in the cap or the block, then set them aside **(see illustration)**. Wipe clean the block and cap bearing recesses, and inspect them for nicks, gouges and scratches.

3 If required, on diesel engines, unbolt and remove the oil/water pump housing from the timing belt end of the engine. The housing is

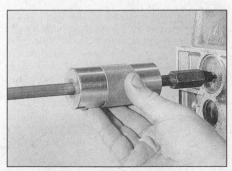
13.1a Unscrew the bolts . . .

13.1b . . . and remove the oil trap and gasket from the front of the cylinder block – 1.4 & 1.6 litre engine

13.2 Marker pens can be used as shown to identify bearing shells without damaging them

13.3 Unbolt the housing from the end of the cylinder block

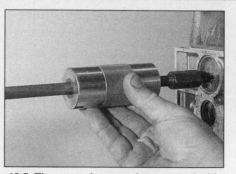

13.5 The core plugs can be removed with a puller – if they are driven into the block, they may be impossible to remove

13.8 All bolt holes in the block should be cleaned and restored with a tap

secured by a number of different types of bolt, so note their locations carefully before removing **(see illustration)**. Recover the metal gasket fitted between the engine and the housing – a new one must be obtained for refitting.

4 Scrape all traces of gasket from the cylinder block/lower crankcase, taking care not to damage the sealing surfaces.

5 Remove all oil gallery plugs (where fitted). The plugs are usually very tight – they may have to be drilled out and the holes re-tapped. Use new plugs when the engine is reassembled. Remove the core plugs by knocking them sideways in their bores with a hammer and a punch, then grasping them with large pliers and pulling them back through their holes. Alternatively, drill a small hose in the centre of each core plug, and pull them out with a car bodywork dent puller **(see illustration)**.

Caution: The core plugs (also known as freeze or soft plugs) may be difficult or impossible to retrieve if they are driven into the block coolant passages.

6 If any of the castings are extremely dirty, they should be steam-cleaned. After the castings are returned from steam-cleaning, clean all oil holes and oil galleries one more time. Flush all internal passages with warm water until the water runs clear, then dry thoroughly, and apply a light film of oil to all machined surfaces, to prevent rusting. If you have access to compressed air, use it to

speed the drying process, and to blow out all the oil holes and galleries (always take safety precautions when using compressed air).

7 If the castings are not very dirty, you can do an adequate cleaning job with hot soapy water (as hot as you can stand!) and a stiff brush. Take plenty of time, and do a thorough job. Regardless of the cleaning method used, be sure to clean all oil holes and galleries very thoroughly, and to dry all components completely; protect the machined surfaces as described above, to prevent rusting.

8 All threaded holes must be clean and dry, to ensure accurate torque readings during reassembly; now is also a good time to clean and check the threads of all principal bolts – however, note that some, such as the cylinder head and flywheel/driveplate bolts, must be renewed as a matter of course whenever they are disturbed. Run the proper-size tap into each of the holes, to remove rust, corrosion, thread sealant or sludge, and to restore damaged threads **(see illustration)**. If possible, use compressed air to clear the holes of debris produced by this operation.

9 When all inspection and repair procedures are complete (see below) and the block is ready for reassembly, apply suitable sealant to the new oil gallery plugs, and insert them into the holes in the block. Tighten them securely. After coating the sealing surfaces of the new core plugs with suitable sealant, install them in the cylinder block/crankcase. Make sure they are driven in straight and

seated properly, or leakage could result. Special tools are available for this purpose, but a large socket with an outside diameter that will just slip into the core plug, used with an extension and hammer, will work just as well **(see illustration)**.

10 Refit the blanking plugs or (new) piston-cooling oil jets (as applicable), tightening their retaining bolts securely. Also refit all other external components removed, referring to the relevant Chapter of this manual for further details where required. Where applicable, refit the main bearing caps and tighten the bolts finger-tight.

11 If the engine is not going to be reassembled right away, cover it with a large plastic bag to keep it clean. Apply a thin coat of engine oil to all machined surfaces to prevent rust.

Inspection

12 Visually check the castings for cracks and corrosion. Look for stripped threads in the threaded holes. If there has been any history of internal coolant leakage, it may be worthwhile having an engine overhaul specialist check the cylinder block/crankcase for cracks with special equipment. If defects are found, have them repaired, if possible, or renew the assembly.

13 Check each cylinder bore for scuffing and scoring.

14 Note: *The cylinder bores must be measured with all the crankshaft main bearing caps bolted in place (without the crankshaft and bearing shells) to the specified torque wrench settings.* Measure the diameter of each cylinder at the top (just under the ridge area), centre and bottom of the cylinder bore, parallel to the crankshaft axis. Next, measure each cylinder's diameter at the same three locations across the crankshaft axis **(see illustration)**. Note the measurements obtained.

15 Measure the piston diameter at right-angles to the gudgeon pin axis, just above the bottom of the skirt; again, note the results **(see illustration)**.

16 If it is wished to obtain the piston-to-bore clearance, measure the bore and piston skirt as described above, and subtract the skirt

13.9 A large socket on an extension can be used to drive the new core plugs into their bores

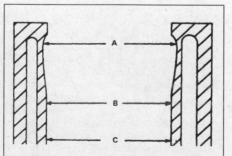

13.14 Measure the diameter of each cylinder just under the wear ridge (A), at the centre (B) and at the bottom (C)

diameter from the bore measurement. If the precision measuring tools shown are not available, the condition of the pistons and bores can be assessed, though not quite as accurately, by using feeler gauges as follows:

a) Select a feeler gauge of thickness equal to the specified piston-to-bore clearance (where given), and slip it into the cylinder along with the matching piston. The piston must be positioned in the correct orientation. The feeler gauge must be between the piston and cylinder on one of the thrust faces (at right-angles to the gudgeon pin bore).

b) The piston should slip down the cylinder (with the feeler gauge in place) with moderate pressure; if it falls through or slides through easily, the clearance is excessive, and a new piston will be required. If the piston binds at the lower end of the cylinder, and is loose toward the top, the cylinder is tapered. If tight spots are encountered as the piston/feeler gauge is rotated in the cylinder, the cylinder is out-of-round (oval).

17 Repeat these procedures for the remaining pistons and cylinder bores.

18 Compare the results with the Specifications at the beginning of this Chapter; if any measurement is beyond the dimensions specified for that class (check the piston crown marking to establish the class of piston fitted), or if any bore measurement is significantly different from the others (indicating that the bore is tapered or out-of-round), the piston or bore is excessively-worn.

19 Worn pistons must be renewed – check for availability with a Ford dealer or engine reconditioning specialist.

20 If any of the cylinder bores are badly scuffed or scored, or if they are excessively-worn, out-of-round or tapered, the usual course of action would be to have the cylinder block/crankcase rebored, and to fit new, oversized, pistons on reassembly. See a Ford dealer or engine reconditioning specialist for advice, as no oversizes are specified.

21 If the bores are in reasonably good condition and not excessively worn, then it may only be necessary to renew the piston rings.

22 If this is the case, the bores should be honed, to allow the new rings to bed-in correctly and provide the best possible seal. Before honing the bores, refit the main bearing caps without the bearing shells, and tighten the bolts to the specified torque wrench setting. **Note:** *If you don't have the tools, or don't want to tackle the honing operation, most engine reconditioning specialists will do it for a reasonable fee.*

23 Two types of cylinder hones are commonly available – the flex hone or 'bottle-brush' type, and the more traditional surfacing hone with spring-loaded stones. Both will do the job and are used with a power drill, but for the less-experienced mechanic, the 'bottle-brush' hone will probably be easier to use.

You will also need some paraffin or honing oil, and rags. Proceed as follows:

a) Mount the hone in the drill, compress the stones, and slip it into the first bore. Be sure to wear safety goggles or a face shield.

b) Lubricate the bore with plenty of honing oil, switch on the drill, and move the hone up and down the bore, at a pace that will produce a fine cross-hatch pattern on the cylinder walls. Ideally, the cross-hatch lines should intersect at approximately a 60° angle **(see illustration)**. Be sure to use plenty of lubricant, and don't take off any more material than is absolutely necessary to produce the desired finish. **Note:** *Piston ring manufacturers may specify a different crosshatch angle – read and follow any instructions included with the new rings.*

c) Don't withdraw the hone from the bore while it's running. Instead, switch off the drill, and continue moving the hone up and down the bore until it comes to a complete stop, then compress the stones and withdraw the hone. If you're using a 'bottle-brush' hone, switch off the drill, then turn the chuck in the normal direction of rotation while withdrawing the hone from the bore.

d) Wipe the oil out of the bore, and repeat the procedure for the remaining cylinders.

e) When all the cylinder bores are honed, chamfer the top edges of the bores with a small file, so the rings won't catch when the pistons are installed. Be very careful not to nick the cylinder walls with the end of the file.

f) The entire cylinder block/crankcase must be washed very thoroughly with warm, soapy water, to remove all traces of the abrasive grit produced during the honing operation. **Note:** *The bores can be considered clean when a lint-free white cloth – dampened with clean engine oil – used to wipe them out doesn't pick up any more honing residue, which will show up as grey areas on the cloth.* Be sure to run a brush through all oil holes and galleries, and flush them with running water.

g) When the cylinder block/crankcase is completely clean, rinse it thoroughly and dry it, then lightly oil all exposed machined surfaces, to prevent rusting.

24 On diesel engines, if the oil/water pump housing was removed, it can be refitted at this stage if wished. Use a new gasket, and before fully tightening the bolts, align the housing faces with those of the engine block.

25 The cylinder block/crankcase should now be completely clean and dry, with all components checked for wear or damage, and repaired or overhauled as necessary. Refit as many ancillary components as possible, for safekeeping. If reassembly is not to start immediately, cover the block with a large plastic bag to keep it clean, and protect the machined surfaces as described above to prevent rusting.

13.15 Measure the piston skirt diameter at right-angles to the gudgeon pin axis, just above the base of the skirt

14 Piston/connecting rod assemblies – inspection

1 Before the inspection process can be carried out, the piston/connecting rod assemblies must be cleaned, and the original piston rings removed from the pistons.

2 The rings should have smooth, polished working surfaces, with no dull or carbon-coated sections (showing that the ring is not sealing correctly against the bore wall, so allowing combustion gases to blow by) and no traces of wear on their top and bottom surfaces. The end gaps should be clear of carbon, but not polished (indicating a too-small end gap), and all the rings (including the elements of the oil control ring) should be free to rotate in their grooves, but without excessive up-and-down movement. If the rings appear to be in good condition, they are probably fit for further use; check the end gaps (in an unworn part of the bore) as described in Section 18.

3 If any of the rings appears to be worn or damaged, or has an end gap significantly different from the specified value, the usual course of action is to renew all of them as a set. **Note:** *While it is usual to renew piston rings when an engine is overhauled, they may be re-used if in acceptable condition. If re-using the rings, make sure that each ring is marked during removal to ensure that it is refitted correctly.*

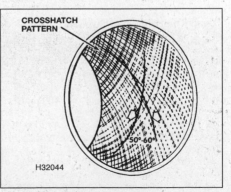

CROSSHATCH PATTERN

50°-60°

H32044

13.23 Cylinder bore honing pattern – typical

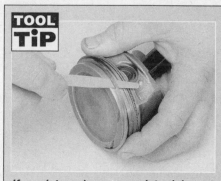

If a piston ring removal tool is not available, the rings can be removed by hand, expanding them over the top of the pistons. The use of two or three old feeler blades will be helpful in preventing the rings dropping into empty grooves.

4 Using a piston ring removal tool, carefully remove the rings from the pistons. Be careful not to nick or gouge the pistons in the process, and mark or label each ring as it is removed, so that its original top surface can be identified on reassembly, and so that it can be returned to its original groove. Take care also with your hands – piston rings are sharp. If a piston ring removal tool is not available, the rings can be removed by hand, expanding them over the top of the pistons **(see Tool Tip)**.

5 Scrape all traces of carbon from the top of the piston. A hand-held wire brush or a piece of fine emery cloth can be used, once the majority of the deposits have been scraped away. Do not, under any circumstances, use a wire brush mounted in a drill motor to remove deposits from the pistons – the piston material is soft, and may be eroded away by the wire brush.

6 Use a piston ring groove-cleaning tool to remove carbon deposits from the ring grooves. If a tool isn't available, but replacement rings have been found, a piece broken off the old ring will do the job **(see illustrations)**. Be very careful to remove only the carbon deposits – don't remove any metal, and do not nick or scratch the sides of the ring grooves. Protect your fingers – piston rings are sharp.

7 Once the deposits have been removed, clean the piston/rod assemblies with solvent, and dry them with compressed air (if available). Make sure the oil return holes in the back sides of the ring grooves, and the oil hole in the lower end of each rod, are clear.

8 If the pistons and cylinder walls aren't damaged or worn excessively and if the cylinder block/crankcase is not rebored, new pistons won't be necessary. Normal piston wear appears as even vertical wear on the piston thrust surfaces, and slight looseness of the top ring in its groove.

9 Carefully inspect each piston for cracks around the skirt, at the pin bosses, and at the ring lands (between the ring grooves).

14.6a The piston ring grooves can be cleaned with a special tool, as shown here . . .

10 Look for scoring and scuffing on the thrust faces of the skirt, holes in the piston, and burned areas at the edge of the crown. If the skirt is scored or scuffed, the engine may have been suffering from overheating and/or abnormal combustion, which caused excessively-high operating temperatures. The cooling and lubrication systems should be checked thoroughly. A hole in the piston is an indication that abnormal combustion (pre-ignition) was occurring. Burned areas at the edge of the piston crown are usually evidence of spark knock (detonation – petrol engines only). If any of the above problems exist, the causes must be corrected, or the damage will occur again. The causes may include faulty injectors, intake air leaks, incorrect fuel/air mixture, incorrect ignition timing, or EGR system malfunctions.

11 Corrosion of the piston, in the form of small pits, indicates that coolant is leaking into the combustion chamber and/or the crankcase. Again, the cause must be corrected, or the problem may persist in the rebuilt engine.

12 Check the piston-to-rod clearance by twisting the piston and rod in opposite directions. Any noticeable play indicates excessive wear, which must be corrected. The piston/connecting rod assemblies should be taken to a Ford dealer or engine reconditioning specialist to have the pistons, gudgeon pins and rods checked, and new components fitted as required.

13 On petrol engines, don't attempt to separate the pistons from the connecting

15.5 Measure the diameter of each crankshaft journal at several points, to detect taper and out-of-round conditions

14.6b . . . or a section of a broken ring, if available

rods. This is a task for a Ford dealer or similar engine reconditioning specialist, due to the special heating equipment, press, mandrels and supports required to do the job. If the piston/connecting rod assemblies do require this sort of work, have the connecting rods checked for bend and twist, since only such engine repair specialists will have the facilities for this purpose.

14 Check the connecting rods for cracks and other damage. Temporarily remove the big-end bearing caps and the old bearing shells, wipe clean the rod and cap bearing recesses, and inspect them for nicks, gouges and scratches. After checking the rods, replace the old shells, slip the caps into place, and tighten the bolts finger-tight.

15 Crankshaft (except 1.4 & 1.6 litre engines) – inspection

1 Clean the crankshaft, and dry it with compressed air if available. Be sure to clean the oil holes with a pipe cleaner or similar probe.

⚠ *Warning: Wear eye protection when using compressed air.*

2 Check the main and crankpin (big-end) bearing journals for uneven wear, scoring, pitting and cracking.

3 Run a fingernail across each journal several times. If the journal feels too rough, it should be reground.

4 Remove all burrs from the crankshaft oil holes with a stone, file or scraper.

5 Using a micrometer, measure the diameter of the main bearing and crankpin (big-end) journals, and compare the results with the Specifications at the beginning of this Chapter, where given **(see illustration)**.

6 By measuring the diameter at a number of points around each journal's circumference, you will be able to determine whether or not the journal is out-of-round. Take the measurement at each end of the journal, near the webs, to determine if the journal is tapered.

7 If the crankshaft journals are damaged, tapered, out-of-round, or worn beyond the limits specified in this Chapter, the crankshaft

must be taken to an engine overhaul specialist, who will regrind it, and who can supply the necessary undersize bearing shells, where available.

8 Check the oil seal journals at each end of the crankshaft for wear and damage. If either seal has worn an excessive groove in its journal, consult an engine overhaul specialist, who will be able to advise whether a repair is possible, or whether a new crankshaft is necessary.

16 Main and big-end bearings – inspection

1 Even though the main and big-end bearing shells should be renewed during the engine overhaul (where possible), the old shells should be retained for close examination, as they may reveal valuable information about the condition of the engine.

2 Bearing failure occurs because of lack of lubrication, the presence of dirt or other foreign particles, overloading the engine, and corrosion **(see illustration)**. Regardless of the cause of bearing failure, it must be corrected before the engine is reassembled, to prevent it from happening again.

3 When examining the bearing shells, remove them from the cylinder block/crankcase and main bearing caps and from the connecting rods and the big-end bearing caps, then lay them out on a clean surface in the same general position as their location in the engine. This will enable you to match any bearing problems with the corresponding crankshaft journal. Do not touch any shell's bearing surface with your fingers while checking it, or the delicate surface may be scratched.

4 Dirt or other foreign matter gets into the engine in a variety of ways. It may be left in the engine during assembly, or it may pass through filters or the crankcase ventilation system. It may get into the oil, and from there into the bearings. Metal chips from machining operations and normal engine wear are often present. Abrasives are sometimes left in engine components after reconditioning, especially when parts are not thoroughly cleaned using the proper cleaning methods. Whatever the source, these foreign objects often end up embedded in the soft bearing material, and are easily recognised. Large particles will not embed in the material, and will score or gouge the shell and journal. The best prevention for this cause of bearing failure is to clean all parts thoroughly, and to keep everything spotlessly-clean during engine assembly. Frequent and regular engine oil and filter changes are also recommended.

5 Lack of lubrication (or lubrication breakdown) has a number of inter-related causes. Excessive heat (which thins the oil), overloading (which squeezes the oil from the

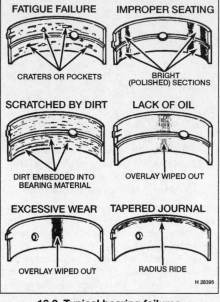

16.2 Typical bearing failures

bearing face) and oil leakage (from excessive bearing clearances, worn oil pump or high engine speeds) all contribute to lubrication breakdown. Blocked oil passages, which usually are the result of misaligned oil holes in a bearing shell, will also starve a bearing of oil, and destroy it. When lack of lubrication is the cause of bearing failure, the bearing material is wiped or extruded from the shell's steel backing. Temperatures may increase to the point where the steel backing turns blue from overheating.

6 Driving habits can have a definite effect on bearing life. Full-throttle, low-speed operation (labouring the engine) puts very high loads on bearings, which tends to squeeze out the oil film. These loads cause the shells to flex, which produces fine cracks in the bearing face (fatigue failure). Eventually, the bearing material will loosen in pieces, and tear away from the steel backing. Short-distance driving leads to corrosion of bearings, because insufficient engine heat is produced to drive off condensed water and corrosive gases. These products collect in the engine oil, forming acid and sludge. As the oil is carried to the engine bearings, the acid attacks and corrodes the bearing material.

7 Incorrect shell refitting during engine assembly will lead to bearing failure as well. Tight-fitting shells leave insufficient bearing running clearance, and will result in oil starvation. Dirt or foreign particles trapped behind a bearing shell result in high spots on the bearing, which lead to failure. Do not touch any shell's bearing surface with your fingers during reassembly; there is a risk of scratching the delicate surface, or of depositing particles of dirt on it.

17 Engine overhaul – reassembly sequence

1 Before reassembly begins, ensure that all new parts have been obtained, and that all necessary tools are available. Read through the entire procedure, to familiarise yourself with the work involved, and to ensure that all items necessary for reassembly of the engine are at hand.

2 In addition to all normal tools and materials, suitable sealant will be required for certain seal surfaces. The various sealants recommended by Ford appear in the relevant procedures in Chapter 2A, 2B or 2C. In all other cases, provided the relevant mating surfaces are clean and flat, new gaskets will be sufficient to ensure joints are oil-tight. *Do not* use any kind of silicone-based sealant on any part of the fuel system or inlet manifold, and *never* use exhaust sealants upstream of the catalytic converter (between the engine and the converter).

Caution: Certain types of high-volatility RTV can foul the oxygen sensor and cause it to fail. Be sure that any RTV used is a low-volatility type and meets Ford specifications for use on engines equipped with an oxygen sensor.

3 In order to save time and avoid problems, engine reassembly can be carried out in the following order:
a) Crankshaft (Section 19).
b) Piston/connecting rod assemblies (Section 20).
c) Oil pump (Chapter 2A, 2B or 2C).
d) Sump (Chapter 2A, 2B or 2C).
e) Flywheel/driveplate (Chapter 2A, 2B or 2C).
f) Injection pump – diesel engines (Chapter 4B). **Note:** *Prior to fitting the injection pump, ensure that the rigid coolant pipe which connects to the oil/water pump housing is fully refitted. Once the injection pump is in place, there is no room to fit this pipe.*
g) Cylinder head (Chapter 2A, 2B or 2C).
h) Timing belt and toothed pulleys (Chapter 2A, 2B or 2C).
i) Engine external components.

4 At this stage, all engine components should be absolutely clean and dry, with all faults repaired. All components should be neatly arranged on a completely clean work surface or in individual containers.

18 Piston rings – refitting

1 Before installing new piston rings, check the end gaps. Lay out each piston set with a piston/connecting rod assembly, and keep them together as a matched set from now on.
2 Insert the top compression ring into the first cylinder, and square it up with the cylinder

18.3 With the ring square in the bore, measure the end gap with a feeler gauge

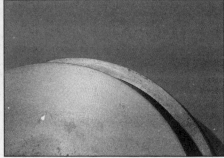

18.6a Look for etched markings (STD – indicating a standard-sized ring) identifying piston ring top surface

walls by pushing it in with the top of the piston. The ring should be near the bottom of the cylinder, at the lower limit of ring travel.

3 To measure the end gap, slip feeler gauges between the ends of the ring, until a gauge equal to the gap width is found **(see illustration)**. The feeler gauge should slide between the ring ends with a slight amount of drag. Compare the measurement to the value given in the Specifications Section of this Chapter; if the gap is larger or smaller than specified, double-check to make sure you have the correct rings before proceeding. If you are assessing the condition of used rings, have the cylinder bores checked and measured by a Ford dealer or similar engine reconditioning specialist, so that you can be sure of exactly which component is worn, and seek advice as to the best course of action to take.

4 If the end gap is still too small, it must be opened up by careful filing of the ring ends using a fine file. If it is too large, very careful checking is required of the dimensions of all components, as well as of the new parts.

5 Repeat the procedure for each ring that will be installed in the first cylinder, and for each

ring in the remaining cylinders. Remember to keep rings, pistons and cylinders matched up.

6 Refit the piston rings as follows. Where the original rings are being refitted, use the marks or notes made on removal, to ensure that each ring is refitted to its original groove and the same way up. New rings generally have their top surfaces identified by markings (often an indication of size, such as STD, or the word TOP) – the rings must be fitted with such markings uppermost **(see illustrations)**. **Note:** *Always follow the instructions printed on the ring package or box – different manufacturers may require different approaches. Do not mix up the top and second compression rings, as they usually have different cross-sections.*

7 The oil control ring (lowest one on the piston) is usually installed first. It is composed of three separate elements. Slip the spacer/expander into the groove. Next, install the lower side rail. Don't use a piston ring installation tool on the oil ring side rails, as they may be damaged. Instead, place one end of the side rail into the groove between the spacer/expander and the ring land, hold it firmly in place, and slide a finger around the piston while pushing the rail into the groove. Next, install the upper side rail in the same manner **(see illustrations)**.

8 After the three oil ring components have been installed, check that both the upper and lower side rails can be turned smoothly in the ring groove.

9 The second compression (middle) ring is installed next, followed by the top compression ring – ensure their marks are uppermost. Don't expand either ring any more than necessary to slide it over the top of the piston.

10 With all the rings in position, space the ring gaps (including the elements of the oil control ring) uniformly around the piston at 120° intervals. Repeat the procedure for the remaining pistons and rings.

19 Crankshaft (except 1.4 & 1.6 litre engines) – refitting and main bearing clearance check

1 Crankshaft refitting is the first major step in engine reassembly. It is assumed at this point that the cylinder block/crankcase and crankshaft have been cleaned, inspected and repaired or reconditioned as necessary. Position the engine upside-down.

2 Remove the main bearing cap bolts, and lift out the caps. Lay the caps out in the proper order, to ensure correct installation.

3 If they're still in place, remove the old bearing shells from the block and the main bearing caps. Wipe the bearing recesses with a clean, lint-free cloth. They must be kept spotlessly clean.

Main bearing running clearance check

4 Clean the backs of the new main bearing shells. Fit the shells with an oil groove in each main bearing location in the block. Note the thrustwashers integral with the No 3 (centre) upper main bearing shell, or the thrustwasher halves fitted either side of No 3 upper main bearing location. Fit the other shell from each bearing set in the corresponding main bearing cap. Make sure the tab on each bearing shell fits into the notch in the block or cap/lower crankcase. Also, the oil holes in the block must line up with the oil holes in the bearing shell **(see illustrations)**. Don't hammer the shells into place, and don't nick or gouge the bearing faces. No lubrication should be used at this time.

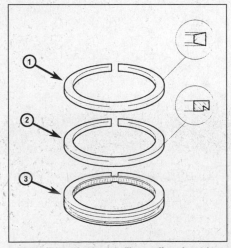

18.6b Piston ring profiles – diesel engine

1 Top compression ring
2 Lower compression ring
3 Oil control ring

18.7a Installing the spacer/expander in the oil control ring groove

18.7b DO NOT use a piston ring installation tool when installing the oil ring side rails

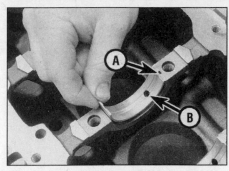

19.4a Ensure that the tab (A) and oil hole (B) are correctly aligned when refitting the shells

19.4b Note the thrustwashers fitted to No 3 main bearing shell

19.6 Lay the Plastigauge strips on the main bearing journals, parallel to the crankshaft centre-line

5 Clean the bearing surfaces of the shells in the block and the crankshaft main bearing journals with a clean, lint-free cloth. Check or clean the oil holes in the crankshaft, as any dirt here will go straight through the new bearings.

6 Once you're certain the crankshaft is clean, carefully lay it in position in the main bearings. Trim several pieces of the appropriate-size Plastigauge (they must be slightly shorter than the width of the main bearings), and place one piece on each crankshaft main bearing journal, parallel with the crankshaft centre-line (see illustration).

7 Clean the bearing surfaces of the caps and shells, then fit the shells to the main bearing caps (see illustration). Install the caps in their respective positions (don't mix them up) with the arrows pointing to the timing belt end of the engine. Don't disturb the Plastigauge.

8 Working on one cap at a time, from the centre main bearing outwards (and ensuring that each cap is tightened down squarely and evenly onto the block), tighten the main bearing cap bolts to the specified torque wrench setting.

9 Remove the bolts, and carefully lift off the main bearing caps. Don't disturb the Plastigauge or rotate the crankshaft. If any of the main bearing caps are difficult to remove, tap them gently from side-to-side with a soft-faced mallet to loosen them.

10 Compare the width of the crushed Plastigauge on each journal with the scale printed on the Plastigauge envelope to obtain the main bearing running clearance (see illustration). Check the Specifications to make sure that the clearance is correct.

11 If the clearance is not as specified, seek the advice of a Ford dealer or similar engine reconditioning specialist – if the crankshaft journals are in good condition, it may be possible simply to renew the shells to achieve the correct clearance. If this is not possible, the crankshaft must be reground by a specialist who can supply the necessary undersized shells. First though, make sure that no dirt or oil was between the bearing shells and the caps or block when the clearance was measured. If the Plastigauge is noticeably wider at one end than the other,

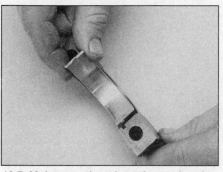

19.7 Make sure the tab on the cap bearing shell engages correctly

the journal may be tapered.

12 Carefully scrape all traces of the Plastigauge material off the main bearing journals and the bearing surfaces. Be very careful not to scratch the bearing – use your fingernail or the edge of a credit card.

Final refitting

13 Carefully lift the crankshaft out of the engine. Clean the bearing surfaces of the shells in the block, then apply a thin, uniform layer of clean molybdenum disulphide-based grease, engine assembly lubricant, or clean engine oil to each surface (see illustration). Coat the thrustwasher surfaces as well.

14 Lubricate the crankshaft oil seal journals with molybdenum disulphide-based grease, engine assembly lubricant, or clean engine oil.

19.10 Compare the width of the crushed Plastigauge to the scale on the envelope to determine the main bearing running clearance

15 Make sure the crankshaft journals are clean, then lay the crankshaft back in place in the block (see illustration).

16 Refit and tighten the main bearing caps as follows:

a) Clean the bearing surfaces of the shells in the caps, then lubricate them. Refit the caps in their respective positions, with the arrows pointing to the timing belt end of the engine.

b) Working on one cap at a time, from the centre main bearing outwards (and ensuring that each cap is tightened down squarely and evenly onto the block), tighten the main bearing cap bolts to the specified torque wrench setting (see illustration).

19.13 Oil the bearing shells before fitting the crankshaft

19.15 Fitting the crankshaft

19.16 Tightening the main bearing caps

17 Rotate the crankshaft a number of times by hand, to check for any obvious binding.
18 Check the crankshaft endfloat (see Section 12). It should be correct if the crankshaft thrustwashers/thrust control bearing(s) aren't worn or damaged, or have been renewed.
19 Refit the crankshaft left-hand oil seal carrier and install a new seal (Chapter 2B or 2C).

20 Piston/connecting rod assemblies – refitting and big-end bearing clearance check

1 Before refitting the piston/connecting rod assemblies, the cylinder bores must be perfectly clean, the top edge of each cylinder must be chamfered, and the crankshaft must be in place.

20.3a The location tab on each big-end bearing shell must engage with the notch in the connecting rod or cap . . .

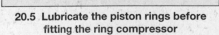

20.5 Lubricate the piston rings before fitting the ring compressor

2 Remove the big-end bearing cap from No 1 cylinder connecting rod (refer to the marks noted or made on removal). Remove the original bearing shells, and wipe the bearing recesses of the connecting rod and cap with a clean, lint-free cloth. They must be kept spotlessly-clean

Big-end bearing running clearance check

3 Clean the back of the new upper bearing shell, fit it to the connecting rod, then fit the other shell of the bearing set to the big-end bearing cap. Make sure the tab on each shell fits into the notch in the rod or cap recess (no tabs are fitted on 1.4 and 1.6 litre engines – ensure that the ends of the shells are flush with the rod/cap mating faces) **(see illustrations)**. Don't lubricate the bearing at this time.
Caution: Don't hammer the shells into place, and don't nick or gouge the bearing face.
4 It's critically important that all mating surfaces of the bearing components are perfectly clean and oil-free when they're assembled.
5 Position the piston ring gaps as described in Section 18, lubricate the piston and rings with clean engine oil, and attach a piston ring compressor to the piston **(see illustration)**. Leave the skirt protruding about a quarter-inch, to guide the piston into the cylinder bore. The rings must be compressed until they're flush with the piston.

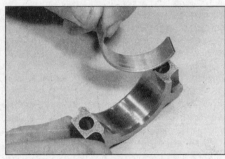

20.3b . . . except on 1.4 & 1.6 litre engines, where the shells must be located centrally, ends flush with the connecting rod/cap mating faces

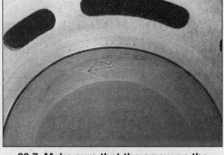

20.7 Make sure that the arrow on the piston crown is facing the timing belt end of the engine

6 Rotate the crankshaft until No 1 crankpin (big-end) journal is at BDC (Bottom Dead Centre), and apply a coat of engine oil to the cylinder walls.
7 Arrange the No 1 piston/connecting rod assembly so that the arrow on the piston crown points to the timing belt end of the engine **(see illustration)**. Gently insert the assembly into the No 1 cylinder bore, and rest the bottom edge of the ring compressor on the engine block.
8 Tap the top edge of the ring compressor to make sure it's contacting the block around its entire circumference.
9 Gently tap on the top of the piston with the end of a wooden hammer handle, while guiding the connecting rod's big-end onto the crankpin. The piston rings may try to pop out of the ring compressor just before entering the cylinder bore, so keep some pressure on the ring compressor **(see illustration)**. Work slowly, and if any resistance is felt as the piston enters the cylinder, stop immediately. Find out what's binding, and fix it before proceeding. Do not, for any reason, force the piston into the cylinder – you might break a ring and/or the piston.
10 To check the big-end bearing running clearance, cut a piece of the appropriate-size Plastigauge slightly shorter than the width of the connecting rod bearing, and lay it in place on the No 1 crankpin (big-end) journal, parallel with the crankshaft centre-line. **Note:** *No big-end running clearance is specified for 1.4 and 1.6 litre engines.*
11 Clean the connecting rod-to-cap mating surfaces, and refit the big-end bearing cap. Make sure the etched number on the cap is on the same side as that on the rod.
12 Tighten each pair of cap bolts first to the specified Stage 1 torque, then through the Stage 2 angle – 90° is the equivalent of a quarter-turn or right-angle, which can easily be judged by assessing the start and end positions of the socket handle or torque wrench used; for accuracy, however, use an angle gauge **(see illustrations)**.
13 Unscrew the bolts and detach the cap, being very careful not to disturb the Plastigauge.

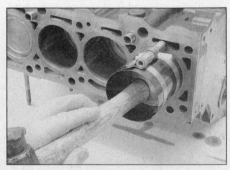

20.9 With the compressor fitted, use the handle of a hammer to gently drive the piston into the cylinder

20.12a Tighten the big-end bearing cap bolts to the specified torque . . .

20.12b . . . then through the specified angle – note the use of an angle gauge

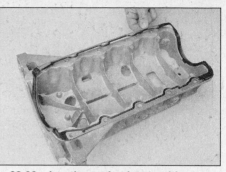

20.22a Lay the gasket into position . . .

14 Compare the width of the crushed Plastigauge to the scale printed on the Plastigauge envelope, to obtain the running clearance. Compare it to the Specifications, to make sure the clearance is correct.

15 If the clearance is not as specified, seek the advice of a Ford dealer or similar engine reconditioning specialist – if the crankshaft journals are in good condition, it may be possible simply to renew the shells to achieve the correct clearance. If this is not possible, the crankshaft must be reground by a specialist, who can also supply the necessary undersized shells. First though, make sure that no dirt or oil was trapped between the bearing shells and the connecting rod or cap when the clearance was measured. Also, recheck the crankpin journal diameter. If the Plastigauge was wider at one end than the other, the crankpin journal may be tapered.

16 Carefully scrape all traces of the Plastigauge material off the journal and the bearing surface. Be very careful not to scratch the bearing – use your fingernail or the edge of a credit card.

Final piston/connecting rod refitting

17 Make sure the bearing surfaces are perfectly clean, then apply a uniform layer of clean molybdenum disulphide-based grease, engine assembly lubricant, or clean engine oil, to both of them. You'll have to push the piston into the cylinder to expose the bearing surface of the shell in the connecting rod.

18 Slide the connecting rod back into place on the crankpin (big-end) journal, refit the big-

end bearing cap, and then tighten the bolts in the stages described above.

19 Repeat the entire procedure for the remaining piston/connecting rod assemblies.

20 The important points to remember are:
a) *Keep the backs of the bearing shells and the recesses of the connecting rods and caps perfectly clean when assembling them.*
b) *Make sure you have the correct piston/rod assembly for each cylinder – use the etched cylinder numbers to identify the front-facing side of both the rod and its cap.*
c) *The arrow on the piston crown must face the timing belt end of the engine.*
d) *Lubricate the cylinder bores with clean engine oil.*
e) *Lubricate the bearing surfaces when refitting the big-end bearing caps after the running clearance has been checked.*

21 After all the piston/connecting rod assemblies have been properly installed, rotate the crankshaft a number of times by hand, to check for any obvious binding.

Except 1.4 and 1.6 litre models

22 Use a little grease to stick the new gasket in place, then offer the lower crankcase into position and loosely secure with the bolts **(see illustrations)**. On diesel engines, the bolts are of two different lengths, with the longer bolts fitted to the 'inside' of the lower crankcase.

23 The lower crankcase must now be aligned with the cylinder block before the bolts are tightened. Using a straight-edge and feeler

20.22b . . . then refit the lower crankcase

blades, check the protrusion or gap all round **(see illustration)**. Spacer shims are available in various thicknesses to correct the alignment – unless new components have been fitted use the same spacers found on removal.

24 Tighten the lower crankcase bolts to the specified torque, ensuring that the alignment with the cylinder block is not lost **(see illustration)**.

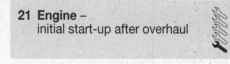

21 Engine – initial start-up after overhaul

1 With the engine refitted in the vehicle, double-check the engine oil and coolant levels. Make a final check that everything has been reconnected, and that there are no tools or rags left in the engine compartment.

2 On petrol models, remove the spark plugs and disable the ignition system by unplugging the ignition coil wiring connectors.

3 On all models, remove fuse No 12 (in the engine compartment fusebox) to disable the fuel pump; this is necessary on petrol models to prevent flooding the catalytic converter with unburnt fuel. On diesel models, the large wiring connector on the injection pump can also be disconnected.

4 Turn the engine on the starter until the oil pressure warning light goes out.

5 As applicable, reconnect all wiring, and refit fuse No 12 and the spark plugs. On petrol models, switch on the ignition and listen for

20.23 Check the alignment of the lower crankcase

20.24 Tighten the lower crankcase bolts to the specified torque

the fuel pump; it will run for a little longer than usual, due to the lack of pressure in the system, but wait until the pump stops running.

6 Start the engine, noting that this also may take a little longer than usual, due to the fuel system components being empty.

7 While the engine is idling, check for fuel, coolant and oil leaks. Don't be alarmed if there are some odd smells and smoke from parts getting hot and burning off oil deposits. The engine may also not idle very well for the first few minutes, until it 'learns' the best idle settings (refer to *Disconnecting the battery*).

8 Keep the engine idling until hot water is felt circulating through the top hose, check that it idles reasonably smoothly and at the usual speed, then switch it off.

9 After a few minutes, recheck the oil and coolant levels, and top-up as necessary (*Weekly checks*).

10 If they were tightened as described, there is no need to re-tighten the cylinder head bolts once the engine has first run after reassembly – in fact, Ford state that the bolts must not be re-tightened.

11 If new components such as pistons, rings or crankshaft bearings have been fitted, the engine must be run-in for the first 500 miles (800 km). Do not operate the engine at full-throttle, or allow it to labour in any gear during this period. It is recommended that the oil and filter be changed at the end of this period.

Chapter 3
Cooling, heating & air conditioning systems

Contents

Degrees of difficulty

Easy, suitable for novice with little experience	Fairly easy, suitable for beginner with some experience	Fairly difficult, suitable for competent DIY mechanic	Difficult, suitable for experienced DIY mechanic	Very difficult, suitable for expert DIY or professional

Specifications

Coolant
Mixture type .... See *Lubricants and fluids*
Cooling system capacity .... See Chapter 1A or 1B

System pressure
Pressure test .... 1.2 bars approximately – see cap for actual value (should hold this pressure for 2 minutes)

Expansion tank filler cap
Pressure rating .... 1.2 bars approximately – see cap for actual value

Thermostat
Petrol engines:
  1.4 litre and 1.6 litre:
    Starts to open .... 82°C
    Fully-open .... 96°C
  1.8 litre and 2.0 litre:
    Starts to open .... 92°C
    Fully-open .... 99°C
Diesel engine:
  Starts to open .... 87°C
  Fully-open .... 102°C

Air conditioning system
Refrigerant R134a
Refrigerant oil capacity when refilling .... 200 cc

Torque wrench settings

	Nm	lbf ft
Air conditioning accumulator/dehydrator-to-subframe bolts	7	5
Air conditioning compressor mounting bolts	24	18
Air conditioning condenser mounting bolts	24	18
Air conditioning high pressure cut-off switch	10	7
Compressor centre pulley bolt	13	10
Coolant pump bolts:		
Petrol engines	9	7
Diesel engines	10	7
Coolant pump housing to cylinder block	18	13
Coolant pump pulley bolts	24	18
Radiator mounting bracket-to-subframe bolts	25	18
Refrigerant line to condenser	8	6
Refrigerant line to compressor	20	15
Refrigerant line connection	8	6
Thermostat housing-to-cylinder head bolts:		
1.8 litre and 2.0 litre petrol engines	20	15
Diesel engines	23	17
Thermostat cover/water outlet-to-thermostat housing bolts	9	7
Timing belt idler pulley (1.8 litre and 2.0 litre petrol engine)	38	28
Timing belt tensioner (diesel engine)	33	24

1 General information

⚠️ **Warning: DO NOT attempt to remove the expansion tank filler cap, or to disturb any part of the cooling system, while it or the engine is hot, as there is a very great risk of scalding. If the expansion tank filler cap must be removed before the engine and radiator have fully cooled down (even though this is not recommended) the pressure in the cooling system must first be released. Cover the cap with a thick layer of cloth, to avoid scalding, and slowly unscrew the filler cap until a hissing sound can be heard. When the hissing has stopped, showing that pressure is released, slowly unscrew the filler cap further until it can be removed; if more hissing sounds are heard, wait until they have stopped before unscrewing the cap completely. At all times, keep well away from the filler opening.**

⚠️ **Warning: Do not allow coolant to come in contact with your skin, or with the painted surfaces of the vehicle. Rinse off spills immediately with plenty of water. Never leave coolant lying around in an open container, or in a puddle in the driveway or on the garage floor. Children and pets are attracted by its sweet smell, but coolant is fatal if ingested.**

⚠️ **Warning: If the engine is hot, the electric cooling fan may start rotating even if the engine is not running, so be careful to keep hands, hair and loose clothing well clear when working in the engine compartment.**

Engine cooling system

All vehicles covered by this manual employ a pressurised engine cooling system with thermostatically-controlled coolant circulation.

The coolant is circulated by an impeller-type pump, bolted to the right-hand end of the cylinder block, inboard of the timing belt. On all models the pump is driven by the crank-shaft pulley via the auxiliary drivebelt. The coolant flows through the cylinder block around each cylinder; in the cylinder head, cast-in coolant passages direct coolant around the inlet and exhaust ports, near the spark plug areas and close to the exhaust valve guides.

A wax type thermostat is located in a housing attached to the engine. During warm-up, the closed thermostat prevents coolant from circulating through the radiator. Instead, it returns through the coolant pipe running across the front of the engine to the radiator or expansion bottle. The supply to the heater is made from the rear of the thermostat housing. As the engine nears normal operating temperature, the thermostat opens and allows hot coolant to travel through the radiator, where it is cooled before returning to the engine.

The radiator is of aluminium construction, and has plastic end tanks. On models with automatic transmission, the fluid cooler is located across the front of the radiator.

The cooling system is sealed by a pressure-type filler cap in the expansion tank. The pressure in the system raises the boiling point of the coolant, and increases the cooling efficiency of the radiator. When the engine is at normal operating temperature, the coolant expands, and the surplus is displaced into the expansion tank. When the system cools, the surplus coolant is automatically drawn back from the tank into the radiator.

The temperature gauge and cooling fan(s) are controlled by the cylinder head temperature (CHT) sensor that transmits a signal to the engine electronic control module (ECU) to operate them.

Fail-Safe cooling system mode

The cooling system is fitted with a fail-safe mode, this comes into operation in stages when the operating temperature of the engine is to high.

Stage 1

The CHT sensor transmits a signal to the engine ECU, which then moves the gauge into the red zone.

If the engine is not switched off and the temperature continues to rise the multi-function warning light will come on.

Stage 2

The engine ECU will control the engine by starting to cut out two cylinders and restricting the engine to below 3000 rpm. When this occurs the engine warning light will also illuminate.

Note: *If the temperature should drop to normal, the ignition will have to be switched off and then on again, to revert back to four cylinders. The warning light can only be extinguished by a fault code reader, see your local dealer.*

Stage 3

If the engine temperature continues to rise, the engine will be totally disabled before major engine damage occurs. The engine warning light will begin to flash, indicating to the driver that the engine will be switched off after 30 seconds.

Heating/ventilation system

The heating system consists of a blower fan and heater matrix (radiator) located in the heater unit, with hoses connecting the heater matrix to the engine cooling system. Hot engine coolant is circulated through the heater matrix. When the heater temperature control on the facia is operated, a flap door opens to expose the heater box to the passenger compartment. When the blower control is operated, the blower fan forces air through the unit according to the setting selected. The heater controls are linked to the flap doors by cables.

Incoming fresh air for the ventilation system passes through a pollen filter mounted below the windscreen cowl panel (see the relevant part of Chapter 1) – this ensures that most particles will be removed before the air enters the cabin. However, it is vital that the pollen filter is changed regularly, since a blocked filter will significantly reduce airflow to the cabin, leading to ineffective de-misting.

The ventilation system air distribution is controlled by cable-operated flap doors on the heater housing. All the vehicles have a recirculated air function, with the flap being controlled by a servo motor.

Air conditioning system

See Section 11.

2 Engine coolant (antifreeze) – general information

⚠️ **Warning: Engine coolant (antifreeze) contains monoethylene glycol and other constituents, which are toxic if taken internally. They can also be absorbed into the skin after prolonged contact.**

Note: Refer to the relevant part of Chapter 1 for further information on coolant renewal.

The cooling system should be filled with a water/monoethylene glycol-based coolant solution, of a strength which will prevent freezing down to at least –25°C, or lower if the local climate requires it. Coolant also provides protection against corrosion, and increases the boiling point.

The cooling system should be maintained according to the schedule described in the relevant part of Chapter 1. If the engine coolant used is old or contaminated it is likely to cause damage, and encourage the formation of corrosion and scale in the system. Use coolant which is to Ford's specification and to the correct concentration.

Before adding the coolant, check all hoses and hose connections, because coolant tends to leak through very small openings. Engines don't normally consume coolant, so if the level goes down, find the cause and correct it.

The engine coolant concentration should be between 40% and 55%. If the concentration drops below 40% there will be insufficient protection, this must then be brought back to specification. Hydrometers are available at most automotive accessory shops to test the coolant concentration.

3 Cooling system hoses – disconnection and renewal

Note: Refer to the warnings given in Section 1 of this Chapter before starting work.

1 If the checks described in the relevant part of Chapter 1 reveal a faulty hose, it must be renewed as follows.

2 First drain the cooling system (see the relevant part of Chapter 1); if the coolant is not due for renewal, the drained coolant may be re-used, if it is collected in a clean container.

3 To disconnect any hose, use a pair of pliers to release the spring clamps (or a screwdriver to slacken screw-type clamps), then move them along the hose clear of the union. Carefully work the hose off its stubs **(see illustration)**. The hoses can be removed with relative ease when new – on an older car, they may have stuck.

4 If a hose proves stubborn, try to release it by rotating it on its unions before attempting to work it off. Gently prise the end of the hose with a blunt instrument (such as a flat-bladed screwdriver), but do not apply too much force, and take care not to damage the pipe stubs or hoses. Note in particular that the radiator hose unions are fragile; do not use excessive force when attempting to remove the hoses. If all else fails, cut the hose with a sharp knife, then slit it so that it can be peeled off in two pieces. While expensive, this is preferable to buying a new radiator. Check first, however, that a new hose is readily available.

5 When refitting a hose, first slide the clamps onto the hose, then work the hose onto its unions. If the hose is stiff, use soap (or washing-up liquid) as a lubricant, or soften it by soaking it in boiling water, but take care to prevent scalding.

6 Work each hose end fully onto its union, then check that the hose is settled correctly and is properly routed. Slide each clip along the hose until it is behind the union flared end, before tightening it securely.

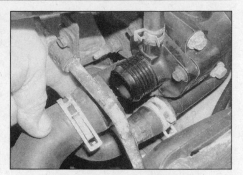

3.3 Removing the coolant hose

7 Refill the system with coolant (see the relevant part of Chapter 1).

8 Check carefully for leaks as soon as possible after disturbing any part of the cooling system.

4 Thermostat – removal, testing and refitting

Note: Refer to the warnings given in Section 1 of this Chapter before starting work.

Removal

1 Disconnect the battery negative (earth) lead (see Chapter 5A, Section 1).

2 Drain the cooling system (see the relevant part of Chapter 1). If the coolant is relatively new or in good condition, drain it into a clean container and re-use it.

1.4 litre and 1.6 litre petrol engines

3 Where required, remove the alternator as described in Chapter 5A.

4 Disconnect the radiator coolant hose and the heater hose from the thermostat housing **(see illustration)**.

5 Unbolt the thermostat cover and withdraw the thermostat **(see illustration)**. Note the position of the air bleed valve, and how the thermostat is installed (ie, which end is facing outwards).

1.8 litre and 2.0 litre petrol engines

6 Slacken and remove the three bolts from the thermostat cover and withdraw from the thermostat housing **(see illustration)**.

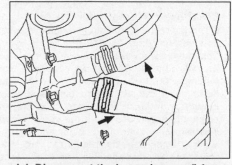

4.4 Disconnect the hoses (arrowed) from the thermostat housing

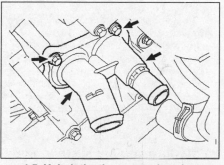

4.5 Unbolt the thermostat housing

4.6 Pull thermostat cover back to remove the thermostat

4.7 Arrow shows the position of the air bleed valve

4.8 Remove the thermostat rubber seal

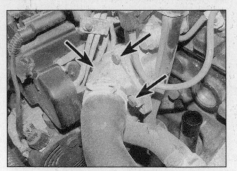

4.11 Undo the three thermostat cover bolts (arrowed)

7 Withdraw the thermostat, noting the position of the air bleed valve **(see illustration)**, and how the thermostat is installed (ie, which end is facing outwards).
8 Remove the thermostat rubber seal **(see illustration)**. (Install a new seal on refitting.)

Diesel engines

Note: *A new thermostat sealing ring will be required on refitting.*

9 Proceed as described in paragraphs 1 and 2. Remove the air inter cooler as described in Chapter 4b, Section 18.
10 Disconnect the radiator coolant hose from the thermostat housing (if required).
11 Unscrew the securing bolts, and lift off the thermostat cover **(see illustration)**.
12 Note the position of the air bleed valve, and how the thermostat is installed (ie, which end is facing outwards). Lift out the thermostat and recover the sealing ring.

Testing

General

13 Before assuming the thermostat is to blame for a cooling system problem, check the coolant level (see *Weekly checks*), the auxiliary drivebelt tension and condition (see the relevant part of Chapter 1) and the temperature gauge operation.
14 If the engine seems to be taking a long time to warm up (based on heater output or temperature gauge operation), the thermostat is probably stuck open. Renew the thermostat.
15 Equally, a lengthy warm-up period might suggest that the thermostat is missing – it may have been removed or inadvertently omitted by a previous owner or mechanic. Don't drive the vehicle without a thermostat – the engine management system's ECU will stay in warm-up mode for longer than necessary, causing emissions and fuel economy to suffer.
16 If the engine runs hot, use your hand to check the temperature of the radiator top hose. If the hose isn't hot, but the engine is, the thermostat is probably stuck closed, preventing the coolant inside the engine from escaping to the radiator – renew the thermostat.
17 If the radiator top hose is hot, it means

that the coolant is flowing and the thermostat is open. Consult the *Fault finding* Section at the end of this manual to assist in tracing possible cooling system faults.

Thermostat test

18 If the thermostat remains in the open position at room temperature, it is faulty, and must be renewed as a matter of course.
19 To test it fully, suspend the (closed) thermostat on a length of string in a container of cold water, with a thermometer beside it; ensure that neither touches the side of the container.
20 Heat the water, and check the temperature at which the thermostat begins to open; compare this value with that specified. Checking the fully-open temperature may not be possible in an open container, if it is higher than the boiling point of water at atmospheric pressure. Remove the thermostat and allow it to cool down; check that it closes fully.
21 If the thermostat does not open and close as described, if it sticks in either position, or if it does not open at the specified temperature, it must be renewed.

Refitting

22 Refitting is the reverse of the removal procedure, noting the following points:
a) *Clean the mating surfaces carefully, and renew the thermostat's sealing ring.*
b) *Fit the thermostat in the same position as noted on removal.*
c) *Tighten the thermostat cover/housing bolts to the specified torque wrench setting.*

5.1 Undo the retaining screw and lift out the resistor

d) *Remake all the coolant hose connections, then refill the cooling system as described in the relevant part of Chapter 1.*
e) *Start the engine and allow it to reach normal operating temperature, then check for leaks and proper thermostat operation.*

5 Radiator electric cooling fan(s) – testing, removal and refitting

Note: *Refer to the warnings given in Section 1 of this Chapter before starting work.*

Testing

1 The radiator cooling fan is controlled by the engine management system's ECU, acting on the information received from the cylinder head temperature sensor. Where twin fans or two-speed fans are fitted, control is through a resistor assembly, secured to the top of the fan shroud – this can be renewed separately if faulty **(see illustration)**.
2 First, check the relevant fuses and relays (see Chapter 12).
3 To test the fan motor, unplug the electrical connector, and use fused jumper wires to connect the fan directly to the battery. If the fan still does not work, renew the motor.
4 If the motor proved sound, the fault lies in the cylinder head temperature sensor (see Section 6), in the wiring loom (see Chapter 12 for testing details) or in the engine management system (see Chapter 4A).

Removal

5 Disconnect the battery negative (earth) lead (see Chapter 5A, Section 1).
6 Unplug the cooling fan electrical connector(s), and release the wiring loom from the fan shroud.
7 Unclip the shroud from its upper radiator mountings, then lift the assembly to disengage it from its lower mountings.
8 Withdraw the fan(s) and shroud as an assembly from underneath the vehicle **(see illustration)**.
9 The fan(s) can be removed from the motor(s) by disengaging the clip **(see illustration)**, then pull the fan off the motor shaft **(see illustration)**.

10 Undo the securing screws from the motor assembly to remove the motor from the shroud **(see illustration)**. The wiring connectors may need to be taken out of the multi-plug to remove the motor(s) from the shroud.

Refitting

11 Refitting is the reverse of the removal procedure, noting the following points:
a) *When refitting the fan to the motor, make sure it has located correctly before refitting the retaining clip.*
b) *Ensure that the shroud is settled correctly at all four mounting points before finally clipping into position.*

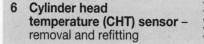

6 Cylinder head temperature (CHT) sensor – removal and refitting

Note: *Refer to the warnings given in Section 1 of this Chapter before starting work.*
1 On 1.4 litre and 1.6 litre petrol engines, the sensor is screwed into the top of the cylinder head between number 2 and 3 spark plugs.
2 On 1.8 litre and 2.0 litre petrol engines, the sensor is screwed into the back of the cylinder head, nearest the timing belt end and below the inlet manifold.
3 On Diesel engines, the sensor is screwed into the gearbox end of the cylinder head.

Removal

1.4 litre and 1.6 litre petrol engines

Note: *A new CHT sensor must be fitted every*

6.4 Remove the cylinder head cover

6.9 Unscrew the sensor arrowed

5.8 Lower the assembly to remove from below the vehicle

5.9b . . . then pull the fan off the motor shaft

time it is removed, as the mating face is distorted when installed.
4 Where applicable, unbolt the cylinder head cover from the spark plug leads **(see illustration)**.

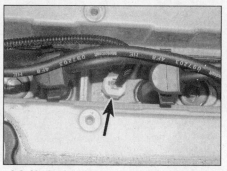

6.6 Undo the sensor arrowed and renew

6.11 Unbolt and remove the crankcase vent

5.9a Using a drift, tap off the retaining clip . . .

5.10 Undo the screws arrowed to remove the fan motor

5 Disconnect the wiring connector from the sensor.
6 Slacken and remove the sensor from the cylinder head **(see illustration)**.

1.8 litre and 2.0 litre petrol engines

7 Remove the alternator as described in Chapter 5A.
8 Disconnect the wiring connector from the sensor.
9 Slacken and remove the sensor from the rear of the cylinder head **(see illustration)**.

Diesel engine

10 Disconnect the battery negative lead with reference to Chapter 5A, Section 1.
11 Unbolt the crankcase vent oil separator from the end of the cylinder head and move to one side **(see illustration)** – the vent hoses may need to be removed to gain better access.
12 Disconnect the wiring connector from the sensor **(see illustration)**.

6.12 Disconnect the wiring connector and remove the sensor (arrowed)

7.2 Unclip the lower radiator cover from the rear of the front bumper

7.4a Using a cable tie (arrowed), to support the condenser and . . .

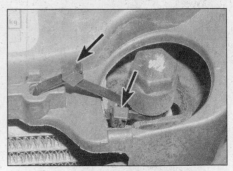

7.4b . . . two cable ties (arrowed) to support the other side

13 Slacken and remove the sensor from the end of the cylinder head.

Refitting

14 Refitting is the reverse of the removal procedure, noting the following points:
a) Screw in the sensor, tighten it securely and reconnect its electrical connector.
b) Refit any hoses and components removed for access.

---

7 Radiator and expansion tank – removal, inspection and refitting

Note: *Refer to the warnings given in Section 1 of this Chapter before starting work.*

Radiator

Removal

Note: *If leakage is the reason for removing the radiator, bear in mind that minor leaks can often be cured using a radiator sealant added to the coolant with the radiator in situ.*

1 Remove the radiator fan and shroud assembly as described in Section 5. **Note:** *On 1.4 litre and 1.6 litre vehicles, the fan and shroud assembly can be removed with the radiator.*

2 To provide greater clearance for the radiator to be lowered and removed, ensure that the handbrake is firmly applied, then raise and support the front of the car on axle stands (see *Jacking and vehicle support*). Remove the radiator lower cover **(see illustration)**.

3 Drain the cooling system (see the relevant part of Chapter 1). Disconnect all the hoses from the radiator.

4 On vehicles with air conditioning, support the condenser from the front top crossmember to keep it in position **(see illustrations)**.

 Warning: Do not disconnect any of the refrigerant hoses.

5 Remove the two bolts (each side) from the mounting bracket below the radiator **(see illustration)** (disconnect the electrical connector on the horn if required); retrieve the bottom mounting rubbers **(see illustration)**, noting which way up they are fitted, and store them carefully.

6 Carefully unclip the radiator from the air conditioning condenser (where fitted) and withdraw it from the vehicle. Leaving the air conditioning condenser in place **(see illustrations)**.

Inspection

7 With the radiator removed, it can be inspected for leaks and damage. If it needs repair, have a radiator specialist or dealer service department perform the work, as special techniques are required.

8 Insects and dirt can be removed from the radiator with a garden hose or a soft brush. Take care not to damage the cooling fins as this is being done.

Refitting

9 Refitting is the reverse of the removal procedure, noting the following points:
a) Be sure the mounting rubbers are seated properly at the base of the radiator.

7.5a Undo the four bolts from the mounting bracket (two arrowed) . . .

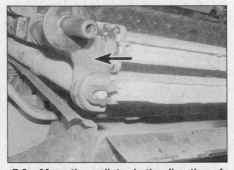

7.6a Move the radiator in the direction of the arrow to unclip from the condenser

b) After refitting, refill the cooling system with the recommended coolant (see the relevant part of Chapter 1).
c) Start the engine, and check for leaks. Allow the engine to reach normal operating temperature, indicated by the radiator top hose becoming hot. Once the engine has cooled (ideally, leave overnight), recheck the coolant level, and add more if required.

Expansion tank

10 With the engine completely cool, remove the expansion tank filler cap to release any pressure, then refit the cap.

11 Disconnect the hoses from the tank **(see illustration)**, upper hose first. As each hose is disconnected, drain the tank's contents into a clean container. If the coolant is not due for renewal, the drained coolant may be re-used, if it is kept clean.

7.5b . . . and remove the bottom mounting rubbers

7.6b Air conditioning condenser supported by cable ties

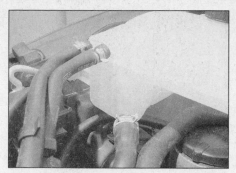

7.11 Disconnect the three hoses from the expansion tank

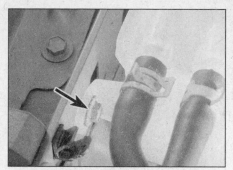

7.12a Remove the mounting bolt (arrowed) . . .

7.12b . . . and lift off locating clip (arrowed)

12 Unscrew the tank's mounting bolt and lift out from the inner strut panel (see illustrations).
13 Wash out the tank, and inspect it for cracks and chafing – renew it if damaged.
14 Refitting is the reverse of the removal procedure. Refill the cooling system with the recommended coolant (see the relevant part of Chapter 1), then start the engine and allow it to reach normal operating temperature, indicated by the radiator top hose becoming hot. Recheck the coolant level and add more if required, then check for leaks.

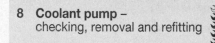

8 Coolant pump –
checking, removal and refitting

Note: *Refer to the warnings given in Section 1 of this Chapter before starting work.*

Checking

1 A failure in the coolant pump can cause serious engine damage due to overheating.
2 There are three ways to check the operation of the coolant pump while it's installed on the engine. If the pump is defective, it should be replaced with a new or rebuilt unit.
3 With the engine running at normal operating temperature, squeeze the radiator top hose. If the coolant pump is working properly, a pressure surge should be felt as the hose is released.

 Warning: Keep your hands away from the radiator electric cooling fan blades.

4 Coolant pumps are equipped with weep or vent holes. If a failure occurs in the pump seal, coolant will leak from the hole. In most cases you'll need a torch to find the hole on the coolant pump from underneath to check for leaks.
5 The coolant pump is at the timing belt end of the engine – to check for a leak, it may be helpful to remove the timing belt covers, as described in Chapter 2A, 2B or 2C.
6 If the coolant pump shaft bearings fail, there may be a howling sound at the drivebelt end of the engine while it's running. Shaft wear can be felt if the coolant pump pulley is rocked up and down.
7 Don't mistake drivebelt slippage, which causes a squealing sound, for coolant pump bearing failure.

Removal

Petrol engines

8 Disconnect the battery negative lead with reference to Chapter 5A, Section 1.
9 Drain the cooling system (see Chapter 1A).
10 Slacken the coolant pump pulley bolts (four bolts on the 1.4 litre and 1.6 litre, three bolts on the 1.8 litre and 2.0 litre).
11 Remove the auxiliary drivebelt as described in Chapter 1A.
12 Undo and remove the coolant pump pulley (see illustration).
13 On the 1.8 litre and 2.0 litre engines, the pump can now be unbolted from the housing (see illustration). If the coolant pump housing requires removing, carry on with the following paragraphs.

14 Remove the timing belt as described in Chapter 2A or 2B. If the belt is fouled with coolant, it must be renewed as a matter of course, also if the belt is approaching its scheduled renewal (see Chapter 1A).
15 On 1.8 litre and 2.0 litre engines, disconnect the coolant hose from the coolant pump housing, and unbolt the timing belt idler pulley.
16 Unscrew the pump/housing retaining bolts and manoeuvre the coolant pump out of the engine compartment (see illustration). Recover the sealing ring or gasket.

Diesel engines

17 Disconnect the battery negative lead with reference to Chapter 5A, Section 1.
18 Drain the cooling system as described in Chapter 1B.
19 Slacken the coolant pump pulley bolts, then remove the auxiliary drivebelt as described in Chapter 1B.
20 Unbolt the coolant pump pulley and remove.
21 Remove the timing belt cover and engine mounting as described in Chapter 2C. The engine must be supported as the engine front mounting is disconnected; support the engine from above with a hoist or engine support bar, if available. If the engine is supported from below with a trolley jack, use a wide block of wood between the jack head and the sump, to spread the load.
22 Remove the four bolts securing the engine front mounting bracket to the block, then lift the engine up by approximately 20 mm.

8.12 Removing the coolant pump pulley (1.8 litre and 2.0 litre petrol engine)

8.13 Undo the four coolant pump retaining bolts (1.8 litre and 2.0 litre petrol engines)

8.16 Coolant pump housing on the 1.8 litre and 2.0 litre

8.23 Removing the coolant pump from the cylinder block

8.24 Fit new coolant pump gasket engines

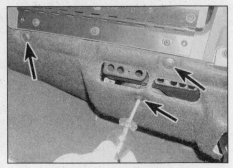

9.2 Undo the three screws (arrowed) to remove the footwell trim

23 Unscrew the seven coolant pump securing bolts and withdraw the pump (see illustration). Recover the gasket.

Refitting

24 Clean the pump mating surfaces carefully; the gasket must be renewed whenever it is disturbed (see illustration). Refit the pump and tighten the bolts to the specified torque wrench setting.

25 The remainder of the refitting procedure is the reverse of dismantling, noting the following points:
a) Tighten all fixings to the specified torque wrench settings (where given).
b) Where applicable, check the timing belt for contamination and renew if required, as described in the relevant part of Chapter 2.
c) On completion, refill the cooling system

as described in the relevant part of Chapter 1.

| 9 | Heater/ventilation components – removal and refitting |

Heater blower motor

Removal

1 Disconnect the battery negative (earth) lead (see Chapter 5A, Section 1).
2 Remove the three screws securing the lower passenger side footwell trim (see illustration), then withdraw the panel from the vehicle.
3 Remove the three screws from the glovebox hinge, and remove the glovebox, pushing in at both sides to release from the facia (see illustrations).

4 Undo the securing screw, and detach the ventilation hose from the motor assembly (see illustrations).
5 Unplug the motor's electrical connector, and undo the three screws securing the motor in place. Remove the motor from the housing (see illustrations).
6 The motor's control resistor can be removed by undoing the screw at one end of the resistor, then pull the resistor out of the heater housing (see illustration).

Refitting

7 Refitting is the reverse of the removal procedure.

Heater matrix

Removal

8 Disconnect the battery negative (earth) lead (see Chapter 5A, Section 1).

9.3a Remove the three lower screws from the glovebox hinge . . .

9.3b . . . then push both sides of the glovebox in to remove

9.4a Remove the screw from the air vent . . .

9.4b . . . and pull out from the heater assembly

9.5a Disconnect the wiring connector and remove the screws . . .

9.5b . . . then lower the heater blower motor from the housing

9.6 The resistor is to the right of the heater blower motor

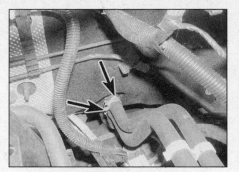

9.10 The two heater hoses must be disconnected (arrowed)

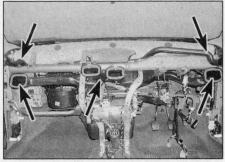

9.12 Undo and remove the five ventilation hoses (arrowed)

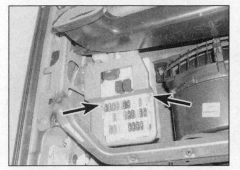

9.14 Undo the two screws (arrowed) from the fusebox

9.15a Undo the three bolts (arrowed) at each end of the crossmember . . .

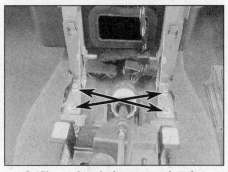

9.15b . . . four bolts arrowed at the centre . . .

9 Apply the handbrake, then raise and support the front of the car on axle stands. Drain the cooling system (see the relevant part of Chapter 1).

10 Disconnect the coolant hoses from the

9.15c . . . and, on the right-hand side, unclip the cap from the front pillar and remove the securing bolt

heater matrix unions protruding through the engine compartment bulkhead (see illustration).

11 Working inside the passenger compartment, remove the facia as described in Chapter 11.

12 Unclip the five ventilation hoses from the crash pad crossmember, and detach them from the heater housing (see illustration).

13 Working your way around the crash pad crossmember, unclip the wiring loom and undo the securing bolts for any earth connections.

14 Remove the two securing bolts from the fusebox (see illustration).

15 Undo the securing bolts from the ends of the crash pad crossmember bracket, including the one inside the right-hand pillar. Undo the centre securing bolts, then remove the crossmember from the bulkhead (see illustrations).

16 Undo the retaining screws and unclip the bottom sections from the heater unit (see illustration).

17 Detach the securing clips from the heater unit casing, and undo the screws to release the heater matrix lower casing (see illustration).

18 Undo the screw to release the retaining bracket from the heater matrix inside the casing (take care not to damage the heater matrix on removal) (see illustration).

Refitting

19 Refitting is the reverse of the removal procedure. Additional metal clips may be required to secure the heater unit's bottom casing to the heater unit as the plastic ones may break on removal.

20 Refill the cooling system with the recommended coolant (see the relevant part of Chapter 1). Start the engine and allow it to

9.16 Remove both parts of the lower heater casing

9.17 Heater matrix comes out with the casing

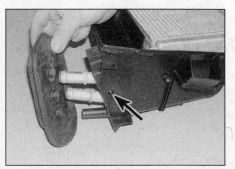

9.18 Remove the foam seal and the securing screw (arrowed)

9.22 Carefully lever out the air vents

9.23 Vent can be pushed out from the rear of the facia

reach normal operating temperature, indicated by the radiator top hose becoming hot. Recheck the coolant level and add more if required, then check for leaks. Check the operation of the heater.

Pollen filter

21 Refer to the relevant part of Chapter 1.

Facia vents

22 Using a flat-bladed instrument, and a pad to protect the facia, prise out the vents from the facia panel (see illustration).
23 It may be necessary to remove: the glovebox (Chapter 11) to aid the removal of the passenger air vent (see illustration); the radio/cassette (Chapter 12) to aid the removal of the centre air vents; and the main light switch (Chapter 12) to aid the removal of the driver's air vent.
24 Refitting is a reversal of removal.

10 Heater/air conditioning controls – removal and refitting

Heater control panel

1 Disconnect the battery negative (earth) lead (see Chapter 5A, Section 1).
2 Remove the radio/cassette player as described in Chapter 12. Pull out and remove the ashtray.
3 Undo the four securing screws from inside the radio/cassette player aperture (see illustration), then carefully unclip the heater control panel from the facia.
4 Taking careful note of all their locations, disconnect the various wiring connectors from the rear of the panel and unclip the heater operating cables from the temperature and direction controls (see illustration).

5 Make sure that nothing remains attached to the panel, then withdraw it from the facia.

Blower, direction and temperature controls

6 Remove the heater control panel as described above.
7 Remove the four securing screws at the back of the control panel and withdraw the control switch assembly. If not already done, pull off the control knobs, then remove the retaining screw from the back of the switch, twist them to release from the switch assembly (see illustrations).
8 Refitting is the reverse of the removal procedure. Check the operation of the controls on completion.

Air conditioning switch

9 Remove the heater control panel as described above.
10 Undo the securing screws from the back of the control panel to release the switch assembly (the air conditioning, air recirculation, heated rear screen and heated front screen switches are a single complete assembly) (see illustration).
11 Refitting is the reverse of the removal procedure. Check the operation of the switches on completion.

11 Air conditioning system – general information and precautions

General information

The air conditioning system consists of a condenser mounted in front of the radiator, an evaporator mounted adjacent to the heater matrix, a compressor driven by an auxiliary drivebelt, an accumulator/dehydrator, and the plumbing connecting all of the above components – this contains a choke (or 'venturi') mounted in the inlet to the evaporator, which creates the drop in pressure required to produce the cooling effect.

A blower fan forces the warmer air of the passenger compartment through the evaporator core (rather like a radiator in reverse), transferring the heat from the air to

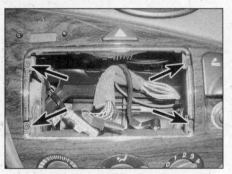

10.3 Undo the four screws (arrowed)

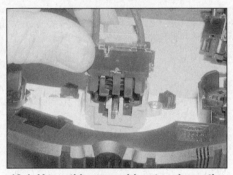

10.4 Use a thin screwdriver to release the heater cable unit

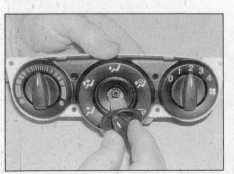

10.7a Pull the control knob off the switch . . .

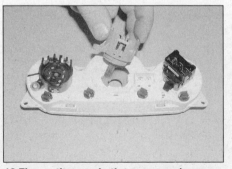

10.7b . . . then undo the screw and remove the switch from its bayonet fitting

10.10 The switches come as a complete assembly

the refrigerant. The liquid refrigerant boils off into low-pressure vapour, taking the heat with it when it leaves the evaporator.

Precautions

⚠ **Warning: The air conditioning system is under high pressure. Do not loosen any fittings or remove any components until after the system has been discharged. Air conditioning refrigerant should be properly discharged at a dealer service department or an automotive air conditioning repair facility capable of handling R134a refrigerant. Always wear eye protection when disconnecting air conditioning system fittings.**

When an air conditioning system is fitted, it is necessary to observe the following special precautions whenever dealing with any part of the system, its associated components, and any items which necessitate disconnection of the system:

a) *While the refrigerant used – R134a – is less damaging to the environment than the previously-used R12, it is still a very dangerous substance. It must not be allowed into contact with the skin or eyes, or there is a risk of frostbite. It must also not be discharged in an enclosed space – while it is not toxic, there is a risk of suffocation. The refrigerant is heavier than air, and so must never be discharged over a pit.*

b) *The refrigerant must not be allowed to come in contact with a naked flame, otherwise a poisonous gas will be created – under certain circumstances, this can form an explosive mixture with air. For similar reasons, smoking in the presence of refrigerant is highly dangerous, particularly if the vapour is inhaled through a lighted cigarette.*

c) *Never discharge the system to the atmosphere – R134a is not an ozone-depleting ChloroFluoroCarbon (CFC) like R12, but is instead a hydrofluorocarbon, which causes environmental damage by contributing to the 'greenhouse effect' if released into the atmosphere.*

d) *R134a refrigerant must not be mixed with R12; the system uses different seals (now green-coloured, previously black) and has different fittings requiring different tools, so that there is no chance of the two types of refrigerant becoming mixed accidentally.*

e) *If for any reason the system must be disconnected, entrust this task to your Ford dealer or a refrigeration engineer.*

f) *It is essential that the system be professionally discharged prior to using any form of heat – welding, soldering, brazing, etc – in the vicinity of the system, before having the vehicle oven-dried at a temperature exceeding 70°C after repainting, and before disconnecting any part of the system.*

12 Air conditioning system components – removal and refitting

⚠ **Warning: The air conditioning system is under high pressure. Do not loosen any fittings or remove any components until after the system has been discharged. Air conditioning refrigerant should be properly discharged into an approved type of container at a dealer service department or an automotive air conditioning repair facility capable of handling R134a refrigerant. Cap or plug the pipe lines as soon as they are disconnected, to prevent the entry of moisture. Always wear eye protection when disconnecting air conditioning system fittings.**
Note: *This Section refers to the components of the air conditioning system itself – refer to Sections 9 and 10 for details of components common to the heating/ventilation system.*

Condenser

1 Have the refrigerant discharged at a dealer service department or an automotive air conditioning repair facility.
2 Disconnect the battery negative (earth) lead (see Chapter 5A, Section 1).
3 Apply the handbrake, then raise the front of the vehicle and support on axle stands.
4 Unclip the radiator undershield and remove.
5 Using the Ford service tool 34-001, disconnect the refrigerant lines from the condenser. Immediately cap the open fittings, to prevent the entry of dirt and moisture.
6 Remove the two bolts from each side of the radiator support bracket (note that the condenser is also mounted on the brackets in front of the radiator), have a jack or pair of axle stands ready to support the weight.
7 Disengage the condenser upper mountings, then unclip it from the radiator and remove it from below. Store it upright, to prevent fluid loss. Take care not to damage the condenser fins.
8 Refitting is the reverse of removal. Renew the O-rings and lubricate with refrigerant oil.
9 Have the system evacuated, charged and leak-tested by the specialist who discharged it.

Evaporator

10 The evaporator is mounted inside the heater housing with the heater matrix. Apart from the need to have the refrigerant discharged, and to use Ford service tools 34-001 and 34-003 to disconnect the lines, the procedure is as described in Section 9 of this Chapter.
11 Unbolt the heater unit assembly from the bulkhead to remove the evaporator. Refitting is the reverse of removal.
12 Have the system evacuated, charged and leak-tested by the specialist who discharged it.

Compressor

13 Have the refrigerant discharged at a dealer service department or an automotive air conditioning repair facility.
14 Disconnect the battery negative (earth) lead (see Chapter 5A, Section 1).
15 Apply the handbrake, then raise the front of the vehicle and support on axle stands.
16 Remove the undershield and the slacken the auxiliary drivebelt as described in Chapter 1.
17 Unscrew the clamping bolt to disconnect the refrigerant lines from the compressor. Plug the line connections to prevent entry of any dirt or moisture.
18 Unbolt the compressor from the cylinder block/crankcase, unplug its electrical connector, then withdraw the compressor from the vehicle. **Note:** *Keep the compressor level during handling and storage. If the compressor has seized, or if you find metal particles in the refrigerant lines, the system must be flushed out by an air conditioning technician, and the accumulator/dehydrator must be renewed.*
19 Prior to installation, turn the compressor clutch centre six times, to disperse any oil that has collected in the head.
20 Refit the compressor in the reverse order of removal; renew all seals disturbed.
21 If you are installing a new compressor, refer to the compressor manufacturer's instructions for adding refrigerant oil to the system.
22 Have the system evacuated, charged and leak-tested by the specialist that discharged it.

Accumulator/dehydrator

23 Have the refrigerant discharged at a dealer service department or an automotive air conditioning repair facility.
24 Disconnect the battery negative (earth) lead (see Chapter 5A, Section 1).
25 The accumulator/dehydrator, which acts as a reservoir and filter for the refrigerant, is located under the right-hand front wing **(see illustration)**. Using the Ford service tool 34-002, disconnect the refrigerant line next to the accumulator/dehydrator from the compressor. Immediately cap the open fittings, to prevent the entry of dirt and

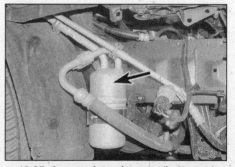

12.25 Accumulator (arrowed) situated under the right-hand front wing

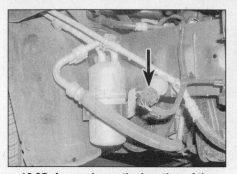

12.35 Arrow shows the location of the high pressure switch

12.42 Low pressure switch (arrowed) in air conditioning pipe by the brake servo

13.1 Cooling system heater booster with three glow plugs fitted

moisture, then unplug the pressure-cycling switch electrical connector.

26 Apply the handbrake, then raise the front of the vehicle and support on axle stands.

27 Remove the right-hand front wheel. Unscrew the inner wheelarch liner and remove from the vehicle.

28 Using the Ford service tool 34-002, disconnect the refrigerant line from the accumulator/dehydrator. Remove the refrigerant line screw-on cap. Immediately cap the open fittings, to prevent the entry of dirt and moisture.

29 Unbolt the accumulator/dehydrator from the front suspension subframe.

30 Withdraw the accumulator/dehydrator.

31 Refit the accumulator/dehydrator in the reverse order of removal; renew all seals disturbed.

32 If you are installing a new accumulator/dehydrator, top-up with new oil to the volume removed, plus 90 cc of extra refrigerant oil.

33 Have the system evacuated, charged and leak-tested by the specialist that discharged it.

High pressure cut-off switch

34 Have the refrigerant discharged at a dealer service department or an automotive air conditioning repair facility.

35 Unplug the switch electrical connector, and unscrew the switch (see illustration).

36 Refitting is the reverse of the removal procedure. Renew the O-rings and lubricate with refrigerant oil.

37 Have the system evacuated, charged and leak-tested by the specialist that discharged it. Check the operation of the air conditioning system.

Low pressure cycling switch

38 Unscrew the carbon canister purge valve

(if fitted), from the bulkhead and move to one side.

39 Pull off the low pressure switch connector.

 Warning: Ensure that the air conditioning system has been filled; otherwise it will be destroyed. Bridge the plug contacts for the air conditioning low pressure switch.

40 Start the engine and switch on the air conditioning.

41 Let the engine idle for 30 seconds, then switch off the engine.

42 Unscrew the low pressure switch (see illustration).

43 Refitting is the reverse of the removal procedure.

44 Check the operation of the air conditioning system.

13 Heater booster (diesel models) – general information, removal and refitting

1 The electrically-operated additional heater is for the European market (except Scandinavia), and is only fitted to the diesel models. The heater booster is positioned in the centre of the bulkhead in the engine compartment (see illustration). It has three glow plugs, which give additional heater settings and is controlled by the engine ECU. The additional heater is deactivated when energy is required to operate other components, to prevent the battery from being drained. For the ECU to control the additional heaters it has to evaluate the following signals:

a) Cylinder head temperature
b) Air intake temperature
c) Alternator charging

Note: The complete heater booster unit must

13.8 Remove the coolant hoses and undo the two securing nuts from the bulkhead

be renewed if there is a fault, as the glow plugs cannot be renewed separately because of the sealing of the unit

Removal

2 Disconnect the battery negative (earth) lead (see Chapter 5A, Section 1).

3 Undo the air intake hose and remove the air filter housing from the vehicle.

4 Undo retaining screw, then unclip the fusebox and move it to one side.

5 Remove the two securing bolts and detach the EGR valve from the top of the bulkhead.

6 Disconnect the wiring connector to the heater booster.

7 Drain the cooling system (see Chapter 1B), then undo the retaining clips and remove the coolant hoses.

8 Undo the two securing nuts from the heater booster bracket and remove from the engine compartment (see illustration).

9 On some models, it may be necessary to remove the front exhaust pipe to remove the heater booster.

Refitting

10 Refitting is a reversal of removal.

Chapter 4 Part A:
Fuel & exhaust systems – petrol models

Contents

Degrees of difficulty

Easy, suitable for novice with little experience	Fairly easy, suitable for beginner with some experience	Fairly difficult, suitable for competent DIY mechanic	Difficult, suitable for experienced DIY mechanic	Very difficult, suitable for expert DIY or professional

Specifications

General

System type	Sequential Electronic Fuel injection (SEFi)
Fuel octane requirement	95 RON unleaded
Idle speed	700 ± 30 rpm (regulated by EEC-V engine management system – no adjustment possible)
CO content at idle	Less than 0.3%

Fuel system data

Note: *The resistance values quoted below are typical, but may be used for guidance. Generally, a faulty component will be indicated by a zero or infinity reading, rather than a slight deviation from the values given. Always have your findings verified before buying a new component (if possible, perform the same test on a new component, and compare the results).*

Fuel pressure regulator

Regulated fuel pressure:	
Pressure regulator hose disconnected	2.7 ± 0.2 bars
Engine running, pressure regulator hose connected	2.1 ± 0.2 bars
Hold pressure – engine stopped after five minutes	1.8 bars minimum

Fuel injectors

Resistance	13.7 to 15.2 ohms

Idle speed control valve

Resistance	6 to 14 ohms

Idle increase solenoid valve

Resistance	50 to 120 ohms

Crankshaft speed/position sensor

Resistance	200 to 450 ohms

Camshaft position sensor

Resistance	200 to 900 ohms

Intake air temperature sensor

Resistance:	
At –40°C	860 to 900 k ohms
At 20°C	35 to 40 k ohms
At 100°C	1.9 to 2.5 k ohms
At 120°C	1.0 to 1.3 k ohms

Fuel system data (continued)

Throttle potentiometer
Resistance – see text . . . .   400 to 6000 ohms

Power steering pressure switch
Operating pressure – green switch body:
    Contacts open – infinite resistance . . . .   31.5 ± 3.5 bars
    Contacts close – 0 to 2.5 ohms resistance . . . .   Between 13.5 and 24.0 bars

Torque wrench settings

	Nm	lbf ft
Camshaft position sensor:		
1.4 and 1.6 litre models	8	6
1.8 and 2.0 litre	20	15
Catalytic converter (1.8 and 2.0 litre models):		
Front support bracket bolts	22	16
Lower support bracket bolts	47	35
To-manifold nuts (renew)	47	35
Crankshaft position sensor	9	7
Cylinder head temperature sensor (renew)	10	7
EGR valve (1.8 and 2.0 litre models)	9	7
Exhaust flange nuts/bolts, clamp nuts	47	35
Exhaust heat shield fasteners	10	7
Exhaust manifold:		
1.4 and 1.6 litre models	53	39
1.8 and 2.0 litre models	15	11
Fuel pressure regulator mounting bolts:		
1.4 and 1.6 litre models	10	7
1.8 and 2.0 litre models	6	4
Fuel rail bolts:		
1.4 and 1.6 litre models	15	11
1.8 and 2.0 litre models	10	7
Fuel supply pipe retaining plate bolts	10	7
Idle speed control valve	10	7
Inlet manifold	18	13
Knock sensor	20	15
Power steering pressure switch	20	15

1 General information and precautions

General information

The fuel system consists of a fuel tank (mounted under the body, beneath the rear seats), fuel hoses, an electric fuel pump mounted in the fuel tank, and a sequential electronic fuel injection system controlled by a EEC-V engine management control module (also called the ECU, or Electronic Control Unit).

The electric fuel pump supplies fuel under pressure to the fuel rail, which distributes fuel to the injectors. A pressure regulator controls the system pressure in relation to inlet tract depression. From the fuel rail, fuel is injected into the inlet ports, just above the inlet valves, by four fuel injectors. The aluminium alloy fuel rail is mounted to the cylinder head on 1.4 and 1.6 litre models, while the fuel rail on 1.8 and 2.0 litre models is mounted on the inlet manifold.

The amount of fuel supplied by the injectors is precisely controlled by the ECU. The module uses the signals from the crankshaft position sensor, and the camshaft position sensor, to trigger each injector separately in cylinder firing order (sequential injection), with benefits in terms of better fuel economy and leaner exhaust emissions.

The ECU is the heart of the entire engine management system, controlling the fuel injection, ignition and emissions control systems. The module receives information from various sensors which is then computed and compared with pre-set values stored in its memory, to determine the required period of injection.

Information on crankshaft position and engine speed is generated by a crankshaft position sensor. The inductive head of the sensor runs just above the engine flywheel and scans a series of 36 protrusions on the flywheel periphery. As the crankshaft rotates, the sensor transmits a pulse to the system's ignition module every time a protrusion passes it. There is one missing protrusion in the flywheel periphery at a point corresponding to 90° BTDC. The ignition module recognises the absence of a pulse from the crankshaft position sensor at this point to establish a reference mark for crankshaft position. Similarly, the time interval between absent pulses is used to determine engine speed. This information is then fed to the ECU for further processing.

The camshaft position sensor is located in the cylinder head so that it registers with a lobe on the camshaft. The camshaft position sensor functions in the same way as the crankshaft position sensor, producing a series of pulses; this gives the ECU a reference point, to enable it to determine the firing order, and operate the injectors in the appropriate sequence.

The mass airflow sensor is based on a 'hot-wire' system, sending the ECU a constantly-varying (analogue) voltage signal corresponding to the mass of air passing into the engine. Since air mass varies with temperature (cold air being denser than warm), measuring air mass provides the module with a very accurate means of determining the correct amount of fuel required to achieve the ideal air/fuel mixture ratio.

The traditional coolant temperature sensor has been replaced by a cylinder head temperature sensor. The new sensor is seated in a blind hole in the cylinder head, and measures the temperature of the metal directly. This component is an NTC (Negative Temperature Coefficient) thermistor – that is, a semi-conductor whose electrical resistance decreases as its temperature increases. It provides the ECU with a constantly-varying (analogue) voltage signal, corresponding to the temperature of the engine. This is used to refine the calculations made by the module, when determining the correct amount of fuel required to achieve the ideal air/fuel mixture ratio.

Inlet air temperature information is supplied by the inlet air temperature sensor built into the airflow sensor. This component is also an NTC thermistor – see the previous paragraph – providing the module with a signal corresponding to the temperature of air passing into the engine. This is used to refine the calculations made by the module, when determining the correct amount of fuel required to achieve the ideal air/fuel mixture ratio.

A throttle position sensor is mounted on the end of the throttle valve spindle, to provide the ECU with a constantly-varying (analogue) voltage signal corresponding to the throttle opening. This allows the module to register the driver's input when determining the amount of fuel required by the engine.

Road speed is monitored by the vehicle speed sensor. This component is a Hall-effect generator, mounted on the transmission's speedometer drive. It supplies the module with a series of pulses corresponding to the vehicle's road speed, enabling the module to control features such as the fuel shut-off on overrun.

The clutch pedal position is monitored by a switch fitted to the pedal bracket. This sends a signal to the ECU.

Where power steering is fitted, a pressure-operated switch is screwed into the power steering system's high-pressure pipe. The switch sends a signal to the ECU to increase engine speed to maintain idle speed when the power steering pump loads up the engine (typically, during parking manoeuvres).

The oxygen sensor in the exhaust system provides the module with constant feedback – 'closed-loop' control – which enables it to adjust the mixture to provide the best possible operating conditions for the catalytic converter.

The air inlet side of the system consists of an air cleaner housing, the mass airflow sensor, an inlet hose and duct, and a throttle housing.

The throttle valve inside the throttle housing is controlled by the driver, through the accelerator pedal. As the valve opens, the amount of air that can pass through the system increases. As the throttle valve opens further, the mass airflow sensor signal alters, and the ECU opens each injector for a longer duration, to increase the amount of fuel delivered to the inlet ports.

Both the idle speed and mixture are under the control of the ECU, and cannot be adjusted.

Precautions

 Warning: Many of the procedures in this Chapter require the removal of fuel lines and connections, which may result in some fuel spillage. Before carrying out any operation on the fuel system, refer to the precautions given in 'Safety first!' at the beginning of this manual, and follow them implicitly. Petrol is a highly-dangerous and volatile liquid, and the precautions necessary when handling it cannot be overstressed.
Note: *Residual pressure will remain in the fuel lines long after the vehicle was last used. When disconnecting any fuel line, first depressurise the fuel system as described in Section 2.*

2 Fuel system – depressurisation

Note: *Refer to the warning note in Section 1 before proceeding.*

⚠️ **Warning: The following procedure will merely relieve the pressure in the fuel system – remember that fuel will still be present in the system components, and take precautions accordingly before disconnecting any of them.**

1 The fuel system referred to in this Chapter is defined as the fuel tank and tank-mounted fuel pump/fuel gauge sender unit, the fuel filter, the fuel injector, fuel pressure regulator, and the metal pipes and flexible hoses of the fuel lines between these components. All these contain fuel, which will be under pressure while the engine is running and/or while the ignition is switched on.

2 The pressure will remain for some time after the ignition has been switched off, and must be relieved before any of these components is disturbed for servicing work.

3 The simplest depressurisation method is to disconnect the fuel pump electrical supply by removing the fuel pump fuse (No 12, in the engine compartment fusebox) and starting the engine **(see illustration)**. If the engine does not start, crank it on the starter for a few seconds, otherwise, allow the engine to idle until it dies through lack of fuel. Turn the engine over once or twice on the starter to ensure that all pressure is released, then switch off the ignition; do not forget to refit the fuse when work is complete.

4 If an adapter is available to fit the Schrader-type valve on the fuel rail pressure test/release fitting (identifiable by its blue plastic cap, and located on the fuel rail), this may be used to release the fuel pressure **(see illustration)**. The Ford adapter (tool number 23-033) operates similar to a drain tap – turning the tap clockwise releases the pressure. If the adapter is not available, place cloth rags around the valve, then remove the cap and allow the fuel pressure to dissipate. Refit the cap on completion.

5 Note that, once the fuel system has been depressurised and drained (even partially), it will take significantly longer to restart the

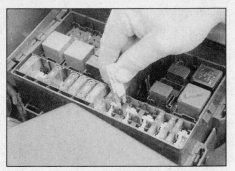

2.3 Removing fuse No 12

engine – perhaps several seconds of cranking – before the system is refilled and pressure restored.

3 Unleaded petrol – general information and usage

The fuel recommended by Ford is given in the Specifications section of this Chapter, followed by the equivalent petrol currently on sale in the UK.

All petrol models are designed to run on fuel with a minimum octane rating of 95 (RON). All models have a catalytic converter, and so must be run on unleaded fuel only. Under no circumstances should leaded or lead-replacement fuel (UK '4-star' or 'LRP') be used, as this will damage the converter.

Super unleaded petrol (98 octane) can also be used in all models if wished, though there is no advantage in doing so.

4 Fuel lines and fittings – general information

Note: *Refer to the warning note in Section 1 before proceeding.*

Disconnecting and connecting couplings

1 Special snap-together couplings are employed at many of the unions in the fuel feed and return lines.

2.4 Schrader valve cap on fuel rail

4.3a Prise out he coloured insert with a small screwdriver . . .

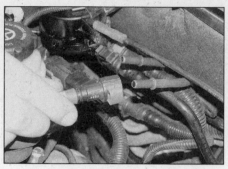

4.3b . . . then separate the coupling

2 Before disconnecting any fuel system component, relieve the residual pressure in the system (see Section 2), and equalise tank pressure by removing the fuel filler cap.

⚠ *Warning: This procedure will merely relieve the increased pressure necessary for the engine to run – remember that fuel will still be present in the system components, and take precautions accordingly before disconnecting any of them.*

3 Release the union by prising out the coloured insert with a small screwdriver and carefully pulling the coupling apart **(see illustrations)**. Use rag to soak up any spilt fuel. Where the unions are colour-coded, the pipes cannot be confused. Where both unions are the same colour, note carefully which pipe is connected where, and ensure that they are correctly reconnected on refitting.

4 To reconnect one of these couplings, press the pipe fully into place, then press in the insert until it snaps into place. Switch the ignition on and off five times to pressurise the system, and check for any sign of fuel leakage around the disturbed coupling before attempting to start the engine.

Checking

5 Checking procedures for the fuel lines are included in Chapter 1A, Section 7.

Component renewal

6 If any damaged sections are to be renewed, use original-equipment replacement hoses or pipes, constructed from exactly the same material as the section being replaced. Do not install substitutes constructed from inferior or inappropriate material; this could cause a fuel leak or a fire.

7 Before detaching or disconnecting any part of the fuel system, note the routing of all hoses and pipes, and the orientation of all clamps and clips. Replacement sections must be installed in exactly the same manner.

8 Before disconnecting any part of the fuel system, be sure to relieve the fuel system pressure (see Section 2), and equalise tank pressure by removing the fuel filler cap. Also disconnect the battery negative (earth) lead – see *Disconnecting the battery*. Cover the fitting being disconnected with a rag, to absorb any fuel that may spray out.

5 Air cleaner assembly and air inlet components – removal and refitting
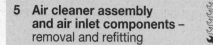

Air cleaner assembly

1 Loosen the clip and disconnect the air inlet duct from the mass airflow sensor on the air cleaner **(see illustration)**.

2 Disconnect the wiring from the airflow sensor **(see illustration)**.

3 Disconnect the breather hose leading to the cylinder head cover **(see illustration)**.

4 Remove the four screws securing the cover to the air cleaner housing **(see illustration)**.

5 Withdraw the cover and remove the filter element.

6 Lift the air cleaner base to release it from the rubber grommets **(see illustration)**.

7 Check the rubber grommets for deterioration and renew them if necessary.

8 Refitting is the reverse of the removal procedure. Ensure that the base pegs seat fully in their rubber grommets, and that the mass airflow sensor is correctly located.

Air inlet components

9 To remove the air inlet duct between the mass airflow sensor and throttle housing, loosen the retaining clips at either end, and carefully ease off the duct **(see illustration)**.

10 To remove the air inlet duct attached to the air cleaner base, first remove the air cleaner assembly as described in paragraphs 1 to 6.

11 Prise up the two clips securing the duct to the engine compartment front panel, then separate the two halves of the duct at the sleeve joint next to the battery. The rear half of the duct is clipped into the engine left-hand

5.1 Loosen the clip on the air inlet duct

5.2 Disconnect the wiring from the airflow sensor

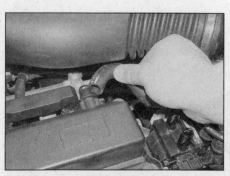

5.3 Disconnect the breather hose from the cylinder head cover

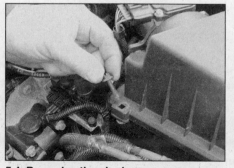

5.4 Removing the air cleaner cover screws

5.6 Removing the air cleaner base

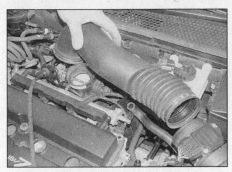

5.9 Removing the air inlet duct – 1.8 litre model

5.11a Prise out the two plastic clips at the front . . .

5.11b . . . then unclip at the rear, and remove the front air inlet duct complete

mounting bracket. The duct can, however, be removed complete, with some manoeuvring **(see illustrations)**.

12 Refitting is a reversal of removal.

6 Accelerator cable – removal, refitting and adjustment

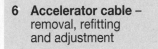

Removal

1 Remove five screws and take out the trim panel above the driver's footwell to gain access to the accelerator pedal; unclip the diagnostic connector plug from the panel as it is removed.

2 Disconnect the inner cable from the top of the pedal by pulling the end of the cable out, and unhooking the inner cable through the slot at the top of the pedal **(see illustration)**.

> **HAYNES HINT** *Attach a length of string to the end of the cable before removing the cable through the bulkhead. If the string is untied once the cable has been fed through and completely removed, the string can then be used to pull the cable back through, preserving the cable routing.*

3 Prise the rubber grommet from the bulkhead, and remove the cable and end fitting through into the engine compartment.

4 Disconnect the inner cable from the quadrant on the throttle housing by extracting the retaining clip, then prising the end fitting off sideways **(see illustrations)**.

5 Release the cable from the supports in the engine compartment, and withdraw it from the engine, noting how it is routed **(see illustrations)**.

Refitting

6 Refitting is a reversal of removal. The rubber grommet must be fitted to the bulkhead first, and the cable end fitting pushed through it. When the cable is reconnected at each end, check its operation as follows.

Adjustment

7 The cable is self-adjusting. Check that the throttle quadrant moves smoothly and easily from the fully-closed to the fully-open position and back again as an assistant depresses and releases the accelerator pedal.

7 Accelerator pedal – removal and refitting

Removal

1 Remove five screws and take out the trim panel above the driver's footwell to gain access to the accelerator pedal; unclip the diagnostic connector plug from the panel as it is removed.

2 Detach the accelerator cable from the pedal (see Section 6), then unscrew the three nuts and remove the accelerator pedal assembly **(see illustration)**.

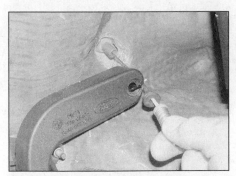

6.2 Unhook the accelerator cable from the pedal

6.4a Extract the securing clip . . .

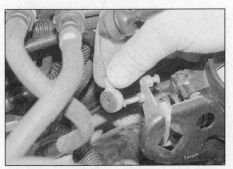

6.4b . . . then prise off the accelerator cable end fitting

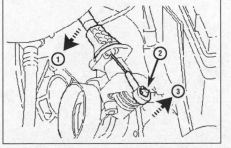

6.5a Twist the cable outer (1), remove the clip (2) and prise off the end fitting (3) – 1.4 & 1.6 litre models

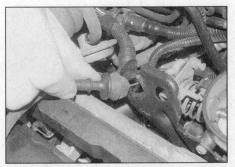

6.5b Removing the cable from the support bracket – 1.8 & 2.0 litre models

7.2 Accelerator pedal, showing cable attachment and mounting nuts

Refitting

3 Refit in the reverse order of removal. On completion, check the action of the pedal and the cable to ensure that the throttle has full unrestricted movement, and fully returns when released.

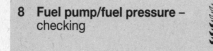

8 Fuel pump/fuel pressure – checking

Note: *Refer to the warning note in Section 1 before proceeding.*

Fuel pump operation check

1 Switch on the ignition, and listen for the fuel pump (the sound of an electric motor running, audible from beneath the rear seats). Assuming there is sufficient fuel in the tank, the pump should start and run for approximately one or two seconds, then stop, each time the ignition is switched on. **Note:** *If the pump runs continuously all the time the ignition is switched on, the electronic control system is running in the backup (or 'limp-home') mode referred to by Ford as 'Limited Operation Strategy' (LOS). This almost certainly indicates a fault in the EEC-V module itself, and the vehicle should therefore be taken for diagnostic testing (see Section 14) – do not waste time or risk damaging the components by trying to test the system without the proper facilities.*

2 Listen for fuel return noises from the fuel pressure regulator. It should be possible to feel the fuel pulsing in the regulator and in the feed hose from the fuel filter.

3 If the pump does not run at all, check the fuse, relay and wiring (see Chapter 12). Check also that the fuel cut-off switch (located in the lower trim panel on the right-hand side of the driver's footwell) has not been activated; if it has, reset it as described below:
a) *Turn off the ignition.*
b) *If the switch has been triggered, the switch tab will be in the raised position. Press the switch in to reset it.*
c) *Turn the ignition switch to position II (so that the instrument panel warning lights come on), then return it to position I. The engine can then be started as normal.*

Note: *The switch must not be reset immediately after an accident if there is a risk of fuel spillage.*

Fuel pressure check

4 A fuel pressure gauge will be required for this check, and should be connected in the fuel line between the fuel filter and the fuel rail, in accordance with the gauge maker's instructions. A pressure gauge equipped with an adapter to suit the Schrader-type valve on the fuel rail pressure test/release fitting (identifiable by its blue plastic cap, and located on the end of the fuel rail – refer to illustration 2.4) will be required. If the Ford special tool 29-033 is available, the tool can be attached to the valve, and a conventional-type pressure gauge attached to the tool.

5 If using the service tool, ensure that its tap is turned fully anti-clockwise, then attach it to the valve. Connect the pressure gauge to the service tool. If using a fuel pressure gauge with its own adapter, connect it in accordance with its maker's instructions.

6 Start the engine and allow it to idle. Note the gauge reading as soon as the pressure stabilises, and compare it with the regulated fuel pressure figures listed in the Specifications.
a) *If the pressure is high, check for a restricted fuel return line. If the line is clear, renew the fuel pressure regulator.*
b) *If the pressure is low, pinch the fuel return line. If the pressure now goes up, renew the fuel pressure regulator. If the pressure does not increase, check the fuel feed line, the fuel pump and the fuel filter.*

7 Detach the vacuum hose from the fuel pressure regulator; the pressure shown on the gauge should increase. Note the increase in

pressure, and compare it with that listed in the *Specifications*. If the pressure increase is not as specified, check the vacuum hose and pressure regulator.

8 Reconnect the regulator vacuum hose, and switch off the engine. Verify that the hold pressure stays at the specified level for five minutes after the engine is turned off.

9 Carefully disconnect the fuel pressure gauge, depressurising the system first as described in Section 2. Be sure to cover the fitting with a rag before slackening it. Mop up any spilt petrol.

10 Run the engine, and check that there are no fuel leaks.

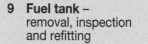

9 Fuel tank – removal, inspection and refitting

Note: *Refer to the warning note in Section 1 before proceeding.*

Removal

1 Run the fuel level as low as possible prior to removing the tank.

2 Relieve the residual pressure in the fuel system (see Section 2), and equalise tank pressure by removing the fuel filler cap.

3 Disconnect the battery negative (earth) lead (see *Disconnecting the battery*).

4 Where possible, syphon or pump out the remaining fuel from the fuel tank (there is no drain plug). The fuel must be emptied into a suitable container for storage.

5 Chock the front wheels, loosen the rear wheel nuts, then jack up the rear of the car and support it on axle stands (see *Jacking and vehicle support*). Remove the rear roadwheels.

6 Unscrew and remove the nuts at the exhaust flange behind the flexible section of pipe at the front, and separate the joint. Have an axle stand or similar support ready, on which the front part of the exhaust can be supported.

7 Unscrew and remove the fasteners securing the exhaust heat shield at the rear **(see illustration)**; remove the heat shield, noting how it is fitted.

8 Unhook the exhaust system mounting rubbers at the front and rear **(see illustrations)**, and allow the exhaust system to rest on the rear suspension crossmember, and

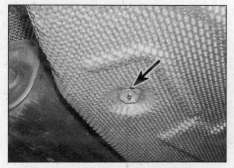

9.7 Exhaust heat shield and 'flat nut' fastener (arrowed)

9.8a Using a dedicated Draper tool to disconnect the exhaust front mounting rubbers

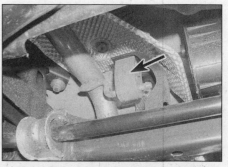

9.8b Exhaust rear mounting rubber (arrowed)

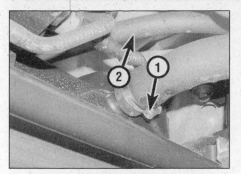

9.9 Fuel tank filler pipe clip (1) and vent hose (2)

9.10a Charcoal canister (arrowed) at the rear of the tank

9.10b Disconnect the charcoal canister pipes (arrowed)

at the front, on an axle stand or similar. There is no need to remove the exhaust from under the car (although this will greatly improve working room) – manoeuvre the exhaust under the car in order to clear the fuel tank.

9 Loosen the clips and disconnect the filler pipe and vent hose from the fuel tank (see illustration). Note the exact fitted positions of the clips, for use when refitting. Do not use any sharp tools to prise the pipes from the tank fittings, or the pipes may be damaged, leading to leakage on completion.

10 At the charcoal canister at the rear of the tank, pull off the vapour pipe at the base, and release the fitting from the pipe at the side (see illustrations). Note the respective positions of the pipes carefully for refitting.

11 Depress the metal clip used to locate the charcoal canister, then lift the canister upwards to free it from the clip, and remove it from under the car (see illustration).

12 Position a container beneath the fuel filter (see illustration), then disconnect the fuel supply hose from the filter inlet by prising out the insert to release the fitting. Be prepared for some loss of fuel.

13 Disconnect the fuel return line at the connector next to the fuel filter. Note that the return pipe is identified by a red colour band.

14 Support the fuel tank using a jack and block of wood.

15 Unscrew and remove the tank strap bolt (see illustrations) and unhook the straps, noting how they are fitted.

16 Taking care that the wiring and fuel lines are not strained, partially lower the fuel tank (see illustration). Release the fuel pipes from the attachments on the tank as necessary. When the tank has been sufficiently lowered, disconnect the fuel pump/gauge sender wiring plug from the top of the tank (see illustration).

17 Lower the fuel tank and withdraw it from under the vehicle. If necessary, disconnect the supply hose from the fuel pump. The filter may also be removed at this time.

Inspection

18 Whilst removed, the fuel tank can be inspected for damage or deterioration. Removal of the fuel pump/fuel gauge sender unit (see Section 10) will allow a partial inspection of the interior. If the tank is contaminated with sediment or water, swill it out with clean fuel. Do not under any circumstances undertake any repairs on a leaking or damaged fuel tank; this work must be carried out by a professional who has experience in this critical and potentially-dangerous work.

19 Whilst the fuel tank is removed from the vehicle, it should be placed in a safe area where sparks or open flames cannot ignite the fumes coming out of the tank. Be especially

9.11 Removing the charcoal canister from behind the fuel tank

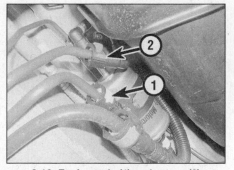

9.12 Fuel supply (1) and return (2) connections

9.15a Tank strap bolt (arrowed) at the front of the tank

9.15b Unscrewing the tank strap bolt

9.16a Lower the fuel tank . . .

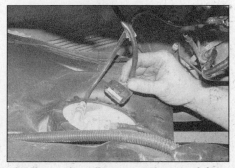

9.16b . . . then disconnect the remaining pipes and wiring

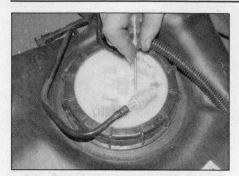

10.2a Release the pipe lugs with a small screwdriver . . .

10.2b . . . and separate the pipes – note the O-rings

10.3a Using a home-made tool to unscrew . . .

10.3b . . . and remove the retaining ring

careful inside garages where a natural-gas type appliance is located, because the pilot light could cause an explosion.

20 Check the condition of the filler pipe and renew it if necessary.

Refitting

21 If a new tank is being fitted, transfer the rollover valves, vent hose and filler pipe to the new tank.

22 Refitting is a reversal of the removal

10.4 Remove the top cover as far as the wiring allows

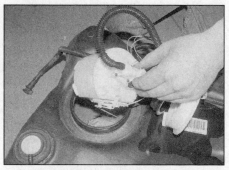

10.5a Twist the pump/sender unit to release the retaining lugs at the base . . .

10.5b . . . then withdraw the cover, pump and rubber seal, without damaging the float arm

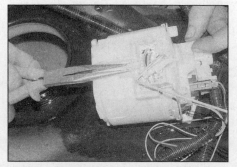

10.7a Squeeze the lugs at the side . . .

procedure. Ensure that all connections are securely fitted. When refitting the quick-release couplings, press them together and secure with the coloured insert. If evidence of contamination was found, do not return any previously-drained fuel to the tank unless it is carefully filtered first.

10 Fuel pump/fuel gauge sender unit – removal and refitting

Note: *Refer to the warning note in Section 1 before proceeding. Ford technicians use a special wrench to unscrew the pump/sender unit retaining ring, but ordinary tools can be used successfully (see text).*

Removal

1 A combined fuel pump and fuel gauge sender unit is located in the top face of the fuel tank. The combined unit can only be detached and withdrawn from the tank after the tank is released and lowered from under the vehicle. Refer to Section 9 and remove the fuel tank, then proceed as follows.

2 With the fuel tank removed, disconnect the fuel supply and return pipes (if still attached to the tank) from their respective stubs by releasing the lugs using a small screwdriver. Note that the fuel supply pipe connector is identified by a white band, and the return pipe connector by a red band. Make sure that both O-rings are recovered from each pipe as they are disconnected **(see illustrations)**.

3 Unscrew and remove the special retaining ring. Ford specify the use of their service tool 310-069 (a large socket/spanner with projecting teeth to engage the fuel pump/sender unit retaining ring's slots) for this task. A large pair of slip-joint pliers, or an oil filter removal strap wrench, may be sufficient for this task, but we used a tool made from two long bolts and two strips of metal **(see illustrations)**.

4 With the retaining ring removed, the pump/sender top cover can be withdrawn. Feed the wiring out through the opening, noting that the cover cannot be completely removed until the pump/sender unit is also removed from the tank **(see illustration)**.

5 Turn the pump/sender unit anti-clockwise inside the tank (this is quite stiff to turn), then carefully withdraw the unit, taking care not to damage the sender unit float or its arm **(see illustrations)**.

6 If not already done, remove the rubber seal from the periphery of the pump. The seal must be renewed whenever the pump/sender unit is removed from the tank.

7 If required, the sender unit can be separated from the pump by squeezing together the lugs below its mounting at the side **(see illustrations)**. It is not clear at the time of writing whether the sender unit is available separately.

Refitting

8 Refitting is a reversal of removal, noting the following points:
   a) Ensure that the pump/sender unit seats fully and squarely in the tank before twisting it clockwise to secure it. Check that the unit is firmly located before proceeding.
   b) Turn the pump/sender top cover so that the arrows on the tank and unit are aligned **(see illustration)**.
   c) Fit a new rubber seal and tighten the retaining ring securely.
   d) Refit the fuel tank as described in Section 9.

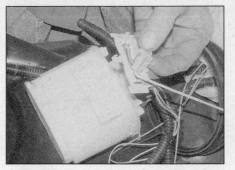
10.7b . . . and remove the sender unit

10.8 Top cover and tank alignment arrows

11 Fuel tank roll-over valves – removal and refitting

Note: *Refer to the warning note in Section 1 before proceeding.*

Removal

1 The roll-over valves are located in rubber grommets in the top of the fuel tank, with hoses leading rearwards to the carbon canister. Their purpose is to prevent fuel loss if the vehicle becomes inverted in a crash.
2 Remove the fuel tank as described in Section 9.
3 Release the vent hose from the clip on the top of the tank.
4 Carefully prise the roll-over valve from the rubber grommet and remove it together with the hose.

5 Check the condition of the rubber grommet and renew it if necessary.

Refitting

6 Refitting is a reversal of removal, but apply a light smear of clean engine oil to the rubber grommet, to ease fitting.

12 Fuel tank filler pipe – removal and refitting

Note: *Refer to the warning note in Section 1 before proceeding.*

Removal

1 Disconnect the battery negative (earth) lead (see *Disconnecting the battery*).
2 Equalise tank pressure by removing the fuel filler cap.

3 Chock the front wheels, loosen the right-hand rear wheel nuts, then jack up the rear of the car and support it on axle stands (see *Jacking and vehicle support*). Remove the right-hand rear roadwheel – this is not absolutely essential, but will make the job easier.
4 Release and remove the various fasteners used to secure the right-hand rear wheelarch liner, then manoeuvre the liner out from the wheelarch **(see illustrations)**.
5 Loosen the clips and disconnect the filler pipe and vent hose from the fuel tank **(see illustrations)**. Note the exact fitted positions of the clips, for use when refitting. Do not use any sharp tools to prise the pipes from the tank fittings, or the pipes may be damaged, leading to leakage on completion.
6 The filler pipe is secured by two bolts (one top and bottom) – remove the bolts to release the pipe. It is now possible to remove the pipe from under the wheelarch **(see illustrations)**.

12.4a The rear wheelarch liner is secured by a combination of screws . . .

12.4b . . . and clips, which can be prised out . . .

12.4c . . . before removing the liner completely

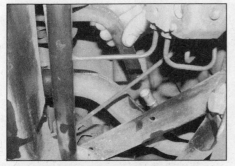
12.5a Disconnect the vent hose . . .

12.5b . . . and filler pipe from the rear of the tank

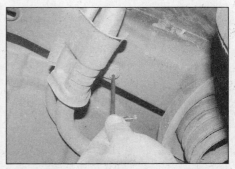
12.6a Remove the pipe retaining bolts at the top . . .

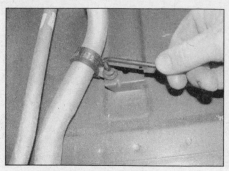

12.6b . . . and at the bottom . . .

12.6c . . . then manoeuvre the filler pipe out from under the wheelarch

7 Check the condition of the filler pipe and hose and renew if necessary.

Refitting

8 Refitting is a reversal of removal. Tighten the rear crossmember bolts to the specified torque (refer to Chapter 10 Specifications).

13 Fuel cut-off switch – removal and refitting

Note: *To reset the switch after it has been triggered, first check that there are no signs that fuel is escaping. Turn off the ignition. If the switch has been triggered, the switch tab will be in the raised position. Press the switch down to reset it. Turn the ignition switch to position II (so that the instrument panel warning lights come on), then return it to position I. The engine can then be started as normal.*

Removal

1 The fuel cut-off (or inertia) switch is located behind the driver's footwell side trim panel. First disconnect the battery negative (earth) lead (see *Disconnecting the battery*).
2 Pull up the weatherstrip from the driver's door aperture, and release it from the side trim.
3 Prise out the two screwhead covers, then unscrew and remove the two screws securing the trim panel. Remove the trim panel for access to the cut-off switch **(see illustration)**.
4 Unscrew and remove the two switch securing screws **(see illustration)**, then

disconnect the wiring plug and remove the switch.

Refitting

5 Refitting is a reversal of removal, but make sure that the switch is reset. Start the engine to prove this.

14 Fuel injection system – checking

Note: *Refer to the warning note in Section 1 before proceeding.*

1 If a fault appears in the fuel injection system, first ensure that all the system wiring connectors are securely connected and free of corrosion – also refer to paragraphs 6 to 9 below. Then ensure that the fault is not due to poor maintenance; ie, check that the air cleaner filter element is clean, the spark plugs are in good condition and correctly gapped, the valve clearances are correct, the cylinder compression pressures are correct, the ignition system wiring is in good condition and securely connected, and the engine breather hoses are clear and undamaged, referring to Chapter 1A, Chapter 2A or 2B and Chapter 5B.
2 If these checks fail to reveal the cause of the problem, the vehicle should be taken to a suitably-equipped Ford dealer for testing. A diagnostic connector is incorporated in the engine management system wiring harness, into which dedicated electronic test equipment can be plugged (the connector is located behind a small panel in the driver's side lower

facia – unclip and remove the panel for access) **(see illustration)**. The test equipment is capable of 'interrogating' the engine management system ECU electronically and accessing its internal fault log (reading fault codes).
3 Fault codes can only be extracted from the ECU using a dedicated fault code reader. A Ford dealer will obviously have such a reader, but they are also available from other suppliers, including Haynes. It is unlikely to be cost-effective for the private owner to purchase a fault code reader, but a well-equipped local garage or auto-electrical specialist will have one.
4 Using this equipment, faults can be pinpointed quickly and simply, even if their occurrence is intermittent. Testing all the system components individually in an attempt to locate the fault by elimination is a time-consuming operation that is unlikely to be fruitful (particularly if the fault occurs dynamically), and carries a high risk of damage to the ECU's internal components.
5 Experienced home mechanics equipped with an accurate tachometer and a carefully-calibrated exhaust gas analyser may be able to check the exhaust gas CO content and the engine idle speed; if these are found to be out of specification, then the vehicle must be taken to a suitably-equipped Ford dealer for assessment. Neither the air/fuel mixture (exhaust gas CO content) nor the engine idle speed are manually adjustable; incorrect test results indicate the need for maintenance (possibly, injector cleaning) or a fault within the fuel injection system.

Limited Operation Strategy – precaution

6 Certain faults, such as failure of one of the engine management system sensors, will cause the system will revert to a backup (or 'limp-home') mode, referred to by Ford as 'Limited Operation Strategy' (LOS). This is intended to be a 'get-you-home' facility only – the engine management warning light will come on when this mode is in operation.
7 In this mode, the signal from the defective sensor is substituted with a fixed value (it would normally vary), which may lead to loss of power, poor idling, and generally-poor running, especially when the engine is cold.

13.3 Removing the footwell side trim panel

13.4 Fuel cut-off switch securing screws (arrowed)

14.2 Diagnostic connector location in driver's lower facia panel

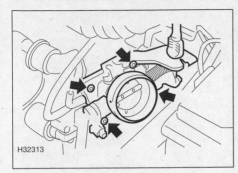

15.5a Throttle body housing bolts (arrowed) – 1.4 & 1.6 litre models . . .

15.5b . . . and 1.8 & 2.0 litre models

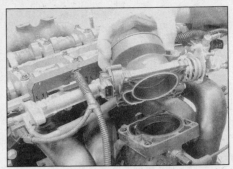

15.5c Removing the throttle body housing – 1.8 & 2.0 litre models

8 However, the engine may in fact run quite well in this situation, and the only clue (other than the warning light) would be that the exhaust CO emissions (for example) will be higher than they should be.

9 Bear in mind that, even if the defective sensor is correctly identified and renewed, the engine will not return to normal running until the fault code is erased, taking the system out of LOS. This also applies even if the cause of the fault was a loose connection or damaged piece of wire – until the fault code is erased, the system will continue in LOS.

15 Fuel injection system components – removal and refitting

Note: *Refer to the warning note in Section 1 before proceeding.*

Throttle body housing

1 The housing is located on the left-hand side of the inlet manifold. First disconnect the battery negative (earth) lead (see *Disconnecting the battery*).

2 Remove the air inlet duct as described in Section 5.

3 Disconnect the accelerator cable from the throttle body housing, using the information in Section 6.

4 Disconnect the throttle position sensor multi-plug.

5 Unscrew and remove the four mounting bolts and withdraw the throttle housing from the inlet manifold **(see illustrations)**. Discard

the rubber gasket and obtain a new one. **Note:** *Take care when cleaning the inside of the housing, as it is treated with a special coating during manufacture, which could be removed by over-enthusiastic cleaning, or by use of powerful solvents.*

6 Refitting is a reversal of removal, but clean the mating faces and fit a new gasket, and tighten the mounting bolts securely **(see illustration)**.

Fuel rail and injectors

7 Relieve the residual pressure in the fuel system (see Section 2), and equalise tank pressure by removing the fuel filler cap.

> ⚠️ *Warning: This procedure will merely relieve the increased pressure necessary for the engine to run – remember that fuel will still be present in the system components, and take precautions accordingly before disconnecting any of them.*

8 Disconnect the battery negative (earth) lead (see *Disconnecting the battery*).

1.4 and 1.6 litre engines

9 Disconnect the breather hose from the cylinder head cover.

10 Disconnect the wiring plugs from the idle speed valve and throttle position sensor, then detach the wiring harness from the clip on the fuel rail.

11 Unclip the fuel lines from the cylinder head cover.

12 Using a small screwdriver, prise up and remove the four wire clips (one on each injector) securing the injector wiring busbar –

use a magnetic holding tool to prevent the wire clips falling down the back of the engine as they are removed. Lift off the wiring busbar, and move it to the rear.

13 Disconnect the vacuum hose from the fuel pressure regulator.

14 Disconnect the fuel supply and return lines, noting their fitted positions. The supply line is colour-coded white, and the return line is colour-coded red.

15 Unscrew and remove the two bolts securing the fuel rail **(see illustration)**. Pulling the fuel rail equally at both ends, remove it squarely from the inlet manifold.

1.8 and 2.0 litre engines

16 Loosen the retaining clips at either end, and remove the air cleaner inlet duct.

17 Disconnect the accelerator cable from the throttle body housing, using the information in Section 6.

18 Using a small screwdriver, prise up and remove the four wire clips (one on each injector) securing the injector wiring busbar – use a magnetic holding tool to prevent the wire clips falling down the back of the engine as they are removed. Lift off the wiring busbar, and move it to the rear **(see illustrations)**.

19 Disconnect the vacuum hose from the fuel pressure regulator **(see illustration)**.

20 Disconnect the fuel supply and return lines, noting their fitted positions. The supply line is colour-coded white, and the return line is colour-coded red.

21 Unscrew and remove the two bolts securing the fuel rail. Pulling the fuel rail

15.6 Fit a new throttle body housing gasket

15.15 Fuel rail mounting bolts (arrowed) – 1.4 & 1.6 litre models

15.18a Use a screwdriver to prise out the wire clips . . .

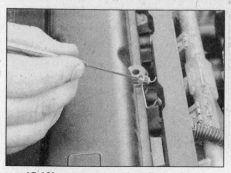

15.18b . . . recover the clips using a magnetic tool . . .

15.18c . . . then lift off the injector wiring busbar

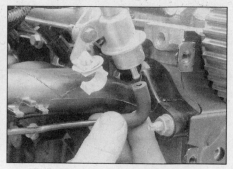

15.19 Disconnect the fuel pressure regulator vacuum hose

equally at both ends, remove it squarely from the inlet manifold **(see illustration)**.

All engines

22 If required, remove the clips and carefully pull the injectors from the fuel rail **(see illustration)**.

23 Using a screwdriver if necessary, prise the O-rings from the grooves at each end of the injectors. Discard the O-rings and obtain new ones **(see illustrations)**.

24 Refitting is the reverse of the removal procedure, noting the following points:

a) *Lubricate the new O-rings with clean engine oil to aid refitting.*

b) *Ensure that the hoses and wiring are routed correctly, and secured on reconnection by any clips or ties provided.*

c) *Refit the accelerator cable as described in Section 6.*

d) *On completion, switch the ignition on to activate the fuel pump and pressurise the system, without cranking the engine. Check for signs of fuel leaks around all disturbed unions and joints before attempting to start the engine.*

Fuel pressure regulator

25 Relieve the residual pressure in the fuel system (see Section 2), and equalise tank pressure by removing the fuel filler cap.

⚠️ **Warning: This procedure will merely relieve the increased pressure necessary for the engine to run – remember that fuel will still be present in the system components, and take precautions accordingly before disconnecting any of them.**

26 Disconnect the battery negative (earth) lead (see *Disconnecting the battery*).

27 Disconnect the fuel supply and return lines, noting their fitted positions **(see illustration)**. The supply line is colour-coded white, and the return line is colour-coded red.

28 Disconnect the vacuum pipe from the fuel pressure regulator (refer to illustration 15.19).

29 Undo the two bolts and remove the fuel pressure regulator from the fuel rail **(see illustration)**.

30 Using a screwdriver if necessary, prise the O-ring from the groove in the fuel pressure regulator **(see illustration)**. Discard the O-ring, and obtain a new one.

31 Refitting is a reversal of removal, but lubricate the new O-ring with clean engine oil to aid installation. Tighten the mounting bolts to the specified torque.

Idle speed control valve

32 The valve is located on the inlet manifold, next to the throttle housing. On 1.8 and 2.0 litre models, the valve is on the inside of the

15.21 Removing the fuel rail

15.22 Prise out the securing clips and remove the injectors

15.23a Removing an injector O-ring

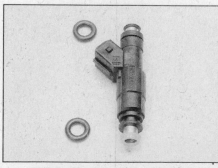

15.23b Fuel injector and O-rings

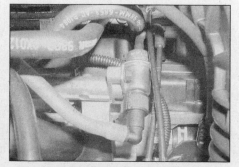

15.27 Fuel pressure regulator – 1.4 litre model

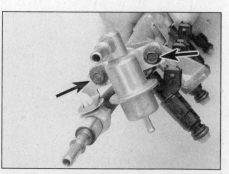

15.29 Fuel pressure regulator mounting bolts (arrowed)

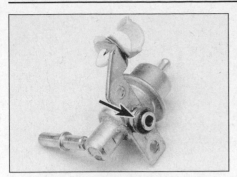
15.30 Always fit a new O-ring (arrowed)

15.32 Idle air control valve on 1.8 litre model – seen with inlet manifold removed

15.34 Idle air control valve wiring plug – 1.8 litre model

inlet manifold, making access especially difficult **(see illustration)**.

33 On 1.8 and 2.0 litre models, loosen the retaining clips at either end, and remove the air cleaner inlet duct.

34 Disconnect the wiring plug from the valve **(see illustration)**.

35 Unscrew the mounting bolts and remove the valve from the inlet manifold **(see illustration)**. On 1.8 and 2.0 litre models, access to the bolts is less easy; remove the alternator as described in Chapter 5A, or ultimately, if suitable tools are not available, it may be simpler to remove the inlet manifold (Section 16) for access.

36 Recover the rubber seal from the valve, and discard it. Obtain a new seal for refitting.

37 Refitting is a reversal of removal, but note the following points.

a) Clean the mating surfaces, and fit a new seal.

15.35 Idle air control valve – 1.4 litre model

b) Tighten the valve bolts to the specified torque.

c) Once the wiring and battery are reconnected, start the engine and allow it to idle. When it has reached normal operating temperature, check that the idle speed is stable, and that no induction (air) leaks are evident. Switch on all electrical loads (headlights, heated rear window, etc), and check that the idle speed is still satisfactory.

Mass airflow sensor

38 Loosen the clip and disconnect the air inlet duct from the mass airflow sensor on the air cleaner cover. If necessary, remove the air cleaner cover for improved access.

39 Disconnect the wiring from the sensor **(see illustration)**.

40 Unscrew the crosshead mounting screws and remove the sensor from the air cleaner cover.

41 Refitting is a reversal of removal.

Inlet air temperature sensor

42 The sensor is an integral part of the mass airflow sensor, and cannot be renewed separately.

Engine management module (ECU)

Note: The module is fragile. Take care not to drop it, or subject it to any other kind of impact. Do not subject it to extremes of temperature, or allow it to get wet. The module

wiring plug must never be disconnected while the ignition is switched on.

43 The engine management module is located behind the facia, on the right-hand side. First disconnect the battery negative (earth) lead (see *Disconnecting the battery*).

Right-hand-drive models

44 Pull up the weatherstrip from the driver's door aperture, and release it from the side trim.

45 Prise off the trim panel fitted between the end of the facia panel and the door aperture, approximately half way up the door aperture.

46 Prise out the two screwhead covers, then unscrew and remove the two screws securing the footwell side trim panel. Remove the trim panel for access to the module (refer to illustration 13.3).

47 Remove the four screws and prise out the plastic clip securing the driver's side lower trim panel. Remove the panel from the facia, and detach the diagnostic connector socket **(see illustrations)**.

Left-hand-drive models

48 Remove the glovebox as described in Chapter 11.

49 Remove the four screws securing the passenger's side lower trim panel. Remove the panel from the facia.

All models

50 Remove the two screws securing the central locking module, and lower the module out of position; there is no need to disconnect the wiring **(see illustration)**.

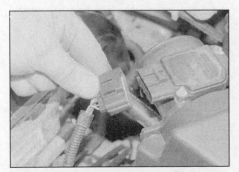
15.39 Disconnect the airflow sensor wiring plug

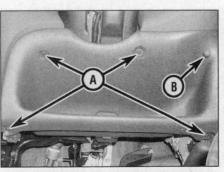
15.47a Lower facia panel is secured by four screws (A) and plastic clip (B)

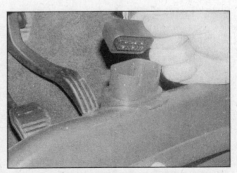
15.47b Remove the panel, and disconnect the diagnostic connector

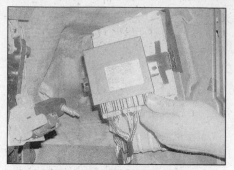

15.50 Removing the central locking module for access to the ECU

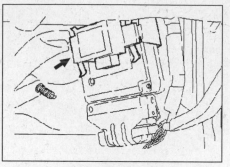

15.51a Unclip the ECU retaining bracket (arrowed) . . .

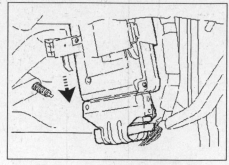

15.51b . . . and remove the ECU downwards

51 Release the spring clips securing the module bracket in position, and remove the module downwards into the footwell (see illustrations).

52 The ECU wiring connector is protected by a tamperproof shield, secured by a shear-bolt and welded nut, which must be drilled to remove the bolt. Great care must be taken not to damage the wiring harness during drilling.

53 First drill a 3 mm pilot hole in the nut, then enlarge the hole using an 8 mm drill until the shear-bolt can be removed.

54 With the shear-bolt removed, slide off the tamperproof shield (see illustration).

55 Remove the wiring connector securing screw, then disconnect the plug from the ECU, and remove the module from the car (see illustration).

56 Refitting is a reversal of removal. Use a new shear-bolt, and tighten it until the head shears off.

Crankshaft position sensor

57 The sensor is located on the front left-hand side of the engine (see illustration). For improved access, apply the handbrake then jack up the front of the vehicle and support it on axle stands (see *Jacking and vehicle support*).

58 Where fitted, unclip the cover from the crankshaft position sensor on the front of the engine, then disconnect the wiring plug.

59 Unscrew the mounting bolt and withdraw the sensor (see illustrations). If a spacer is fitted between the sensor and engine, it is vital that this is refitted when refitting the sensor, or the sensor head will hit the rotor teeth.

60 Refitting is a reversal of removal. Tighten the sensor retaining bolt to the specified torque.

Camshaft position sensor

61 The camshaft position sensor is located at

the rear of the cylinder head – on the right-hand side on 1.4 and 1.6 litre models, and on the left-hand side on 1.8 and 2.0 litre models (left and right as seen from the driver's seat).

62 On 1.8 and 2.0 litre models, loosen the retaining clips at either end, and remove the air cleaner inlet duct. Disconnect the breather hose from the cylinder head cover.

63 Disconnect the wiring connector from the sensor, then unscrew the sensor retaining bolt and withdraw the sensor from the cylinder head (see illustrations).

64 Refitting is a reversal of removal. Tighten the sensor retaining bolt to the specified torque.

Cylinder head temperature sensor

65 The sensor is located in the centre of the head, between Nos 2 and 3 spark plugs, on 1.4 and 1.6 litre models, and on the right-hand end of the head on 1.8 and 2.0 litre models.

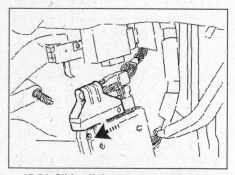

15.54 Slide off the tamperproof shield

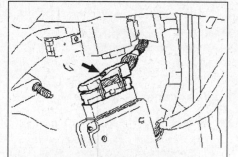

15.55 ECU wiring connector securing screw (arrowed)

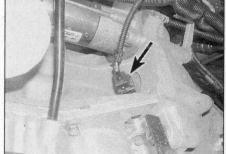

15.57 Crankshaft position sensor (arrowed) – 1.4 litre model

15.59a Unscrew the mounting bolt . . .

15.59b . . . and withdraw the sensor

15.63a Disconnect the wiring plug – 1.8 litre model . . .

15.63b . . . then remove the sensor from the cylinder head

15.68a Disconnecting the cylinder head temperature sensor wiring plug – 1.4 litre model . . .

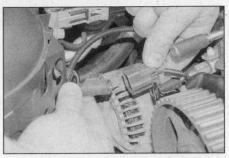

15.68b . . . on 1.8 & 2.0 litre models, the wiring plug is clipped to the timing belt upper cover

There is no need to drain the coolant, as the sensor measures the temperature of the metal directly.

66 On 1.4 and 1.6 litre models, disconnect the HT leads from the spark plugs as necessary for access – make sure that the leads are numbered for position (with No 1 at the timing belt end). Prise out the rubber bung used to secure the sensor wiring.

67 On 1.8 and 2.0 litre models, remove the alternator as described in Chapter 5A.

68 Disconnect the wiring from the temperature sensor **(see illustrations)**.

69 Unscrew and remove the sensor **(see illustration)**. Note: *On 1.4 and 1.6 litre engines, the sensor cannot be re-used – a new one must be fitted, since the mating face of the sensor is deformed when fully tightened, to ensure a good contact with the cylinder head. If the old sensor were re-used, it would result in inaccurate readings.*

70 Refitting is a reversal of removal. Clean the sensor mounting hole, then fit the sensor and tighten it to the specified torque.

Throttle position sensor

71 The sensor is located on the side of the throttle body housing. First disconnect the sensor wiring plug **(see illustrations)**.

72 Remove the retaining screws, and withdraw the unit from the throttle housing. *Do not* force the sensor's centre to rotate past its normal operating sweep; the unit will be seriously damaged.

73 Refitting is a reversal of removal, but ensure that the sensor is correctly orientated,

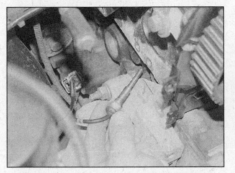

15.69 Removing the temperature sensor – 1.8 litre model

by locating its centre on the D-shaped throttle shaft (throttle closed), and aligning the sensor body so that the screws pass easily into the throttle housing.

Vehicle speed sensor

74 Refer to Chapter 7A.

Output shaft speed sensor

75 Refer to Chapter 7B, Section 5.

Clutch pedal position switch

76 Remove five screws and take out the trim panel above the driver's footwell to gain access to the clutch pedal; unclip the diagnostic connector plug from the panel as it is removed.

77 Reach up and disconnect the wiring from the clutch switch at the top of the pedal, then twist the switch anti-clockwise and remove it from the pedal bracket **(see illustration)**.

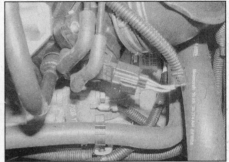

15.71a Throttle position sensor wiring plug – 1.4 litre model . . .

78 Refitting is a reversal of removal.

Power steering pressure switch

79 The switch is screwed into the power steering system's high-pressure pipe at the front right-hand side of the engine compartment **(see illustration)**. On some models, access is improved by removing the radiator grille as described in Chapter 11.

80 Releasing its clip, unplug the switch's electrical connector, then unscrew the switch from the power steering high pressure pipe. Place a wad of rag underneath, to catch any spilt fluid. If a sealing washer is fitted, renew it if it is worn or damaged.

81 Refitting is the reverse of the removal procedure, noting the following points:

a) *Tighten the switch to the specified torque.*
b) *Top-up the fluid reservoir (see 'Weekly checks') to replace any fluid lost from the system.*

15.71b . . . disconnecting the plug on a 1.8 litre model

15.77 Removing the clutch pedal switch

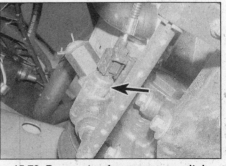

15.79 Power steering pressure switch (arrowed)

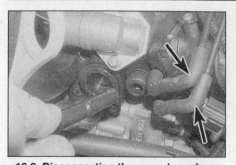

16.6 Disconnecting the servo hose from the manifold – also note charcoal canister and pressure regulator hoses (arrowed)

c) *If a significant amount of fluid was lost, bleed the power steering system as described in Chapter 10.*

Oxygen sensor

82 Refer to Chapter 4C.

16 Manifolds –
removal and refitting

Note: *Refer to the warning note in Section 1 before proceeding.*

Inlet manifold

Removal – 1.4 and 1.6 litre models

1 Depressurise the fuel system as described in Section 2, then disconnect the battery negative (earth) lead (see *Disconnecting the battery*).

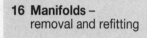

16.14 Disconnecting the injection harness wiring plug

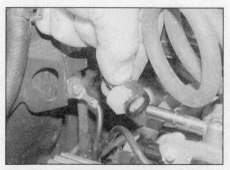

16.15b . . . then disconnect the return line from the fuel rail

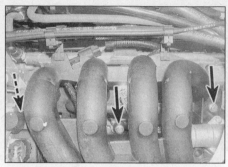

16.9 Three of the eight manifold securing bolts (arrowed)

2 Unclip the power steering reservoir from its mounting bracket, and move it to one side without disconnecting the hoses.
3 Remove the auxiliary drivebelt as described in Chapter 1A.
4 Remove the air cleaner and inlet duct as described in Section 5, and disconnect the accelerator cable using the information in Section 6.
5 Unclip the wiring harness from the inlet manifold, and disconnect the wiring plugs from the following (refer to Section 15):

a) *Ignition coil.*
b) *Idle speed control valve.*
c) *Throttle position sensor.*
d) *Knock sensor.*

6 Disconnect the crankcase ventilation hose next to the idle speed valve, the vacuum hose from the fuel pressure regulator, and the brake servo vacuum hose from the inlet manifold **(see illustration)**.

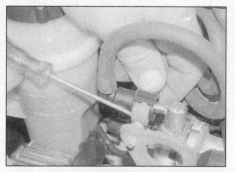

16.15a Prise out the coloured insert with a screwdriver . . .

16.15c Disconnecting the fuel supply line

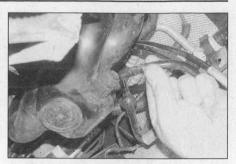

16.13 Disconnecting the brake servo vacuum hose from the inlet manifold – seen from below

7 Remove the fuel rail and injectors as described in Section 15.
8 Unbolt the dipstick tube and wiring plug support brackets from the front of the inlet manifold.
9 Unscrew and remove the eight manifold retaining nuts/bolts, noting that some of them are not easily accessible **(see illustration)** – it may be necessary to jack up the front of the car (see *Jacking and vehicle support*) and gain access from below.
10 Carefully withdraw the manifold from the cylinder head, and disconnect the charcoal canister vacuum pipe from the manifold as it becomes accessible. Recover the two-part manifold gasket, and discard it – a new gasket must be used when refitting.

Removal – 1.8 and 2.0 litre models

11 Depressurise the fuel system as described in Section 2, then disconnect the battery negative (earth) lead (see *Disconnecting the battery*).
12 Remove the air cleaner and inlet duct as described in Section 5, and disconnect the accelerator cable using the information in Section 6.
13 Disconnect the brake servo vacuum hose from the base of the manifold – squeeze the end fitting and pull to release it **(see illustration)**.
14 Trace the injection wiring harness back to the large multi-plug located behind the power steering fluid reservoir, and disconnect the plug **(see illustration)**. Also disconnect the wiring plug from the camshaft position sensor, located at the rear of the cylinder head, at the transmission end.
15 Disconnect the fuel supply and return lines from the fuel rail, noting their fitted positions. The supply line is colour-coded white, and the return line is colour-coded red **(see illustrations)**. The manifold is removed complete with the fuel rail. **Note:** *Protect the alternator from fuel spillage with rags or a plastic bag.*
16 Unscrew and remove the seven manifold retaining bolts, and the nut at either end, noting that some of them are not easily accessible – it may be necessary to jack up the front of the car (see *Jacking and vehicle support*) and gain access from below. Note that the right-hand nut also secures a wiring support bracket –

16.16 Removing one of the inlet manifold studs

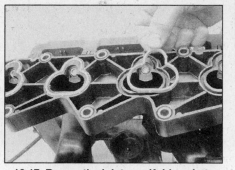

16.17 Renew the inlet manifold gaskets

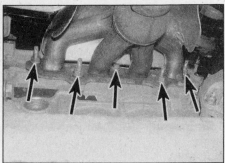

16.25 Exhaust manifold securing nuts (arrowed) – seen from below

unclip the wiring before removing the bracket. Once the two nuts have been removed, unscrew their studs from the cylinder head – the studs have Torx end fittings to make removal easier **(see illustration)**.

17 Check that there is nothing else attached to the manifold which would prevent its removal. Withdraw the manifold from the engine, keeping it as level as possible, to reduce fuel spillage from the fuel rail. Recover the four gaskets, and discard them – new ones must be used on refitting **(see illustration)**.

Refitting – all models

18 Refitting is a reversal of removal, but note the following additional points:
a) Clean the mating faces of the inlet manifold and cylinder head, and use new gaskets.
b) Tighten the nuts/bolts to the specified torque.
c) When the engine is fully warmed-up, check for signs of fuel, intake and/or vacuum leaks.
d) Road test the vehicle and check for proper operation of all disturbed components.

Exhaust manifold

⚠️ **Warning: The engine (and exhaust) must be completely cold before starting this procedure. Ideally, the vehicle should have been left to cool overnight.**

Removal – 1.4 and 1.6 litre models

19 Disconnect the battery negative (earth) lead (see *Disconnecting the battery*).
20 Apply the handbrake, then jack up the front of the car and support it on axle stands (see *Jacking and vehicle support*).
21 Disconnect the wiring plug from the oxygen sensor in the exhaust front pipe. Loosen the union nut at the end of the EGR pipe, and release the pipe connection.
22 To prevent possible damage to the flexible section of pipe behind the first flange joint, Ford technicians cable-tie two strips of thick metal on either side, down the length of the flexible section.
23 Loosen and remove the nuts/bolts, and separate the exhaust at the front flange joint. Recover the gasket, and discard it – a new one must be used when refitting.

24 Working from above, remove the three bolts securing the exhaust manifold heat shield, noting that one of them also secures the engine earth strap.
25 Unscrew the five manifold securing nuts/bolts **(see illustration)**, withdraw the manifold from the cylinder head, and recover the gasket. Remove the assembly from above, taking care that the oxygen sensor is not knocked or damaged.

Removal – 1.8 and 2.0 litre models

26 Disconnect the battery negative (earth) lead (see *Disconnecting the battery*).
27 Apply the handbrake, then jack up the front of the car and support it on axle stands (see *Jacking and vehicle support*).
28 Disconnect the wiring plug from the oxygen sensor in the exhaust front pipe; the wiring plug is located above the radiator, and is bright green **(see illustration)**.

16.28 Disconnect the oxygen sensor wiring plug

16.29b ... and lift off the exhaust manifold heat shield

29 Unscrew the four bolts securing the exhaust manifold heat shield, and lift the shield off **(see illustrations)**. It is quite likely that difficulty will be experienced removing the bolts, as corrosion may have effectively rounded-off the bolt heads – be sure to use a close-fitting socket or ring spanner from the outset. If the bolts cannot be removed, as a last resort, the heat shield will have to be destroyed to remove it – take care, however, that the wiring for the oxygen sensor (fitted just below the heat shield) is not damaged during this operation.
30 Under the car, unscrew and remove the bolts securing the exhaust front pipe/catalytic converter support brackets – one bracket in front of the catalytic converter-to-centre section joint, and one securing the catalytic converter clamp to the cylinder block **(see illustrations)**.

16.29a Remove the four bolts (arrowed) ...

16.30a View of the rear clamp, at the exhaust front joint ...

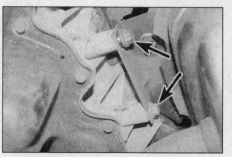

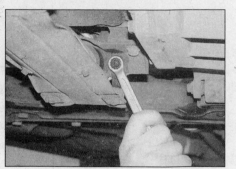

16.30b . . . and the two clamp bolts to be undone (arrowed)

16.30c Catalytic converter clamp-to-cylinder block bolts (arrowed) – seen from below

16.31a Unscrew the two nuts . . .

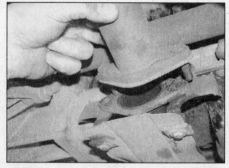

16.31b . . . and separate the exhaust front joint

16.31c Recover the joint gasket

16.32 Removing one of the power steering pipe brackets

31 Remove the nuts and separate the catalytic converter-to-centre section joint; recover the gasket **(see illustrations)**. Position a jack underneath the front pipe, to

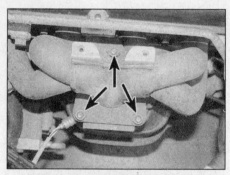

16.33a Loosen the three manifold-to-catalytic converter nuts (arrowed) . . .

16.33b . . . then carefully lower the converter assembly

support it when the manifold-to-catalytic converter joint is separated.
32 Returning to the engine compartment, remove the two power steering pipe mounting brackets at either side of the manifold **(see illustration)**.
33 Check that the jack under the front pipe is supporting its weight, then slowly loosen and remove the three nuts securing the catalytic

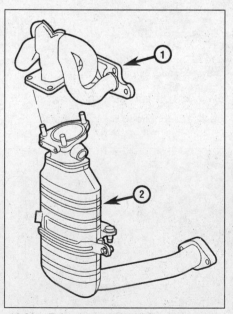

16.33c Exhaust manifold (1) and catalytic converter (2)

converter to the manifold (new nuts must be used when refitting). Use the jack to lower the front section of exhaust until the three studs are clear of the manifold, then recover the ring gasket and discard it. Lower the catalytic converter completely, and remove it from under the car **(see illustrations)**. Treat the converter assembly with care – if handled roughly, the ceramic element inside may be fractured.
34 Unscrew and remove the six bolts and three nuts securing the manifold to the cylinder head. Withdraw the manifold from the studs; recover the metal gasket and the two plastic sleeves from the outer studs **(see illustrations)**.
35 Before lifting the converter into position, loosen the two bolts at the base of the front support bracket so that the rear half of the bracket is free to slide – once the converter is fully refitted, these bolts can be tightened.

16.34a Remove the manifold from the studs . . .

16.34b . . . then recover the plastic sleeves . . .

16.34c . . . and the metal gasket

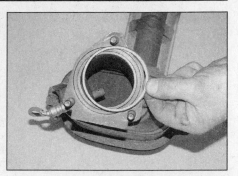

16.36 Fit a new ring gasket to the manifold joint

Refitting – all models

36 Refitting is a reversal of removal, but fit new gaskets and tighten all nuts and bolts to the specified torque **(see illustration)**.

17 Exhaust system –
general information, removal and refitting

General information

1 On 1.4 and 1.6 litre models, the system comprises the manifold and downpipe, and an original factory-fitted one-piece rear section containing the catalytic converter and two silencers. To fit new centre or rear silencers, the original rear section has to be cut through, mid-way along the connecting pipe; service sections can then be fitted.
2 On 1.8 and 2.0 litre models, the catalytic converter is mounted vertically, below the manifold. A short intermediate pipe, containing a flexible section, connects the converter to the factory-fitted one-piece rear section, which contains the centre and rear silencers. To renew either silencer, the original rear section must be cut through mid-way between the centre and rear silencers.
3 Before making any cut, offer up the replacement exhaust section for comparison, and if necessary, adjust the cutting points as required. Bear in mind that there must be some 'overlap' allowance, as the original and replacement sections are sleeved together.
4 The system is suspended throughout its entire length by rubber mountings. On 1.8 and 2.0 litre models, a rigid two-part clamp arrangement supports the catalytic converter.
5 To remove a part of the system, first jack up the front or rear of the car, and support it on axle stands (see *Jacking and vehicle support*). Alternatively, position the car over an inspection pit, or on car ramps.
6 Ford recommend that all nuts (such as flange joint nuts, clamp joint nuts, or converter-to-manifold nuts) are renewed on reassembly – given that they may be in less-than-perfect condition as a result of corrosion, this seems a good idea, especially as it will make subsequent removal easier.

Catalytic converter

Removal – 1.4 and 1.6 litre models

Note: *Later models may be fitted with an oxygen sensor in the front section of pipe, behind the catalytic converter, as well as the sensor in the front downpipe. On these models, unclip the wiring plug from the mounting plate on the underside of the car, and separate the plug halves before proceeding – refer to Chapter 4C if necessary.*
7 To prevent possible damage to the flexible section of pipe behind the flange joint, Ford technicians cable-tie two strips of thick metal on either side, down the length of the flexible section.
8 Remove the four bolts and washers securing the heat shield below the converter, and lower the shield out of position.
9 If the original exhaust rear section has never been disturbed, it will be necessary to cut the pipe behind the converter. The cutting point is 795 mm back from the front flange face; take care to cut the pipe at right-angles to the pipe (and to **only** cut the pipe); clean up any rough edges.
10 If a new centre silencer has been fitted, loosen the clamp bolts securing the converter to the centre silencer. Do not try to separate the joint at this stage.
11 Loosen and remove the nuts, and separate the exhaust at the front flange joint **(see illustration)**. Recover the gasket, and discard it – a new one must be used when refitting.
12 Unhook the converter from the two

mounting rubbers under the car **(see illustration)**. Note that these mountings are a different colour (typically, red) to the others, indicating their different temperature rating. If fitting new rubbers, ensure that the correct ones are used.
13 If a clamp is used at the rear of the converter, separate the pipes by twisting them relative to each other, and pull the sleeved joint apart.
14 Remove the converter from under the car, taking great care not to drop it or knock it, as the internals are fragile.

Removal – 1.8 and 2.0 litre models

15 Refer to Section 16, paragraphs 28 to 33 inclusive.
16 Before refitting the converter, loosen the two bolts at the base of the front support bracket so that the rear half of the bracket is free to slide – once the converter is fully refitted, these bolts can be tightened.

Refitting – all models

17 Refitting is a reversal of removal. Clean up any sleeve joints before mating them together. Use new gaskets, nuts and bolts as necessary, and tighten all fasteners to the specified torque **(see illustration overleaf)**.
Note: *Exhaust sealant paste should not be used on any part of the exhaust system upstream of the catalytic converter (between the engine and the converter) – even if the sealant does not contain additives harmful to the converter, pieces of it may break off and foul the element, causing local overheating.*

17.11 Exhaust front flange joint

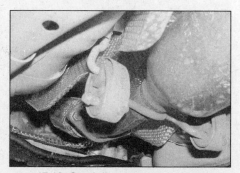

17.12 Catalytic converter rubber mountings

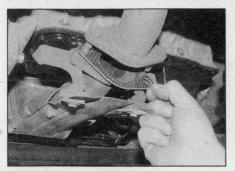

17.17 Fitting a new exhaust front joint gasket

Intermediate pipe – 1.8 and 2.0 litre models

Removal

18 To prevent possible damage to the flexible section of pipe in front of the second flange joint, Ford technicians cable-tie two strips of thick metal on either side, down the length of the flexible section.

19 Loosen and remove the nuts at the flange joints at either end of the pipe (new nuts should be used when refitting). When both ends are free, separate the joints.

20 Taking care not to bend or strain the flexible section excessively, lower the rear end of the pipe and withdraw it over the subframe and out from under the car. Recover the gasket at either end of the pipe, and discard them – new ones must be used when refitting.

Refitting

21 Refitting is a reversal of removal. Use new gaskets and nuts, and tighten the flange joint nuts to the specified torque.

Centre silencer

Removal – 1.4 and 1.6 litre models

22 If the original rear section has not been disturbed, it will be necessary to cut the exhaust rear section in two places to renew the centre silencer. The first cutting point is at 795 mm from the face of the front flange, with the second at 2144 mm; take care to cut the pipe at right-angles to the pipe (and to **only** cut the pipe); clean up any rough edges.

23 If the exhaust has already been repaired, the centre silencer may have clamped sleeve joints at one or both ends. Loosen the clamp nuts, unhook the silencer from its mounting rubbers, then twist and pull the sections of pipe to separate the sleeve joints.

24 Remove the silencer from under the car.

Removal – 1.8 and 2.0 litre models

25 If the original rear section is still intact, it must be cut at a point between the centre and rear silencers. The cutting point is 2033 mm back from the face of the flange joint in front of the centre silencer; take care to cut the pipe at right-angles to the pipe (and to **only** cut the pipe); clean up any rough edges.

26 If a new rear silencer has been fitted, there will be a clamped sleeve joint at the rear of the centre silencer. Loosen the clamp nuts, but do not try to separate the sleeve joint at this stage.

27 Loosen and remove the nuts, and separate the exhaust at the flange joint in front of the centre silencer (use new nuts when refitting). Recover the gasket, and discard it – a new one must be used when refitting.

28 Unhook the centre silencer from its rubber mountings. If a sleeve joint is used at the rear, twist and pull the pipes to separate the joint. Remove the centre silencer from under the car.

Refitting – all models

29 Refitting is a reversal of removal. Clean up any sleeve joints before mating them together. Use new gaskets and nuts, and tighten all fasteners to the specified torque.

Rear silencer

Removal

30 If the original exhaust rear section is still fitted, it will be necessary to cut the pipe between the centre and rear silencers to fit the service replacement section. The cutting points are as follows:
- a) 1.4 and 1.6 litre models – 2144 mm behind the front face of the front flange.
- b) 1.8 and 2.0 litre models – 2033 mm behind the face of the flange in front of the centre silencer.

31 Bear in mind the advice in paragraph 3 before making any cut; take care to cut the pipe at right-angles to the pipe (and to **only** cut the pipe); clean up any rough edges.

32 Unhook the rear silencer from its mounting rubber(s).

33 If the rear silencer has been renewed previously, loosen the clamp nuts until the joint is free, then twist and pull the pipes relative to each other, to free and separate the sleeve joint.

34 Remove the rear silencer from under the car.

Refitting

35 Refitting is a reversal of removal. Clean up any sleeve joints before mating them together. Use new nuts (or a new clamp), and tighten the nuts to the specified torque.

Heat shield(s)

36 The heat shields are secured to the underside of the body by special nuts, or by bolts. A shield is fitted below the catalytic converter, to reduce the risk of fire when parking over dry grass or leaves, for example – otherwise, the shields are fitted above the exhaust, to reduce radiated heat affecting the cabin or fuel tank.

37 Each shield can be removed separately, but note that some overlap each other, making it necessary to loosen another section first. If a shield is being removed to gain access to a component located behind it, it may prove sufficient in some cases to remove the retaining nuts and/or bolts, and simply lower the shield, without disturbing the exhaust system. Otherwise, remove the exhaust section as described earlier.

Chapter 4 Part B:
Fuel & exhaust systems – diesel models

Contents

Degrees of difficulty

Easy, suitable for novice with little experience	**Fairly easy,** suitable for beginner with some experience	**Fairly difficult,** suitable for competent DIY mechanic	**Difficult,** suitable for experienced DIY mechanic	**Very difficult,** suitable for expert DIY or professional

Specifications

General

System type	Bosch VP-30 combined lift and injection pump, chain-driven from crankshaft. Direct injection via five-hole, pencil-type injectors, electronic pump control unit (PCU) linked to revised EEC-V engine management module (ECU)
Application	1.8 litre Endura-DI engine
Firing order	1 – 3 – 4 – 2 (No 1 at timing belt end)
Idle speed	800 ± 50 rpm (regulated by EEC-V engine management system – no adjustment possible)

Fuel

Fuel type	Commercial diesel fuel for road vehicles (DERV)

Injection pump

Make and type	Bosch VP-30 electronic, distributor-type
Rotation (viewed from crankshaft pulley end)	Clockwise
Drive	By twin 'gemini' chains from crankshaft
Injection pump timing	By timing pin, at TDC

Injectors

Type	Pencil-type, five-hole

Glow plugs

Type	No Bosch recommendation

Turbocharger

Type	Garrett GT15, integral with exhaust manifold. Air-to-air intercooler

Torque wrench settings

	Nm	lbf ft
Alternator bracket bolts	25	18
Alternator/air conditioning compressor bolts	25	18
Catalytic converter-to-manifold nuts (renew)	47	35
Crankshaft position sensor bolt	10	7
Cylinder head temperature sensor	20	15
EGR cooler lower bolts	23	17
EGR tube/cooler clamp nut/bolt (renew)	9	7
EGR valve flange bolts	20	15
Engine rear mounting bolts	48	35
Exhaust front flange nuts (renew)	48	35
Exhaust front pipe support bracket bolt	25	18
Exhaust heat shield fasteners	10	7
Exhaust manifold	25	18
Glow plugs	15	11
Injection pump bracket bolts	22	16
Injection pump locking screw	12	9
Injection pump oil seal housing nuts	10	7
Injection pump rear mounting bolts	20	15
Injection pump timing belt sprocket bolts (use locking fluid)	42	31
Injection pump-to-drive pulley bolts	33	24
Injector clamp bolt (renew)	23	17
Injector pipe unions	28	21
Inlet manifold	23	17
Turbocharger oil return (or feed/return) flange bolts	10	7

1 General information and precautions

General information

The fuel system consists of a fuel tank (mounted under the body, beneath the rear seats), fuel filter, electronic fuel injection pump with pump control unit, injectors, fuel lines and hoses, fuel gauge sender unit mounted in the fuel tank, and EEC-V engine management control module (ECU).

Fuel is drawn from the tank by the transfer pump incorporated in the injection pump. It then passes through the fuel filter, located in the engine bay, where foreign matter and water are removed. The injection pump is driven from the crankshaft via a twin-row ('gemini') chain and supplies fuel under very high pressure to each injector in turn as it is needed. The camshaft is driven from the injection pump via a toothed timing belt.

The Endura-DI engine is very much a 'state-of-the-art' unit, in that it features a full electronic engine management system, very similar to that fitted to the Focus petrol models. An extensive array of sensors is fitted, which supply information on many different parameters to the ECU.

Information on crankshaft position and engine speed is generated by a crankshaft position sensor. The inductive head of the sensor runs just above the engine flywheel, and scans a series of 36 protrusions on the flywheel periphery. As the crankshaft rotates, the sensor transmits a pulse every time a protrusion passes it. There is one missing protrusion in the flywheel periphery at a point corresponding to 90° BTDC. The ECU recognises the absence of a pulse from the crankshaft position sensor at this point to establish a reference mark for crankshaft position. Similarly, the time interval between absent pulses is used to determine engine speed.

Information on the quantity and temperature of the inlet air is derived from the MAP sensor and the inlet air temperature sensors. The manifold absolute pressure (or MAP) sensor is connected to the inlet manifold by a vacuum hose, and measures the pressure in the inlet system. Two air temperature sensors are fitted – one before the turbocharger, and one after the intercooler. The temperature and quantity of air has a direct bearing on the quantity of fuel to be injected for optimum efficiency.

The traditional coolant temperature sensor has been replaced by a cylinder head temperature sensor. The new sensor is seated in a blind hole in the cylinder head, and measures the temperature of the metal directly. Information on engine temperature is critical for accurate fuelling calculations, and is also used to control the pre-heating system for cold starts.

The clutch pedal sensor informs the ECU whether the clutch is engaged or disengaged. When the clutch pedal is depressed, the quantity of fuel injected is momentarily reduced, to make gearchanging smoother.

The stop-light switch and separate brake pedal sensor inform the ECU when the brakes are applied – when this signal is received, the ECU puts the engine into idle mode until a signal is received from the accelerator position sensor.

The amount of fuel delivered is determined by the pump's internal quantity and timing solenoid valves, which are controlled by the pump control unit (PCU), mounted on top of the pump. The pump is internally equipped with a pulse ring fitted to the main rotor, and an angle sensor determines the pump rotor's position and speed, in much the same way as the crankshaft position sensor and engine flywheel, except that there are four gaps in the pump rotor 'teeth' – one for each cylinder. The pump control unit is supplied with information from the 'main' engine management module (ECU), and from this, is able to calculate the most appropriate values for injection timing and quantity (injection duration). The electronically-controlled pump internals enable these calculated values to be delivered with great accuracy, for improved efficiency and reduced emissions.

No accelerator cable is fitted on the Endura-DI engine – instead, a sensor located next to the accelerator pedal informs the ECU of the accelerator position, and this information is used to determine the most appropriate fuelling requirements from the injection pump. The engine idle speed is also controlled by the ECU, and cannot be adjusted. From the signals it receives from the various sensors, the ECU can control the idle speed very accurately, compensating automatically for additional engine loads or unfavourable ambient/engine temperatures.

Rigid pipes connect the pump to the four injectors. Each injector has five holes, to disperse the fuel evenly, and sprays fuel directly into the combustion chamber as its piston approaches TDC on the compression stroke. This system is known as direct injection. The pistons have an off-centre recess machined into their crowns, the shape of which has been calculated to improve 'swirl' (fuel/air mixing). The injectors open in two stages, to promote smoother combustion – the rate of opening is fixed by two internal springs. Lubrication is provided by allowing a small quantity of fuel to leak back past the injector internal components. The leaked-back fuel is returned to the pump and then to the fuel tank.

Cold-starting performance is automatically controlled by the ECU and pump control unit. Under cold start conditions, the injection pump timing is advanced by the pump control unit, while the ECU operates the glow plug system. The pre-heater or 'glow' plugs fitted to each cylinder are electrically heated before, during and immediately after starting, and are particularly effective during a cold start. A warning light illuminates when the ignition is switched on, showing that the glow plugs are in operation. When the light goes out, pre-heating is complete and the engine can be started. In very cold conditions, the glow plugs remain on after the engine has started (post-heating) – this helps the engine to run more smoothly during warm-up, and reduces exhaust emissions.

Older diesel engines, including the previous Endura-DE, had injection pumps which were equipped with a solenoid valve to cut the fuel supply when the ignition switch is turned off, to stop the engine (the valve was usually known as a 'stop' solenoid). The Endura-DI injection pump does not have a stop solenoid – instead, the ECU is able to 'switch off' the injection pump via the pump control unit, and this forms part of the vehicle immobiliser system.

The fuel system has a built-in 'strategy' to prevent it from drawing in air, should the car run low on fuel. The ECU monitors the level of fuel in the tank, via the gauge sender unit. After switching on the low fuel level warning light, it will eventually induce a misfire as a further warning to the driver, and lower the engine's maximum speed until the engine stops.

The fuel system on diesel engines is normally very reliable. Provided that clean fuel is used and the specified maintenance is conscientiously carried out, no problems should be experienced. The injection pump

and injectors may require overhaul after a high mileage has been covered, but this cannot be done on a DIY basis.

Precautions

⚠️ **Warning: It is necessary to take certain precautions when working on the fuel system components, particularly the fuel injectors. Before carrying out any operations on the fuel system, refer to the precautions given in 'Safety first!' at the beginning of this manual, and to any additional warning notes at the start of the relevant Sections. In particular, note that the injectors on direct injection diesel engines operate at extremely high pressures (approximately 1100 bar/16 000 psi on the Endura-DI), making the injector spray extremely hazardous.**

2 Fuel system – priming and bleeding

1 As this system is intended to be 'self-bleeding', no hand-priming pump or separate bleed screws/nipples are fitted.

2 When any part of the system has been disturbed therefore, air must be purged from the system by cranking the engine on the starter motor until it starts. When it has started, keep the engine running for approximately 5 minutes to ensure that all air has been removed from the system. To minimise the strain on the battery and starter motor when trying to start the engine, crank it in 10-second bursts, pausing for 30 seconds each time, until the engine starts.

3 Depending on the work that has been carried out, it may be possible to partially prime the system so as to spare the battery by reducing as much as possible the amount of cranking time required to start the engine. To spare the battery, fill the filter with clean fuel via its vent screw opening, but it is essential that no dirt is introduced into the system and that no diesel fuel is poured over vulnerable components when doing this.

4 If a hand-operated vacuum pump is available, this can be connected to the pump's fuel return union and used to suck fuel through the supply lines and filter. This will obviously save the battery a good deal of work. If a long length of clear plastic tubing is used to connect the vacuum pump to the injection pump union, it will be easier to see when fuel emerges free from air bubbles. Turn the ignition switch to position II so that fuel can pass through the pump.

5 If air has entered the injector pipes, slacken each union at the injectors and crank the engine until fuel emerges, then tighten securely all unions and mop up the spilt fuel. Start the engine and keep it running for a few minutes to ensure that all air has been expelled.

3 Fuel system – contamination problems

1 If, at any time, sudden fuel filter blockage, poor starting or otherwise unsatisfactory engine performance should be traced to the appearance of black sludge or slime within the fuel system, this may be due to corrosion caused by the presence of various micro-organisms in the fuel. These can live in the fuel tank if water is allowed to remain there in significant quantities, their waste products causing corrosion of steel and other metallic components of the fuel system.

2 If the fuel system is thought to be contaminated in this way, immediately seek the advice of a Ford dealer or diesel specialist. Thorough treatment is required to cure the problem and to prevent it from occurring again.

3 If you are considering treating the vehicle on a DIY basis, proceed as follows. Do not re-use the contaminated fuel.

4 First drain and remove the fuel tank, flush it thoroughly with clean diesel fuel, and use a torch to examine as much as possible of its interior. If the contamination is severe, the tank must be steam-cleaned internally and then flushed again with clean diesel fuel.

5 Disconnect the fuel feed and return hoses from the injection pump, remove the fuel filter element and flush through the system's feed and return lines with clean diesel fuel.

6 Renew the filter element, refit the fuel tank and reconnect the fuel lines, then fill the tank with clean diesel fuel and bleed the system as described above. Watch carefully for signs of the problem occurring again.

7 While it is unlikely that such contamination will be found beyond the fuel filter, if it is thought to have reached the injection pump, the pump may require cleaning. This is a task only for the local diesel specialist. Do not attempt to disturb any part of the pump or to clean it yourself.

8 The most common cause of excessive quantities of water being in the fuel is condensation from the water vapour in the air. Diesel fuel tanks (whether underground storage tanks or that in the vehicle) are more susceptible to this problem than petrol tanks because of petrol's higher vapour pressure. Water formation in the vehicle's tank can be minimised by keeping the tank as full as possible at all times, and by using the vehicle regularly.

9 Note that proprietary additives are available to inhibit the growth of micro-organisms in vehicle fuel tanks or storage tanks. Modern diesel fuels should by now contain these additives in any case.

10 If you buy all your fuel from the same source and suspect that to be the source of the contamination, the owner or operator should be advised. Otherwise, the risk of taking on contaminated fuel can be minimised by using only reputable filling stations which have a good turnover.

4.1 Disconnect the inlet air temperature sensor wiring plug

4.4a Lift out the air cleaner assembly . . .

4 Air cleaner assembly and air inlet components – removal and refitting

Air cleaner assembly

1 Disconnect the wiring from the inlet air temperature sensor **(see illustration)**.
2 Release the hose clip and disconnect the air inlet duct from the air cleaner cover. Note that the hose clip may not be of the screw type, and will have to be separated by prising the crimped section with a small screwdriver. The clip can be re-used if care is taken, but it may be preferable to fit a screw-drive clip when refitting.
3 Disconnect the breather hose leading to the cylinder head cover.
4 Lift the air cleaner to release it from the rubber grommets, and disconnect the hose from the port underneath **(see illustrations)**.
5 Check the rubber grommets for deterioration and renew them if necessary.
6 Refitting is the reverse of the removal procedure. Ensure that the air cleaner pegs seat fully in their rubber grommets.

Air inlet components

7 If removing the inlet duct between the air cleaner and turbocharger, first ensure that the engine is cool. Release the hose clip and carefully ease the duct off the turbocharger. Note that the hose clip may not be of the screw type, and will have to be separated by prising the crimped section with a small

screwdriver. The clip can be re-used if care is taken, but it may be preferable to fit a screw-drive clip when refitting.
8 To remove the air inlet duct attached to the air cleaner base, first remove the air cleaner assembly as described in paragraphs 1 to 4.
9 Prise up the two clips securing the duct to the engine compartment front panel, then separate the two halves of the duct at the sleeve joint next to the battery. The rear half of the duct is clipped into the engine left-hand mounting bracket. The duct can, however, be removed complete, with some manoeuvring **(see illustration)**.
10 Refitting is a reversal of removal.

5 Accelerator pedal – removal and refitting
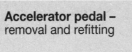

Removal

1 Remove five screws and take out the trim panel above the driver's footwell to gain access to the accelerator pedal; unclip the datalink connector plug from the panel as it is removed.
2 Disconnect the wiring plug from the accelerator position sensor, then unscrew the bolts and remove the accelerator pedal assembly.

Refitting

3 Refit in the reverse order of removal. On completion, check the action of the pedal with the engine running.

4.4b . . . and disconnect the hose underneath

4.9 Removing the air cleaner front inlet duct

6 Fuel tank – removal, inspection and refitting

Note: *Refer to the warning note in Section 1 before proceeding.*
1 Refer to Chapter 4A, Section 9. The basic procedure for tank removal on diesel models is much the same as that for petrol versions, but ignore the references to the charcoal canister and the fuel filter. The fuel supply and return connections are at the front of the tank, approximately where the fuel filter is located on petrol models.

7 Fuel gauge sender unit – removal and refitting

Note: *Refer to the warning note in Section 1 before proceeding. Ford technicians use a special wrench to unscrew the pump/sender unit retaining ring, but ordinary tools can be used successfully (see text).*
1 The fuel gauge sender unit is located in the top face of the fuel tank. The unit can only be detached and withdrawn from the tank after the tank is released and lowered from under the vehicle.
2 Removing the fuel gauge sender unit is a very similar procedure to that for removing the combined fuel pump and sender unit fitted to petrol models, described in Chapter 4A, Section 10.

8 Fuel tank roll-over valves – removal and refitting

1 Refer to Chapter 4A, Section 11 (remove the fuel tank as described in Section 6 of this Chapter).

9 Fuel tank filler pipe – removal and refitting

1 Refer to Chapter 4A, Section 12.

10 Diesel injection system – checking

Note: *Refer to the warning note in Section 1 before proceeding.*
1 If a fault appears in the diesel injection system, first ensure that all the system wiring connectors are securely connected and free of corrosion. Then ensure that the fault is not due to poor maintenance; ie, check that the air cleaner filter element is clean, the valve clearances are correct, the cylinder compression pressures are correct, the fuel

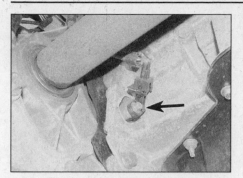

11.1 The crankshaft position sensor is located at the rear of the engine (arrowed)

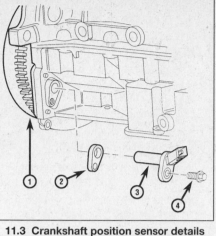

11.3 Crankshaft position sensor details

1 *Flywheel*
2 *Spacer*
3 *Crankshaft position sensor*
4 *Mounting bolt*

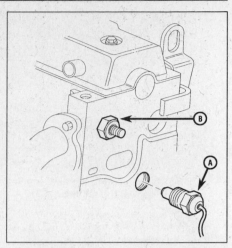

11.5 Cylinder head temperature sensor (A) is fitted below oil pressure switch (B)

filter has been drained (or changed) and the engine breather hoses are clear and undamaged, referring to Chapter 1B or Chapter 2C.

2 If these checks fail to reveal the cause of the problem, the vehicle should be taken to a suitably-equipped Ford dealer for testing. A diagnostic connector is incorporated in the engine management system wiring harness, into which dedicated electronic test equipment can be plugged (the connector is located behind a small panel in the driver's side lower facia – unclip and remove the panel for access). The test equipment is capable of 'interrogating' the engine management system ECU electronically and accessing its internal fault log (reading fault codes).

3 Fault codes can only be extracted from the ECU using a dedicated fault code reader. A Ford dealer will obviously have such a reader, but they are also available from other suppliers, including Haynes. It is unlikely to be cost-effective for the private owner to purchase a fault code reader, but a well-equipped local garage or auto-electrical specialist will have one.

4 Using this equipment, faults can be pinpointed quickly and simply, even if their occurrence is intermittent. Testing all the system components individually in an attempt to locate the fault by elimination is a time-consuming operation that is unlikely to be fruitful (particularly if the fault occurs dynamically), and carries a high risk of damage to the ECU's internal components.

5 Experienced home mechanics equipped with a diesel tachometer or other diagnostic equipment may be able to check the engine idle speed; if found to be out of specification, the vehicle must be taken to a suitably-equipped Ford dealer for assessment. The engine idle speed is not manually adjustable; incorrect test results indicate the need for maintenance (possibly, injector cleaning or recalibration) or a fault within the injection system.

6 If excessive smoking or knocking is evident, it may be due to a problem with the fuel injectors. Proprietary treatments are available which can be added to the fuel, in order to clean the injectors. Injectors do deteriorate

with prolonged use, however, and it is reasonable to expect them to need reconditioning or renewal after 60 000 miles (100 000 km) or so. Accurate testing, overhaul and calibration of the injectors must be left to a specialist.

11 Diesel injection system electronic components – removal and refitting

Crankshaft position sensor

1 The sensor is located at the flywheel end of the engine, low down at the rear **(see illustration)**. For improved access, apply the handbrake then jack up the front of the vehicle and support it on axle stands (see *Jacking and vehicle support*).

2 Where fitted, unclip the cover from the crankshaft position sensor, then disconnect the wiring plug.

3 Unscrew the mounting bolt and withdraw the sensor. If a spacer is fitted between the sensor and engine, it is vital that this is refitted when refitting the sensor, or the sensor head will hit the rotor teeth **(see illustration)**.

4 Refitting is a reversal of removal.

Cylinder head temperature (CHT) sensor

5 The switch is screwed into the left-hand (flywheel) end of the cylinder head, behind the vacuum pump and below the oil pressure warning light switch **(see illustration)**.

6 Open the bonnet and disconnect the battery negative (earth) lead – see *Disconnecting the battery*.

7 To improve access to the switch, it will be necessary to remove (or partially remove) the air cleaner inlet duct and the intercooler right-hand air duct, referring to Sections 4 and 18.

8 It will also be helpful to release the hoses and remove the crankcase ventilation system oil separator from the left-hand end of the cylinder head, as described in Chapter 4C, Section 3.

9 Trace the wiring from the sensor, and disconnect it at the plug, which is clipped to the brake vacuum pump at the front of the engine **(see illustration)**.

10 The sensor can now be unscrewed and removed **(see illustration)**. However, access to the sensor is such that great difficulty may be experienced in getting a tool to fit onto it. Ultimately, it may be necessary to cut the sensor wiring, unscrew the sensor using a thin-wall socket or box spanner, then re-make the wiring after fitting, using a suitable connector.

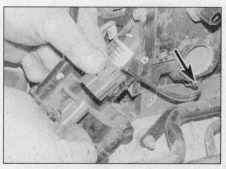

11.9 Unclip and disconnect the wiring plug, then remove the sensor (arrowed)

11.10 Cylinder head temperature sensor (arrowed)

11.13a Disconnecting the air temperature sensor at the air cleaner . . .

11.13b . . . and the other sensor at the intercooler

11.16 MAP sensor location on engine compartment bulkhead

11 Refitting is a reversal of removal. Clean the threads of the sensor and mounting hole, then refit the sensor and tighten it to the specified torque.

Inlet air temperature sensors

12 Two sensors are fitted to the Endura-DI engine – one on the air cleaner inlet duct, and one on the intercooler duct leading to the inlet manifold, behind the right-hand headlight. The removal and refitting procedure for either sensor is identical.
13 Disconnect the wiring from the sensor, then twist the sensor anti-clockwise and remove it (see illustrations).
14 Refitting is a reversal of removal.

Vehicle speed sensor

15 Refer to Chapter 7A.

Manifold absolute pressure (MAP) sensor

16 The MAP sensor is mounted on the engine compartment bulkhead, next to the brake/clutch fluid reservoir (see illustration).
17 Disconnect the vacuum hose from the port at the base of the sensor, then disconnect the wiring plug behind it.
18 Unscrew and remove the two mounting bolts, and withdraw the sensor from the bulkhead.
19 Prior to refitting, remove the vacuum hose from the inlet manifold connection (see illustration), and check it for signs of perishing or splitting, especially at the pipe ends.
20 Refitting is a reversal of removal, ensuring

that the wiring plug and vacuum hose are securely reconnected.

Fuel control valve

21 The control valve is fitted to the top of the fuel filter (at the right-hand rear corner of the engine compartment), and contains a bi-metal strip. Its function is to close the fuel return to the fuel tank at low fuel temperatures, allowing fuel which has been warmed by passing through the injection pump to flow back into the filter, thus warming the fuel being drawn from the tank.
22 Noting their positions for refitting, disconnect the fuel supply and outlet pipes from the connections at the fuel filter (see illustration).
23 Extract the wire clip securing the control valve and return pipe, and release it from the top of the filter (see illustration). Once again noting the fitted positions of the fuel pipes, disconnect them from each end of the valve (note that the return pipe may in this case be black, and smaller in diameter than the supply pipe).
24 Refitting is a reversal of removal. Ensure that the pipe connections are correctly and securely remade, then run the engine and check for signs of fuel leakage.

EGR vacuum regulator solenoid

25 Refer to Chapter 4C.

Clutch pedal position switch

26 Remove five screws and take out the trim panel above the driver's footwell to gain access to the clutch pedal; unclip the datalink

connector plug from the panel as it is removed.
27 Reach up and disconnect the wiring from the clutch switch at the top of the pedal, then twist the switch anti-clockwise and remove it from the pedal bracket.
28 Refitting is a reversal of removal.

Stop-light and brake pedal position switches

29 These are two separate switches, both fitted at the top of the brake pedal. Remove five screws and take out the trim panel above the driver's footwell to gain access to the brake pedal; unclip the datalink connector plug from the panel as it is removed.
30 Reach up and disconnect the wiring from the switch at the top of the pedal; if both switches are removed at once, take care to note which wiring plug serves which switch (see illustration). Twist the switch through 90° and remove it from the pedal bracket. The stop-light switch (upper) is removed by twisting anti-clockwise, while the brake pedal position switch (lower) is twisted clockwise to remove.

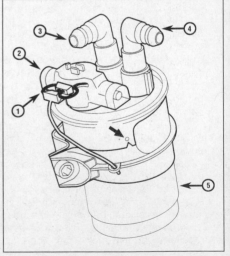

11.23 Fuel control valve and related components

1 Retaining wire clip
2 Fuel control valve
3 Filter outlet
4 Filter inlet
5 Fuel filter

11.19 MAP sensor vacuum connection (arrowed) at inlet manifold

11.22 Overhead view of the fuel filter, showing pipe layout

31 Refitting is a reversal of removal.

Accelerator pedal sensor

32 The accelerator pedal sensor is integral with the pedal assembly, which is removed as described in Section 5.

Injection pump control unit (PCU)

33 The pump control unit is integral with the injection pump, and cannot be separated from it. If a new injection pump is fitted, the PCU must be electronically 'matched' to the engine management module (ECU), otherwise the pump will not function correctly (or even at all, if the immobiliser function is not correctly set up) – this is a task for a Ford dealer, as specialised electronic equipment is required.

Engine management module (ECU)

Note: *The module is fragile. Take care not to drop it, or subject it to any other kind of impact. Do not subject it to extremes of temperature, or allow it to get wet. The module wiring plug must never be disconnected while the ignition switch is on.*
34 The engine management module is located behind the facia, on the right-hand side. First disconnect the battery negative (earth) lead (see *Disconnecting the battery*).

Right-hand-drive models

35 Pull up the weatherstrip from the driver's door aperture, and release it from the side trim.
36 Prise off the trim panel fitted between the end of the facia panel and the door aperture, approximately half way up the door aperture.
37 Prise out the two screwhead covers, then unscrew and remove the two screws securing the footwell side trim panel. Remove the trim panel for access to the module.
38 Remove the four screws securing the driver's side lower trim panel. Remove the panel from the facia, and detach the data link connector socket.

Left-hand-drive models

39 Remove the glovebox as described in Chapter 11.
40 Remove the four screws securing the passenger's side lower trim panel. Remove the panel from the facia.

All models

41 Disconnect the small wiring plug from the central security module **(see illustration)**.
42 Release the spring clips securing the main module in position, and remove the module downwards into the footwell.
43 The ECU wiring connector is protected by a tamperproof shield, secured by a shear-bolt and welded nut, which must be drilled to remove the bolt. Great care must be taken not to damage the wiring harness during drilling.
44 First drill a 3 mm pilot hole in the nut, then enlarge the hole using an 8 mm drill until the shear-bolt can be removed.

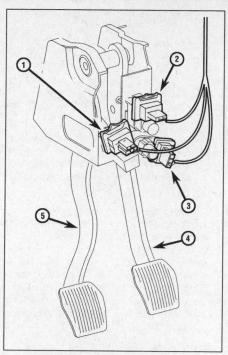

11.30 Foot pedal switch details

1	*Clutch pedal switch*	*3*	*Brake pedal position switch*
2	*Brake stop-light switch*	*4*	*Brake pedal*
		5	*Clutch pedal*

45 With the shear-bolt removed, slide off the tamperproof shield.
46 Remove the wiring connector securing screw, then disconnect the plug from the ECU, and remove the module from the car.
47 Refitting is a reversal of removal. Use a new shear-bolt, and tighten it until the head shears off.

---

12 Fuel injection pump timing – checking and adjustment

Injection pump timing is carried using the TDC setting method described in Section 13. It would appear that no further checking or setting of the pump timing is possible – at least, not without dedicated test equipment.

13.4 Unbolt the alternator mounting bracket

11.41 Unclip the security module before removing the main ECU module

Where necessary, the injection pump should be checked and adjusted by a Ford dealer or diesel engine specialist.

---

13 Fuel injection pump – removal and refitting

Caution: *Be careful not to allow dirt into the injection pump or injector pipes during this procedure.*
Note: *If a new injection pump is fitted, there is a possibility that the engine may not run properly (or even at all) until both the engine management module (ECU) and the new pump control unit have been electronically 'configured' using Ford diagnostic equipment. In particular, the immobiliser may not function correctly, leading to the engine not starting.*

Removal

1 Disconnect the battery negative (earth) lead (see *Disconnecting the battery*).
2 Remove the timing belt as described in Chapter 2C.
3 Remove the injection pipes as described in Section 14.
4 Remove the alternator as described in Chapter 5A, then unbolt and remove the alternator mounting bracket, which is secured by five bolts **(see illustration)**.
5 On models with air conditioning, remove the four bolts securing the air conditioning compressor, using the information in Chapter 3 if necessary. The refrigerant lines **must not** be disconnected – unbolt the compressor, and tie it up to one side.
6 If the car was raised to remove the alternator, refit the front wheel (where removed) and lower the car to the ground.
7 Unbolt and remove the injection pump rear mounting bracket, which is secured by four bolts and one nut **(see illustration)**.
8 Slacken the three bolts securing the injection pump sprocket, and remove the sprocket from the pump. The sprocket may need to be prevented from turning as this is done – it should prove sufficient to select a gear and apply the handbrake, but it may be necessary to jam the flywheel ring gear as

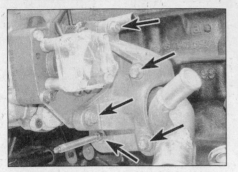

13.7 Undo the four bolts and the one retaining nut (arrowed)

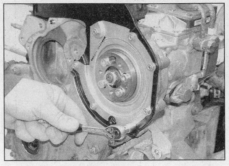

13.9 Remove the seal housing retaining nuts

13.13 Undo the three pump retaining bolts (arrowed)

described in Chapter 2C, Section 6. The sprocket is sealed to the inner pulley using RTV sealant, and may need to be prised free; recover the metal gasket.

9 Remove the seven nuts which secure the injection pump oil seal housing, and withdraw the seal housing from around the pump inner pulley **(see illustration)**. Withdraw the timing belt backplate from the oil pump housing studs, noting which way round it fits.

10 Noting their positions for refitting, prise out the plastic retaining clips and disconnect the fuel supply and return pipes from the connections at the pump. The supply pipe is marked with a white band, and the return pipe has a red band.

11 Disconnect the wiring connector from the pump control unit, on top of the injection pump. The connector is secured by a clip, which slides forwards to release.

Caution: As with any ECU, take care while the wiring connector is unplugged that the pump control unit is not damaged by static discharge across the exposed wiring pins – it may be advisable to cover the pins with a strip of paper, taped in place (do not use tape directly, as this may contaminate the pins).

12 Unscrew and remove the four bolts securing the injection pump to the drive pulley. As with removal of its timing belt sprocket, it may be necessary to prevent the pulley from turning as the bolts are loosened.

13 The three pump mounting bolts can now be slackened, and the pump removed **(see illustration)**. The bolts are accessible through the elongated holes in the drive pulley – support the pump as the bolts are unscrewed, noting that the bolts cannot be removed completely. When the bolts have been fully slackened, carefully withdraw the pump from the engine. Recover the metal gasket from the pump mounting face.

Refitting

14 Ensure that the engine is still set at TDC, using the information in Chapter 2C, Section 3, if necessary.

15 Offer the pump into position, with a new gasket, and fit the three mounting bolts, tightening them to the specified torque. Using a 6 mm drill bit, align the hole in the pump drive pulley with the hole in the pump rotor mounting face **(see illustration)**.

16 Keeping the drill bit in position, refit the four pump drive pulley bolts, and tighten them to the specified torque.

17 If a new pump is being fitted, note that a new pump is supplied locked in the TDC position. The locking is achieved by a small screw near the pump control unit – remove the screw, fit the small horseshoe spacer provided with the new pump, and tighten the screw to the specified torque **(see illustration)**.

18 Refit the timing belt backplate over the oil pump housing studs.

19 Before fitting the new injection pump oil seal housing, fit the plastic protector sleeve (which should be included with the oil seal

housing) over the shoulder of the injection pump drive pulley.

20 Fit the new oil seal housing over the protector sleeve, and secure with the seven nuts. Note that the PTFE oil seal should not be oiled in any way prior to fitting. Tighten the seven nuts in a diagonal sequence to the specified torque, then remove the protector sleeve **(see illustration)**.

21 Fit a new metal gasket to the pump drive pulley. Apply a coating of Loctite RTV 5910 sealant to the pulley (avoiding the three sprocket bolt holes). The three bolts should be cleaned, then lightly coated with Loctite 518 locking fluid. Offer up the timing belt sprocket, aligning the bolt holes carefully, then fit the three bolts and tighten to the specified torque.

22 Refit the injection pump rear mounting bracket, and tighten the four bolts and nut to the specified torque.

23 Refit the alternator, and (where applicable) the air conditioning compressor, using the information in Chapter 5A and Chapter 3 respectively.

24 Remove the covers from the injection pump unions, and from the injectors. Install the injector pipe assembly (Ford state that a new pipe assembly must be fitted whenever it is disturbed), and tighten the unions at the pump to the specified torque. Fit the unions to the injectors, screwing them all the way on, but tightening them by hand only at this stage.

25 Reconnect the wiring plug to the pump control unit, and secure it in position with the locking catch.

26 Refit the fuel supply pipe (colour-coded white) to the injection pump, and secure by pressing the plastic retaining clip fully home.

27 Before reconnecting the return pipe, the injection pump should be primed with fuel, to reduce the length of time spent cranking the engine at start-up. If a new pump has been fitted (or the old pump has been off the engine for some time), priming with fuel is essential, as the fuel lubricates the pump internals, which may otherwise be dry. Follow the procedures in Section 2. If a vacuum pump is not available, a new pump can be partially primed by pouring in clean fuel via the fuel supply and return connections – take precautions against fuel spillage on delicate

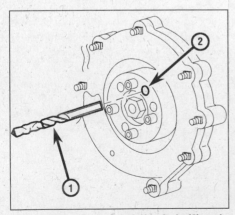

13.15 Injection pump timing hole (2) and 6 mm drill bit (1)

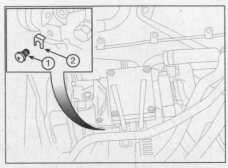

13.17 Injection pump locking screw (1) and horseshoe spacer (2)

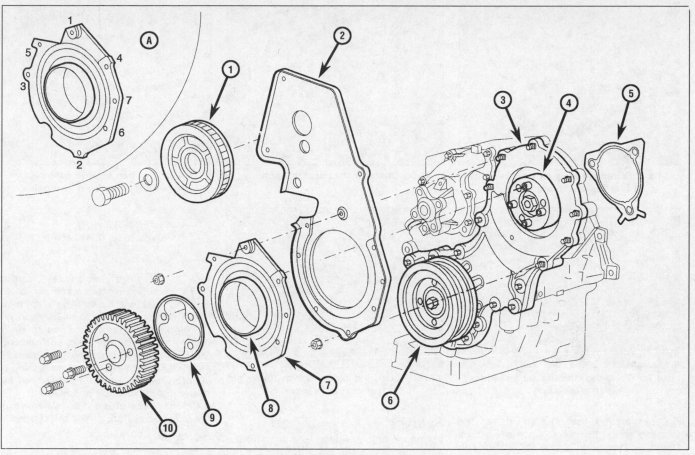

13.20 Fuel injection pump oil seal housing and related components

1 Camshaft pulley
2 Timing belt backplate
3 Oil pump housing
4 Fuel injection pump rotor
5 Metal gasket
6 Crankshaft pulley
7 Fuel injection pump oil seal housing
8 Protector sleeve
9 Metal gasket
10 Fuel injection pump sprocket
A Oil seal housing bolt tightening sequence

components by covering the surrounding area with clean rags, and be very careful not to introduce dirt into the pump.

28 Refit the fuel return pipe (colour-coded red) to the injection pump, and secure by pressing the plastic retaining clip fully home.

29 Refit the timing belt as described in Chapter 2C.

30 Making sure that the fuel pipe unions at the injectors are fully screwed on but only hand-tight, place some clean rags around each union, to reduce the fuel spray. Keeping well clear of the injectors, crank the engine on the starter until fuel (probably preceded by air) emerges from all four pipe unions. If the engine starts, or tries to start, switch off immediately.

31 Clean up any spilt fuel, then tighten the injector pipe unions to the specified torque.

32 Start the engine, and let it idle, noting that it may take a while before a stable idle speed is achieved, as the engine management module (ECU) may have to re-learn some of the 'adaptive' values. As the engine warms-up, check for signs of leakage from the fuel unions. If no leakage is evident, take the car

for a short journey (of at least 5 miles) to allow the ECU to complete its 'learning' process.

33 If a new injection pump has been fitted, refer to the Note at the start of this Section. Otherwise, if fuel is present at the injector unions (see paragraph 30), and the pump control unit wiring has been reconnected, the engine should start. If the engine shows signs of firing, but will not run, a push-start or tow-start may coax it to life, but this should only

14.4 Removing the insulation cover from the injection pump

be attempted by the experienced DIY mechanic. If the battery has been weakened by repeated attempts to start, charge it using a battery charger before continuing.

14 Injection pipes – removal and refitting

Caution: Be careful not to allow dirt into the injection system during this procedure.

Removal

1 The injection pipes should be removed as a set. At the time of writing, it is not clear whether individual pipes are available – if so, the pipes can be separated after releasing the anti-rattle clips.

2 Disconnect the battery negative (earth) lead (see *Disconnecting the battery*).

3 Remove the intercooler as described in Section 18.

4 Cut the cable-ties securing the insulation cover fitted over the pump, and remove the cover **(see illustration)**.

14.5 Unscrewing the pipe unions at the injector pump

14.6a Unscrew the injector unions . . .

14.6b . . . then remove each pair of injection pipes from the engine

14.7a Cover the injection pump unions with a plastic bag . . .

14.7b . . . and the injectors with fingers cut from a rubber glove

15 Fuel injectors –
removal, testing and refitting

> ⚠ *Warning: Exercise extreme caution when working on the fuel injectors. Never expose the hands or any part of the body to injector spray, as the high working pressure can cause the fuel to penetrate the skin, with possibly fatal results. You are strongly advised to have any work which involves testing the injectors under pressure carried out by a dealer or fuel injection specialist.*
> *Caution: Be careful not to allow dirt into the injection system during this procedure.*

Removal

5 Clean around the pipe unions at the injectors and at the pump. Counter-hold the pump adapters with one spanner, and unscrew the pipe union nuts with another **(see illustration)**.
6 Unscrew the injector union nuts, then remove each pair of pipes from the engine **(see illustrations)**.
7 Plug or cap all open unions to keep fuel in and dirt out – we used a plastic bag taped over the pump, and fingers cut from old rubber gloves over the injectors **(see illustrations)**.
8 Ford state that new pipes must be used when refitting – consult a Ford dealer or diesel specialist for advice on this point, but it would seem prudent to fit new pipes if a new pump is being installed.

Refitting

9 When refitting, make sure that all the anti-rattle clips are in place. Do not bend or strain the pipes. Blow through the pipes with compressed air (from an air line or a foot pump) to expel any debris.
10 Refit the pipe assemblies to both the injectors and injection pump, initially hand-tightening the union nuts. With the assembly in place, fully tighten the nuts to the specified torque.
11 Reconnect the battery negative (earth) lead (see *Disconnecting the battery*).
12 If only the pipes have been removed, there should be no need to bleed the system (Section 2).
13 Run the engine and check the disturbed unions for leaks.

1 Disconnect the battery negative (earth) lead (see *Disconnecting the battery*). Clean around the injectors and the injection pipe unions.
2 Remove the injection pipes as described in Section 14.
3 Unscrew the retaining bolts and remove the injector clamp plates, noting how they are fitted over the flat section of the injectors **(see illustration)**. New clamp bolts must be obtained for refitting.
4 The injectors are released by turning them 90° clockwise, then pulling them upwards and out. Recover the copper heat shield washers from each injector **(see illustration)**, and discard them – new washers must be used on reassembly.
5 Take care not to drop the injectors, nor allow the needles at their tips to become damaged.

Testing

6 Testing of injectors requires a special high-pressure test rig, and is best left to a professional. If the skin is exposed to spray from the injectors, the pressure is high enough for diesel fuel to penetrate the skin, with potentially fatal results.
7 Defective injectors should be renewed or professionally repaired. DIY repair is not a practical proposition.

Refitting

8 Commence refitting by inserting new heat shield washers, domed faces downwards, to the injector bores.

15.3 Undo the retaining bolt and remove the injector clamp plate

15.4 Recover the copper washer from the injector recess in the cylinder head

9 Insert the injectors and turn them anti-clockwise to secure.
10 Refit the injector clamps, tightening the new retaining bolts to the specified torque **(see illustration)**.
11 Refit the injection pipes with reference to Section 14 **(see illustration)**.

16 Glow plugs –
testing, removal and refitting

Testing

1 If the system malfunctions, testing is ultimately by substitution of known good units, but some preliminary checks may be made as follows.
2 Connect a voltmeter or 12-volt test light between the glow plug supply cable and earth (engine or vehicle metal) **(see illustration)**. Make sure that the live connection is kept clear of the engine and bodywork.
3 Have an assistant switch on the ignition and check that voltage is applied to the glow plugs. Note that, after a certain number of seconds, the system cuts out automatically if the engine is not started, to prevent battery drain. Switch off the ignition.
4 If an ammeter of suitable range (0 to 50 amp approx) is available, connect it between the glow plug feed wire and the busbar (the wire which connects the four plugs together). During the pre-heating period, the ammeter should show a current draw of approximately

16.2 Glow plug supply connection (arrowed)

15.10 Tighten the injector clamp bolts to the specified torque

8 amps per working plug, ie, 32 amps if all four plugs are working. If one or more plugs appear not to be drawing current, remove the busbar and check each plug separately with a continuity tester or self-powered test light.
5 If there is no supply at all to the glow plugs, the associated wiring may be at fault. Otherwise, this points to a defective cylinder head temperature sensor (see Section 11), or to a problem with the ECU.
6 To locate a defective glow plug, disconnect the main feed wire and the interconnecting busbar from the top of the glow plugs. Be careful not to drop the nuts and washers.
7 Use a continuity tester, or a 12-volt test light connected to the battery positive terminal, to check for continuity between each glow plug terminal and earth. The resistance of a glow plug in good condition is very low (less than 1 ohm), so if the test light does not come on or the continuity tester shows a high resistance, the glow plug is certainly defective.
8 If an ammeter is available, the current draw of each glow plug can be checked. After an initial surge of around 15 to 20 amps, each plug should draw around 10 amps. Any plug which draws much more or less than this is probably defective.
9 As a final check the glow plugs can be removed and inspected as described below.

Removal

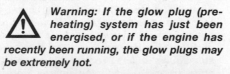 **Warning: If the glow plug (pre-heating) system has just been energised, or if the engine has recently been running, the glow plugs may be extremely hot.**

15.11 Refit the injection pipes, tightening the unions up evenly

10 Access to the glow plugs is poor, and (although not essential) will be made much easier if the injection pipes are removed as described in Section 14.
11 Remove the screw securing the feed wire in front of the dipstick tube **(see illustration)**.
12 Unscrew the nut securing each glow plug connector, then lift the wiring away from the plugs **(see illustration)**. Note that the wiring feeds under the thermostat housing, but the wiring need not be removed completely for access to the plugs.
13 Unscrew the glow plugs, and remove them from the engine for inspection **(see illustration)**.
14 Inspect the glow plug stems for signs of damage. A badly burned or charred stem may be an indication of a faulty fuel injector – consult a diesel specialist for advice if necessary. Otherwise, if one plug is found to be faulty and the engine has completed a high mileage, it is probably worth renewing all four plugs as a set.

Refitting

15 Refitting is a reversal of removal, noting the following points:

a) Apply a little anti-seize compound (or copper brake grease) to the glow plug threads.
b) Make sure when re-making the glow plug wiring connections that the contact surfaces are clean.
c) Tighten the glow plugs to the specified torque.

16.11 Unscrewing the glow plug feed wire

16.12 Number 4 glow plug and wiring

16.13 Check glow plugs for signs of burning

17.13 Turbocharger oil feed union (arrowed)

17 Turbocharger – general information, removal and refitting

General information

1 The turbocharger increases engine efficiency by raising the pressure in the inlet manifold above atmospheric pressure. Instead of the air simply being sucked into the cylinders, it is forced in. Additional fuel is supplied by the injection pump, in proportion to the increased amount of air.

2 Energy for the operation of the turbocharger comes from the exhaust gas. The gas flows through a specially-shaped housing (the turbine housing) and in so doing, spins the turbine wheel. The turbine wheel is attached to a shaft, at the end of which is another vaned wheel, known as the compressor wheel. The compressor wheel spins in its own housing, and compresses the inducted air on the way to the inlet manifold.

3 Between the turbocharger and the inlet manifold, the compressed air passes through an intercooler (see Section 18 for details). The purpose of the intercooler is to remove from the inducted air some of the heat gained in being compressed. Because cooler air is denser, removal of this heat further increases engine efficiency.

4 Boost pressure (the pressure in the inlet manifold) is limited by a wastegate, which diverts the exhaust gas away from the turbine wheel in response to a pressure-sensitive actuator.

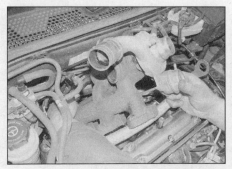

17.16 With the inlet manifold removed, the exhaust manifold can be lifted out

17.15 Exhaust manifold removed to the rear of the engine compartment

5 The turbo shaft is pressure-lubricated by its own dedicated oil feed pipe. The shaft 'floats' on a cushion of oil. Oil is returned to the sump via a return pipe that connects to the sump.

6 The turbocharger on the Endura-DI engine is integral with the exhaust manifold, and is not available separately.

Precautions

7 The turbocharger operates at extremely high speeds and temperatures. Certain precautions must be observed to avoid premature failure of the turbo, or injury to the operator.

Do not operate the turbo with any parts exposed. Foreign objects falling onto the rotating vanes could cause excessive damage and (if ejected) personal injury.

Cover the turbocharger air inlet ducts to prevent debris entering, and clean using lint-free cloths only.

Do not race the engine immediately after start-up, especially if it is cold. Give the oil a few seconds to circulate.

Always allow the engine to return to idle speed before switching it off – do not blip the throttle and switch off, as this will leave the turbo spinning without lubrication.

Allow the engine to idle for several minutes before switching off after a high-speed run.

Observe the recommended intervals for oil and filter changing, and use a reputable oil of the specified quality. Neglect of oil changing, or use of inferior oil, can cause carbon formation on the turbo shaft and subsequent failure. Thoroughly clean the area around all oil pipe unions before disconnecting them, to prevent the ingress of dirt. Store dismantled components in a sealed container to prevent contamination.

Removal

8 The turbocharger should only be removed with the engine completely cool. Disconnect the battery negative lead (see *Disconnecting the battery*).

9 Remove the air cleaner and inlet duct as described in Section 4.

10 Using the information in Section 18 if necessary, disconnect the intercooler air ducts from the turbocharger and inlet manifold, and remove them from the top of

the engine – there is no absolute need to remove the intercooler itself.

11 Remove the EGR tube or cooler, as described in Chapter 4C, Section 4.

12 Using the information in Section 20, remove the catalytic converter.

13 Anticipating some oil spillage, disconnect the oil feed and return pipes from the turbocharger as described below:

a) *Models up to June 1999 have the oil feed pipe secured by a banjo bolt at the top (see illustration), with a separate oil return connection flange on the underside of the housing, secured by two bolts. Recover the copper washers from the banjo bolt, and the O-ring seal from the connection flange.*

b) *On models after June 1999, the oil feed pipe shares the same connection flange as the return pipe, on the underside of the housing, again secured by two bolts. Recover the gasket from the flange.*

14 Remove the four exhaust manifold bolts which can be accessed from above.

15 Support the manifold from below, then remove the remaining two manifold bolts and two nuts, and withdraw the assembly rearwards from the cylinder head. Place the assembly securely at the rear of the engine compartment **(see illustration)**.

16 In order to withdraw the exhaust manifold, the easiest option we found was to remove the inlet manifold as described in Section 19. This allows the exhaust manifold assembly to be withdrawn upwards **(see illustration)**.

17 It is not advisable to separate the wastegate assembly from the turbocharger without first consulting a Ford dealer or turbocharger specialist, as the setting may be lost. Interfering with the wastegate setting may lead to a reduction in performance, or could result in engine damage.

18 If on inspection, there are any signs of internal oil contamination on the turbine or compressor wheels, this indicates failure of the turbocharger oil seals. Renewing these seals is a job best left to a turbocharger specialist. In the event of any problem with the turbocharger, one of these specialists will usually be able to rebuild a defective unit, or offer a rebuilt unit on an exchange basis, either of which will prove cheaper than a new unit.

Refitting

19 Refitting is a reversal of removal, noting the following points:

a) *Clean the mating surfaces, use a new exhaust manifold gasket, and tighten the manifold bolts to the specified torque.*

b) *Refit and tighten the engine rear mounting bolt to the specified torque.*

c) *On models up to June 1999, use new copper washers on the oil feed pipe banjo bolt, and tighten the bolt securely. Fit a new O-ring seal to the oil return flange, and tighten the bolts to the specified torque.*

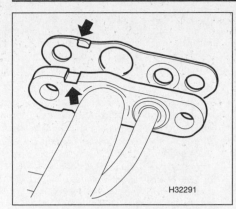

17.19 Turbocharger oil feed/return flange gasket locating tab and notch (arrows)

d) *On models after June 1999, use a new gasket on the oil feed/return flange connection, fitting the gasket according to its locating tab (see illustration). Tighten the flange bolts to the specified torque.*

e) *When refitting the EGR tube/cooler, offer it into position, and hand-tighten the bolts. Position the new clamp as noted on removal, tighten the clamp nut/bolt to the specified torque, then tighten the remaining bolts.*

f) *Refer to Section 20 when refitting the catalytic converter.*

g) *On models with the EGR cooler, top-up the cooling system as necessary (see 'Weekly checks').*

18 Intercooler –
general information, removal and refitting

General information

1 The intercooler is effectively an 'air radiator', used to cool the pressurised inlet air before it enters the engine.

2 When the turbocharger compresses the inlet air, one side-effect is that the air is heated, causing the air to expand. If the inlet air can be cooled, a greater effective volume of air will be inducted, and the engine will produce more power.

3 The compressed air from the turbocharger,

18.5a Undo the two screws (arrowed) . . .

which would normally be fed straight into the inlet manifold, is instead ducted forwards around the left side of the engine to the base of the intercooler. The intercooler is mounted at the front of the car, in the airflow. The heated air entering the base of the unit rises upwards, and is cooled by the airflow over the intercooler fins, much as with the radiator. When it reaches the top of the intercooler, the cooled air is then ducted rearwards around the right side into the inlet manifold.

Removal

4 Disconnect the battery negative lead, and position the lead away from the battery (also see *Disconnecting the battery*).

5 Remove the two screws and lift off the intercooler cover **(see illustrations)**.

6 Slacken the hose clips and disconnect the intercooler air inlet pipe from the left-hand

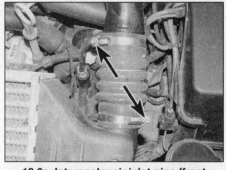

18.6a Intercooler air inlet pipe (front section) hose clips – arrowed

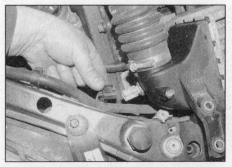

18.7 Disconnect the air temperature sensor wiring plug

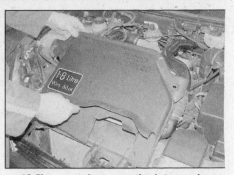

18.5b . . . and remove the intercooler cover

side of the unit (left as seen from the driver's seat). If required, the inlet pipe can be removed completely – remove the nut securing it to the cylinder head cover, loosen the clip securing it to the turbocharger, and remove it **(see illustrations)**.

7 Disconnect the wiring plug from the inlet air temperature sensor, fitted to the outlet pipe on the right-hand side of the unit **(see illustration)**.

8 Slacken the hose clip and disconnect the intercooler air outlet pipe. Again, if required, the pipe can be removed completely, after loosening the clip at the inlet manifold and removing the nut securing the pipe to the cylinder head cover **(see illustrations)**.

9 Remove the four bolts (two each side) securing the intercooler to the engine compartment front panel. Lift the intercooler out of the engine compartment, and place it

18.6b Loosening the hose clip at the inlet manifold

18.8a Loosen the hose clip at the inlet manifold . . .

18.8b . . . then unbolt the rigid section from the cylinder head cover and remove it

18.9a Unscrew the two bolts each side . . .

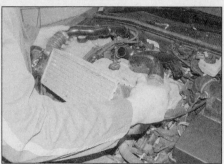

18.9b . . . then lift out the intercooler and remove it

somewhere safe (remember that the intercooler fins are just as vulnerable to damage as those on the radiator) **(see illustrations)**.

Refitting

10 Refitting is a reversal of removal. Check the inlet and outlet pipes for signs of damage, and make sure that the pipe clips are securely tightened.

19 Manifolds – removal and refitting

Inlet manifold

Removal

1 Remove the turbocharger and exhaust manifold to the rear of the engine compart-

19.2 Loosening one of the EGR valve flange bolts

19.6a Unscrew the stud nearest the power steering pump . . .

ment as described in Section 17.
2 Unscrew the two flange bolts underneath the EGR valve, and separate the joint **(see illustration)**. Recover the gasket.
3 Disconnect the wiring plug from the EGR valve on top of the inlet manifold.
4 Noting their positions carefully for refitting, disconnect the vacuum hose from the EGR valve, and the MAP sensor vacuum hose from the inlet manifold **(see illustration)**. Note that the EGR valve is an integral part of the inlet manifold, and does not appear to be available separately.
5 Unbolt the two brackets at the rear of the engine which support the power steering fluid pipe, and move the pipe clear of the inlet manifold.
6 Unscrew and remove the two nuts and six bolts securing the inlet manifold, then unscrew the stud nearest the power steering pump bracket – the stud has a Torx end

19.4 Disconnecting EGR vacuum hose – MAP sensor hose just visible below

19.6b . . . then withdraw the manifold and EGR valve from the engine

fitting, to make unscrewing it easier. Withdraw the manifold from the cylinder head **(see illustrations)**. Recover the manifold gasket, and discard it – a new one should be obtained for refitting.

Refitting

7 Refitting is a reversal of the removal procedure, noting the following points:
  a) *Ensure that the mating faces are clean.*
  b) *Ensure that a new gasket is fitted between the manifold and the cylinder head, and at the EGR flange.*
  c) *With the manifold in place, refit and tighten the stud next to the power steering pump.*
  d) *Tighten the retaining nuts and bolts to the specified torque, working from the centre outwards to avoid warping the manifold.*
  e) *Refit the turbocharger as described in Section 17.*

Exhaust manifold

8 The exhaust manifold is removed with the turbocharger, as described in Section 17. The turbocharger housing is integral with the exhaust manifold.

20 Exhaust system – general information and component renewal

General information

1 The catalytic converter is mounted at an angle, directly below the exhaust manifold. Immediately below the converter is a short flexible section of pipe, connecting to the factory-fitted one-piece rear section, which contains the centre and rear silencers. To renew either silencer, the original rear section must be cut through mid-way between the centre and rear silencers.
2 Before making any cut, offer up the replacement exhaust section for comparison, and if necessary, adjust the cutting points as required. Bear in mind that there must be some 'overlap' allowance, as the original and replacement sections are sleeved together.
3 The system is suspended throughout its entire length by rubber mountings, with a rigid support bracket fitted below the catalytic converter.
4 To remove a part of the system, first jack up the front or rear of the car, and support it on axle stands (see *Jacking and vehicle support*). Alternatively, position the car over an inspection pit, or on car ramps.
5 Ford recommend that all nuts (such as flange joint nuts, clamp joint nuts, or converter-to-manifold nuts) are renewed on reassembly – given that they may be in less-than-perfect condition as a result of corrosion, this seems a good idea, especially as it will make subsequent removal easier.
6 At least on the car seen in our workshop, no gaskets appear to be used on the exhaust

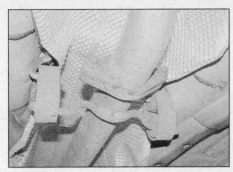

20.9 Separate the exhaust at this flange joint

20.10a View of the catalytic converter support bracket from below – through-bolt arrowed . . .

20.10b . . . the bracket can be removed completely if preferred

system mating surfaces. Make sure that the mating faces of the exhaust system joints are cleaned thoroughly before assembling.

Catalytic converter

Removal

7 To prevent possible damage to the flexible section of pipe behind the flange joint, Ford technicians cable-tie two strips of thick metal on either side, down the length of the flexible section.

8 Remove the four nuts securing the converter to the exhaust manifold.

9 Loosen and remove the nuts at the flange joint just in front of the first exhaust mounting rubbers (the flange joint at the base of the converter is less accessible) **(see illustration)**. Do not attempt to separate the joint at this stage.

10 Support the converter, then remove the through-bolt from the support bracket at the base of the converter. Alternatively, remove the support bracket completely **(see illustrations)**.

11 With the converter supported, separate the flange joint, and feed the converter rearwards out through the heat-shielded 'tunnel' under the car, taking great care not to drop it or knock it, as the internals are fragile **(see illustrations)**. The converter is a bulky component, and it may be necessary to rotate it as it is withdrawn – try not to bend the flexible section if possible.

Refitting

12 Refitting is a reversal of removal. Use new nuts and bolts as necessary, and tighten all fasteners to the specified torque. **Note:** *Exhaust sealant paste should not be used on any part of the exhaust system upstream of the catalytic converter (between the engine and the converter) – even if the sealant does not contain additives harmful to the converter, pieces of it may break off and foul the element, causing local overheating.*

Centre silencer

Removal

13 If the original rear section is still intact, it must be cut at a point between the centre and rear silencers. The cutting point is 2033 mm back from the face of the front flange joint. Bear in mind the advice in paragraph 2 before making any cut; take care to cut the pipe at right-angles to the pipe (and to **only** cut the pipe); clean up any rough edges.

14 If a new rear silencer has been fitted, there will be a clamped sleeve joint at the rear of the centre silencer. Loosen the clamp nuts, but do not try to separate the sleeve joint at this stage.

15 Loosen and remove the nuts, and separate the exhaust at the flange joint in front of the centre silencer (use new nuts when refitting).

16 Unhook the centre silencer from its rubber mountings. If a sleeve joint is used at the rear, twist and pull the pipes to separate the joint. Remove the centre silencer from under the car.

Refitting

17 Refitting is a reversal of removal. Clean up any sleeve joints before mating them together. Use new nuts, and tighten all fasteners to the specified torque.

Rear silencer

Removal

18 If the original rear section is still intact, it must be cut at a point between the centre and rear silencers. The cutting point is 2033 mm back from the face of the front flange joint. Bear in mind the advice in paragraph 2 before making any cut; take care to cut the pipe at

right-angles to the pipe (and to **only** cut the pipe); clean up any rough edges.

19 Unhook the rear silencer from its mounting rubber(s).

20 If the rear silencer has been renewed previously, loosen the clamp nuts until the joint is free, then twist and pull the pipes relative to each other, to free and separate the sleeve joint.

21 Remove the rear silencer from under the car.

Refitting

22 Refitting is a reversal of removal. Clean up any sleeve joints before mating them together. Use new nuts (or a new clamp), and tighten the nuts to the specified torque.

Heat shield(s)

23 The heat shields are secured to the underside of the body by special nuts, or by bolts. The shields are fitted above the exhaust, to reduce radiated heat affecting the cabin or fuel tank.

24 Each shield can be removed separately, but note that some overlap each other, making it necessary to loosen another section first. If a shield is being removed to gain access to a component located behind it, it may prove sufficient in some cases to remove the retaining nuts and/or bolts, and simply lower the shield, without disturbing the exhaust system. Otherwise, remove the exhaust section as described earlier.

20.11a Feed the converter and flexible section downwards . . .

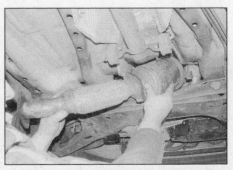

20.11b . . . and out from under the car

Notes

Chapter 4 Part C:
Emission control systems

Contents

Degrees of difficulty

Easy, suitable for novice with little experience	**Fairly easy,** suitable for beginner with some experience	**Fairly difficult,** suitable for competent DIY mechanic	**Difficult,** suitable for experienced DIY mechanic	**Very difficult,** suitable for expert DIY or professional

Specifications

Torque wrench settings	Nm	lbf ft
EGR clamp nut	9	7
EGR cooler mounting bolts	23	17
EGR pipe flange bolts	20	15
EGR pipe union nuts	40	30
EGR valve mounting bolts	20	15
Oxygen sensor:		
1.4 and 1.6 litre models	42	31
1.8 and 2.0 litre models	48	35

1 General information

Emission control systems – petrol-engined models

All petrol models are designed to use unleaded petrol, and are controlled by the Ford EEC-V engine management system to give the best compromise between driveability, fuel consumption and exhaust emission production. In addition, a number of systems are fitted that help to minimise other harmful emissions. A crankcase emission control system is fitted, which reduces the release of pollutants from the engine's lubrication system, and a catalytic converter is fitted which reduces exhaust gas pollutants. An evaporative loss emission control system is fitted which reduces the release of gaseous hydrocarbons from the fuel tank. On 1.4 and 1.6 litre models, an exhaust gas recirculation (EGR) system is fitted, to further reduce emissions.

Crankcase emission control

To reduce the emission of unburned hydrocarbons from the crankcase into the atmosphere, the engine is sealed and the blow-by gases and oil vapour are drawn from inside the crankcase, through a wire-mesh oil separator, into the inlet tract to be burned by the engine during normal combustion.

Under all conditions, the gases are forced out of the crankcase by the (relatively) higher crankcase pressure.

Exhaust emission control

To minimise the amount of pollutants which escape into the atmosphere, all petrol models are fitted with a three-way catalytic converter in the exhaust system. The fuelling system is of the closed-loop type, in which an oxygen (lambda) sensor in the exhaust system provides the engine management system ECU with constant feedback, enabling the ECU to adjust the air/fuel mixture to optimise combustion. Removal of the catalytic converter is covered in Chapter 4A or Chapter 4B.

The oxygen sensor has a built-in heating element, controlled by the ECU through the oxygen sensor relay, to quickly bring the sensor's tip to its optimum operating temperature. The sensor's tip is sensitive to oxygen, and sends a voltage signal to the ECU that varies according on the amount of oxygen in the exhaust gas. If the inlet air/fuel mixture is too rich, the exhaust gases are low in oxygen so the sensor sends a low-voltage signal, the voltage rising as the mixture weakens and the amount of oxygen rises in the exhaust gases. Peak conversion efficiency of all major pollutants occurs if the inlet air/fuel mixture is maintained at the chemically-correct ratio for the complete combustion of petrol of 14.7 parts (by weight) of air to 1 part of fuel (the stoichiometric ratio). The sensor output voltage alters in a large step at this point, the ECU using the signal change as a reference point and correcting the inlet air/fuel mixture accordingly by altering the fuel injector pulse width.

Some later models are fitted with two sensors, one before and one after the converter. This allows a more accurate monitoring of the exhaust gas, and a faster reaction time from the ECU; the efficiency of the converter can also be monitored.

An Exhaust Gas Recirculation (EGR) system is also fitted to 1.4 and 1.6 litre models. This reduces the level of nitrogen oxides produced during combustion by introducing a proportion of the exhaust gas back into the inlet manifold, under certain engine operating conditions, via a plunger valve. The system is controlled electronically by the engine management ECU.

Evaporative emission control

To minimise the escape of unburned hydrocarbons into the atmosphere, an evaporative loss emission control system is fitted to all petrol models. The fuel tank filler cap is sealed and a charcoal canister is mounted behind the fuel tank to collect the petrol vapours released from the fuel contained in the fuel tank. It stores them until

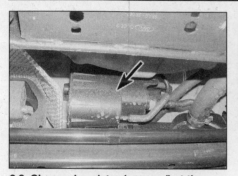

2.2 Charcoal canister (arrowed) at the rear of the tank

2.3 Canister purge valve in the engine compartment

they can be drawn from the canister (under the control of the fuel injection/ignition system ECU) via the purge valve(s) into the inlet tract, where they are then burned by the engine during normal combustion.

To ensure that the engine runs correctly when it is cold and/or idling and to protect the catalytic converter from the effects of an over-rich mixture, the purge control valve(s) are not opened by the ECU until the engine has warmed-up, and the engine is under load; the valve solenoid is then modulated on and off to allow the stored vapour to pass into the inlet tract.

Emission control systems – diesel-engined models

Diesel models are also equipped with the Ford EEC-V engine management system to give the best compromise between driveability, fuel consumption and exhaust emission production. In addition, a number of systems are fitted that help to minimise other harmful emissions. A crankcase emission control system is fitted, which reduces the release of pollutants from the engine's lubrication system, and a catalytic converter is fitted which reduces exhaust gas pollutants. An exhaust gas recirculation (EGR) system is fitted, to further reduce emissions.

Crankcase emission control

To reduce the emission of unburned hydrocarbons from the crankcase into the atmosphere, the engine is sealed and the blow-by gases and oil vapour are drawn from inside the crankcase, through a wire mesh oil

separator, into the inlet tract to be burned by the engine during normal combustion.

Under all conditions ,the gases are forced out of the crankcase by the (relatively) higher crankcase pressure. All diesel engines have a ventilation valve in the camshaft cover, to control the flow of gases from the crankcase.

Exhaust emission control

An oxidation catalyst is fitted in the exhaust system of all diesel-engined models. This has the effect of removing a large proportion of the gaseous hydrocarbons, carbon monoxide and particulates present in the exhaust gas.

An Exhaust Gas Recirculation (EGR) system is fitted to all diesel-engined models. This reduces the level of nitrogen oxides produced during combustion by introducing a proportion of the exhaust gas back into the inlet manifold, under certain engine operating conditions, via a plunger valve. The system is controlled electronically by the engine management system.

2 Evaporative loss emission control system (petrol models) – component renewal

1 The evaporative loss emission control system fitted to petrol models consists of the purge valve, the activated charcoal filter canister and a series of connecting vacuum hoses. Little is possible by way of routine maintenance, except to check that the vacuum hoses are clear and undamaged. Careless servicing work may lead to the hoses

becoming crushed – always take care to route these and other hoses correctly.

2 The canister is located behind the fuel tank, under the car **(see illustration)**. Removal of the components is described as part of the fuel tank removal procedure, in Chapter 4A, Section 9.

3 The purge valve is located at the right-hand rear of the engine compartment (right as seen from the driver's seat) **(see illustration)**. Disconnect the hoses (noting their positions) and wiring plug from the valve, then release it from its mounting bracket. Refitting is a reversal of removal.

3 Crankcase emission system – component renewal

1 The crankcase emission control (or positive crankcase ventilation – PCV) system consists of hoses connecting the crankcase to the air cleaner or inlet manifold. Oil separator units are fitted to some petrol engines, usually at the left-hand end or on the front of the engine.

2 The system requires no attention other than to check at regular intervals that the hoses, valve and oil separator are free of blockages and in good condition.

PCV valve

1.4 and 1.6 litre engines

3 To remove the PCV valve fitted at the front of the engine, proceed as follows (note that this valve is not fitted in all markets).

4 Remove the alternator as described in Chapter 5A.

5 Disconnect the two crankcase ventilation hoses from the inlet manifold, noting their fitted positions.

6 Trace the ventilation hose down to the PCV valve, and disconnect the hose from the valve.

7 Pull the valve from its location, and remove it from the engine compartment **(see illustration)**. If required, the oil separator housing can also be removed, after removing the seven retaining bolts.

1.8 and 2.0 litre petrol engines

8 To remove the PCV valve fitted at the left-hand side of the engine (left as seen from the driver's seat), proceed as follows.

9 Access to the PCV valve is not easy. The valve is located behind the catalytic converter, and below the thermostat housing, in a raised section of the engine block at the far left-hand end of the engine, adjacent to the transmission. Trace the ventilation hose to the valve, and disconnect it.

10 The valve can be removed from its location by pulling it out **(see illustration)**.

11 If the hose connecting the PCV valve to the inlet manifold is damaged, the thermostat housing must be removed for access, as described in Chapter 3.

3.7 PCV valve location on 1.4 and 1.6 litre engines

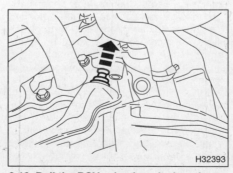

3.10 Pull the PCV valve from its location to remove it

3.17a Unscrew the three retaining bolts (arrowed) . . .

3.17b . . . and remove the oil separator

3.19 When refitting the oil separator, use a new gasket

Diesel engines

12 The PCV valve fitted to diesel engines is incorporated in the camshaft cover. It does not appear that the valve is available separately.

All engines

13 Wash the valve in suitable solvent (such as engine degreaser), and ensure that all passages are clear. Check the hoses for signs of damage, especially at the hose ends. Where an O-ring is used to seal the valve into its location, check the condition of the O-ring before refitting.

14 Refitting is a reversal of removal. Make sure that the hoses are securely and correctly refitted, and that the hoses are routed as before.

Oil separator

1.8 and 2.0 litre petrol engines

15 The oil separator is located on the front of the engine block, behind the exhaust manifold and catalytic converter. To gain access, the exhaust manifold and catalytic converter will almost certainly have to be removed, as described in Chapter 4A.

16 Either disconnect the hose leading to the separator, or pull out the PCV valve.

17 The separator is secured by three bolts. Unscrew the bolts and remove the separator, recovering the gasket (see illustrations).

18 If not already done, remove the PCV valve from the separator. Wash out the oil separator using a suitable solvent (such as engine degreaser), and ensure that its passages are clear.

3.22 Disconnect the oil pressure warning light switch

19 Refitting is a reversal of removal. Use a new gasket, and tighten the retaining bolts securely (see illustration).

Diesel engines

20 The oil separator is located at the left-hand end of the cylinder head. To improve access, remove the air cleaner and inlet duct, as described in Chapter 4B.

21 Disconnect the two upper hoses from the oil separator, noting their locations.

22 To make removing the separator easier, disconnect the wiring plug from the oil pressure warning light switch (see illustration).

23 Unscrew and remove the bolt securing the separator to the cylinder head, and move the separator to gain access to the lower hose. Disconnect the lower hose from the separator, and remove the separator from the engine (see illustrations).

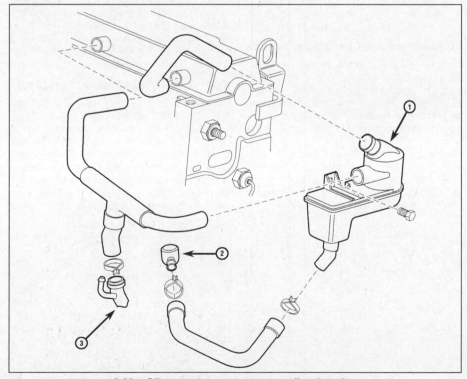

3.23a Oil separator components – diesel engine

1 Oil separator
2 Dipstick guide
3 Crankcase ventilation connection

3.23b Unscrew the mounting bolts . . .

3.23c . . . and remove the separator from the engine

24 Wash out the oil separator using a suitable solvent (such as engine degreaser), and ensure that its passages are clear. Check the hoses for signs of damage, especially at the hose ends.

25 Refitting is a reversal of removal. Make sure that the hoses are securely and correctly refitted, and that the hoses are routed as before.

4 Exhaust Gas Recirculation (EGR) system – component removal

1 The EGR system fitted to 1.4 and 1.6 litre engines, and to the diesel engine, consists of the EGR valve, the modulator (solenoid) valve and a series of connecting vacuum hoses. Some 1.4 and 1.6 litre engines for certain markets have a differential pressure feedback sensor, while diesel engines may additionally be fitted with an EGR cooler, supplied from the engine cooling system.

2 On petrol models, the EGR valve is mounted on a flange joint at the exhaust manifold, and is connected to a second flange joint at the throttle housing by a metal pipe.

3 On diesel models, the EGR valve is part of the inlet manifold. The valve is connected to the exhaust manifold by a large metal tube, which on some models incorporates the EGR cooler.

EGR solenoid

4 The EGR solenoid is mounted centrally at

the rear of the engine compartment, on the bulkhead **(see illustration)**.

5 Disconnect the vacuum hoses from the valve, noting their locations – the top hose leads to a connection at the air cleaner, while the two smaller hoses connect to the EGR valve itself and into the brake servo vacuum hose. Disconnect the wiring plug from the unit, then unscrew the two mounting bolts and remove it from the bulkhead.

6 Refitting is a reversal of removal.

EGR valve

7 On diesel engines, the EGR valve is part of the inlet manifold. Refer to Chapter 4B for manifold removal details.

8 On 1.4 and 1.6 litre engines, the EGR valve is fitted above the exhaust manifold; removal and refitting is as follows.

9 Disconnect the vacuum hose from the top of the valve **(see illustration)**, then loosen the clamp nut on the metal pipe at the base of the valve, and release the pipe connection (it may not be possible to fully separate the joint until the valve is removed).

10 Unscrew and remove the two valve mounting bolts, and withdraw the valve from its location. Recover the gasket, and discard it – a new one must be used when refitting.

11 Refitting is a reversal of removal, noting the following points:

a) *Offer the valve into position, using a new gasket, and fit the mounting bolts hand-tight.*

b) *Tighten the pipe union nut to the specified torque, then tighten the mounting bolts to the specified torque.*

EGR differential pressure sensor

12 The differential pressure sensor (where fitted) is located on the engine compartment bulkhead, next to the EGR solenoid.

13 Note the positions of the vacuum hoses for refitting (they are of different diameter), then disconnect them from the ports on the sensor.

14 Disconnect the sensor wiring plug, then unscrew the sensor mounting bolts and remove the sensor from its location.

15 Refitting is a reversal of removal, making sure that the hoses are correctly refitted.

EGR pipework (petrol engines)

Exhaust manifold-to-EGR valve pipe

16 Loosen the pipe union nuts at either end of the pipe, and disconnect the vacuum hoses from the feed pipe connections halfway along the main pipe.

17 Withdraw the pipe from the rear of the engine.

18 Refitting is a reversal of removal. Tighten the union nuts to the specified torque.

EGR valve supply pipe

19 Remove the EGR valve as described previously in this Section.

20 Unscrew and remove the two bolts securing the pipe flange below the EGR valve location, and separate the joint.

21 Unbolt and remove the engine lifting eye fitted next to the ignition coil, then loosen the EGR pipe clamp bolt also located next to the coil.

22 Disconnect wiring plugs from the ignition coil, and from the throttle position sensor. Also release the brake servo vacuum pipe connection at the front of the throttle housing by depressing the locking collar.

23 Unscrew and remove the two bolts securing the pipe flange at the throttle housing, and separate the joint **(see illustration)**. Recover the O-ring seal, and discard it – a new one must be used when refitting.

24 Withdraw the pipe from the engine, feeding it carefully past any obstructions, and noting how the various pipes and hoses are routed around it, for use when refitting.

25 Refitting is a reversal of removal. Use a new O-ring seal at the front flange joint, and tighten all bolts to the specified torque.

EGR tube/cooler (diesel engine)

26 Depending on market, the EGR system on diesel models may be fitted with a cooler (supplied from the cooling system), which reduces the temperature of the exhaust gas being recycled; the cooler is effectively a water jacket around the pipe connecting the exhaust manifold and the EGR valve. Models without the cooler have a simple connecting tube between the exhaust manifold and EGR valve.

4.4 EGR solenoid valve location on engine compartment bulkhead

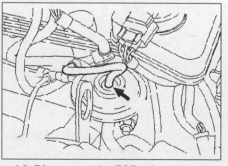

4.9 Disconnect the EGR valve vacuum hose (arrowed) – 1.4 and 1.6 litre engines

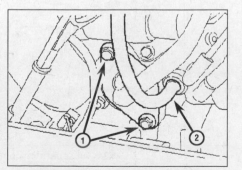

4.23 EGR pipe flange bolts (1) and brake servo vacuum pipe connection (2)

4.27 Using pliers to release the EGR cooler upper hose clip

4.28 Unscrewing one of the EGR valve flange bolts

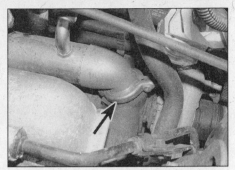

4.29 EGR cooler clamp (arrowed) fitted position

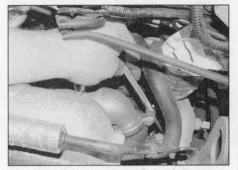

4.30a Loosen the EGR cooler clamp bolt . . .

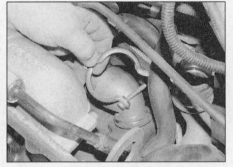

4.30b . . . then unhook it from the cooler and remove it

4.31 EGR cooler-to-exhaust manifold bolts (arrowed) – seen from below, with exhaust removed

27 On models with the cooler, access is improved by removing the intercooler hose from the inlet manifold (see Chapter 4B if necessary). Disconnect the upper coolant hose (anticipate some coolant spillage) and position the hose ends upwards, or insert plugs, to minimise further coolant loss (see illustration). The lower coolant hose is more easily disconnected as the cooler is being removed.

28 Unscrew and remove the two flange bolts underneath the EGR valve, and separate the joint (see illustration). Recover the gasket.

29 Before removing the clamp securing the EGR tube/cooler to the exhaust manifold, make a careful note of its orientation, as the new clamp must be fitted exactly the same way – this is to allow access to the catalytic converter flange nuts. On models with the cooler, when viewed from above, the clamp 'hinge' should be obscured by the cooler (see illustration).

30 Loosen the clamp nut and bolt, and free the clamp from the exhaust manifold (see illustrations). Recover the clamp, and discard it – a new one must be obtained for reassembly.

31 On models with the cooler, remove the two small bolts at the base of the cooler body. These are actually easier to see from below (see illustration).

32 Remove the tube/cooler from the EGR valve and exhaust manifold. As the cooler is withdrawn, disconnect the lower coolant pipe – again, arrange the pipe to minimise coolant loss (see illustrations).

4.32a Once the cooler is clear, disconnect the lower coolant hose . . .

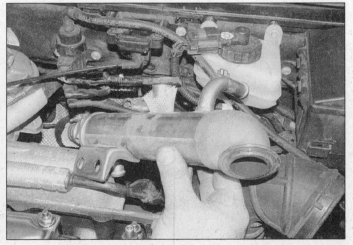

4.32b . . . then remove the cooler completely

33 Refitting is a reversal of removal, noting the following points:

a) *When refitting the EGR tube/cooler, offer it into position, and hand-tighten the bolts. Position the new clamp as noted on removal, tighten the clamp nut/bolt to the specified torque, then tighten the remaining bolts.*

b) *Reconnect the cooler hoses correctly, and top-up the cooling system as necessary.*

5 Oxygen sensor (petrol models) – removal and refitting

Note: *Some later models are fitted with two sensors – one before and one after the catalytic converter. This enables more efficient monitoring of the exhaust gas, allowing a faster response time. The overall efficiency of the converter itself can also be checked.*

Removal

1 On 1.4 and 1.6 litre models, access to the sensor in the front downpipe can be gained from above, but access to the second sensor fitted to later models can only be gained with the car raised and supported (see *Jacking and vehicle support*).

2 On 1.8 and 2.0 litre models, remove the four bolts securing the heat shield fitted over the exhaust manifold, and lift away the heat shield for access to the sensor.

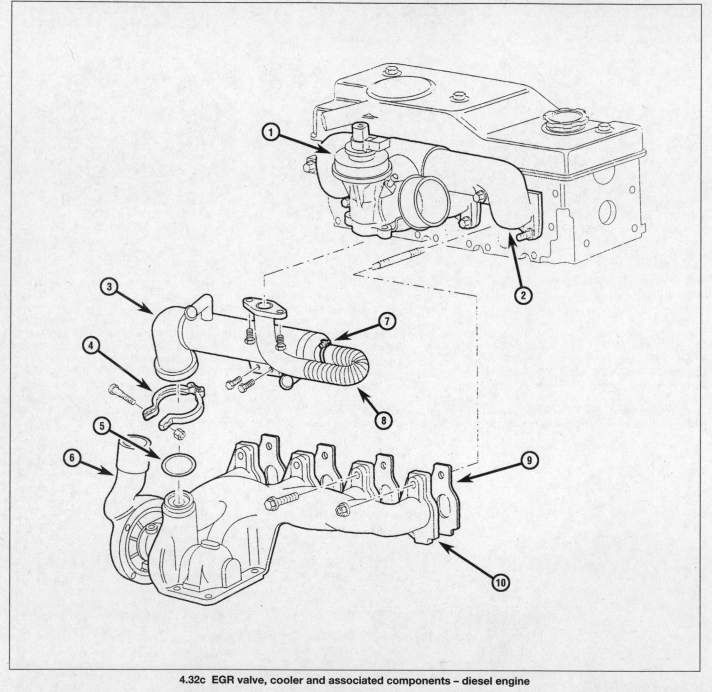

4.32c EGR valve, cooler and associated components – diesel engine

1 EGR valve	3 EGR cooler	5 Gasket	7 Clamp	9 Manifold gasket
2 Inlet manifold	4 Clamp	6 Turbocharger	8 Connecting pipe	10 Exhaust manifold

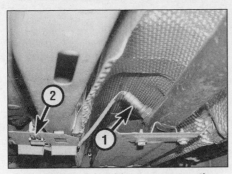

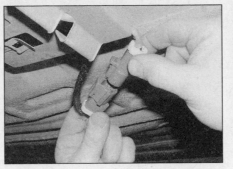

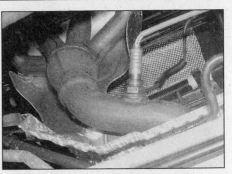

5.3a On models with two sensors, the sensor (1) is at the rear of the converter, with the wiring plug (2) alongside

5.3b Disconnecting the second sensor wiring plug

5.4 Typical sensor location in exhaust downpipe – 1.4 litre model

3 Trace the wiring from the sensor body back to its wiring plug, and disconnect it. On models with two sensors, the wiring plug for the rearmost sensor is clipped to a metal plate attached to the underside of the car **(see illustrations)**. Note how the wiring is routed, as it must not come into contact with hot exhaust components.

4 Unscrew the sensor from its location, and remove it **(see illustration)**. Once removed, take great care that the sensor is not dropped or damaged. Keep the sensor tip clean while it is removed.

Refitting

5 It may be beneficial to clean the sensor before refitting it, especially if the sensor tip appears to be contaminated. However, great care must be exercised, as the tip will be damaged by any abrasives, and by certain solvents. Seek the advice of a Ford dealer before cleaning the sensor.

6 Refitting is a reversal of removal, noting the following points:

a) Apply a little anti-seize compound to the sensor threads, taking care not to allow any on the sensor tip, and tighten the sensor to the specified torque.

b) Reconnect the wiring, ensuring that it is routed clear of any hot exhaust components.

c) If required, proof that the sensor is working can be gained by having the exhaust emissions checked, and compared with the figure quoted in Chapter 4A. Remember that a faulty sensor will have generated a fault code – if this code is still logged in the ECU electronic memory, the engine management system may still be in LOS (refer to Chapter 4A, Section 14).

6 Catalytic converter – general information, removal and refitting

General information

1 The catalytic converter reduces harmful exhaust emissions by chemically converting

the more poisonous gases to ones which (in theory at least) are less harmful. The chemical reaction is known as an 'oxidising' reaction, or one where oxygen is 'added'.

2 Inside the converter is a honeycomb structure, made of ceramic material and coated with the precious metals palladium, platinum and rhodium (the 'catalyst' which promotes the chemical reaction). The chemical reaction generates heat, which itself promotes the reaction – therefore, once the car has been driven several miles, the body of the converter will be very hot.

3 The ceramic structure contained within the converter is understandably fragile, and will not withstand rough treatment. Since the converter runs at a high temperature, driving through deep standing water (in flood conditions, for example) is to be avoided, since the thermal stresses imposed when plunging the hot converter into cold water may well cause the ceramic internals to fracture, resulting in a 'blocked' converter – a common cause of failure. A converter which has been damaged in this way can be checked by shaking it (do not strike it) – if a rattling noise is heard, this indicates probable failure.

Precautions

4 The catalytic converter is a reliable and simple device which needs no maintenance in itself, but there are some facts of which an owner should be aware if the converter is to function properly for its full service life:

Petrol models

a) DO NOT use leaded petrol (or lead-replacement petrol) in a car equipped with a catalytic converter – the lead (or other additives) will coat the precious metals, reducing their converting efficiency and will eventually destroy the converter.

b) Always keep the ignition and fuel systems well-maintained in accordance with the manufacturer's schedule (see Chapter 1A).

c) If the engine develops a misfire, do not drive the car at all (or at least as little as possible) until the fault is cured.

d) DO NOT push- or tow-start the car – this

will soak the catalytic converter in unburned fuel, causing it to overheat when the engine does start.

e) DO NOT switch off the ignition at high engine speeds – ie, do not 'blip' the throttle immediately before switching off the engine.

f) DO NOT use fuel or engine oil additives – these may contain substances harmful to the catalytic converter.

g) DO NOT continue to use the car if the engine burns oil to the extent of leaving a visible trail of blue smoke.

h) Remember that the catalytic converter operates at very high temperatures. DO NOT, therefore, park the car in dry undergrowth, over long grass or piles of dead leaves after a long run.

i) As mentioned above, driving through deep water should be avoided if possible. The sudden cooling effect may fracture the ceramic honeycomb, damaging it beyond repair.

j) Remember that the catalytic converter is FRAGILE – do not strike it with tools during servicing work, and take care handling it when removing it from the car for any reason.

k) In some cases, a sulphurous smell (like that of rotten eggs) may be noticed from the exhaust. This is common to many catalytic converter-equipped cars, and has more to do with the sulphur content of the brand of fuel being used than the converter itself.

l) If a substantial loss of power is experienced, remember that this could be due to the converter being blocked. This can occur simply as a result of high mileage, but may be due to the ceramic element having fractured and collapsed internally (see paragraph 3). A new converter is the only cure in this instance.

m) The catalytic converter, used on a well-maintained and well-driven car, should last for between 50 000 and 100 000 miles – if the converter is no longer effective, it must be renewed.

Diesel models

5 The catalytic converter fitted to diesel models is simpler than that fitted to petrol

models, but it still needs to be treated with respect to avoid problems:

a) DO NOT use fuel or engine oil additives – these may contain substances harmful to the catalytic converter.

b) DO NOT continue to use the car if the engine burns (engine) oil to the extent of leaving a visible trail of blue smoke.

c) Remember that the catalytic converter operates at very high temperatures. DO NOT, therefore, park the car in dry undergrowth, over long grass or piles of dead leaves after a long run.

d) As mentioned above, driving through deep water should be avoided if possible. The sudden cooling effect will fracture the ceramic honeycomb, damaging it beyond repair.

e) Remember that the catalytic converter is FRAGILE – do not strike it with tools during servicing work, and take care handling it when removing it from the car for any reason.

f) If a substantial loss of power is experienced, remember that this could be due to the converter being blocked. This can occur simply as a result of high mileage, but may be due to the ceramic element having fractured and collapsed internally (see paragraph 3). A new converter is the only cure in this instance.

g) The catalytic converter, used on a well-maintained and well-driven car, should last for between 50 000 and 100 000 miles – if the converter is no longer effective, it must be renewed.

Removal and refitting

6 The catalytic converter is part of the exhaust system – refer to the relevant Section of Chapter 4A or 4B.

Chapter 5 Part A:
Starting and charging systems

Contents

Degrees of difficulty

Easy, suitable for novice with little experience	**Fairly easy,** suitable for beginner with some experience	**Fairly difficult,** suitable for competent DIY mechanic	**Difficult,** suitable for experienced DIY mechanic	**Very difficult,** suitable for expert DIY or professional

Specifications

Battery
Type .... Lead-calcium (marked Ca)

Alternator
Type (typical):
  Petrol engine .... Magneti Marelli A1151-80A 98AB10300DD
  Diesel engine .... Magneti Marelli A1151M90A 98AB10300JA
Rated output:
  Petrol engine 80A
  Diesel engine 90A
Minimum brush length .... 5.0 mm
Regulated voltage at 4000 rpm and 3 to 7 amp load – all types ...... 13.5 to 14.6 volts

Starter motor
Type (typical):
  Petrol engine .... Motorcraft XS7U – 11000 – C3A (9221BA)
  Diesel engine .... Motorcraft 98AB – 11000 – AC (9028CA)
Minimum brush length .... 8.0 mm
Armature endfloat .... 0.25 mm

Torque wrench settings	Nm	lbf ft
Alternator:		
Coupling bolts (diesel engine)	12	9
Mounting bolts:		
Petrol engine	45	33
Diesel engine	25	18
Mounting nuts (petrol engine)	45	33
Pulley bracket bolts (diesel engine)	25	18
Battery:		
Hold-down clamp	12	9
Tray securing bolts	12	9
Earth cable-to-engine bolt	35	26
Starter motor mounting bolts	35	26

1 General information, precautions and battery disconnection

General information

The engine electrical systems include all ignition, charging and starting components. Because of their engine-related functions, these components are discussed separately from body electrical devices such as the lights, the instruments, etc (which are included in Chapter 12).

Precautions

Always observe the following precautions when working on the electrical system:

a) Be extremely careful when servicing engine electrical components. They are easily damaged if handled, connected or checked improperly.

b) Never leave the ignition switched on for long periods of time when the engine is not running.

c) Do not disconnect the battery leads while the engine is running.

d) Maintain correct polarity when connecting a battery lead from another vehicle during jump starting – see the 'Jump starting' Section at the front of this manual.

e) Always disconnect the negative lead first, and reconnect it last, or the battery may be shorted by the tool being used to loosen the lead clamps.

It's also a good idea to review the safety-related information regarding the engine electrical systems located in the 'Safety first!' section at the front of this manual, before beginning any operation included in this Chapter.

Battery disconnection

Several systems fitted to the vehicle require battery power to be available at all times, either to ensure their continued operation (such as the clock) or to maintain control unit memories (such as that in the engine management system's ECU) which would be wiped if the battery were to be disconnected. Whenever the battery is to be disconnected, first note the following, to ensure that there are no unforeseen consequences of this action:

a) First, on any vehicle with central locking, it is a wise precaution to remove the key from the ignition, and to keep it with you, so that it does not get locked in if the central locking should engage accidentally when the battery is reconnected.

b) The engine management system's ECU will lose the information stored in its memory – referred to by Ford as the 'KAM' (Keep-Alive Memory) – when the battery is disconnected. This includes idling and operating values, and any fault codes detected – in the case of the fault codes, if it is thought likely that the system has developed a fault for which the corresponding code has been logged, the vehicle must be taken to a Ford dealer for the codes to be read, using the special diagnostic equipment necessary for this (see Chapter 4A, Section 14). Whenever the battery is disconnected, the information relating to idle speed control and other operating values will have to be re-programmed into the unit's memory. The ECU does this by itself, but until then, there may be surging, hesitation, erratic idle and a generally inferior level of performance. To allow the ECU to relearn these values, start the engine and run it as close to idle speed as possible until it reaches its normal operating temperature, then run it for approximately two minutes at 1200 rpm. Next, drive the vehicle as far as necessary – approximately 5 miles of varied driving conditions is usually sufficient – to complete the relearning process.

c) If the battery is disconnected while the alarm system is armed or activated, the alarm will remain in the same state when the battery is reconnected. The same applies to the engine immobiliser system (where fitted).

d) If a trip computer is in use, any information stored in memory will be lost.

e) If a Ford Keycode audio unit is fitted, and the unit and/or the battery is disconnected, the unit will not function again on reconnection until the correct security code is entered. Details of this procedure, which varies according to the unit and model year, are given in the Ford Audio Systems Operating Guide supplied with the vehicle when new, with the code itself being given in a Radio Passport and/or a Keycode Label at the same time. Ensure you have the correct code before you disconnect the battery. For obvious security reasons, the procedure is not given in this manual. If you do not have the code or details of the correct procedure, but can supply proof of ownership and a legitimate reason for wanting this information, the vehicle's selling dealer may be able to help.

2.3 Undo battery retaining bolt (arrowed)

Devices known as 'memory-savers' (or 'code-savers') can be used to avoid some of the above problems. Precise details vary according to the device used. Typically, it is plugged into the cigarette lighter, and is connected by its own wires to a spare battery; the vehicle's own battery is then disconnected from the electrical system, leaving the 'memory-saver' to pass sufficient current to maintain audio unit security codes and ECU memory values, and also to run permanently-live circuits such as the clock, all the while isolating the battery in the event of a short-circuit occurring while work is carried out.

⚠️ **Warning: Some of these devices allow a considerable amount of current to pass, which can mean that many of the vehicle's systems are still operational when the main battery is disconnected. If a 'memory-saver' is used, ensure that the circuit concerned is actually 'dead' before carrying out any work on it.**

2 Battery – removal, refitting, testing and charging

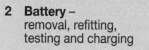

Removal

1 Unclip the battery cover and remove.

2 Disconnect the battery leads, negative (earth) lead first – see Section 1.

3 Remove the battery hold-down strap **(see illustration)**.

4 Lift out the battery.
Caution: The battery is heavy.

5 Whilst the battery is out, inspect and clean the battery tray (see *Weekly checks*).

6 If you are renewing the battery, make sure that you get one that's identical, with the same dimensions, amperage rating, cold cranking rating, etc. Dispose of the old battery in a responsible fashion. Most local authorities have facilities for the collection and disposal of such items – batteries contain sulphuric acid and lead, and should not be simply thrown out with the household rubbish.

Refitting

7 Refitting is the reverse of the removal procedure. **Note:** *After the battery has been disconnected, the engine management system requires approximately 5 miles of driving to relearn its optimum settings. During this period, the engine may not perform normally.*

Testing

Standard and low maintenance battery

8 If the vehicle covers a small annual mileage it is worthwhile checking the specific gravity of the electrolyte every three months to determine the state of charge of the battery.

Use a hydrometer to make the check and compare the results with the following table.

Ambient temperature:

	above 25°C (77°F)	below 25°C (77°F)
Fully charged	1.210 to 1.230	1.270 to 1.290
70% charged	1.170 to 1.190	1.230 to 1.250
Discharged	1.050 to 1.070	1.110 to 1.130

Note that the specific gravity readings assume an electrolyte temperature of 15°C (60°F); for every 10°C (18°F) below 15°C (60°F) subtract 0.007. For every 10°C (18°F) above 15°C (60°F) add 0.007.

9 If the battery condition is suspect, first check the specific gravity of electrolyte in each cell. A variation of 0.040 or more between any cells indicates loss of electrolyte or deterioration of the internal plates.

10 If the specific gravity variation is 0.040 or more, the battery should be renewed. If the cell variation is satisfactory but the battery is discharged, it should be charged, as described later in this Section.

Maintenance-free battery

11 In cases where a 'sealed for life' maintenance-free battery is fitted, topping-up and testing of the electrolyte in each cell is not possible. The condition of the battery can therefore only be tested using a battery condition indicator or a voltmeter.

12 Certain models my be fitted with a maintenance-free battery, with a built-in charge condition indicator. The indicator is located in the top of the battery casing, and indicates the condition of the battery from its colour. On Ford batteries, if the indicator shows green, then the battery is in a good state of charge. If the indicator shows red, then the battery requires charging, as described later in this Section. Other battery manufacturers use different colour-coding – refer to their information.

All battery types

13 If testing the battery using a voltmeter, connect the voltmeter across the battery. The test is only accurate if the battery has not been subjected to any kind of charge for the previous six hours. If this is not the case, switch on the headlights for 30 seconds, then wait four to five minutes before testing the battery after switching off the headlights. All other electrical circuits must be switched off, so check that the doors and tailgate are fully shut when making the test.

14 If the voltage reading is less than 12 volts, then the battery is discharged, whilst a reading of 12 to 12.4 volts indicates a partially discharged condition.

15 If the battery is to be charged, remove it from the vehicle and charge it as described later in this Section.

Charging

Note: *The following is intended as a guide only. Always refer to the manufacturer's recommendations (often printed on a label attached to the battery) before charging a battery.*

Standard and low maintenance battery

16 Charge the battery at a rate equivalent to 10% of the battery capacity (eg, for a 45Ah battery, charge at 4.5A) and continue to charge the battery at this rate until no further rise in specific gravity is noted over a four hour period.

17 Alternatively, a trickle charger charging at the rate of 1.5 amps can safely be used overnight.

18 Specially rapid 'boost' charges which are claimed to restore the power of the battery in 1 to 2 hours are not recommended, as they can cause serious damage to the battery plates through overheating.

19 While charging the battery, note that the temperature of the electrolyte should never exceed 37.8°C (100°F).

Maintenance-free battery

20 This battery type takes considerably longer to fully recharge than the standard type, the time taken being dependent on the extent of discharge, but it can take anything up to three days.

21 A constant voltage type charger is required, to be set, when connected, to 13.9 to 14.9 volts with a charger current below 25 amps. Using this method, the battery should be re-usable within three hours, giving a voltage reading of 12.5 volts, but this is for a partially discharged battery and, as mentioned, full charging can take considerably longer.

22 If the battery is to be charged from a fully discharged state (condition reading less than 12.2 volts), have it recharged by your Ford dealer or local automotive electrician, as the charge rate is higher and constant supervision during charging is necessary.

3 Charging system – general information and precautions

General information

The charging system includes the alternator, an internal voltage regulator, a no-charge (or 'ignition') warning light, the battery, and the wiring between all the components. The charging system supplies electrical power for the ignition system, the lights, the radio, etc. The alternator is driven by the auxiliary drivebelt at the front of the engine.

The purpose of the voltage regulator is to limit the alternator's voltage to a pre-set value. This prevents power surges, circuit overloads, etc, during peak voltage output.

The charging system doesn't ordinarily require periodic maintenance. However, the drivebelt, battery and wires and connections should be inspected at the intervals outlined in Chapter 1A or 1B.

The dashboard warning light should come on when the ignition key is turned to positions

II or III, then should go off immediately the engine starts. If it remains on, or if it comes on while the engine is running, there is a malfunction in the charging system. If the light does not come on when the ignition key is turned, and the bulb is in working condition, there is a fault in the alternator.

Precautions

Be very careful when making electrical circuit connections to a vehicle equipped with an alternator, and note the following:
a) *When reconnecting wires to the alternator from the battery, be sure to note the polarity.*
b) *Before using arc-welding equipment to repair any part of the vehicle, disconnect the wires from the alternator and the battery terminals.*
c) *Never start the engine with a battery charger connected.*
d) *Always disconnect both battery leads before using a battery charger.*
e) *The alternator is driven by an engine drivebelt which could cause serious injury if your hand, hair or clothes become entangled in it with the engine running.*
f) *Because the alternator is connected directly to the battery, it could arc or cause a fire if overloaded or shorted-out.*
g) *If steam-cleaning or pressure-washing the engine, wrap a plastic bag over the alternator or any other electrical component and secure them with rubber bands (**Do not forget to remove, before re-starting the engine**).*
h) *Never disconnect the alternator terminals while the engine is running.*

4 Charging system – testing

1 If a malfunction occurs in the charging circuit, don't automatically assume that the alternator is causing the problem. First check the following items:
a) *Check the tension and condition of the auxiliary drivebelt – renew it if it is worn or deteriorated (see the relevant part of Chapter 1).*
b) *Ensure the alternator mounting bolts and nuts are tight.*
c) *Inspect the alternator wiring harness and the electrical connections at the alternator; they must be in good condition, and tight.*
d) *Check the large main fuses in the engine compartment (see Chapter 12). If any are blown, determine the cause, repair the circuit and renew the fuse (the vehicle won't start and/or the accessories won't work if the fuse is blown).*
e) *Start the engine and check the alternator for abnormal noises – for example, a shrieking or squealing sound may indicate a badly-worn bearing or brush.*

5.3 Disconnecting the wiring connector

f) Make sure that the battery is fully-charged – one bad cell in a battery can cause overcharging by the alternator.

g) Disconnect the battery leads (negative first, then positive). Inspect the battery

posts and the lead clamps for corrosion. Clean them thoroughly if necessary (see 'Weekly checks'). Reconnect the leads.

2 Using a voltmeter, check the battery voltage with the engine off. It should be approximately 12 volts.

3 Start the engine and check the battery voltage again. Increase engine speed until the voltmeter reading remains steady; it should now be approximately 13.5 to 14.6 volts.

4 Switch on as many electrical accessories as possible (eg, the headlights, heated rear window and heater blower), and check that the alternator maintains the regulated voltage at around 13 to 14 volts. The voltage may drop and then come back up; it may also be necessary to increase engine speed slightly, even if the charging system is working properly.

5 If the voltage reading is greater than the specified charging voltage, renew the voltage regulator.

6 If the voltmeter reading is less than that specified, the fault may be due to worn brushes, weak brush springs, a faulty voltage regulator, a faulty diode, a severed phase winding, or worn or damaged slip rings. The brushes and slip rings may be checked, but if the fault persists, the alternator should be renewed or taken to an auto-electrician for testing and repair.

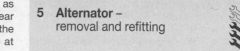

5 Alternator – removal and refitting

Removal

1 Disconnect the battery negative (earth) lead (see Section 1).

2 Remove the auxiliary drivebelt as described in the relevant part of Chapter 1.

1.4 litre and 1.6 litre petrol engine

3 Remove the plastic cover, unscrew the nut and disconnect the wiring from the alternator **(see illustration)**.

4 Remove the lower mounting bolt, and also the upper securing bolt and nut from the alternator **(see illustration)**.

5 Carefully lift the alternator upwards from the engine. Take care not to damage the surrounding components, as there is little room to manoeuvre the alternator.

1.8 litre and 2.0 litre petrol engine

6 Undo the securing bolt from the coolant expansion tank, lift out from securing clip and move to one side (see Chapter 3, Section 7).

7 Lift the power steering reservoir from its retaining bracket and move to one side **(see illustration)**.

8 Undo the securing bolt from the wiring loom bracket, and move the wiring to one side (disconnect the multi-plug) **(see illustrations)**.

9 Undo the bolt from the power steering reservoir bracket to release the earth cable (to aid the removal of the alternator, carefully bend the earth bracket down) **(see illustrations)**.

10 Undo the two retaining bolts from the canister purge valve and move to one side **(see illustration)**.

5.4 Undo the upper securing bolt and nut

5.7 Lift reservoir from the retaining bracket

5.8a Unbolt the wiring clip . . .

5.8b . . . then disconnect the block connector

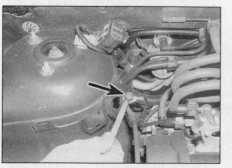

5.9a Unbolt the earth cable (arrowed) . . .

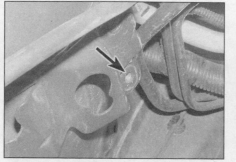

5.9b . . . then carefully bend the bracket down (arrow)

5.10 Disconnect the wiring connector, and move the canister to one side

5.12a Remove the bolt (arrowed) . . .

5.12b . . . and remove the lower bolt as far the inner wing

5.13 Turn and lift the alternator out with the pulley facing upwards

5.17a Undo the two pulley bolts . . .

5.17b . . . loosen the three coupling bolts . . .

5.17c . . . and remove the coupling from the alternator

11 Remove the plastic cover, unscrew the nut and disconnect the wiring from the back of the alternator.
12 Unscrew and remove the alternator mounting bolt nearest the engine (see illustration). Unscrew the other retaining bolt until it has fully disengaged from the bracket (it will not be possible to remove the bolt from the alternator at this stage) (see illustration).
13 Carefully lift the alternator from the engine, turning it with the pulley facing upwards. Take care not to damage the surrounding components on removal, as there is little room to manoeuvre the alternator (see illustration).

Diesel engine

14 Remove the engine undershield.
15 On vehicles with air conditioning, undo the four bolts from the air conditioning compressor and remove to one side.
16 Remove the plastic cover, unscrew the nut and disconnect the wiring from the alternator.
17 Undo the two pulley bracket bolts, then loosen the three generator coupling bolts and remove the coupling (see illustrations).
18 Unscrew the alternator mounting bolts and carefully lift the alternator from the engine

All models

19 If you are renewing the alternator, take the old one with you when purchasing a replacement unit. Make sure that the new or rebuilt unit is identical to the old alternator. Look at the terminals – they should be the

same in number, size and location as the terminals on the old alternator. Finally, look at the identification markings – they will be stamped in the housing, or printed on a tag or plaque affixed to the housing. Make sure that these numbers are the same on both alternators.
20 Many new/rebuilt alternators do not have a pulley installed, so you may have to switch the pulley from the old unit to the new/rebuilt one. When buying an alternator, ask about the installation of pulleys – some auto-electrical specialists will perform this service free of charge.

Refitting

Note: *One of the mounting bolts on the 1.8 litre and 2.0 litre petrol engine will need to be put in place before refitting the alternator (see paragraph 12).*

6.2 Remove the end cover from the alternator

21 Refitting is the reverse of the removal procedure, referring where necessary to the relevant Chapters of this manual. Tighten all nuts and bolts to the specified torque wrench settings.

6 Alternator brushes and voltage regulator – renewal

Note: *This procedure assumes that replacement parts of the correct type have been obtained. At the time of writing, no individual alternator components were available as separate replacement Ford parts. An auto-electrical specialist should be able to supply parts such as brushes.*
Note: *The following procedure is for the Magneti Marelli unit fitted to the project vehicles – the procedure is essentially the same for any other alternators that may be fitted to other models.*

Removal

1 Remove the alternator from the vehicle (see Section 5) and place it on a clean workbench.
2 Remove the four securing nuts, and withdraw the plastic end cover from the alternator (see illustration).
3 Unclip the plastic cover at the centre from the brushes (see illustration).
4 Remove the voltage regulator/brush holder mounting screws and nuts (see illustration).

6.3 Lift off the centre cover

6.4 Remove the screws and nuts arrowed

6.5 Lift the regulator assembly from the alternator

5 Remove the regulator/brush holder from the rear of the alternator housing **(see illustration)**.
6 Measure the exposed length of each brush, and compare it to the minimum length listed in this Chapter's Specifications. If the length of either brush is less than the specified minimum, renew the assembly.
7 Make sure that each brush moves smoothly in the brush holder.
8 Check that the slip rings – the ring of copper on which each brush bears – are clean. Wipe them with a solvent-moistened cloth; if either appears scored or blackened, take the alternator to a repair specialist for advice.

Refitting

9 Refitting is the reverse of the removal procedure.
10 Fit the voltage regulator/brush holder, ensuring that the brushes bear correctly on the slip rings, and that they compress into their holders. Tighten the screws securely.
11 Install the rear cover, and tighten the screws securely.
12 Refit the alternator as described in Section 5.

7 Starting system – general information and precautions

General information

The sole function of the starting system is to turn over the engine quickly enough to allow it to start.

The starting system consists of a gear reduced starter motor, battery, ignition switch, relay and the wires connecting them. The solenoid is mounted directly on the starter motor.

The solenoid/starter motor assembly is installed in line with the engine, bolting onto the transmission bellhousing. The relay for the starter circuit is in the fusebox inside the vehicle (relay No 17).

When the ignition key is turned to position III, the starter relay is actuated providing voltage to the starter motor solenoid. The starter motor solenoid engages the drive pinion with the ring gear on the flywheel. The solenoid then switches the battery current to the starter motor, to turn the engine. The starter motor remains engaged until the ignition switch is released.

The starter motor on a vehicle equipped with automatic transmission can be operated only when the selector lever is in Park or Neutral (P or N).

If the alarm system is armed or activated, the starter motor cannot be operated. The same applies with the engine immobiliser system (where fitted).

Precautions

Always observe the following precautions when working on the starting system:
a) *Excessive cranking of the starter motor can overheat it, and cause serious damage. Never operate the starter motor for more than 15 seconds at a time without pausing to allow it to cool for at least two minutes. Excessive starter operation will also risk unburned fuel collecting in the catalytic converter's element, causing it to overheat when the engine does start.*
b) *The starter is connected by a cable directly from the battery, and could arc or cause a fire if mishandled, overloaded or shor- circuited.*
c) *Always detach the lead from the negative terminal of the battery before working on the starting system (see Section 1).*

8 Starting system – testing

Note: *Before diagnosing starter problems, make sure that the battery is fully charged, and ensure that the alarm/engine immobiliser system is not activated.*
1 If the starter motor does not turn at all when the switch is operated, make sure that, on automatic transmission models, the selector lever is in Park or Neutral (P or N).
2 Make sure that the battery is fully charged, and that all leads, both at the battery and starter solenoid terminals, are clean and secure.

3 If the starter motor spins but the engine is not cranking, the overrunning clutch or (when applicable) the reduction gears in the starter motor may be slipping, in which case the starter motor must be overhauled or renewed. (Other possibilities are that the starter motor mounting bolts are very loose, or that teeth are missing from the flywheel/driveplate ring gear.)
4 If, when the switch is actuated, the starter motor does not operate at all but the solenoid clicks, then the problem lies with either the battery, the main solenoid contacts, or the starter motor itself (or the engine is seized).
5 If the solenoid plunger cannot be heard to click when the switch is actuated, the battery is faulty, there is a fault in the circuit, or the solenoid itself is defective.
6 To check the solenoid, connect a fused jumper lead between the battery (+) and the ignition switch terminal (the small terminal) on the solenoid. If the starter motor now operates, the solenoid is OK, and the problem is in the ignition switch, selector lever position sensor (automatic transmission) or in the wiring.
7 If the starter motor still does not operate, remove it. The brushes and commutator may be checked, but if the fault persists, the motor should be renewed or taken to an auto-electrician for testing and repair.
8 If the starter motor cranks the engine at an abnormally-slow speed, first make sure that the battery is charged, and that all terminal connections are tight. If the engine is partially seized, or has the wrong viscosity oil in it, it will crank slowly.
9 Run the engine until normal operating temperature is reached, then switch off and disable the ignition system by unplugging the ignition coil's electrical connector; remove fuse 12 to disconnect the fuel pump.
10 Connect a voltmeter positive lead to the battery positive terminal, and connect the negative lead to the negative terminal.
11 Crank the engine, and take the voltmeter readings as soon as a steady figure is indicated. Do not allow the starter motor to turn for more than 15 seconds at a time. A reading of 10.5 volts or more, with the starter motor turning at normal cranking speed, is normal. If the reading is 10.5 volts or more but

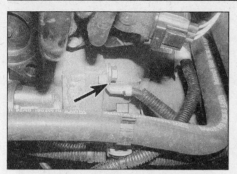

9.3 Earth lead (arrowed) on starter mounting bolt

9.5 Remove the wiring connectors from the starter motor

9.6 Undo the lower starter mounting bolt (arrowed)

the cranking speed is slow, the solenoid contacts are burned, the motor is faulty, or there is a bad connection. If the reading is less than 10.5 volts and the cranking speed is slow, the starter motor is faulty or there is a problem with the battery.

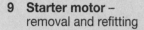

9 Starter motor –
removal and refitting

1 Disconnect the battery negative (earth) lead – see Section 1.

1.4 litre and 1.6 litre petrol engine, and diesel engine

Removal

2 Remove the air cleaner as described in Chapter 4A.
3 Unscrew the upper two starter motor mounting bolts, noting that one also secures an earth lead **(see illustration)**.
4 Apply the handbrake, then jack up the front of the vehicle and support it on axle stands (see *Jacking and vehicle support*).
5 Unscrew the nuts to disconnect the wiring from the starter/solenoid terminals **(see illustration)**.
6 Remove the remaining starter motor mounting bolt **(see illustration)**. Remove the starter.

9.9 Withdraw the starter from the transmission housing

Refitting

7 Refitting is the reverse of the removal procedure. Tighten the bolts to the specified torque wrench settings.

1.8 litre and 2.0 litre petrol engine

Removal

8 Apply the handbrake, then jack up the front of the vehicle and support it on axle stands (see *Jacking and vehicle support*).
9 Unscrew the mounting bolts from the starter motor, then release the starter motor from the dowels on the transmission housing and withdraw from the engine **(see illustration)**.
10 Disconnect the wiring from the starter motor as the starter is being withdrawn **(see illustration)**.

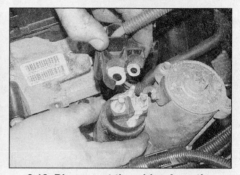

9.10 Disconnect the wiring from the starter motor

Refitting

11 Refitting is a reversal of removal. Tighten the bolts to the specified torque wrench settings.

10 Starter motor –
testing and overhaul

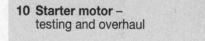

If the starter motor is thought to be suspect, it should be removed from the vehicle and taken to an auto-electrician for testing. Most auto-electricians will be able to supply and fit brushes at a reasonable cost. However, check on the cost of repairs before proceeding as it may prove more economical to obtain a new or exchange motor.

Chapter 5 Part B:
Ignition system – petrol models

Contents

Degrees of difficulty

Easy, suitable for novice with little experience	Fairly easy, suitable for beginner with some experience	Fairly difficult, suitable for competent DIY mechanic	Difficult, suitable for experienced DIY mechanic	Very difficult, suitable for expert DIY or professional

Specifications

General

System type	Electronic distributorless ignition system (DIS) with ignition module controlled by EEC-V engine management module (ECU)
Firing order	1-3-4-2
Location of No 1 cylinder	Timing belt end

Ignition system data

Ignition timing	Controlled by the ECU
Ignition coil resistances (typical):	
Primary windings	0.4 to 0.6 ohms
Secondary windings	10 500 to 16 500 ohms

Torque wrench settings

	Nm	lbf ft
Ignition coil mounting bolts	6	4
Knock sensor mounting bolt	20	15

1 General information and precautions

General information

The ignition system is integrated with the fuel injection system to form a combined engine management system under the control of the Ford EEC-V engine management module or Electronic Control Unit (ECU) – see Chapter 4A for further information. The main ignition system components include the ignition switch, the battery, the crankshaft speed/position sensor, knock sensor, the ignition coil, and the spark plugs and HT leads.

A Distributorless Ignition System (DIS) is fitted, where the main functions of the conventional distributor are replaced by a computerised module within the ECU. The coil unit operates on the 'wasted spark' principle. The coil unit in fact contains two separate coils – one for cylinders 1 and 4, the other for cylinders 2 and 3. Each of the two coils produces an HT voltage at both outputs every time its primary coil voltage is interrupted – ie, cylinders 1 and 4 always 'fire' together, then 2 and 3 'fire' together. When this happens, one of the two cylinders concerned will be on the compression stroke (and will ignite the fuel/air mixture), while the other one is on the exhaust stroke – because the spark on the exhaust stroke has no effect, it is effectively 'wasted', hence the term 'wasted spark'.

Because there is no distributor to adjust, the ignition timing cannot be altered by conventional means, and the advance and retard functions are carried out by the ECU.

The basic operation is as follows: the ECU supplies a voltage to the input stage of the ignition coil, which causes the primary windings in the coil to be energised. The supply voltage is periodically interrupted by the ECU and this results in the collapse of primary magnetic field, which then induces a much larger voltage in the secondary coil, called the HT voltage. This voltage is directed (via the HT leads) to the spark plug in the cylinder. The spark plug electrodes form a gap small enough for the HT voltage to arc across, and the resulting spark ignites the fuel/air mixture in the cylinder. The timing of this sequence of events is critical, and is regulated solely by the ECU.

The ECU calculates and controls the ignition timing primarily according to engine speed, crankshaft position, camshaft position, and inlet airflow rate information, received from sensors mounted on and around the engine. Other parameters that affect ignition timing are throttle position and rate of opening, inlet air temperature, engine temperature and engine knock, all monitored via sensors mounted on the engine. Note that most of these sensors have a dual role, in that the information they provide is equally useful in determining the fuelling requirements as in deciding the optimum ignition or firing point – therefore, removal of some of the sensors mentioned below is described in Chapter 4A.

The ECU computes engine speed and crankshaft position from toothed impulse rotor attached to the engine flywheel, with an engine speed sensor whose inductive head runs just above rotor. As the crankshaft (and flywheel) rotate, the rotor 'teeth' pass the engine speed sensor, which transmits a pulse to the ECU every time a tooth passes it. At the top dead centre (TDC) position, there is one missing tooth in the rotor periphery, which results in a longer pause between signals from the sensor. The ECU recognises the absence of a pulse from the engine speed sensor at this point, and uses it to establish the TDC position for No 1 piston. The time interval between pulses, and the location of the missing pulse, allow the ECU to accurately determine the position of the crankshaft and its speed. The camshaft position sensor enhances this information by detecting whether a particular piston is on an inlet or an exhaust cycle.

Information on engine load is supplied to the ECU via the air mass meter, and from the throttle position sensor. The engine load is determined by computation based on the quantity of air being drawn into the engine. Further engine load information is sent to the ECU from the knock sensor. The sensor is sensitive to vibration, and detect the knocking which occurs when the engine starts to 'pink' (pre-ignite). If pre-ignition occurs, the ECU retards the ignition timing of the cylinder that is pre-igniting in steps until the pre-ignition ceases. The ECU then advances the ignition timing of that cylinder in steps until it is restored to normal, or until pre-ignition occurs again.

Sensors monitoring engine temperature, throttle position, vehicle road speed, and (where applicable) automatic transmission gear position and air conditioning system operation, provide additional input signals to the ECU on vehicle operating conditions. From all this constantly-changing data, the ECU selects, and if necessary modifies, a particular ignition advance setting from a map of ignition characteristics stored in its memory.

In the event of a fault in the system due to loss of a signal from one of the sensors, the ECU reverts to an emergency ('limp-home') program. This will allow the car to be driven, although engine operation and performance will be limited – the ignition timing, for instance, will be set to a fixed value. A warning light on the instrument panel will illuminate if the fault is likely to cause an increase in harmful exhaust emissions.

It should be noted that comprehensive fault diagnosis of all the engine management systems described in this Chapter is only possible with dedicated electronic test equipment. In the event of a sensor failing or

other fault occurring, a fault code will be stored in the ECU's fault log, which can only be extracted from the ECU using a dedicated fault code reader. A Ford dealer will obviously have such a reader, but they are also available from other suppliers, including Haynes. It is unlikely to be cost-effective for the private owner to purchase a fault code reader, but a well-equipped local garage or auto-electrical specialist will have one. Once the fault has been identified, the removal/refitting sequences detailed in the following Sections will then allow the appropriate component(s) to be renewed as required.

Precautions

The following precautions must be observed, to prevent damage to the ignition system components and to reduce risk of personal injury.

a) Do not keep the ignition on for more than 10 seconds if the engine will not start.
b) Ensure that the ignition is switched off before disconnecting any of the ignition wiring.
c) Ensure that the ignition is switched off before connecting or disconnecting any ignition test equipment, such as a timing light.
d) Do not earth the coil primary or secondary circuits.

⚠️ **Warning: Voltages produced by an electronic ignition system are considerably higher than those produced by conventional ignition systems. Extreme care must be taken when working on the system with the ignition switched on. Persons with surgically-implanted cardiac pacemaker devices should keep well clear of the ignition circuits, components and test equipment.**

2 Ignition system – testing

General

1 The components of the ignition system are normally very reliable; most faults are far more likely to be due to loose or dirty connections, or to 'tracking' of HT voltage due to dirt, dampness or damaged insulation, than to the failure of any of the system's components. **Always** check all wiring thoroughly before condemning an electrical component, and work methodically to eliminate all other possibilities before deciding that a particular component is faulty.
2 The old practice of checking for a spark by holding the live end of an HT lead a short distance away from the engine is **not** recommended; not only is there a high risk of a powerful electric shock, but the ECU, HT coil, or power stage may be damaged. Similarly, **never** try to 'diagnose' misfires by pulling off one HT lead at a time.

3 The following tests should be carried out when an obvious fault such as non-starting or a clearly detectable misfire exists. Some faults, however, are more obscure and are often disguised by the fact that the ECU will adopt an emergency program ('limp-home') mode to maintain as much driveability as possible. Faults of this nature usually appear in the form of excessive fuel consumption, poor idling characteristics, lack of performance, knocking or 'pinking' noises from the engine under certain conditions, or a combination of these conditions. Where problems such as this are experienced, the best course is to refer the car to a suitably-equipped garage for diagnostic testing using dedicated test equipment.

Engine will not start

Note: *Remember that a fault with the anti-theft alarm or immobiliser will give rise to apparent starting problems. Make sure that the alarm or immobiliser has been deactivated, referring to the vehicle handbook for details.*
4 If the engine either will not turn over at all, or only turns very slowly, check the battery and starter motor. Connect a voltmeter across the battery terminals (meter positive probe to battery positive terminal) then note the voltage reading obtained while turning the engine over on the starter for (no more than) ten seconds. If the reading obtained is less than approximately 9.5 volts, first check the battery, starter motor and charging system as described in Part A of this Chapter.
5 If the engine turns over at normal speed but will not start, check the HT circuit.
6 Connect a timing light (following its manufacturer's instructions) and turning the engine over on the starter motor; if the light flashes, voltage is reaching the spark plugs, so these should be checked first. If the light does not flash, check the HT leads themselves using the information given in Chapter 1A. If there is a spark, continue with the checks described in Section 3 of this Chapter.
7 If there is still no spark, check the condition of the coil(s), if possible by substitution with a known good unit, or by checking the primary and secondary resistances. If the fault persists, the problem lies elsewhere; if the fault is now cleared, a new coil is the obvious cure. However, check carefully the condition of the LT connections themselves before obtaining a new coil, to ensure that the fault is not due to dirty or poorly-fastened connectors.
8 If the coil is in good condition, the fault is probably within the power stage (built into the ECU), one of the system sensors, or related components (as applicable). In this case, a fault code should be logged in the diagnostic unit, which could be read using a fault code reader **(see illustration)**.
9 Fault codes can only be extracted from the ECU using a dedicated fault code reader. A

2.8 Diagnostic connector socket location on driver's lower facia panel

Ford dealer will obviously have such a reader, but they are also available from other suppliers, including Haynes. It is unlikely to be cost-effective for the private owner to purchase a fault code reader, but a well-equipped local garage or automotive electrical specialist will have one.

Engine misfires

10 An irregular misfire is probably due to a loose connection to one of the ignition coils or system sensors.

11 With the ignition switched off, check carefully through the system, ensuring that all connections are clean and securely fastened.

12 Check the condition of the spark plug HT leads. Ensure that the leads are routed and clipped so that they come into contact with fewest possible metal surfaces, as this may encourage the HT voltage to 'leak', via poor or damaged insulation. If there is any sign of damage to the insulation, renew the leads as a set.

13 Unless the HT leads are known to have been recently renewed, it is considered good practice to eliminate the HT leads from fault diagnosis in cases of misfiring by fitting a new set as a matter of course.

14 When fitting new leads, remove one lead at a time, so that confusion over their fitted positions does not arise. If the old leads were damaged, take steps to ensure that the new leads do not become similarly damaged.

15 If the HT leads are sound, regular misfiring indicates a problem with the ignition coil or spark plugs. Fit new plugs as described in Chapter 1A, or test the coil(s) as described in Section 4. A dirty or faulty crankshaft sensor could also be to blame – see Chapter 4A.

16 Any further checking of the system components should be carried out after first checking the ECU for fault codes – see paragraph 9.

3 Fault finding –
general information
and preliminary checks

Note: *Both the ignition and fuel systems must ideally be treated as one inter-related engine management system. Although the contents of this section are mainly concerned with the ignition side of the system, many of the components perform dual functions, and some of the following procedures of necessity relate to the fuel system.*

General information

1 The fuel and ignition systems on all engines covered by this manual incorporate an on-board diagnostic system to facilitate fault finding and system testing. Should a fault occur, the ECU stores a series of signals (or fault codes) for subsequent read-out via the diagnostic connector (see the Section on checking the fuel injection system in Chapter 4A).

2 If driveability problems have been experienced and engine performance is suspect, the on-board diagnostic system can be used to pinpoint any problem areas, but this requires special test equipment. Once this has been done, further tests may often be necessary to determine the exact nature of the fault; ie, whether a component itself has failed, or whether it is a wiring or other inter-related problem.

3 Apart from visually checking the wiring and connections, any testing will require the use of a fault code reader at least. A Ford dealer will obviously have such a reader, but they are also available from other suppliers, including Haynes. It is unlikely to be cost-effective for the private owner to purchase a fault code reader, but a well-equipped local garage or automotive electrical specialist will have one.

Preliminary checks

Note: *When carrying out these checks to trace a fault, remember that if the fault has appeared only a short time after any part of the vehicle has been serviced or overhauled, the first place to check is where that work was carried out, however unrelated it may appear, to ensure that no carelessly-refitted components are causing the problem.*

If you are tracing the cause of a 'partial' engine fault, such as lack of performance, in addition to the checks outlined below, check the compression pressures. Check also that the fuel filter and air cleaner element have been renewed at the recommended intervals. Refer to Chapter 1A and the appropriate Part of Chapter 2 for details of these procedures.

Remember that any fault codes which have been logged will have to be cleared from the ECU memory using a dedicated fault code reader (see paragraph 3) before you can be certain the cause of the fault has been fixed.

4 Open the bonnet and check the condition of the battery connections – remake the connections or renew the leads if a fault is found. Use the same techniques to ensure that all earth points in the engine compartment provide good electrical contact through clean, metal-to-metal joints, and that all are securely fastened **(see illustration)**.

5 Next work methodically around the engine compartment, checking all visible wiring, and the connections between sections of the wiring loom. What you are looking for at this stage is wiring that is obviously damaged by chafing against sharp edges, or against moving suspension/transmission components and/or the auxiliary drivebelt, by being trapped or crushed between carelessly-refitted components, or melted by being forced into contact with hot engine castings, coolant pipes, etc. In almost all cases, damage of this sort is caused in the first instance by incorrect routing on reassembly after previous work has been carried out (see the note at the beginning of this sub-Section).

6 Obviously, wires can break or short together inside the insulation so that no visible evidence

betrays the fault, but this usually only occurs where the wiring loom has been incorrectly routed so that it is stretched taut or kinked sharply; either of these conditions should be obvious on even a casual inspection. If this is thought to have happened and the fault proves elusive, the suspect section of wiring should be checked very carefully during the more detailed checks which follow.

7 Depending on the extent of the problem, damaged wiring may be repaired by rejoining the break or splicing-in a new length of wire, using solder to ensure a good connection, and remaking the insulation with adhesive insulating tape or heat-shrink tubing, as desired. If the damage is extensive, given the implications for the vehicle's future reliability, the best long-term answer may well be to renew that entire section of the loom, however expensive this may appear.

8 When the actual damage has been repaired, ensure that the wiring loom is re-routed correctly, so that it is clear of other components, is not stretched or kinked, and is secured out of harm's way using the plastic clips, guides and ties provided.

9 Check all electrical connectors, ensuring that they are clean, securely fastened, and that each is locked by its plastic tabs or wire clip, as appropriate. If any connector shows external signs of corrosion (accumulations of white or green deposits, or streaks of 'rust'), or if any is thought to be dirty, it must be unplugged and cleaned using electrical contact cleaner. If the connector pins are severely corroded, the connector must be renewed; note that this may mean the renewal of that entire section of the loom.

10 If the cleaner completely removes the corrosion to leave the connector in a satisfactory condition, it would be wise to pack the connector with a suitable material which will exclude dirt and moisture, and prevent the corrosion from occurring again; a Ford dealer may be able to recommend a suitable product.

11 All models have an inductive sensor which determines crankshaft speed and TDC position. On an older engine, it is possible that the tip of the sensor may become contaminated with oil and/or dirt, interfering with its operation and giving rise to a misfire.

3.4 Check all engine compartment earth points for corrosion

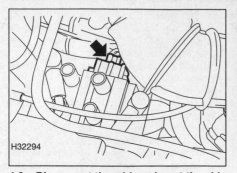

4.2a Disconnect the wiring plug at the side of the coil – 1.4 and 1.6 litre models . . .

4.2b . . . the coil wiring plug is at the front on 1.8 and 2.0 litre models

4.3 The HT leads can be disconnected from the coil, but it is better to disconnect them at the spark plugs

Refer to Chapter 4A, Section 15, for sensor removal and refitting information.

12 Working methodically around the engine compartment, check carefully that all vacuum hoses and pipes are securely fastened and correctly routed, with no signs of cracks, splits or deterioration to cause air leaks, or of hoses that are trapped, kinked, or bent sharply enough to restrict airflow. Check with particular care at all connections and sharp bends, and renew any damaged or deformed lengths of hose.

13 Check the crankcase breather hoses for splits, poor connections or blockages. Details of the breather system vary according to which engine is fitted, but all models have at least one hose running from the top of the engine connected to the air inlet duct or inlet manifold. The breather hoses run from the engine block (or from the oil filler tube) and carry oil fumes into the engine, to be burned with the fuel/air mixture. A variety of poor-running problems (especially unstable idling) can result from blocked or damaged breather hoses.

14 Working from the fuel tank, via the filter, to the fuel rail (and including the feed and return), check the fuel lines, and renew any that are found to be leaking, trapped or kinked. Check particularly the ends of the hoses – these can crack and perish sufficiently to allow leakage.

15 Check that the accelerator cable is correctly secured and adjusted, and that it is routed with as few sharp turns as possible. Renew the cable if there is any doubt about its condition, or if it appears to be stiff or jerky in operation. Refer to Chapter 4A for further information, if required.

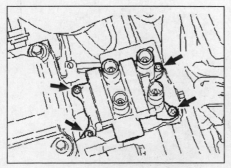

4.4 Ignition coil mounting bolts (arrowed)

16 Remove the air cleaner cover as described in Chapter 1A, and check that the air filter is not clogged or soaked. A clogged air filter will obstruct the inlet airflow, causing a noticeable effect on engine performance. Renew the filter if necessary.

17 Start the engine and allow it to idle.

Caution: Working in the engine compartment while the engine is running requires great care if the risk of personal injury is to be avoided; among the dangers are burns from contact with hot components, or contact with moving components such as the radiator cooling fan or the auxiliary drivebelt. Refer to 'Safety first!' at the front of this manual before starting, and ensure that your hands, and any long hair or loose clothing, are kept well clear of hot or moving components at all times.

18 Working from the air inlet, via the air cleaner assembly and the airflow sensor (or air mass meter) to the throttle housing and inlet manifold (and including the various vacuum hoses and pipes connected to these), check for air leaks. Usually, these will be revealed by sucking or hissing noises, but minor leaks may be traced by spraying a solution of soapy water on to the suspect joint; if a leak exists, it will be shown by the change in engine note and the accompanying air bubbles (or sucking-in of the liquid, depending on the pressure difference at that point). If a leak is found at any point, tighten the fastening clamp and/or renew the faulty components, as applicable.

19 Similarly, work from the cylinder head, via the manifold to the tailpipe, to check that the exhaust system is free from leaks. The simplest way of doing this, if the vehicle can be raised and supported safely and with complete security while the check is made, is to temporarily block the tailpipe while listening for the sound of escaping exhaust gases; any leak should be evident. If a leak is found at any point, tighten the fastening clamp bolts and/or nuts, renew the gasket, and/or renew the faulty section of the system, as necessary, to seal the leak.

20 It is possible to make a further check of the electrical connections by wiggling each electrical connector of the system in turn as the engine is idling; a faulty connector will be immediately evident from the engine's response as contact is broken and remade. A faulty connector should be renewed to ensure that the future reliability of the system; note that this may mean the renewal of that entire section of the loom.

21 If the preliminary checks have failed to reveal the fault, the car must be taken to a Ford dealer or suitably-equipped garage for diagnostic testing using electronic test equipment.

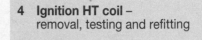

4 Ignition HT coil –
   removal, testing and refitting

Removal

1 The ignition coil is bolted to the left-hand end of the cylinder head; on 1.8 and 2.0 litre engines, the coil is mounted on a separate bracket.

2 Make sure the ignition is switched off, then disconnect the wiring plug from the coil **(see illustrations)**.

3 Check the coil terminals to see whether they are marked for cylinder numbering – if not, make your own marks to ensure that the HT leads are correctly refitted. Identify the HT leads for position if necessary, then carefully pull them from the coil terminals **(see illustration)**. The coil can be removed with the HT leads attached, but in this case, the HT leads must be disconnected from the spark plugs.

4 Unscrew the mounting bolts and remove the ignition coil from the engine compartment **(see illustration)**.

5 Alternatively, on 1.8 and 2.0 litre models, disconnect the wiring plug from the radio suppressor; the coil and its mounting bracket can now be removed after unscrewing the three Torx mounting bolts **(see illustrations)**.

Testing

6 Using an ohmmeter, measure the resistances of the ignition coil's primary and secondary windings and compare with the information given in the Specifications. Renew the coil if necessary.

4.5a Disconnect the radio suppressor wiring plug . . .

4.5b . . . unscrew the three Torx bolts (two above, one below) . . .

4.5c . . . and remove the coil and mounting bracket

Refitting

7 Refitting is a reversal of removal. Take great care that the HT leads are correctly refitted, and tighten the coil mounting bolts to the specified torque.

5 Ignition system sensors – removal and refitting

Knock sensor

Refitting

1 A knock sensor is only fitted to 1.4 and 1.6 litre engines, and is bolted to the front of the cylinder block **(see illustration)**.
2 The knock sensor wiring plug is clipped to a bracket next to the engine oil dipstick **(see illustration)**. Slide the wiring plug downwards to remove it from the clip, then separate the two halves of the wiring plug.
3 Trace the wiring down to the knock sensor, then unscrew the centre bolt and remove the sensor from the engine.

Removal

4 Refitting is a reversal of removal, noting the following points:

a) Clean the sensor and its location on the engine.
b) The sensor must be positioned so that it does not contact the cylinder head, nor the crankcase ventilation system oil separator housing (where applicable) **(see illustration)**.
c) The sensor bolt **must** be tightened to the specified torque, as this is critical to the sensor's correct operation.

Crankshaft position sensor

5 Refer to Chapter 4A, Section 15.

6 Ignition timing – checking and adjustment

Due to the nature of the ignition system, the ignition timing is constantly being monitored and adjusted by the engine management ECU, and nominal values cannot be given. Therefore, it is not possible for the home mechanic to check the ignition timing.

The only way in which the ignition timing can be checked is using special electronic test equipment, connected to the engine management system diagnostic connector

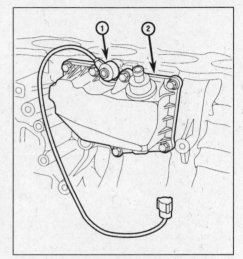

5.1 Knock sensor location on front of engine (seen with cylinder head removed)

1 Knock sensor
2 Oil separator housing

(refer to Chapter 4A). No adjustment of the ignition timing is possible. Should the ignition timing be incorrect, then a fault must be present in the engine management system.

5.3 Knock sensor wiring plug

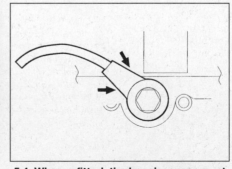

5.4 When refitted, the knock sensor must clear the cylinder head and oil separator housing at the points arrowed

Notes

Chapter 6
Clutch

Contents

Degrees of difficulty

Easy, suitable for novice with little experience	Fairly easy, suitable for beginner with some experience	Fairly difficult, suitable for competent DIY mechanic	Difficult, suitable for experienced DIY mechanic	Very difficult, suitable for expert DIY or professional

Specifications

General

Transmission type:
  1.4, 1.6 and 1.8 litre petrol models iB5
  2.0 litre petrol and 1.8 litre diesel models . . . . MTX 75

Note: *Throughout this Chapter, it is often necessary (and more convenient) to refer to the clutch components by the type of transmission fitted.*

Clutch

Friction disc diameter:
  iB5 transmission models . . . . 210 mm
  MTX 75 transmission models . . . . 228 mm
Lining thickness (wear limit) . . . . 7.0 mm
Pedal stroke (not adjustable) . . . . 133 ± 3.0 mm

Torque wrench settings

	Nm	lbf ft
Clutch bleed nipple:		
iB5 transmission models	10	7
MTX 75 transmission models	14	10
Clutch cover/pressure plate to flywheel*	29	21
Clutch master/slave cylinder mounting nuts/bolts	10	7
Clutch release lever clamp bolt	25	18

Use new bolts on models with MTX 75 transmission.

1 General information

All manual transmission models are equipped with a single dry plate diaphragm spring clutch assembly. The cover assembly consists of a steel cover (doweled and bolted to the flywheel face), the pressure plate, and a diaphragm spring.

The friction disc is free to slide along the splines of the transmission input shaft, and is held in position between the flywheel and the pressure plate by the pressure of the diaphragm spring. Friction lining material is riveted to the friction disc (driven plate), which has a spring-cushioned hub, to absorb transmission shocks and help ensure a smooth take-up of the drive.

The clutch release bearing contacts the fingers of the diaphragm spring. Depressing the clutch pedal pushes the release bearing against the diaphragm fingers, so moving the centre of the diaphragm spring inwards. As the centre of the spring is pushed inwards, the outside of the spring pivots outwards, so moving the pressure plate backwards and disengaging its grip on the friction disc.

When the pedal is released, the diaphragm spring forces the pressure plate back into contact with the friction linings on the friction disc. The disc is now firmly held between the pressure plate and the flywheel, thus transmitting engine power to the transmission.

All Focus models have a hydraulically-operated clutch. A master cylinder is mounted below the clutch pedal, and takes its hydraulic fluid supply from a separate chamber in the brake fluid reservoir. Depressing the clutch pedal operates the master cylinder pushrod, and the fluid pressure is transferred along the fluid lines to a slave cylinder mounted inside the bellhousing. The slave cylinder is incorporated into the release bearing – when the slave cylinder operates, the release bearing moves against the diaphragm spring fingers and disengages the clutch.

The hydraulic clutch offers several advantages over a cable-operated clutch – it is completely self-adjusting, requires less pedal effort, and is less subject to wear problems.

Since many of the procedures covered in this Chapter involve working under the vehicle, make sure that it is securely supported on axle stands placed on a firm, level floor (see *Jacking and vehicle support*). **Note:** *Throughout this Chapter, it is often necessary (and more convenient) to refer to the clutch components by the type of transmission fitted – refer to the Specifications at the start of this Chapter.*

Warning: The hydraulic fluid used in the system is brake fluid, which is poisonous. Take care to keep it off bare skin, and in particular out of your eyes. The fluid also attacks paintwork, and may discolour carpets, etc – keep spillages to a minimum, and wash any off immediately with cold water. Finally, brake fluid is highly inflammable, and should be handled with the same care as petrol.

2 Clutch – checking

1 The following checks may be performed to diagnose a clutch problem:

  a) Check the fluid lines from the clutch master cylinder into the bellhousing for damage, signs of leakage, or for kinks or dents which might restrict fluid flow.

  b) To check 'clutch spin-down time', run the engine at normal idle speed with the transmission in neutral (clutch pedal up). Disengage the clutch (pedal down), wait several seconds, then engage reverse. No grinding noise should be heard. A grinding noise would most likely indicate a problem in the pressure plate or the friction disc. Remember, however, that the MTX 75 transmission reverse gear has synchromesh fitted to it, so the probable symptom of a clutch fault would be a slight rearwards movement (or attempted movement) of the vehicle. If the check is made on level ground with the handbrake released, the movement would be more noticeable

  c) To check for complete clutch release, run the engine at idle, and hold the clutch pedal approximately half an inch from the floor. Shift between 1st gear and reverse several times. If the shift is not smooth, or if the vehicle attempts to move forwards or backwards, component failure is indicated.

  d) Slow or poor operation may be due to air being present in the fluid. This is most likely after servicing work has been carried out, as the system is self-bleeding in normal use. If the system has not been disturbed, air in the system may well be the result of a leak. The system can be bled of air as described in Section 7.

  e) Check the clutch pedal for excessive wear of the bushes, and for any obstructions which may restrict the pedal movement.

  f) If clutch failure is apparent after prolonged driving in very wet weather or (particularly) flooding, the clutch friction disc may have corroded to the input shaft, and will therefore not release even when the clutch is depressed. This condition can arise in a very short time after the engine is switched off. Before attempting to free it, consult a Ford dealer or garage – starting the engine in gear with the clutch depressed may lead to component damage. The likelihood of this problem arising can be reduced by always greasing the input shaft splines when fitting clutch components.

Pedal stroke – checking

2 Turn the steering wheel (from the straight-ahead position) to the left by about 30°.

3 Using tape or a cable-tie, attach the end lip of a measuring tape to the clutch pedal rubber. Alternatively, have an assistant hold the measuring tape in place – either way, make sure that the end of the tape does not move from one measurement to the next.

4 Without touching the pedal, read off and record the distance measured from the pedal to the front of the steering wheel rim (dimension A).

5 Now press the pedal down to its stop, and record the new distance (dimension B). Make sure that the pedal action is not hindered by the carpets or floor mats, or by incorrect fitting of the master cylinder.

6 The pedal stroke C is obtained by subtracting dimension A from dimension B:

  C (stroke) = B (depressed dimension) minus A (released dimension)

7 Check that the dimension is within the tolerance given in the Specifications. No adjustment of the pedal stroke is possible – providing the clutch is working satisfactorily, even a dimension outside the tolerance is arguably acceptable. An incorrect pedal stroke combined with poor clutch operation points to a component failure – check the pedal and master cylinder first.

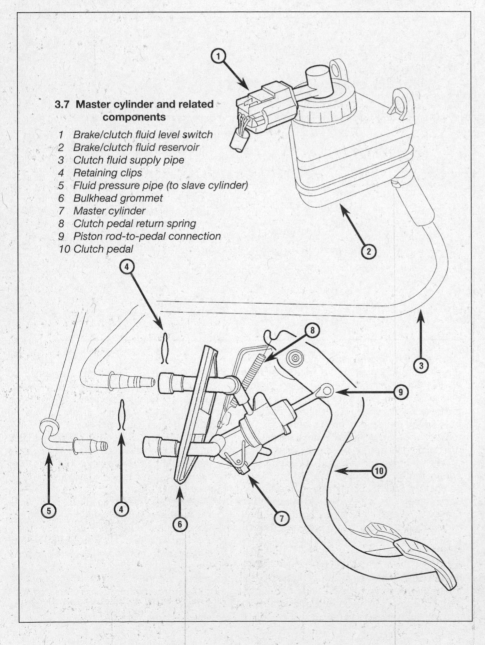

3.7 Master cylinder and related components

1 Brake/clutch fluid level switch
2 Brake/clutch fluid reservoir
3 Clutch fluid supply pipe
4 Retaining clips
5 Fluid pressure pipe (to slave cylinder)
6 Bulkhead grommet
7 Master cylinder
8 Clutch pedal return spring
9 Piston rod-to-pedal connection
10 Clutch pedal

3 Clutch master cylinder – removal and refitting

Note: *Refer to the warning in Section 1 concerning the dangers of hydraulic fluid before proceeding.*

Removal

1 Disconnect the battery negative lead, and position the lead away from the terminal.

2 Working inside the vehicle, move the driver's seat fully to the rear, to allow maximum working area. Remove the fasteners securing the driver's side lower facia trim panel, and remove the panel from the car, unclipping the diagnostic connector plug as the panel is removed.

3 Although not essential, removing the clutch pedal as described in Section 4 will make removing the master cylinder considerably easier.

4 Before proceeding, anticipate some spillage of hydraulic (brake) fluid. If sufficient fluid comes into contact with the carpet, it may be discoloured or worse. Place a good quantity of clean rags below the clutch pedal, and have a container ready in the engine compartment.

5 Remove the brake fluid reservoir cap, and then tighten it down over a piece of polythene or cling film, to obtain an airtight seal. This may help to reduce the spillage of fluid when the lines are disconnected.

6 To gain access to the fluid connections where they pass through the engine compartment bulkhead, jack up the front of the car, and support it on axle stands (see *Jacking and vehicle support*).

7 Working in the engine compartment, or from below, pull out the securing clip from the top of the fluid supply connection (the larger-diameter pipe). Pull the pipe fitting from the master cylinder; anticipate some fluid loss, and plug or clamp the hose end if possible **(see illustration opposite)**.

8 To remove the (smaller) fluid pressure pipe, first release it from the support bracket adjacent to the bulkhead. Pull out the securing clip from above, then pull the pipe fitting out of the base of the cylinder. Again,

3.9 Removing the pipe flange clip

plug or tape over the pipe end, to avoid losing fluid, and to prevent dirt entry.

9 Returning to the driver's footwell, first unscrew the nut (or pull off the metal clip) which secures the pipe flange to the bulkhead **(see illustration)**.

10 Remove the two bolts which secure the master cylinder body to the pedal bracket **(see illustration)**.

11 Unclip the master cylinder sideways from the pedal bracket, then carefully prise off the piston rod from the top of the clutch pedal. Taking care not to tilt the master cylinder (to avoid further fluid spillage), remove it from the footwell.

Refitting

12 Refitting is a reversal of removal, noting the following points:

a) Tighten the mounting bolts to the specified torque.

b) If necessary, fit new clips when reconnecting the fluid pipes.

c) Refit the clutch pedal (if removed) as described in Section 4.

d) Remove the polythene from under the fluid reservoir cap, and top-up the fluid level (see 'Weekly checks').

e) Refer to Section 7 and bleed the clutch hydraulic system.

f) If the fluid level in the reservoir fell sufficiently, it may be necessary to bleed the braking system also – refer to Chapter 9.

g) On completion, operate the clutch a few times without starting the engine, then check for signs of fluid leakage at the bulkhead connections in the engine compartment.

3.10 Master cylinder-to-pedal bracket bolts (arrowed)

h) Start the engine, and check for correct clutch operation.

4 Clutch pedal – removal and refitting

Removal

1 Disconnect the battery negative lead, and position the lead away from the terminal.

2 Working inside the vehicle, move the driver's seat fully to the rear, to allow maximum working area. Remove the fasteners securing the driver's side lower facia trim panel, and take out the panel, unclipping the diagnostic connector plug as the panel is removed.

3 Unscrew the nut from the end of the pedal pivot shaft, and withdraw the pedal pivot shaft sufficiently through the mounting bracket **(see illustration)**. Unless the brake pedal is also to be removed, the shaft need only be partially withdrawn.

4 Carefully prise off the master cylinder piston rod from the top of the clutch pedal, then unhook and remove the clutch pedal return spring **(see illustration)**.

5 Remove the clutch pedal; recover the clutch pedal metal sleeve, and the plastic bushes if they are loose.

6 With the pedal removed, inspect and renew the components as necessary **(see illustration)**. Also check the rubber pad which contacts the clutch pedal switch.

4.3 Unscrew the pivot shaft nut

4.4 Removing the master cylinder piston rod

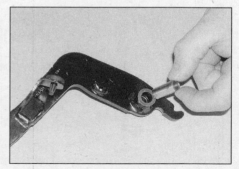

4.6 Remove the pedal bush and check its condition

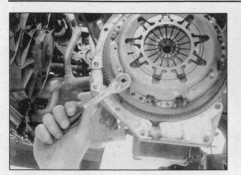

5.3 Loosen the clutch cover (pressure plate) retaining bolts

5.4 Remove the clutch cover, and take out the friction disc

Refitting

7 Prior to refitting the pedal, apply a little grease to the pivot shaft, sleeve and pedal bushes.

8 Refitting is a reversal of the removal procedure, making sure that the bushes and sleeve are correctly located.

9 Check the clutch operation and the pedal stroke, as described in Section 2.

5 Clutch components – removal, inspection and refitting

 Warning: Dust created by clutch wear and deposited on the clutch components may contain asbestos, which is a health hazard. DO NOT blow it out with compressed air, and do not inhale any of it. DO NOT use petrol or petroleum-based solvents to clean off the dust. Brake system cleaner or methylated spirit should be used to flush the dust into a suitable receptacle. After the clutch components are wiped clean with rags, dispose of the contaminated rags and cleaner in a sealed, marked container.

Removal

1 Access to the clutch may be gained in one of two ways. The engine/transmission unit can be removed, as described in Chapter 2D, and the transmission separated from the engine on the bench. Alternatively, the engine may be

5.12 Refitting the friction disc

left in the vehicle and the transmission removed independently, as described in Chapter 7A.

2 Having separated the transmission from the engine, check if there are any marks identifying the relation of the clutch cover to the flywheel. If not, make your own marks using a dab of paint or a scriber. These marks will be used if the original cover is refitted, and will help to maintain the balance of the unit. A new cover may be fitted in any position allowed by the locating dowels.

3 Unscrew the six clutch cover retaining bolts, working in a diagonal sequence, and slackening the bolts only a turn at a time **(see illustration)**. If necessary, the flywheel may be held stationary using a wide-bladed screwdriver, inserted in the teeth of the starter ring gear and resting against part of the cylinder block. Ford state that, on models with the MTX 75 transmission, new cover bolts must be used when refitting.

4 Ease the clutch cover off its locating dowels. Be prepared to catch the clutch friction disc, which will drop out as the cover is removed **(see illustration)**. Note which way round the friction disc is fitted.

Inspection

5 The most common problem which occurs in the clutch is wear of the clutch friction disc (driven plate). However, all the clutch components should be inspected at this time, particularly if the engine has covered a high mileage. Unless the clutch components are known to be virtually new, it is worth renewing them all as a set (disc, pressure plate and release bearing). Renewing a worn friction disc by itself is not always satisfactory, especially if the old disc was slipping and causing the pressure plate to overheat.

6 Examine the linings of the friction disc for wear and loose rivets, and the disc hub and rim for distortion, cracks, broken torsion springs, and worn splines. The surface of the friction linings may be highly glazed, but as long as the friction material pattern can be clearly seen, and the rivet heads are at least 1 mm below the lining surface, this is satisfactory. The disc must be renewed if the lining thickness has worn down to, or just above, the level of the rivet heads.

7 If there is any sign of oil contamination, indicated by shiny black discoloration, the disc must be renewed, and the source of the contamination traced and rectified. This will be a leaking crankshaft oil seal or transmission input shaft oil seal. The renewal procedure for the former is given in the relevant Part of Chapter 2. Renewal of the transmission input shaft oil seal should be entrusted to a Ford dealer, as it involves dismantling the transmission, and (where applicable) the renewal of the clutch release bearing guide tube, using a press.

8 Check the machined faces of the flywheel and pressure plate. If either is grooved, or heavily scored, renewal is necessary. The pressure plate must also be renewed if any cracks are apparent, or if the diaphragm spring is damaged or its pressure suspect. Pay particular attention to the tips of the spring fingers, where the release bearing acts upon them.

9 With the transmission removed, it is also advisable to check the condition of the release bearing, as described in Section 6. Having got this far, it is almost certainly worth renewing it. Note that the release bearing is integral with the slave cylinder – the two must be renewed together; however, given that access to the slave cylinder is only possible with the transmission removed, not to renew it at this time is probably a false economy.

Refitting

10 It is important that no oil or grease is allowed to come into contact with the friction material of the friction disc or the pressure plate and flywheel faces. To ensure this, it is advisable to refit the clutch assembly with clean hands, and to wipe down the pressure plate and flywheel faces with a clean dry rag before assembly begins.

11 Ford technicians use a special tool for centralising the friction disc at this stage. The tool holds the disc centrally on the pressure plate, and locates in the middle of the diaphragm spring fingers. If the tool is not available, it will be necessary to centralise the disc after assembling the cover loosely on the flywheel, as described in the following paragraphs.

12 Place the friction disc against the flywheel, ensuring that it is the right way round **(see illustration)**. It may be marked FLYWHEEL SIDE, but if not, position it so that the raised hub with the cushion springs is facing away from the flywheel.

13 Place the clutch cover over the dowels. Refit the retaining bolts (fit new ones on MTX 75 transmission models), and tighten them finger-tight so that the friction disc is gripped lightly, but can still be moved.

14 The friction disc must now be centralised so that, when the engine and transmission are mated, the splines of the gearbox input shaft will pass through the splines in the centre of the friction disc hub.

15 Centralisation can be carried out by inserting a round bar through the hole in the centre of the friction disc, so that the end of the bar rests in the hole in the rear end of the crankshaft. Move the bar sideways or up-and-down, to move the friction disc in whichever direction is necessary to achieve centralisation. Centralisation can then be checked by removing the bar and viewing the friction disc hub in relation to the diaphragm spring fingers, or by viewing through the side apertures of the cover, and checking that the disc is central in relation to the outer edge of the pressure plate.

16 An alternative and more accurate method of centralisation is to use a commercially-available clutch-aligning tool, obtainable from most accessory shops **(see illustration)**.

17 Once the clutch is centralised, progressively tighten the cover bolts in a diagonal sequence to the torque setting given in the Specifications **(see illustration)**.

18 Ensure that the input shaft splines and friction disc splines are clean. Apply a thin smear of high melting-point grease to the input shaft splines – do not apply excessively, however, or it may end up on the friction disc, causing the new clutch to slip.

19 Refit the transmission to the engine.

---

6   Clutch release bearing (and slave cylinder) – removal, inspection and refitting

Removal

1 Separate the engine and transmission as described in the previous Section.

2 The release bearing and slave cylinder are combined into one unit, and cannot be separated **(see illustrations)**.

3 On models with the MTX 75 transmission, remove the cylinder bleed screw dust cap, and prise out the sealing grommet from the bellhousing as the cylinder is removed – a new grommet (and suitable sealant) must be obtained for refitting.

4 Remove the three mounting bolts, and withdraw the slave cylinder and release bearing from the transmission bellhousing **(see illustrations)**.

Inspection

5 Check the bearing for smoothness of operation, and renew it if there is any sign of harshness or roughness as the bearing is spun. Do not attempt to dismantle, clean or lubricate the bearing.

6 It is worth renewing the release bearing as a matter of course, unless it is known to be in perfect condition. Ford specifically say not to re-use the slave cylinder (and therefore the release bearing) on MTX 75 transmission models.

7 Check the condition of all O-ring seals, and renew if necessary. Considering the difficulty

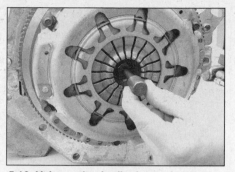

5.16 Using a clutch-aligning tool to centre the friction disc

in gaining access to some of the seals if they fail, it would be wise to renew these as a precaution.

Refitting

8 Refitting of the clutch release bearing is a reversal of the removal procedure, noting the following points:

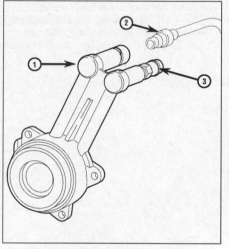

6.2a Release bearing and slave cylinder – iB5 transmission

1 *Release bearing/slave cylinder*
2 *Fluid supply pipe (from master cylinder)*
3 *Bleed screw*

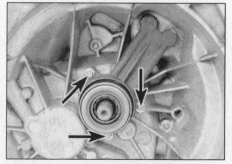

6.4a Undo the three bolts (arrowed) . . .

5.17 Tightening the clutch cover bolts

a) *Tighten the mounting bolts to the specified torque.*
b) *On models with the MTX 75 transmission, fit a new sealing grommet to the bellhousing, and seal/secure it in position using a suitable sealant.*
c) *On completion, bleed the system and check for leaks from the slave cylinder fluid connection.*

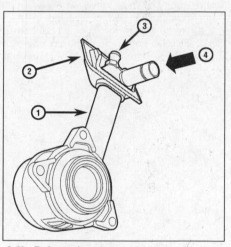

6.2b Release bearing and slave cylinder – MTX 75 transmission

1 *Release bearing/slave cylinder*
2 *Plastic grommet/boot*
3 *Bleed screw*
4 *Fluid supply (from master cylinder)*

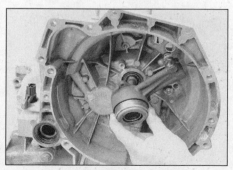

6.4b . . . and remove the slave cylinder/release bearing

7.3 Clutch bleed screw (arrowed)

7 Clutch hydraulic system – bleeding

1 The clutch hydraulic system will not normally require bleeding, and this task should only be necessary when the system has been opened for repair work. However, as with the brake pedal, if the clutch pedal feels at all soggy or unresponsive in operation, this may indicate the need for bleeding.

2 Air in the clutch system could be the result of a leak. Do not overlook the possibility of a leak in the system, for the following reasons:

a) *Leaking fluid will damage paintwork and/or carpets.*

b) *The clutch system shares its fluid with the braking system, so a clutch system leak could result in brake failure from low fluid level.*

c) *Equally, fluid loss affecting the clutch system could be the result of a braking system fluid leak.*

3 The system bleed screw is located on top of the transmission bellhousing, next to the fluid pressure pipe **(see illustration)**.

4 Remove the air cleaner and inlet duct as described in the Chapter 4A, and the battery and battery tray, as described in Chapter 5A.

5 Move the pipework and wiring harness to one side as necessary to reach the bleed screw.

6 Remove the bleed screw cap.

Models with iB5 transmission

7 Ford technicians use a special tool which enables them to use a 'reverse' bleeding technique. For information, this technique is described below. However, Ford also say that conventional brake bleeding techniques can be used, so if this special tool is not available, proceed as described in paragraphs 10.

8 The Ford tool is a pressurised container of brake fluid, which is held at a level below the bleed screw. The fluid reservoir is first drained to the MIN level, then the tool is used to force brake fluid **in** via a tube connected to the bleed screw, until the fluid level in the reservoir reaches the MAX mark.

Models with MTX 75 transmission

9 Before bleeding the clutch system, it is recommended that the braking system is bled first, as described in Chapter 9.

10 Bleeding the clutch is much the same as bleeding the brakes – refer to Chapter 9 for the various methods which may be used. Ensure that the level in the brake fluid reservoir is maintained well above the MIN mark at all times, otherwise the clutch and brake hydraulic systems will both need bleeding.

All transmissions

11 On completion, tighten the bleed screw securely, and top-up the brake fluid level to the MAX mark. If possible, test the operation of the clutch before refitting all the components removed for access.

12 Failure to bleed correctly may point to a leak in the system, or to a worn master or slave cylinder. At the time of writing, it appears that the master and slave cylinders are only available as complete assemblies – overhaul is not possible.

Chapter 7 Part A:
Manual transmission

Contents

Degrees of difficulty

Easy, suitable for novice with little experience	**Fairly easy,** suitable for beginner with some experience	**Fairly difficult,** suitable for competent DIY mechanic	**Difficult,** suitable for experienced DIY mechanic	**Very difficult,** suitable for expert DIY or professional

Specifications

General

Transmission type . . . . Five forward speeds, one reverse. Synchromesh on all forward gears (and reverse gear, on MTX 75 transmission). Gearchange linkage operated by twin cables

Transmission code:
1.4, 1.6 and 1.8 litre petrol engine models iB5
2.0 litre petrol and 1.8 litre diesel engine models . . . . MTX 75
Transmission oil type . . . . See end of *Weekly checks*
Transmission oil capacity . . . . See Chapter 1A or 1B Specifications

Gear ratios

iB5 transmission (typical)
1st 3.583:1
2nd 1.926:1
3rd 1.281:1
4th 0.951:1
5th 0.756:1
Reverse 3.615:1

MTX 75 transmission – 2.0 litre petrol models
1st 3.417:1
2nd 2.136:1
3rd 1.483:1
4th 1.114:1
5th 0.854:1
Reverse 3.462:1

MTX 75 transmission – 1.8 litre diesel models
1st 3.666:1
2nd 2.047:1
3rd 1.258:1
4th 0.864:1
5th 0.674:1
Reverse 3.462:1

Final drive ratios
1.4 litre engine models 3.610:1
1.6 litre engine models 3.824:1
1.8 litre petrol engine models 4.059:1
1.8 litre diesel engine models 3.560:1
2.0 litre engine models 4.060:1

Torque wrench settings

	Nm	lbf ft
iB5 transmission		
Battery tray bolts	25	18
Engine/transmission left-hand mounting lower section	80	59
Engine/transmission left-hand mounting upper section:		
Centre nut	133	98
Four outer nuts	48	35
Engine/transmission rear mounting through-bolts	48	35
Fluid filler/level plug	35	26
Gearchange cable bracket bolts	20	15
Gearchange cable bushing	9	7
Gearchange mechanism to floor	9	7
Reversing light switch	18	13
Selector lever securing bolt	25	18
Slave cylinder pressure pipe bracket	28	21
Transmission to engine	48	35
MTX 75 transmission		
Battery tray bolts	25	18
Coolant pipe to transmission	30	22
Engine/transmission left-hand mounting lower section	80	59
Engine/transmission left-hand mounting upper section:		
Centre nut	133	98
Four outer nuts	48	35
Engine/transmission rear mounting through-bolts	48	35
Fluid drain plug	45	33
Fluid filler/level plug	45	33
Reversing light switch	10	7
Selector mechanism to transmission	23	17
Starter motor mounting bolts	35	26
Transmission to engine	48	35

1 General information

The vehicles covered by this manual are equipped with either a 5-speed manual or a 4-speed automatic transmission. This Part of Chapter 7 contains information on the manual transmission. Service procedures for the automatic transmission are contained in Part B.

The transmission is contained in a cast-aluminium alloy casing bolted to the engine's left-hand end, and consists of the gearbox and final drive differential – often called a transaxle. The transmission unit type is stamped on a plate attached to the transmission. The 5-speed manual transmissions used in the Focus are the iB5 and MTX 75 types – refer to the Specifications for application details.

The iB5 unit is identical to that used in the previous Escort range, with the exception that it is newly equipped with a cable-actuated gearchange linkage. The MTX 75 transmission, previously seen in the Mondeo range, also has a cable gearchange linkage.

Drive is transmitted from the crankshaft via the clutch to the input shaft, which has a splined extension to accept the clutch friction disc. From the input shaft, drive is transmitted to the output shaft, from where the drive is transmitted to the differential crownwheel, which rotates with the differential and planetary gears, thus driving the sun gears and driveshafts. The rotation of the planetary gears on their shaft allows the inner roadwheel to rotate at a slower speed than the outer roadwheel when the car is cornering.

The input and output shafts are arranged side-by-side, parallel to the crankshaft and driveshafts, so that their gear pinion teeth are in constant mesh. In the neutral position, the output shaft gear pinions rotate freely, so that drive cannot be transmitted to the crownwheel.

Gear selection is via a floor-mounted lever and selector cable mechanism.

The transmission selector mechanism causes the appropriate selector fork to move its respective synchro-sleeve along the output shaft, to lock the gear pinion to the synchro-hub. Since the synchro-hubs are splined to the output shaft, this locks the pinion to the shaft, so that drive can be transmitted. To ensure that gearchanging can be made quickly and quietly, a synchromesh system is fitted to all forward gears, consisting of baulk rings and spring-loaded fingers, as well as the gear pinions and synchro-hubs. The synchromesh cones are formed on the mating faces of the baulk rings and gear pinions. The MTX 75 has synchromesh on reverse gear, and dual synchromesh on 1st, 2nd and 3rd gears, for even smoother gearchanging.

Transmission overhaul

Because of the complexity of the assembly, possible unavailability of replace-ment parts and special tools necessary, internal repair procedures for the transmission are not recommended for the home mechanic. The bulk of the information in this Chapter is devoted to removal and refitting procedures.

2 Gearchange cables – adjustment

iB5 transmission

Note: A 3 mm drill bit will be required for this adjustment.

1 Inside the car, move the gear lever to neutral.
2 Carefully unclip the surround panel at the base of the gear lever gaiter, and move the panel aside for access to the base of the gear lever, disconnecting the switch wiring if necessary.
3 Insert a 3 mm drill bit into the gear lever base mechanism, making sure that it is fully inserted **(see illustration)**.

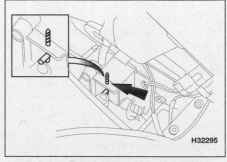

2.3 Insert a 3 mm drill bit to adjust the cables

2.5 Removing the cover from the selector mechanism

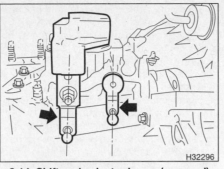

2.14 Shift and selector levers (arrowed) should be vertical when in neutral

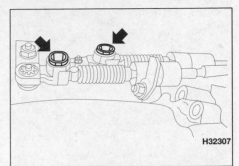

2.15 Press the plastic locking sliders as indicated to release them for adjustment

4 Apply the handbrake, then jack up the front of the car, supporting it on axle stands (see *Jacking and vehicle support*). Where applicable, remove the engine undershield.

5 At the front face of the transmission housing, remove the selector mechanism cover by working around the edge, releasing a total of seven clips **(see illustration)**.

6 Only the selector cable is to be adjusted during this procedure – this is the cable which comes to the lowest point on the front of the transmission, with its end fitting nearest the engine.

7 Unlock the selector cable by pressing the coloured insert towards the engine, and move the transmission selector lever (**not** the gear lever inside the car) to its centre position by moving it up or down as necessary.

8 Now move the transmission selector lever fully to its left- and right-hand stop positions, and release it. Lock the selector cable in the final position by moving the coloured insert away from the engine.

9 Refit the selector mechanism cover, ensuring that the clips engage correctly, and lower the car to the ground.

10 Inside the car, remove the drill bit from the gear lever base mechanism, and refit the surround panel.

11 Start the engine, keeping the clutch pedal depressed, and check for correct gear selection.

MTX 75 transmission

Note 1: *The special Ford tool 16-088A will be required in order to carry out the following adjustment. This tool locks the gear lever in the neutral position during adjustment. If the tool is not available, adjustment is still possible by proceeding on a trial-and-error basis, preferably with the help of an assistant to hold the gear lever in the neutral position.*

Note 2: *On some models with the MTX 75 transmission, access to the gearchange cables (at the rear of the transmission) is far from easy, and may in fact only be at all possible from above. If this is found to be the case, removing the air cleaner and the auxiliary fusebox will improve working room.*

12 Apply the handbrake, then jack up the front of the car, supporting it on axle stands (see *Jacking and vehicle support*). Where

applicable, remove the engine undershield and left-hand wheelarch liner.

13 Inside the car, move the gear lever to neutral.

14 Under the car, the shift and selector levers on the transmission should be vertical when neutral is selected **(see illustration)**. On some models, it may only be possible to view the cables from above, and even then, not easily.

15 If adjustment is required, release the adjusters on the cables by depressing the tabs on the sides of the red plastic locking sliders **(see illustration)**.

16 If using the special tool, inside the car, prise out the gear lever gaiter frame and pull the gaiter up onto the gear knob. Lock the gear lever in neutral.

17 If the special tool is not available, have an assistant place the gear lever in the approximate neutral position, and hold it there.

18 With the levers on the transmission in neutral, lock the red plastic locking sliders by pressing them in.

19 Where applicable, remove the special tool, and refit the gaiter to the gearchange lever.

20 Lower the car to the ground. Start the engine, keeping the clutch pedal depressed, and check for correct gear selection.

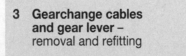

3 Gearchange cables and gear lever – removal and refitting

Note: *On some models with the MTX 75*

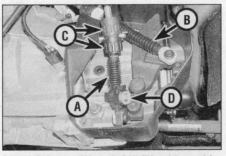

3.7a Selector (A) and shift (B) cables, with support bracket collars (C) and cable adjuster securing clip (D) – iB5 transmission

transmission, access to the gearchange cables (at the rear of the transmission) is far from easy, and may in fact only be at all possible from above. If this is found to be the case, removing the air cleaner and the auxiliary fusebox will improve working room.

Removal

1 Disconnect the battery negative (earth) lead (see *Disconnecting the battery*).

2 Inside the car, place the gear lever in neutral.

3 Apply the handbrake, then loosen the front wheel nuts. Jack up the front of the vehicle and support it on axle stands (see *Jacking and vehicle support*). Remove both wheels.

4 Remove the engine undershield (where applicable) and the left-hand wheelarch liner.

5 Remove the front section of the exhaust pipe, referring to Chapter 4A or 4B as necessary. Note particularly that the flexible section of the exhaust must not be bent too far during removal.

6 Remove the washer-type fasteners, and lower the exhaust heat shield from the vehicle underside.

7 At the transmission, unclip the cover (where fitted) from the selector mechanism. Remove the cables from the support brackets by twisting the spring-loaded knurled collars clockwise (iB5) or anti-clockwise (MTX 75). Release the coloured plastic clips which secure the cable adjuster(s), and remove the cables from the transmission levers – note their fitted locations **(see illustrations)**. Withdraw the cables downwards from the engine compartment.

3.7b Remove the selector cable – MTX 75 transmission

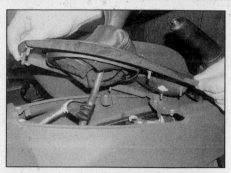

3.8 Unclip the gear lever surround for access to the cables

8 Unclip and remove the gear lever surround panel, then lift it upwards and disconnect the switch wiring, noting its fitted locations **(see illustration)**.

9 Remove the centre console as described in Chapter 11.

10 Disconnect the shift (white) and selector (black) inner cables from the gear lever by prising off the end fittings. Disconnect the cable outers from the floor brackets by twisting the collars clockwise (iB5) or anticlockwise against each other (MTX 75) **(see illustrations)**.

11 Remove the fasteners securing the heater air duct to the floor, and remove the duct.

12 Unscrew the fasteners securing the side cover panels fitted between the centre section of the facia panel and the floor, and remove the panels. Behind these panels, release the clips and remove the screws securing the heater side panels, and remove the panels.

13 Fold back the carpet and insulation material under the centre part of the facia for access to the selector cable floor grommet. Remove the two screws and release the grommet from the floor.

> **HAYNES HiNT**
> *Before withdrawing the cables, tie some string to their ends, and feed the string through as the cables are removed. Once the cables are completely removed, untie the string, leaving it in position until the new cables are fitted – the string can then be used to pull the new cables into the position, preserving the correct routing.*

14 Pass the cables down through the vehicle floor, and remove them from under the car.

15 If required, the gear lever can be removed by unscrewing the mounting bolts, or the complete selector mechanism can be removed by unscrewing the four nuts **(see illustration)**.

Refitting

16 Refitting is a reversal of removal. Use new

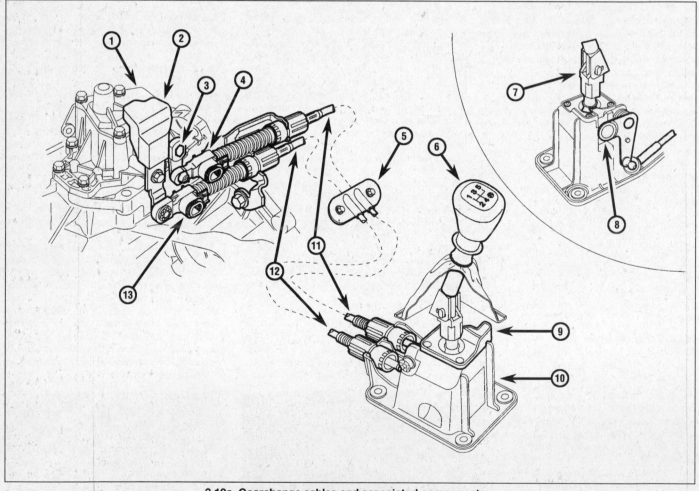

3.10a Gearchange cables and associated components – MTX 75 transmission

1 Internal shift mechanism housing	5 Grommet	10 External shift mechanism housing
2 Balance weight	6 Gear lever	11 Selector cable (black)
3 Selector lever shaft	7 Reverse gear lock	12 Shift cable (white)
4 Selector cable adjuster	8 Angle lever	13 Shift cable adjuster
	9 Reverse gear locking mechanism	

3.10b Gear lever and cables with centre console removed

3.10c Prise the inner cable end fittings with a screwdriver . . .

3.10d . . . and disconnect them from the lever

clips when reconnecting the gearchange cables, and adjust the cables as described in Section 2.

4 Vehicle speed sensor – removal and refitting

1 The Focus has an electronic speedometer, rather than the older, cable-driven mechanical type. An electronic sensor is fitted to the transmission (in place of the older speedometer drive pinion), and the speed signal from this sensor is passed to the instrument panel via the engine management ECU. Besides driving the speedometer, the speed sensor signal is used by the ECU as one of the parameters for fuel system-related calculations.

Removal

2 Access to the speed sensor is easiest from below. Apply the handbrake, then loosen the left-hand front wheel nuts. Jack up the front of the car and support it on axle stands (see *Jacking and vehicle support*).
3 Remove the left-hand front wheel and the wheelarch liner – the sensor is located next to the right-hand driveshaft, at the rear of the transmission (see illustration).
4 Disconnect the wiring plug from the top of the sensor.
5 Using thin-nose pliers, pull out the retaining pin at the base of the sensor, noting how it is fitted (see illustration).
6 Pull the sensor out of its location in the transmission – be prepared for a little oil spillage. Recover the O-ring seal – fit a new seal if the old one is in poor condition.

Refitting

7 Refitting is a reversal of the removal procedure, but lightly oil the O-ring before inserting the assembly in the transmission casing.

5 Reversing light switch – removal and refitting

iB5 transmission

1 The switch is located on the front of the transmission, next to the selector cable front

3.10e Release the cable outers from the floor brackets by twisting the knurled collars

cover (see illustration). To improve access, jack up the front left-hand side of the car (see *Jacking and vehicle support*).
2 Disconnect the wiring plug from the switch (see illustration).

4.3 Vehicle speed sensor (arrowed) – seen from below

5.1 Reversing light switch – iB5 transmission

3.15 Selector mechanism mounting nuts

3 Unscrew and remove the switch from the front of the transmission – anticipate a little oil spillage as this is done.
4 Refitting is a reversal of removal. Tighten the switch to the specified torque.

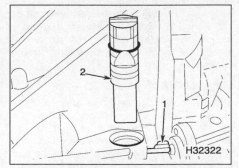

4.5 Pull out the retaining pin (1) and remove the speed sensor (2)

5.2 Disconnecting the reversing light switch wiring plug

5.6 Disconnect the multi-plug, then undo the two retaining bolts (arrowed) – MTX 75 transmission

MTX 75 transmission

5 The switch is located on top of the transmission. Remove the air cleaner as described in Chapter 4A or 4B, and the battery and battery tray, as described in Chapter 5A.
6 Disconnect the wiring leading to the reversing light switch on the top of the transmission **(see illustration)**.
7 Unscrew the mounting bolts and remove the reversing light switch from the cover housing on the transmission.
8 Refitting is a reversal of the removal procedure.

6 Oil seals – renewal

1 Oil leaks frequently occur due to wear or deterioration of the driveshaft oil seals, vehicle speed sensor O-ring, or the selector shaft oil seal (iB5). Renewal of these seals is relatively easy, since the repairs can be performed without removing the transmission from the vehicle.

Driveshaft oil seals

2 The driveshaft oil seals are located at the sides of the transmission, where the driveshafts enter the transmission. If leakage at the seal is suspected, raise the vehicle and support it securely on axle stands. If the seal is leaking, oil will be found on the side of the transmission below the driveshaft.

6.4 Prise out the oil seal with a suitable lever

3 Refer to Chapter 8 and remove the appropriate driveshaft.
4 Using a large screwdriver or lever, carefully prise the oil seal out of the transmission casing, taking care not to damage the transmission casing **(see illustration)**.

> **HAYNES HINT** *If an oil seal is difficult to remove, it sometimes helps to drive the seal into the transmission a little way, applying force at one point only (at the top, for instance). This can have the effect of swivelling the opposite side of the seal out of the casing, and it can then be pulled out.*

5 Wipe clean the oil seal seating in the transmission casing.
6 Dip the new oil seal in clean oil, then press it a little way into the casing by hand, making sure that it is square to its seating.
7 Using suitable tubing or a large socket, carefully drive the oil seal fully into the casing until it contacts the seating **(see illustration)**.
8 When refitting the left-hand driveshaft on the iB5 transmission, use the protective sleeve which should be provided with Ford parts. The sleeve is fitted into the seal, and the driveshaft is then fitted through it – the sleeve is then withdrawn and cut free.
9 Refit the driveshaft (see Chapter 8).

Vehicle speed sensor oil seal

10 The procedure is covered in Section 4.

Selector shaft oil seal (iB5)

11 Apply the handbrake, then jack up the front of the car, supporting it on axle stands (see *Jacking and vehicle support*).
12 At the front face of the transmission housing, remove the selector mechanism cover by working around the edge, releasing a total of seven clips.
13 Prise off the retaining clips, then pull the shift and selector cables from the transmission levers, and detach them from the cable support brackets by turning the knurled collars clockwise.
14 Unscrew and remove the four bolts securing the selector mechanism rear cover to the transmission housing.

6.7 Drive in the oil seal using a socket

15 Remove the transmission shift lever by prising off the protective cap and extracting the retaining clip.
16 With the shift lever removed, unscrew the securing bolt and take off the selector lever and dust cover.
17 The selector shaft oil seal can now be prised out of its location. If using a screwdriver or similar sharp tool, take great care not to mark or gouge the selector shaft or the seal housing as this is done, or the new seal will also leak.
18 Before fitting the new oil seal, carefully clean the visible part of the selector shaft, and the oil seal housing. Wrap a little tape around the end of the shaft, to protect the seal lips as they pass over it.
19 Smear the new oil seal with a little oil, then carefully fit it over the end of the selector shaft, lips facing inwards (towards the transmission).
20 Making sure that the seal stays square to the shaft, press it fully along the shaft (if available, a 16 mm ring spanner is ideal for this).
21 Press the seal fully into its housing, again using the ring spanner or perhaps a deep socket. Remove the tape from the end of the shaft.
22 Further refitting is a reversal of removal. Tighten the selector lever securing bolt to the specified torque, and use new clips when reconnecting the gearchange cables.
23 On completion, check and if necessary adjust the cables as described in Section 2.

7 Transmission oil – draining and refilling

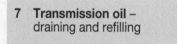

Note: *Although not included in the maintenance schedule by the manufacturers, it is a good idea to drain and renew the manual transmission oil on a regular basis. The frequency with which this needs to carried out can be left to the individual, but it is certainly advisable on a vehicle that has covered a high mileage.*

iB5 transmission

1 The iB5 transmission has no drain plug; the most effective way to drain the oil is to remove one or both driveshafts, as described in Chapter 8.
2 When refilling the transmission, remember that the vehicle must be level for the oil level to be correct. Refill the transmission using the information in Chapter 1A – refer to the table at the end of *Weekly checks* for the type of oil to be used.

MTX 75 transmission

3 The drain plug is located in the base of the differential housing – like the oil filler/level plug, a special hexagonal socket (or large Allen key) will be required for removal.

8.3a Prise up the locking clip . . .

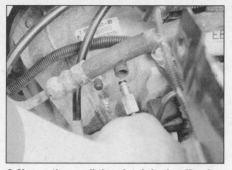

8.3b . . . then pull the clutch hydraulic pipe out

8.4 Unclip the hydraulic pipe from the bracket on top of the transmission

4 The oil is best drained when the transmission is hot, but bear in mind the risk of burning yourself on hot exhaust components, etc. Apply the handbrake, then jack up the front of the car, and support it on axle stands (see *Jacking and vehicle support*).

5 Where applicable, remove the engine undershield. Position a suitable container under the transmission drain plug, then unscrew and remove it, and allow the oil to drain.

6 When the flow of oil stops, clean and refit the drain plug, and tighten it to the specified torque.

7 When refilling the transmission, remember that the vehicle must be level for the oil level to be correct. Refill the transmission using the information in Chapter 1A or 1B – refer to the table at the end of *Weekly checks* for the type of oil to be used.

---

8 Transmission –
removal and refitting

⚠️ *Warning: The hydraulic fluid used in the clutch system is brake fluid, which is poisonous. Take care to keep it off bare skin, and in particular out of your eyes. The fluid also attacks paintwork, and may discolour carpets, etc – keep spillages to a minimum, and wash any off immediately with cold water. Finally, brake fluid is highly inflammable, and should be handled with the same care as petrol.*

Note: *Read through this procedure before starting work to see what is involved, particularly in terms of lifting equipment. Depending on the facilities available, the home mechanic may prefer to remove the engine and transmission together, then separate them on the bench, as described in Chapter 2D. The help of an assistant is highly recommended if the transmission is to be removed (and later refitted) on its own.*

Removal – iB5 transmission

1 Remove the air cleaner and inlet duct as described in Chapter 4A.

2 Remove the battery and battery tray as described in Chapter 5A, and the ignition coil, as described in Chapter 5B.

3 Make sure that the gear lever is in neutral. Taking adequate precautions against brake fluid spillage (refer to the *Warning* at the start of this Section), pull out the securing clip, then pull the pipe fitting out of the clutch slave cylinder at the top of the transmission **(see illustrations)**. Plug or tape over the pipe end, to avoid losing fluid, and to prevent dirt entry.

4 Unclip the slave cylinder fluid pipe from the support bracket, and move it clear of the transmission **(see illustration)**.

5 Remove the plastic cap from the top of each front suspension strut, at the inner wing mounting in the engine compartment. Holding the piston rod against rotation using an Allen key, loosen each strut's centre nut by five full turns using a large ring spanner.

6 Before jacking up the front of the car, loosen the front wheel nuts, and if possible, the driveshaft retaining nuts.

7 Apply the handbrake, and chock the rear wheels. Jack up the front of the car, and support it on axle stands (see *Jacking and vehicle support*). There must be sufficient clearance below the car for the transmission to be lowered and withdrawn. Remove the front wheels and, where applicable, the engine undershield.

8 Disconnect the wiring plugs from the reversing light switch, and from the vehicle speed sensor, referring to Sections 4 and 5 if necessary.

9 At the front of the transmission, unclip the cover from the selector mechanism **(see illustration)**. Remove the cables from the support brackets by twisting the spring-loaded knurled collars clockwise. Release the coloured plastic clip securing the selector cable adjuster, and remove the cables from the transmission levers – note their fitted locations. Release the cables from the clips on top of the transmission, and move the cables clear.

10 Working from below, remove the two fasteners securing the auxiliary drivebelt lower cover, and remove the cover from the engine.

11 Remove both driveshafts from the transmission as described in Chapter 8.

12 Remove the starter motor as described in Chapter 5A. Note that an earth cable is attached to the upper mounting bolt, and the transmission cable support bracket is secured to the rear bolt **(see illustrations)**. As far as possible, pull the wiring loom through and to one side of the transmission.

13 Unscrew and remove the two nuts/bolts, and separate the exhaust front pipe at the first

8.9 Unclip and remove the plastic cover from the front of the transmission

8.12a Unscrew the starter motor mounting bolts . . .

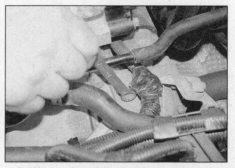

8.12b . . . the wiring harness and earth point is attached to this bolt . . .

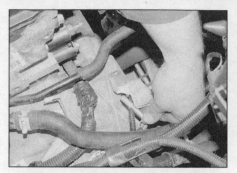

8.12c . . . and the transmission cable support bracket is fitted to this one

8.14 Removing the engine/transmission rear mounting

8.18 Lift off the top section of the left-hand mounting

flange joint under the car. Unhook the exhaust pipe from the rubber mountings.

14 Unscrew the two through-bolts and remove the engine/transmission rear mounting from the subframe **(see illustration)**.

15 The engine/transmission must now be supported, as the left-hand mounting must be dismantled and removed. Ford technicians use a support bar which locates in the tops of the inner wings – proprietary engine support bars are available from tool outlets.

16 If a support bar is not available, an engine hoist should be used. With an engine hoist, the engine/transmission can be manoeuvred more easily and safely. In the workshop, we found the best solution was to move the engine to the required position, and support it from below – using the hoist on the transmission then gave excellent manoeuvrability, and total control for lowering out.

17 Supporting both the engine and transmission from below should be considered a last resort, and should only be done if a heavy-duty hydraulic ('trolley') jack is used, with a large, flat piece of wood on the jack head to spread the load and avoid damage to the sump. A further jack will be needed to lower the transmission out. **Note:** *Always take care when using a hydraulic jack, as it is possible for this type to collapse under load – generally, a scissor-type jack avoids this problem, but is also less stable, and offers no manoeuvrability.*

18 With the engine securely supported, progressively unscrew and remove the nuts securing the top section of the engine left-hand mounting, and lift it off **(see illustration)**.

19 Remove the bolts securing the engine left-hand mounting brace, and remove the brace from the engine mounting **(see illustration)**.

20 Remove three further nuts, and remove

the lower section of the engine left-hand mounting – note that one of the nuts secures the clutch hydraulic pipe support bracket **(see illustrations)**.

21 Unscrew and remove the uppermost transmission-to-engine flange bolts – do not remove all the flange bolts at this stage.

22 Taking care that nothing which is still attached to the engine is placed under strain, lower the transmission as far as possible.

23 Remove the transmission-to-engine lower flange bolts, noting that, on some models, one of the bolts also retains the power steering pipe support bracket **(see illustration)**. The flange bolts are of different lengths, so note their positions carefully for refitting.

24 On 1.4 and 1.6 litre engines, swing the transmission forwards, and wedge it in position with a stout piece of wood, about 300 mm long, between the engine and the subframe.

25 Check that, apart from the remaining flange bolts, there is nothing preventing the transmission from being lowered and removed. Make sure that any wiring or hoses lying on top of the transmission are not going to get caught up and stretched as the transmission is lowered.

> **HAYNES HiNT** *Before removing the transmission from the engine, it is helpful for refitting to paint or scratch an alignment mark or two across the engine/transmission, so that the transmission can be offered up in approximately the right alignment to engage the dowels.*

26 Unscrew the remaining flange bolts. If the transmission does not separate on its own, it must be rocked from side-to-side, to free it from the locating dowels. As the transmission is withdrawn from the engine, make sure its weight is supported at all times – the transmission input shaft (or the clutch) may otherwise be damaged as it is withdrawn through the clutch assembly bolted to the engine flywheel. Recover the adapter plates fitted between the engine and transmission, as they may fall out when the two are separated.

8.19 Unscrew the two bolts (arrowed) securing the mounting brace

8.20a Unscrew the three nuts (arrowed) . . .

8.20b . . . and remove the lower section of the left-hand mounting

8.23 This transmission-to-engine bolt (arrowed) also locates the power steering fluid pipe – 1.4 litre model

27 Keeping the transmission steady, carefully lower it down and remove it from under the car **(see illustration)**. On 1.8 litre engine models, the transmission will have to be moved forwards to clear the subframe as it is lowered – if the transmission is being supported from below, take care that it is kept steady.

28 The clutch components can now be inspected with reference to Chapter 6, and renewed if necessary. Unless they are virtually new, it is worth renewing the clutch components as a matter of course, even if the transmission has been removed for some other reason.

Removal – MTX 75 transmission

Petrol models

29 Remove the air cleaner and inlet duct as described in Chapter 4A. Also remove the air intake from the front panel, and the resonator and air inlet tube.

30 Remove the battery and battery tray as described in Chapter 5A, and the ignition coil as described in Chapter 5B.

31 Unscrew the bolt and disconnect the main earth lead next to the screenwash reservoir filler neck.

32 If available, fit the Ford special tool to the gear lever as described in Section 2.

33 Make sure that the gear lever is in neutral. Prise off the retaining clips, and pull the shift and selector cable end fittings from the transmission levers. Release the coloured locking sliders by pressing them in. Disconnect the cable outers from the support brackets by turning the knurled collars anti-clockwise. Move the cables clear of the transmission.

34 Taking adequate precautions against brake fluid spillage (refer to the **Warning** at the start of this Section), pull out the securing clip, then pull the pipe fitting out of the clutch slave cylinder at the top of the transmission. Plug or tape over the pipe end, to avoid losing fluid, and to prevent dirt entry.

35 Move the slave cylinder fluid pipe clear of the transmission.

36 Remove the plastic cap from the top of each front suspension strut, at the inner wing mounting in the engine compartment. Holding the piston rod against rotation using an Allen key, loosen each strut's centre nut by five full turns using a large ring spanner.

37 Before jacking up the front of the car, loosen the front wheel nuts, and if possible, the driveshaft retaining nuts.

38 Apply the handbrake, and chock the rear wheels. Jack up the front of the car, and support it on axle stands (see *Jacking and vehicle support*). There must be sufficient clearance below the car for the transmission to be lowered and withdrawn. Remove the front wheels and where applicable, the engine undershield.

39 Disconnect the wiring plugs from the reversing light switch, and from the vehicle speed sensor, referring to Sections 4 and 5 if necessary.

40 Working from below, remove the two fasteners securing the auxiliary drivebelt lower cover, and remove the cover from the engine.

41 Remove both driveshafts from the transmission as described in Chapter 8.

42 Remove the starter motor as described in Chapter 5A.

43 Unscrew the flange nuts/bolts at either end, and remove the flexible section of exhaust pipe from under the car.

44 Unscrew the two through-bolts and remove the engine/transmission rear mounting from the subframe.

45 The engine/transmission must now be supported, as the left-hand mounting must be dismantled and removed. Ford technicians use a support bar which locates in the tops of the inner wings – proprietary engine support bars are available from tool outlets.

46 If a support bar is not available, an engine hoist should be used. With an engine hoist, the engine/transmission can be manoeuvred more easily and safely. In the workshop, we found the best solution was to move the engine to the required position, and support it from below – using the hoist on the transmission then gave excellent manoeuvrability, and total control for lowering out.

47 Supporting both the engine and transmission from below should be considered a last resort, and should only be done if a heavy-duty hydraulic ('trolley') jack is used, with a large, flat piece of wood on the jack head to spread the load and avoid damage to the sump. A further jack will be needed to lower the transmission out. **Note:** *Always take care when using a hydraulic jack, as it is possible for this type to collapse under load – generally, a scissor-type jack avoids this problem, but is also less stable, and offers no manoeuvrability.*

48 With the engine securely supported, progressively unscrew and remove the nuts securing the top section of the engine left-hand mounting, and lift it off.

49 Remove three further nuts/bolts, and remove the lower section of the engine left-hand mounting.

50 Unscrew and remove the two uppermost transmission-to-engine flange bolts – do not remove all the flange bolts at this stage. The flange bolts are of different lengths, so note their positions carefully for refitting.

51 Swing the transmission forwards, and wedge it in position with a stout piece of wood, about 350 mm long, between the engine and the subframe.

52 Check that, apart from the remaining flange bolts, there is nothing preventing the transmission from being lowered and removed. Make sure that any wiring or hoses lying on top of the transmission are not going to get caught up and stretched as the transmission is lowered.

8.27 Lowering out the transmission

> **HAYNES HiNT** *Before removing the transmission from the engine, it is helpful for refitting to paint or scratch an alignment mark or two across the engine/transmission, so that the transmission can be offered up in approximately the right alignment to engage the dowels.*

53 Unscrew the remaining flange bolts. If the transmission does not separate on its own, it must be rocked from side-to-side, to free it from the locating dowels. As the transmission is withdrawn from the engine, make sure its weight is supported at all times – the transmission input shaft (or the clutch) may otherwise be damaged as it is withdrawn through the clutch assembly bolted to the engine flywheel. Recover the adapter plates fitted between the engine and transmission, as they may fall out when the two are separated.

54 Keeping the transmission steady, carefully lower it down and remove it from under the car.

55 The clutch components can now be inspected with reference to Chapter 6, and renewed if necessary. Unless they are virtually new, it is worth renewing the clutch components as a matter of course, even if the transmission has been removed for some other reason.

Diesel models

56 Remove the battery and battery tray as described in Chapter 5A.

57 Remove the intercooler as described in Chapter 4B.

58 Remove the air cleaner and inlet duct as described in Chapter 4B. Also remove the air intake from the front panel, and the air inlet tube.

59 Disconnect the following wiring from the following components:

   a) *Alternator.*
   b) *Injection pump.*
   c) *Glow plug supply cable.*
   d) *Radiator cooling fan (unclip harness from front panel).*
   e) *Unclip the battery wiring harness.*
   f) *Vehicle speed sensor.*

g) *Reversing light switch.*

h) *Transmission harness connector.*

60 Remove the radiator cooling fan as described in Chapter 3.

61 Remove the plastic cap from the top of each front suspension strut, at the inner wing mounting in the engine compartment. Holding the piston rod against rotation using an Allen key, loosen each strut's centre nut by five full turns using a large ring spanner.

62 If available, fit the Ford special tool to the gear lever as described in Section 2.

63 Before jacking up the front of the car, loosen the front wheel nuts, and if possible, the driveshaft retaining nuts.

64 Apply the handbrake, and chock the rear wheels. Jack up the front of the car, and support it on axle stands (see *Jacking and vehicle support*). There must be sufficient clearance below the car for the transmission to be lowered and withdrawn. Remove the front wheels and, where applicable, the engine undershield.

65 Unscrew the four nuts, and separate the catalytic converter from the exhaust manifold. Referring to Chapter 4B if necessary, remove the catalytic converter and flexible pipe completely.

66 Remove the starter motor as described in Chapter 5A.

67 Make sure that the gear lever is in neutral. Prise off the retaining clips, and pull the shift and selector cable end fittings from the transmission levers. Release the coloured locking sliders by pressing them in. Disconnect the cable outers from the support brackets by turning the knurled collars anti-clockwise. Move the cables clear of the transmission.

68 Working from below, remove the two fasteners securing the auxiliary drivebelt lower cover, and remove the cover from the engine.

69 Remove both driveshafts from the transmission as described in Chapter 8.

70 Taking adequate precautions against brake fluid spillage (refer to the *Warning* at the start of this Section), pull out the securing clip, then pull the pipe fitting out of the clutch slave cylinder at the top of the transmission. Plug or tape over the pipe end, to avoid losing fluid, and to prevent dirt entry.

71 Unclip the clutch fluid pipe from its support bracket, and tie it up out of the way.

72 Locate the power steering fluid pipe support bracket near the clutch fluid pipe. Remove the bracket securing bolt, and move the pipe clear of the transmission.

73 The oil separator at the transmission end of the cylinder head must now be removed.

Release the spring clips and disconnect the hoses, then disconnect the wiring connectors in front of the unit. Unscrew the mounting bolt, and remove the separator from the cylinder head.

74 Release the clip securing the transmission wiring harness to the top of the transmission, and move the wiring aside as far as possible.

75 Unscrew the coolant pipe support bracket from the transmission, and tie the coolant pipe up out of the way.

76 The remainder of the removal procedure is the same as given for petrol engine models, described in paragraphs 44 to 55 inclusive.

Refitting

77 If removed, refit the clutch components (see Chapter 6). Also ensure that the engine-to-transmission adapter plates are in position on the engine.

78 Where a block of wood was used to wedge the engine forwards for transmission removal, make sure that it is in place for refitting.

79 With the transmission secured to the hoist/trolley jack as on removal, raise it into position, and then carefully slide it onto the engine, at the same time engaging the input shaft with the clutch friction disc splines. If marks were made between the transmission and engine on removal, these can be used as a guide to correct alignment.

80 Do not use excessive force to refit the transmission – if the input shaft does not slide into place easily, readjust the angle of the transmission so that it is level, and/or turn the input shaft so that the splines engage properly with the disc. If problems are still experienced, check that the clutch friction disc is correctly centred (Chapter 6).

81 Once the transmission is successfully mated to the engine, insert as many of the flange bolts as possible, and tighten them progressively, to draw the transmission fully onto the locating dowels.

82 Refit the lower section of the engine left-hand mounting, and tighten the nuts to the specified torque. On the iB5 transmission, refit the mounting brace/pipe support bracket, and tighten the mounting bolts.

83 Where applicable, remove the wedge fitted between the engine and subframe. Raise the transmission into position, then refit the upper section of the engine left-hand mounting. Tighten the nuts to the specified torque, noting that the centre nut is tightened considerably more than the four outer ones.

84 Refit the remaining transmission-to-engine bolts, and tighten all of them to the specified torque.

85 Refit the engine/transmission rear mounting to the subframe, and tighten the through-bolts to the specified torque.

86 Once the engine/transmission mountings have been refitted, the support bar, engine hoist or supporting jack can be removed.

87 Further refitting is a reversal of removal, noting the following points:

a) *Refit the starter motor as described in Chapter 5A.*

b) *Refit the driveshafts as described in Chapter 8.*

c) *On completion, adjust the gear cables as described in Section 2.*

9 Transmission overhaul – general information

The overhaul of a manual transmission is a complex (and often expensive) engineering task for the DIY home mechanic to undertake, which requires access to specialist equipment. It involves dismantling and reassembly of many small components, measuring clearances precisely and if necessary, adjusting them by the selection shims and spacers. Internal transmission components are also often difficult to obtain and in many instances, extremely expensive. Because of this, if the transmission develops a fault or becomes noisy, the best course of action is to have the unit overhauled by a specialist repairer or to obtain an exchange reconditioned unit.

Nevertheless, it is not impossible for the more experienced mechanic to overhaul the transmission if the special tools are available and the job is carried out in a deliberate step-by-step manner, to ensure that nothing is overlooked.

The tools necessary for an overhaul include internal and external circlip pliers, bearing pullers, a slide hammer, a set of pin punches, a dial test indicator, and possibly a hydraulic press. In addition, a large, sturdy workbench and a vice will be required.

During dismantling of the transmission, make careful notes of how each component is fitted to make reassembly easier and accurate.

Before dismantling the transmission, it will help if you have some idea of where the problem lies. Certain problems can be closely related to specific areas in the transmission which can make component examination and renewal easier. Refer to *Fault finding* at the end of this manual for more information.

Chapter 7 Part B:
Automatic transmission

Contents

Degrees of difficulty

Easy, suitable for novice with little experience	**Fairly easy,** suitable for beginner with some experience	**Fairly difficult,** suitable for competent DIY mechanic	**Difficult,** suitable for experienced DIY mechanic	**Very difficult,** suitable for expert DIY or professional

Specifications

General

Transmission type .... Electronically-controlled automatic, four forward speeds (one overdrive) and reverse. Selectable overdrive function, torque converter lock-up in 3rd and 4th gears

Transmission code 4F27E

Gear ratios

1st	2.816:1
2nd	1.498:1
3rd	1.000:1
4th	0.726:1
Reverse	2.649:1

Torque wrench settings

	Nm	lbf ft
Engine/transmission left-hand mounting lower section	80	59
Engine/transmission left-hand mounting upper section:		
Centre nut	133	98
Four outer nuts	48	35
Engine/transmission rear mounting bolts	48	35
Fluid cooler union nuts	25	18
Fluid pan bolts	7	5
Roadwheel nuts	85	63
Torque converter to driveplate (use new nuts)	37	27
Transmission lever bolt	10	7
Transmission range sensor bolts	10	7
Transmission to engine	48	35

1 General information

Available only on 1.6 litre Focus models, the 4F27E automatic transmission is controlled electronically by the engine management electronic control unit. This is an all-new four-speed unit, featuring an overdrive top gear and a lock-up torque converter. This unit, which was developed by Mazda and is built in the USA, has been designed specifically for front-wheel-drive applications, and is particularly light and compact.

The transmission control system is known as ESSC (electronic synchronous shift control) contained within a specially-modified EEC-V engine management system module, only used on Focus automatic models. The electronic control system has a fail-safe mode, which gives the transmission limited operation in order to drive the vehicle home or to a repair garage. A warning light on the instrument panel tells the driver when this occurs. The EEC-V module uses all the information available from the various transmission and engine management-related sensors (also see Chapters 4A and 5B) to determine the optimum gearshift points for

smoothness, performance and economy. Depending on throttle position and vehicle speed, the module can 'lock-up' the torque converter in 3rd and 4th gear, eliminating torque converter 'slip' and improving fuel consumption.

The transmission features a selectable overdrive top gear. When this is enabled (using a pushbutton on the underside of the selector lever), a fourth, extra-high ratio can be selected automatically; otherwise, the transmission will only use three forward speeds. An O/D OFF warning light is illuminated when the overdrive function is disabled.

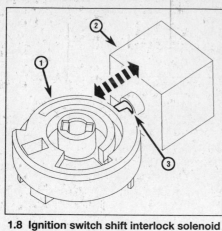

1.8 Ignition switch shift interlock solenoid details

1 *Ignition barrel rotor*   2 *Solenoid*
                              3 *Locking pin*

The unit has been designed to have a low maintenance requirement, the fluid level being checked periodically (see Chapter 1A). The fluid is intended to last the life of the transmission, and is cooled by a separate cooler located next to the radiator.

There is no kickdown switch, as kickdown is controlled by the throttle position sensor in the engine management system.

The gear selector includes the normal P, R, N, D, 2, and 1 positions.

As is normally the case with automatic transmissions, a starter inhibitor relay is fitted, which prevents the engine from being started (by interrupting the supply to the starter solenoid) when the selector is in any position other than P or N. The intention is to prevent the car moving, which might otherwise happen if the engine were started in position D, for example. The inhibitor system is controlled by the EEC-V module, based on signals received from the engine and transmission sensors. For more details on relay locations, see Chapter 12.

As a further safety measure, the ignition key can only be removed from the ignition switch when the selector is in P; it is also necessary for the ignition to be on, and for the brake pedal and selector lever locking button (on the side of the lever) to be depressed in order to move the selector from position P **(see illustration)**. If the vehicle battery is discharged, the selector lever release solenoid will not function. If it is required to move the vehicle in this state, insert a pen or a similar small instrument into the aperture on the left-hand side of the centre console. Push the locking lever downwards and move the selector lever to the required position.

2 Fault finding – general

In the event of a fault occurring on the transmission, first check that the fluid level is correct (see Chapter 1A). If there has been a loss of fluid, check the oil seals as described in Section 6. Also check the hoses to the fluid cooler in the radiator for leaks. The only other tasks possible for the home mechanic are the renewal of the various transmission sensors (Section 5); however, it is not advisable to go ahead and renew any sensor until the fault has been positively identified by reading the transmission fault codes.

Any serious fault which occurs will result in the transmission entering the fail-safe mode, and a fault code (or several codes) will be logged in the control module. These codes can be read using an electronic fault code reader. A Ford dealer will obviously have such a reader, but they are also available from other suppliers, including Haynes. It is unlikely to be cost-effective for the private owner to purchase a fault code reader, but a well-equipped local garage or auto-electrical specialist will have one.

If the fault still persists, it is necessary to determine whether it is of an electrical, mechanical or hydraulic nature; to do this, special test equipment is required. It is therefore essential to have the work carried out by an automatic transmission specialist or Ford dealer if a transmission fault is suspected.

Do not remove the transmission from the vehicle for possible repair before professional fault diagnosis has been carried out, since most tests require the transmission to be in the vehicle.

3 Selector cable – removal, refitting and adjustment

Removal

1 Loosen the left-hand front wheel nuts. Apply the handbrake, jack up the front of the vehicle and support it on axle stands. Remove the left-hand front wheel.

2 Remove the front section of the exhaust pipe, referring to Chapter 4A as necessary. Note particularly that the flexible section of the exhaust must not be bent too far during removal.

3 Remove the 'flat nut' fasteners, and lower the exhaust heat shield from the vehicle underside.

4 Locate the end of the selector cable, which is on the front of the transmission **(see illustration)**.

5 Disconnect the cable end fitting by prising it off the transmission selector lever.

6 Unclip the cable outer from the bracket on the transmission – the cable is secured by a locking collar which must be turned through 90° anti-clockwise to remove **(see illustration)**.

7 Trace the cable back from the selector lever, releasing it from the various clips

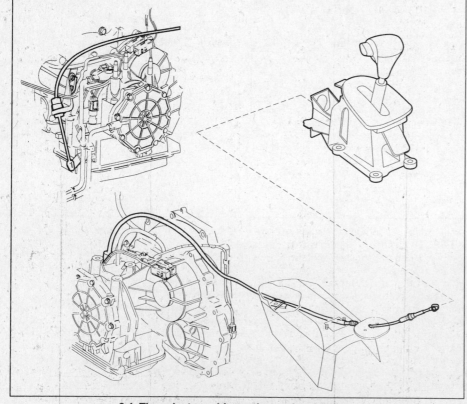

3.4 The selector cable routing and end fittings

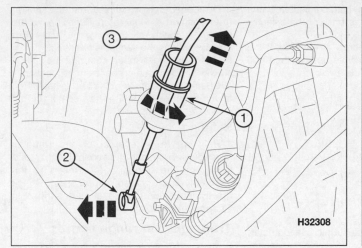

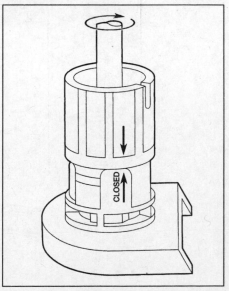

3.6 Selector cable attachment at the transmission end

1 Locking collar 3 Outer cable
2 Inner cable end fitting

3.9 Selector cable attachment at selector lever

1 Selector lever 3 Outer cable
2 Inner cable end fitting

attaching it to the transmission and underside of the car. Remove the heat shield, then prise out the grommet from the vehicle floor where the cable passes into the car.

8 Remove the centre console as described in Chapter 11.

9 Move the selector lever to P. Working through the front of the selector housing, disconnect the cable inner from the lever by prising the end fitting sideways, then unclip the cable outer from the floor bracket by pulling upwards **(see illustration)**.

10 Remove the fasteners securing the heater air duct to the floor, and remove the duct.

11 Unscrew the fasteners securing the side cover panels fitted between the centre section of the facia panel and the floor, and remove the panels. Behind these panels, release the clips and remove the screws securing the heater side panels, and remove the panels.

12 Fold back the carpet and insulation material under the centre part of the facia, for access to the selector cable floor grommet. Remove the two screws and release the grommet from the floor.

 Before withdrawing the selector cable, tie some string to its end, and feed the string through as the cable is removed. Once the cable is completely removed, untie the string, leaving it in position until the new cable is fitted – the string can then be used to pull the new cable into the position, preserving the correct routing.

13 Pass the cable down through the vehicle floor, and remove it from under the car.

Refitting

14 Refitting is a reversal of removal, noting the following points:

a) Once the cable has been reconnected to the selector lever, shift the lever to

position D before reconnecting the cable end fitting at the transmission lever.

b) Before securing the cable to the transmission bracket or transmission lever, check the cable adjustment as described below.

Adjustment

15 Inside the vehicle, move the selector lever to position D.

16 With the inner cable disconnected from the lever on the transmission, check that the transmission lever is in the D position. To do this, it will be necessary to move the lever slightly up and down until it is positioned correctly. A further check can be made by observing that the D mark on the selector lever position sensor is correctly aligned with the mark on the transmission lever **(see illustration)**.

17 Check that the cable locking collar beneath the vehicle is still unlocked (ie, turned anti-clockwise by 90°).

18 With both the selector levers inside the vehicle and on the side of the transmission in position D, refit the cable end fitting to the transmission lever, then turn the locking collar

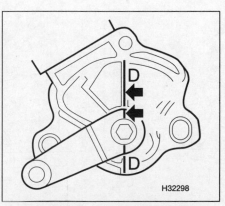

3.16 Selector lever position sensor/ transmission lever alignment markings

90° clockwise to lock it. The arrowhead markings on the collar should line up when the collar is locked **(see illustration)**.

19 Refit the left-hand front wheel, then lower the vehicle to the ground. Tighten the wheel nuts to the specified torque.

20 Road test the vehicle to check the operation of the transmission.

4 Selector components – removal and refitting

Selector assembly

Removal

1 Remove the centre console as described in Chapter 11.

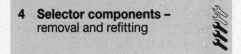

3.18 Cable end fitting arrowhead markings in locked position

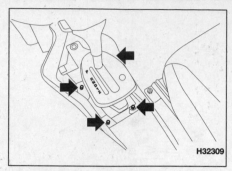

4.4 Selector lever mounting nuts (arrowed)

2 Working through the front of the selector housing, disconnect the cable inner from the lever as described in Section 3.
3 Disconnect the multi-plug wiring connectors at the rear of the assembly, noting their positions, and move the wiring harness clear.
4 Unscrew the four mounting nuts, and withdraw the selector lever assembly **(see illustration)**.
5 If required, the assembly can be further dismantled (after removing the selector lever knob, as described below) by unclipping the top cover and removing the illumination bulb and inner cover.

Refitting

6 Refitting is a reversal of the removal procedure, but adjust the selector cable as described in Section 3.

Selector lever knob

Removal

7 Remove the centre console as described in Chapter 11.

8 Disconnect the multi-plug connector for the overdrive switch, at the base of the selector lever.
9 Remove the grub screw at the side of the knob, below the overdrive button, then pull the knob upwards off the lever.

Refitting

10 Refitting is a reversal of removal.

---

5 Transmission sensors – removal and refitting

Vehicle/output shaft speed sensor

1 The Focus has an electronic speedometer, rather than the older, cable-driven mechanical type. An electronic sensor is fitted to the transmission (in place of the older speedometer drive pinion), and the speed signal from this sensor is passed to the instrument panel via the engine management ECU. Besides driving the speedometer, the speed sensor signal is used by the ECU as one of the parameters for fuel system-related calculations, and for determining transmission gearshift points.

Removal

2 Access to the speed sensor is easiest from below. Apply the handbrake, then loosen the left-hand front wheel nuts. Jack up the front of the car and support it on axle stands (see *Jacking and vehicle support*).
3 Remove the left-hand front wheel and the wheelarch liner – the sensor is located at the rear of the transmission, behind the driveshafts **(see illustration)**.

4 Disconnect the wiring plug from the sensor, then position a suitable container below the sensor, to catch any transmission fluid which may be spilt as the sensor is removed.
5 Unscrew the sensor securing bolt, and slowly withdraw the sensor from its location.
6 Check the condition of the O-ring seal fitted to the sensor body – fit a new seal if the old one is in poor condition.

Refitting

7 Refitting is a reversal of the removal procedure, but clean the sensor location and lightly oil the O-ring before inserting the assembly in the transmission casing. Check the transmission fluid level as described in Chapter 1A on completion.

Transmission range sensor

8 The transmission range sensor is effectively a selector position sensor, the signal from which is used by the EEC-V module to modify the operation of the transmission, dependent on which 'gear' is selected. For example, besides controlling gearshift points, depending on the signal received, the module may actuate the starter inhibitor relay, the reversing lights, or the ignition key lock.

Removal

Note: *To set the range sensor in its working position, Ford special tool 307415 is required. If this tool is not available, the sensor position must be carefully marked before removal.*

9 Access to the range sensor is easiest from below – the sensor is at the front of the transmission, near the transmission selector lever **(see illustration)**. Apply the handbrake, then jack up the front of the car and support it on axle stands (see *Jacking and vehicle support*).

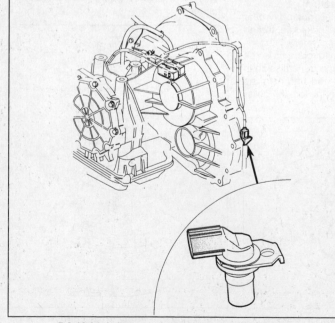

5.3 Vehicle/output shaft speed sensor location

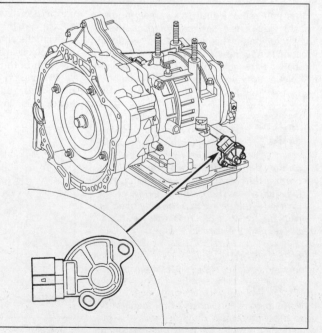

5.9 Transmission range sensor location

10 Prise the selector cable end fitting off the transmission lever, and disconnect the wiring plug from the sensor.
11 Hold the transmission lever against rotation, then unscrew the lever retaining bolt, and remove the lever from the sensor.
Caution: If the lever is not held as its bolt is undone, the force required to loosen the bolt will be transmitted to the sensor itself, which may well lead to the sensor being damaged. The same applies when retightening the bolt on completion.
12 Before removing the sensor, make a couple of alignment marks between the sensor and the transmission, for use when refitting.
13 Take precautions against the possible spillage of transmission fluid. Unscrew the two sensor retaining bolts, and withdraw the sensor from the transmission.

Refitting

14 Clean the sensor location in the transmission, and the sensor itself. If a new sensor is being fitted, transfer the alignment marks from the old unit to the new one – this will provide an approximate setting, which should allow the car to be driven.
15 Refit the sensor, and secure it loosely in position with the two bolts, tightened by hand only at this stage.
16 Ford special tool 307415 must now be used to set the sensor in its working position. If the tool is not available, realign the marks made prior to removal. When correctly aligned, tighten the two sensor retaining bolts to the specified torque.
17 Refit the transmission lever. Tighten the lever retaining bolt to the specified torque, holding the lever against rotation as the bolt is tightened (refer to the Caution earlier in this Section).
18 Reconnect the selector cable to the transmission lever, and check the cable adjustment as described in Section 3.
19 On completion, lower the car to the ground.

Turbine (input) shaft speed sensor

20 The turbine shaft speed sensor is located on top of the transmission, and is an inductive pick-up sensor which senses the speed of rotation of the input shaft (see illustration). This information is used by the ECU to control gearchanging and the torque converter lock-up clutch. Removal and refitting details are similar to the output shaft speed sensor described earlier in this Section.

Brake pedal position switch

21 The signal from the switch is used by the ECU to disengage the torque converter lock-up, and to allow the selector lever to be moved from the P position when starting the engine. Removal and refitting details for the switch will be the same as for the stop-light switch, in Chapter 9.

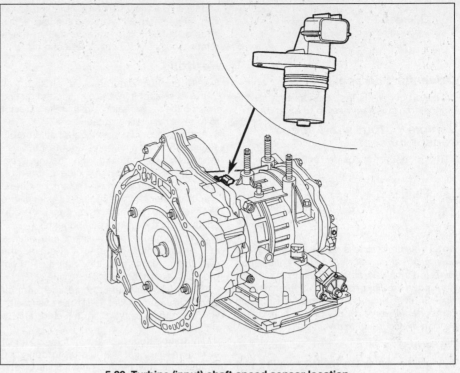

5.20 Turbine (input) shaft speed sensor location

Brake pedal shift interlock actuator

22 This unit part of the system used to lock the selector lever in P when the ignition key is removed, and is incorporated in the selector lever itself.
23 Remove the selector knob as described in Section 4. With the knob removed, the actuator pushrod can be pulled out and removed (see illustration).
24 Refitting is a reversal of removal. Check the operation of the system on completion.

Selector lever shift interlock solenoid

25 The main solenoid controlling the shift interlock system (used to lock the selector lever in P when the ignition key is removed) is located at the base of the selector lever (see illustration). For access to the solenoid, remove the centre console as described in Chapter 11. At the time of writing, no further removal details were available from Ford.

Transmission fluid temperature sensor

26 The fluid temperature sensor signal is used by the ECU to determine whether to allow the operation the torque converter lock-up clutch, and the selection of the overdrive 4th gear. The sensor is located among the transmission solenoid valves inside the fluid pan – no renewal procedure is suggested by Ford, so any suspected problems should be referred to a Ford dealer.

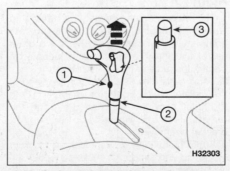

5.23 Brake pedal shift interlock actuator details

1 Selector knob retaining screw
2 Selector knob
3 Actuator pushrod

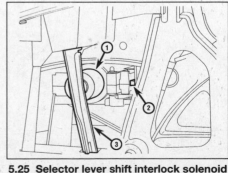

5.25 Selector lever shift interlock solenoid details

1 Solenoid
2 Locking pin
3 Manual release mechanism

6 Oil seals – renewal

Driveshaft oil seals

The procedure is the same as that for the manual transmission (refer to Chapter 7A).

Vehicle/output shaft speed sensor oil seal

The procedure is covered in Section 5.

7 Fluid pan – removal and refitting

Note: *This procedure is provided principally to cure any leak developing from the fluid pan joint. It is not advisable for the DIY mechanic to remove the fluid pan for any other reason, since it gives access to internal transmission components, servicing of which is considered beyond the scope of this Manual.*

Removal

1 Apply the handbrake, then jack up the front of the car and support it on axle stands (see *Jacking and vehicle support*).
2 Place a suitable container below the pan, as most of the contents of the transmission will drain when the pan is removed.
3 Progressively unscrew and remove the fluid pan bolts.
4 The fluid pan is 'stuck' to the base of the transmission by a bead of sealant, so it is unlikely that the pan will fall off once the bolts are removed. Care must now be taken to break the sealant without damaging the mating surfaces. Do not prise the pan down, as this may bend it, or damage the sealing

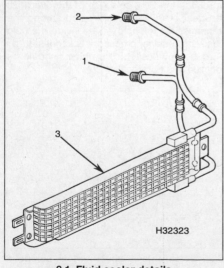

8.1 Fluid cooler details

1 Return hose   3 Fluid cooler
2 Supply hose

surfaces. The most successful method found is to run a sharp knife around the joint – this should cut through sufficiently to make removal possible without excess effort.

Refitting

5 With the fluid pan removed, clean off all traces of sealant from the pan and the mating face on the transmission. Again, take care not to mark either mating surface.
6 Apply a 1.5 mm thick bead of suitable sealant (Ford recommend Loctite 5699, or equivalent) to the fluid pan mating face, running the bead on the inside of the bolt holes. Do not apply excess sealant, or a bead much thicker than suggested, since the excess could end up inside the pan, and contaminate the internal components.
7 Offer the pan up into position, and insert a few of the bolts to locate it. Refit all the remaining bolts, and tighten them progressively to the specified torque.
8 Give the sealant time to cure, then trim off any excess with a knife. Refill the transmission via the dipstick tube, with reference to Chapter 1A.
9 On completion, take the car for a run of several miles to get the fluid up to operating temperature, then re-check the fluid level, and check for signs of leakage.

8 Fluid cooler – removal and refitting

Note 1: *If a leak is discovered at the fluid cooler connections to the transmission, do not try to cure it by overtightening the unions, as damage will almost certainly result.*
Note 2: *On models with air conditioning, the condenser in front of the radiator must be removed to allow removal of the fluid cooler. Since this entails disconnecting the refrigerant lines from the condenser, this part of the procedure must be entrusted to an air conditioning specialist – do not attempt to disconnect the refrigerant lines yourself (refer to the warnings in Chapter 3).*

Removal

1 This procedure should only be attempted when the engine and transmission are completely cool, otherwise there is a great risk of scalding. The fluid cooler is mounted in front of the radiator **(see illustration)**.
2 Using cable-ties or string, tie either end of the radiator to the front crossmember, using the holes provided – this is to support the radiator later on, when its lower support bracket is removed.
3 Apply the handbrake, then jack up the front of the car and support it on axle stands (see *Jacking and vehicle support*).
4 Remove the three screws securing the radiator lower splash shield, and remove the shield from under the car.
5 On models with air conditioning,

disconnect the wiring plug from the horn unit (at the left-hand side of the radiator). Unclip the compressor wiring from the radiator support bracket.
6 Ensure that the radiator is supported as described in paragraph 2, then unscrew the bolts at either side, and remove the radiator lower support bracket.
7 Place a container below the fluid cooler connections, to catch the escaping fluid; also note that, if the engine is still warm, the fluid may be extremely hot. Note the positions of the hose connections for refitting, then slacken the hose clips and detach the hoses from the cooler. Tie the hoses up out of the way, and plug the hose ends to prevent the ingress of dirt.
8 On models with air conditioning, the condenser must now be removed as described in Chapter 3, Section 12.
9 Remove the self-locking nuts from the fluid cooler mounting brackets (two brackets on the right, and one on the left-hand side), then lift the cooler upwards and out. Try to keep the fluid connections end uppermost, to reduce further fluid loss.
10 If required, the fluid cooler hoses can be removed by unscrewing the union nuts at the transmission fittings. Trace the hoses around the engine compartment, unclipping them as necessary and noting how the hoses are routed for refitting.

Refitting

11 Clean the fluid cooler fins of any debris as necessary, using a small brush – do not use any other tools, as the fins can easily be damaged.
12 Refitting is a reversal of removal, noting the following points:
 a) If the fluid hoses were removed, tighten the union nuts at the transmission to the specified torque.
 b) Use new self-locking nuts when refitting the cooler to the mounting brackets.
 c) Where applicable, the air conditioning system must be recharged by a specialist once the condenser has been refitted.
 d) Top up the transmission fluid level using the information in Chapter 1A.
 e) Start the engine and check for signs of fluid leakage from the disturbed connections.

9 Automatic transmission – removal and refitting

Removal

1 Remove the air cleaner and inlet duct as described in Chapter 4A. Also remove the air intake from the front panel, and the resonator and air inlet tube.
2 Remove the battery and battery tray as described in Chapter 5A.
3 Disconnect the vacuum hose from the EGR

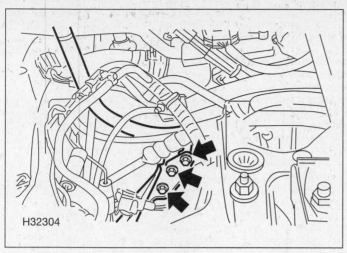

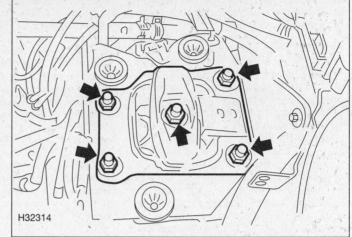

9.5 Selector cable/fluid filler tube support bracket bolts (arrowed)

9.18 Engine/transmission left-hand mounting upper section nuts (arrowed)

valve (at the transmission end of the engine – refer to Chapter 4C, Section 4, for more details).

4 Remove the plastic cap from the top of each front suspension strut, at the inner wing mounting in the engine compartment. Holding the piston rod against rotation using an Allen key, loosen each strut's centre nut by five full turns using a large ring spanner.

5 Remove the three bolts securing the selector cable/fluid filler tube support bracket to the front of the transmission **(see illustration)**. Move the bracket to one side, clear of the transmission.

6 Before jacking up the front of the car, loosen the front wheel nuts, and if possible, the driveshaft retaining nuts.

7 Apply the handbrake, and chock the rear wheels. Jack up the front of the car, and support it on axle stands (see *Jacking and vehicle support*). There must be sufficient clearance below the car for the transmission to be lowered and withdrawn. Remove the front wheels.

8 Disconnect the selector cable end fitting from the transmission lever as described in Section 3.

9 Disconnect the wiring plugs from the vehicle/output shaft speed sensor, turbine shaft speed sensor and transmission range sensor, as described in Section 5.

10 Remove the front section of the exhaust pipe, referring to Chapter 4A as necessary. Note particularly that the flexible section of the exhaust must not be bent too far during removal.

11 Remove both driveshafts from the transmission as described in Chapter 8.

12 Wipe clean around the fluid supply and return pipes on the front of the transmission. It is essential that no dirt is introduced into the transmission.

13 Noting their respective positions, unscrew the union nuts and disconnect the fluid pipes from the transmission. Be prepared for loss of fluid, and cover the pipe ends and

transmission pipe fittings, to prevent further loss or dirt entry.

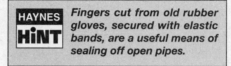

HAYNES HiNT *Fingers cut from old rubber gloves, secured with elastic bands, are a useful means of sealing off open pipes.*

14 Remove the starter motor as described in Chapter 5A. Note that one of the mounting bolts also secures the transmission earth strap.

15 Working from below, unscrew the through-bolts and remove the engine/transmission rear mounting.

16 The engine/transmission must now be supported, as the left-hand mounting must be dismantled and removed. Ford technicians use a support bar which locates in the tops of the inner wings – proprietary engine support bars are available from tool outlets.

17 If a support bar is not available, an engine hoist should be used. Supporting the engine from below should be considered a last resort, and should only be done if a heavy-duty hydraulic ('trolley') jack is used, with a large, flat piece of wood on the jack head to spread the load and avoid damage to the

9.19 Engine/transmission left-hand mounting lower section nuts (arrowed)

sump. Note that a further jack will be needed to lower the transmission out.

18 With the engine securely supported, progressively unscrew and remove the nuts securing the top section of the engine/transmission left-hand mounting, and lift it off **(see illustration)**.

19 Remove three further nuts/bolts, and remove the lower section of the engine left-hand mounting **(see illustration)**.

20 Locate the transmission fluid filler tube, and remove the screw at its base where it enters the transmission. Pull the tube out of its location, and remove it.

21 Remove the cover (where fitted) from the base of the transmission bellhousing, for access to the four large torque converter nuts. It will be necessary to turn the engine (using a spanner or socket on the crankshaft pulley bolt) in order to bring each of the nuts into view. It may also prove necessary to jam the driveplate ring gear with a suitable tool, to prevent the engine turning as the nuts are unscrewed. Before removing the last nut, paint an alignment mark between the converter and driveplate, to use when refitting. New nuts must be obtained for refitting.

22 Swing the transmission forwards, and wedge it in position with a stout piece of wood, about 300 mm long, between the engine and the subframe.

23 Support the transmission from below, ideally using a transmission jack (if one is not available, a sturdy jack with a large, flat piece of wood on top of the jack head will suffice). Have an assistant ready, to help steady the transmission as the flange bolts are removed – attempting to remove the transmission single-handed is not recommended, as it is a heavy assembly which can be awkward to handle.

24 Check that, apart from the remaining flange bolts, there is nothing preventing the transmission from being lowered and removed. Make sure that any wiring or hoses

lying on top of the transmission are not going to get caught up and stretched as the transmission is lowered.

 Before removing the transmission from the engine, it is helpful for refitting to paint or scratch an alignment mark or two across the engine/transmission, so that the transmission can be offered up in approximately the right alignment to engage the dowels.

25 Unscrew and remove the flange bolts – there are three inserted from the transmission side, and six from the engine side **(see illustration)**. Note the bolt locations carefully, as they are of different lengths. If the transmission does not separate on its own, it must be rocked from side-to-side, to free it from the locating dowels. As the transmission is withdrawn from the engine, make sure its weight is supported at all times – care must be taken that the torque converter (which is a large, heavy, circular component) does not fall out.
26 Keeping the transmission steady on the jack head, and maintaining a supporting hand on the torque converter, carefully lower it and remove it from under the car.
27 Once the transmission has been fully lowered and steadied, bolt a strip of wood or metal across the bellhousing face, with suitable packing, to secure the torque converter firmly in position. The converter centre spigot should be 25 mm below the bellhousing face – this can be determined by placing a straight-edge across the bellhousing, and measuring between it and the centre of the converter **(see illustration)**.

Refitting
28 Prior to refitting, clean the contact surfaces

of the driveplate and torque converter.
29 Check that the torque converter is fully entered in the transmission, as described in paragraph 27.
Caution: This procedure is important, to ensure that the torque converter is engaged with the fluid pump. If it is not fully engaged, serious damage will occur.
30 As for removal, use a block of wood to wedge the engine forwards for refitting.
31 With the help of an assistant, raise the transmission, and locate it on the rear of the driveplate. The torque converter must remain in full engagement during the fitting procedure. Use the markings made prior to removal to help align the transmission.
32 Refit the transmission-to-engine flange bolts to the locations noted on removal, and tighten them progressively, to draw the transmission fully onto the locating dowels.
33 Align the mark made on removal between the torque converter and driveplate. Refit and tighten the torque converter-to-driveplate nuts to the specified torque – new nuts must be used. Turn the engine as necessary to bring each nut into view, and lock the ring gear to prevent it turning as the nuts are tightened.
34 Refit the lower section of the engine left-hand mounting, and tighten the nuts to the specified torque.
35 Remove the wedge fitted between the engine and subframe. Raise the transmission into position, then refit the upper section of the engine left-hand mounting. Tighten the nuts to the specified torque, noting that the centre nut is tightened considerably more than the four outer ones.
36 Working from below, refit the through-bolts to the engine/transmission rear mounting, and tighten them to the specified torque.

37 Once the engine/transmission mountings have been refitted, the support bar, engine hoist or supporting jack can be removed.
38 Further refitting is a reversal of removal, noting the following points:
a) Refit the starter motor as described in Chapter 5A.
b) Refit the driveshafts as described in Chapter 8.
c) Tighten all fasteners to the specified torque (where given).
d) On completion, adjust the selector cable as described in Section 3, and top-up the fluid level as described in Chapter 1A.
e) Re-check the transmission fluid level once the car has been driven.
f) Note that, since the battery has been disconnected, the ECU will take time to 're-learn' various settings which will have an adverse effect on how the transmission performs. After the car has completed a few miles of varied driving, however, the ECU's adaptive values should have been re-established.

10 Automatic transmission overhaul – general information

Overhaul of the automatic transmission should be left to an automatic transmission specialist or a Ford dealer. Refer to the information given in Section 2 before removing the unit.

Note that, if the vehicle is still within the warranty period, in the event of a fault it is important to take it to a Ford dealer, who will carry out a comprehensive diagnosis procedure using specialist equipment. Failure to do this will invalidate the warranty.

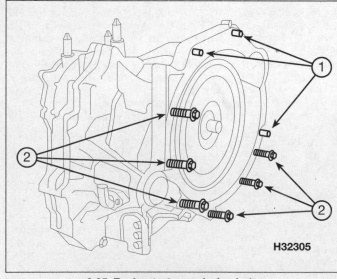

9.25 Engine-to-transmission bolts
1 Three bolt inserted from transmission side
2 Six bolts inserted from engine side

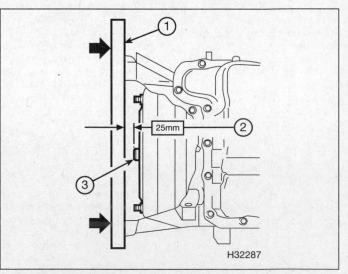

9.27 Checking that the torque converter is fully entered into the transmission
1 Straight-edge
2 Depth = 25 mm
3 Torque converter centre spigot

Chapter 8
Driveshafts

Contents

Degrees of difficulty

Easy, suitable for novice with little experience	**Fairly easy,** suitable for beginner with some experience	**Fairly difficult,** suitable for competent DIY mechanic	**Difficult,** suitable for experienced DIY mechanic	**Very difficult,** suitable for expert DIY or professional

Specifications

Driveshaft grease*

Outer constant velocity joint:
New gaiter 60g
New joint 100g
Inner tripod joint:
iB5 manual transmission 100g
MTX 75 manual transmission 125g
Automatic transmission . . . . No specified capacity available at time of writing – consult a dealer
* **Note:** *Outer grease part number XS4C-M1C230-AA; Inner grease part number XS4C-M1C230-BA. A good quality molybdenum disulphide may be used if these are not available.*

Torque wrench settings

	Nm	lbf ft
Driveshaft/hub nut	316	233
Lower arm balljoint clamp bolt	47	35
Rear engine mounting bolt	48	35
Right-hand intermediate shaft bearing	25	18
Roadwheel nuts	85	63
Suspension strut upper mounting nut	48	35

1 General information

Drive is transmitted from the transmission differential to the front wheels by means of two driveshafts. The right-hand driveshaft is in two sections, and incorporates a support bearing. The inner driveshaft gaiters are made of rubber, and the outer driveshaft gaiters are made of thermoplastic. This gives the outer gaiter a good resistance to external effects, like road chippings and permanent loading when the steering is being turned.

Each driveshaft consists of three main components: the sliding (tripod type) inner joint, the driveshaft itself, and the outer CV (constant velocity) joint. The inner end of the left-hand tripod joint is secured in the differential side gear by the engagement of a circlip. The inner tripod of the right-hand driveshaft is located in the intermediate shaft tripod housing. The intermediate shaft is held in the transmission by the support bearing, which in turn is supported by a bracket bolted to the rear of the cylinder block. The outer CV joint on both driveshafts is of ball-bearing type, and is secured in the front hub by the driveshaft nut.

2 Driveshafts – removal and refitting

Removal

1 Remove the wheel cover (or centre cover) from the wheel, apply the handbrake, and engage 1st gear or P. Loosen the driveshaft nut about half a turn **(see illustration)**. This nut is very tight – use only high-quality, close-fitting tools, and take adequate precautions against personal injury when loosening it.
2 Retain the suspension strut piston with an Allen key, then loosen the strut upper mounting nut and unscrew it by five complete turns.

 Warning: Do not remove this nut, it must still be left on the threads at least the full depth of the nut.
3 To avoid spillage when the driveshafts are separated from the MTX 75 transmission, drain the transmission fluid, as described in Chapter 7A. On models with no draining facilities, use a suitable container to catch the oil/fluid when the driveshaft has been removed.

2.1 Loosen the driveshaft nut, before jacking up the vehicle

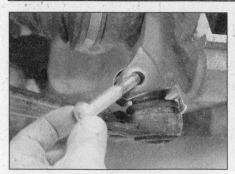

2.5a Remove the lower balljoint bolt . . .

2.5b . . . then lever the lower arm down using a suitable bar . . .

2.5c . . . and disengage the balljoint from the hub

4 Loosen the front wheel retaining nuts. Apply the handbrake, jack up the front of the vehicle and support it on axle stands. Remove the wheel.

5 Note which way round the lower arm balljoint clamp bolt is fitted, then unscrew it from the hub carrier. Lever the balljoint down from the hub carrier; if it is tight, carefully prise the clamp open using a large flat-bladed tool **(see illustrations)**. Take care not to damage the balljoint seal during the separation procedure.

6 Completely unscrew the driveshaft nut. **Note:** *The nut is of special laminated design, and should only be re-used a maximum of 4 times. (It is a good idea to file a small notch in the nut every time it is removed.)* Obtain a new nut if necessary.

7 Press the driveshaft through the front hub and hub carrier by pulling the hub carrier

outwards **(see illustration)**. When the driveshaft is free, support it on an axle stand, making sure that the inner tripod joint is not turned through more than 18° (damage may occur if the joint is turned through too great an angle).

Left-hand side

8 Insert a lever or slide hammer between the inner driveshaft joint and the transmission case **(see illustration)**. Prise free the inner joint from the differential, taking care not to damage the casing.

9 Take care not to damage the adjacent components and, in particular, make sure that the driveshaft oil seal in the differential is not damaged. If the transmission was not drained, be prepared for oil spillage.

10 On manual transmissions only, note that if the right-hand driveshaft has already been

removed, it is possible to release the left-hand driveshaft by inserting a forked drift from the right-hand side. However, care must be taken to prevent damage to the differential gears, particularly if the special Ford tool is not used.

11 Withdraw the driveshaft from under the vehicle.

12 Extract the circlip from the groove on the inner end of the driveshaft, and obtain a new one.

Right-hand side

13 The right-hand driveshaft may either be removed complete with the intermediate shaft from the transmission, or it may be disconnected from the outer end of the intermediate shaft.

14 If the latter course of action is taken, remove the retaining clip from around the larger end of the inner gaiter, and withdraw the inner tripod joint from the intermediate shaft.

15 If the complete driveshaft is to be removed, proceed as follows. Unscrew the nuts securing the driveshaft support bearing bracket to the rear of the cylinder block **(see illustration)**. On automatic models, it may be necessary to remove the bolt from the rear engine/gearbox mounting **(see illustration)**, and lever the engine forwards slightly.

16 Withdraw the complete driveshaft from the transaxle and from the bearing bracket, and remove it from under the vehicle **(see illustration)**. If the transmission was not drained, be prepared for oil spillage.

2.7 Pull hub/strut assembly outwards, to disengage driveshaft

2.8 Disengaging the driveshaft using a slide hammer

2.15a Undo the two retaining nuts (arrowed)

2.15b On automatics, remove the bolt (arrowed)

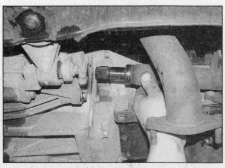

2.16 Withdraw the driveshaft from the transaxle

Both sides

17 Check the condition of the differential oil seals, and if necessary renew them as described in Chapter 7A (manual transmission) or Chapter 7B (automatic transmission). Check the support bearing, and if necessary renew it as described in Section 5.

Refitting

Right-hand side

18 If the intermediate shaft has not been removed, proceed to paragraph 21. Otherwise, proceed as follows.
19 Carefully refit the complete driveshaft in the support bearing and into the transmission, taking care not to damage the oil seal. Turn the driveshaft until it engages the splines on the differential gears.
20 Tighten the bolts securing the support bearing to the bracket on the cylinder block to the specified torque. Proceed to paragraph 26.
21 Locate the inner tripod joint of the driveshaft into the intermediate shaft.
22 After packing the joint with new grease (see Specifications at the beginning of this Chapter), refit the gaiter and tighten retaining clip.

Left-hand side

23 Locate the new circlip in the groove on the inner end of the driveshaft **(see illustration)**.
24 Use a special sleeve to protect the differential oil seal as the driveshaft is inserted. If the sleeve is not used, take great care to avoid damaging the seal. (Installation sleeves are supplied with new oil seals, where required.)
25 Insert the driveshaft into the transmission, making sure that the circlip is fully engaged.

Both sides

26 Pull the hub carrier outwards, and insert the outer end of the driveshaft through the hub. Turn the driveshaft to engage the splines in the hub, and fully push on the hub. Ford use a special tool to draw the driveshaft into the hub, but it is unlikely that the splines will be tight. However, if they are, it will be necessary to obtain the tool, or to use a similar home-made tool.
27 Screw on the driveshaft nut finger-tight.
28 Locate the front suspension lower arm balljoint stub in the bottom of the hub carrier, making sure balljoint shield is in place **(see illustration)**. Insert the clamp bolt in the previously-noted position, screw on the nut, and tighten it to the specified torque.
29 Tighten the suspension strut upper mounting nut to the specified torque.
30 Fill the transmission with oil or fluid, and check the level as described in the relevant part of Chapter 1.
31 Refit the wheel, and lower the vehicle to the ground. Tighten the wheel retaining nuts to the specified torque.
32 Fully tighten the driveshaft nut to the specified torque. Finally, refit the wheel cover (or centre cover).

2.23 Fit a new retaining clip to the end of the shaft

3 Driveshaft inner tripod joint gaiter – renewal

1 The inner sliding tripod joint gaiter is renewed by disconnecting the driveshaft from the inner joint housing at the transmission (left-hand side) or intermediate shaft (right-hand side). The work can be carried out either with the driveshaft removed from the vehicle, or with it *in situ*. If it is wished to fully remove the driveshaft, refer to Section 2 first. Note that if both the inner and outer gaiters are being renewed at the same time, the outer gaiter can be removed from the inner end of the driveshaft. As the only nut holding the driveshaft in place is the driveshaft retaining nut on the hub, then it would be easier to work on the shaft with it removed.

Renewal without removing the driveshaft

2 Loosen the front wheel nuts on the appropriate side. Apply the handbrake, jack up the front of the vehicle and support it on axle stands. Remove the wheel.
3 Note which way round the front suspension lower arm balljoint clamp bolt is fitted, then unscrew it from the hub carrier. Lever the balljoint down from the hub carrier; if it is tight, prise the clamp open carefully using a large flat-bladed tool. Take care not to damage the balljoint seal during the separation procedure.
4 Mark the driveshaft in relation to the joint housing, to ensure correct refitting.

2.28 Refitting balljoint shield

5 Note the fitted location of both of the inner joint gaiter retaining clips. Release the clips from the gaiter, and slide the gaiter back along the driveshaft (away from the transmission) a little way.
6 Pull the front suspension strut outwards, while guiding the tripod joint out of the joint housing. Support the inner end of the driveshaft on an axle stand.
7 Check that the inner end of the driveshaft is marked in relation to the splined tripod hub. If not, carefully centre-punch the two items, to ensure correct refitting. Alternatively, use dabs of paint on the driveshaft and one end of the tripod.
8 Extract the circlip retaining the tripod on the driveshaft.
9 Using a suitable puller, remove the tripod from the end of the driveshaft, and slide off the gaiter.
10 If the outer gaiter is also to be renewed, remove it with reference to Section 4.
11 Clean the driveshaft, and obtain a new tripod retaining circlip. The gaiter retaining clips must also be renewed.
12 Slide the new gaiter on the driveshaft, together with new clips.
13 Refit the tripod on the driveshaft splines, if necessary using a soft-faced mallet to drive it fully onto the splines. It must be fitted with the chamfered edge leading (towards the driveshaft), and with the previously-made marks aligned. Secure it in position using the new circlip. Ensure that the circlip is fully engaged in its groove.
14 With the front suspension strut pulled outwards, guide the tripod joint into the joint housing, making sure that the previously-made marks are aligned. Pack the joint with new grease (see Specifications at the beginning of this Chapter).
15 Slide the gaiter along the driveshaft, and locate it on the joint housing. The small-diameter end of the gaiter must be located in the groove on the driveshaft.
16 Ensure that the gaiter is not twisted or distorted, then insert a small screwdriver under the lip of the gaiter at the housing end. This will allow trapped air to escape during the next step.
17 Push the tripod fully into the housing, then pull it out by 20 mm. Remove the screwdriver, then fit the retaining clips and tighten them.
18 Reconnect the front suspension lower arm balljoint to the hub carrier. Refit and tighten the clamp nut and bolt to its specified torque.
19 Refit the wheel, and lower the vehicle to the ground. Tighten the wheel nuts to their specified torque.

Renewal with the driveshaft on the bench

20 Mount the driveshaft in a vice.
21 Mark the driveshaft in relation to the joint housing, to ensure correct refitting.
22 Note the fitted location of both of the inner joint gaiter retaining clips, then release the

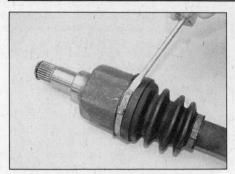

3.22 Remove the gaiter securing clips

3.23 Withdrawing the joint housing from the tripod joint

3.25 Using circlip pliers to remove the circlip from the shaft

clips from the gaiter **(see illustration)**, and slide the gaiter back along the driveshaft a little way.

23 Remove the inner joint housing from the tripod **(see illustration)**.

24 Check that the inner end of the driveshaft is marked in relation to the splined tripod hub. If not, carefully centre-punch the two items, to ensure correct refitting. Alternatively, use dabs of paint on the driveshaft and one end of the tripod.

25 Extract the circlip retaining the tripod on the driveshaft **(see illustration)**.

26 Using a puller, remove the tripod from the end of the driveshaft **(see illustration)**, and slide off the gaiter.

27 If the outer gaiter is also to be renewed, remove it with reference to Section 4.

28 Clean the driveshaft, and obtain a new joint retaining circlip. The gaiter retaining clips must also be renewed.

29 Slide the new gaiter on the driveshaft, together with new clips **(see illustration)**.

30 Refit the tripod on the driveshaft splines, if necessary using a soft-faced mallet and a suitable socket to drive it fully onto the splines. It must be fitted with the chamfered edge leading (towards the driveshaft), and with the previously-made marks aligned **(see illustration)**. Secure it in position using a new circlip. Ensure that the circlip is fully engaged in its groove.

31 Scoop out all of the old grease from the joint housing, then pack the joint with new grease (see Specifications at the beginning of this Chapter). Guide the joint housing onto the tripod joint, making sure that the previously-made marks are aligned.

32 Slide the gaiter along the driveshaft, and locate it on the tripod joint housing. The small-diameter end of the gaiter must be located in the groove on the driveshaft.

33 Ensure that the gaiter is not twisted or distorted, then insert a small screwdriver under the lip of the gaiter at the housing end. This will allow trapped air to escape during the next step.

34 Push the housing fully on the tripod, then pull it out by 20 mm. Remove the screwdriver, then fit the retaining clips and tighten them **(see illustration)**.

4 Driveshaft outer CV joint gaiter – renewal

1 The outer CV joint gaiter can be renewed by removing the inner gaiter first as described in Section 3, or after removing the driveshaft complete as described in Section 2. If the driveshaft is removed, then the inner gaiter need not necessarily be removed. It is impractical to renew the outer gaiter by dismantling the outer joint with the driveshaft in position in the vehicle. The following paragraphs describe renewal of the gaiter on the bench.

2 If required, mount the driveshaft in a vice.

3 Mark the driveshaft in relation to the CV joint housing, to ensure correct refitting.

4 Note the fitted location of both of the outer joint gaiter retaining clips, then release the clips from the gaiter, and slide the gaiter back along the driveshaft a little way.

5 Using a brass drift or a copper hammer, carefully drive the outer CV joint hub from the splines on the driveshaft **(see illustration)**. Initial resistance will be felt until the internal

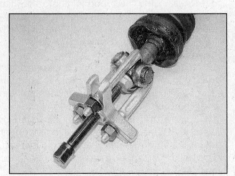

3.26 Using a puller to remove the tripod

3.29 Slide the gaiter and the clips onto the shaft

3.30 Align the marks when refitting the tripod

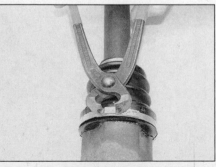

3.34 Using pincers/pliers to tighten the securing clips

4.5 Using a copper hammer to remove the outer CV joint

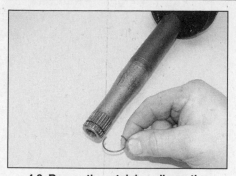

4.6 Renew the retaining clip on the driveshaft

4.12 Make sure clip (arrowed) engages fully when CV joint is refitted

4.15 Using pincers/pliers to tighten the securing clips

circlips are released. Take care not to damage the bearing cage.

6 Extract the circlip from the end of the driveshaft **(see illustration)**.

7 Slide the gaiter, and remove it from the driveshaft together with the clips.

8 Clean the driveshaft, and obtain a new joint retaining circlip. The gaiter retaining clips must also be renewed.

9 Slide the new gaiter (together with new clips) onto the driveshaft.

10 Fit a new circlip to the groove in the end of the driveshaft.

11 Scoop out all of the old grease, then pack the joint with new grease (see Specifications at the beginning of this Chapter). Take care that the fresh grease does not become contaminated with dirt or grit as it is being applied.

12 Locate the CV joint on the driveshaft so that the splines are aligned, then push the joint until the internal circlip is fully engaged **(see illustration)**.

13 Move the gaiter along the driveshaft, and locate it over the joint and onto the outer CV joint housing. The small-diameter end of the gaiter must be located in the groove on the driveshaft.

14 Ensure that the gaiter is not twisted or distorted, then insert a small screwdriver under the lip of the gaiter at the housing end, to allow any trapped air to escape.

15 Remove the screwdriver, fit the retaining clips in their previously-noted positions, and tighten them **(see illustration)**.

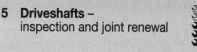

5 Driveshafts –
inspection and joint renewal

1 If any of the checks described in the relevant part of Chapter 1 reveal apparent excessive wear or play in any driveshaft joint, first remove the wheel cover (or centre cover), and check that the driveshaft nut is tightened to the specified torque. Repeat this check on the other side of the vehicle.

2 Road test the vehicle, and listen for a metallic clicking from the front as the vehicle is driven slowly in a circle on full-lock. If a clicking noise is heard, this indicates wear in the outer constant velocity joint, which means that the joint must be renewed; reconditioning is not possible.

3 To renew an outer CV joint, remove the driveshaft as described in Section 2, then separate the joint from the driveshaft with reference to Section 4. In principle, the gaiter can be left on the driveshaft, provided that it is in good condition; in practice, it makes sense to renew the gaiter in any case, having got this far.

4 If vibration, consistent with road speed, is felt through the car when accelerating, there is a possibility of wear in the inner tripod joints.

5 To renew an inner tripod joint, remove the driveshaft as described in Section 2, then separate the joint from the driveshaft with reference to Section 3.

6 Continual noise from the right-hand driveshaft, increasing with road speed, may indicate wear in the support bearing. To renew this bearing, the driveshaft and intermediate shaft must be removed, and the bearing extracted using a puller.

7 Remove the bearing dust cover, and obtain a new one.

8 Drive or press on the new bearing, applying the pressure to the inner race only. Similarly drive or press on the new dust cover.

8•6 Notes

Chapter 9
Braking system

Contents

Degrees of difficulty

Easy, suitable for novice with little experience	**Fairly easy,** suitable for beginner with some experience	**Fairly difficult,** suitable for competent DIY mechanic	**Difficult,** suitable for experienced DIY mechanic	**Very difficult,** suitable for expert DIY or professional

Specifications

Front brakes

Type	Ventilated disc, with single sliding piston caliper
Disc diameter	258.0 mm
Disc thickness:	
New	22.0 mm
Minimum	20.0 mm
Maximum disc thickness variation	0.020 mm
Maximum disc/hub run-out (installed)	0.050 mm
Caliper piston diameter	54.0 mm

Rear drum brakes

Type	Leading and trailing shoes, with automatic adjusters
Drum diameter:	
New	203.0 mm
Maximum	204.3 mm
Shoe width	36.0 mm
Wheel cylinder bore diameter:	
Estate with 1.4 litre & 1.6 litre engine and manual transmission	22.2 mm
3-door, 4-door & 5-door with diesel engine and manual transmission	19.05 mm
All other models	20.64 mm

Rear disc brakes

Type	Solid disc, with single piston floating caliper
Disc diameter	252.7 mm
Disc thickness:	
New	10.0 mm
Minimum	8.0 mm
Maximum disc thickness variation	0.020 mm
Maximum disc/hub runout (installed)	0.050 mm
Caliper piston diameter	34.0 mm

Torque wrench settings

	Nm	lbf ft
ABS hydraulic unit bracket to body	25	18
ABS hydraulic unit to bracket	9	7
ABS wheel sensor securing bolts	9	7
Brake pipe to master cylinder	17	13
Brake pipe to hydraulic control unit	11	8
Brake pipe unions	15	11
Front caliper guide bolts	28	21
Handbrake lever mountings	20	15
Master cylinder to servo mountings	20	15
Pedal bracket to servo mountings	23	17
Rear caliper bracket	55	41
Rear caliper guide bolts	35	26
Rear drum brake backplate/disc shield	66	49
Rear hub nut	235	173
Roadwheel nuts	85	63
Vacuum pump (diesel models):		
Pump-to-cylinder head bolts	22	16
Vacuum line to pump union	18	13
Intercooler securing bolts	5	4
Cylinder cover securing bolts	5	4
Yaw rate sensor to bracket	8	6
Yaw rate sensor bracket to body	5	4

1 General information

The braking system is of diagonally-split, dual-circuit design, with ventilated discs at the front, and drum or disc brakes (according to model) at the rear. The front calipers are of single sliding piston design, and (where fitted) the rear calipers are of a single-piston floating design, using asbestos-free pads. The rear drum brakes are of the leading and trailing shoe type, and are self-adjusting during foot-brake operation. The rear brake shoe linings are of different thicknesses, in order to allow for the different proportional rates of wear.

The vacuum servo unit uses inlet manifold depression (generated only when a petrol engine is running) to boost the effort applied by the driver at the brake pedal and transmits this increased effort to the master cylinder pistons. Because there is no throttling of the inlet manifold on a diesel engine, it is not a suitable source of vacuum for brake servo operation. Vacuum is therefore derived from a separate vacuum pump, driven via a pushrod operated by an eccentric on the camshaft.

Pressure conscious regulator valves (PCRVs) are fitted to the rear brakes, to prevent rear wheel lock-up under hard braking. The valves are sometimes referred to as pressure control relief valves. On non-ABS models, they are fitted in the master cylinder rear brake outlet ports; on models with ABS, they are located in the ABS hydraulic unit. On Estate models without ABS there is a load sensing valve (LAV) for the rear wheels, which is connected to the rear suspension cross-member. It controls the brake fluid pressure to each of the rear wheels, depending on vehicle loading.

The handbrake is cable-operated, and acts on the rear brakes. On rear drum brake models, the cables operate on the rear trailing brake shoe operating levers; on rear disc brake models, they operate on levers on the rear calipers. The handbrake lever incorporates an automatic adjuster, which will adjust the cable when the handbrake is operated several times.

Where fitted, the anti-lock braking system (ABS) uses the basic conventional brake system, together with an ABS hydraulic unit fitted between the master cylinder and the four brake units at each wheel. The hydraulic unit consists of a hydraulic actuator, an ABS brake pressure pump, an ABS module with built-in relay box, and two pressure-control relief valves. Braking at each of the four wheels is controlled by separate solenoid valves in the hydraulic actuator. If wheel lock-up is detected by one of the wheel sensors, when the vehicle speed is above 3 mph, the valve opens. Releasing pressure to the relevant brake, until the wheel regains a rotational speed corresponding to the speed of the vehicle. The cycle can be repeated many times a second. In the event of a fault in the ABS system, the conventional braking system is not affected. Diagnosis of a fault in the ABS system requires the use of special equipment, and this work should therefore be left to a Ford dealer.

There are two traction control systems available for the Focus: brake traction control system (BTCS) which is fitted to the 1.4 litre petrol and diesel models; and the full speed traction control (TCS), sometimes called Spark Fuel Traction Control (SFTC), which is fitted to the 1.6 litre, 1.8 litre and the 2.0 litre models. The systems are integrated with the ABS, and use the same wheel sensors. The hydraulic control unit has additional solenoid valves incorporated to enable control of the wheel brake pressure.

The BTCS system is only active at speeds up to 85 km/h (53 mph) – when the system is active the warning light on the instrument panel illuminates to warn the driver. This uses controlled braking of the spinning driving wheel, when the grip at the driven wheels are different. The spinning wheel is braked by the ABS system, transferring a greater proportion of the engine torque through the differential to the other driven wheel, which increases the use of the available traction control.

The TCS system uses all the features of the BTCS system, plus it also reduces the engine torque to improve directional stability. If the driving wheels are spinning, the ABS/TCS module calculates the required engine torque during traction control and sends this request to the engine ECU. This then calculates the required ignition timing and the number of fuel injectors to be deactivated in order to achieve the required engine torque.

The advantages of the TCS system over the BTCS system are:

a) *Reduces the load on the braking system.*
b) *Reduces the load on the engine.*
c) *Improves directional stability.*
d) *Shortens reaction time.*
e) *Operates at all vehicle speeds.*

On the 2.0 litre Zetec model there is an Electronic Stability Program (ESP) available, this system supports the vehicles stability and steering through a combination of ABS and traction control operations. There is a switch on the centre console, so that if required the system can be switched off. This will then illuminate the warning light on the instrument panel, to inform the driver that the ESP is not in operation. The stability of the vehicle is measured by Yaw rate and Accelerometer sensors, which sense the movement of the vehicle about its vertical axis, and also lateral acceleration.

Note: *When servicing any part of the system, work carefully and methodically; also observe*

2.2 Prise the pad retaining clip from the caliper

2.3a Prise the covers off to locate the caliper guide bolts . . .

2.3b . . . then slacken and remove the bolts

scrupulous cleanliness when overhauling any part of the hydraulic system. Always renew components (in axle sets, where applicable) if in doubt about their condition, and use only genuine Ford replacement parts, or at least those of known good quality. Note the warnings given in 'Safety first!' and at relevant points in this Chapter concerning the dangers of asbestos dust and hydraulic fluid.

2 Front brake pads – renewal

⚠️ **Warning: Disc brake pads must be renewed on BOTH front wheels at the same time – never renew the pads on only one wheel, as uneven braking may result. Although genuine Ford linings are asbestos-free, the dust created by wear of non-genuine pads may contain asbestos, which is a health hazard. Never blow it out with compressed air, and don't inhale any of it. DO NOT use petroleum-based solvents to clean brake parts; use brake cleaner or methylated spirit only. DO NOT allow any brake fluid, oil or grease to contact the brake pads or disc. Also refer to the warning at the start of Section 14 concerning brake fluid.**

1 Apply the handbrake. Loosen the front wheel nuts, then jack up the front of the vehicle and support it on axle stands. Remove the front wheels. Work on one brake assembly at a time, using the assembled brake for reference if necessary.

2 Using a flat-bladed screwdriver, prise the outer brake pad retaining clip from the caliper **(see illustration)**. Hold the clip with a pair of pliers as this is done, to avoid personal injury.
3 Prise the plastic covers from the ends of the two guide pins then, using a 7 mm Allen key, unscrew the guide bolts securing the caliper to the carrier bracket **(see illustrations)**.
4 Withdraw the caliper from the disc **(see illustration)**, and support it on an axle stand to avoid straining the hydraulic hose.
5 Pull the inner pad from the piston in the caliper, then remove the outer pad from the caliper by sliding the pad out of the caliper with its securing clip, noting their fitted positions **(see illustrations)**.
6 Brush all dust and dirt from the caliper, pads and disc, but do not inhale it, as it may be harmful to health. Scrape any corrosion from the edge of the disc, taking care not to damage the friction surface.
7 Inspect the front brake disc for scoring and cracks. If a detailed inspection is necessary, refer to Section 4.
8 The piston must be pushed back into the caliper bore, to provide room for the new brake pads. Use a C-clamp to accomplish this. As the piston is depressed to the bottom of the caliper bore, the fluid in the master cylinder will rise slightly. Make sure that there is sufficient space in the brake fluid reservoir to accept the displaced fluid, and if necessary, syphon some off first. Any brake fluid spilt on paintwork should be washed off with clean water, without delay – brake fluid is also a highly-effective paint-stripper.

⚠️ **Warning: Do not syphon the fluid by mouth; it is poisonous.**

9 Fit the new pads using a reversal of the removal procedure, and tighten the guide bolts to the torque wrench setting given in the Specifications at the beginning of this Chapter.
10 On completion, firmly depress the brake pedal a few times, to bring the pads to their normal working position. Check the level of the brake fluid in the reservoir, and top-up if necessary.
11 Give the vehicle a short road test, to make sure that the brakes are functioning correctly, and to bed-in the new linings to the contours of the disc. New linings will not provide maximum braking efficiency until they have bedded-in; avoid heavy braking as far as possible for the first hundred miles or so.

3 Front brake caliper – removal, overhaul and refitting

Note: Refer to the warning at the beginning of the previous Section before proceeding.

Removal

1 Apply the handbrake. Loosen the front wheel nuts, then jack up the front of the vehicle and support it on axle stands. Remove the appropriate front wheel.
2 Fit a brake hose clamp to the flexible hose leading to the caliper **(see illustration)**. This will minimise brake fluid loss during subsequent operations.

2.4 Withdraw the caliper, complete with brake pads

2.5a Unclip the inner pad from the piston . . .

2.5b . . . then unclip the outer pad from the caliper

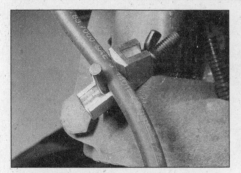

3.2 Brake hose clamp fitted to the front flexible brake hose

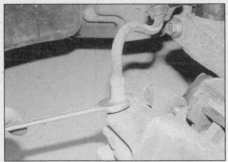

3.3 Slacken the brake hose at the caliper

3.15 Tightening the carrier bracket mounting bolts

3 Loosen the union on the caliper end of the flexible brake hose **(see illustration)**. Once loosened, do not try to unscrew the hose at this stage.

4 Remove the brake pads as described in Section 2.

5 Support the caliper in one hand, and prevent the hydraulic hose from turning with the other hand. Unscrew the caliper from the hose, making sure that the hose is not twisted unduly or strained. Once the caliper is detached, plug the open hydraulic unions in the caliper and hose, to keep out dust and dirt.

6 If required, the caliper carrier bracket can be unbolted from the hub carrier.

Overhaul

Note: *Before starting work, check on the availability of parts (caliper overhaul kit/seals).*

7 With the caliper on the bench, brush away all traces of dust and dirt, but take care not to inhale any dust, as it may be harmful to your health.

8 Pull the dust cover rubber seal from the end of the piston.

9 Apply low air pressure to the fluid inlet union, to eject the piston. Only low air pressure is required for this, such as is produced by a foot-operated tyre pump.

Caution: The piston may be ejected with some force. Position a thin piece of wood between the piston and the caliper body, to prevent damage to the end face of the piston, in the event of it being ejected suddenly.

10 Using a suitable blunt instrument, prise the piston seal from the groove in the cylinder bore. Take care not to scratch the surface of the bore.

11 Clean the piston and caliper body with methylated spirit, and allow to dry. Examine the surfaces of the piston and cylinder bore for wear, damage and corrosion. If the piston alone is unserviceable, a new piston must be obtained, along with seals. If the cylinder bore is unserviceable, the complete caliper must be renewed. The seals must be renewed, regardless of the condition of the other components.

12 Coat the piston and seals with clean brake fluid, then manipulate the piston seal into the groove in the cylinder bore.

13 Push the piston squarely into its bore, taking care not to damage the seal.

14 Fit the dust cover rubber seal onto the piston and caliper, then depress the piston fully.

Refitting

15 Refit the caliper by reversing the removal operations. Make sure that the flexible brake hose is not twisted. Tighten the mounting bolts and wheel nuts to the specified torque **(see illustration)**.

16 Bleed the brake circuit according to the procedure given in Section 14, remembering to remove the brake hose clamp from the flexible hose. Make sure there are no leaks from the hose connections. Test the brakes carefully before returning the vehicle to normal service.

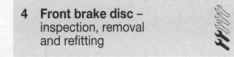

4 Front brake disc – inspection, removal and refitting

Note: *To prevent uneven braking, BOTH front brake discs should be renewed or reground at the same time.*

Inspection

1 Apply the handbrake. Loosen the relevant wheel nuts, jack up the front of the vehicle and support it on axle stands. Remove the appropriate front wheel.

2 Remove the front brake caliper from the disc with reference to Section 2, and undo the two carrier bracket securing bolts. Do not disconnect the flexible hose. Support the caliper on an axle stand, or suspend it out of the way with a piece of wire, taking care to avoid straining the flexible hose.

3 Temporarily refit two of the wheel nuts to diagonally-opposite studs, with the flat sides of the nuts against the disc **(see illustration)**. Tighten the nuts progressively, to hold the disc firmly.

4 Scrape any corrosion from the disc. Rotate the disc, and examine it for deep scoring, grooving or cracks. Using a micrometer, measure the thickness of the disc in several places **(see illustration)**. The minimum thickness is stamped on the disc hub. Light wear and scoring is normal, but if excessive, the disc should be removed, and either reground by a specialist, or renewed. If regrinding is undertaken, the minimum thickness must be maintained. Obviously, if the disc is cracked, it must be renewed.

5 Using a dial gauge or a flat metal block and feeler gauges, check that the disc run-out 10 mm from the outer edge does not exceed the limit given in the Specifications. To do this, fix the measuring equipment, and rotate the disc, noting the variation in measurement as the disc is rotated **(see illustration)**. The difference between the minimum and maximum measurements recorded is the disc run-out.

6 If the run-out is greater than the specified amount, check for variations of the disc thickness as follows. Mark the disc at eight positions 45° apart then, using a micrometer,

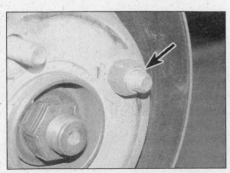

4.3 Nut holding the disc on firmly (arrowed)

4.4 Using a micrometer to measure the thickness of the brake disc

4.5 Measuring the disc run-out with a dial gauge

4.10 Withdraw the disc from the hub

measure the disc thickness at the eight positions, 15 mm in from the outer edge. If the variation between the minimum and maximum readings is greater than the specified amount, the disc should be renewed.

7 The hub face run-out can also be checked in a similar way. First remove the disc as described later in this Section, fix the measuring equipment, then slowly rotate the hub, and check that the run-out does not exceed the amount given in the Specifications. If the hub face run-out is excessive, this should be corrected (by renewing the hub bearings – see Chapter 10) before rechecking the disc run-out.

Removal

8 With the wheel and caliper removed, remove the wheel nuts which were temporarily refitted in paragraph 3.

9 Mark the disc in relation to the hub, if it is to be refitted.

10 Remove the washer/retaining clip(s) (where fitted), and withdraw the disc over the wheel studs (see illustration).

Refitting

11 Make sure that the disc and hub mating surfaces are clean, then locate the disc on the wheel studs. Align the previously-made marks if the original disc is being refitted.

12 Refit the washer/retaining clip(s), where fitted.

13 Refit the brake caliper and carrier bracket with reference to Section 2.

14 Refit the wheel, and lower the vehicle to the ground. Tighten wheel nuts to their specified torque.

15 Test the brakes carefully before returning the vehicle to normal service.

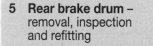

5 Rear brake drum – removal, inspection and refitting

Note: Refer to the warning at the beginning of Section 6 before proceeding.
Note: To prevent uneven braking, BOTH rear brake drums should be renewed at the same time.

Removal

1 Chock the front wheels, release the handbrake and engage 1st gear (or P). Loosen the relevant wheel nuts, jack up the rear of the vehicle and support it on axle stands. Remove the appropriate rear wheel.

2 Remove the dust cap from the centre of the drum, and remove the retaining nut (see illustrations). This nut is very tight – use only high-quality, close-fitting tools, and take adequate precautions against personal injury when loosening it. Note: The driveshaft/hub nut is of special laminated design, and should only be re-used a maximum of 4 times. (It is a good idea to mark the nut every time it is removed.) Obtain a new nut if necessary.

3 If the drum will not pull off easily, make sure the handbrake cable is released fully, then use a suitable puller to draw the drum and bearing assembly off the stub axle.

4 With the brake drum removed, clean the dust from the drum, brake shoes, wheel cylinder and backplate, using brake cleaner or methylated spirit. Take care not to inhale the dust, as it may contain asbestos.

Inspection

5 Clean the inside surfaces of the brake drum, then examine the internal friction surface for signs of scoring or cracks. If it is cracked, deeply scored, or has worn to a diameter greater than the maximum given in the Specifications, then it should be renewed, together with the drum on the other side (see illustration).

6 Regrinding of the brake drum is not recommended.

Refitting

7 The wheel bearings may have been damaged on drum removal, if necessary renew the bearings as described in Chapter 10.

8 Refitting is a reversal of removal, tightening relevant bolts to their specified torque.

9 Test the brakes carefully before returning the vehicle to normal service.

6 Rear brake shoes – renewal

 Warning: Drum brake shoes must be renewed on BOTH rear wheels at the same time – never renew the shoes on only one wheel, as uneven braking may result. Also, the dust created by wear of the shoes may contain asbestos, which is a health hazard. Never blow it out with compressed air, and don't inhale any of it. An approved filtering mask should be worn when working on the brakes. DO NOT use petroleum-based solvents to clean brake parts; use brake cleaner or methylated spirit only.

1 Chock the front wheels, release the handbrake and engage 1st gear (or P). Loosen the relevant wheel nuts, jack up the rear of the vehicle and support it on axle stands. Remove the rear wheels. Work on one brake assembly at a time, using the assembled brake for reference if necessary.

2 Disconnect the ABS wiring connector (if fitted).

5.2a Remove the dust cap . . .

5.2b . . . and undo the hub nut

5.5 Checking the drum for wear

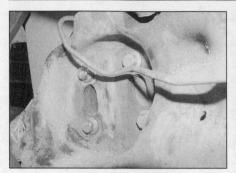

6.3a Undo the four bolts . . .

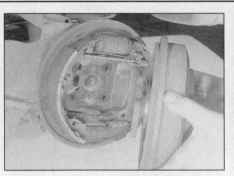

6.3b . . . and remove the hub/drum assembly

6.4 Note the position of the springs

3 Remove the rear brake drum and hub assembly by unscrewing the four bolts at the rear of the hub assembly **(see illustrations)**. This is to prevent any damage to the wheel bearings on removal of the drum.

4 Note the fitted position of the springs and the brake shoes, then clean the components with brake cleaner, and allow to dry **(see illustration)**. Position a tray beneath the backplate, to catch the fluid and residue.

5 Remove the two shoe hold-down springs, use a pair of pliers to depress the ends so that they can be withdrawn off the pins. Remove the hold-down pins from the backplate **(see illustrations)**.

6 Disconnect the top ends of the shoes from the wheel cylinder, taking care not to damage the rubber boots.

7 To prevent the wheel cylinder pistons from being accidentally ejected, fit a suitable

elastic band or wire lengthways over the cylinder/pistons. DO NOT press the brake pedal while the shoes are removed.

8 Pull the bottom end of the brake shoes from the bottom anchor **(see illustration)** (use pliers or an adjustable spanner over the edge of the shoe to lever it away, if required).

9 Pull the handbrake cable spring back from the operating lever on the rear of the trailing shoe. Unhook the cable end from the cut-out in the lever, and remove the brake shoes **(see illustration)**.

10 Working on a clean bench, move the bottom ends of the brake shoes together, and unhook the lower return spring from the shoes, noting the location holes.

11 Pull the leading shoe from the strut and brake shoe adjuster **(see illustration)**, unhook the upper return spring from the shoes, noting the location holes.

12 Pull the adjustment strut to release from the trailing brake shoe, and remove the strut support spring **(see illustration)**.

13 If the wheel cylinder shows signs of fluid leakage, or if there is any reason to suspect it of being defective, inspect it now, as described in the next Section.

14 Clean the backplate, and apply small amounts of high-melting-point brake grease to the brake shoe contact points. Be careful not to get grease on any friction surfaces **(see illustration)**.

15 Lubricate the sliding components of the brake shoe adjuster with a little high-melting-point brake grease, but leave the serrations on the eccentric cam clean.

16 Fit the new brake shoes using a reversal of the removal procedure, but set the eccentric cam at its lowest position before assembling it to the trailing shoe.

6.5a Unclip the brake shoe hold-down springs . . .

6.5b . . ..and pull out the pins from the backplate

6.8 Pull brake shoe from the bottom anchor

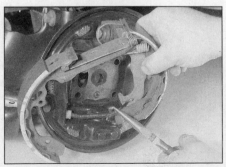

6.9 Use pliers to disengage cable from lever

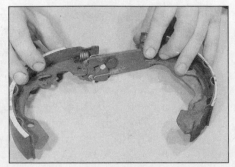

6.11 Disengage the leading brake shoe

6.12 Disengage the adjustment strut

6.14 Grease the brake shoe contact points on the backplate

17 Before refitting the brake drum, it should be inspected as described in Section 5.
18 With the drum in position and all the securing bolts and nuts tightened to their specified torque, refit the wheel. then carry out the renewal procedure on the remaining rear brake.
19 Lower the vehicle to the ground, and tighten the wheel nuts to the specified torque.
20 Depress the brake pedal several times, in order to operate the self-adjusting mechanism and set the shoes at their normal operating position.
21 Make several forward and reverse stops, and operate the handbrake fully two or three times (adjust handbrake as required). Give the vehicle a road test, to make sure that the brakes are functioning correctly, and to bed-in the new shoes to the contours of the drum. Remember that the new shoes will not give full braking efficiency until they have bedded-in.

7 Rear wheel cylinder – removal, overhaul and refitting

Note: *Before starting work, check on the availability of parts (wheel cylinder, or overhaul kit/seals). Also bear in mind that if the brake shoes have been contaminated by fluid leaking from the wheel cylinder, they must be renewed. The shoes on BOTH sides of the vehicle must be renewed, even if they are only contaminated on one side. The wheel cylinders fitted to Estate models are of larger diameter than those fitted to the Saloon and Hatchback. Be sure to order the correct parts, and be sure that the same size of wheel cylinder is fitted to both sides, or uneven braking could result.*

Removal

1 Remove the brake drum as described in Section 6 paragraphs 1 to 3.
2 Minimise fluid loss either by removing the master cylinder reservoir cap, and then tightening it down onto a piece of polythene to obtain an airtight seal, or by using a brake hose clamp, a G-clamp, or similar tool, to clamp the flexible hose at the nearest convenient point to the wheel cylinder.

3 Pull the brake shoes apart at their top ends, so that they are just clear of the wheel cylinder. The automatic adjuster will hold the shoes in this position, so that the cylinder can be withdrawn.
4 Wipe away all traces of dirt around the hydraulic union at the rear of the wheel cylinder, then undo the union nut.
5 Unscrew the two bolts securing the wheel cylinder to the backplate **(see illustration)**.
6 Withdraw the wheel cylinder from the backplate so that it is clear of the brake shoes. Plug the open hydraulic unions, to prevent the entry of dirt, and to minimise further fluid loss whilst the cylinder is detached.

Overhaul

7 No overhaul procedures or parts were available at the time of writing, check availability of spares before dismantling. Replacing a wheel cylinder as a unit is recommended.

Refitting

8 Wipe clean the backplate and remove the plug from the end of the hydraulic pipe. Fit the cylinder onto the backplate and screw in the hydraulic union nut by hand, being careful not to cross-thread it.
9 Tighten the mounting bolts, then fully tighten the hydraulic union nut.
10 Retract the automatic brake adjuster mechanism, so that the brake shoes engage with the pistons of the wheel cylinder. To do this, prise the shoes apart slightly, turn the automatic adjuster to its minimum position, and release the shoes.
11 Remove the clamp from the flexible brake hose, or the polythene from the master cylinder (as applicable).
12 Refit the brake drum with reference to Section 6.
13 Bleed the hydraulic system as described in Section 14. Providing suitable precautions were taken to minimise loss of fluid, it should only be necessary to bleed the relevant rear brake.
14 Test the brakes carefully before returning the vehicle to normal service.

8.3 Disconnect the handbrake cable from the caliper arm

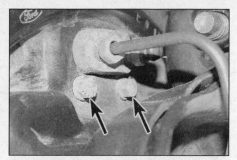

7.5 Loosen the brake pipe union nut, before removing the two securing bolts (arrowed)

8 Rear brake pads – renewal

⚠️ *Warning: Disc brake pads must be renewed on BOTH rear wheels at the same time – never renew the pads on only one wheel, as uneven braking may result. Although genuine Ford linings are asbestos-free, the dust created by wear of non-genuine pads may contain asbestos, which is a health hazard. Never blow it out with compressed air, and don't inhale any of it. DO NOT use petroleum-based solvents to clean brake parts; use brake cleaner or methylated spirit only. DO NOT allow any brake fluid, oil or grease to contact the brake pads or disc.*

1 Chock the front wheels, and engage 1st gear (or P). Loosen the rear wheel nuts, then jack up the rear of the vehicle and support it on axle stands. Remove the rear wheels, and release the handbrake.
2 Work on one brake assembly at a time, using the assembled brake for reference if necessary.
3 Push back the caliper handbrake arm to obtain some slack in the cable, pull up and disconnect the cable from the caliper arm **(see illustration)**. Once the cable has been disconnected, don't operate the handbrake arm excessively, as this will make refitting the cable more difficult.
4 Unscrew and remove the two caliper retaining bolts **(see illustration)**. Withdraw

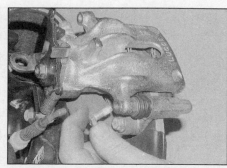

8.4 Removing the second bolt from the caliper

8.5a Remove the inner . . .

8.5b . . . and outer pad from the caliper bracket

8.7 Using a special tool to screw the piston back into the caliper

8.8 One of the cut-outs (arrowed) must line up with the lug on the brake pad

8.10 Arrow shows the lug on the rear of the brake pad

and support the caliper on an axle stand, or tie it to one side with wire. Do not allow it to hang down unsupported, as this will strain the brake hose.

5 Remove the pads from the carrier bracket, noting their fitted positions (see illustrations). Brush all dust and dirt from the caliper, pads and disc, but do not inhale it, as it may be harmful to health. Scrape any corrosion from the edge of the disc.

6 Inspect the rear brake disc as described in Section 4.

7 Before fitting the new pads, screw the caliper piston fully into its bore (see illustration), at the same time pressing the piston fully to the bottom of the bore. Special tools are available for this operation, although it may be possible to use long-nosed pliers engaged with the cut-outs in the piston. Brake fluid will be displaced into the master cylinder reservoir, so check first that there is enough

space to accept the fluid. If necessary, syphon off some of the fluid. Any brake fluid spilt on paintwork should be washed off with clean water, without delay – brake fluid is also a highly-effective paint-stripper.

⚠️ **Warning: Do not syphon the fluid by mouth; it is poisonous.**

8 The caliper piston must be rotated so that one of the cut-outs is positioned to engage with the lug on the back of the inner pad (see illustration).

9 Fit the new pads, applying a little copper-based brake grease to the contact areas on the pad backing plates, and taking care not to get any on the friction material.

10 Refit the caliper back into position making sure the flexible brake hose is not twisted, engage the piston cut-out with the lug on the back of the inner pad (see illustration), and secure with the two securing bolts. Do not

depress the brake pedal until the handbrake cable has been reconnected, since the extra pad-to-disc clearance makes reconnecting the cable easier.

11 Reconnect the cable to the caliper operating arm, noting the points made in Section 26.

12 Firmly depress the brake pedal a few times, to bring the pads to their normal working position. Check the level of the brake fluid in the reservoir, and top-up if necessary.

13 Give the vehicle a road test, to make sure that the brakes are functioning correctly, and to bed-in the new linings to the contours of the disc. Remember that full braking efficiency will not be obtained until the new linings have bedded-in.

9 Rear brake caliper – removal, overhaul and refitting

Removal

1 Chock the front wheels, and engage 1st gear (or P). Loosen the rear wheel nuts, jack up the rear of the vehicle and support it on axle stands. Remove the appropriate rear wheel.

2 Fit a brake hose clamp to the flexible hose leading to the caliper (see illustration 3.2). This will minimise brake fluid loss during subsequent operations.

3 Slacken (but do not completely unscrew) the union on the caliper end of the flexible hose.

4 Remove the brake pads as described in Section 8.

5 Unscrew the caliper from the hydraulic brake hose, making sure that the hose is not twisted or strained unduly (see illustration). Plug the open hydraulic unions to keep dust and dirt out.

6 If necessary, unbolt the carrier bracket from the hub carrier (see illustration).

Overhaul

7 No overhaul procedures, or parts, were available at the time of writing. Check the availability of spares before dismantling the caliper. Do not attempt to dismantle the

9.5 Remove caliper, and unscrew from brake hose

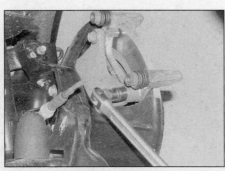

9.6 Undo and remove the two carrier securing bolts

10.2 Remove the caliper carrier bracket

10.3a Prise off the retaining clip . . .

10.3b . . . and withdraw the disc from the rear hub

handbrake mechanism inside the caliper; if the mechanism is faulty, the complete caliper assembly must be renewed.

Refitting

8 Refit the caliper, and where applicable the carrier bracket, by reversing the removal operations. Refer to the points made in Section 26 when reconnecting the handbrake cable. Tighten the mounting bolts and wheel nuts to the specified torque, and do not forget to remove the brake hose clamp from the flexible brake hose.

9 Bleed the brake circuit according to the procedure given in Section 14. Make sure there are no leaks from the hose connections. Test the brakes carefully before returning the vehicle to normal service.

10 Rear brake disc – inspection, removal and refitting

Removal

1 Remove the rear caliper and pads as described in Section 8.

2 Unbolt the caliper carrier bracket from the hub **(see illustration)**, then mark the disc in relation to the hub, if it is to be refitted.

3 Remove the retaining clip from the wheel stud (where fitted), and withdraw the disc over the wheel studs **(see illustrations)**.

4 Procedures for inspection of the rear brake discs are the same as the front brake discs as described in Section 4.

Refitting

5 Refitting is a reversal of removal, as described in the relevant Sections.

11 Master cylinder – removal and refitting

⚠ *Warning: Brake fluid is poisonous. Take care to keep it off bare skin, and in particular not to get splashes in your eyes. The fluid also attacks paintwork and plastics – wash off spillages immediately with cold water.*

Finally, brake fluid is highly inflammable, and should be handled with the same care as petrol.

Removal

Master cylinder (RHD models)

1 Exhaust the vacuum in the servo by pressing the brake pedal a few times, with the engine switched off.

2 Disconnect the battery negative lead. **Note:** *Before disconnecting the battery, refer to Chapter 5A, Section 1, for precautions.*

3 Disconnect the low fluid level warning light multi-plug from the fluid reservoir. Unscrew the cap.

4 Draw off the hydraulic fluid from the reservoir, using an old battery hydrometer or similar. Alternatively raise the vehicle and remove the wheels. Slacken the front bleed nipples and drain the fluid from the reservoir.

11.5 Undo the two evaporation emission canister purge valve securing bolts (petrol engines)

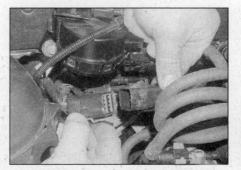

11.7 Disconnect the wiring multi-plug

⚠ *Warning: Do not syphon the fluid by mouth; it is poisonous. Any brake fluid spilt on paintwork should be washed off with clean water, without delay – brake fluid is also a highly-effective paint-stripper.*

5 Lower the vehicle and, on petrol models, remove the evaporation emission canister purge valve **(see illustration)**.

6 On diesel models, detach the fuel filter from its bracket and move to one side **(see illustration)**.

7 Disconnect the wiring harness electrical connector from in front of the master cylinder and its retaining bracket **(see illustration)**.

8 Detach the fuel vapour lines from the bulkhead.

9 Release the fuel line from the bulkhead below the brake servo.

10 Release the clip and disconnect the fluid supply hose from the brake fluid reservoir to the master cylinder **(see illustration)**. Detach

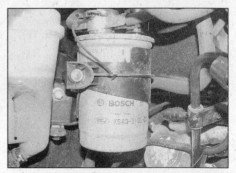

11.6 Undo the retaining screw to remove the fuel filter (diesel engines)

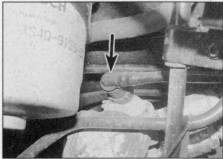

11.10 Release the supply hose (arrowed) from the master cylinder

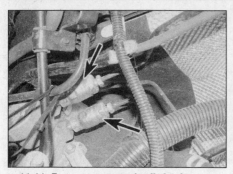

11.11 Pressure-control relief valves on non-ABS models

11.15 Release the wiring harness bracket, when removing the master cylinder securing nuts

11.19 Removing the air filter housing

the hose from the bulkhead, keeping the end higher than the reservoir level, and plug or cap the hose, to prevent fluid loss or dirt entry.

11 Identify the locations of each brake pipe on the master cylinder. On non-ABS models, there are four pipes; the two rear brake pipes are attached to pressure-control relief valves on the master cylinder (see illustration). On ABS models, there are only two pipes, which lead to the ABS hydraulic unit.

12 Place rags beneath the master cylinder to catch spilt hydraulic fluid.

13 Clean around the hydraulic union nuts. Unscrew the nuts, and disconnect the hydraulic lines from the master cylinder. If the nuts are tight, a split ring spanner should be used in preference to an open-ended spanner. Cap the end of the pipes and the master cylinder to prevent any dirt contamination.

14 On vehicles with Stability Assist, disconnect the pressure sensors electrical connector.

15 Undo the master cylinder securing nuts, and withdraw the master cylinder from the studs on the servo unit (see illustration).

16 Recover the gasket/seal from the master cylinder.

17 If the master cylinder is faulty, it must be renewed. At the time of writing, no overhaul kits were available.

Master cylinder (LHD models)

18 Carry out the procedures as described in paragraphs 1 to 4.

19 Lower the vehicle. Undo the securing bolts from the air filter housing and intake tube, then remove from the vehicle (see illustration).

20 Disconnect the electrical connector from the auxiliary fusebox (see illustration). Remove the retaining screw, and detach the fusebox from its bracket. Move the fusebox to the air filter housing position temporarily.

21 Carry out the procedures as described in paragraphs 10 to 17.

Brake fluid reservoir

22 The reservoir is not part of the master cylinder. Disconnect the electrical connector from the filler cap. Unscrew the cap, and using an old battery hydrometer or similar, empty the brake fluid. Refit the cap.

23 Detach the wiring harness from the lower part of the reservoir (see illustration).

24 Undo the two securing screws from the reservoir and detach it from the bulkhead (see illustration).

25 Release the clip and disconnect the fluid supply hoses for the brake and clutch fluid reservoir.

Refitting

26 Refitting is a reversal of the removal procedure, noting the following points:

a) *Clean the contact surfaces of the master cylinder and servo, and locate a new gasket on the master cylinder.*

b) *Refit and tighten the nuts to the specified torque.*

c) *Carefully insert the brake pipes in the apertures in the master cylinder, then tighten the union nuts. Make sure that the nuts enter their threads correctly.*

d) *Fill the reservoir with fresh brake fluid.*

e) *Bleed the brake hydraulic system as described in Section 14.*

f) *Test the brakes carefully before returning the vehicle to normal service.*

12 Brake pedal – removal and refitting

Removal

1 Working inside the vehicle, move the driver's seat fully to the rear, to allow maximum working area.

2 Undo the four screws and prise out the retaining clip to remove the driver's side facia lower panel. Unclip the multi-plug from the trim panel.

3 Disconnect the electrical connectors to the brake/clutch pedal switches. Remove the switches by turning them, then pulling them out of the pedal bracket (see illustration).

4 Slacken the four retaining nuts on the pedal bracket assembly.

5 Detach the clutch master cylinder, by unscrewing the securing bolts and unclipping from the pedal bracket (see illustration).

11.20 Release the wiring connectors from the base of the fusebox

11.23 Unclip the wiring harness (arrowed) from the reservoir

11.24 Disconnect the wiring plug, and undo the two securing bolts

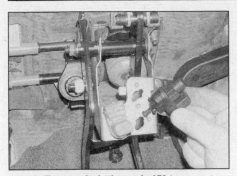

12.3 Turn switch through 45° to remove

12.5 Remove the two bolts (arrowed)

12.6a Undo the pedal pivot shaft bolt

12.6b Withdraw the clutch actuator rod, and release the return spring (arrowed)

12.7a Remove the two clips . . .

12.7b . . . and slacken the securing bolt arrowed (facia removed for clarity)

6 Remove the clutch pedal pivot shaft nut, and slide the pivot shaft bolt out far enough to remove the clutch pedal. Release the return spring from the clutch pedal, and unclip the clutch actuator rod from the pedal **(see illustrations)**. (Make note of the position of the clutch pedal bushes and spacer on removal.)
7 On vehicles built 1/1999 onwards, remove the two clips to release the brake pedal from the pedal assembly, the upper bracket bolt may need to be slackened **(see illustrations)**.
8 Depress the clip and remove the pin from the servo actuator rod **(see illustrations)**.
9 Slide the pivot shaft bolt out to remove the brake pedal **(see illustration)**. (Prise out the bushes from the brake pedal pivot to renew.) Renew the components as necessary.

Refitting
10 Prior to refitting the pedal, apply a little

grease to the pivot shaft, pedal bushes and actuator rods.
11 Refitting is a reversal of the removal procedure, but make sure that the pedal bushes and actuator rods are correctly located.
12 Before fitting the stop-light switch, pull the plunger on the switch out to its full extent. Depress the brake pedal, then fit the switch in place on the bracket. Slowly release the brake pedal, and check the operation of the brake lights.

13 Hydraulic pipes and hoses – inspection, removal and refitting

Note: *Refer to the warning at the start of Section 14 concerning the dangers of brake fluid.*

Inspection
1 Jack up the front and rear of the vehicle, and support on axle stands. Making sure the vehicle is safely supported on a level surface.
2 Check for signs of leakage at the pipe unions, then examine the flexible hoses for signs of cracking, chafing and fraying.
3 The brake pipes should be examined carefully for signs of dents, corrosion or other damage. Corrosion should be scraped off, and if the depth of pitting is significant, the pipes renewed. This is particularly likely in those areas underneath the vehicle body where the pipes are exposed and unprotected.
4 Renew any defective brake pipes and/or hoses.

Removal
5 If a section of pipe or hose is to be removed, loss of brake fluid can be reduced

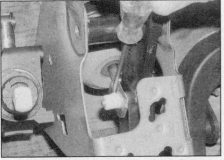

12.8a Using screwdriver to depress clip . . .

12.8b . . . and pull out the pin from the brake actuator rod

12.9 Pull out the pedal pivot shaft bolt

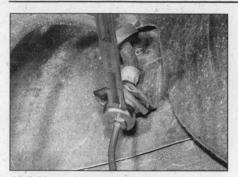

13.7 Unscrewing a brake pipe union using a split ring spanner

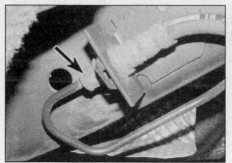

13.9a Slacken the union nut (arrowed) before . . .

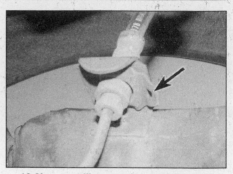

13.9b . . . pulling out the retaining clip (arrowed)

by unscrewing the filler cap, and completely sealing the top of the reservoir with cling film or adhesive tape. Alternatively, the reservoir can be emptied (see Section 11).

6 To remove a section of pipe, hold the adjoining hose union nut with a spanner to prevent it from turning, then unscrew the union nut at the end of the pipe, and release it. Repeat the procedure at the other end of the pipe, then release the pipe by pulling out the clips attaching it to the body.

7 Where the union nuts are exposed to the full force of the weather, they can sometimes be quite tight. If an open-ended spanner is used, burring of the flats on the nuts is not uncommon, and for this reason, it is preferable to use a split ring (brake) spanner **(see illustration)**, which will engage all the flats. If such a spanner is not available, self-locking grips may be used as a last resort; these may well damage the nuts, but if the pipe is to be renewed, this does not matter.

8 To further minimise the loss of fluid when disconnecting a flexible brake line from a rigid pipe, clamp the hose as near as possible to the pipe to be detached, using a brake hose clamp or a pair of self-locking grips with protected jaws.

9 To remove a flexible hose, first clean the ends of the hose and the surrounding area, then unscrew the union nuts from the hose ends. Remove the spring clip, and withdraw the hose from the serrated mounting in the support bracket. Where applicable, unscrew the hose from the caliper **(see illustrations)**.

10 Brake pipes supplied with flared ends and

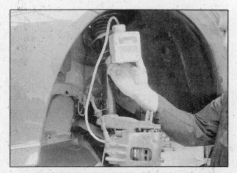

14.7 Hold the container up, to maintain fluid pressure

union nuts can be obtained individually or in sets from Ford dealers or accessory shops. The pipe is then bent to shape, using the old pipe as a guide, and is ready for fitting. Be careful not to kink or crimp the pipe when bending it; ideally, a proper pipe-bending tool should be used.

Refitting

11 Refitting of the pipes and hoses is a reversal of removal. Make sure that all brake pipes are securely supported in their clips, and ensure that the hoses are not kinked. Check also that the hoses are clear of all suspension components and underbody fittings, and will remain clear during movement of the suspension and steering.

12 On completion, bleed the hydraulic system as described in Section 14.

14 Hydraulic system – bleeding

⚠ Warning: Brake fluid contains polyglycol ethers and polyglycols which are poisonous. Take care to keep it off bare skin, and in particular not to get splashes in your eyes. Wash hands thoroughly after handling and if fluid contacts the eyes, flush out with cold running water. If irritation persists get medical attention immediately. The fluid also attacks paintwork and plastics – wash off spillages immediately with cold water. Finally, brake fluid is highly inflammable, and should be handled with the same care as petrol.

Note: On vehicles with ABS, disconnect the battery negative (earth) lead (Chapter 5A, Section 1).

1 If the master cylinder has been disconnected and reconnected, then the complete system (all circuits) must be bled of air. If a component of one circuit has been disturbed, then only that particular circuit need be bled.

2 Bleeding should commence on the furthest bleed nipple from the master cylinder, followed by the next one until the bleed nipple remaining nearest to the master cylinder is bled last.

3 There are a variety of do-it-yourself 'one-man' brake bleeding kits available from motor accessory shops, and it is recommended that one of these kits be used wherever possible, as they greatly simplify the brake bleeding operation. Follow the kit manufacturer's instructions in conjunction with the following procedure. If a pressure-bleeding kit is obtained, then it will not be necessary to depress the brake pedal in the following procedure.

4 During the bleeding operation, do not allow the brake fluid level in the reservoir to drop below the minimum mark. If the level is allowed to fall so far that air is drawn in, the whole procedure will have to be started again from scratch. **Note:** On models fitted with ABS, if air enters the hydraulic unit, the unit must be bled using special Ford test equipment. Only use new fluid for topping-up, preferably from a freshly-opened container. Never re-use fluid bled from the system.

5 Before starting, check that all rigid pipes and flexible hoses are in good condition, and that all hydraulic unions are tight. Take great care not to allow hydraulic fluid to come into contact with the vehicle paintwork, otherwise the finish will be seriously damaged. Wash off any spilt fluid immediately with cold water.

6 If a brake bleeding kit is not being used, gather together a clean jar, a length of plastic or rubber tubing which is a tight fit over the bleed screw, and a new container of the specified brake fluid (see Lubricants and fluids). The help of an assistant will also be required.

7 Clean the area around the bleed screw on the rear brake unit to be bled (it is important that no dirt be allowed to enter the hydraulic system), and remove the dust cap. Connect one end of the tubing to the bleed screw, and immerse the other end in the jar. This should be held at least 300mm above the bleed nipple to maintain fluid pressure to the caliper **(see illustration)**. The jar should be filled with sufficient brake fluid to keep the end of the tube submerged.

8 Open the bleed screw by one or two turns, and have the assistant depress the brake pedal to the floor. Tighten the bleed screw at the end of the down stroke, then have the assistant release the pedal. Continue this

procedure until clean brake fluid, free from air bubbles, can be seen flowing into the jar. Finally tighten the bleed screw with the pedal in the fully-depressed position.

9 Remove the tube, and refit the dust cap. Top-up the master cylinder reservoir if necessary, then repeat the procedure on the opposite rear brake.

10 Repeat the procedure on the front brake furthest from the master cylinder, followed by the brake nearest to the master cylinder.

11 Check the feel of the brake pedal – it should be firm. If it is spongy, there is still some air in the system, and the bleeding procedure should be repeated.

12 When bleeding is complete, top-up the master cylinder reservoir and refit the cap.

13 On models with a hydraulically-operated clutch, check the clutch operation on completion; it may be necessary to bleed the clutch hydraulic system as described in Chapter 6.

15 Vacuum servo unit – testing, removal and refitting

Testing

1 To test the operation of the servo unit, depress the footbrake four or five times to dissipate the vacuum, then start the engine while keeping the footbrake depressed. As the engine starts, there should be a noticeable give in the brake pedal as vacuum builds up. Allow the engine to run for at least two minutes, and then switch it off. If the brake pedal is now depressed again, it should be possible to hear a hiss from the servo when the pedal is depressed. After four or five applications, no further hissing should be heard, and the pedal should feel harder.

2 Before assuming that a problem exists in the servo unit itself, inspect the non-return valve as described in the next Section.

Removal

RHD models

Note: *Where fitted, the air conditioning system will have to be ecacuated.*

15.10 Air conditioning low pressure switch (arrowed)

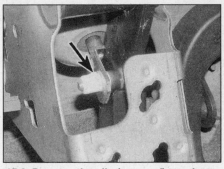
15.6 Depress the clip (arrowed) to release the pivot pin

3 Refer to Section 11 and remove the master cylinder.

4 On vehicles with Stability Assist, disconnect the electrical connector from the brake servo solenoid.

5 Inside the vehicle, remove the driver's side facia lower panel for access to the brake pedal. Disconnect the electrical connectors to the brake pedal switches.

6 Depress the clip and remove the pin from the servo actuator rod **(see illustration)**, then remove the four nuts from the servo unit mounting bracket above the pedals.

7 Under the bonnet, unclip the wiring harness and brake lines from the retaining clips on the bulkhead.

8 Detach the power steering reservoir from its retaining bracket and move to one side **(see illustration)**.

9 On 1.8 litre and 2.0 litre models disconnect the fuel lines from the bulkhead.

10 On vehicles with air conditioning, disconnect the electrical connector from the pressure switch **(see illustration)**.

11 Apply the handbrake. Loosen the right-hand front wheel nuts, then jack up the front of the vehicle and support it on axle stands. Remove the right-hand front wheel.

12 Undo the securing screws from the wheelarch liner and remove from under the right-hand wing.

13 Evacuate the air conditioning as described in Chapter 3. When disconnecting the air conditioning pipes, cap the ends to prevent any contamination.

14 Using a special tool, disconnect the

15.16 On petrol engines, undo the mounting bolt (arrowed)

15.8 Lift the power steering reservoir of its mounting bracket

accumulator air conditioning pipe from the evaporator. Also disconnect the condenser pipe from the evaporator and remove from the vehicle.

15 Unclip the air conditioning pipes, from their brackets under the right-hand wing. Unscrew the bracket and remove the air conditioning pipes from the engine compartment.

16 Undo the bolt from the rear support insulator mounting on the transaxle (except diesels) **(see illustration)**. Refit the wheel and lower the vehicle.

17 Undo the securing bolt from the coolant expansion tank, and move to one side.

18 On 1.4 litre and 1.6 litre models, support the engine with an engine hoist. Undo the three securing bolts from the engine mounting and remove from the vehicle. Move the engine forward about 20mm, taking care not to place excessive force on the remaining engine mountings.

19 On 1.8 litre and 2.0 litre models, remove the alternator as described in Chapter 5A.

20 Withdraw the servo unit from the bulkhead, and remove it from the engine compartment, taking care not to damage any other components **(see illustration)**.

21 Note that the servo unit cannot be dismantled for repair or overhaul and, if faulty, must be renewed.

LHD models

22 Carry out the procedures as described in paragraphs 1 to 4.

23 Release the cover on the hydraulic control unit and disconnect the electrical connector.

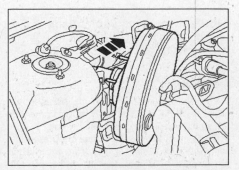
15.20 Withdraw the servo unit from the bulkhead

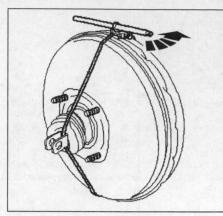

15.31 Compress the brake servo actuator rod before installation

24 Undo the brake pipes to the hydraulic control unit. Cap the end of the pipes and the hydraulic unit to prevent any dirt contamination.
25 Undo the securing bolts from the hydraulic unit and remove from the vehicle.
26 Unclip the brake lines from the retaining clips on the bulkhead.
27 Remove the driver's side facia lower panel for access to the brake pedal.
28 Depress the clip and remove the pin from the servo actuator rod, then remove the four nuts from the servo unit mounting bracket above the pedals.
29 Withdraw the servo unit from the bulkhead, and remove it from the engine compartment, taking care not to damage any other components.
30 Note that the servo unit cannot be dismantled for repair or overhaul and, if faulty, must be renewed.

Refitting

31 Refitting is a reversal of the removal procedure, noting the following points:
 a) *Refer to the relevant Sections/Chapters for details of refitting the other components removed.*
 b) *Compress the actuator rod into the brake servo, before refitting (see illustration).*
 c) *Make sure the gasket is correctly positioned on the servo.*
 d) *Test the brakes carefully before returning the vehicle to normal service.*

16 Vacuum servo unit vacuum hose and non-return valve – removal, testing and refitting

Removal

1 With the engine switched off, depress the brake pedal four or five times, to dissipate any remaining vacuum from the servo unit.
2 Disconnect the vacuum hose adapter at the servo unit, by pulling it free from the rubber grommet. If it is reluctant to move, prise it free, using a screwdriver with its blade inserted under the flange.

16.5 Non-return valve in brake vacuum hose

3 Detach the vacuum hose from the inlet manifold connection, pressing in the collar to disengage the tabs, then withdrawing the collar slowly.
4 If the hose or the fixings are damaged or in poor condition, they must be renewed.

Testing

5 Examine the non-return valve **(see illustration)** for damage and signs of deterioration, and renew it if necessary. The valve may be tested by blowing through its connecting hoses in both directions. It should only be possible to blow from the servo end towards the inlet manifold.

Refitting

6 Refitting is a reversal of the removal procedure. If fitting a new non-return valve, ensure that it is fitted the correct way round.

17 Pressure-conscious regulator valve (non-ABS models) – removal and refitting

Note: *Refer to the warning at the start of Section 14 concerning the dangers of brake fluid.*

Removal

1 On non-ABS models, the two pressure-conscious regulator valves are located on the master cylinder outlets to the rear brake circuits **(see illustration)**.
2 Unscrew the fluid reservoir filler cap, and draw off the fluid – see Section 11.

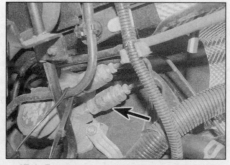

17.1 Pressure-conscious control relief valves (arrowed)

3 Position some rags beneath the master cylinder, to catch any spilled fluid.
4 Clean around the valve to be removed. Hold the valve stationary with one spanner, and unscrew the hydraulic pipe union nut with another spanner. Pull out the pipe, and bend it slightly away from the valve, taking care not to kink the pipe.
5 Unscrew the valve from the master cylinder and plug the master cylinder to prevent dirt contamination.

Refitting

6 Refitting is a reversal of the removal procedure. On completion, bleed the hydraulic system as described in Section 14.

18 Pressure-conscious regulator valves (ABS models) – general information

1 The pressure conscious regulator valves are built into the ABS hydraulic unit.
2 Electronic brake force distribution (EBD) takes the place of the pressure-conscious regulator valves (PCRVs) and load-sensing valves (LAVs) used in the conventional braking systems.
3 The EBD function is an additional programme (software) to the conventional ABS programme that allows greater use of the rear brakes up to the point of ABS operation.
4 The EBD function can come into operation during regular braking, depending on the loading of the vehicle and the surface friction.
5 In contrast to the PCRVs or LAVs, during the EBD control the brake force is determined not by the brake pressure or the vehicle speed but by the wheel slip.

19 ABS hydraulic unit – removal and refitting

Note: *At the time of writing, no parts for the ABS hydraulic unit (see illustration opposite) where available, and it must therefore be renewed as an assembly. Refer to the warning at the start of Section 14 concerning the dangers of brake fluid.*

Removal

1 Disconnect the battery negative lead. **Note:** *Before disconnecting the battery, refer to Chapter 5A, Section 1, for precautions.*
2 Disconnect the low fluid level warning light multi-plug from the fluid reservoir. Unscrew the cap.
3 Draw off the hydraulic fluid from the reservoir, using an old battery hydrometer or similar. Alternatively raise the vehicle and remove the wheels. Slacken the front bleed nipples and drain the fluid from the reservoir.
4 Lower the vehicle. Undo the securing bolts from the air filter housing and intake tube, then remove from the vehicle.

5 Disconnect the electrical connector from the auxiliary fusebox. Remove the retaining screw, and detach the fusebox from its bracket. Move the fusebox to the air filter housing position temporarily.

6 Release the cover on the hydraulic control unit and disconnect the electrical connector.

7 Undo the six brake pipes to the hydraulic control unit. Cap the end of the pipes and the hydraulic unit to prevent any dirt contamination. Unclip the brake lines from the retaining clips on the bulkhead.

8 On LHD models, disconnect the brake pipes from the master cylinder.

9 Detach the wiring loom from the suspension turret.

10 Undo the securing bolts from the brake hydraulic unit, and withdraw from the bulkhead. Remove it from the engine compartment, taking care not to damage any other components.

Refitting

11 Refitting is a reversal of removal. Ensure that the multi-plug is securely connected, and that the brake pipe unions are tightened to the specified torque. On completion, bleed the hydraulic system as described in Section 14. **Note:** *If air enters the hydraulic unit, the unit must be bled using special Ford test equipment.*

20 ABS wheel sensor –
testing, removal and refitting

Testing

1 Checking of the sensors is done before removal, connecting a voltmeter to the disconnected sensor multi-plug. Using an analogue (moving coil) meter is not practical, since the meter does not respond quickly enough. A digital meter having an ac facility may be used to check that the sensor is operating correctly.

2 To do this, raise the relevant wheel then

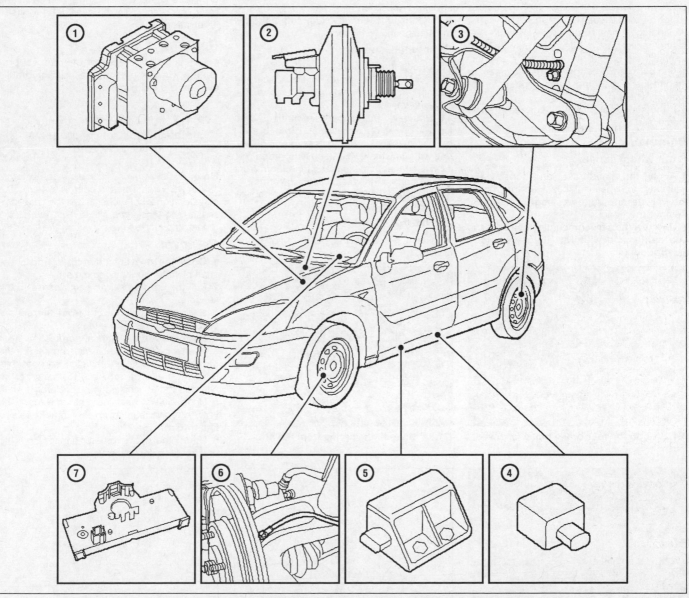

19.1 ABS – Stability Assist components (LHD shown)

1 ABS Hydraulic Control Unit
2 Brake servo and master cylinder
3 Rear wheel sensor
4 Lateral acceleration sensor
5 Yaw rate sensor
6 Front wheel sensor
7 Steering wheel rotation sensor

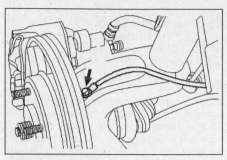

20.7 Undo the mounting bolt (arrowed) to remove the front wheel sensor

disconnect the wiring to the ABS sensor and connect the meter to it.

3 Spin the wheel and check that the output voltage is between 1.5 and 2.0 volts, depending on how fast the wheel is spun.

4 Alternatively, an oscilloscope may be used to check the output of the sensor – an alternating current will be traced on the screen, of magnitude depending on the speed of the rotating wheel.

5 If the sensor output is low or zero, renew the sensor.

Removal
Front wheel sensor

6 Apply the handbrake and loosen the relevant front wheel nuts. Jack up the front of the vehicle and support it on axle stands. Remove the wheel.

7 Unscrew the sensor mounting bolt from the hub carrier and withdraw the sensor (see illustration).

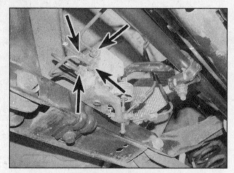

21.2 Undo the four brake pipes (arrowed)

21.3b . . . then undo the securing bolt (arrowed)

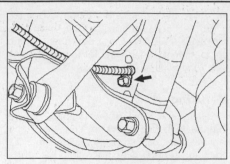

20.11 Undo the mounting bolt (arrowed) to remove the rear wheel sensor

8 Remove the sensor wiring loom from the support brackets on the front suspension strut and wheelarch.

9 Disconnect the multi-plug, and withdraw the sensor and wiring loom.

Rear wheel sensor

10 Chock the front wheels, and engage 1st gear (or P). Jack up the rear of the vehicle and support it on axle stands. Remove the relevant wheel.

11 Unscrew the sensor mounting bolt, located on the brake backplate (drum brakes) or rear suspension hub carrier (disc brakes), and withdraw the sensor (see illustration).

12 Disconnect the sensor wiring loom from the supports on the rear suspension arms.

13 Disconnect the multi-plug, and withdraw the sensor and wiring loom.

Refitting

14 Refitting is a reversal of the removal procedure.

21.3a Unhook the spring from the arm . . .

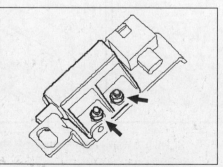

22.5 Undo the two nuts (arrowed) to remove the yaw rate sensor

21 Load-sensing valve (LAV) – removal and refitting

Note: *This Section only applies to the Estate model without ABS.*

Removal

1 Disconnect the battery negative (earth) lead (see Chapter 5A, Section 1).

2 Slacken and remove the four brake pipe unions from the side of the valve (see illustration). Cap the ends of the brake lines to minimise fluid loss.

3 Disengage the spring from the adjusting arm, and undo the securing bolt from the retaining bracket to remove the valve (see illustrations).

Refitting

4 Refitting is a reversal of the removal procedure. On completion, bleed the hydraulic system as described in Section 14.

22 Traction control/Electronic stability control components – removal and refitting

Note: *This system uses the same components as the ABS and Traction control system. The only additional components are the 'yaw rate' sensor and 'accelerometer sensor', which are mounted on the same bracket on the inner sill.*

Removal

1 Open the relevant door, then unclip the scuff plate trim from along the sill.

2 Pull the carpet back to gain access to the sensors.

3 Undo the retaining bolt from the sensor bracket and detach from the sill.

4 Disconnect the electrical connectors from the sensor. One connector is to measure the movement about the vehicles vertical axis (yaw rate) and the other is to measure the vehicles lateral acceleration (accelerometer).

5 Undo the two retaining nuts, to remove the yaw rate sensor from the bracket (see illustration).

6 Unclip the Accelerometer sensor from the bracket (see illustration).

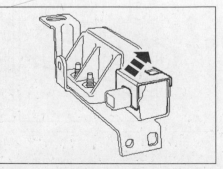

22.6 Unclip the accelerometer sensor (arrowed) from the mounting bracket

Refitting

7 Refitting is a reversal of the removal procedure.

23 Traction control system – general information

1 The Traction control system is an expanded version of the ABS system. It is integrated with the ABS, and uses the same wheel sensors. It also uses the hydraulic control unit, which incorporates additional internal solenoid valves.
2 To remove the hydraulic unit or wheel sensors, carry out the procedures as described in Sections 19 and 20.

24 Stop-light switch – removal, refitting and adjustment

Removal

1 Disconnect the battery negative (earth) lead (see Chapter 5A, Section 1).
2 Undo the four screws and prise out the retaining clip to remove the facia lower panel. Unclip the multi-plug from the trim panel.
3 Disconnect the wiring connector from the brake light switch.
4 Rotate the switch clockwise by a quarter-turn, and withdraw it from the pedal bracket. (If the switch is fitted in the upper part of the pedal bracket then rotate the switch anti-clockwise to remove.)

26.2 Unclip the handbrake gaiter

26.3 Slacken off the cable adjustment

25.3 Disconnecting the electrical connector from the switch

Refitting and adjustment

5 With the switch removed, reset it by fully extending its plunger.
6 Depress the brake pedal and hold in this position, then refit the stop-light switch to the mounting bracket.
7 With the switch securely clipped in position, release the brake pedal, and gently pull it fully back to the at-rest position. This will automatically set the adjustment of the stop-light switch.
8 Reconnect the wiring connector and the battery, and check the operation of the switch prior to refitting the facia lower panel.

25 Handbrake lever – removal and refitting

Removal

1 Chock the front wheels, and engage 1st gear (or P).
2 Remove the centre console as described in Chapter 11.
3 Disconnect the electrical connector from the handbrake switch (see illustration).
4 Undo the lock nut and slacken the handbrake adjusting nuts (see illustration).
5 Unscrew the two mounting bolts securing the handbrake lever to the floor.
6 Withdraw the handbrake from inside the vehicle.

Refitting

7 Refitting is a reversal of removal.

26.4 Move the heat shield along the exhaust

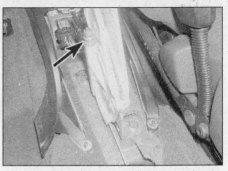
25.4 Undo the nuts (arrowed) to slacken the handbrake cable

8 When refitting the lever, it will be necessary to reset the mechanism, as follows.
9 Lift the handbrake lever up four notches, then tighten the adjustment nut until the slack in the cable has been taken up. Refit the locking nut.
10 Check the operation of the handbrake several times before returning the vehicle to normal service.

26 Handbrake cables – removal and refitting

Removal

1 Chock the front wheels, and engage 1st gear (or P). Loosen the wheel nuts on the relevant rear wheel, then jack up the rear of the vehicle and support it on axle stands. Fully release the handbrake lever.
2 Unclip the gaiter from around the handbrake lever and remove (see illustration).
3 Undo the locking nut and slacken off the handbrake adjusting nut (see illustration).
4 Working beneath the vehicle, unbolt the exhaust heat shield(s) from the underbody (see illustration). Move them along the exhaust to gain access to the cables.
5 If required, release the exhaust system from the rubber mountings. Lower the exhaust system as far as possible, supporting it on blocks or more axle stands.
6 Remove the relevant rear wheel and unclip the handbrake outer cable from its retaining clips (see illustration).

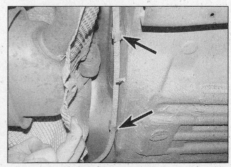
26.6 Unclip the cable from the retaining clips (arrowed)

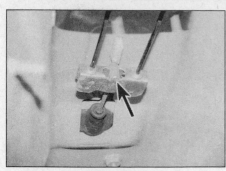

26.7a Twist the cable (arrowed) to disengage

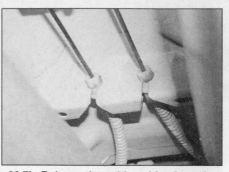

26.7b Release the cable guides from the bracket

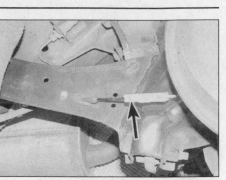

26.9 Release the cable from the sleeve (arrowed)

26.11 Remove the bolt arrowed to release the cable guide

7 Turn the cable through 90° to unhook the relevant cable from the equaliser bar. Lever the plastic cable guide from its bracket **(see illustrations)**.

8 On vehicles with ABS disconnect the brake system sensor.

9 On drum brake models, unclip the handbrake cable from the sleeve in front of the brake drum **(see illustration)**. On some models you may need to remove the rear brake shoes on the relevant side as described in Section 6, then remove the cable outer from the backplate by compressing the retaining lugs and pushing the cable through.

10 On disc brake models, push the caliper handbrake arm towards the front of the car, and unhook the end of the cable inner from the arm. Remove the cable outer from the caliper bracket.

11 Unbolt the outer cable guide from the tie-bar, then disconnect it from its retaining clip

(see illustration). Withdraw the cable from beneath the vehicle.

Refitting

12 Refitting is a reversal of the removal procedure, noting the following points:
  a) *Adjust the cable as described in Section 25.*
  b) *Make sure that the cable end fittings are correctly located*
  c) *Check the operation of the handbrake. Make sure that both wheels are locked, then free to turn, as the handbrake is operated.*

27 Vacuum pump (diesel models) – removal and refitting

Removal

1 Disconnect the battery negative lead (see Chapter 5A, Section 1).

2 Remove the air intake/intercooler as described in Chapter 4B.

3 Unscrew the union nut and disconnect the vacuum line from the top of the pump **(see illustration)**.

4 Release the retaining clips and disconnect the oil separator/return hose(s) from the cylinder head cover.

5 Unbolt the air intake hoses from the top of the cylinder head cover, and detach the breather hoses.

6 Unbolt and remove the cylinder head camshaft cover.

7 Using a suitable socket or spanner on the crankshaft pulley bolt, turn the crankshaft until the vacuum pump pushrod (operated by the eccentric on the camshaft end) is fully retracted into the cylinder head.

8 Disconnect the electrical connectors from the heater/glow plug, the engine temperature sensor and the oil pressure switch.

9 Release the retaining clips and disconnect the oil separator/return hose(s) from the pump. Be prepared for some oil spillage as the hose is disconnected and mop up any spilt oil.

10 Evenly and progressively slacken the bolts securing the pump to the front of the cylinder head **(see illustration)**. Note that there is no need to remove the lower bolt completely, as the lower end of the pump is slotted.

11 Remove the pump from the engine compartment, along with its sealing ring **(see illustration)**. Discard the sealing ring, a new one should be used on refitting.

Refitting

12 Refitting is a reversal of removal, noting the following points:
  a) *Ensure the pump and cylinder head mating surfaces are clean and dry. Fit the new sealing ring to the pump recess.*
  b) *Start the engine and check for correct operation of the pump (check brakes have servo action) as described in Section 16.*
  c) *Make sure all the hose connections are secure, and check for leaks.*

27.3 Undo the vacuum pipe from the top of the pump

27.10 Loosen the bolts of evenly, then remove the top bolt

27.11 Renew the sealing ring when refitting the brake vacuum pump

28 Vacuum pump (diesel models) – testing and overhaul

Note: *A vacuum gauge will be required for this check*.

1 The operation of the braking system vacuum pump can be checked using a vacuum gauge.

2 Disconnect the vacuum pipe from the pump, and connect the gauge to the pump union using a suitable length of hose.

3 Start the engine and allow it to idle, then measure the vacuum created by the pump. As a guide, after one minute, a minimum of approximately 500 mm Hg should be recorded. If the vacuum registered is significantly less than this, it is likely that the pump is faulty. However, seek the advice of a Ford dealer before condemning the pump.

4 Overhaul of the vacuum pump is not possible, since no components are available separately. If faulty, the complete pump assembly must be renewed.

Notes

Chapter 10
Suspension and steering systems

Contents

Degrees of difficulty

Easy, suitable for novice with little experience	**Fairly easy,** suitable for beginner with some experience	**Fairly difficult,** suitable for competent DIY mechanic	**Difficult,** suitable for experienced DIY mechanic	**Very difficult,** suitable for expert DIY or professional

Specifications

Front wheel alignment
Toe setting:
  Tolerance allowed before resetting required . . . .   1.5 mm toe-in to 1.5 mm toe-out (0°15' toe-in to 0°15' toe-out)
  Adjustment setting (if required) . . . .   1.0 mm toe-in to 1.0 mm toe-out (0°10' toe-in to 0°10' toe-out)

Rear wheel alignment
Toe setting:
  Tolerance allowed before resetting required . . . .   5.0 mm toe-in to 0.8 mm toe-in (0°49' toe-in to 0°08' toe-in)
  Adjustment setting (if required) . . . .   2.9 mm toe-in ± 1.2 mm (0°28' toe-in ± 0°12')

Roadwheels and tyres
Wheel sizes:
  Steel . . . .   14 x 5 1/2
  Alloy . . . .   15 x 6
  Alloy (option pack) . . . .   16 x 6
Tyre sizes:
  Wheel size 14 x 5 1/2 . . . .   175/70R14T or 185/65R14H
  Wheel size 15 x 6 . . . .   195/55R15H or 195/60R15V
  Wheel size 16 x 6 . . . .   205/50R16V
Tyre pressures . . . .   See *Weekly checks*

Torque wrench settings

	Nm	lbf ft
Front suspension		
Anti-roll bar clamp bolts:		
Stage 1	50	37
Stage 2	70	52
Anti-roll bar link	50	37
Brake caliper guide bolts	28	21
Driveshaft/hub retaining nut	316	233
Front subframe/crossmember:		
Front bolts (two)	115	85
Rear bolts (four)	200	148
Insulator support bracket-to-transaxle centre bolt	50	37
Lower arm balljoint-to-steering knuckle clamp bolt	50	37
Lower arm to subframe:		
Stage 1 (inner rear nut)	100	74
Stage 2 (inner rear nut)	Tighten through further 60°	
Stage 3 (outer rear nut)	120	89
Stage 4 (front bolt)	120	89
Stage 5 (front bolt)	Tighten through further 90°	
Stage 6 (front bolt)	Check front bolt torque is between 170 and 230	125 and 170
Suspension strut thrust bearing retaining nut	48	35
Suspension strut-to-steering knuckle pinch-bolt	90	66
Suspension strut upper mounting nuts (three)	25	18
Rear suspension		
Anti-roll bar clamp bolts	48	35
Anti-roll bar link to lower arm	15	11
Brake caliper bracket bolts	55	41
Brake caliper guide bolts	35	26
Crossmember mounting bolts	115	85
Front lower arm mounting bolts	115	85
Hub nut	235	173
Rear lower arm to crossmember	115	85
Rear lower arm to knuckle	115	85
Shock absorber to knuckle	115	85
Shock absorber upper bolt (Estate)	115	85
Shock absorber upper nut (except Estate)	18	13
Spindle/hub retaining bolts	66	49
Tie-bar/control blade front mounting bracket securing bolts	115	85
Upper arm mounting bolts	115	85
Steering		
Flexible coupling-to-pinion shaft clamp bolt:		
Two bolts – early models	25	18
One bolt – later models	28	21
Power steering pipe unions-to-valve body clamp plate bolt	23	17
Roadwheel nuts	85	63
Steering column retaining locknuts	18	13
Steering column Torx bolt	23	17
Steering coupling-to-steering gear clamp bolt	35	26
Steering gear mounting bolts	80	59
Steering pump mounting bolts	23	17
Steering pump pressure line union	65	48
Steering wheel	50	37
Track rod end locknut	63	46
Track rod end balljoint to steering knuckle	47	35

1 General information

The independent front suspension is of MacPherson strut type, incorporating coil springs, integral telescopic shock absorbers, and an anti-roll bar. The struts are attached to steering knuckles at their lower ends, and the knuckles are in turn attached to the lower suspension arm by balljoints. The anti-roll bar is bolted to the rear of the subframe/crossmember, and is connected to the front suspension struts by links.

The new fully independent rear suspension is of a Control Blade multi-link type. There are three arms on each side: one forged upper arm, and two pressed-steel lower side arms. The Control Blade on the Focus is used in place of the Mondeo's trailing arm and cast knuckle, and are of a one-piece pressed steel construction. As well as being substantially lighter, the single pressing makes it easier to assemble. The coil springs are separate from the shock absorbers and a rear anti-roll bar is fitted to all models **(see illustrations)**.

A Power steering type rack-and-pinion steering gear is fitted, together with a conventional column and telescopic coupling, incorporating a universal joint. The power steering has a relatively 'quick' rack with just 2.9 turns lock-to-lock and a turning circle of 10.9 metres. A power steering system fluid cooler is fitted in front of the cooling system radiator on the crossmember.

When working on the suspension or steering, you may come across nuts or bolts which seem impossible to loosen. These nuts and bolts on the underside of the vehicle are continually subjected to water, road grime, mud, etc, and can become rusted or seized, making them extremely difficult to remove. In order to unscrew these stubborn nuts and bolts without damaging them (or other components), use lots of penetrating oil, and allow it to soak in for a while. Using a wire brush to clean exposed threads will also ease removal of the nut or bolt, and will help to prevent damage to the threads. Sometimes, a sharp blow with a hammer and punch will break the bond between a nut and bolt, but care must be taken to prevent the punch from slipping off and ruining the threads. Using a

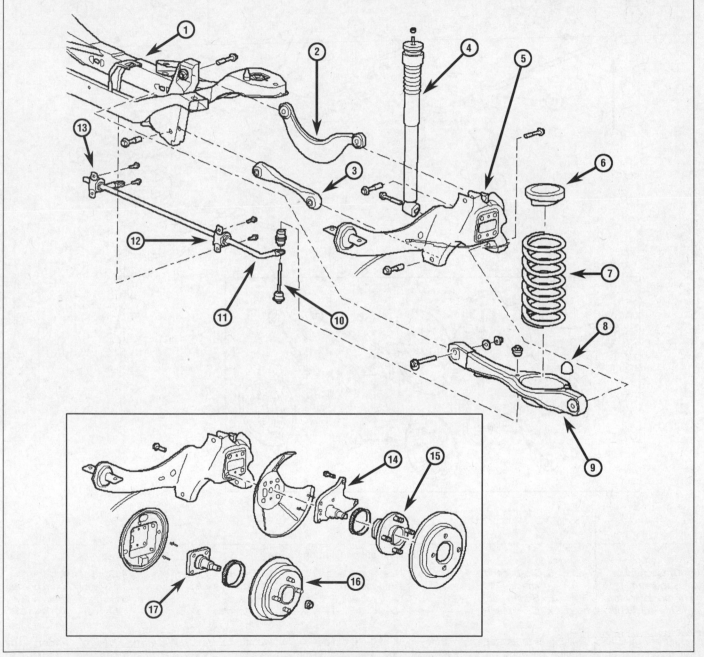

1.2a Rear suspension on Hatchback and Saloon

1 Crossmember	5 Tie-bar and knuckle	9 Rear lower arm	13 Anti-roll bar clamp	16 Drum and hub
2 Upper arm	6 Spring pad	10 Anti-roll bar link	14 Stub axle (disc	assembly (drum brakes)
3 Front lower arm	7 Coil spring	11 Anti-roll bar	brakes)	17 Stub axle (drum
4 Shock absorber (damper)	8 Rubber bump stop	12 Anti-roll bar bush	15 Hub (disc brakes)	brakes)

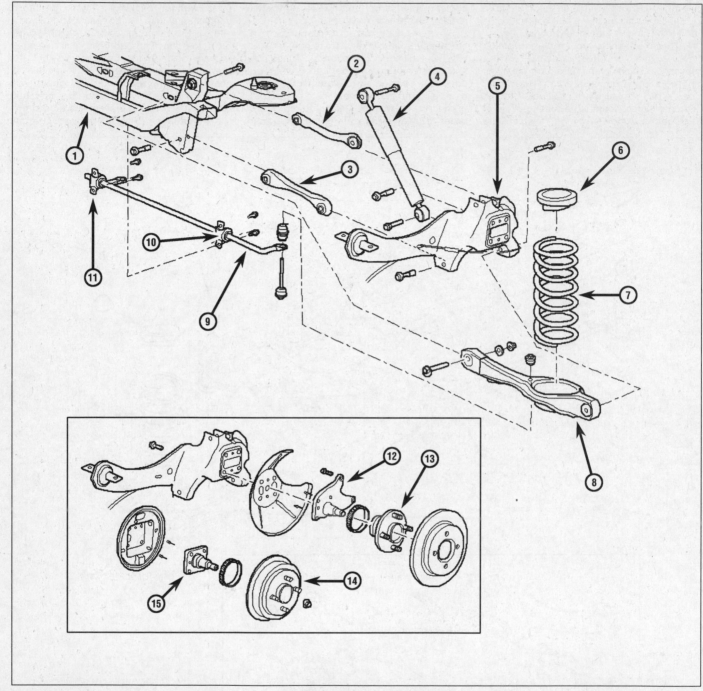

1.2b Rear suspension on Estate

1 Crossmember	5 Tie-bar and	8 Rear lower arm	11 Anti-roll bar clamp	14 Drum and hub
2 Upper arm	knuckle	9 Anti-roll bar	12 Stub axle (disc	assembly (drum brakes)
3 Front lower arm	6 Spring pad	10 Anti-roll bar	brakes)	15 Stub axle (drum
4 Shock absorber (damper)	7 Coil spring	bush	13 Hub (disc brakes)	brakes)

longer bar or spanner will increase leverage, but never use an extension bar/pipe on a ratchet, as the internal mechanism could be damaged. Actually *tightening* the nut or bolt slightly first, may help to break it loose. Nuts or bolts which have required drastic measures to remove them should always be renewed.

Since most of the procedures dealt with in this Chapter involve jacking up the vehicle and working underneath it, a good pair of axle stands will be needed. A hydraulic trolley jack is the preferred type of jack to lift the vehicle, and it can also be used to support certain components during removal and refitting operations.

⚠️ **Warning: Never, under any circumstances, rely on a jack to support the vehicle while working beneath it. It is not recommended, when jacking up the rear of the vehicle, to lift beneath the rear crossmember.**

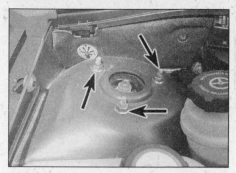

2.2 Loosen the three nuts (arrowed), but do not remove

2.4 Leave the nut on a couple of turns to save damaging the threads

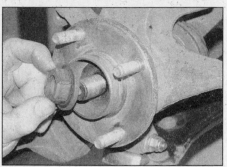

2.7 Unscrew the driveshaft/hub nut

The nut can only be re-used up to four times

2 Steering knuckle and hub assembly – removal and refitting

Removal

1 Apply the handbrake. Remove the wheel cover from the relevant front wheel, and loosen (but do not remove) the driveshaft/hub nut. This nut is very tight – use only good quality, close fitting tools, and take adequate precautions against personal injury when loosening the hub nut.

2 Loosen the three top strut nuts by at least five turns (but do not remove) **(see illustration)**.

3 Loosen the front wheel nuts, jack up the front of the vehicle and support it on axle stands. Remove the front wheel.

4 Unscrew the track rod end balljoint nut, and detach the rod from the arm on the steering knuckle using a conventional balljoint removal tool **(see illustration)**. Take care not to damage the balljoint seal.

5 Remove the ABS sensor (when fitted) as described in Chapter 9.

6 Remove the brake caliper and brake disc as described in Chapter 9. Suspend the caliper from a suitable point under the wheelarch, taking care not to damage or strain the hose.

7 Unscrew and remove the driveshaft/hub nut **(see illustration)**. **Note:** *The nut is of special*

laminated design, and should only be re-used a maximum of 4 times. (It is a good idea to file a small notch on the nut every time it is removed.) Obtain a new nut if necessary.

8 Note which way round the lower arm balljoint clamp bolt is fitted, then unscrew and remove it from the knuckle assembly **(see illustration)**. Lever the balljoint down from the knuckle; if it is tight, prise the clamp open using a large flat-bladed tool. Take care not to damage the balljoint seal during the separation procedure.

9 Pull the steering knuckle and hub assembly from the driveshaft splines **(see illustration)**. If it is tight, connect a universal puller to the hub flange, and withdraw it from the driveshaft. When the driveshaft is free, support it on an axle stand, or suspend it from a suitable point under the wheelarch, making sure that the inner constant velocity joint is not turned through more than 18°. (Damage may occur if the joint is turned through too great an angle.)

10 Unscrew and remove the pinch-bolt securing the steering knuckle assembly to the front suspension strut, noting which way round it is fitted **(see illustration)**. Prise open the clamp using a wedge-shaped tool, and release the knuckle from the strut. If necessary, tap the knuckle downwards with a soft-headed mallet to separate the two components.

Refitting

11 Locate the assembly on the front

suspension strut. Insert the pinch-bolt with its head facing the same way as removal. Fit the nut and tighten it to the specified torque.

12 Pull the steering knuckle/hub assembly outwards, and insert the driveshaft to engage the splines in the hub. Ford use a special tool to draw the driveshaft into the hub, but it is unlikely that the splines will be tight. However, if they are, it will be necessary to obtain the tool, or to use a similar home-made tool.

13 Refit the lower arm balljoint to the knuckle assembly, and insert the clamp bolt with its head facing the same way as removal. Refit the nut and tighten it to the specified torque.

14 Refit the driveshaft/hub nut, and tighten it moderately at this stage. Final tightening of the nut is made with the vehicle lowered to the ground.

15 Refit the brake caliper and brake disc as described in Chapter 9. Refitting the brake hose support bracket to the strut.

16 Where fitted, refit the ABS sensor as described in Chapter 9.

17 Reconnect the track rod end balljoint to the steering knuckle, and tighten the nut to the specified torque.

18 Refit the front wheel, and lower the vehicle to the ground. Tighten the three top strut mounting bolts to the specified torque.

19 Tighten the driveshaft/hub nut and wheel nuts to their specified torque, then refit the wheel cover.

2.8 Removing the bolt from the bottom balljoint

2.9 Carefully pull driveshaft from the hub and support it on an axle stand

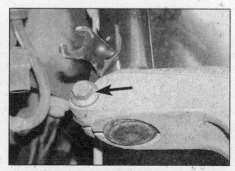

2.10 Steering knuckle to strut pinch-bolt (arrowed)

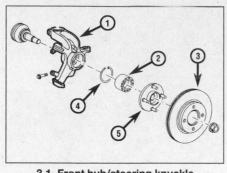

3.1 Front hub/steering knuckle components

1	Steering	3	Brake disc
	knuckle	4	Circlip
2	Wheel bearing	5	Hub

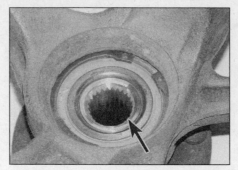

3.5 Press the centre hub (arrowed) out of the bearing

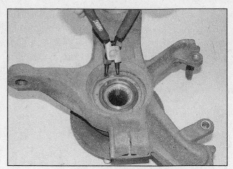

3.8 Removing the circlip from the steering knuckle

---

3 Front hub and bearings – inspection and renewal

Inspection

1 The front hub bearings are non-adjustable, and are supplied already greased (see illustration).
2 To check the bearings for excessive wear, apply the handbrake, jack up the front of the vehicle and support it on axle stands.
3 Grip the front wheel at the top and the bottom, and attempt to rock it. If excessive movement is noted, it may be that the hub bearings are worn. Do not confuse wear in the

driveshaft outer joint or front suspension lower arm balljoint with wear in the bearings. Hub bearing wear will show up as roughness or vibration when the wheel is spun; it will also be noticeable as a rumbling or growling noise when driving.
Note: *Removal of the front hub may damage the bearings, and render them unserviceable for future use. When renewing the hub, the bearing assembly must always be renewed.*

Renewal

4 Remove the steering knuckle and hub assembly as described in Section 2.
5 The hub must now be removed from the bearing inner races. It is preferable to use a press to do this, but it is possible to drive out the hub using a length of metal tube of suitable diameter (see illustration).
6 Part of the inner race may remain on the hub, and this should be removed using a puller.

7 Note that when renewing the hub, the wheel bearing will have to be renewed also, as it may be damaged on removal.
8 Using circlip pliers, extract the circlip securing the hub bearing in the steering knuckle (see illustration).
9 Press or drive out the bearing, using a length of metal tubing of diameter slightly less than the bearing outer race.
10 Clean the bearing seating faces in the steering knuckle.
11 Using a length of metal tube of diameter slightly less than the outer race, press or drive the new bearing into the knuckle until it is fully located. Do not apply any pressure to the inner race. **Note:** *The black side of the bearing must face towards the ABS wheel speed sensor.*
12 Locate the circlip into the groove in the knuckle, taking care not to cover the wheel speed sensor with the circlip.
13 Support the inner race on a length of metal tube, then press or drive the hub fully into the bearing.
14 Refit the steering knuckle and hub assembly as described in Section 2.

---

4 Front suspension strut assembly – removal and refitting

Removal

1 Disconnect the brake hose from the bracket on the strut (see illustration).
2 Remove the nut from the anti-roll bar link and disconnect it from the strut (see illustration). On models fitted with ABS, disconnect the wheel sensor wiring.
3 Unscrew and remove the pinch-bolt securing the steering knuckle assembly to the front suspension strut, noting which way round it is fitted. Lever the steering knuckle/hub assembly down and release it from the strut (see illustrations). If necessary, tap the knuckle downwards with a soft-headed mallet to separate the two components. **Note:** *Support the steering knuckle/hub assembly when released from the strut, to prevent any damage to the driveshaft.*
4 Support the strut/spring assembly under the wheelarch, then remove the upper mounting nuts (see illustration).

4.1 Unclip the brake hose from the strut

4.2 Undo the anti-roll bar link rod securing nut

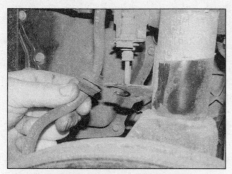

4.3a Lever the hub assembly down . . .

4.3b . . . and disengage the strut

4.4 Remove the three upper mounting nuts

5.3 Make sure spring compressor tool is on securely

5.4 Slacken and remove the retaining nut

5 Lower the suspension strut from under the wheelarch, withdrawing it from the vehicle.

Refitting

6 Refitting is a reversal of removal. Making sure that all the relevant bolts are tightened to their specified torque.

5 Front suspension strut – overhaul

⚠ *Warning: Before attempting to dismantle the front suspension strut, a tool to hold the coil spring in compression must be obtained. Do not attempt to use makeshift methods. Uncontrolled release of the spring could cause damage and personal injury. Use a high-quality spring compressor, and*

carefully follow the tool manufacturer's instructions provided with it. After removing the coil spring with the compressor still fitted, place it in a safe, isolated area.

1 If the front suspension struts exhibit signs of wear (leaking fluid, loss of damping capability, sagging or cracked coil springs) then they should be dismantled and overhauled as necessary. The struts themselves cannot be serviced, and should be renewed if faulty; the springs and related components can be renewed individually. To maintain balanced characteristics on both sides of the vehicle, the components on both sides should be renewed at the same time.

2 With the strut removed from the vehicle (see Section 4), clean away all external dirt, then mount it in a vice.

3 Fit the coil spring compressor tools (ensuring that they are fully engaged), and compress the spring until all tension is

relieved from the upper mounting **(see illustration)**.

4 Hold the strut piston rod with an Allen key, and unscrew the thrust bearing retaining nut with a ring spanner **(see illustration)**.

5 Withdraw the top mounting, thrust bearing, upper spring seat and spring, followed by the gaiter and the bump stop **(see illustrations)**.

6 If a new spring is to be fitted, the original spring must now be carefully released from the compressor. If it is to be re-used, the spring can be left in compression.

7 With the strut assembly now completely dismantled, examine all the components for wear and damage, and check the bearing for smoothness of operation. Renew components as necessary **(see illustration)**.

8 Examine the strut for signs of fluid leakage. Check the strut piston rod for signs of pitting along its entire length, and check the strut body for signs of damage. Test the operation of the strut, while holding it in an upright position, by moving the piston through a full stroke, and then through short strokes of 50 to 100 mm. In both cases, the resistance felt should be smooth and continuous. If the resistance is jerky, uneven, or if there is any visible sign of wear or damage to the strut, renewal is necessary.

5.5a Remove the upper bearing and spring seat . . .

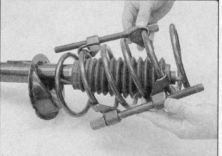

5.5b . . . then carefully remove the spring . . .

5.5c . . . followed by the gaiter . . .

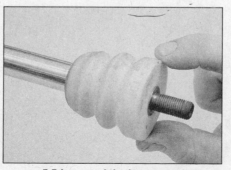

5.5d . . . and the bump stop

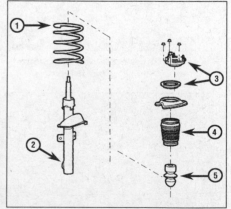

5.7 Front suspension strut components

1 Coil Spring	4 Gaiter
2 Strut	5 Rubber bump
3 Upper mounting	stop
with bearing	

9 Reassembly is a reversal of dismantling, noting the following points:
  a) *Make sure that the coil spring ends are correctly located in the upper and lower seats before releasing the compressor* **(see illustration)**.
  b) *Check that the bearing is correctly fitted to the piston rod seat.*
  c) *Tighten the thrust bearing retaining nut to the specified torque.*
  d) *The coil springs must be installed with the paint mark at the bottom.*

6 Front crossmember/ anti-roll bar and links – removal and refitting

Removal

Note: *Before disconnecting the battery, refer to Chapter 5A, Section 1.*

1 Disconnect the battery negative terminal.
2 Apply the handbrake, jack up the front of the vehicle and support it on axle stands.
3 Centre the steering wheel and lock in position. Remove both the front wheels.
4 Undo the track rod end balljoint nuts on both sides of the vehicle, and detach the rods from the arms on the steering knuckles using a conventional balljoint removal tool **(see illustration)**. Take care not to damage the balljoint seals.
5 Undo the connecting link bottom balljoint nuts, and disconnect them from the anti-roll bar on both sides of the vehicle **(see illustration)**. Use a balljoint removal tool if required taking care not to damage the balljoint seal.
6 Disconnect the steering column shaft from the pinion extension; by removing the securing bolt at the lower part of the steering column the shaft will then pull apart **(see illustration)**. On very early models there are two bolts, remove the lower bolt and loosen the upper bolt to disconnect the steering column shaft.
7 On diesel models remove the engine undertray.
8 Remove the bolt from the insulator support bracket on the rear of the transaxle unit **(see illustration)**.
9 Using a suitable jack, support the crossmember. Remove the six crossmember securing bolts **(see illustrations)**, and carefully lower the crossmember to gain access to the anti-roll bar clamps. There is a special tool to align the bolt holes in the crossmember on refitting. If this is not available mark the mounting points, so as to refit in the correct position.
10 Unscrew and remove the anti-roll bar mounting bolts from the crossmember on both sides of the vehicle **(see illustration)**.
11 Withdraw the anti-roll bar from the crossmember, taking care not to damage the surrounding components.
12 To remove the anti-roll bar connecting links from the strut assembly, undo the top balljoint nuts and detach from the strut bracket **(see illustration)**.
13 If the crossmember requires removing completely, remove the lower suspension arms and steering rack as described in Sections 7 and 20.

5.9 Spring located in the lower seat (arrowed)

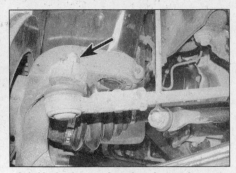
6.4 Undo the track rod end securing nut (arrowed)

6.5 Undo the connecting link bottom balljoint (arrowed)

6.6 Remove the securing bolt and disconnect the steering column shaft

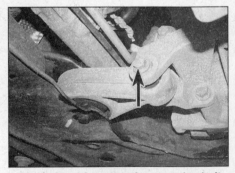
6.8 Undo and remove the mounting bolt (arrowed)

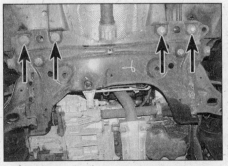
6.9a Slacken and remove the four rear crossmember bolts (arrowed) . . .

6.9b . . . and the two front crossmember bolts (arrowed), left-hand side shown

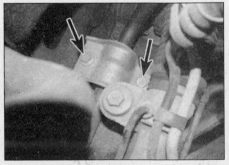
6.10 Undo the anti-roll bar securing bolts (arrowed)

Refitting

14 When fitting the anti-roll bar bushes make sure they are located correctly on the flats of the anti-roll bar with **no** lubricant **(see illustration)**.

15 Set the anti-roll bar to the design height setting of 98mm and support it in that position **(see illustration)**.

16 Refit the clamps to the anti-roll bar, installing the rear bolts first and tightening to 30 Nm. Then install the front bolts and tighten to 30 Nm. Further tighten the bolts in two stages as given in the Specifications.

17 Remove the anti-roll bar support for the design height.

18 Jack the crossmember up, into the correct position on the chassis (using the aligning tool if available). Make sure the crossmember ball-bearing washers are installed correctly before tightening the new bolts.

19 Renew the crossmember bolts and tighten them to their specified torque.

20 Refitting is then a reversal of the removal procedure. Making sure that all the relevant bolts are renewed and tightened to their specified torque.

---

7 Front suspension lower arm – removal, overhaul and refitting

Removal

1 Apply the handbrake, jack up the front of the vehicle and support it on axle stands. Remove the appropriate wheel.

2 Where applicable, remove the undertray from under the engine compartment and disconnect from the wheelarch.

3 Note which way round the front suspension lower arm balljoint clamp bolt is fitted, then unscrew and remove it from the knuckle assembly. Lever the balljoint down from the knuckle; if it is tight, prise the joint open carefully using a large flat-bladed tool. Take care not to damage the balljoint seal during the separation procedure.

4 Unscrew and remove the lower arm rear mounting clamp nuts, also undo the front mounting bolt and remove **(see illustrations)**.

7.4a Undo the two rear mounting nuts (arrowed) . . .

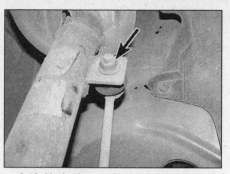

6.12 Undo the nut (arrowed) from the upper connecting link balljoint

5 Remove the lower arm from the subframe, and withdraw it from the vehicle.

Overhaul

6 Examine the rubber bushes and the suspension lower balljoint for wear and damage. At the time of writing the manual the balljoint and rubber bushes could not be renewed on the lower arm. Renew the complete lower arm if there is any wear or damage.

Refitting

Note: *The bolts, nuts and bearing washers securing the lower arm to the subframe must be renewed after removal.*

7 Locate the lower arm on the subframe, and insert the front mounting bolt and nut. Fit the clamp and nuts to the rear mounting and tighten them in stages **(see illustration)**.

8 Refit the front suspension lower arm balljoint to the knuckle assembly, and insert the clamp bolt with its head facing in the same direction as removal. Refit the nut and tighten to the specified torque.

9 Refit the wheel, and lower the vehicle to the ground. Making sure that all the relevant bolts are tightened to their specified torque.

---

8 Front suspension lower arm balljoint – renewal

Note: *If the lower arm balljoint is worn, the complete lower arm must be renewed. At the time of writing the manual the balljoint could*

7.4b . . . then undo the front mounting bolt (arrowed)

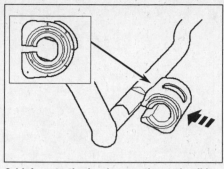

6.14 Locate the bushes on the anti-roll bar

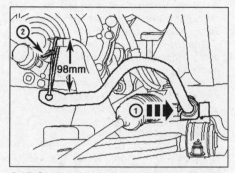

6.15 Setting the design height for the anti-roll bar

1 Locate the anti-roll bar bushes into the mounting clamps
2 Set the height to 98mm

not be renewed separately from the lower arm.

1 Remove and refit the front suspension lower arm as described in Section 7.

---

9 Rear hub and bearings – inspection and renewal

Inspection

1 The rear hub bearings are non-adjustable **(see illustration)**.

2 To check the bearings for excessive wear,

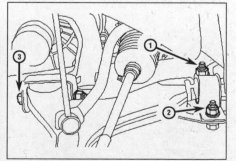

7.7 Tighten the nuts and bolts in the sequence given in the Specifications

1 Inner rear nut	*3 Front bolt*
2 Outer rear nut	

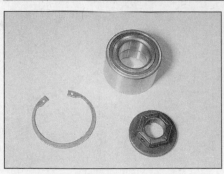

9.1 The wheel bearing is not adjustable

9.5a Remove the dust cap . . .

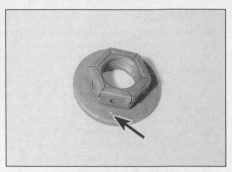

9.5b . . . and mark the nut (arrowed) each time it is removed

chock the front wheels, then jack up the rear of the vehicle and support it on axle stands. Fully release the handbrake.

3 Grip the rear wheel at the top and bottom, and attempt to rock it. If excessive movement is noted, or if there is any roughness or vibration felt when the wheel is spun, it is indicative that the hub bearings are worn.

Renewal

4 Remove the rear wheel.

5 Tap off the dust cap and unscrew the hub nut **(see illustration)**. **Note:** *The nut is of special laminated design, and should only be re-used a maximum of 4 times. It is a good idea to mark the nut every time it is removed.* Obtain a new one if necessary **(see illustration)**.

6 Remove the rear brake drum **(see illustration)**. If the drum will not pull off easily, use a suitable puller to draw the drum and

9.6 Pull the brake drum from the stub axle

bearing assembly off the stub axle.

7 On models fitted with rear brake discs, remove the rear brake disc as described in Chapter 9.

Use a suitable puller to draw the hub and bearing assembly off the stub axle.

8 Part of the inner race may remain on the stub axle, this should be removed using a puller.

9 Remove the ABS sensor ring from the hub/drum assembly (where fitted). This must be renewed when refitting.

10 Using circlip pliers, extract the circlip securing the bearing in the hub/drum **(see illustration)**.

11 Press or drive out the bearing, using a length of metal tubing of diameter slightly less than the bearing outer race.

12 Clean the bearing seating faces in the hub/drum.

13 Using the length of metal tubing, Press or drive the new bearing into the hub/drum until it is fully located **(see illustration)**. Do not apply any pressure to the inner race.

14 Locate the circlip into the groove in the hub/drum to secure the bearing in place.

15 Press the new ABS sensor ring onto the hub assembly slowly and squarely, as damage to the new ring will cause failure of the ABS system (where fitted).

16 Locate the new rear hub/drum and bearing assembly on the stub axle, then refit the hub nut and tighten it to the specified torque **(see illustration)**. Rotate the hub assembly in the opposite direction when tightening the hub retaining nut to prevent damage to the bearing.

17 Tap the dust cap fully onto the hub. If the dust cap was damaged on removal then a new one must be fitted.

18 On models fitted with rear brake discs, refit the rear brake disc as described in Chapter 9.

19 Refit the rear wheel, and lower the vehicle to the ground. Tighten all bolts and nuts to their specified torque.

10 Rear shock absorber – removal, testing and refitting

Removal

Saloon & Hatchback models

1 Open the tailgate/boot and remove the interior trim panel to gain access to the shock absorber top mounting nut.

2 Using an Allen key to hold the piston rod, undo the shock absorber upper mounting nut **(see illustration)**.

3 Chock the front wheels, then jack up the rear of the vehicle and support it on axle stands. Remove the wheels as required.

4 Place a jack under the lower suspension arm/coil spring to support it. Unscrew and remove the shock absorber lower mounting bolt, then withdraw the shock absorber from under the vehicle.

Estate models

5 Chock the front wheels, then jack up the rear of the vehicle and support it on axle stands. Remove the wheels as required.

9.10 Removing the circlip

9.13 Using a threaded bar and a tube to press the bearing in

9.16 Refitting the hub nut

10.2 Undo the upper mounting nut on the shock absorber

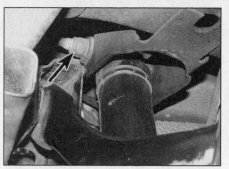

10.7a Remove the upper bolt (arrowed) . . .

10.7b . . . and the lower bolt (arrowed)

6 On the left-hand shock absorber, undo the rear exhaust silencer heat shield bolts. Remove it from the vehicle, so as to gain access to the upper mounting nut.

7 Place a jack under the lower suspension arm/coil spring to support it. Unscrew and remove the upper mounting bolt, then the lower mounting bolt **(see illustrations)**. Withdraw the shock absorber from under the vehicle.

Testing

8 Check the mounting rubbers for damage and deterioration. If they are worn, they may be able to be renewed separately from the shock absorber body (check the availability of parts).

9 Mount the shock absorber in a vice, gripping it by the lower mounting. Examine the shock absorber for signs of fluid leakage. Test the operation of the shock absorber by

moving it through a full stroke, and then through short strokes of 50 to 100 mm. In both cases, the resistance felt should be smooth and continuous. If the resistance is jerky or uneven, the shock absorber should be renewed.

Refitting

10 Refitting is a reversal of the removal procedure, tightening the mounting bolts to their specified torque. **Note:** *The supporting jack under the lower suspension arm/coil spring can be raised or lowered to refit the shock absorber if required.*
Note: *The final tightening of the mounting bolts must be carried out with the vehicle weight on the road wheels.*

11 Rear anti-roll bar and links – removal and refitting

⚠ *Warning: Before the final tightening of any components on the rear suspension, it must be set to the Design Height setting on both sides of the vehicle (see below).*

Removal

1 Remove the rear coil spring as described in Section 12.
2 Undo the nuts and bolts securing the anti-roll bar links to the rear lower arms, then remove the washers and bushes **(see illustration)**.
3 Unscrew the bolts securing the anti-roll bar

mounting clamps to the rear suspension crossmember **(see illustration)**; release the clamps (one each side), and withdraw the anti-roll bar from under the vehicle.

4 Examine the rubber bushes for the mounting clamps and links, and if necessary renew them. The links are available individually.

Refitting

5 When fitting the bushes to the anti-roll bar, make sure they are located correctly on the flats of the anti-roll bar with **no** lubricant (except water if required). Make sure the nipple is on the left-hand side of the bush when fitted **(see illustration)**.
6 Locate the anti-roll bar on the rear crossmember, then refit the clamps and tighten the bolts to the specified torque.
7 Refit the anti-roll bar links to the rear lower arms, together with the bushes and washers.
8 Carry out the procedures for the rear suspension Design Height setting (see below).

Suspension Design Height setting

9 Remove the rear coil springs as described in Section 12.
10 Use a jack to raise the lower arm until the fabricated spacer (dimensions as below) can be put between the lower arm and crossmember in a vertical position **(see illustrations)**, this is then the Design Height setting. (On the Saloon and Hatchback it will

11.2 Remove the nut and bolt (arrowed)

11.3 Rear anti-roll bar clamp bolts (arrowed)

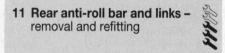

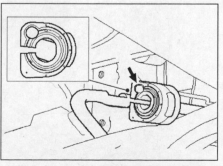

11.5 Arrow shows the position of the nipple when fitted

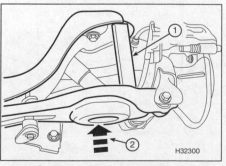

11.10a Rear suspension Design Height setting

1 Fabricated spacer
2 Jack to raise lower arm

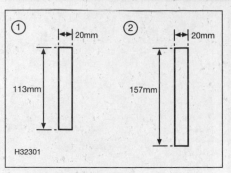

11.10b Fabricated spacers for Design Height (dimensions in mm)

1 Saloon and Hatchbacks
2 Estates

be necessary to remove the bump-stop to locate the spacer vertically.)

11 When set in this position on both sides, all the rear suspension bolts can be tightened to their specified torques.

12 The spacers can then be removed and the coil springs refitted as described in Section 12.

13 Refit the rear wheels, and lower the vehicle to the ground.

12 Rear coil spring – removal and refitting

Warning: Before attempting to remove the rear suspension coil spring, a tool to hold the coil spring in compression must be obtained. Careful use of conventional coil spring compressors must be taken at all times to avoid personal injury. A dealer's spring compressor tool may be required for the removal of the spring.

Removal

1 Chock the front wheels, then jack up the rear of the vehicle so the wheels are clear from the ground. Support the vehicle on axle stands. Remove the wheels as required.

2 Fit the coil spring compressor tool (ensuring that it is fully engaged), and compress the coil spring until all tension is relieved from the mounting **(see illustration)**.

3 Withdraw the coil spring from under the vehicle, taking care to keep the compressor tool in full engagement with the coil spring.

4 If a new coil spring is to be fitted, the original coil spring must be released from the compressor. If it is to be re-used, the coil spring can be left in compression.

Refitting

5 Refitting is a reversal of the removal procedure, but make sure that the coil spring is located correctly in the upper and lower seats. The coil springs must be installed with the paint mark at the bottom. **Note:** *If there is a rattle from the rear springs, check that a sleeve is fitted to the top end of the coil spring. This sleeve can be purchased from a dealer.*

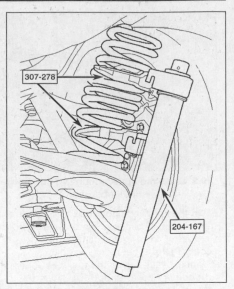

12.2 Ford spring compressor (part numbers shown)

Refitting

5 Refitting is a reversal of the removal procedure. Delay fully tightening the lower arm mounting bolts, until the suspension Design Height setting procedure has been carried out as described in Section 11. The wheel alignment will also require checking, see Section 26.

13 Rear suspension rear lower arm – removal and refitting

Removal

Note: *The bushes in the suspension arms cannot be renewed separately; renew the complete arm if there is any wear or damage.*

1 Remove the rear suspension coil spring as described in Section 12.

2 Undo and remove the nut securing the anti-roll bar link to the lower arm **(see illustration)**.

3 Unscrew and remove the bolt securing the rear lower arm to the crossmember, and the bolt to the hub assembly **(see illustrations)**.

4 Withdraw the rear lower arm from under the vehicle.

14 Rear suspension front lower arm – removal and refitting

Removal

Note: *The bushes in the suspension arms cannot be renewed separately; renew the complete arm if there is any wear or damage.*

1 Remove the rear suspension coil spring as described in Section 12. (This is to achieve the Design Height setting.)

2 Unscrew and remove the bolt securing the front lower arm to the crossmember.

3 Unscrew and remove the bolt securing the front lower arm to the hub assembly **(see illustration)**, and withdraw the arm from under the vehicle.

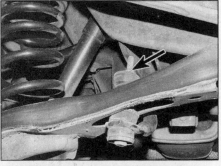

13.2 Remove the bolt (arrowed) to disconnect the anti-roll bar

13.3a Remove rear lower arm-to-crossmember bolt . . .

13.3b . . . and bolt-to-hub assembly (arrowed)

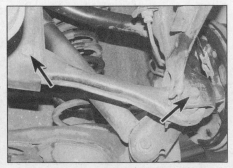

14.3 Remove the two mounting bolts (arrowed)

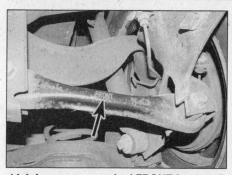

14.4 Lower arm marked FRONT (arrowed)

Refitting

4 Refitting is a reversal of the removal procedure, make sure the arm (marked FRONT) is fitted correctly **(see illustration)**. Delay fully tightening the lower arm mounting bolts, until the suspension Design Height setting procedure has been carried out as described in Section 11.

15 Rear suspension upper arm – removal and refitting

Removal

Note: *The bushes in the suspension arms cannot be renewed separately; renew the complete arm if there is any wear or damage.*
1 Remove the rear suspension coil spring as described in Section 12. (This is to achieve the Design Height setting.)
2 Unscrew and remove the bolt securing the upper arm to the hub assembly.
3 Unscrew and remove the bolt securing the upper arm to the crossmember **(see illustration)**, and withdraw the arm from under the vehicle taking note of the way it was fitted for installation purposes.

Refitting

4 Refitting is a reversal of the removal procedure, make sure the arm is fitted the right way around. Delay fully tightening the upper arm mounting bolts, until the suspension Design Height setting procedure has been carried out as described in Section 11.

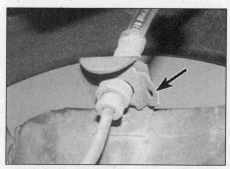

16.3 Slacken the brake pipe and remove the securing clip (arrowed)

15.3 Remove the two mounting bolts (arrowed) – Estate

16 Rear suspension tie-bar (control blade) – removal and refitting

Removal

1 Remove the rear suspension coil spring as described in Section 12.
2 Detach the handbrake cable guide from the tie-bar, and pull the cable clear of the tie-bar.
3 Fit a brake hose clamp to the rear flexible brake pipe, and disconnect the brake pipe union. Using a pair of pliers pull out the clip securing the brake pipe to the body **(see illustration)**.
4 Remove the rear brake drum/disc assembly as described in Chapter 9.
5 Unscrew and remove the bolt securing the lower part of the rear shock absorber to the tie-bar assembly.
6 Where applicable, release the ABS wheel sensor lead from the tie-bar.
7 Unscrew and remove the front and rear lower arm bolts from the tie-bar assembly.
8 Unscrew and remove the upper arm bolt from the tie-bar assembly.
9 Unbolt the tie-bar front mounting bracket from the underbody **(see illustration)**, and withdraw the assembly from under the vehicle.

Refitting

10 Refitting is a reversal of the removal procedure. Delay fully tightening all the mounting bolts, until the suspension Design Height setting procedure has been carried out as described in Section 11. Bleed the brake hydraulic system as described in Chapter 9.

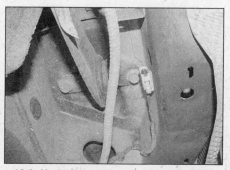

16.9 Undo the two front mounting bolts from the tie-bar

17 Rear suspension crossmember – removal and refitting

Removal

1 Remove the rear suspension coil spring as described in Section 12.
2 Support the hub assemblies on both sides of the vehicle using axle stands.
3 Remove the anti-roll bar as described in Section 11.
4 Remove the upper arm and lower arms as described in Sections 13, 14, and 15.
5 Detach and lower the exhaust system from its hanger, supporting it to prevent any damage.
6 Using a trolley jack, support the crossmember.
7 Unscrew the mounting bolts (three bolts each side), and lower the crossmember to the ground **(see illustration)**.

Refitting

8 Refitting is a reversal of the removal procedure, noting the following points:
a) *When raising the crossmember, note that locating pins are provided to ensure correct alignment.*
b) *Delay fully tightening the suspension mounting bolts until the suspension Design Height setting procedure has been carried out as described in Section 11.*
c) *Tighten all bolts to the specified torque.*
d) *Check, and if necessary adjust, the rear wheel toe setting as described in Section 26.*

18 Steering wheel – removal and refitting

⚠️ **Warning: All models are equipped with an airbag system. Make sure that the safety recommendations given in Chapter 12 are followed, to prevent personal injury.**

Removal

1 Disconnect the battery negative (earth) lead (refer to Chapter 5A, Section 1).

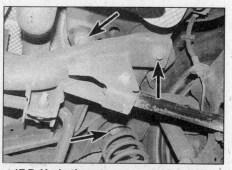

17.7 Undo the rear crossmember bolts (arrowed), left-hand side shown

18.5 Holding steering wheel, while slackening the retaining bolt

18.6 Wiring connector (arrowed) stays in place

18.8 Refitting the retaining bolt

⚠️ *Warning: Before proceeding, wait a minimum of 5 minutes, as a precaution against accidental firing of the airbag unit. This period ensures that any stored energy in the back-up capacitor is dissipated.*

2 Remove the airbag module (see Chapter 12).

⚠️ *Warning: Position the airbag module in a safe place, with the mechanism facing downwards as a precaution against accidental operation.*

3 Centralise the steering wheel so that the front wheels are in the straight-ahead position. Remove the keys and lock the steering in position.

4 Disconnect the speed cruise control electrical connector (where fitted)

5 Unscrew the retaining bolt from the centre of the steering wheel. Mark the position of the steering wheel on the steering column shaft for refitting (see illustration).

6 Remove the steering wheel from the top of the column, while pushing the wiring connector through the hole, so as to stay in position on the steering column (see illustration).

Refitting

7 Make sure that the front wheels are still facing straight-ahead, then locate the steering wheel on the top of the steering column. Align the marks made on the removal.

8 Refit the retaining bolt (see illustration), and tighten it to the specified torque while holding the steering wheel. Do not tighten the bolt with the steering lock engaged, as this may damage the lock.

9 Reconnect the wiring connector(s) for the horn and airbag.

10 Locate the airbag module on the steering wheel as described in Chapter 12, then insert the securing screws and tighten them.

11 Reconnect the battery negative lead.

19 Steering column – removal, inspection and refitting

⚠️ *Warning: All models are equipped with an airbag system. Make sure that the safety recommendations given in Chapter 12 are followed, to prevent personal injury.*

Removal

1 Disconnect the battery negative (earth) lead (refer to Chapter 5A, Section 1).

⚠️ *Warning: Before proceeding, wait a minimum of 5 minutes, as a precaution against accidental firing of the airbag unit. This period ensures that any stored energy in the back-up capacitor is dissipated.*

2 Remove the steering wheel as described in Section 18.

3 Undo the four screws and unclip the retaining clip to remove the facia lower panel. Unclip the multi-plug from the trim panel (see illustrations).

4 Lower the steering column locking lever. Remove the steering column upper shroud, release the two retaining clips with a thin-bladed screwdriver. Using the same screwdriver, unclip the radio control switch and disconnect the wiring connector (see illustrations).

5 Undo the three screws from the lower shroud and remove from the steering column (see illustration).

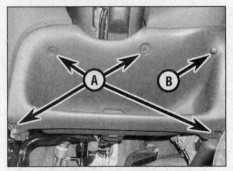

19.3a Remove the four screws (A) and retaining clip (B)

19.3b Withdraw the multi-plug from the trim

19.4a Unclip the upper shroud with a thin screwdriver (arrowed) . . .

19.4b . . . then lift off shroud

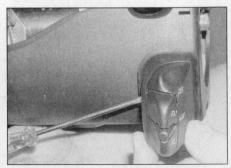

19.4c Unclip the remote from the lower shroud . . .

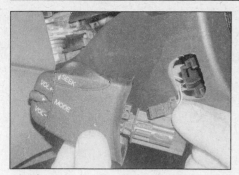

19.4d . . . and unplug the wiring connector

19.5 Unscrew the three screws from the lower shroud

19.6a Disconnect the wiring from the left . . .

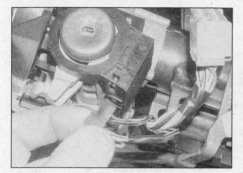

19.6b . . . and right of the steering column

19.8 Unclip the wiring bracket from the steering column

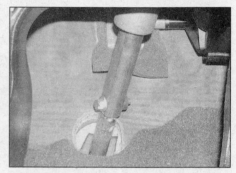

19.9 Unscrew the bolt to disengage the column from the rack

6 Disconnect the electrical connectors from the right and left-hand side of the steering column switches (see illustrations).
7 On vehicles with stability assistance fitted, disconnect the steering wheel rotation sensor electrical connector.
8 Release the locating clips to detach the wiring harness from the steering column (see illustration).
9 Remove the securing bolt from the sleeve which joins the lower part of the steering column to the steering rack (see illustration). On very early models there are two securing bolts, in this case slacken the upper bolt and remove the lower bolt before pulling the column upwards.
10 Unscrew and remove the three steering column mounting locking nuts and one Torx bolt (see illustration). Slide the column upwards to disengage from the sleeve to the steering rack (see illustration), and withdraw it from inside the vehicle.

Inspection

Note: *The first tests are performed with the column in the vehicle.*
11 With the steering lock disengaged, attempt to move the steering wheel up-and-down and also to the left-and-right without turning the wheel, to check for steering column bearing wear, steering column shaft joint play and steering wheel or steering column being loose. The steering column cannot be repaired, if any faults are detected install a new column.
12 Examine the height adjustment lever mechanism for wear and damage.

13 With the steering column removed, check the universal joints for wear, and examine the column upper and lower shafts for any signs of damage or distortion. Where evident, the column should be renewed complete.

Refitting

14 Refitting is a reversal of removal, noting the following points:
a) Make sure the wheels are still in the straight-ahead position when the steering column is installed.
b) Fit new locking nuts to the steering column mounting bracket.
c) Fit new pinch-bolt to the steering column sleeve, which joins to the steering rack.
d) Tighten bolts to their specified torque.
e) See Chapter 12 before refitting the airbag.
f) If the electronic stability program warning light (if fitted), comes on after installing the steering column the system will need

19.10a Undo the three nuts and one Torx bolt arrowed . . .

19.10b . . . then lift the column upwards from the steering rack

re-configuring at a Ford dealer using the FDS 2000.

20 Power steering rack – removal and refitting

Removal

1 Centralise the steering wheel so that the front wheels are in the straight-ahead position. Remove the keys and lock the steering in position.
2 From inside the vehicle, remove the securing bolt from the sleeve which joins the column to the steering rack. On very early models there are two securing bolts, in this case slacken the upper bolt and remove the lower bolt before pulling away from the splines.

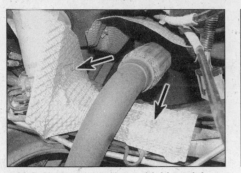

20.8 Undo the two heat shield retaining bolts (arrowed)

20.10 Slacken the bolt (1), and rotate the pipe clamp (2)

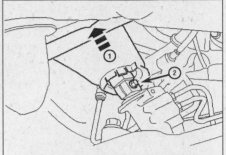

20.12 Unclip seal (1) from the pinion housing, and remove bolt (2) from the pinion shaft

3 Apply the handbrake, then jack up the front of the vehicle and support it on axle stands. Remove both front wheels.

4 Unscrew the track rod end nuts, and detach the rods from the arms on the steering knuckles using a conventional balljoint removal tool. Take care not to damage the balljoint seals.

5 Remove the connecting links from the struts and anti-roll bar, taking care not to damage the balljoint seals.

6 On diesel models remove the undershield from the engine.

7 Remove the bolt from the support bracket on the transaxle unit.

8 Unbolt and remove the heat shield from the steering rack **(see illustration)**.

9 Undo the screw securing the hose support clamp to the housing on the steering gear pinion.

10 Position a container beneath the steering rack, then unscrew the bolt securing the power steering pipes to the steering rack. Identify the lines for position, then rotate the clamp **(see illustration)**, disconnect the pipes and check the O-ring seals for any damage. Allow the fluid to drain into the container. Cover the apertures in the steering rack and also the ends of the fluid pipes, to prevent the ingress of dust and dirt into the hydraulic circuit.

11 Using a trolley jack, support the front crossmember, and remove the six retaining

bolts. There is a special tool to align the crossmember on refitting. If this is not available, mark the mounting points, so as to refit in the correct position.

12 Lower the crossmember, disconnecting the steering pinion drive and the floor seal from the steering column pinion housing. Remove the lower securing bolt from the steering column extension when visible **(see illustration)**.

13 Unscrew and remove the steering rack mounting bolts **(see illustrations)**.

14 Withdraw the steering rack from the crossmember taking care not to damage any components on removal.

15 With the steering rack removed, the bushes can be renewed in the housing. If the special tool is not available, use a long bolt with a metal tube and washers to press the new bush into the housing. Make sure the bushes are fitted to the correct depth.

Refitting

16 Refitting is a reversal of removal, noting the following points:

a) *Check the O-rings on the steering fluid pipes for damage or perishing, renew if necessary.*

b) *Make sure the pressure valve is correctly located in the valve body.*

c) *Check the steering column floor seal for damage. Make sure it is correctly located on the pinion housing.*

d) *Jack the crossmember up, into the correct position on the chassis using the aligning tool (if available). Make sure the crossmember ball-bearing washers are installed correctly, before tightening the bolts to their specified torque.*

e) *Renew the pinch bolt(s) in the steering pinion sleeve.*

f) *Fill and bleed the system with steering fluid as described in Section 22.*

g) *Check the front wheel alignment as described in Section 26.*

21 Power steering gear rubber gaiters – renewal

1 Remove the track rod end and its locknut from the track rod, as described in Section 25. Make sure that a note is made of the exact position of the track rod end on the track rod, in order to retain the front wheel alignment setting on refitting.

2 Release the outer and inner retaining clips, and disconnect the gaiter from the steering gear housing **(see illustration)**.

3 Disconnect the breather from the gaiter, then slide the gaiter off the track rod.

4 Apply grease to the track rod inner joint. Wipe clean the seating areas on the steering gear housing and track rod.

5 Slide the new gaiter onto the track rod and

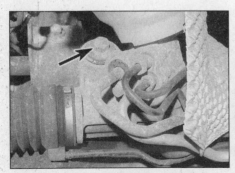

20.13a Undo the right-hand steering rack mounting bolt . . .

20.13b . . . and the left-hand mounting bolt (arrowed)

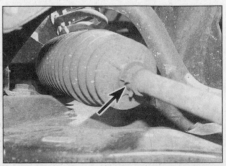

21.2 Release the retaining clip (arrowed) from the gaiter

21.5 Reconnect the breather pipe (arrowed) to the gaiter

steering gear housing, and reconnect the breather (see illustration).
6 Fit a new inner and outer retaining clips.
7 Refit the track rod end as described in Section 25.
8 Have the front wheel alignment checked, and if necessary adjusted, at the earliest opportunity (refer to Section 26).

22 Power steering hydraulic system – bleeding

 Warning: Do not hold the steering wheel against the full lock stops for more than five seconds, as damage to the steering pump may result.

1 Following any operation in which the power steering fluid lines have been disconnected, the power steering system must be bled, to remove any trapped air.
2 With the front wheels in the straight-ahead position, check the power steering fluid level in the reservoir and, if low, add fresh fluid until it reaches the MAX or MAX COLD mark. Pour the fluid slowly, to prevent air bubbles forming, and use only the specified fluid (refer to *Weekly checks*).
3 Start the engine and slowly turn the steering from lock-to-lock.
4 Stop the engine, and check the hoses and connections for leaks. Check the fluid level and add more if necessary. Make sure the fluid in the reservoir does not fall below the MIN mark, as air could enter the system.
5 Start the engine again, allow it to idle, then bleed the system by slowly turning the steering wheel from side-to-side several times. This should purge the system of all internal air. However, if air remains in the system (indicated by the steering operation being very noisy), leave the vehicle overnight, and repeat the procedure again the next day.
6 If air still remains in the system, it may be necessary to resort to the Ford method of bleeding, which uses a vacuum pump. Turn the steering to the right until it is near the stop, then fit the vacuum pump to the fluid reservoir, and apply 0.15 bars of vacuum. Maintain the vacuum for a minimum of 5 minutes, then repeat the procedure with the steering turned until it is near to the left stop.

7 Keep the fluid level topped-up throughout the bleeding procedure; note that, as the fluid temperature increases, the level will rise.
8 On completion, switch off the engine, and return the wheels to the straight-ahead position. Check for any leaks.

23 Power steering pump – removal and refitting

Note: *The power steering pump can be of an aluminium or cast iron construction, which are similar in the removal and refitting procedure. On the 1.8 and 2.0 models, the pulley can be removed from the pump on the vehicle (by means of a puller). The other models require the pump to be removed from the vehicle before removing the pulley. The power steering pump is positioned at the front of the engine, except on diesels and 1.4 litre & 1.6 litre petrol engines with air conditioning, where it is positioned at the rear of the engine.*

Petrol models

Removal

1 Disconnect the battery negative (earth) lead (refer to Chapter 5A, Section 1).
2 Remove the auxiliary drivebelt as described in Chapter 1A.
3 Position a suitable container beneath the power steering pump, to catch any spilt fluid.
4 Remove the fluid cooler hose (except 1.4 litre & 1.6 litre without air conditioning). Insert a special tool into the end of the hose along the pipe to release the locking tangs (see illustration). Allow the fluid to drain into container.
5 On 1.4 litre & 1.6 litre vehicles with air conditioning, lower the vehicle and detach the power steering reservoir from its retaining bracket, disconnect the hose and drain the fluid into the container.
6 Slacken the clip, and disconnect the fluid supply hose from the pump inlet. Plug the hose, to prevent the ingress of dust and dirt (see illustration).
7 Unscrew and remove the bolt securing the high pressure fluid line support to the pump mounting bracket (not fitted on 1.4 litre & 1.6 litre vehicles with air conditioning). Unscrew

23.6 Disconnect the supply hose (arrowed) from the pump

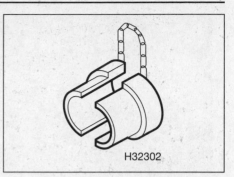

23.4 Special tool: Slide into the ends of the fluid cooling hose to disengage

the union nut, and disconnect the high-pressure line from the pump (see illustration). Allow the fluid to drain into the container.
8 Disconnect the power steering pressure (PSP) switch electrical connector by depressing the locking tab (the PSP switch is in the high-pressure pipe on 1.4 litre).
9 Unscrew and remove the four mounting bolts (three bolts on 1.4 litre & 1.6 litre vehicles with air conditioning), and withdraw the power steering pump from its bracket.

Diesel models

Removal

10 Disconnect the battery negative (earth) lead (refer to Chapter 5A, Section 1).
11 Remove the auxiliary drivebelt as described in Chapter 1B.
12 Remove the engine undershield and position a suitable container beneath the power steering pump, to catch any spilt fluid.
13 Remove the fluid cooler hose. Insert a special tool into the end of the hose along the pipe to release the locking tangs (see illustration 23.4). Allow the fluid to drain into container.
14 Lower the vehicle and undo the securing clips at each end of the charge air cooler (CAC)-to-intake manifold hose (see illustration). Undo the nut securing the hose across the camshaft cover to remove.
15 Unscrew the bolt securing the high pressure fluid line support to the pump mounting bracket.
16 Undo the screw securing the diesel fuel

23.7 Disconnect the high pressure pipe (arrowed)

23.14 Undo the securing clip on the air intake hose

23.16 Remove the screw (arrowed) to move the fuel filter

23.21 Withdrawing the pump from its mounting bracket

filter, and move the filter to one side to gain access to pump **(see illustration)**.

17 Unscrew the union nut, and disconnect the high-pressure line from the pump. Allow the fluid to drain into the container.

18 Unscrew and remove the two upper mounting bolts from the power steering pump bracket.

19 Raise the vehicle and support on axle stands.

20 Loosen the clip, and disconnect the fluid supply hose from the pump inlet. Plug the hose, to prevent the ingress of dust and dirt.

21 Unscrew and remove the two lower mounting bolts from the power steering pump bracket. Withdraw the power steering pump downwards from its bracket **(see illustration)**.

Refitting

22 Refitting is a reversal of removal, noting the following points.

24.6 The fluid cooler is positioned across the front of the radiator

25.2 Slackening locknut

a) Tighten the bolts and unions to the specified torque.
b) Where fitted, the O-ring on the high-pressure outlet should be renewed. Use a special tool or a tapered tube to slide the New o-ring onto the pipe union.
c) Bleed the power steering hydraulic system as described in Section 22.
d) When renewing the pump, remove the power steering pressure switch and high pressure pipes, where fitted.

24 Power steering fluid cooler – removal and refitting

Removal

1 Detach the power steering reservoir from its retaining bracket, disconnect the hose and drain the fluid into a suitable container.

2 Unclip the hose from the retaining bracket.

3 Apply the handbrake, then jack up the front of the vehicle and support it on axle stands.

4 Undo the securing screws from the splash shield under the radiator and remove shield. (Disconnect the temperature sensor electrical connector, if fitted).

5 Remove the fluid cooler hose. Insert a special tool into the end of the hose along the pipe to release the locking tangs (see illustration 23.4). Allow the fluid to drain into container.

6 Undo the fluid cooler securing bolts and remove the cooler from the vehicle **(see illustration)**.

Refitting

7 Refitting is a reversal of removal. Bleed the power steering hydraulic system as described in Section 22.

25 Track rod end – renewal

Removal

1 Apply the handbrake, then jack up the front of the vehicle and support it on axle stands. Remove the appropriate front roadwheel.

2 Slacken the locknut on the track rod by a quarter-turn **(see illustration)**. Hold the track rod end stationary with another spanner engaged with the special flats while loosening the locknut.

3 Unscrew and remove the track rod end balljoint retaining nut.

4 To release the tapered shank of the balljoint from the steering knuckle arm, use a balljoint separator tool **(see illustration)** (if the balljoint is to be re-used, take care not to damage the dust cover when using the separator tool).

5 Count the number of exposed threads visible on the inner section of the track rod, and record this figure.

6 Unscrew the track rod end from the track rod, counting the number of turns necessary to remove it. If necessary, hold the track rod stationary with grips.

Refitting

7 Screw the track rod end onto the track rod by the number of turns noted during removal, until it just contacts the locknut.

8 Engage the shank of the balljoint with the steering knuckle arm, and refit the nut. Tighten the nut to the specified torque. If the balljoint shank turns while the nut is being tightened, use an Allen key **(see illustration)** to hold the shank or press up on the balljoint. The tapered fit of the shank will lock it, and prevent rotation as the nut is tightened.

9 Now tighten the locknut on the track rod, while holding the track rod end as before.

10 Refit the roadwheel, and lower the vehicle to the ground.

25.4 Use ball joint separator tool to release balljoint

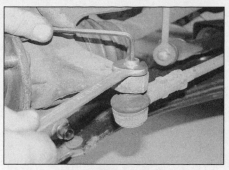

25.8 Use Allen key to prevent shank from turning

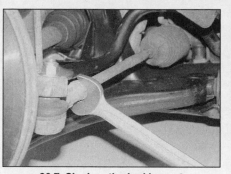

26.7 Slacken the locking nut

26.9 Eccentric bolt/washer to adjust rear suspension

11 Finally check, and if necessary adjust, the front wheel alignment as described in Section 26.

26 Wheel alignment and steering angles – general information

1 Accurate front wheel alignment is essential to provide positive steering, and to prevent excessive tyre wear. Before considering the steering/suspension geometry, check that the tyres are correctly inflated, that the front wheels are not buckled, and that the steering linkage and suspension joints are in good order, without slackness or wear.

2 Wheel alignment consists of four factors:

Camber is the angle at which the front wheels are set from the vertical, when viewed from the front of the vehicle. 'Positive camber' is the amount (in degrees) that the wheels are tilted outward at the top of the vertical.

Castor is the angle between the steering axis and a vertical line, when viewed from each side of the car. 'Positive castor' is when the steering axis is inclined rearward at the top.

Steering axis inclination is the angle (when viewed from the front of the vehicle) between the vertical and an imaginary line drawn through the suspension strut upper mounting and the lower suspension arm balljoint.

Toe setting is the amount by which the distance between the front inside edges of the roadwheels (measured at hub height) differs from the diametrically-opposite distance measured between the rear inside edges of the roadwheels.

3 With the exception of the toe setting, all other steering angles are set during manufacture, and no adjustment is possible. It can be assumed, therefore, that unless the vehicle has suffered accident damage, all the pre-set steering angles will be correct. Should there be some doubt about their accuracy, it will be necessary to seek the help of a Ford dealer, as special gauges are needed to check the steering angles.

4 Two methods are available to the home mechanic for checking the toe setting. One method is to use a gauge to measure the distance between the front and rear inside edges of the roadwheels. The other method is to use a scuff plate, in which each front wheel is rolled across a movable plate which records any deviation, or scuff, of the tyre from the straight-ahead position as it moves across the plate. Relatively-inexpensive equipment of both types is available from accessory outlets.

5 If, after checking the toe setting using whichever method is preferable, it is found that adjustment is necessary, proceed as follows.

6 Turn the steering wheel onto full-left lock, and record the number of exposed threads on the right-hand track rod. Now turn the steering onto full-right lock, and record the number of threads on the left-hand track rod. If there are the same number of threads visible on both sides, then subsequent adjustment can be made equally on both sides. If there are more threads visible on one side than the other, it will be necessary to compensate for this during adjustment. *After adjustment, there should be the same number of threads visible on each track rod. This is most important.*

7 To alter the toe setting, slacken the locknut on the track rod **(see illustration)**, and turn the track rod using self-locking pliers to achieve the desired setting. When viewed from the side of the car, turning the rod clockwise will increase the toe-in, turning it anti-clockwise will increase the toe-out. Only turn the track rods by a quarter of a turn each time, and then recheck the setting.

8 After adjustment, tighten the locknuts. Reposition the steering gear rubber gaiters, to remove any twist caused by turning the track rods.

9 The rear wheel toe-setting may also be checked and adjusted. This setting is adjusted by turning the eccentric bolt/washer securing the rear lower arms to the rear axle crossmember **(see illustration)**. **Note:** *Once the rear suspension bolts have been slackened, the suspension Design Height setting procedure has to be carried out as described in Section 11, before re-tightening.*

10 This bolt has to be slackened, then tightened up to 8 Nm. The eccentric bolt/washer can now be turned clockwise or anti-clockwise to adjust the rear wheel alignment. When the wheel alignment is correct, the eccentric bolt/washer can be re-tightened back up to 115 Nm.

11 The rear wheel toe-setting additionally requires alignment with the front wheels, therefore it would be best left to a Ford garage or specialist having the correct equipment for wheel alignment.

Chapter 11
Bodywork and fittings

Contents

Degrees of difficulty

Easy, suitable for novice with little experience	**Fairly easy,** suitable for beginner with some experience	**Fairly difficult,** suitable for competent DIY mechanic	**Difficult,** suitable for experienced DIY mechanic	**Very difficult,** suitable for expert DIY or professional

Specifications

Torque wrench settings	Nm	lbf ft
Bonnet hinge bolts to body	22	16
Bonnet hinge bolts to bonnet	10	7
Boot lid hinge bolts	22	16
Bumper mounting nuts	10	7
Door check strap-to-body bolts	22	16
Door check strap-to-door bolts	6	4
Door hinge-to-body bolts	35	26
Door hinge-to-door bolts	47	35
Door striker plate bolts	20	15
Front seat mounting bolts	28	21
Rear seat backrest catch retaining bolts	30	22
Rear seat hinge pins	20	15
Seat belt mounting nuts and bolts	38	28
Tailgate hinge-to-body bolts	22	16
Tailgate hinge-to-body nuts	8	6
Tailgate hinge-to-tailgate bolts	10	7
Wiper arm securing nuts	18	13

1 General information

The bodyshell and underframe on all models feature variable thickness steel. Achieved by laser-welded technology, used to join steel panels of different gauges. This gives a stiffer structure, with mounting points being more rigid, which gives an improved crash performance.

An additional safety crossmember is incorporated between the A-pillars in the upper area of the bulkhead, and the facia and steering column are secured to it. The lower bulkhead area is reinforced by additional systems of members connected to the front of the vehicle. The body side rocker panels (sills) have been divided along the length of the vehicle by internal reinforcement, this functions like a double tube which increases its strength. All doors are reinforced and incorporate side impact protection, which is secured in the door structure. There are additional impact absorbers to the front and rear of the vehicle, behind the bumper assemblies.

All sheet metal surfaces which are prone to corrosion are galvanised. The painting process includes a base colour which closely matches the final topcoat, so that any stone damage is not as noticeable. The front wings are of a bolt-on type to ease their replacement if required.

Automatic seat belts are fitted to all models, and the front seat safety belts are equipped with a pyrotechnic pretension seat belt buckle, which is attached to the seat frame of each front seat. In the event of a serious front impact, the system is triggered and pulls the stalk buckle downwards to tension the seat belt. It is not possible to reset the tensioner once fired, and it must therefore be renewed. The tensioners are fired by an explosive charge similar to that used in the airbag, and are triggered via the airbag control module. The safety belt retractor, which is fitted in the base of the B-pillar, has a device to control the seat belt, if the deceleration force is enough to activate the airbags.

In the UK, central locking is standard on all models. In other countries, it is available on certain models only. Where double-locking is fitted, the lock mechanism is disconnected (when the system is in use) from the interior door handles, making it impossible to open any of the doors or the tailgate/bootlid from inside the vehicle. This means that, even if a thief should break a side window, he will not be able to open the door using the interior handle. Models with the double-locking system are fitted with a control module located beneath the facia on the right-hand side. In the event of a serious accident, a crash sensor unlocks all doors if they were previously locked.

Many of the procedures in this Chapter require the battery to be disconnected. Refer to Chapter 5A, Section 1, first.

2 Maintenance – bodywork and underframe

The general condition of a vehicle's bodywork is the one thing that significantly affects its value. Maintenance is easy, but needs to be regular. Neglect, particularly after minor damage, can lead quickly to further deterioration and costly repair bills. It is important also to keep watch on those parts of the vehicle not immediately visible, for instance the underside, inside all the wheelarches, and the lower part of the engine compartment.

The basic maintenance routine for the bodywork is washing – preferably with a lot of water, from a hose. This will remove all the loose solids which may have stuck to the vehicle. It is important to flush these off in such a way as to prevent grit from scratching the finish. The wheelarches and underframe need washing in the same way, to remove any accumulated mud, which will retain moisture and tend to encourage rust. Paradoxically enough, the best time to clean the underframe and wheelarches is in wet weather, when the mud is thoroughly wet and soft. In very wet weather, the underframe is usually cleaned of large accumulations automatically, and this is a good time for inspection.

Periodically, except on vehicles with a wax-based underbody protective coating, it is a good idea to have the whole of the underframe of the vehicle steam-cleaned, engine compartment included, so that a thorough inspection can be carried out to see what minor repairs and renovations are necessary. Steam-cleaning is available at many garages, and is necessary for the removal of the accumulation of oily grime, which sometimes is allowed to become thick in certain areas. If steam-cleaning facilities are not available, there are some excellent grease solvents available which can be brush-applied; the dirt can then be simply hosed off. Note that these methods should not be used on vehicles with wax-based underbody protective coating, or the coating will be removed. Such vehicles should be inspected annually, preferably just prior to Winter, when the underbody should be washed down, and any damage to the wax coating repaired. Ideally, a completely fresh coat should be applied. It would also be worth considering the use of such wax-based protection for injection into door panels, sills, box sections, etc, as an additional safeguard against rust damage, where such protection is not provided by the vehicle manufacturer.

After washing paintwork, wipe off with a chamois leather to give an unspotted clear finish. A coat of clear protective wax polish will give added protection against chemical pollutants in the air. If the paintwork sheen has dulled or oxidised, use a cleaner/polisher combination to restore the brilliance of the shine. This requires a little effort, but such dulling is usually caused because regular washing has been neglected. Care needs to be taken with metallic paintwork, as special non-abrasive cleaner/polisher is required to avoid damage to the finish. Always check that the door and ventilator opening drain holes and pipes are completely clear, so that water can be drained out. Brightwork should be treated in the same way as paintwork. Windscreens and windows can be kept clear of the smeary film which often appears, by the use of proprietary glass cleaner. Never use any form of wax or other body or chromium polish on glass.

3 Maintenance – upholstery and carpets

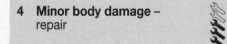

Mats and carpets should be brushed or vacuum-cleaned regularly, to keep them free of grit. If they are badly stained, remove them from the vehicle for scrubbing or sponging, and make quite sure they are dry before refitting. Seats and interior trim panels can be kept clean by wiping with a damp cloth. If they do become stained (which can be more apparent on light-coloured upholstery), use a little liquid detergent and a soft nail brush to scour the grime out of the grain of the material. Do not forget to keep the headlining clean in the same way as the upholstery. When using liquid cleaners inside the vehicle, do not over-wet the surfaces being cleaned. Excessive damp could get into the seams and padded interior, causing stains, offensive odours or even rot.

Caution: If the inside of the vehicle gets wet accidentally, it is worthwhile taking some trouble to dry it out properly, particularly where carpets are involved. Do not leave oil or electric heaters inside the vehicle for this purpose.

4 Minor body damage – repair

Repairs of minor scratches in bodywork

If the scratch is very superficial, and does not penetrate to the metal of the bodywork, repair is very simple. Lightly rub the area of the scratch with a paintwork renovator, or a very fine cutting paste, to remove loose paint from the scratch, and to clear the surrounding bodywork of wax polish. Rinse the area with clean water.

Apply touch-up paint to the scratch using a fine paint brush; continue to apply fine layers of paint until the surface of the paint in the scratch is level with the surrounding paintwork. Allow the new paint at least two weeks to harden, then blend it into the surrounding paintwork by rubbing the scratch area with a paintwork renovator or a very fine cutting paste. Finally, apply wax polish.

Where the scratch has penetrated right through to the metal of the bodywork, causing the metal to rust, a different repair technique is required. Remove any loose rust from the bottom of the scratch with a penknife, then apply rust-inhibiting paint to prevent the formation of rust in the future. Using a rubber or nylon applicator, fill the scratch with bodystopper paste. If required, this paste can be mixed with cellulose thinners to provide a very thin paste which is ideal for filling narrow scratches. Before the stopper-paste in the scratch hardens, wrap a piece of smooth cotton rag around the top of a finger. Dip the finger in cellulose thinners, and quickly sweep it across the surface of the stopper-paste in the scratch; this will ensure that the surface of the stopper-paste is slightly hollowed. The scratch can now be painted over as described earlier in this Section.

Repairs of dents in bodywork

When deep denting of the vehicle's bodywork has taken place, the first task is to pull the dent out, until the affected bodywork almost attains its original shape. There is little point in trying to restore the original shape completely, as the metal in the damaged area will have stretched on impact, and cannot be reshaped fully to its original contour. It is better to bring the level of the dent up to a point which is about 3 mm below the level of the surrounding bodywork. In cases where the dent is very shallow anyway, it is not worth trying to pull it out at all. If the underside of the dent is accessible, it can be hammered out gently from behind, using a mallet with a wooden or plastic head. Whilst doing this, hold a suitable block of wood firmly against the outside of the panel, to absorb the impact from the hammer blows and thus prevent a large area of the bodywork from being 'belled-out'.

Should the dent be in a section of the bodywork which has a double skin, or some other factor making it inaccessible from behind, a different technique is called for. Drill several small holes through the metal inside the area – particularly in the deeper section. Then screw long self-tapping screws into the holes, just sufficiently for them to gain a good purchase in the metal. Now the dent can be pulled out by pulling on the protruding heads of the screws with a pair of pliers.

The next stage of the repair is the removal of the paint from the damaged area, and from an inch or so of the surrounding 'sound' bodywork. This is accomplished most easily by using a wire brush or abrasive pad on a power drill, although it can be done just as effectively by hand, using sheets of abrasive paper. To complete the preparation for filling, score the surface of the bare metal with a screwdriver or the tang of a file, or alternatively, drill small holes in the affected area. This will provide a really good 'key' for the filler paste.

To complete the repair, see the Section on filling and respraying.

Repairs of rust holes or gashes in bodywork

Remove all paint from the affected area, and from an inch or so of the surrounding 'sound' bodywork, using an abrasive pad or a wire brush on a power drill. If these are not available, a few sheets of abrasive paper will do the job most effectively. With the paint removed, you will be able to judge the severity of the corrosion, and therefore decide whether to renew the whole panel (if this is possible) or to repair the affected area. New body panels are not as expensive as most people think, and it is often quicker and more satisfactory to fit a new panel than to attempt to repair large areas of corrosion.

Remove all fittings from the affected area, except those which will act as a guide to the original shape of the damaged bodywork (e.g. headlight shells etc). Then, using tin snips or a hacksaw blade, remove all loose metal and any other metal badly affected by corrosion. Hammer the edges of the hole inwards, in order to create a slight depression for the filler paste.

Wire-brush the affected area to remove the powdery rust from the surface of the remaining metal. Paint the affected area with rust-inhibiting paint, if the back of the rusted area is accessible, treat this also.

Before filling can take place, it will be necessary to block the hole in some way. This can be achieved by the use of aluminium or plastic mesh, or aluminium tape.

Aluminium or plastic mesh, or glass-fibre matting, is probably the best material to use for a large hole. Cut a piece to the approximate size and shape of the hole to be filled, then position it in the hole so that its edges are below the level of the surrounding bodywork. It can be retained in position by several blobs of filler paste around its periphery.

Aluminium tape should be used for small or very narrow holes. Pull a piece off the roll, trim it to the approximate size and shape required, then pull off the backing paper (if used) and stick the tape over the hole; it can be overlapped if the thickness of one piece is insufficient. Burnish down the edges of the tape with the handle of a screwdriver or similar, to ensure that the tape is securely attached to the metal underneath.

Bodywork repairs – filling and respraying

Before using this Section, see the Sections on dent, deep scratch, rust holes and gash repairs.

Many types of bodyfiller are available, but generally speaking, those proprietary kits which contain a tin of filler paste and a tube of resin hardener are best for this type of repair. A wide, flexible plastic or nylon applicator will be found invaluable for imparting a smooth and well-contoured finish to the surface of the filler.

Mix up a little filler on a clean piece of card or board – measure the hardener carefully (follow the maker's instructions on the pack), otherwise the filler will set too rapidly or too slowly. Using the applicator, apply the filler paste to the prepared area; draw the applicator across the surface of the filler to achieve the correct contour and to level the surface. As soon as a contour that approximates to the correct one is achieved, stop working the paste – if you carry on too long, the paste will become sticky and begin to 'pick-up' on the applicator. Continue to add thin layers of filler paste at 20-minute intervals, until the level of the filler is just proud of the surrounding bodywork.

Once the filler has hardened, the excess can be removed using a metal plane or file. From then on, progressively-finer grades of abrasive paper should be used, starting with a 40-grade production paper, and finishing with a 400-grade wet-and-dry paper. Always wrap the abrasive paper around a flat rubber, cork, or wooden block – otherwise the surface of the filler will not be completely flat. During the smoothing of the filler surface, the wet-and-dry paper should be periodically rinsed in water. This will ensure that a very smooth finish is imparted to the filler at the final stage.

At this stage, the 'dent' should be surrounded by a ring of bare metal, which in turn should be encircled by the finely 'feathered' edge of the good paintwork. Rinse the repair area with clean water, until all of the dust produced by the rubbing-down operation has gone.

Spray the whole area with a light coat of primer – this will show up any imperfections in the surface of the filler. Repair these imperfections with fresh filler paste or bodystopper, and once more smooth the surface with abrasive paper. Repeat this spray-and-repair procedure until you are satisfied that the surface of the filler, and the feathered edge of the paintwork, are perfect. Clean the repair area with clean water, and allow to dry fully.

The repair area is now ready for final spraying. Paint spraying must be carried out in a warm, dry, windless and dust-free atmosphere. This condition can be created artificially if you have access to a large indoor working area, but if you are forced to work in the open, you will have to pick your day very carefully. If you are working indoors, dousing the floor in the work area with water will help to settle the dust which would otherwise be in the atmosphere. If the repair area is confined to one body panel, mask off the surrounding panels; this will help to minimise the effects of a slight mis-match in paint colours. Bodywork fittings (e.g. chrome strips, door handles etc) will also need to be masked off. Use genuine masking tape, and several thicknesses of newspaper, for the masking operations.

6.4a Disconnect the indicator wiring . . .

6.4b . . . and the foglight wiring (arrowed)

Before commencing to spray, agitate the aerosol can thoroughly, then spray a test area (an old tin, or similar) until the technique is mastered. Cover the repair area with a thick coat of primer; the thickness should be built up using several thin layers of paint, rather than one thick one. Using 400-grade wet-and-dry paper, rub down the surface of the primer until it is really smooth. While doing this, the work area should be thoroughly doused with water, and the wet-and-dry paper periodically rinsed in water. Allow to dry before spraying on more paint.

Spray on the top coat, again building up the thickness by using several thin layers of paint. Start spraying at one edge of the repair area, and then, using a side-to-side motion, work until the whole repair area and about 2 inches of the surrounding original paintwork is covered. Remove all masking material 10 to 15 minutes after spraying on the final coat of paint.

Allow the new paint at least two weeks to harden, then, using a paintwork renovator, or a very fine cutting paste, blend the edges of the paint into the existing paintwork. Finally, apply wax polish.

Plastic components

With the use of more and more plastic body components by the vehicle manufacturers (e.g. bumpers. spoilers, and in some cases major body panels), rectification of more serious damage to such items has become a matter of either entrusting repair work to a specialist in this field, or renewing complete

components. Repair of such damage by the DIY owner is not really feasible, owing to the cost of the equipment and materials required for effecting such repairs. The basic technique involves making a groove along the line of the crack in the plastic, using a rotary burr in a power drill. The damaged part is then welded back together, using a hot-air gun to heat up and fuse a plastic filler rod into the groove. Any excess plastic is then removed, and the area rubbed down to a smooth finish. It is important that a filler rod of the correct plastic is used, as body components can be made of a variety of different types (e.g. polycarbonate, ABS, polypropylene).

Damage of a less serious nature (abrasions, minor cracks etc) can be repaired by the DIY owner using a two-part epoxy filler repair material. Once mixed in equal proportions, this is used in similar fashion to the bodywork filler used on metal panels. The filler is usually cured in twenty to thirty minutes, ready for sanding and painting.

If the owner is renewing a complete component himself, or if he has repaired it with epoxy filler, he will be left with the problem of finding a suitable paint for finishing which is compatible with the type of plastic used. At one time, the use of a universal paint was not possible, owing to the complex range of plastics encountered in body component applications. Standard paints, generally speaking, will not bond to plastic or rubber satisfactorily. However, it is now possible to obtain a plastic body parts finishing kit which consists of a pre-primer treatment, a primer

and coloured top coat. Full instructions are normally supplied with a kit, but basically, the method of use is to first apply the pre-primer to the component concerned, and allow it to dry for up to 30 minutes. Then the primer is applied, and left to dry for about an hour before finally applying the special-coloured top coat. The result is a correctly-coloured component, where the paint will flex with the plastic or rubber, a property that standard paint does not normally posses.

5 Major body damage – repair

Where serious damage has occurred, or large areas need renewal due to neglect, it means that complete new panels will need welding-in; this is best left to professionals. If the damage is due to impact, it will also be necessary to check completely the alignment of the bodyshell; this can only be carried out accurately by a Ford dealer, using special jigs. If the body is left misaligned, it is primarily dangerous, as the car will not handle properly, and secondly, uneven stresses will be imposed on the steering, suspension and possibly transmission, causing abnormal wear or complete failure, particularly to items such as the tyres.

6 Bumpers – removal and refitting

Note: *Headlamp washers are fitted to some models; as the bumper is being removed, disconnect as required.*

Removal

Front bumper

1 Apply the handbrake, jack up the front of the vehicle and support it on axle stands.
2 Remove the radiator grille as described in Section 7.
3 Remove the two front headlamps as described in Chapter 12, Section 7.
4 Disconnect the wiring connectors from the indicator and foglight units **(see illustrations)**.
5 Undo the screws securing the wheelarch liners to the front bumper (one each side), and the screws (three each side) securing the bumper to the front wings **(see illustrations)**.
6 Release the six securing clips from the top of the bumper cover, and the three clips from the bottom of the bumper cover **(see illustrations)**.
7 With the help of an assistant to support one end of the bumper, withdraw the bumper forwards from the vehicle, at the same time pulling the sides away from the body to prevent damage to paintwork **(see illustration)**.

6.5a Removing bumper-to-wheelarch lining screw . . .

6.5b . . . and bumper-to-wing bolts

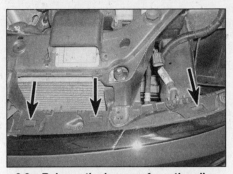

6.6a Release the bumper from the clips (arrowed) . . .

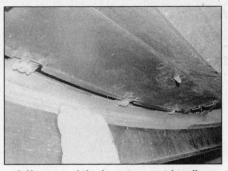

6.6b . . . and the lower cover trim clips

6.7 Disengage locating pegs from the wing

Rear bumper – except Estate

8 Chock the front wheels, jack up the rear of the vehicle and support it on axle stands. Open up the boot/tailgate.

6.10 Undo the wheelarch lining-to-bumper retaining screw

9 Remove the four retaining screws from the upper part of the bumper.
10 Remove the screws securing the wheelarch liners to the rear bumper (see illustration).
11 Using a flat-bladed screwdriver, unclip the clips from the lower part of the bumper (see illustration).
12 On the Saloon model, unscrew the trims from inside the light units and remove. Undo the bumper securing nuts from behind the trims (three each side).
13 With the help of an assistant to support one end of the bumper, withdraw the bumper rearwards from the vehicle, at the same time pulling the sides away from the body to prevent damage to paintwork.
14 Disconnect the electrical connectors from the rear foglight and reversing lamp, where fitted.

Rear bumper – Estate

15 Chock the front wheels, jack up the rear of the vehicle and support it on axle stands.
16 Open the tailgate, and open the two pockets on the side panels, one on the left and one on the right (see illustrations).
17 Remove the two screws from the top of the plastic First Aid kit holder, in the right-hand pocket, then unclip from the aperture. Undo the bumper securing nut from behind the trim (see illustrations).
18 Unclip the plastic tray from inside the left-hand pocket, and undo the bumper securing nut from behind the trim (see illustration).
19 Remove the four retaining screws from the upper part of the bumper (see illustration).
20 Remove the screws securing the wheelarch liners to the rear bumper (see illustration).

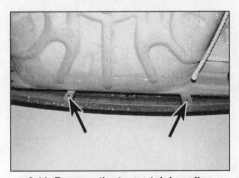

6.11 Remove the two retaining clips (arrowed)

6.16a Open the left-hand compartment . . .

6.16b . . . the right-hand compartment

6.17a Unscrew and remove the plastic trim . . .

6.17b . . . then undo the bumper securing nut (arrowed)

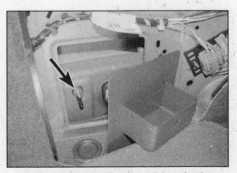

6.18 Unclip plastic tray and undo the bumper securing nut (arrowed)

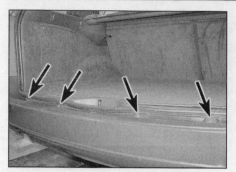

6.19 Undo the four upper bumper screws
(arrowed)

6.20 Undo the wheelarch lining-to-bumper
retaining screw

21 Behind the wheelarch liners at each corner of the bumper, undo the securing nuts and also pull off the rubber buffers (one on each side).
22 With the help of an assistant to support

7.2 Remove air deflector

one end of the bumper, withdraw the bumper rearwards from the vehicle.

Refitting

23 Refitting is a reversal of the removal procedure. Make sure that, where applicable, the bumper guides are located correctly. Check all electrical components that have been disconnected.

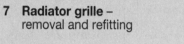

7 Radiator grille –
removal and refitting

Removal

1 Support the bonnet in the open position.
2 Undo the four securing screws from the radiator air deflector and remove (see illustration).

3 Unscrew the two radiator grille lower mounting bolts (see illustration).
4 Release the clips at the top ends of the radiator grille, unclip the centre of the grille from the lock assembly and lift out from the front panel to remove (see illustration).

Refitting

5 Refitting is a reversal of the removal procedure.

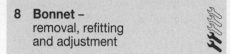

8 Bonnet –
removal, refitting
and adjustment

Removal

1 Open the bonnet, and support it in the open position using the stay.
2 Disconnect the battery negative (earth) lead (Chapter 5A, Section 1).
3 Disconnect the windscreen washer hoses from the bottom of the jets, and unclip from the bonnet (see illustrations).
4 Disconnect the windscreen washer wiring connector from the bottom of the jets, and unclip from the bonnet (see illustrations).
5 To assist in correctly realigning the bonnet when refitting it, mark the outline of the hinges with a soft pencil. Loosen the two hinge retaining bolts on each side (see illustration).
6 With the help of an assistant, unscrew the four bolts, release the stay, and lift the bonnet from the vehicle.

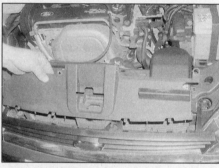

7.3 Undo the two securing bolts
(one each side)

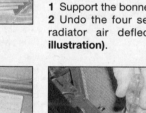

7.4 Unclip grill at the centre

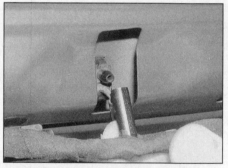

8.3a Pull hose from the washer jet . . .

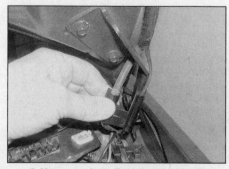

8.3b . . . and unclip from the hinge

8.4a Unplug wiring connectors . . .

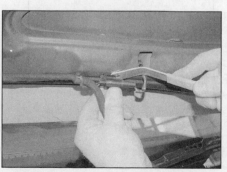

8.4b . . . and unclip from bonnet

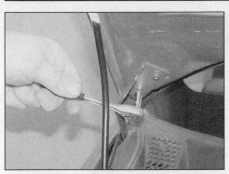

8.5 Undo the hinge bolts

9.4 Lower radiator (on vehicles with air conditioning)

9.5a Unbolt the lock . . .

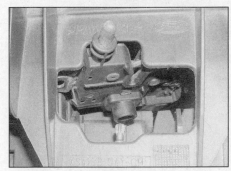

9.5b . . . and disengage from the lock cylinder

9.6 Disconnect the wiring connector

9.7 Withdraw the lock cylinder from the housing

Refitting and adjustment

7 Refitting is a reversal of the removal procedure, noting the following points:
  a) *Position the bonnet hinges within the outline marks made during removal, but if necessary alter its position to provide a uniform gap all round.*
  b) *Adjust the front height by repositioning the lock (see Section 9) and turning the rubber buffers on the engine compartment front cross panel up or down to support the bonnet.*

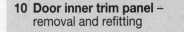

9 Bonnet lock – removal, refitting and adjustment

Removal

1 Remove the radiator grille as described in Section 7.
2 Ensure that the handbrake is firmly applied, then raise and support the front of the car on axle stands (see *Jacking and vehicle support*).
3 On vehicles with air conditioning, unclip the radiator lower cover from the bottom of the radiator support bracket.
4 On vehicles with air conditioning, unbolt the radiator support bracket from the bottom of the radiator. Replace the four securing bolts with pieces of threaded rod and nuts **(see illustration)**, so as to lower the radiator (approx 75mm) to gain access to the bonnet lock securing bolts.

5 Mark the position of the lock on the crossmember. Unscrew the securing bolts and withdraw the lock, unclipping it from the lock cylinder **(see illustrations)**.
6 Disconnect the wiring connector from the lock assembly, as it is being removed **(see illustration)**.
7 Push the lock cylinder from the housing, using a screwdriver to unclip it **(see illustration)**.

Refitting and adjustment

8 Refitting is a reversal of the removal procedure, starting by positioning the lock as noted before removal.
9 If the front of the bonnet is not level with the front wings, the lock may be moved up or down within the mounting holes. After making an adjustment, raise or lower the rubber buffers to support the bonnet correctly.

10 Door inner trim panel – removal and refitting

Removal

Front

1 Disconnect the battery negative (earth) lead (Chapter 5A, Section 1).
2 Insert a screwdriver into a hole under the door grab handle, then twist it to unclip the cover trim. Undo the two screws from behind the cover inside the door pull handle **(see illustrations)**.
3 Carefully prise out the plastic screw cover from the inner door handle cavity, using a small screwdriver. Remove the screw, and ease the bezel from around the door handle **(see illustrations)**.

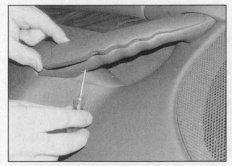

10.2a Unclip grab handle trim . . .

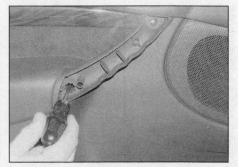

10.2b . . . and remove the two screws

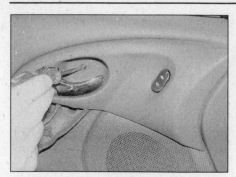

10.3a Undo the retaining screw . . .

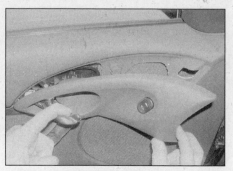

10.3b . . . and withdraw the bezel from the trim panel

10.4 Disconnecting the wiring connector

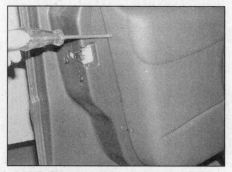

10.5 Remove all the retaining screws around the trim

10.6 Lift the trim panel from the door

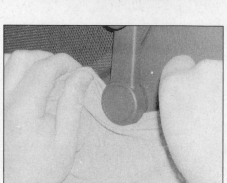

10.7 Using a cloth to disengage spring clip from the handle

4 Disconnect the wiring connector from the window operating switch **(see illustration)**.
5 Working around the outer edge of the door inner trim panel, undo all the securing screws **(see illustration)**.

6 Pull the trim panel away from the door, then rotate upwards at the rear to remove from the vehicle **(see illustration)**.

Rear

7 Carry out the procedures as described for the front doors, except on models fitted with manual (ie, non-electric) rear windows, fully shut the window, and note the position of the regulator handle. Release the spring clip by inserting a clean cloth between the handle and the door trim. Using a 'sawing' action, pull the cloth against the open ends of the clip to release it, at the same time pulling the handle from the regulator shaft splines. Withdraw the handle (and where fitted, the spacer) and recover the clip **(see illustration)**.

Refitting

8 Refitting is a reversal of the removal procedure. On the rear manual windows, fit the retaining clip to the winder handle before

refitting the winder handle to the regulator shaft **(see illustration)**.

10.8 Position of the clip, before refitting the handle

11 Door window glass – removal and refitting

Removal

Front

1 Remove the door inner trim panel as described in Section 10.
2 Rotate the side impact bolster anti-clockwise to remove it from its retaining clips, then pull out the retaining clips from the door panel **(see illustrations)**.
3 Undo the four screws from the speaker and remove from the door, disconnect the wiring as it becomes accessible **(see illustrations)**.

11.2a Unclip the impact bolster . . .

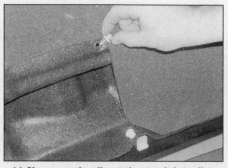

11.2b . . . and pull out the retaining clips

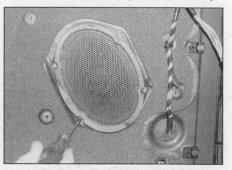

11.3a Remove the four screws . . .

11.3b . . . and disconnect the wiring connector

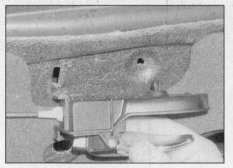

11.4 Disengage the door release handle

11.5 Carefully cut the sealer from around the weathershield

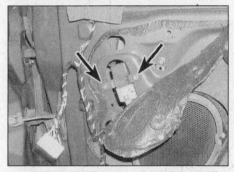

11.6 Remove the two screws (arrowed)

4 Detach the door release handle from the door by unclipping it from the front end, then slide the handle out in a forwards direction **(see illustration)**. (The door handle at this point can be left attached to the cable.)

5 Using a knife or scraper, cut through the butyl strip to enable the weather shield to be peeled back from the door panel. Take care not to damage the weathershield or door panel **(see illustration)**. (Do not touch the adhesive as re-bonding will be impaired.)

6 On the driver's door only, undo the two retaining screws to remove the 'one-touch down' relay (if required) **(see illustration)**.

7 Temporarily refit the window operating switch to its electrical connector.

8 Lower the window until the glass support bracket bolts align with the holes in the door panel,

then slacken the bolts in the support bracket

(see illustration). (Do not remove the bolts.)

9 Lift the window glass from the door while tilting it up at the rear, and withdraw it from the outside of the door frame **(see illustration)**.

Rear

10 Carry out the procedures as described in paragraphs 1 to 5 for the front door.

11 Unclip the triangle inner trim panel from the window frame **(see illustration)**.

12 Slacken the two retaining screws for the window runner guide, and lift up from inside the rear door aperture to remove from door panel **(see illustrations)**.

13 Temporarily refit the regulator handle on its splines, or the window operating switch to its electrical connector.

14 Lower the window until the glass support bracket securing sleeve/pin aligns with the hole in the door panel **(see illustration)**.

15 Using a punch, push out the pin in the securing sleeve, then push out the sleeve to release the window glass from the support bracket. Retrieve the pin and sleeve from inside the door for refitting.

11.8 Slacken the two bolts (arrowed)

11.9 Lifting the glass out from the door frame

11.11 Unclip the trim from the window frame

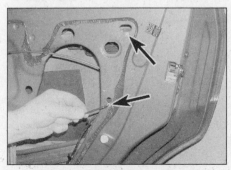

11.12a Slacken the two screws (arrowed) . . .

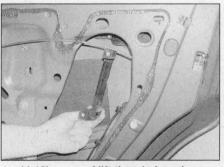

11.12b . . . and lift the window glass runner out

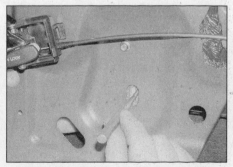

11.14 Align the sleeve/pin for removal

11.17 Lifting the glass out from the door frame

16 Temporarily refit the regulator handle on its splines, or the window operating switch to its electrical connector to lower the window support bracket.

17 Lift the glass from the door while tilting it inwards, and withdraw it from the inside of the door **(see illustration)**.

Refitting

18 Refitting is a reversal of the removal procedure, making sure that the glass is correctly located in the support brackets. **Note:** *On the rear window, relocate the securing sleeve/pin in the window glass before refitting (see illustration), ensuring they project equally either side of the glass. Guide the window into the door so that the securing sleeve/pin locates into the window lifting support bracket. Lightly tap the top of the window to locate the sleeve/pin into the lifting support bracket.*

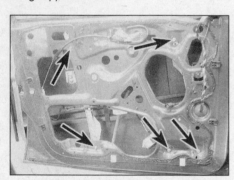

12.2 Undo the bolts (arrowed)

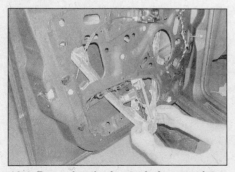

12.4 Removing the front window regulator from the door

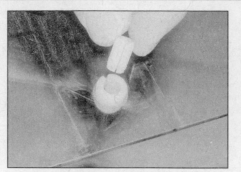

11.18 Press the sleeve/pin into glass before refitting

12 Door window regulator – removal and refitting

Removal

Front

1 Carry out the procedures to remove the window glass as described in Section 11, paragraphs 1 to 9.

2 Loosen and remove the regulator/electric motor mounting bolts **(see illustration)**.

3 Disconnect the wiring multi-plug from the window regulator motor **(see illustration)**.

4 Unclip the regulator cables from inside the door panel, then withdraw the window regulator mechanism downwards and out through the hole in the inner door panel **(see illustration)**.

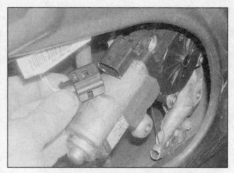

12.3 Unplug the wiring connector

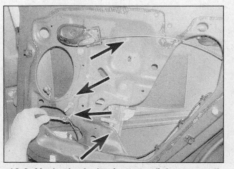

12.6 Undo the bolts (arrowed) for manual windows

Rear

5 Carry out the procedures to remove the window glass as described in Section 11.

6 Loosen and remove the regulator and manual winder/electric motor mounting bolts **(see illustration)**.

7 On electric windows, disconnect the wiring multi-plugs from the window regulator motor.

8 Withdraw the window regulator mechanism from inside the door, through the hole in the inner door panel **(see illustration)**.

Refitting

9 Refitting is a reversal of the removal procedure.

13 Door handle and lock components – removal and refitting

⚠ *Warning: before working on any electrical components, disconnect the battery negative (earth) lead (Chapter 5A, Section 1).*

Removal

Exterior handle – front

1 Remove the door inner trim panel as described in Section 10.

2 Rotate the side impact bolster anti-clockwise to remove it from its retaining clips, then pull out the retaining clips from the door panel.

3 Undo the four screws from the speaker and remove from the door, disconnect the wiring as it becomes accessible.

4 Detach the inner door release handle from the door by unclipping it from the front end, then slide the handle out in a forwards direction. (The door handle at this point can be left attached to the cable.)

5 Using a knife or scraper, cut through the butyl strip to enable the weather shield to be peeled back from the door panel. Take care not to damage the weather shield or door panel. (Do not touch the adhesive as re-bonding will be impaired.)

6 To remove the outer lock cylinder bezel, undo the retaining screw from the inside of the door handle assembly. (It is not necessary to fully remove this screw.) Unclip and remove the bezel from the lock cylinder **(see illustrations)**.

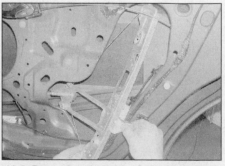

12.8 Removing the rear window regulator from the door

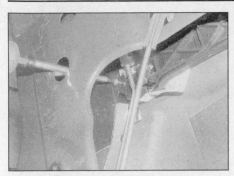

13.6a Slacken the retaining screw . . .

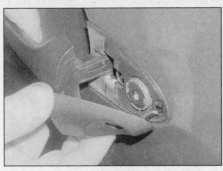

13.6b . . . and remove the lock cylinder bezel

inside the rear door aperture and remove from door panel.

10 Remove the grommet from the access hole on the inside of the door assembly **(see illustration)**.

11 Slacken the retaining screw through the access hole, to remove the outer door handle bezel **(see illustrations)**. (It is not necessary to fully remove this screw.)

12 Loosen but do not remove the screw from the inside of the door, for the exterior handle. Slide the handle back, and pull out from the door **(see illustrations)**. Unclip the door handle seals from the door panel.

Interior handle

13 Remove the door inner trim panel Section 10.

14 Detach the door release handle from the door by unclipping it from the front end, then slide the handle out in a forwards direction **(see illustration)**.

7 Loosen but do not remove the screw from the inside of the door for the exterior handle. Slide the handle back, and pull out from the door. Unclip the door handle seals from the door panel **(see illustrations)**.

Exterior handle – rear

8 Carry out the procedures as described for the front door exterior handle (paragraphs 1 to 5).

9 Unscrew the window runner guide from

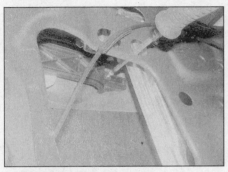

13.7a Slacken the retaining screw

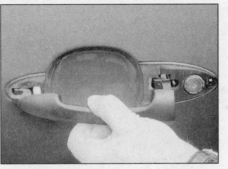

13.7b . . . unclip the door handle . . .

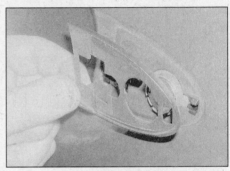

13.7c . . . and remove the door handle seals

13.10 Remove grommet to access screw

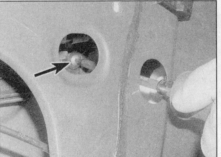

13.11a Slacken the retaining screw (arrowed) . . .

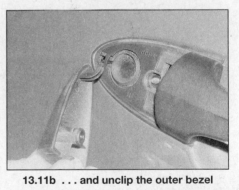

13.11b . . . and unclip the outer bezel

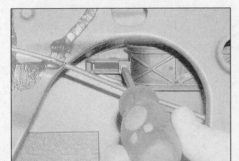

13.12a Slacken the retaining screw . . .

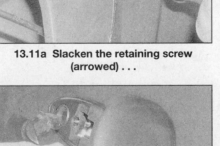

13.12b . . . and unclip the door handle

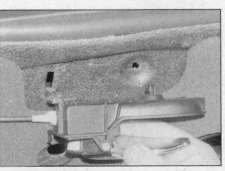

13.14 Unclip the handle from the door

13.16 Unclip the outer cable, then release the inner cable

13.19 Undo the lock mounting bolts

13.20 Withdraw the lock mechanism from the door

15 Before you can remove the cable from the handle, set the lever switch in the locked position.

16 Using a thin-bladed screwdriver unclip the outer cable locating clip, then release the inner operating cable from the handle assembly **(see illustration)**.

Lock motor/module – front

17 Remove the exterior handle as described earlier in this Section.

18 Disconnect the electrical connector from the door lock motor, using a small screwdriver to release the retaining clip.

19 Slacken and remove the three Torx bolts from the lock assembly at the rear edge of the door **(see illustration)**.

20 Unclip the door lock/handle reinforcement bracket from the door panel. Manoeuvre the assembly out through the door inner frame,

complete with the door lock mechanism **(see illustration)**.

21 With the door lock assembly on a work top, unclip the trim from the back of the security shield then undo the two securing screws to remove from the door lock assembly **(see illustrations)**.

22 Release the adjustment locking clip from the remote control rod **(see illustration)**. Measure the amount of thread at the top of the rod before removing the clip as this will adjust the linkage on refitting. (The clip may break on removal so a new one will be required.)

23 Unhook the connecting rod from the door lock cylinder lever, by turning it through a quarter-turn.

24 Unclip the outer cable from the lock housing (note position of the outer cable in the

lock housing), then turn the inner cable through a quarter-turn to remove it from the door lock linkage **(see illustration)**.

Lock cylinder

25 Remove the lock/module as described earlier in this Section.

26 Prise out the cylinder retaining tab from the handle reinforcement bracket, using a small screwdriver **(see illustration)**.

27 Insert the key, and turn it so that it engages the cylinder, then pull out the lock cylinder **(see illustration)**.

Lock motor/module – rear

28 Remove the exterior handle as described earlier in this Section.

29 Slacken and remove the three Torx bolts, from the lock assembly at the rear edge of the door **(see illustration)**.

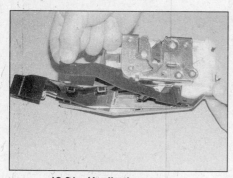

13.21a Unclip the cover . . .

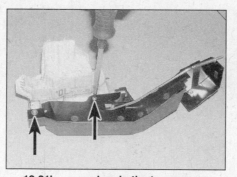

13.21b . . . and undo the two screws (arrowed)

13.22 Lever out the locking clip (a new one may be needed)

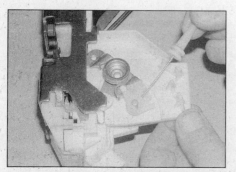

13.24 Unclip the outer cable, then release the inner cable

13.26 Release the locking tab

13.27 Pull out the lock cylinder

13.29 Unscrew the lock mounting bolts

13.30 Removing the lock assembly from the door

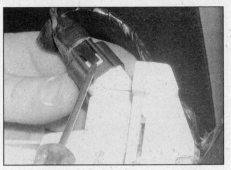

13.31 Unclip the wiring connector

30 Unclip the door lock/handle reinforcement bracket from the door panel. Manoeuvre assembly out through the door inner frame, complete with the door lock mechanism **(see illustration)**.

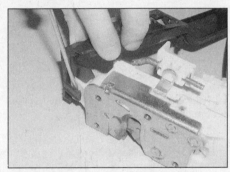

13.32 Unclip the bracket from the lock

31 Disconnect the wiring connector from the door lock motor, using a small screwdriver to release the retaining clip **(see illustration)**.
32 With the door lock assembly on a work top, unclip the handle reinforcement bracket from the lock motor **(see illustration)**.
33 Remove the connecting rod/adjusting clip from the door lock assembly. Measure the amount of thread at the top of the rod before removing the clip as this will adjust the linkage on refitting. Turn the rod/adjusting clip through a quarter-turn to remove **(see illustration)**.
34 Unclip the outer cable from the lock housing (note the position of the outer cable in the lock housing), then turn the inner cable through a quarter-turn to remove it from the door lock linkage **(see illustration)**.

Striker/contact switch

35 Using a pencil, mark the position of the striker/contact switch on the pillar.

36 Undo the mounting screws using a Torx key, and remove the striker/contact switch. Disconnect the wiring connector **(see illustrations)**.

Check strap

37 Using a Torx key, unscrew and remove the check strap mounting bolt from the door pillar **(see illustration)**.
38 Prise the rubber grommet from the door aperture, then unscrew the mounting nuts and withdraw the check strap from the door **(see illustrations)**.

Refitting

Handles (exterior and interior)

39 Refitting is a reversal of the removal procedure. (When refitting operating cable, make sure the outer cable is located into the correct recess.)

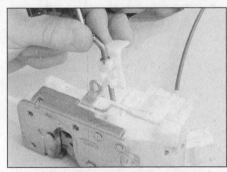

13.33 Disengage the clip from the lock lever

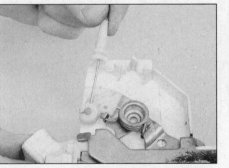

13.34 Unclip the outer cable, then release the inner cable

13.36a Remove the securing bolts . . .

13.36b . . . and disconnect the wiring connector

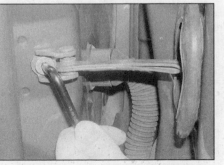

13.37 Unscrew the mounting bolt

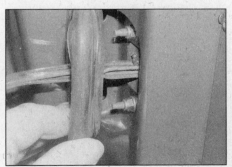

13.38a Remove the rubber cover . . .

13.38b ... and undo the check strap mounting nuts

Lock cylinder

40 Check that the retaining clip is fitted correctly.

41 Align the grooves on the cylinder with the grooves on the reinforcement plate, then

14.2 Undo the mounting bolt

14.3 Disconnect the wiring plug

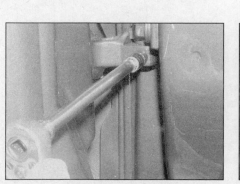

14.5 Slacken the hinge grub screws

carefully push the cylinder into the handle until it engages the clip.

42 The remaining refitting procedure is a reversal of removal.

Lock motor

43 Refitting is a reversal of the removal procedure. (A new adjusting clip may need to be fitted; do not fully clip together until the final adjustment is made.)

Striker

44 Refitting is a reversal of the removal procedure, but check that the door lock passes over the striker centrally. If necessary, reposition the striker before fully tightening the mounting screws.

Check strap

45 Refitting is a reversal of the removal procedure.

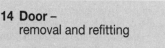

14 Door –
removal and refitting

Removal

1 Disconnect the battery negative (earth) lead (Chapter 5A, Section 1).

2 Using a Torx key, unscrew and remove the check strap mounting bolt from the door pillar **(see illustration)**.

3 On the front doors, disconnect the wiring connector by twisting it anti-clockwise **(see illustration)**.

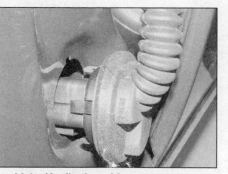

14.4a Unclip the rubber grommet . . .

15.2 Unclip the mirror bezel

4 On the rear doors, unclip the rubber grommet and disconnect the wiring block connector **(see illustrations)**.

5 Using a Torx socket, slacken the retaining screws in the top and bottom hinges **(see illustration)**.

6 Carefully lift the door from the hinges.

Refitting

7 Refitting is a reversal of the removal procedure, but check that the door lock passes over the striker centrally. If necessary, reposition the striker. When refitting the wiring connector to the font doors, the line and the white dot on the connector should be in line.

15 Exterior mirror and glass –
removal and refitting

Removal

Mirror

1 Where electric mirrors are fitted, disconnect the battery negative (earth) lead (Chapter 5A, Section 1).

2 Unclip the quarter bezel from the front of the window opening and remove **(see illustration)**.

3 On manual mirrors, detach the adjustment lever by turning the rubber gaiter to disengage from the bezel **(see illustration)**.

4 On electric mirrors, disconnect the wiring multi-plug from the mirror control switch.

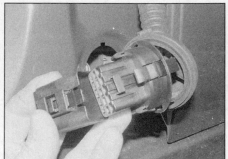

14.4b . . . and disconnect the wiring connector

15.3 Turn the switch to disengage

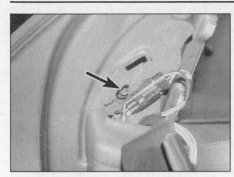

15.4 Unclip the wiring connector to access the mirror securing bolt (arrowed)

15.6 Press the mirror glass in the direction of the arrow to remove

15.7 Disconnect the wiring connectors

Release the clip and detach the electrical connector to gain access to the retaining bolt **(see illustration)**.

5 Unscrew the mirror mounting bolt, then withdraw the mirror from the outside of the door. Recover the mirror seal as the wiring/cable is being drawn through the rubber grommet.

Mirror glass

6 Press the mirror glass from the inner side outwards and unclip from the retaining bracket **(see illustration)**.

7 Withdraw the mirror glass and disconnect the wiring connectors for the heated mirrors **(see illustration)**.

Refitting

8 Refitting is a reversal of the removal procedure. Take care not to drop the rubber grommet inside the door panel when removing the mirror, as the interior door trim will have to be removed to retrieve it.

16 Interior mirror – removal and refitting

1 Lift up the retaining clip at the base of the mirror bracket, and slide the mirror assembly upwards off the mounting attached to the windscreen **(see illustrations)**.

2 Refitting is the reversal of the removal procedure.

16.1a Lift up the retaining clip (arrowed) . . .

17 Boot lid – removal and refitting

Removal

1 Disconnect the battery negative (earth) lead (Chapter 5A, Section 1), and open the boot lid.

2 On the left-hand hinge, pull off the trim covering, and release the wiring on the hinge arm. Prise out the grommet to free the wiring **(see illustration)**.

3 Remove the trim from inside the boot lid **(see illustration)**.

4 Disconnect the wiring at the connectors visible through the boot lid inner skin aperture.

5 Attach a length of strong cord to the end of the wires in the aperture, to act as an aid to guiding the wiring through the lid when it is refitted.

16.1b . . . and slide mirror upwards off the windscreen mounting

6 Withdraw the wiring loom through the boot lid apertures. Untie the cord, and leave it in place in the boot lid for refitting the wiring loom.

7 Using a small screwdriver, prise off the clips securing the struts to the boot lid. Pull the sockets from the ball-studs, and move the struts downwards **(see illustration)**.

8 Mark the position of the hinge arms with a pencil. Place rags beneath each corner of the boot lid, to prevent damage to the paintwork.

9 With the help of an assistant, unscrew the mounting bolts and lift the boot lid from the car.

Refitting

10 Refitting is a reversal of the removal procedure, noting the following points:
a) *Check that the boot lid is correctly aligned with the surrounding bodywork, with an equal clearance around its edge.*

17.2 Pull grommet out to remove the wiring

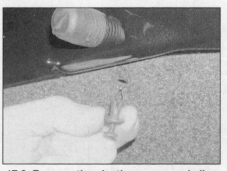

17.3 Remove the plastic screws and clips

17.7 Prise off clip to release the strut

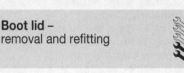

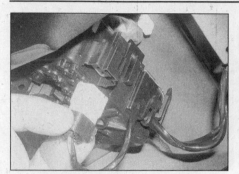

18.3 Unplug the wiring connector

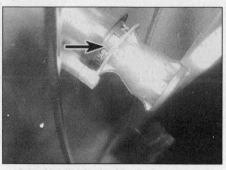

18.4a Unclip the lock cylinder surround (arrowed from inside)

18.4b . . . and remove from boot lid

b) *Adjustment can be made by loosening the hinge bolts, and moving the boot lid within the elongated mounting holes.*
c) *Check that the lock enters the striker centrally when the boot lid is closed.*

18.5 Unscrew the lock mounting bolts

18 Boot lid lock components – removal and refitting

Removal

1 Disconnect the battery negative (earth) lead (Chapter 5A, Section 1).
2 With the boot lid open, undo the plastic screws from the boot liner trim and remove.
3 Disconnect the wiring plug from the lock assembly **(see illustration)**.
4 Unclip the rubber grommet from around the lock cylinder on the inside of the boot lid **(see illustrations)**.
5 Using a Torx key, unscrew the lock mounting screws, and withdraw the lock and lock cylinder **(see illustration)**.
6 With the lock assembly on a suitable work bench; file down the lock cylinder housing to expose the spring and plunger **(see illustrations)**.
7 Remove the spring and plunger, then turn the lock cylinder and pull out of the lock housing **(see illustration)**. (The spring is NOT used on refitting.)

Refitting

8 Refitting is a reversal of the removal procedure, noting when refitting the lock cylinder :
a) *Use an M6 tap to cut a thread in the lock cylinder housing, where the plunger had been removed (see illustration).*
b) *Install the lock cylinder, then turn to locate into place.*
c) *Push the plunger into the hole, then fit retaining screw (M6 x 6.5mm) to secure the plunger (see illustrations) (use Loctite sealer on the threads).*

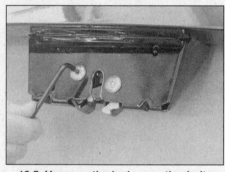

18.6a File down the lock cylinder housing (arrowed) . . .

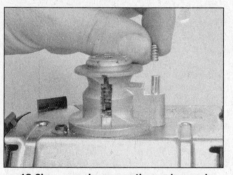

18.6b . . . and remove the spring and plunger

18.7 Turn lock cylinder to disengage from the lock assembly

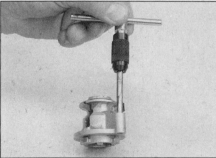

18.8a Use an M6 tap to cut a thread . . .

18.8b . . . refit the lock cylinder, and insert the plunger . . .

18.8c . . . then fit the retaining screw, using Loctite sealer on the threads

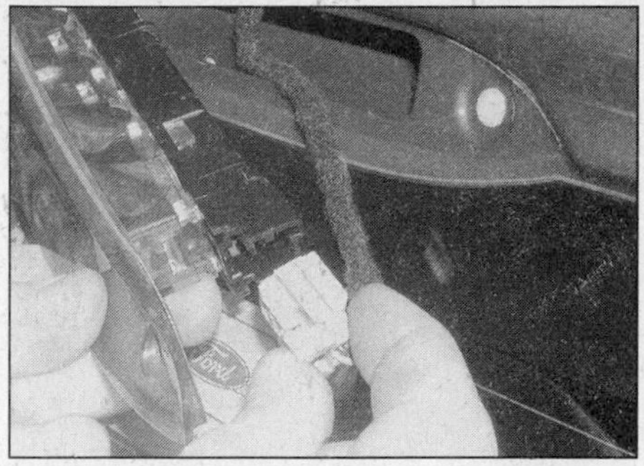

19.3a Disconnect the wiring connector . . .

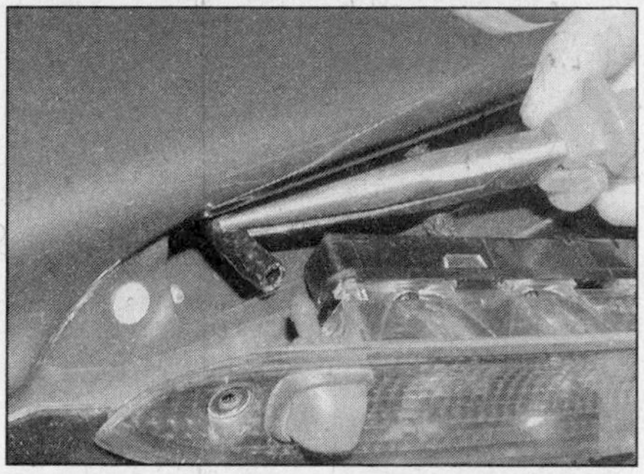

19.3b . . . and the rear washer pipe

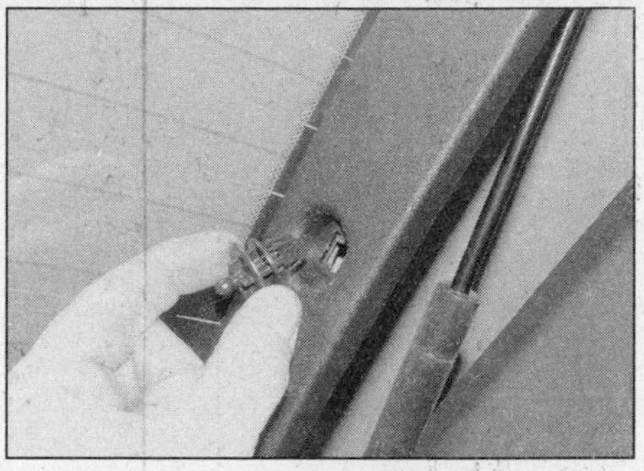

19.4a On Hatchback models pull out the rear shelf cord posts . . .

19 Tailgate – removal and refitting

Removal

1 Disconnect the battery negative (earth) lead (Chapter 5A, Section 1).

2 The tailgate may be unbolted from the hinges and the hinges left in position.

3 Remove the two screws from the high-level rear brake light cover, and disconnect the bulbholder wiring and washer pipe **(see illustrations)**.

4 Undo the retaining screws, then unclip the tailgate trim. Carefully unclip the upper tailgate trims from around the rear screen. On Hatchback models unclip the rear shelf cord posts from the upper tailgate trims **(see illustrations)**.

5 Disconnect the wiring loom connectors through the tailgate inner skin aperture including the earth wiring. Attach a strong fine cord to the end of the wiring loom, to act as an aid to guiding the wiring through the tailgate when it is refitted.

6 Prise the rubber grommet from the left-hand side of the tailgate aperture **(see illustration)**, and pull out the wiring loom. Untie the cord, leaving it in position in the tailgate for guiding the wire through on refitting.

7 Have an assistant support the tailgate in its open position.

8 Using a small screwdriver, prise off the clip securing the struts to the tailgate. Pull the sockets from the ball-studs, and move the struts downwards **(see illustration)**.

9 Unscrew and remove the hinge bolts (two each side) from the tailgate **(see illustration)**. Withdraw the tailgate from the body aperture, taking care not to damage the paintwork.

10 If the hinges are to be removed from the roof panel, unscrew the retaining screws (one each side), from the bottom of the D-pillar trim panels **(see illustration)**. Unclip the trims from both sides and remove from the pillars.

11 Carefully pull down the rear edge of the headlining for access to the nuts and bolts. Take care not to damage the headlining **(see illustration)**.

12 Unscrew the mounting nuts and bolts for the hinges from the rear roof panel.

Refitting

13 Refitting is a reversal of the removal procedure, but check that the tailgate is located centrally in the body aperture, and that the striker enters the lock centrally. If necessary, loosen the mounting nuts and reposition the tailgate as required.

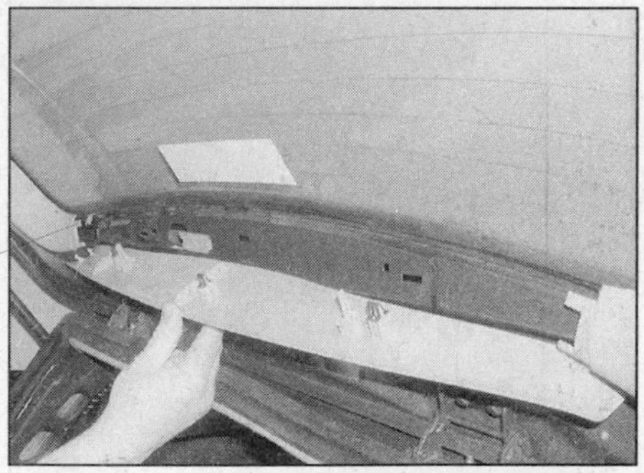

19.4b . . . then unclip the upper tailgate trims

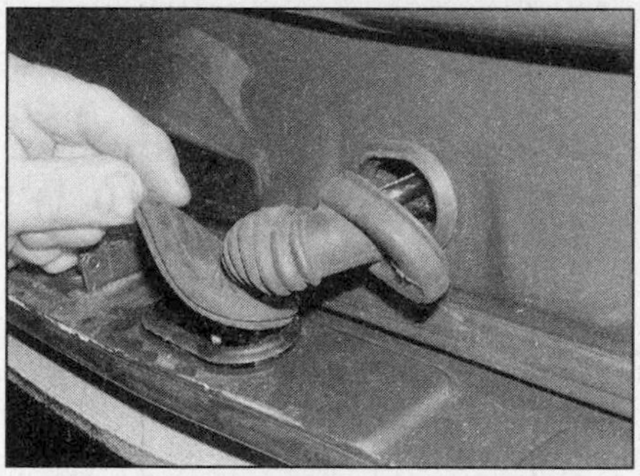

19.6 Unclip the rubber wiring grommet

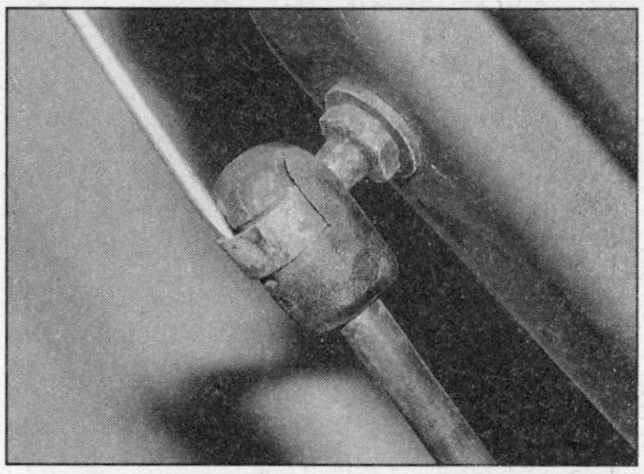

19.8 Prise off clip to release the strut

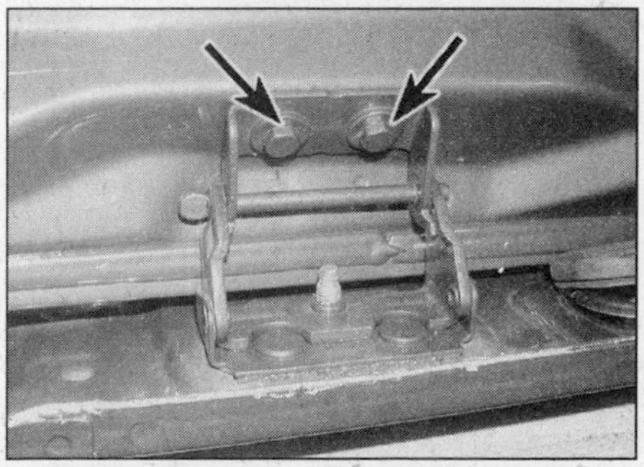

19.9 Undo the two securing bolts (arrowed)

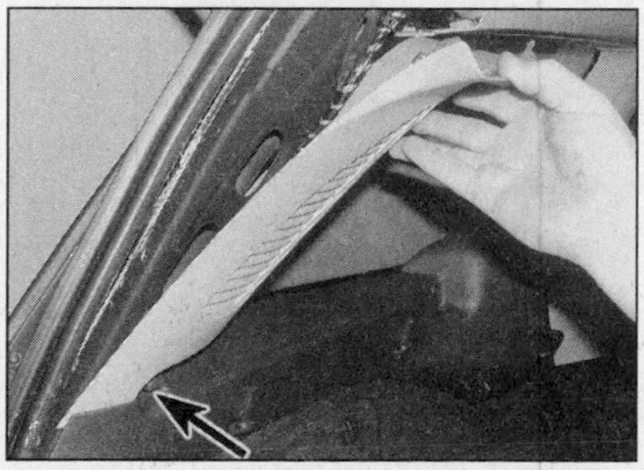

19.10 Remove the screw (arrowed) and unclip trim

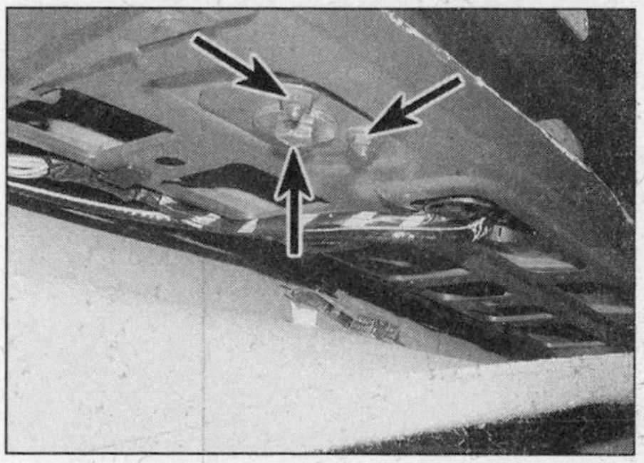

19.11 Undo the nuts and bolt (arrowed) to remove hinge

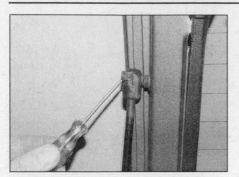

20.2a Use a thin screwdriver to release the securing clip . . .

20.2b . . . then pull the strut off the ball-stud

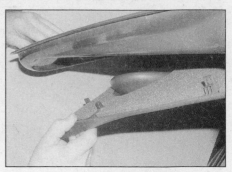

21.2 Unclip the tailgate trim

20 Support struts – removal and refitting

Removal

1 Have an assistant support the tailgate, boot or bonnet in its open position.
2 Prise off the upper spring clip securing the strut to the tailgate, boot or bonnet, then pull the socket from the ball-stud **(see illustrations)**.
3 Similarly prise off the bottom clip, and pull the socket from the ball-stud. Withdraw the strut.

Refitting

4 Refitting is a reversal of the removal procedure, making sure that the strut is fitted the same way up as it was removed.

21 Tailgate lock components – removal and refitting

Removal

Lock assembly – Estate

1 Disconnect the battery negative (earth) lead (Chapter 5A, Section 1).
2 With the tailgate open, undo the two plastic screws and unclip the trim panel from the tailgate **(see illustration)**.
3 Disconnect the electrical connector from the tailgate lock assembly **(see illustration)**.
4 Disengage the operating cable from the rear of the lock cylinder. Unclip the outer cable, then rotate the cable to disengage the inner cable **(see illustration)**.

5 Undo the two lock securing bolts and remove the lock assembly, complete with the operating cable **(see illustration)**.

Lock assembly – Hatchback

6 Disconnect the battery negative (earth) lead (Chapter 5A, Section 1).
7 With the tailgate open, undo the retaining screws and unclip the trim panel from the tailgate **(see illustration)**.
8 Disconnect the electrical connector from the tailgate lock assembly **(see illustration)**.
9 Unclip the rubber grommet from around the lock cylinder on the inside of the tailgate **(see illustrations)**.
10 Using a Torx key, unscrew the lock mounting screws, and withdraw the lock assembly **(see illustration)**.

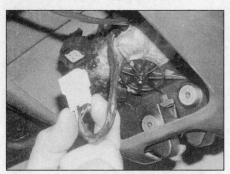

21.3 Disconnect the wiring connector from the lock

21.4 Unclip the outer cable, then release the inner cable

21.5 Undo the two securing bolts and remove the lock

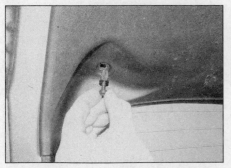

21.7 Remove the retaining screws from the tailgate trim

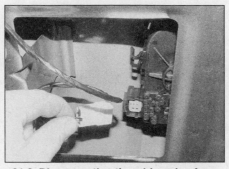

21.8 Disconnecting the wiring plug from the lock assembly

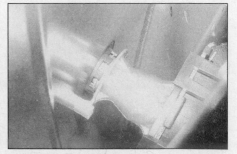

21.9a Arrow shows the rubber grommet clipped onto the lock assembly inside tailgate . . .

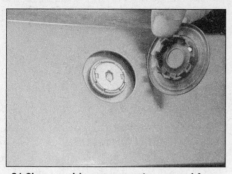

21.9b ... rubber grommet removed from the lock assembly

21.10 Withdrawing the lock assembly from the tailgate

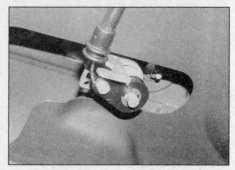

21.13 Unclip the outer cable, then release the inner cable

Lock cylinder – Estate

11 Disconnect the battery negative (earth) lead (Chapter 5A, Section 1).

12 With the tailgate open, undo the two

21.14 Prise trim away from the tailgate, after removing securing nuts

plastic screws and unclip the trim panel from the tailgate.

13 Disengage the operating cable from the rear of the lock cylinder **(see illustration)**.

14 Undo the three securing nuts from the rear number plate light trim and remove from the tailgate **(see illustration)**, disconnect the wiring connectors (if required) as they come into view. Double-sided sticking tape will be required on the ends of the trim for refitting.

15 Slacken and remove the two lock cylinder securing nuts **(see illustration)**.

16 Prise the lock cylinder from the sealing gasket on the tailgate to remove **(see illustration)**. Fit new sealing gasket when refitting.

Lock cylinder – Hatchback

17 With the lock assembly removed

(paragraphs 6 to 10), and on a suitable work bench. File down the lock cylinder housing to expose the spring and plunger **(see illustrations)**.

18 Remove the spring and plunger, then turn the lock cylinder and pull out of the lock housing **(see illustration)**. (The spring is NOT used on refitting.)

Refitting

19 Refitting is a reversal of the removal procedure, noting when refitting the lock cylinder :

a) Use an M6 tap to cut a thread in the lock cylinder housing, where the plunger had been removed **(see illustration)**.

b) Install the lock cylinder, then turn to locate into place.

21.15 Undo the two securing nuts

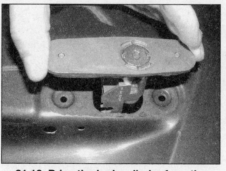

21.16 Prise the lock cylinder from the tailgate

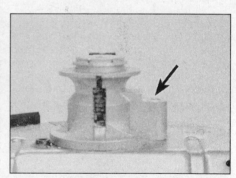

21.17a File down the lock cylinder housing (arrowed) ...

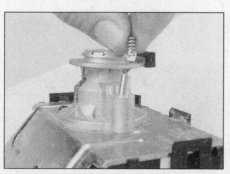

21.17b ... then remove the spring and plunger

21.18 Turn the lock cylinder, to disengage from the lock assembly

21.19a Use an M6 tap to cut a thread in the lock cylinder body

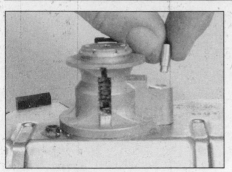

21.19b Put plunger into hole, then fit retaining screw

c) *Push the plunger into the hole (see illustration), then fit retaining screw (M6 x 6.5mm) to secure the plunger (use Loctite sealer on the threads).*

22 Central locking system components – testing, removal and refitting

Testing

1 The central locking/alarm system incorporates a self-test function, which can be activated by operating one of the door interior light switches six times within 8 seconds **(see illustration)**. During the check, the indicators will flash to acknowledge the input, then the indicators should flash every time a door, bonnet or tailgate is opened. If there is an alarm fitted, then the horn will sound along with the indicators flashing. If the doors are double-locked, and the vehicle is fitted with interior sensors, the signal will occur when something is moved within the passenger compartment. A more comprehensive test can be made using the Ford FDS 2000 diagnostic tester.

Removal

Central locking/alarm module

2 To remove the module, first remove the lower right A-pillar trim **(see illustration)**.
3 Disconnect the battery negative (earth) lead (Chapter 5A, Section 1).

4 Undo the securing screws, and remove the module from the bracket **(see illustration)**.
5 Disconnect the wiring multi-plugs, and withdraw the module from inside the vehicle.

Door motors

6 This procedure is covered in Section 13.

Bootlid/tailgate motor

7 Remove the lock as described in Section 18 or 21, as applicable.
8 Remove the two motor securing screws, then manoeuvre the motor assembly out from the body, disconnecting the wiring plug.

Refitting

9 In all cases, refitting is a reversal of the removal procedure.

23 Windscreen and fixed windows – removal and refitting

1 The windscreen and rear window on all models are bonded in place with special mastic, as are the rear side windows. Special tools are required to cut free the old units and fit replacements; special cleaning solutions and primer are also required. It is therefore recommended that this work is entrusted to a Ford dealer or windscreen replacement specialist.

24 Body side-trim mouldings and adhesive emblems – removal and refitting

Removal

1 Body side trims and mouldings are attached either by retaining clips or adhesive bonding. On bonded mouldings, insert a length of strong cord (fishing line is ideal) behind the moulding or emblem concerned. With a sawing action, break the adhesive bond between the moulding or emblem and the panel.
2 Thoroughly clean all traces of adhesive from the panel using methylated spirit, and allow the location to dry.

22.1 The interior light switch is built into the door catch

3 On mouldings with retaining clips, unclip the mouldings from the panel, taking care not to damage the paintwork.

Refitting

4 Peel back the protective paper from the rear face of the new moulding or emblem. Carefully fit it into position on the panel concerned, but take care not to touch the adhesive. When in position, apply hand pressure to the moulding/emblem for a short period, to ensure maximum adhesion to the panel.
5 Replace any broken retaining clips before refitting trims or mouldings.

25 Sunroof – general information and adjustment

Removal

Glass panel

1 Slide back the sun blind, and set the glass panel in the tilt position.
2 Remove the four securing screws (two each side) **(see illustration)**.
3 Lift up or remove the aerial antenna, then lift the sunroof glass panel out from the vehicle.

Sun blind

4 Remove the glass panel as described in paragraphs 1 to 3.
5 Wind the roof opening mechanism to the rear, making sure the glass panel guides do not disengage from the guide rails.

22.2 Undo the retaining screws/clips to remove trim

22.4 Undo screws and remove module

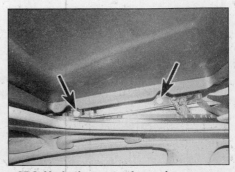

25.2 Undo the sunroof securing screws (arrowed), two screws each side

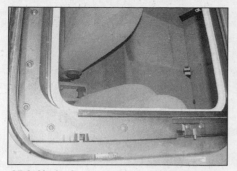

25.6 Undo the screws around the sunroof frame

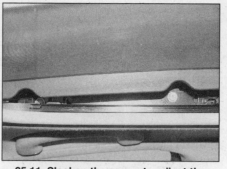

25.11 Slacken the screw to adjust the height of the glass panel

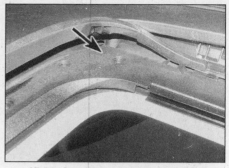

25.15 One of the front drain tubes (arrowed)

6 Undo and remove the 16 screws from around the sun blind panel **(see illustration)**.
7 Slide the sun blind out from the guide rails, taking care not to disturb the cable guides in their runners. Prevent any ingress of dirt into the cable mechanism.

Refitting

8 Refitting is a reversal of removal. Lubricate the cables and guides on assembly.

Adjustment

9 The sunroof should operate freely, without sticking or binding, as it is opened and closed. When in the closed position, check that the panel is flush with the surrounding roof panel.
10 If adjustment is required, slide back the sun blind, but leave the glass panel in the closed position.
11 Loosen the rear securing screws (one each side). Adjust the glass panel up or down, so that it is flush at its back edge with the roof panel **(see illustration)**.
12 Loosen the front securing screws (one each side). Adjust the glass panel up or down, so that it is flush at its front edge with the roof panel.
13 Retighten the four securing screws.
14 Check the roof seal for wind noise and water leaks.

Checking

Drain tubes

15 There are four drain tubes, one located in

25.16 Remove the electrical unit to check the drain tube

each corner of the sunroof aperture **(see illustration)**.
16 The front drain tubes go down the front A-pillars; remove the lower trim panel and electrical junction box or ECU to gain access to the drain tube **(see illustration)**.
17 The rear drain tubes go down the C-pillars; remove the rear side trims to gain access **(see illustration)**.

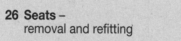

26 Seats –
removal and refitting

Removal

Front seat

1 On models with electrically-operated or heated seats, or with side airbags, disconnect

25.17 Rear drain tube (arrowed)

the battery negative lead, and position the lead away from the battery (see Chapter 5A, Section 1).

⚠ *Warning: Where side airbags are fitted, before proceeding, wait a minimum of 5 minutes, as a precaution against accidental firing of the airbag unit. This period ensures that any stored energy in the back-up capacitor is dissipated.*

2 Slide the seat fully backwards.
3 Remove the trim cover from the outer seat runner **(see illustration)**.
4 Undo the two front seat runner bolts and remove **(see illustration)**.
5 Slide the seat fully forwards, then undo the two rear seat runner bolts and remove.
6 On models with electrically-operated or heated seats, disconnect the various seat wiring multi-plugs from the seat base, noting their fitted positions **(see illustration)**.

26.3 Unclip the runner trim

26.4 Undo the seat mounting bolts

26.6 Disconnect any wiring connectors

26.8 Unbolt the rear seat cushion hinge

26.10 Remove the back seat retaining bolts

26.12 Unclip the cover to access securing screws

26.13 Unclip the release cable from under the parcel shelf

Rear seat cushion

7 On some models, unclip the plastic trim from the hinges at the front of each seat cushion.
8 Unscrew and remove the mounting bolts

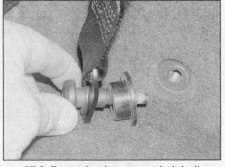

27.2 Removing lower seat belt bolt

from the hinges (see illustration), then withdraw the seat cushion from inside the vehicle.

Rear seat backrest

9 Fold the rear seat cushion forwards (if not already removed). Remove the headrests and fold the backrest forward.
10 Undo and remove the four bolts from the rear of the backrest (see illustration).
11 Release the rear backrest from the locating brackets, and withdraw the backrest from inside the vehicle.

Rear seat backrest catch and release cable

12 Fold the seat backrest forward, unclip the cover from the backrest catch (see illustration).
13 From inside the boot, unclip the backrest release cable from under the rear shelf (see illustration).

14 Undo the backrest catch securing screws and remove the catch complete with the release cable.

Refitting

15 Refitting is a reversal of the removal procedure, tighten the mounting bolts to the specified torque.

27 Seat belts – removal and refitting

⚠ **Warning: Be careful when handling the seat belt tensioning device, it contains a small explosive charge (pyrotechnic device) similar to the one used to deploy the airbag(s). Clearly, injury could be caused if these are released in an uncontrolled fashion. Once fired, the tensioner cannot be reset, and must be renewed. Note also that seat belts and associated components which have been subject to impact loads must be renewed.**

Removal – front seat belt

1 Disconnect the battery negative lead, and position the lead away from the battery (see Chapter 5A, Section 1).

⚠ **Warning: Before proceeding, wait a minimum of 5 minutes, as a precaution against accidental firing of the seat belt tensioner. This period ensures that any stored energy in the back-up capacitor is dissipated.**

4-door & 5-door models

2 Undo and remove the bolt for the lower seat belt anchorage (see illustration).
3 Unclip the upper trim panel from the B-pillar, and pass the seat belt lower anchorage through the trim panel (see illustration).
4 Unscrew the Torx bolt securing the seat belt guide to the B-pillar (see illustration).
5 Remove the two securing screws, then unclip the lower trim panel from the B-pillar (see illustration).
6 Slide the guide loop forwards, then down to detach from the pillar (see illustration).
7 Unscrew the mounting bolt, and lift seat

27.3 Unclip the upper pillar trim

27.4 Undo upper seat belt bolt

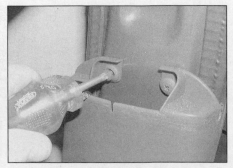

27.5 Remove screws from the lower trim panel

27.6 Slide the seat belt guide loop from the door pillar

27.7 Undo mounting bolt and lift out the seat belt reel

27.8 Remove anchorage rail bolt

belt reel unit to remove from the base of the pillar **(see illustration)**.

3-door models

8 Undo the anchorage rail bolt and slide the belt off **(see illustration)**.

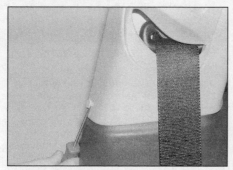

27.9a Prise out the retaining clip . . .

9 Prise out the retaining clip, then unclip the upper trim panel from the B-pillar. Pass the seat belt lower anchorage through the trim panel **(see illustrations)**.
10 Unscrew the Torx bolt securing the seat belt guide to the B-pillar.
11 Remove the rear seat cushion and backrest as described in Section 26. Remove the two retaining clips and unclip the rear side trim panel, for access to the seat belt reel unit **(see illustration)**.
12 Unscrew the mounting bolt, and lift seat belt reel unit to remove from the base of the pillar.

⚠️ *Warning: There is a potential risk of the seat belt tensioning device firing during removal, so it should be handled carefully. Once removed, treat it with care – do not allow use chemicals on or near it, and do not expose it to high temperatures, or it may detonate.*

Removal – rear side seat belt
Estate

13 Fold the rear seat cushions forward, and unscrew the seat belt, lower anchorage bolt.
14 Fold the rear seat backrest forward. Undo the four securing screws from the luggage side cover trim, and unclip the cover trim from the seat belt reel unit **(see illustration)**.
15 Unscrew the mounting bolt securing the seat belt reel unit, and withdraw from the vehicle **(see illustration)**.

3-door & 5-door models

16 Fold the rear seat cushions forward, and unscrew the seat belt, lower anchorage bolt.
17 From inside the boot, undo the retaining screw from the seat belt reel cover trim **(see illustration)**.
18 Unclip the cover trim from around the seat belt reel **(see illustration)**.

27.9b . . . and unclip the upper pillar trim

27.11 Remove retaining clips and lift out side trim panel

27.14 Unclip the side trim from the luggage compartment

27.15 Undo the seat belt reel mounting bolt

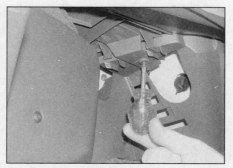

27.17 Undo screw to release seat belt reel cover

27.18 Unclip the cover trim

27.19 Undo the seat belt reel mounting bolt (arrowed)

27.21 Unclip the seat belt trim cover

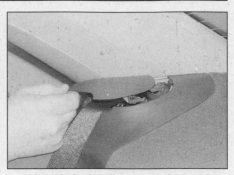

27.22 Undo the trim securing screws

19 Unscrew the mounting bolt securing the seat belt reel unit, and withdraw from the vehicle **(see illustration)**.

Saloon

20 Fold the rear seat cushions forward, and unscrew the seat belt lower anchorage bolt.
21 Fold the rear seat backrest forward, then unclip the small cover trim from the seat belt **(see illustration)**.
22 Undo the two securing screws from the C-pillar intermediate trim panel and unclip from around the seat belt reel unit **(see illustration)**.
23 Unclip the C-pillar upper trim panel, detaching it from the rear parcel shelf **(see illustration)**.

24 Unscrew the mounting bolt securing the seat belt reel unit, and withdraw from the vehicle **(see illustration)**.

Removal – rear centre seat belt

Estate, 3-door & 5 door models

25 The centre rear seat belt reel is attached to the rear seat backrest **(see illustration)**, but removal requires that the seat fabric be removed, so this operation should be referred to a Ford dealer or competent specialist.

Saloon

26 Fold the rear seat backrests forward, then unclip the cover trims from the seat catches **(see illustration)**.

27 Unclip the cover trim from around the seat belt reel **(see illustration)**.
28 Slide the parcel shelf trim forwards to remove.
29 Unscrew the mounting bolt securing the seat belt reel unit to the parcel shelf, and withdraw from the vehicle.

Removal – seat belt stalks

30 The front seat belt stalks are bolted to the seat frame **(see illustration)** and can be removed after removing the front seat as described in Section 26.
31 The rear seat belt stalks can be removed by folding the rear seat cushions forward, then unscrew the seat belt stalk anchorage bolts **(see illustration)**.

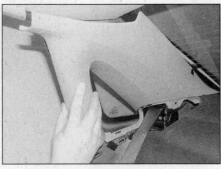

27.23 Unclip the upper trim panel

27.24 Undo the seat belt reel mounting bolt

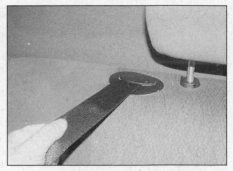

27.25 Centre seat belt fitted in the backrest of the rear seat

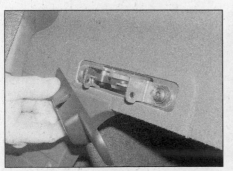

27.26 Unclip the seat catch cover trims

27.27 Unclip the trim from around the seat belt

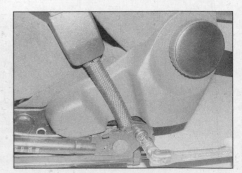

27.30 Undo the mounting bolt on the seat frame

27.31 Unbolt the rear seat belt stalks

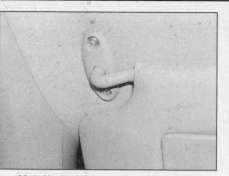

28.1 Undo the two retaining screws

28.3 Lift the plastic cover to remove the screw

Refitting

32 Refitting is a reversal of the removal procedure, noting the following points:

a) Tighten the mounting nuts and bolts to the specified torque.
b) Make sure the seat belt reel locating dowel is correctly positioned.
c) Refit spacers in their correct position.
d) On 3-door models, make sure the anchor rail is located correctly.

28 Interior trim panels – removal and refitting

Note : This section covers the removal and installation of the interior trim panels. It may be necessary to remove an overlapping trim before you can remove the one required. For more information on trim removal, look at relevant Chapters and Sections, where the trims may need to be removed to carry out any other procedures (eg, to remove the steering column you will need to remove the shrouds).

Removal

Sun visor

1 Unscrew the mounting screws and remove the visor (see illustration).
2 Disconnect the wiring for the vanity mirror light, where fitted.
3 Prise up the cover, unscrew the inner bracket mounting screws, and remove the bracket (see illustration).

Passenger grab handle

4 Prise up the covers, then unscrew the mounting screws and remove the grab handle (see illustration).

A-pillar trim

5 To remove the lower A-pillar trim, undo the two securing screws, and unclip from the vehicle complete with the facia side trim (see illustration).
6 Carefully press the A-pillar upper trim away from the retaining clips, and pull the trim upwards.
7 Release the phone microphone electrical connector from the upper trim clips (where fitted).

B-pillar trim – 4-door and Estate

8 Unscrew the seat belt mounting bolt from its lower anchorage point.
9 Carefully separate the upper trim from the lower trim, and unclip from the B-pillar (see illustration). Pass the seat belt lower anchorage through the lower trim panel.
10 Undo the two securing screws from the lower trim panel, then unclip from the B-pillar (see illustration).

C-pillar trim – Hatchback

11 Remove the rear parcel shelf
12 Fold the rear seat backrest cushion forwards.
13 Prise out the retaining clip, and remove the seat belt trim panel cover.
14 Undo the retaining screws from the parcel shelf support, disconnect the electrical connector from the interior light if fitted (see illustration).
15 Release the clips and locating tangs, and detach the upper trim.

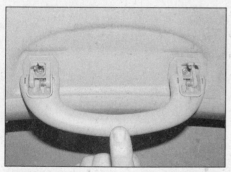

28.4 Lift the plastic covers to remove the screws

28.5 Undo the retaining screws and remove trim

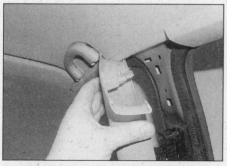

28.9 Unclip the upper trim from the B-pillar

28.10 Undo the two retaining screws from the lower trim

28.14 Undo the retaining screws from the rear side trims

28.23 Undo the retaining screws from the lower side trims

28.24 Unclip the upper trim panel

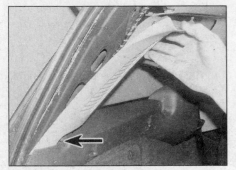

28.25 Undo screw (arrowed) and unclip upper trim panel

28.26 Unclip the sill trim from the inner sill

C-pillar trim – Estate

16 Remove the rear parcel shelf.
17 Fold the rear seat backrest forwards.
18 Unclip and remove the seat belt trim panel cover.

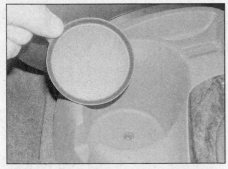

29.2 Lift out cup holder and remove screw

19 Undo the retaining screws from the parcel shelf support.
20 Unclip and remove the upper trim from the C-pillar.

C-pillar trim – Saloon

21 Fold the rear seat backrest cushion forwards.
22 Unclip and remove the seat belt trim panel cover.
23 Undo the two securing screws, and remove the lower trim from around the seat belt reel unit **(see illustration)**.
24 Unclip the C-pillar upper trim panel, detaching it from the rear parcel shelf **(see illustration)**.

D-pillar trim – Estate

25 Slacken and remove the securing screws from the luggage compartment side trim, then unclip the trim from the D-pillar **(see illustration)**.

Sill trim

26 Unclip the sill trims at each end from the pillar trims, and from the inner sill **(see illustration)**.

Steering column shrouds

27 To release the upper shroud from the lower shroud, insert a thin screwdriver into a hole at each side of the column. Lift the upper shroud from the column and unclip from the bottom of the instrument panel.
28 Using a thin screwdriver unclip the radio control switch from the lower shroud.
29 Release the steering column height lever. Undo the three securing screws from the lower shroud, and remove from the column.

Lower facia panel

30 Undo the four securing screws from the lower panel and one retaining clip, and withdraw from the facia. Press out the wiring multi-plug from the panel.

Refitting

31 Refitting is a reversal of the removal procedure. Where seat belt fastenings have been disturbed, make sure that they are tightened to the specified torque. Renew any broken clips as required.

---

29 Centre console – removal and refitting

Removal

Manual transmission models

1 Disconnect the battery negative (earth) lead (Chapter 5A, Section 1).
2 Lift out the cup holders out from the front of the console, and undo the two retaining screws (one each side) **(see illustration)**.
3 On some models pull the cup holder out from the rear of the console, and undo the securing screws.
4 Unclip the ashtray from the rear of the centre console, then lift cover to remove the securing screw from underneath **(see illustrations)**.
5 Unclip the gear lever surround trim from the centre console, then unclip the gaiter from the

29.4a Lift out the rear ashtray . . . .

29.4b . . . and plastic screw cover, to remove screw

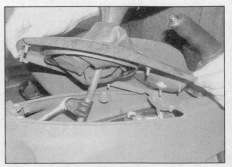

29.5a Unclip the gear lever surround from the console . . .

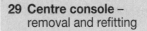

29.5b . . . then unclip the gaiter from the surround

29.7 Unclip the handbrake gaiter from the console

29.8 Withdraw the console over the gear lever and handbrake

surround trim leaving the gaiter on the gear lever (see illustrations).
6 Remove the electrical connectors from any switches.
7 Unclip the handbrake gaiter from the centre console and remove it from the handbrake lever (see illustration).
8 Fully apply the handbrake lever to withdraw the centre console from the vehicle (see illustration).

Automatic transmission models

9 This procedure is the same as given above for manual transmission models, exept for the following.
10 Remove the screw on the side of the selector lever which secures the lever knob.
11 Using a screwdriver, carefully prise out the selector lever surround trim, and remove the selector lever knob and trim.
12 Detach and disconnect the wiring plugs inside the centre console. Cut any cable-ties as necessary.

Refitting

13 Refitting is a reversal of the removal procedure.

---

30 Overhead console – removal and refitting

Removal

1 Disconnect the battery negative (earth) lead (Chapter 5A, Section 1).
2 On models with an electrically-operated sunroof, remove the sunroof switch (Chapter 12, Section 4).
3 On models with a manual sunroof, remove the sunroof handle, after undoing the securing screw (see illustration).
4 Unclip the interior light and disconnect the electrical connector (see illustration).
5 Undo and remove the two retaining screws from the console and disengage from the roof panel.

Refitting

6 Refitting is a reversal of the removal procedure.

31 Glovebox – removal and refitting

Removal

1 Pull back the carpet trim (where fitted), and undo the three retaining screws from the glovebox hinge (see illustration).
2 Withdraw the glovebox by pushing in at both sides (see illustration).

Refitting

3 Refitting is a reversal of the removal procedure, making sure that the glovebox is located correctly before tightening the screws.

30.3 Undo retaining screw and remove the sunroof handle

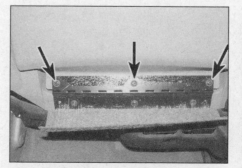

31.1 Undo the three screws (arrowed) to remove the glovebox lid

32 Facia – removal and refitting

Removal

1 Disconnect the battery negative (earth) lead (Chapter 5A, Section 1).
2 Remove the centre console as described in Section 29.
3 Release the two retaining clips from the rear of the air ducting under the centre console and remove from the heater housing (see illustration).
4 Undo the four securing screws from the facia lower centre trim and remove trim from the facia panel (see illustration).
5 Remove the steering column (Chapter 10).

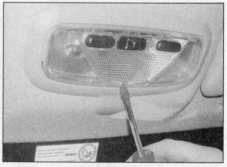

30.4 Carefully unclip the interior light

31.2 Push the sides in to remove the glovebox

32.3 Withdraw the air ducting

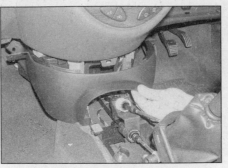

32.4 Withdraw the facia lower centre trim

32.7 Unclip the wiring loom

6 Remove the instrument panel, radio/
cassette player and, where applicable, the
passenger airbag, as described in Chapter 12.
7 Remove the glovebox (Section 31). Unclip
the wiring loom from the lower area of the
glovebox aperture **(see illustration)**.
8 Remove the heater control panel (Chapter 3).
9 Remove the main headlight control switch
(Chapter 12, Section 4).
10 Undo the securing screws/clips from the

lower side trim panels, at the base of the A-
pillars on each side of the vehicle. Unclip and
remove the trim panels to gain access to the
facia side-mounting screws **(see illustration)**.
11 Unscrew the facia side-mounting screws
(two each side) **(see illustration)**.
12 Screw a bolt into the retaining clip in the
air vent, in the top of the facia (there are three
retaining clips, one in the centre and one at
each side). When the bolt is tight in the
retaining clip, pull on the bolt to remove the
clips **(see illustrations)**. Carefully lever the
upper part of the facia panel from its position.
13 Unscrew the facia centre-mounting screw
from behind the heater control panel **(see
illustration)**.
14 Unscrew the two screws from behind the
instrument panel **(see illustration)**.
15 Unscrew the two screws from behind the
passenger airbag **(see illustration)**.

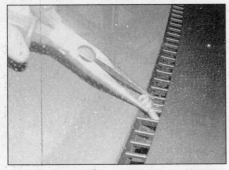

**32.10 Withdraw the lower A-pillar trim
panels**

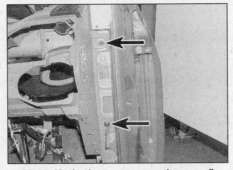

32.11 Undo the two screws (arrowed)

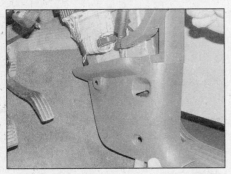

32.12a Using pliers to pull out the bolt . . .

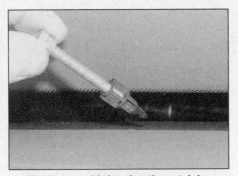

**32.12b . . . withdrawing the retaining
clip . . .**

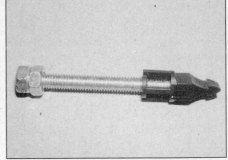

**32.12c . . . then unscrew retaining clip
from the bolt for refitting**

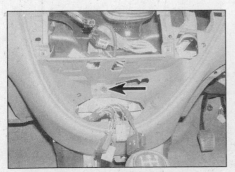

**32.13 Undo the facia centre-mounting
screw (arrowed)**

**32.14 Undo the facia mounting screws
(arrowed)**

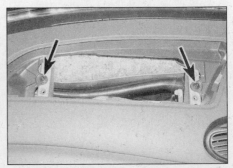

**32.15 Undo the facia mounting screws
(arrowed)**

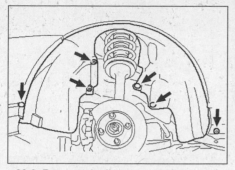

33.2 Remove the liner screws (arrowed)

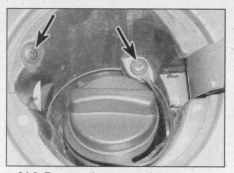

34.2 Remove the two retaining screws (arrowed)

34.4 Prise the lock from the fuel filler flap

16 Withdraw the facia from the bulkhead, and out from the vehicle.

Refitting

17 Refitting is a reversal of the removal procedure. On completion, check the operation of all electrical components.

33 Wheelarch liner – removal and refitting

Removal

Front

1 Apply the handbrake. If the wheel is to be removed (to improve access), loosen the wheel nuts. Jack up the front of the vehicle and support it on axle stands. Remove the front wheel.
2 Unscrew the screws securing the liner to

the inner wheelarch panel **(see illustration)**.
3 Remove the screws and clips securing the liner to the outer edge of the wheelarch and bumper. Withdraw the liner from under the vehicle.

Rear

4 Chock the front wheels, and engage 1st gear (or P). If the wheel is to be removed (to improve access), loosen the wheel nuts. Jack up the rear of the vehicle and support it on axle stands. Remove the rear wheel.
5 Undo the screws securing the liner to the outer edge of the wheelarch and bumper.
6 Remove the clips securing the liner to the inner wheelarch, and withdraw the liner from under the vehicle.

Refitting

7 Refitting is a reversal of the removal procedure. If the wheels were removed, tighten the wheel nuts to the specified torque.

34 Fuel filler flap and lock – removal and refitting

Removal

1 Remove the fuel filler neck as described in the relevant part of Chapter 4.
2 Undo the retaining screws in the plastic housing around the filler neck **(see illustration)**.
3 Carefully twist the fuel flap and plastic housing from the vehicle and pull it from the aperture in the rear wing.
4 If required, the filler flap lock can be prised out of the flap – take care, as the flap is made of plastic **(see illustration)**.

Refitting

5 Refitting is a reversal of removal.

Notes

Chapter 12
Body electrical system

Contents

Degrees of difficulty

Easy, suitable for novice with little experience	Fairly easy, suitable for beginner with some experience	Fairly difficult, suitable for competent DIY mechanic	Difficult, suitable for experienced DIY mechanic	Very difficult, suitable for expert DIY or professional

Specifications

Fuses
Refer to the wiring diagrams at the end of this Chapter
Note: *Fuse ratings and circuits are liable to change from year to year. Consult the handbook supplied with the vehicle, or consult a Ford dealer, for the latest information.*

Relays (auxiliary fusebox in engine compartment)

Relay	Colour	Circuit(s)
R1	Black	Ignition
R2	Not Used	
R3	Black	Heated front screen
R4	Blue	Headlight washer system
R5	Black	Main beam headlights
R6	Black	Dipped beam headlights
R7	Black	Fuel pump, diesel injection pump
R8	Black	Engine Management
R9	Black	Diesel glow plugs
R10	Not Used	
R11	Black	Air conditioning
R12	Black	Daytime running lights
R13	Black	Heated front screen/Diesel fuel heater
R14	Black	Brake lights (ESP)
R15	Black	Engine cooling fan Level 2 (air conditioning)
R16	Dark Green	Engine cooling fan Level 1

Relays (central/main fusebox in passenger compartment)

Relay	Colour	Circuit(s)
R17	Black	Starter inhibitor
R18/19	Black	Front and Rear screen, intermittent wipe
R20	Not Used	
R21	Not Used	
R22	Not Used	
R23	Black	Horn
R24	Black	Battery saver
R25	Black	Heated rear screen and mirrors

Bulbs

	Wattage	Type
Direction indicator lights	21	Bayonet
Front foglight	55	H1 Halogen
Headlight dipped beam	50	H4L Halogen
Headlight main beam	55	H4L Halogen
High-level stop-light (5 bulbs)	5	Wedge
Interior light	10	Festoon
Luggage compartment	5	Wedge
Number plate lights	5	Festoon
Reading light	5	Wedge
Rear foglight	21	Bayonet
Rear tail light/stop-light	5/21	Bayonet
Reversing lights	21	Bayonet
Side repeater direction indicator lights	5	Wedge
Sidelights	5	Wedge

Torque wrench settings

	Nm	lbf ft
Horn unit mounting bracket bolt	12	9
Windscreen wiper motor bolts	8	6
Wiper arm nuts:		
Front	25	18
Rear	20	15
Wiper lever nut on front wiper motor	20	15

1 General information

⚠️ **Warning: Before carrying out any work on the electrical system, read through the precautions given in 'Safety first!' at the beginning of this manual.**

The electrical system is of 12-volt negative earth type. Power for the lights and all electrical accessories is supplied by a lead-acid battery which is charged by the alternator.

This Chapter covers repair and service procedures for the various electrical components not associated with the engine. Information on the battery, alternator and starter motor can be found in Chapter 5A; the ignition system is covered in Chapter 5B.

All models are fitted with a driver's airbag, which is designed to prevent serious chest and head injuries to the driver during an accident. A similar bag for the front seat passenger is also available. The electronic control module for the airbag is located under the centre console inside the vehicle. It contains two frontal impact micro machine sensors, a crash sensor, and a safety sensor. The crash sensor and safety sensor are connected in series, and if they both sense a deceleration in excess of a predetermined limit, the electronic airbag

control module will operate the airbag. The airbag is inflated by a gas generator, which forces the bag out of the module cover in the centre of the steering wheel. A sliding contact ring ensures that a good electrical connection is maintained with the airbag at all times as the steering wheel is turned in each direction. There is also a coiled spring, that is able to 'wind-up' and 'unwind' as the steering wheel is turned, maintaining the electronic contact at all times.

As an optional extra, some models can be equipped with side airbags, which are built into the sides of the front seats. The intention of the side airbags is principally to offer greater passenger protection in a side impact. The side airbags are linked to the 'front' airbags, and are also controlled by the electronic control module under the centre console. The side air bags are also controlled by the sensors located under the carpet and sill trims inside the vehicle.

All models are fitted with an ignition immobiliser, which is built into the key and ignition lock. The alarm system is an optional extra on purchasing the car from new. On vehicles with alarms fitted the horn is located on the left-hand side of the luggage compartment, or on Estate models, it is on the right-hand side.

All models are fitted with a headlight levelling system, which is controlled by a knob on the facia. On position 0, the headlights are in their

base position, and on position 5, the headlights are in their maximum inclined angle.

It should be noted that, when portions of the electrical system are serviced, the lead should be disconnected from the battery negative terminal, to prevent electrical shorts and fires.

Caution: When disconnecting the battery for work described in the following Sections, refer to Chapter 5A, Section 1.

2 Electrical fault finding – general information

Note: *Refer to the precautions given in 'Safety first!' before starting work. The following tests relate to testing of the main electrical circuits, and should not be used to test delicate electronic circuits (such as engine management systems, anti-lock braking systems, etc), particularly where an electronic control module is used. Also refer to the precautions given in Chapter 5A, Section 1.*

General

1 A typical electrical circuit consists of an electrical component, any switches, relays, motors, fuses, fusible links or circuit breakers related to that component, and the wiring and connectors which link the component to both the battery and the chassis. To help to pinpoint a problem in an electrical circuit, wiring diagrams are included at the end of this Chapter.

2 Before attempting to diagnose an electrical fault, first study the appropriate wiring diagram, to obtain a complete understanding of the components included in the particular circuit concerned. The possible sources of a fault can be narrowed down by noting if other components related to the circuit are operating properly. If several components or circuits fail at one time, the problem is likely to be related to a shared fuse or earth connection.

3 Electrical problems usually stem from simple causes, such as loose or corroded connections, a faulty earth connection, a blown fuse, a melted fusible link, or a faulty relay (refer to Section 3 for details of testing relays). Visually inspect the condition of all fuses, wires and connections in a problem circuit before testing the components. Use the wiring diagrams to determine which terminal connections will need to be checked in order to pinpoint the trouble-spot.

4 The basic tools required for electrical fault finding include a circuit tester or voltmeter (a 12-volt bulb with a set of test leads can also be used for certain tests); an ohmmeter (to measure resistance and check for continuity); a battery and set of test leads; and a jumper wire, preferably with a circuit breaker or fuse incorporated, which can be used to bypass suspect wires or electrical components. Before attempting to locate a problem with test instruments, use the wiring diagram to determine where to make the connections.

5 To find the source of an intermittent wiring fault (usually due to a poor or dirty connection, or damaged wiring insulation), a 'wiggle' test can be performed on the wiring. This involves wiggling the wiring by hand to see if the fault occurs as the wiring is moved. It should be possible to narrow down the source of the fault to a particular section of wiring. This method of testing can be used in conjunction with any of the tests described in the following sub-Sections.

6 Apart from problems due to poor connections, two basic types of fault can occur in an electrical circuit – open-circuit, or short-circuit.

7 Open-circuit faults are caused by a break somewhere in the circuit, which prevents current from flowing. An open-circuit fault will prevent a component from working.

8 Short-circuit faults are caused by a 'short' somewhere in the circuit, which allows the current flowing in the circuit to 'escape' along an alternative route, usually to earth. Short-circuit faults are normally caused by a breakdown in wiring insulation, which allows a feed wire to touch either another wire, or an earthed component such as the bodyshell. A short-circuit fault will normally cause the relevant circuit fuse to blow.

Finding an open-circuit

9 To check for an open-circuit, connect one lead of a circuit tester or the negative lead of a voltmeter either to the battery negative terminal or to a known good earth.

10 Connect the other lead to a connector in the circuit being tested, preferably nearest to the battery or fuse. At this point, battery voltage should be present, unless the lead from the battery or the fuse itself is faulty (bearing in mind that some circuits are live only when the ignition switch is moved to a particular position).

11 Switch on the circuit, then connect the tester lead to the connector nearest the circuit switch on the component side.

12 If voltage is present (indicated either by the tester bulb lighting or a voltmeter reading, as applicable), this means that the section of the circuit between the relevant connector and the switch is problem-free.

13 Continue to check the remainder of the circuit in the same fashion.

14 When a point is reached at which no voltage is present, the problem must lie between that point and the previous test point with voltage. Most problems can be traced to a broken, corroded or loose connection.

Finding a short-circuit

15 To check for a short-circuit, first disconnect the load(s) from the circuit (loads are the components which draw current from a circuit, such as bulbs, motors, heating elements, etc).

16 Remove the relevant fuse from the circuit, and connect a circuit tester or voltmeter to the fuse connections.

17 Switch on the circuit, bearing in mind that some circuits are live only when the ignition switch is moved to a particular position.

18 If voltage is present (indicated either by the tester bulb lighting or a voltmeter reading, as applicable), this means that there is a short-circuit.

19 If no voltage is present during this test, but the fuse still blows with the load(s) reconnected, this indicates an internal fault in the load(s).

Finding an earth fault

20 The battery negative terminal is connected to 'earth' – the metal of the engine/transmission unit and the vehicle body – and many systems are wired so that they only receive a positive feed, the current returning via the metal of the car body. This means that the component mounting and the body form part of that circuit. Loose or corroded mountings can

21 Loose or corroded mountings can therefore cause a range of electrical faults, ranging from total failure of a circuit, to a puzzling partial failure. In particular, lights may shine dimly (especially when another circuit sharing the same earth point is in operation), motors (eg, wiper motors or the radiator cooling fan motor) may run slowly, and the operation of one circuit may have an apparently-unrelated effect on another.

22 Note that on many vehicles, earth straps are used between certain components, such as the engine/transmission and the body, usually where there is no metal-to-metal contact between components, due to flexible rubber mountings, etc.

23 To check whether a component is properly earthed, disconnect the battery (refer to Chapter 5A, Section 1) and connect one lead of an ohmmeter to a known good earth point. Connect the other lead to the wire or earth connection being tested. The resistance reading should be zero; if not, check the connection as follows.

24 If an earth connection is thought to be faulty, dismantle the connection, and clean both the bodyshell and the wire terminal (or the component earth connection mating surface) back to bare metal. Be careful to remove all traces of dirt and corrosion, then use a knife to trim away any paint, so that a clean metal-to-metal joint is made.

25 On reassembly, tighten the joint fasteners securely; if a wire terminal is being refitted, use serrated washers between the terminal and the bodyshell, to ensure a clean and secure connection.

26 When the connection is remade, prevent the onset of corrosion in the future by applying a coat of petroleum jelly or silicone-based grease, or by spraying on (at regular intervals) a proprietary water-dispersant lubricant.

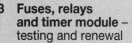

3 Fuses, relays and timer module – testing and renewal

Note: *It is important to note that the ignition switch and the appropriate electrical circuit must always be switched off before any of the fuses (or relays) are removed and renewed. If electrical components/units have to be removed, the battery earth lead must be disconnected. When reconnecting the battery, reference should be made to Chapter 5A.*

1 Fuses are designed to break a circuit when a predetermined current is reached, in order to protect components and wiring which could be damaged by excessive current flow. Any excessive current flow will be due to a fault in the circuit, usually a short-circuit (see Section 2). The main central fusebox, which also carries some relays, is located inside the vehicle behind the glovebox **(see illustration)**.

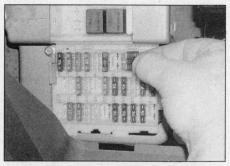

3.1 The central fusebox is behind the glovebox

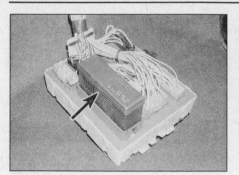

3.2 Central timer module fitted to the rear of the fusebox

3.3 Auxiliary fusebox under bonnet

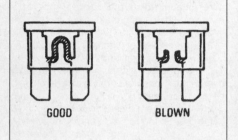

3.4 The fuses can be visually checked to determine if they are blown

3.7 'One touch down' window relay in the driver's door

2 A central timer module (CTM) is located in the back of the main central fusebox **(see illustration)**. This module contains the time control elements for the heated rear window, interior lights and intermittent wiper operation (front and rear). The module also activates a warning buzzer/chime when the vehicle is left with the lights switched on, or if a vehicle fitted with automatic transmission is not parked with the selector in position P.
3 The auxiliary fusebox is located in the engine compartment **(see illustration)**, against the bulkhead next to the air cleaner, and is accessed by unclipping and removing the cover. The auxiliary fusebox also contains some relays.
4 Each circuit is identified by numbers on the main fusebox and on the inside of the auxiliary fusebox cover. Reference to the wiring diagrams at the end of this Chapter will indicate the circuits protected by each fuse.

Plastic tweezers are attached to the auxiliary fusebox to remove and refit the fuses and relays. To remove a fuse, use the tweezers provided to pull it out of the holder, then slide the fuse sideways from the tweezers. The wire within the fuse is clearly visible, and it will be broken if the fuse is blown **(see illustration)**.
5 Always renew a fuse with one of an identical rating. Never substitute a fuse of a higher rating, or make temporary repairs using wire or metal foil; more serious damage, or even fire, could result. The fuse rating is stamped on top of the fuse. Never renew a fuse more than once without tracing the source of the trouble.
6 Note that if the vehicle is to be laid up for a long period, there is a 'battery saver' relay fitted to the central fusebox to prevent the ancillary electrical components from discharging the battery.
7 Relays are electrically-operated switches,

which are used in certain circuits. The various relays can be removed from their respective locations by carefully pulling them from the sockets. Some of the relays in the fuseboxes have a plastic bar on its upper surface to enable the use of the tweezers. The locations and functions of the various relays are given in the specifications **(see illustration)**.
8 If a component controlled by a relay becomes inoperative and the relay is suspect, listen to the relay as the circuit is operated. If the relay is functioning, it should be possible to hear it click as it is energised. If the relay proves satisfactory, the fault lies with the components or wiring of the system. If the relay is not being energised, then either the relay is not receiving a switching voltage, or the relay itself is faulty. (Do not overlook the relay socket terminals when tracing faults.) Testing is by the substitution of a known good unit, but be careful; while some relays are identical in appearance and in operation, others look similar, but perform different functions.

4   Switches –
     removal and refitting

Note: *Before removing any electrical switches, disconnect the battery negative (earth) lead (refer to Chapter 5A, Section 1).*

Removal

Ignition switch and lock barrel

1 Remove the steering column shrouds and lower facia panel, as described in (Chapter 11, Section 28).
2 Insert the ignition key, and turn it to the accessory position. Using a small screwdriver or twist drill through the hole in the side of the lock housing, depress the locking plunger and withdraw the lock barrel **(see illustration)**.
3 The switch which is on the opposite side of the steering column, may be removed by disconnecting the multi-plug, then use a screwdriver to release the switch retaining tabs at the top and bottom **(see illustrations)**.
4 On models with the PATS ('Safeguard') immobiliser, remove the immobiliser

4.2 Depress the locking plunger and withdraw the lock

4.3a Disconnect the multi-plug ...

4.3b ... and unclip the switch

4.4a Disconnect the wiring connector . . .

4.4b . . . and undo the screw (arrowed) to remove

4.5 Unclipping the upper shroud

transceiver from around the lock barrel by disconnecting the wiring plug and removing the securing screw **(see illustrations)**.

Direction indicator and windscreen wiper multi-function switches

5 Release the steering column upper shroud from the lower shroud by inserting a thin screwdriver into a hole at each side of the column. Lift the upper shroud from the column and unclip from the bottom of the instrument panel **(see illustration)**.
6 Depress the plastic tab at the top of the switch with a screwdriver. Lift the switch assembly from the steering column, disconnecting the switch multi-plug on removal **(see illustration)**.

Main light, auxiliary foglight and rear foglight combination switch

7 Undo the four retaining screws and prise

out the one securing clip, to remove the driver's side lower facia panel.
8 Undo the retaining screw from the bottom of the light switch surround/air vent and unclip from the facia **(see illustration)**.
9 Unscrew the three mounting screws from the switch unit **(see illustration)**.
10 Withdraw the switch from the facia panel and disconnect the multi-plug **(see illustration)**.

Instrument light rheostat

11 Carry out the procedures as described in paragraphs 7 to 10.

Headlight aim adjustment control

12 Carry out the procedures as described in paragraphs 7 to 10.

Door mirror control switch

13 Carefully prise the mirror bezel from the door frame.

14 Disconnect the multi-plug and withdraw the switch from the bezel **(see illustration)**.

Hazard warning switch

15 Remove the radio/cassette player as described in Section 22.
16 Undo the four securing screws from inside the radio/cassette player aperture **(see illustration)**, then carefully unclip the heater control panel from its three retaining clips in the facia.
17 Undo the retaining screws from the rear of the switch, withdraw the switch assembly from the panel, then disconnect the multi-plug.

Horn switch

⚠ *Warning: Before carrying out any work on airbags, read through the precautions given in section 26.*

4.6 Unclip the switch, and slide it upwards to remove

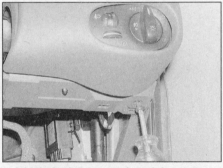

4.8 Undo the surround retaining screw

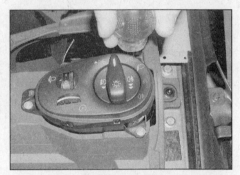

4.9 Undo the three switch mounting screws

4.10 Disconnect the multi-plug on removal

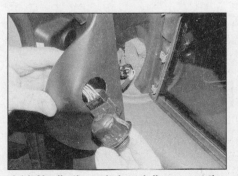

4.14 Unclip the switch and disconnect the wiring plug

4.16 Undo the four retaining screws

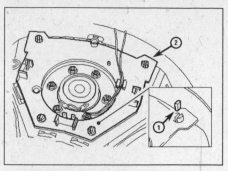

4.20 Lift out the wedges (1) and remove the contact plate (2)

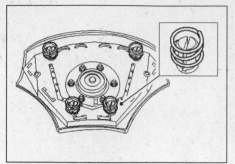

4.21 Locate the springs on the pegs for refitting

4.23 Use a thin screwdriver to unclip the radio switch

18 Remove the airbag unit from the steering wheel as described in Section 26.

19 Disconnect the wiring connectors from the contact plate, releasing the locking tangs to remove.

20 Carefully lift out the four wedges, located in the pegs for the contact plate under the airbag **(see illustration)**.

21 Lift the contact plate off the locating pegs and remove from the airbag unit. **Note:** *There are four springs under the contact plate (one on each of the locating pegs). Take care, to note the position of the four springs, before refitting the contact plate (see illustration).*

Radio remote control switch

22 Release the upper shroud from the lower shroud, by inserting a thin screwdriver into a hole at each side of the column. Lift the upper shroud from the column and unclip from the bottom of the instrument panel.

23 Depress the retaining lug at the rear of the radio switch and withdraw from the lower shroud **(see illustration)**, disconnect the wiring connector.

Cruise control switches

24 Refer to Section 20.

Electrically-operated window switches

25 Carefully prise out the plastic screw cover from the inner door handle cavity, using a small screwdriver. Remove the screw, and ease the bezel from around the door handle **(see illustration)**.

26 Depress the retaining lug and unclip the window operating switches from the bezel **(see illustration)**, disconnect the wiring connector.

Electrically-operated sunroof switch

27 Where fitted, prise out the switch with a

screwdriver, using a cloth pad to prevent damage to the trim.

28 Disconnect the multi-plug and remove the switch.

Handbrake-on warning switch

29 Remove the centre console as described in Chapter 11, Section 29.

30 Disconnect the wiring connector and undo the securing screw to remove the switch from the handbrake lever mounting bracket **(see illustration)**.

Overdrive mode switch (automatic transmission models)

31 The overdrive switch is located on the gear selector lever, for further information (refer to Chapter 7B, Section 4).

Heated windscreen and rear window switch

32 Remove the radio/cassette player as described in Section 22.

33 Undo the four securing screws from inside the radio/cassette player aperture, then carefully unclip the heater control panel from its three retaining clips in the facia.

34 Disconnect the wiring connectors from the switches as the control panel is being removed.

35 Undo the securing screws from the rear of the panel, and withdraw the switch assembly **(see illustration)**.

Seat height adjustment switch

36 Push the switch out from the trim, at the bottom of the seat cushion on the front seats.

37 Disconnect the multi-plug to disengage the switch **(see illustration)**.

4.25 Undo the screw and remove the bezel

4.26 Unclip the switch from the bezel

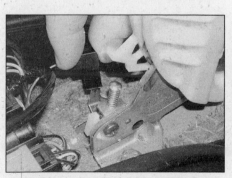

4.30 Disconnect the wiring terminal and undo screw (arrowed)

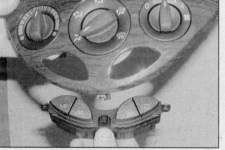

4.35 Switches come free as a complete assembly

4.37 Release the tang to disengage the multi-plug

4.43 The switch is part of the striker plate

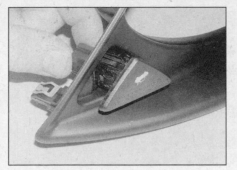

4.47 Press out the boot switch

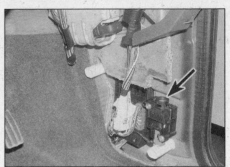

4.50 Fuel cut-off switch (arrowed)

Heated front seat switch

38 Remove the centre console as described in Chapter 11, Section 29.
39 Disconnect the electrical connector from the switch, then press the switch out from the console.

Traction control system (TCS) switch

40 Remove the centre console as described in Chapter 11, Section 29.
41 Disconnect the electrical connector from the switch, then press the switch out from the console.

Courtesy light door switch

42 Open the door, then using a pencil, mark the position of the door striker/contact switch on the pillar.
43 Undo the two securing screws to remove the striker/contact switch, then disconnect the electrical connector **(see illustration)**.

Boot/tailgate opening switch

44 Lower the steering column locking lever and release the retaining clips with a thin-bladed screwdriver to remove the steering column upper shroud (Chapter 10, Section 19).
45 Undo the upper retaining screws from the instrument panel surround, then unclip it from the facia.
46 As the surround is withdrawn, remove the electrical connector from the luggage compartment release switch and trip computer (where fitted).
47 Press the switch out from the surround **(see illustration)**.

Boot light switch

48 Removing the switch will entail removing the lock components to gain access to the switch and its wiring plug – refer to the relevant Sections of Chapter 11 for lock removal details.
49 The switch is part of the lock assembly, and at the time of writing could not be purchased separately.

Fuel cut-off switch

50 The switch is located, behind the driver's side kick panel/lower A-pillar trim **(see illustration)**. Refer to Chapter 4A.

Air conditioning and air recirculation switch

51 Remove the radio/cassette player as described in Section 22.
52 Undo the four securing screws from inside the radio/cassette player aperture, then carefully unclip the heater control panel from its three retaining clips in the facia.
53 Disconnect the wiring connectors from the switches as the control panel is being removed.
54 Undo the securing screws from the rear of the panel, and withdraw the switch assembly **(see illustration 4.35)**.

Refitting

55 Refitting of all switches is a reversal of the removal procedure.

5 Bulbs (exterior lights) – renewal

1 Whenever a bulb is renewed, note the following points:
a) *Switch off all exterior lights, and disconnect the battery negative lead before starting work (see Chapter 5A, Section 1).*
b) *Remember that if the light has just been in use, the bulb may be extremely hot.*
c) *Always check the bulb contacts and holder, ensuring that there is clean metal-to-metal contact between the bulb and its live(s) and earth. Clean off any corrosion*

or dirt before fitting a new bulb.
d) *Wherever bayonet-type bulbs are fitted, ensure that the live contact(s) bear firmly against the bulb contact.*
e) *Always ensure that the new bulb is of the correct rating and that it is completely clean before fitting it; this applies particularly to headlight/foglight bulbs.*
f) *Do not touch the glass of halogen-type bulbs (headlights, front foglights) with the fingers, as this may lead to rapid blackening and failure of the new bulb; if the glass is accidentally touched, clean it with methylated spirit.*
g) *If renewing the bulb does not cure the problem, check the relevant fuse and relay with reference to the Specifications, and to the wiring diagrams at the end of this Chapter.*

Headlight (dipped and main beam)

2 At the rear of the headlight unit, release the clip and remove the cover for access to the bulb **(see illustration)**.
3 Disconnect the wiring plug from the rear of the bulb **(see illustration)**.
4 Release the wire clip securing the bulb, and remove the bulb. Note how the tabs fit in the slots on the rear of the headlight **(see illustration)**.
5 Fit the new bulb using a reversal of the removal procedure. Have the headlight beam alignment checked as described later in this Chapter.

5.2 Unclip the headlight rear cover

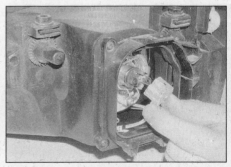

5.3 Disconnect the wiring plug from the bulb

5.4 Withdraw the headlight bulb

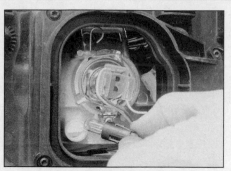

5.7 Withdraw the sidelight bulb

Front direction indicator

9 Undo and remove the screw located in the front direction indicator unit **(see illustration)**.
10 Withdraw the front direction indicator light unit from the bumper assembly.
11 Rotate the bulbholder anti-clockwise, and withdraw it from the light unit **(see illustration)**.
12 Twist the bulb anti-clockwise, and remove it from the bulbholder.
13 Fit the new bulb using a reversal of the removal procedure, but before refitting the retaining screw, make sure the light unit is located correctly **(see illustration)**.

Direction indicator side repeaters

14 Slide the side repeater assembly downwards, and remove it from the front wing **(see illustration)**.
15 Turn the bulbholder anti-clockwise, and disconnect it from the repeater unit **(see illustration)**.
16 Pull the wedge-type bulb from the holder.
17 Fit the new bulb using a reversal of the removal procedure.

5.9 Undo the light unit retaining screw

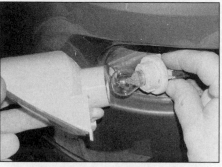

5.11 Removing the bulbholder from the light unit

7 Pull the bulbholder out from the rear of the headlight unit **(see illustration)**. Pull the wedge-type bulb from the bulbholder.
8 Fit the new bulb using a reversal of the removal procedure.

Front foglight

18 Release the retaining spring from the rear of the foglight unit and disconnect the wiring connector **(see illustrations)**.
19 Twist off the rear cover from the light unit, and disconnect the wiring terminal **(see illustration)**.

Front sidelight

6 At the rear of the headlight unit, release the clip and remove the cover for access to the bulb.

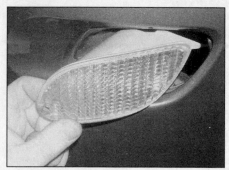

5.13 Locate the peg on the light unit (arrowed)

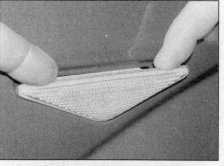

5.14 Push repeater down to remove

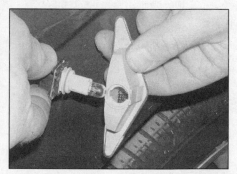

5.15 Removing the bulbholder from the repeater

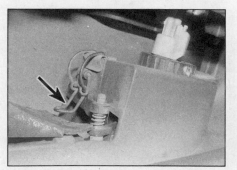

5.18a Unclip the spring clip (arrowed) . . .

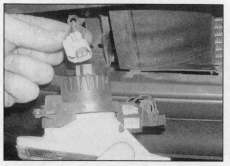

5.18b . . . and disconnect the wiring connector

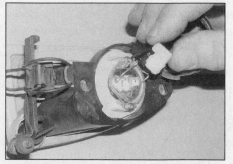

5.19 Disconnecting the terminal from the bulb

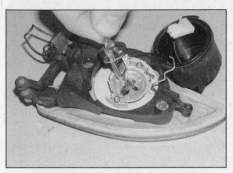

5.20 Withdraw the foglight bulb

5.23 Turn the bulbholder to remove

5.26a Undo the rear light retaining screw . . .

5.26b . . . and the plastic retaining nut inside the luggage compartment

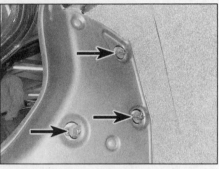

5.27 Undo the three plastic retaining nuts (arrowed)

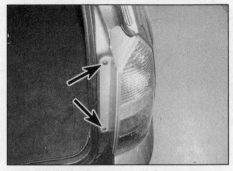

5.28 Undo the two retaining screws (arrowed)

20 Release the wire clip, and take out the bulb, noting its direction of fitting (see illustration).
21 Fit the new bulb using a reversal of the removal procedure. An adjustment screw is located at the bottom corner of the light unit.

Rear foglight/reversing light (Hatchback)

22 To remove the rear light unit push down the clip at the rear of the light unit, and withdraw from the bumper.
23 Turn the bulbholder anti-clockwise to remove from the light unit (see illustration).
24 Depress and twist the bulb anti-clockwise to remove it from the bulbholder.
25 Fit the new bulb using a reversal of the removal procedure. Make sure that the light unit is located correctly.

Rear light cluster

26 On Hatchback models, with the tailgate open. Remove the securing nut from the inside of the light cluster, and the securing screw, on the outside of the light cluster (see illustrations).
27 On Saloon models, from inside the luggage compartment. Remove the three turn-fasteners from the rear the light cluster (see illustration).
28 On Estate models, with the tailgate open. Undo the two securing screws from the side of the light cluster and unclip the light unit outwards to remove (see illustration).
29 Carefully remove the light cluster from the vehicle.
30 On Estate and Saloon models, lift the

retaining clips to separate the bulbholder from the light cluster (see illustration).
31 On Hatchback models, twist the appropriate bulbholder anti-clockwise and pull out from the light cluster (see illustration).
32 Depress and twist the appropriate bulb anti-clockwise to remove it from the bulbholder (see illustration).
33 Fit the new bulb using a reversal of the removal procedure. Make sure that the rear light cluster is located correctly.

Number plate light

34 Insert a flat-bladed screwdriver in the recess on the left of the number plate light, and carefully prise out the light unit (see illustration).

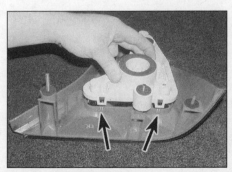

5.30 Lift the retaining clips (arrowed) to release the bulbholder

5.31 Twist bulbholder to release from the light unit

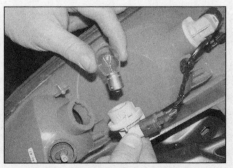

5.32 Push in and twist the bulb anti-clockwise to remove

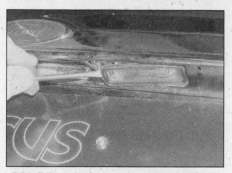

5.34 Prise out the number plate light unit

5.35 Withdraw the bulb from the number plate light

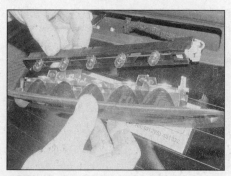

5.39 Unclipping the bulbholder (Estate)

5.40 Pulling out the bulb (Saloon)

35 Release the festoon-type bulb from the contact springs **(see illustration)**.
36 Fit the new bulb using a reversal of the removal procedure. Make sure that the tension of the contact springs is sufficient to hold the bulb firmly.

High-level stop-light

37 On Hatchback and Estate models, undo the two securing screws and remove the light cover.

38 On Saloon models, open the luggage compartment and remove the carpet trim from behind the light unit.
39 Unclip the bulbholder from the reflector **(see illustration)**.
40 Pull out the relevant wedge-type bulb from the holder **(see illustration)**.
41 Fit the new bulb, and refit the light unit using a reversal of the removal procedure.

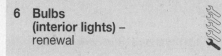

6 Bulbs (interior lights) – renewal

1 Whenever a bulb is renewed, note the following points:
  a) *Switch off all lights, and disconnect the battery negative lead before starting work (see Chapter 5A, Section 1)*
  b) *Remember that if the light has just been in use, the bulb may be extremely hot.*
  c) *Always check the bulb contacts and holder, ensuring that there is clean metal-to-metal contact between the bulb and its live(s) and earth. Clean off any corrosion or dirt before fitting a new bulb.*
  d) *Wherever bayonet-type bulbs are fitted, ensure that the live contact(s) bear firmly against the bulb contact.*
  e) *Always ensure that the new bulb is of the correct rating and that it is completely clean before fitting it.*

Interior/map reading lights

2 Ensure that the interior light is switched off by locating the switch in its correct position. Using a small screwdriver, carefully prise out the light assembly at the side opposite the switch **(see illustrations)**.
3 Disconnect the wiring connector, then lift up and unclip the reflector from the light unit. Release the festoon-type bulb from the contact springs **(see illustrations)**.
4 If map reading lights are fitted, bulbholders are fitted each side of the reflector. Remove the bayonet fitting bulbs by twisting them out of their holders **(see illustration)**.
5 Fit the new bulbs using a reversal of the removal procedure. Make sure that the tension of the contact springs is sufficient to hold the bulbs firmly.

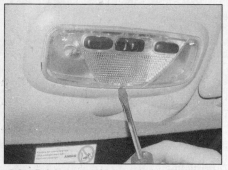

6.2a Prising out the front interior light . . .

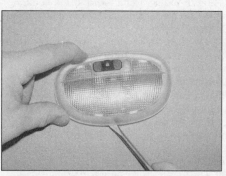

6.2b . . . and prising out the rear interior light

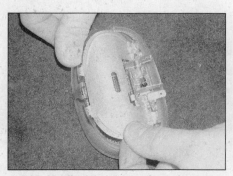

6.3a Unclip the reflector from the rear interior light . . .

6.3b . . . and remove the festoon bulb

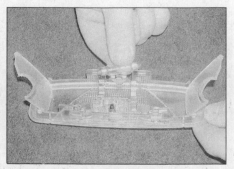

6.3c Removing the bulb from the front interior light

6.4 Removing the bayonet fitting bulb from the map reading light

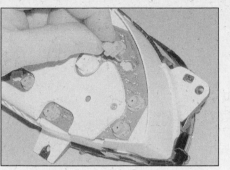

6.7 Turn the bulbholder to remove

6.15 Turn the bulbholder to remove

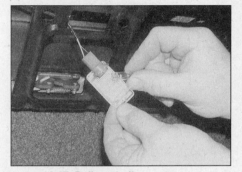

6.17 Pull out bulb to remove

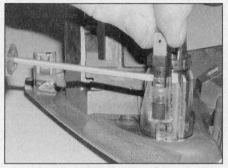

6.20a Unclip the bulbholder . . .

6.20b . . . and remove the bulb

Instrument panel illumination and warning lights

6 Remove the instrument panel as described in Section 10.
7 Twist the bulbholder anti-clockwise to remove it **(see illustration)**.
8 Fit the new bulbholder using a reversal of the removal procedure.

Hazard warning light

9 Remove the switch as described in Section 4.

Main headlight/foglight switch illumination

10 Remove the light switch as described in Section 4.

Automatic transmission selector panel illumination

11 Prise out the panel from around the selector lever on the centre console.
12 Disconnect the bulbholder and pull out the wedge-type bulb.
13 Fit the new bulb using a reversal of the removal procedure.

Clock illumination

Note: *On later models, the clock illumination bulb is not readily renewable. The clock may have to be removed and taken to a Ford dealer or automotive electrician for bulb renewal.*
14 Remove the clock as described in Section 12.

Heater control/fan switch illumination

15 Remove the heater control panel as

described in Chapter 3, Section 10. To remove the bulb from the rear of the panel twist the bulbholder and pull out **(see illustration)**.

Luggage compartment light

16 With the light switched off (the battery negative lead disconnected), prise out the light using a small screwdriver.
17 Pull the wedge type bulb out to remove **(see illustration)**.
18 Fit the new bulb using a reversal of the removal procedure.

Cigar lighter illumination

19 Remove the heater control panel as described in Chapter 3, Section 10.
20 Unclip the bulbholder from the rear of the cigar lighter, and pull out the bulb **(see illustrations)**.

7.3 Undo the lower headlamp mounting bolt (arrowed)

21 Fit the new bulb using a reversal of the removal procedure.

7 Exterior light units – removal and refitting

1 Before removing any light unit, note the following points:
a) *Ensure that the light is switched off, and disconnect the battery negative lead before starting work (see Chapter 5A, Section 1).*
b) *Remember that if the light has just been in use, the bulb and lens may be extremely hot.*

Headlight unit

2 Apply the handbrake, jack up the front of the vehicle and support it on axle stands.
3 From under the vehicle, undo and remove the headlamp bottom securing bolt **(see illustration)**.
4 Lower the vehicle, and with the bonnet supported in its open position, remove the radiator grille as described in Chapter 11, Section 7.
5 Disconnect the wiring multi-plug for the headlight unit.
6 Unscrew the mounting bolts from the top of the headlight unit, and withdraw the unit from the front of the vehicle **(see illustrations)**.
7 Refitting is a reversal of removal. Have the headlight alignment checked as described in the next Section.

7.6a Undo the upper mounting bolts . . .

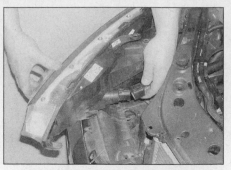

7.6b . . . and remove the headlamp, disconnecting the wiring

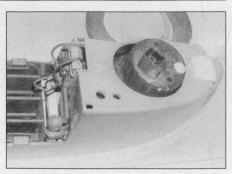

7.15 Retaining clip at the rear of the bumper

Front direction indicator

8 Undo and remove the screw located in the front direction indicator unit.

9 Withdraw the front direction indicator light unit from the bumper assembly.

10 Rotate the bulbholder anti-clockwise, and withdraw it from the light unit. Alternatively, the wiring plug can be disconnected from the bulbholder, leaving the bulb in position. Remove the light unit (for illustrations, see bulb renewal in Section 5).

11 Refitting is a reversal of removal.

Direction indicator side repeaters

12 Slide the side repeater assembly downwards, and remove it from the front wing (see illustration 5.14).

13 Turn the bulbholder anti-clockwise, and disconnect it from the repeater unit (see illustration 5.15).

7.16 Disconnect the wiring from the foglight

14 Fit the new repeater using a reversal of the removal procedure.

Front foglight

15 Release the retaining clip from the rear of the foglight unit, and remove the foglight unit (see illustration).

16 Twist off the rear cover from the light unit, and disconnect the wiring connector (see illustration).

17 Release the wire clip, and take out the bulb, noting its direction of fitting.

18 Refitting is a reversal of the removal procedure. An adjustment screw is located at the bottom corner of the light unit.

Rear foglight/reversing light (Hatchback)

19 Push the clip up under the rear of the light unit, then press the light unit out from the bumper (see illustrations).

20 Disconnect the wiring connector. Turn the bulbholder anti-clockwise to remove from the light unit.

21 Fit the new light unit using a reversal of the removal procedure. Make sure that the light unit is located correctly.

Rear light cluster

22 On Hatchback models, with the tailgate open. Remove the securing nut from the inside of the light cluster, and the securing screw, on the outside of the light cluster (see illustrations 5.26a and 5.26b).

23 On Saloon models, from inside the luggage compartment. Remove the three

turn-fasteners from the rear of the light cluster (see illustration 5.27).

24 On Estate models, with the tailgate open. Remove the two securing screws from the side of the light cluster (see illustration 5.28).

25 Carefully remove the light cluster from the vehicle.

26 On Estate and Saloon models, lift the retaining clips to separate the bulbholder from the light cluster (see illustration 5.30).

27 On Hatchback models, twist the bulbholders anti-clockwise and pull out from the light cluster (see illustration 5.31).

28 Fit the new light cluster unit using a reversal of the removal procedure. Make sure that the rear light cluster is located correctly.

Number plate light assembly

29 Insert a flat-bladed screwdriver in the recess on the left of the number plate light, and carefully prise out the light unit (see illustration).

30 Release the festoon-type bulb from the contact springs.

31 Fit the new light unit using a reversal of the removal procedure.

High-level stop-light

32 On Hatchback and Estate models, undo the two securing screws and remove the light cover.

33 On Saloon models, open the luggage compartment and remove the carpet trim from behind the light unit.

34 Unclip the bulbholder from the reflector and disconnect the wiring (see illustration).

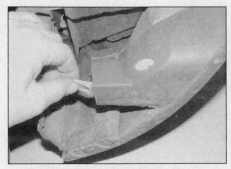

7.19a Unclip the rear light unit . . .

7.19b . . . and remove from the rear bumper

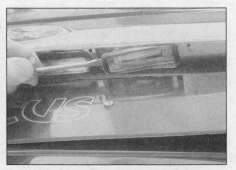

7.29 Unclipping number plate light

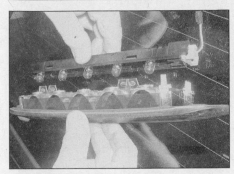

7.34 Unclip the bulbholder from the reflector (Estate)

35 On Saloon models, undo the securing screws inside the boot lid from the light unit and remove from the vehicle **(see illustration)**.
36 Fit the new light unit using a reversal of the removal procedure.

8 Headlight and front foglight beam alignment – checking and adjustment

1 Accurate adjustment of the headlight or front foglight beams is only possible using optical beam-setting equipment. This work should therefore be carried out by a Ford dealer, or other service station with the necessary facilities.
2 Temporary adjustment can be made after renewal of a bulb or light unit, or as an

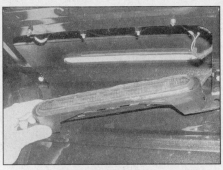

7.35 Unscrew the reflector from inside the boot (Saloon)

emergency measure if the alignment is incorrect following accident damage.
3 To adjust the headlight aim, turn the adjustment screws on the top of the headlight unit to make the adjustment **(see illustration)**. (One of the screws are for vertical alignment, and the other one is for horizontal alignment.)
4 Adjustment of the front foglight beam is carried out using the small screw visible at the bottom corner of the surround trim **(see illustration)**.
5 Before making any adjustments to the settings, it is important that the tyre pressures are correct, and that the vehicle is standing on level ground with no additional load in the vehicle.
6 Bounce the front of the vehicle a few times to settle the suspension. Ideally, somebody of average size should sit in the driver's seat during the adjustment, and the vehicle should have half a tank of fuel.

7 Where a vehicle is fitted with a headlight beam levelling system, set the switch to the 0 position before making any adjustments.
8 Whenever temporary adjustments are made, the settings must be checked and if necessary reset by a Ford dealer or other qualified person as soon as possible.

9 Headlight levelling motor – removal and refitting

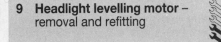

Removal

1 Make sure the beam adjustment switch is in the 0 position.
2 Remove the headlight unit as described in Section 7.
3 Unscrew and remove the securing screws from the cover on the rear of the headlight unit **(see illustration)**.
4 Turn the headlight levelling motor from its bayonet fitting, then unclip the motor spindle balljoint from its socket and pull out from the headlight reflector **(see illustration)**.
5 Disconnect the wiring multi-plug from the motor as it is removed from the headlight unit **(see illustration)**.

Refitting

6 Refitting is a reversal of the removal procedure, noting the following points:
a) *Make sure the beam adjustment switch is still in the 0 position.*
b) *Check the adjuster balljoint engages in its socket correctly* **(see illustration)**.

8.3 Headlamp adjusting screws (arrowed)

8.4 Foglight adjusting screw (arrowed)

9.3 Remove the rear headlamp cover

9.4 Turn motor to withdraw from headlamp

9.5 Disconnect the motor wiring plug

9.6 Recess to locate the balljoint (arrowed)

10.3a Upper steering shroud clips into the slots (arrowed) in the instrument panel surround

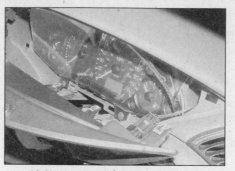

10.3b Unclip the instrument panel surround

10.5 Four screws for instrument panel (arrowed)

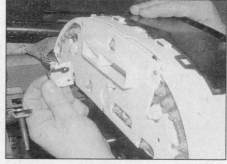

10.6 Disconnecting the multi-plug from the instrument panel

c) On completion, test the operation of the system, and have the beam alignment checked as described in Section 8.

10 Instrument panel – removal and refitting

⚠️ *Warning: The instrument panel must be kept in the upright position, to avoid silicone liquid leaking from the gauges.*

Removal

1 Disconnect the battery negative (earth) lead (refer to Chapter 5A, Section 1).
2 Lower the steering column locking lever and release the retaining clips with a thin-bladed screwdriver to remove the steering column upper shroud (Chapter 10, Section 19).
3 Undo the upper retaining screws from the instrument panel surround, then unclip it from the facia **(see illustrations)**.
4 As the surround is withdrawn, remove the electrical connector from the luggage compartment release switch and trip computer (where fitted).
5 Unscrew the four mounting screws from the instrument panel assembly **(see illustration)**.
6 Disconnect the multi-plug(s) from the rear of the instrument panel, as it is withdrawn from the facia. **(see illustration)**.

Refitting

7 Refitting is a reversal of the removal procedure.

11 Instrument panel components – removal and refitting

⚠️ *Warning: The instrument panel must be kept in the upright position, to avoid silicone liquid leaking from the gauges.*

The instrument panel should not be stripped, as no components were available at the time of writing. In the event of a faulty gauge, remove the instrument panel as described in Section 10, and take it to a Ford dealer for diagnosis. If a warning light or an illumination bulb has failed, remove the bulbholder by twisting it anti-clockwise and pulling it out from the instrument cluster. The wedge type bulb can then be pulled out from the holder.

12 Clock – removal and refitting

Removal

1 Disconnect the battery negative (earth) lead (see Chapter 5A, Section 1).
2 Remove the radio/cassette player as described in Section 22. Pull out and remove the ashtray.
3 Undo the four securing screws from inside the radio/cassette player aperture, then carefully unclip the heater control panel from its three retaining clips in the facia **(see illustration)**.
4 Disconnect the multi-plugs from the rear of the control panel (where required). Undo the two retaining screws and withdraw the clock.
5 On some models, the bulb can be removed by twisting it anti-clockwise; on others, the clock should be taken to a Ford dealer or automotive electrical specialist for bulb renewal.

Refitting

6 Refitting is a reversal of the removal procedure. Reset the clock on completion.

13 Horn – removal and refitting

Removal

Note: *On most models there are two horns fitted.*
1 Apply the handbrake, jack up the front of the vehicle and support it on axle stands.
2 Disconnect the electrical connector(s) from the horn terminal **(see illustrations)**.
3 Unscrew the mounting bolt(s), and withdraw the horn with its mounting bracket from under the vehicle .

12.3 Undo the four screws (arrowed) to remove panel

13.2a Horns fitted behind bumper on the left-hand side

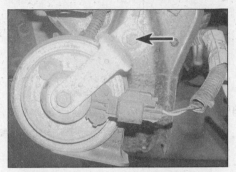

13.2b Disconnect the wiring connector and undo the bolt (arrowed)

Refitting

4 Refitting is a reversal of the removal procedure. Tighten the horn unit mounting bolt to the specified torque, making sure the mounting bracket is located correctly.

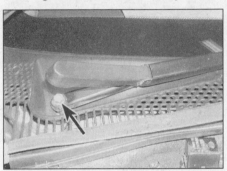

14.3 Loosen the wiper arm retaining nut (arrowed)

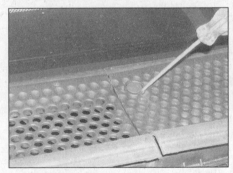

15.3 Prise off the screw cap

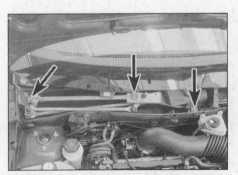

15.6 Wiper motor/linkage mounting bolts (arrowed)

14 Wiper arms – removal and refitting

Removal

1 Disconnect the battery negative (earth) lead (refer to Chapter 5A, Section 1).
2 With the wiper(s) 'parked' (ie, in the normal at-rest position), mark the positions of the blade(s) on the screen, using a wax crayon or strips of masking tape.
3 With the bonnet open (for the front wipers), lift up the plastic cap from the bottom of the wiper arm, and loosen the nut one or two turns **(see illustration)**.
4 Lift the wiper arm, and carefully release it from the taper on the spindle by moving it from side-to-side.
5 Completely remove the nut, and withdraw

14.5 Removing the wiper arm from the spindle

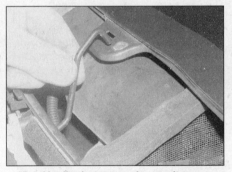

15.4 Unclip the stay and move it to one side

15.7 Withdraw the assembly from the bulkhead

the wiper arm from the spindle **(see illustration)**.

Refitting

6 Refitting is a reversal of the removal procedure. Make sure that the arm is fitted in the previously-noted position before tightening its nut to the specified torque.

15 Windscreen wiper motor and linkage – removal and refitting

Removal

1 Disconnect the battery negative (earth) lead (refer to Chapter 5A, Section 1).
2 Remove the wiper arms (Section 14).
3 Release the grille panel from just in front of the windscreen, by prising off the caps and unscrewing the retaining screws **(see illustration)**.
4 Unclip the small stay from the bulkhead, and disconnect the wiper motor multi-plug **(see illustration)**.
5 Undo the securing bolts from behind the scuttle cowling, and pull cowling forwards to allow removal of the wiper motor/linkage **(see illustration)**.
6 Unscrew the three mounting bolts securing the wiper motor and linkage to the bulkhead **(see illustration)**.
7 Withdraw the wiper motor, complete with the linkage, from the bulkhead **(see illustration)**.
8 Unclip the cover from the wiper motor, and

15.5 Undo the scuttle cowling bolts

15.8a Unclip the wiper motor cover . . .

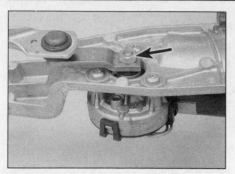

15.8b . . . and undo the nut arrowed (note the position of the arm for refitting)

15.10 Carefully lever the linkage to release the ball and socket

15.11a Unclip the circlip, remove the washer . . .

15.11b . . . and slide the spindle from the linkage

15.12a Make sure the grommet is fitted in the bulkhead

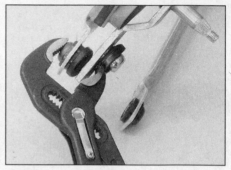

15.12b Press the ball and socket firmly together

mark the position of the motor arm on the mounting plate. Unscrew the centre nut from the wiper motor spindle **(see illustrations)**.

9 Undo the three securing screws, and separate the motor from the mounting plate.

10 If the linkages need to be removed, use a flat-bladed screwdriver to lever the ball and sockets apart **(see illustration)**.

11 The wiper arm spindles can be removed by unclipping the circlip, then lift off the washer and slide the spindle from the wiper linkage **(see illustrations)**.

Refitting

12 Refitting is a reversal of the removal procedure, noting the following points:
  a) *Tighten the wiper motor mounting bolts to their specified torque.*
  b) *Make sure that the wiper motor is in its 'parked' position before fitting the motor*

arm, and check that the wiper linkage is in line with the motor arm.
  c) *When installing the wiper motor and linkage to the bulkhead, make sure the rubber grommet is in place to locate the wiper motor in the bulkhead* **(see illustration)**.
  d) *Use a pair of grips to press the ball and sockets firmly together* **(see illustration)**.
  e) *Use grease to lubricate the wiper spindle and linkages when re-assembling.*

16 Tailgate wiper motor assembly – removal and refitting

Removal

1 Disconnect the battery negative (earth) lead

(refer to Chapter 5A, Section 1).

2 Remove the tailgate wiper arm as described in Section 14.

3 Remove the tailgate inner trim panel by unscrewing the securing screws, then pull the trim off its retaining clips.

4 Release the wiper motor multi-plug from the retaining clip, then disconnect it from the motor **(see illustration)**.

5 Undo the securing bolt and disconnect the wiper motor earth lead **(see illustration)**.

6 Unscrew the three mounting bolts, and remove the wiper motor from inside the tailgate **(see illustration)**.

7 Undo the retaining screws to remove the mounting plate from the motor. If necessary, remove the mounting rubbers for renewal **(see illustration)**.

8 The rubber grommet can be removed from the rear screen by first pulling out the plastic

16.4 Disconnecting the wiper motor multi-plug

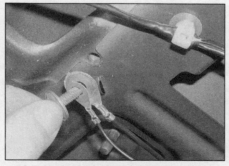

16.5 Undo the bolt to release the earth terminal

16.6 Wiper motor mounting bolts (Estate)

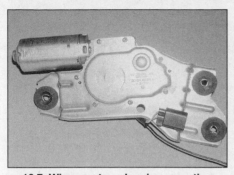

16.7 Wiper motor, showing mounting bracket retaining screws and mounting rubbers

16.8 Pull out the plastic sleeve, so as to remove the rubber grommet

computer (see Section 17). This has a washer reservoir level warning light and also a frost warning light.

Component renewal

3 The following paragraphs describe brief removal procedures for the auxiliary warning system components. Disconnect the battery negative (earth) lead before commencing work (refer to Chapter 5A, Section 1). Refitting procedures are a reversal of removal.

Central Timer Module (CTM)

4 Open the glovebox, press both sides of the glovebox in to release from the facia.
5 Hinge the glovebox downwards to gain access to the fusebox.
6 Undo the two securing bolts from the fusebox, and remove it downwards from the facia bracket (see illustrations).
7 Pull the timer module from the back of the fusebox (see illustration).

Display module

8 Remove the instrument panel surround, referring to Section 10.
9 Disconnect the multi-plug from the trip computer, then release the trip computer from the instrument panel surround.

Low air temperature warning sender unit

The location of the sender unit may vary on the age of the vehicle (the front bumper or the door mirror are the more usual places used).
10 If fitted in the front bumper, remove the bumper as described in Chapter 11, section 6.
11 Unclip the sender unit from the bumper and disconnect the multi-plug.
12 If fitted in the door mirror, remove the mirror as described in Chapter 11, Section 15.

Low washer fluid switch

13 Remove the washer reservoir as described in Section 21.
14 Disconnect the multi-plug from the washer fluid reservoir.
15 Using a screwdriver, lever out the switch from the reservoir.
16 After refitting the switch, refill the reservoir with reference to *Weekly checks*.

sleeve, then pull out the grommet (see illustration).

Refitting

9 Refitting is a reversal of the removal procedure. Make sure that the wiper motor is in its 'parked' position before fitting the wiper arm.

17 Trip computer module – removal and refitting

1 The trip computer (Information and Message Centre) is only available on certain models, and is incorporated in the instrument panel surround. The computer has the following functions:
a) Average speed.
b) Instantaneous fuel consumption.
c) Average fuel consumption.
d) Range to empty.
e) Ambient temperature.
The Information Message Centre activates the warning lamp when insufficient water is in the washer reservoir, and also illuminates the frost warning lamp when the ambient temperature falls to +4°C or (40°F).
2 To remove the trip computer, remove the instrument panel surround as described in Section 10.
3 Disconnect the multi-plug from the trip computer, then release the trip computer from the instrument panel surround.

Refitting

4 Refitting is a reversal of the removal procedure.

18 Auxiliary warning system – general information and component renewal

1 All models have a Central Timer Module (CTM), which is located in the back of the central fusebox. This module controls the timed features in the vehicle and also the acoustic signals.

Functions of the CTM standard version
a) Intermittent wipe, front and rear.
b) Windscreen washer with wiper function, front and rear.
c) Heated rear window and windscreen.
d) Entry illumination.
e) Power saving relay.
f) Lights-on warning chime.
g) Acoustic signal from trip computer module, anti-theft warning system/double locking module and airbag module.

Additional functions for vehicles with automatic transmission
a) Safety belt warning.
b) Reverse gear warning.
c) Ignition key warning.
d) Gear lever not in park position.
2 Some models are fitted with an auxiliary warning system, which is built into the trip

18.6a Undo the two retaining screws . . .

18.6b . . . and lower fusebox to remove

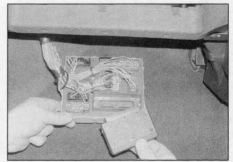

18.7 Timer module fitted to the rear of the fusebox

19.3 Wiring connector for the transceiver unit

19.6 The central locking/security module (arrowed)

19.10 Door catch incorporates the interior light switch

19 Anti-theft alarm system – general information

1 As an optional extra, all models can be fitted with an active anti-theft alarm system, which protects all doors, including the bonnet and bootlid/tailgate. It is activated when the vehicle is locked, either with the key or remote transmitter. When the alarm has been activated, the horn will sound for 30 seconds and the indicators will operate for 5 minutes. The system will then reset, to an armed state, so that if there is another intrusion it will be activated again.

2 All models are fitted with a Passive Anti-theft System (or PATS), which is fully passive in operation and requires no procedure to arm or disarm the system. The PATS circuit is separate from the alarm, meaning that the car is immobilised even if the alarm is not set. This function is incorporated in the engine management ECU to prevent the vehicle from starting.

3 The PATS transceiver unit is fitted around the ignition switch (see illustration), and it 'reads' the code from a microchip in the ignition key to activate, and deactivate. This means that any replacement or duplicate keys must be obtained through a Ford dealer – any cut locally will not contain the microchip, and will therefore not disarm the immobiliser. If an incorrect code, or no code is received then the ECU will immobilise the engine

4 The radio/cassette unit is incorporated into the alarm system – if an attempt is made to remove the unit while the alarm is active, the alarm will sound.

5 Where fitted, the movement sensors on the system consist of two ultrasonic units, located in the B-pillars, incorporating transmitters and receivers. The receivers check that the echo frequency matches the original frequency. If there is any significant difference, the system triggers the alarm.

6 The Central locking/Central Security Module (CSM) has five versions of module depending on vehicle specification:
 1) Central locking.
 2) Central locking and remote control.
 3) Central locking, double locking and remote control.
 4) Central locking, double locking, remote control and alarm system.
 5) Central locking, double locking, remote control and alarm system with infrared interior scanning.

This module is mounted on a bracket beneath the right-hand side of the facia at the bottom of the A-pillar (see illustration).

7 If the tailgate or bootlid are opened using the key or remote transmitter, the alarm will not activate due to an inhibit switch fitted to the lock. This suppresses the alarm system until the tailgate or boot lid is closed again.

8 The remote central door locking is operated by radio frequency, and can be operated from approximately 10 metres. The key has three buttons, depending on the sequence of the buttons pressed, it will lock and unlock the doors, arm the alarm, and also lock and unlock the tailgate.

9 The alarm system (where fitted) has its own horn. On Hatchback and Saloon models, it is located on the left-hand side of the luggage compartment; on Estate models, it is located on the right-hand side of the luggage compartment.

10 The CSM incorporates a self-test function, to activate this the ignition must be in the OFF position. Operate one of the door light switches (see illustration) six times within eight seconds, once the self-test mode has been entered the module will sound the horn (where fitted) and the hazard lights will flash once to acknowledge the input. The horn (where fitted) should sound, and hazard lights flash every time a door, bonnet or tailgate is opened. If the doors are double locked, and interior scanning is fitted, the signal will occur when something is moved within the passenger compartment. A more comprehensive test can be made using the Ford FDS 2000 diagnostic tester, used by your Ford Dealer.

11 The following are inputs to the CSM that can be tested while in the self-test mode:-
 a) Remote transmitter.
 b) Hood switch.
 c) Driver's door interior light switch.
 d) Passenger door interior light switch.
 e) Tailgate interior light switch.
 f) Driver's door lock motor set/reset switch.
 g) Passenger's door lock motor set/reset switch.
 h) Tailgate anti-theft inhibit switch.
 i) Integrated lock/unlock switches within power door lock actuator.
 j) ignition switch.
 k) Radio disconnect trigger.
 l) Tailgate release switch.

20 Cruise control system – general information and component renewal

1 Cruise control is available as an option on certain models.

2 The system is active at road speeds above 30 mph, and comprises of:
 a) Electronic speed control servo.
 b) Driver-operated switches.
 c) A speed control cable.
 d) Brake and clutch pedal switches.
 e) Vehicle speed sensor.

3 The driver-operated switches are mounted on the steering wheel, and allow the driver to control the various functions.

4 The vehicle speed sensor is mounted on the transmission, and generates pulses which are fed to the speed control unit.

5 The stop-light switch, brake pedal switch and (when applicable) clutch pedal switch are used to disable the cruise control system. The stop-light switch is activated when the brake pedal is applied gently, and the brake pedal switch is activated when the brake pedal is applied forcibly.

6 An indicator light on the instrument panel is illuminated when the system is in operation.

7 The following paragraphs describe brief removal procedures for the cruise control system components. The battery negative (earth) lead should be disconnected before commencing work (refer to Chapter 5A, Section 1). Refitting is a reversal of removal.

Steering wheel switches

8 Remove the airbag unit from the steering wheel as described in Section 26.

9 Disconnect the wiring plugs, noting the location of each plug and how the wiring is routed for refitting.

10 Remove the two screws each side securing the operating switches, and remove them as required from the steering wheel.

Brake and clutch pedal switches

11 Undo the four retaining screws and prise out the one securing clip, to remove the driver's side lower facia panel.

12 Disconnect the wiring connectors from the clutch switch, brake pedal switch and stop-light switch.

13 To remove the clutch and brake pedal switches, twist them to release from the pedal assembly.

14 Refitting is the reverse of removal. To ensure correct operation of the brake pedal switches, reset the switch by fully extending its plunger. Depress the pedal and hold the pedal in this position, clip the switch securely into position and gently raise the pedal to the at-rest position. This will automatically set the position of the switch.

Speed control actuator

15 Undo the two retaining clips and remove the air intake pipe, from between the air cleaner and the throttle body.

16 Disconnect the actuator cable from the throttle linkage on the throttle housing, by releasing the inner cable end fitting from the segment and unclipping the outer cable from the bracket.

17 Disconnect the actuator multi-plug, then unscrew the actuator mounting bolts, and remove the actuator from the bulkhead.

18 Remove the four securing bolts to remove the actuator from its bracket.

19 Depress the actuating cable cap locking arm, and remove the cap by turning it anti-clockwise.

20 Gently raise the cable retaining lug by a maximum of 0.5 mm, and push the cable end out of the slot in the pulley.

21 When refitting, make sure that the cable end locks into the slot in the pulley.

22 To locate the cable cap onto the actuator pulley, keep the cable taut and in the pulley groove, and pull the throttle linkage end of the cable to draw the cable cap onto the pulley.

23 To refit the cable cap, keep the cable taut and the pulley still, then refit the cable cap tabs into the actuator slots; turn the cap clockwise until the locking arm locates on the locking stop. **Note:** *Incorrect assembly of the cable onto the pulley may result in a high idle speed. Check that the throttle lever is in its idle position after refitting the actuator.*

21.1 Mounting bolt for filler neck (arrowed)

21.4b . . . and slide the bottle out of the slot in the inner wing (arrowed)

21 Windscreen/tailgate washer system components – removal and refitting

Removal

Washer reservoir and pump

1 Open up the bonnet, and remove the securing bolt for the washer bottle filler neck **(see illustration)**. Pull the filler neck up, to disengage from the washer reservoir.

2 Apply the handbrake and loosen the left-hand front wheel nuts. Jack up the front of the car and support on axle stands. Remove the front wheel.

3 Undo the retaining screws, and release the wheelarch liner as necessary for access to the reservoir.

4 Unscrew the mounting bolts, and slide the

21.4a Undo the mounting bolts (lower bolt arrowed) . . .

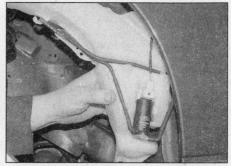
21.5 Disconnect the washer hoses and wiring from the washer pump

reservoir forwards to release it from the inner wing panel **(see illustrations)**.

5 Disconnect the washer hoses and wiring connector from the washer pump as the reservoir is being removed **(see illustration)**. (Anticipate some loss of fluid by placing a container beneath the reservoir.)

6 Pull the windscreen washer pump, and (where applicable) the headlight washer pump, from the reservoir **(see illustration)**.

7 Remove the rubber seal/filter to clean out and check for damage **(see illustration)**.

Washer jet (windscreen)

8 With the bonnet supported in its open position, carefully disconnect the washer tube from the bottom of the jet.

9 Where necessary, disconnect the wiring for the jet heater. Prise the jet out from the bonnet, taking care not to damage the paintwork **(see illustrations)**.

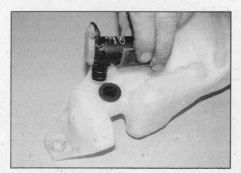
21.6 Pull out the washer motor

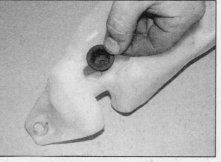
21.7 Check filter is not blocked

21.9a Disconnect the wiring connector for the jet heater (where fitted) . . .

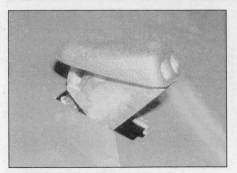

21.9b . . . then carefully prise the jet from the bonnet

21.10 Undo the retaining screws from the high-level stop-light

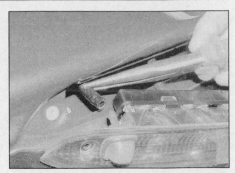

21.11 Pull the washer hose from the washer jet

Washer jet (rear window)

10 On Hatchback and Estate models, undo the two securing screws and remove the high-level stop-light unit **(see illustration)**.

11 Pull the washer tube from the jet **(see illustration)**. (Check with a dealer to find if the washer jet is available separately from the rear light lens.)

Headlight washer jet (where fitted)

12 Remove the front bumper as described in Chapter 11.

13 Disconnect the washer tube from the base of the jet.

14 Pull off the jet retaining clip/screw and withdraw the jet from the bumper.

Refitting

15 Refitting is a reversal of the removal procedure, noting the following points:
   a) *In the case of the screen washer jets, press them in firmly until they are fully engaged.*
   b) *After refitting the headlight washer jet, refit the front bumper as described in Chapter 11.*

22 Radio/cassette player (Audio Unit) – removal and refitting

Note: *Special tools are required to remove the audio unit.*

1 A Ford Keycode anti-theft system is featured in the audio unit, if the unit and/or the battery is disconnected, the audio unit will not

function again on reconnection until the correct security code is entered. Details of this procedure are given in the Ford Audio Systems Operating Guide supplied with the vehicle when new, with the code itself being given in a Radio Passport and/or a Keycode Label at the same time. The units have a detachable front bezel that can be removed when the vehicle is not in use **(see illustration)**. The RDS/EON audio units also allow the registration of the vehicle, or the Vehicle Identification Number (VIN) to be entered into the memory.

2 For obvious security reasons, the re-coding procedure is not given in this manual – if you do not have the code or details of the correct procedure, but can supply proof of ownership and a legitimate reason for wanting this information, the vehicle's selling dealer may be able to help.

3 Note that these units will allow only ten attempts at entering the code – any further attempts will render the unit permanently inoperative until it has been reprogrammed by Ford themselves. At first, three consecutive attempts are allowed; if all three are incorrect, a 30-minute delay is required before another attempt can be made. Each of any subsequent attempts (up to the maximum of ten) can be made only after a similar delay.

Removal

4 Disconnect the battery negative (earth) lead.

5 In order to release the audio unit retaining clips, the U-shaped tools must be inserted into the special holes on each side of the unit.

If possible, it is preferable to obtain purpose-made tools from an audio specialist, as these have cut-outs which snap firmly into the clips so that the unit can be pulled out.

6 Lightly push the U-shaped tools outwards as the audio unit is being removed **(see illustration)**. Pull the unit squarely from its aperture, or it may jam.

7 With the audio unit withdrawn, disconnect the feed, earth, aerial and speaker leads **(see illustration)**. Where applicable, also detach and remove the plastic support bracket from the rear of the unit.

Refitting

8 Refitting is a reversal of removal. With the leads reconnected to the rear of the unit, press it into position until the retaining clips are felt to engage. Reactivate the unit by entering the correct code in accordance with the maker's instructions.

23 Compact disc autochanger – removal and refitting

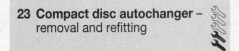

Note: *The Ford 6000 RDS/EON is a radio and single disc CD player, and can be removed as described in Section 22.*

1 A compact disc (CD) player autochanger is available as an optional extra, which is compatible with the Ford 5000 RDS/EON radio cassette player. This autochanger is mounted under the passenger front seat and can hold 6 compact discs.

22.1 Press the securing button to release the bezel

22.6 Using the U-shaped tools to remove the radio

22.7 Disconnecting the multi-plugs and aerial lead

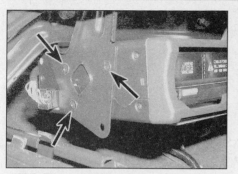

23.5 Three mounting screws each side (arrowed)

24.2 Rear speaker on 3-door model

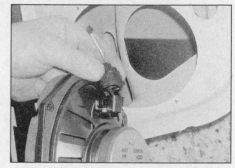

24.3 Disconnecting the speaker wiring connector

Removal

2 The battery negative (earth) lead should be disconnected before commencing work.

3 The CD autochanger unit is mounted in a bracket below the front passenger's seat.

⚠ *Warning: If air bags are fitted to the seat, read warnings in Section 26 of this Chapter before removal.*

4 Remove the front passenger seat as described in Chapter 11, Section 26.

5 Remove the unit mounting screws (three each side), and disconnect the wiring plug **(see illustration)**. Slide the player out of the brackets below the seat, and remove it from the car.

Refitting

6 Refitting is a reversal of the removal procedure.

24 Speakers – removal and refitting

Removal

1 Remove the front or rear door trim panel as described in Chapter 11.

2 Unscrew the four cross-head screws, and withdraw the speaker from the inner panel **(see illustration)**.

3 Disconnect the electrical connector on removal of the speaker **(see illustration)**.

Refitting

4 Refitting is a reversal of the removal procedure.

25 Radio aerial – removal and refitting

Removal

1 If just the aerial mast is to be removed, this can be unscrewed from the base from outside **(see illustration)**.

2 To remove the aerial base, prise out the interior light and remove the two retaining screws from the light surround **(see illustration)**.

3 Unscrew the retaining screw from the base of the aerial **(see illustration)**, disconnect the aerial lead, and remove the base and gasket from outside.

Refitting

4 Refitting is a reversal of the removal procedure.

26 Airbag units – removal and refitting

⚠ *Warning: Handle any airbag unit with extreme care, as a precaution against personal injury, and always hold it with the cover facing away from the body. If in doubt concerning any proposed work involving an airbag unit or its control circuitry, consult a Ford dealer or other qualified specialist.*

⚠ *Warning: Stand any airbag in a safe place with the cover uppermost, and do not expose it to heat sources in excess of 100°C.*

⚠ *Warning: Do not attempt to open or repair an airbag unit, or apply any electrical current to it. Do not use any airbag unit which is visibly damaged or which has been tampered with.*

Driver's airbag

1 Disconnect the battery negative (earth) lead (refer to Chapter 5A, Section 1).

⚠ *Warning: Before proceeding, wait a minimum of 5 minutes, as a precaution against accidental firing of the airbag unit. This period ensures that any stored energy in the back-up capacitor is dissipated.*

2 Rotate the steering wheel so that one of the airbag mounting bolt holes (at the rear of the steering wheel boss) is visible above the steering column upper shroud.

3 Unscrew and remove the first mounting bolt **(see illustration)**, then turn the steering wheel through 180° and remove the remaining mounting bolt.

4 Carefully withdraw the airbag unit from the steering wheel far enough to disconnect the wiring multi-plugs, then remove it from inside the vehicle **(see illustration)**. Stand the airbag in a safe place with the cover uppermost as soon as possible.

5 Refitting is a reversal of the removal procedure.

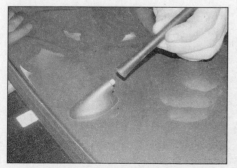

25.1 Unscrew the aerial mast from the base

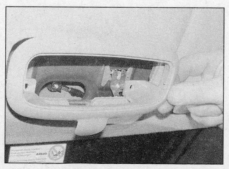

25.2 Withdraw the interior light surround

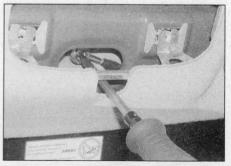

25.3 Undo the aerial mounting screw

26.3 Unscrewing an air bag mounting bolt

26.4 Disconnecting the airbag wiring multi-plug

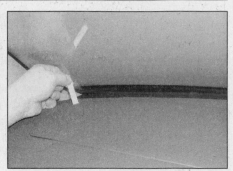

26.7a Work around the trim to unclip from the facia . . .

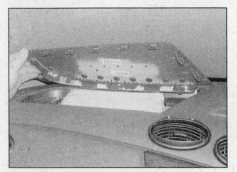

26.7b . . . hinge trim towards the windscreen to access airbag

26.8 Undo the four mounting bolts (arrowed)

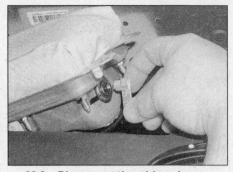

26.9a Disconnect the wiring plug . . .

Passenger's airbag

6 Disconnect the battery negative (earth) lead (refer to Chapter 5A, Section 1).

⚠️ **Warning: Before proceeding, wait a minimum of 5 minutes, as a precaution against accidental firing of the airbag unit. This period ensures that any stored energy in the back-up capacitor is dissipated.**

7 Using a flat-bladed tool, release the clips on the airbag module trim cover. Start at the outer edge and work your way around, carefully disengaging the trim from the facia, and hinge up towards the windscreen **(see illustrations)**.

8 Remove the four airbag unit mounting screws, and withdraw the unit from the facia **(see illustration)**.

9 Disconnect the wiring multi-plug from the airbag unit as it comes into view. A long-nosed pair of pliers may be required to release the connector **(see illustrations)**.

10 Refitting is a reversal of removal.

Side airbag

11 The side airbag units are built into the front seats, and their removal requires that the seat fabric be removed. This is not considered to be a DIY operation, and should be referred to a Ford dealer.

27 Airbag control module – removal and refitting

Removal

1 Disconnect the battery negative (earth) lead (refer to Chapter 5A, Section 1).

⚠️ **Warning: Before proceeding, wait a minimum of 5 minutes, as a precaution against accidental firing of the airbag unit. This period ensures that any stored energy in the back-up capacitor is dissipated.**

2 Remove the centre console and air ducting as described in Chapter 11.

3 Press the retaining lugs and disconnect the multi-plug(s) from the module.

4 Unscrew the mounting bolts and remove the module from the vehicle **(see illustration)**.

Refitting

5 Refitting is a reversal of the removal procedure.

28 Airbag sliding contact – removal and refitting

Removal

1 Remove the driver's airbag unit as described in Section 26.

2 Disconnect the horn switch wiring connector.

3 If fitted, disconnect the multi-plugs for the cruise control switches.

4 Remove the steering wheel and column shrouds as described in Chapter 10.

5 Detach the steering column multi-function switches by depressing the plastic retaining tabs with a flat-bladed screwdriver.

6 Using a small screwdriver, release the two retaining tabs, then remove the sliding contact

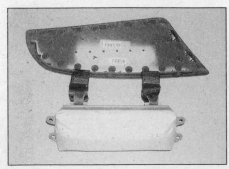

26.9b . . . and remove the airbag complete with trim

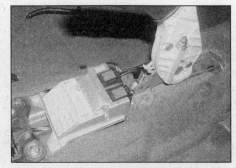

27.4 Airbag control module located under centre console

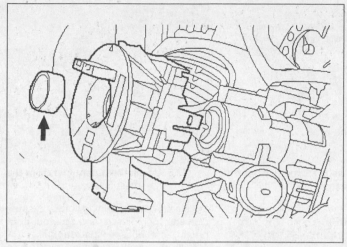

28.6 Note the position of the spacing collar (arrowed)

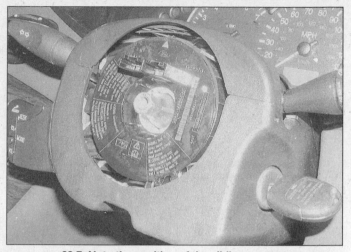

28.7 Note the position of the sliding contact

from the steering column. Note the position of the spacing collar within the centre of the sliding contact **(see illustration)**.

Refitting

7 Refitting is a reversal of the removal procedure, noting the following points:
  a) *Make sure that the front wheels are still pointing straight-ahead.*
  b) *The sliding contact must be fitted in its central position, with the special alignment marks aligned and the arrow mark to the top* **(see illustration)**.
  c) *Make sure the spacing collar is fitted.*

29 Parking sensor system – general information

Offered as an option, the park reverse aid is an ultrasonic proximity detection system, intended to help avoid rear collisions when reversing.

The system consists of ultrasonic sensors mounted in the rear bumper, a display/buzzer unit mounted in the C-pillar trim panel, and an ECU mounted behind the left-hand side trim panel in the luggage compartment.

The system is only operational when reverse gear is engaged; changing audible and visual signals warn the driver of impending contact as the car reverses towards an object in its path.

The sensors in the bumper can be unclipped and disconnected once the rear bumper is removed as described in Chapter 11. To remove the display/buzzer unit, remove the C-pillar trim panel as described in Chapter 11, Section 28.

The system ECU can be disconnected once the luggage area left-hand trim panel is removed.

Caution is required when reversing in heavy rain or similar adverse conditions, as the sensors may not always measure close obstacles accurately. Care must also be taken if a tow bar has been installed.

30 Traveller Assist System (TAS) – general information

Ford HelpNet 5100 RDS EON

This telematic system is an audio system with a traveller assistance service (TAS) using an integral mobile telephone and a Global Positioning System (GPS) receiver. There are two versions of audio available, which have different features offered.

When buying a vehicle, the customer signs the card agreement and is supplied with a SIM card. This is inserted into a slot behind a detachable rocker switch (SEEK button) on the audio unit. When the card is first inserted a commissioning operation will be initiated, during which data specific to the territory and the code for transmission of the GPS co-ordinates are loaded by means of the telephone, this takes about ten minutes to initiate. During the initialisation of the card, the vehicle should be stationary and in open ground. The system automatically loads necessary updates through the telephone.

The telematic system allows the driver to:
  a) *obtain route guidance.*
  b) *ask for traffic information.*
  c) *establish the position of the vehicle.*

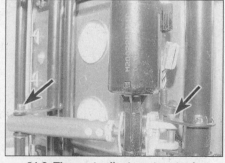

31.8 The seat adjustment motor is secured by roll-pins (arrowed)

  d) *make emergency calls (SOS).*
  e) *hold telephone conversations (PHONE).*
  f) *use services (such as hotel reservations).*
  g) *call up a break down service ('towing vehicle' symbol).*

Any problems with the system should be referred to a Ford dealer for diagnosis.

31 Electric seat components – removal and refitting

⚠️ **Warning: If side airbags are fitted, see Section 26 (Airbag units – removal and refitting) before removing the front seats.**

Heated seats

1 If heated seats are fitted, both driver's and front passenger seats have heating elements built into the seat cushion and backrest.
2 No repairs can be made to the heating elements without dismantling the seat and removing the seat fabric – therefore this work should be left to a Ford dealer or other specialist.
3 The heated seat switches are removed as described in Section 4.
4 For further diagnosis of any problems with the system, refer to Sections 2 and 3, and to the wiring diagrams at the end of this Chapter.

Seat adjustment components

5 Only the driver's seat is equipped with seat adjustment motors, on the highest specification models.
6 To gain access to the motors, remove the driver's seat as described in Chapter 11.
7 The motors are bolted to a mounting frame, which in turn is bolted to the seat base. Before removing a motor, trace its wiring back from the motor to its wiring plug, and disconnect it.
8 Remove the roll-pins from the motor mounting adjusting bar, and remove from the seat base **(see illustration)**.

32.3 Unclip and slide out the metal insert

32.4 Release the plastic surround from the panel

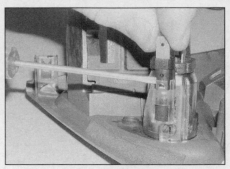

32.5 Unclip the bulbholder from the plastic surround

9 Refitting is a reversal of removal. It is worth periodically greasing the worm-drive components and seat runners, to ensure trouble-free operation.

10 The seat adjustment switches are removed as described in Section 4.

11 For further diagnosis of any problems with the system, refer to Sections 2 and 3, and to the wiring diagrams at the end of this Chapter.

32 Cigarette lighter – removal and refitting

Removal

1 Disconnect the battery negative (earth) lead (refer to Chapter 5A, Section 1).

2 Remove the heater control panel as described in Chapter 3, Section 10.

3 Release the retaining clips inside the cigarette lighter insert, and slide out from the plastic surround (see illustration).

4 Push the plastic surround out to release from the control panel (see illustration).

5 To remove the bulb, unclip the bulbholder from the plastic surround (see illustration).

Refitting

6 Refitting is a reversal of the removal procedure.

FORD FOCUS 1998 on

Diagram 1

Key to symbols

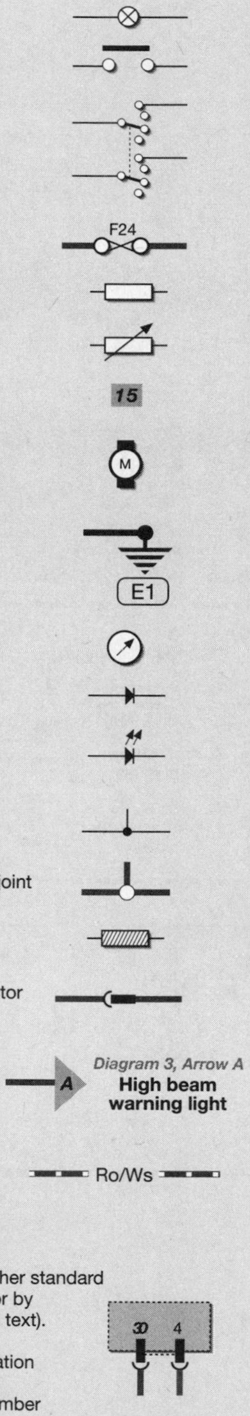

Bulb

Switch

Multiple contact
switch (ganged)

Fuse/fusible link

F24

Resistor

Variable resistor

Item no.

15

Pump/motor

M

Earth and location
(via lead)

E1

Gauge/meter

Diode

Light emitting diode
(LED)

Internal connection
(connecting wires)

Wire splice or soldered joint

Solenoid actuator

Plug and socket connector

Connections to other
circuits. Direction of
arrow denotes current
flow.

A *Diagram 3, Arrow A*
**High beam
warning light**

Wire colour
(Red wire/white tracer) Ro/Ws

Box shape denotes part
of a larger component.
Terminal identified by either standard
termination (bold *italic*) or by
connector number (plain text).

30 4

30 Terminal identification
(i.e. battery +ve)
4 Connector pin number

Earth locations

E1	Battery ground strap		**E7**	LH "A" pillar
E2	RH "A" pillar (1)		**E8**	Tailgate
E3	LH front engine compartment		**E9**	LH luggage compartment
E4	RH "A" pillar (2)		**E10**	LH engine bulkhead
E5	LH side engine compartment (1)		**E11**	RH engine bulkhead
E6	LH side engine compartment (2)			

Key to circuits

Diagram 1	Information for wiring diagrams
Diagram 2	Starting, charging, airbag, horn and clock
Diagram 3	Zetec SE engine management system (manual transmission)
Diagram 4	Zetec SE engine management system (auto. transmission)
Diagram 5	Zetec SE engine management system (auto. transmission) cont. and fuel pump
Diagram 6	Zetec E engine management system
Diagram 7	Endura-DI diesel engine management system
Diagram 8	Endura-DI diesel engine management cont. engine cooling and electric mirrors
Diagram 9	Cruise control, heated rear window, heated seats and power steering
Diagram 10	Electric windows and Wipe/wash
Diagram 11	Central locking, cigarette lighter and radio
Diagram 12	Exterior lights and reversing lights
Diagram 13	Headlights and indicators
Diagram 14	Brake lights, interior lights and heating
Diagram 15	Heating continued and trip computer
Diagram 16	ABS with traction control and central timer
Diagram 17	Instrument display

Engine fuse box

Fuse	Rating	Circuit protected		Fuse	Rating	Circuit protected
F1	40A	Main supply		F18	10A	Cat sensor
F4	50A	Heated windscreen		F19	10A	Side lights
F5	60A	Diesel glow plug		F20	10A	ECU
F6	30A	Engine cooling (air con.)		F21	20A	ABS
F7	40A	Main supply		F22	15A	Running lights (side lights)
F8	30A	Ignition		F23	20A	Diesel aux. heater
F9	20A	ECU		F26	10A	LH main beam
F10	10A	Diagnostics, voltage sensor		F27	10A	RH main beam
F11	30A	ABS		F28	10A	Heated windscreen, diesel
F12	15A	Fuel pump, diesel injector pump				engine and fuel fired heater
F13	30A	Headlight washer		F29	30A	Engine cooling fan (air con.)
F14	10A	Running lights		F64	30A	Heater blower motor
F16	10A	LH dipped beam		F65	30A	Engine cooling fan
F17	10A	RH dipped beam				

Central fuse box

Fuse	Rating	Circuit protected		Fuse	Rating	Circuit protected
F30	7.5A	ABS		F50	7.5A	Radio, central timer,
F31	15A	Radio				instruments
F32	10A	Light switch		F51	7.5A	Heated mirrors
F33	15A	Hazard flasher		F53	10A	Reversing light, heated
F34	7.5A	Horn, electric seats				washer jets
F35	7.5A	Interior lights, mirrors		F54	15A	Brake lights
F36	20A	Clock, electronic modules		F55	20A	Front wiper
F37	25A	Electric windows		F56	25A	Front electric windows
F39	10A	Reverse light, rear wiper		F58	7.5A	Air con. recirculated air
F40	25A	Electric windows		F59	7.5A	Instruments, electronic
F43	15A	Electric windows, rear wiper				modules
F44	20A	Fog lights		F60	7.5A	Air bags
F46	15A	Cigarette lighter		F61	7.5A	Light switch
F47	7.5A	LH side lights		F62	15A	Heated seats
F48	7.5A	RH side lights		F63	20A	Central locking
F49	25A	Heated rear window				

MTS
H31973

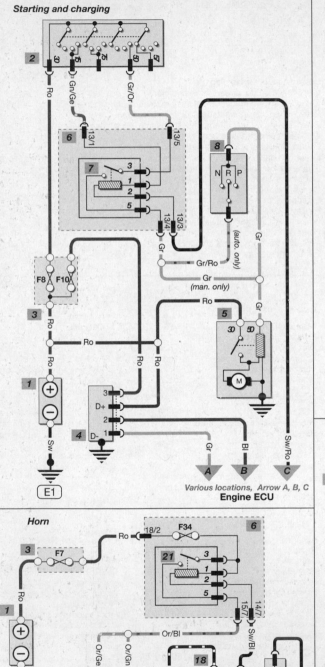

Wire colours

Bl	Blue	Or	Orange
Br	Brown	Pk	Pink
Ge	Yellow	Ro	Red
Gr	Grey	Sw	Black
Gn	Green	Vi	Violet
LGn	Light green	Ws	White

Key to items

1 Battery
2 Ignition switch
3 Engine fuse box
4 Alternator
5 Starter motor
6 Central fuse box
7 Starter relay
8 Starter inhibitor switch
9 Diagnostic connector
10 Airbag module
11 Central timer module
12 Drivers airbag
13 Passenger airbag
14 LH side airbag
15 RH side airbag
16 LH crash sensor
17 RH crash sensor
18 Steering wheel clock spring
19 Drivers seatbelt pretensioner
20 Passenger seatbelt pretensioner
21 Horn relay
22 Horn
23 Second horn
24 Horn switch
25 Clock

Focus 1998 on - Diagram 2

Note: prefix 1/ = C423 multi plug
prefix 2/ = C424 multi plug

H31974

Starting and charging

Airbag system

Clock

Horn

Wire colours

Bl	Blue	**Or**	Orange
Br	Brown	**Pk**	Pink
Ge	Yellow	**Ro**	Red
Gr	Grey	**Sw**	Black
Gn	Green	**Vi**	Violet
LGn	Light green	**Ws**	White

Key to items

1 Battery
2 Ignition switch
3 Engine fuse box
9 Diagnostic connector
26 Engine management control unit
27 Main relay
28 Ignition amplifier
29 Ignition coil
30 Spark plugs
31 Pre-cat oxygen sensor
32 Post-cat oxygen sensor
33 Canister purge solenoid valve
34 Clutch pedal switch
35 Vehicle speed sensor
36 Idle speed control valve
37 Fuel injector cylinder 1
38 Fuel injector cylinder 2
39 Fuel injector cylinder 3
40 Fuel injector cylinder 4
41 Knock sensor
42 Camshaft position sensor
43 Crankshaft position sensor
44 Cylinder head temp. sensor
45 Throttle position sensor
46 Mass airflow sensor
47 Power steering pressure switch

Focus 1998 on - Diagram 3

MTS H31975

Engine management system Zetec SE models with manual transmission

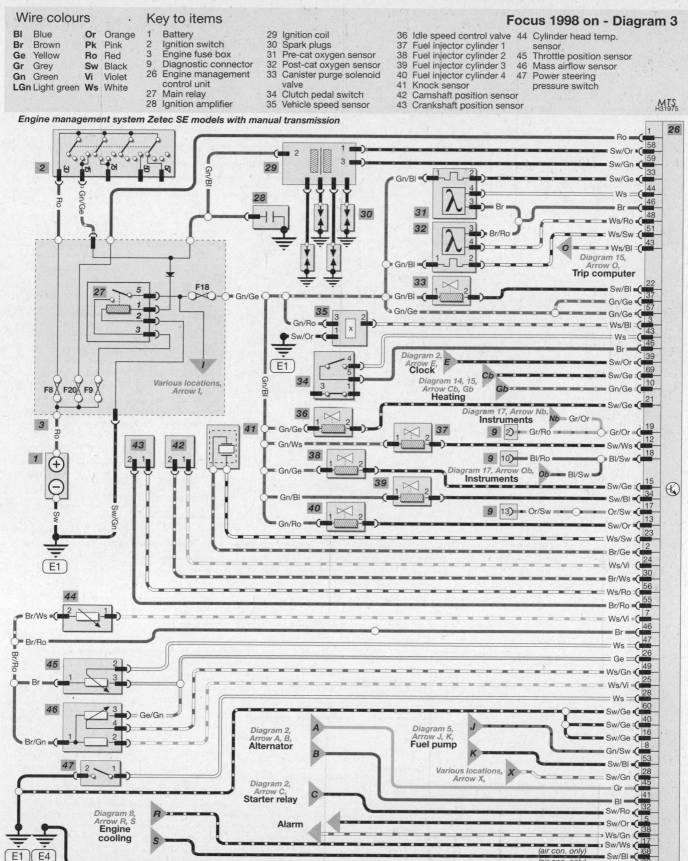

Wire colours

Bl	Blue	**Or**	Orange
Br	Brown	**Pk**	Pink
Ge	Yellow	**Ro**	Red
Gr	Grey	**Sw**	Black
Gn	Green	**Vi**	Violet
LGn	Light green	**Ws**	White

Key to items

1 Battery
2 Ignition switch
3 Engine fuse box
9 Diagnostic connector
26 Engine management control unit
27 Main relay
28 Ignition amplifier
29 Ignition coil
30 Spark plugs
31 Pre-cat oxygen sensor
32 Post-cat oxygen sensor
33 Canister purge solenoid valve
34 Clutch pedal switch
35 Vehicle speed sensor
36 Idle speed control valve
37 Fuel injector cylinder 1
38 Fuel injector cylinder 2
39 Fuel injector cylinder 3
40 Fuel injector cylinder 4
41 Knock sensor
42 Camshaft position sensor
43 Crankshaft position sensor
44 Cylinder head temp. sensor
45 Throttle position sensor
47 Power steering pressure switch
48 Mass airflow sensor
49 Exhaust gas pressure differential sensor

Focus 1998 on - Diagram 4

MTS
H31976

Engine management system Zetec SE models with automatic transmission

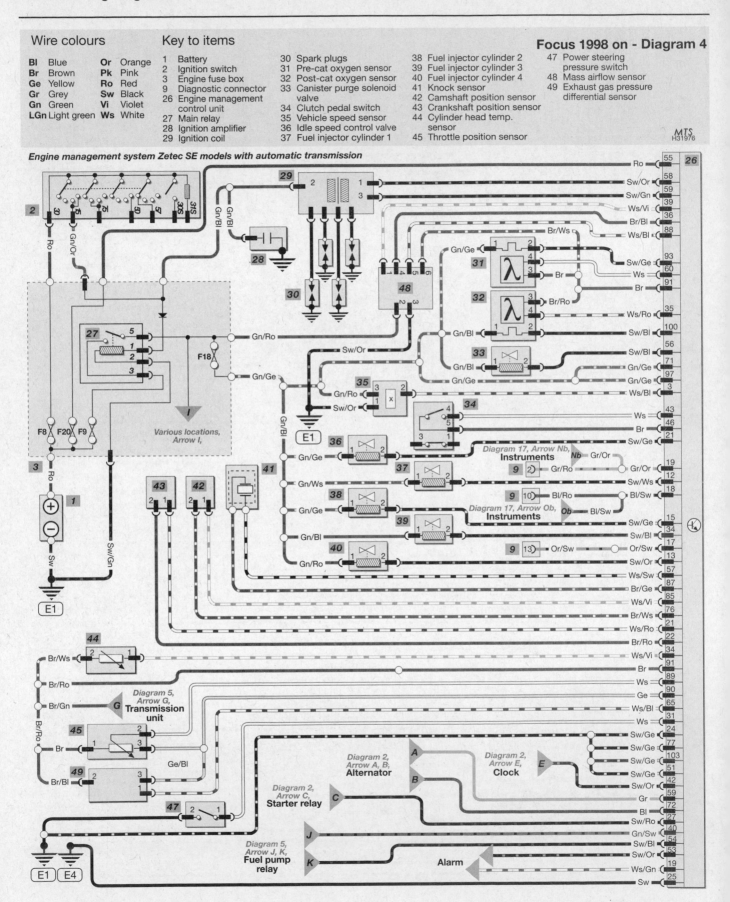

Wire colours

Bl	Blue	Or	Orange
Br	Brown	Pk	Pink
Ge	Yellow	Ro	Red
Gr	Grey	Sw	Black
Gn	Green	Vi	Violet
LGn	Light green	Ws	White

Key to items

1 Battery
2 Ignition switch
3 Engine fuse box
6 Central fuse box
26 Engine management control unit
27 Main relay
50 Ignition relay
52 Gear selector switch
53 Transmission range sensor
54 Turbine shaft speed sensor
55 Output shaft speed sensor
56 Transmission solenoid valve block
57 Fuel pump relay
58 Inertia switch
59 Fuel pump and gauge sender

Focus 1998 on - Diagram 5

MTS
H31977

Engine management system Zetec SE models with automatic transmission continued

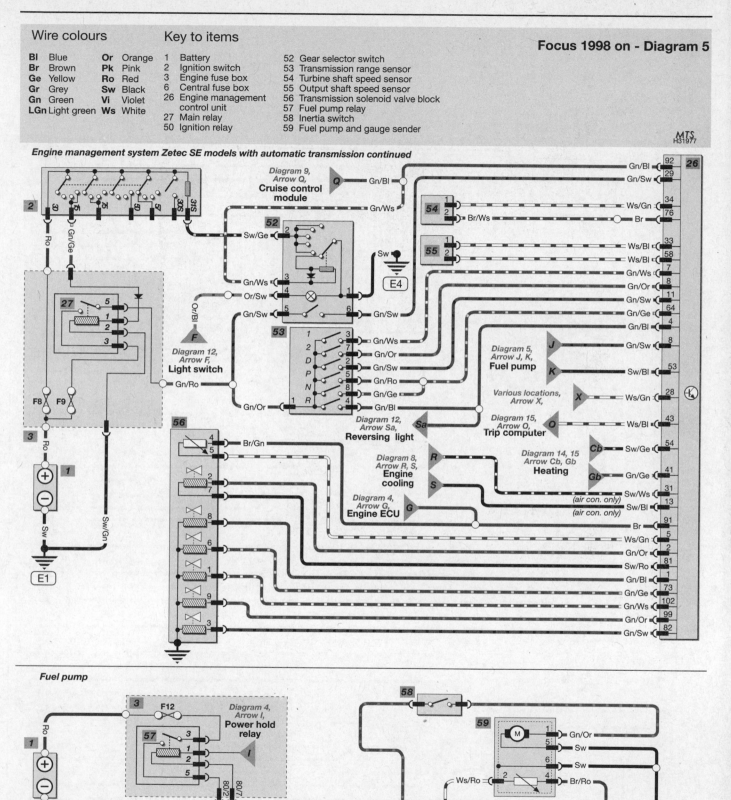

Diagram 9, Arrow Q,
Cruise control module

Diagram 12, Arrow F,
Light switch

Diagram 12, Arrow Sa,
Reversing light

Diagram 5, Arrow J, K,
Fuel pump

Various locations, Arrow X,

Diagram 15, Arrow O,
Trip computer

Diagram 8, Arrow R, S,
Engine cooling

Diagram 14, 15 Arrow Cb, Gb
Heating

Diagram 4, Arrow G,
Engine ECU

(air con. only)
(air con. only)

Fuel pump

Diagram 4, Arrow I,
Power hold relay

Various locations, Arrow K,
Engine ECU

Various locations, Arrow J,
Engine ECU

Diagram 15, 17 Arrow L,
Trip computer, instruments

Diagram 15, 17 Arrow M,
Trip computer, instruments

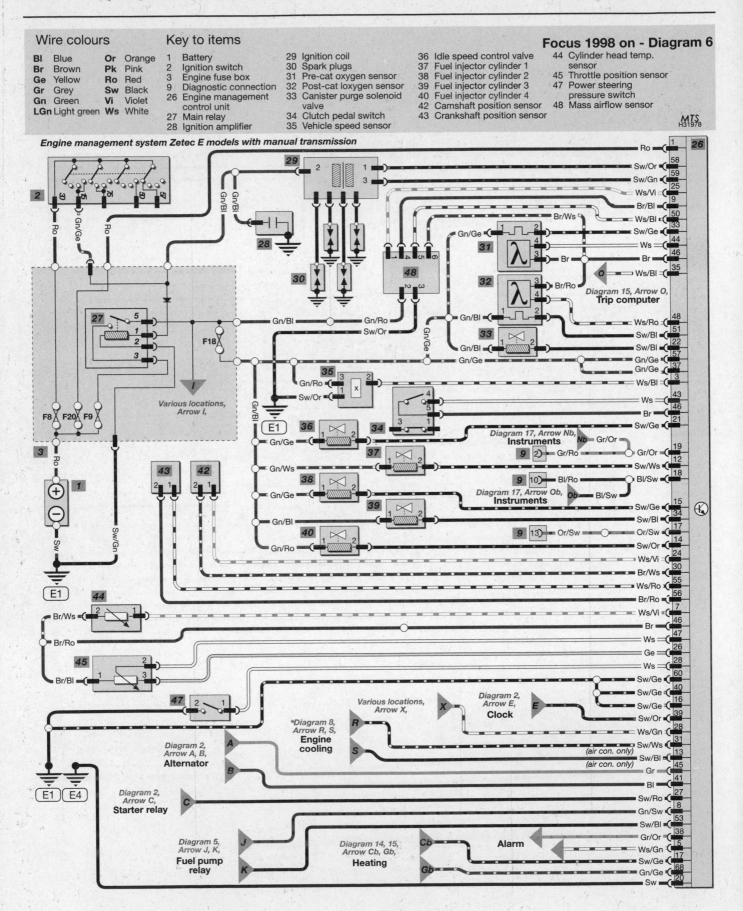

Wire colours

Bl	Blue	**Or**	Orange
Br	Brown	**Pk**	Pink
Ge	Yellow	**Ro**	Red
Gr	Grey	**Sw**	Black
Gn	Green	**Vi**	Violet
LGn	Light green	**Ws**	White

Key to items

1 Battery
2 Ignition switch
3 Engine fuse box
9 Diagnostic connection
26 Engine management control unit
27 Main relay
28 Ignition amplifier
29 Ignition coil
30 Spark plugs
31 Pre-cat oxygen sensor
32 Post-cat loxygen sensor
33 Canister purge solenoid valve
34 Clutch pedal switch
35 Vehicle speed sensor
36 Idle speed control valve
37 Fuel injector cylinder 1
38 Fuel injector cylinder 2
39 Fuel injector cylinder 3
40 Fuel injector cylinder 4
42 Camshaft position sensor
43 Crankshaft position sensor
44 Cylinder head temp. sensor
45 Throttle position sensor
47 Power steering pressure switch
48 Mass airflow sensor

Focus 1998 on - Diagram 6

Engine management system Zetec E models with manual transmission

Wire colours

Bl	Blue	Or	Orange
Br	Brown	Pk	Pink
Ge	Yellow	Ro	Red
Gr	Grey	Sw	Black
Gn	Green	Vi	Violet
LGn	Light green	Ws	White

Key to items

1 Battery
2 Ignition switch
3 Engine fuse box
9 Diagnostic connector
34 Clutch pedal switch
35 Vehicle speed sensor
43 Crankshaft sensor

44 Cylinder head temp. sensor
60 Diesel engine management control unit
61 Injection pump relay
62 Engine run relay
63 Glowplug heater relay 1

64 Glowplug heater relay 2
65 Preglow relay
66 Injection pump control unit
67 Booster heater
68 Aux. coolant heater 1
69 Aux. coolant heater 2
70 Aux. coolant heater 3

71 Vacuum regulator valve
72 Battery temp. sensor
73 Intake air temp. sensor
74 Glow plugs
75 Dual pressure switch

Focus 1998 on - Diagram 7

MTS
H31979

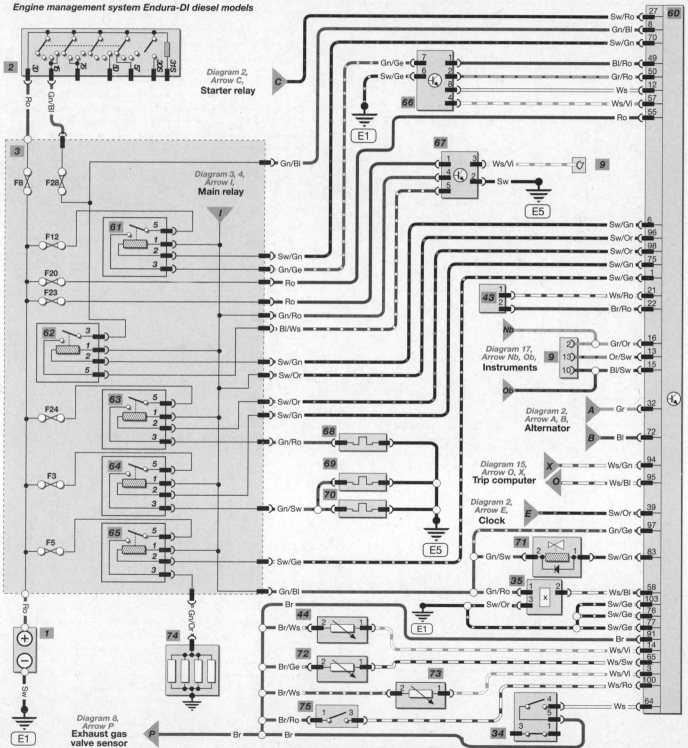

Engine management system Endura-DI diesel models

Wire colours

Bl	Blue	Or	Orange
Br	Brown	Pk	Pink
Ge	Yellow	Ro	Red
Gr	Grey	Sw	Black
Gn	Green	Vi	Violet
LGn	Light green	Ws	White

Key to items

1 Battery
2 Ignition switch
3 Engine fuse box
6 Central fuse box
60 Diesel engine management
   control unit
76 MAP sensor
78 Exhaust gas recirculation sensor
79 Accelerator pedal sensor
80 High speed fan relay (air con. only)
81 Engine cooling fan relay
82 Engine cooling fan
83 Battery saver relay
84 Mirror adjustment switch
85 LH mirror a)up/down
   b) left/right
86 RH mirror (as 85)
87 Rear window heater relay

Focus 1998 on - Diagram 8

MTS
H31980

Engine management system Endura-DI diesel models continued

Engine cooling fan

Electric mirrors

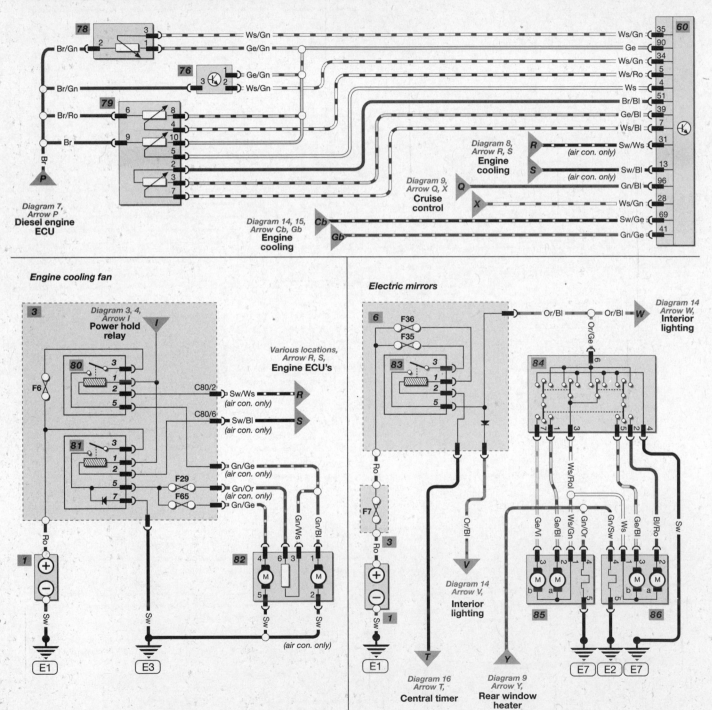

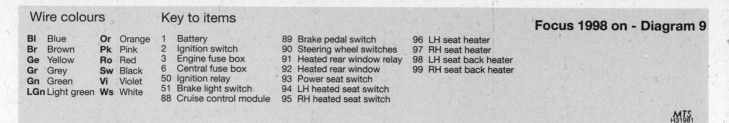

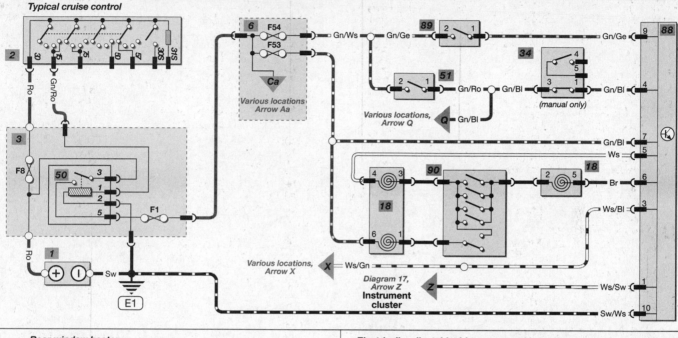

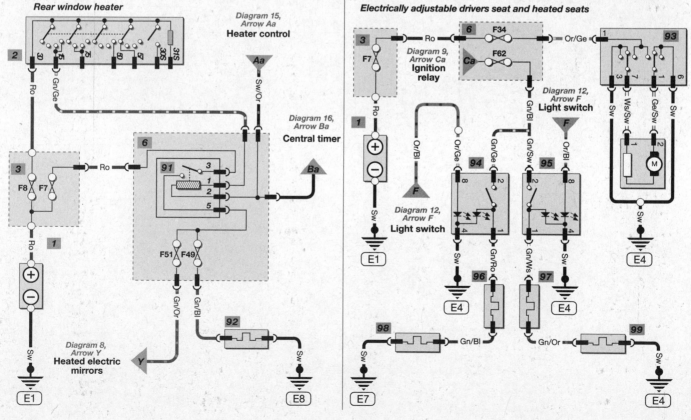

Wire colours

Bl	Blue	**Or**	Orange
Br	Brown	**Pk**	Pink
Ge	Yellow	**Ro**	Red
Gr	Grey	**Sw**	Black
Gn	Green	**Vi**	Violet
LGn	Light green	**Ws**	White

Key to items

1 Battery
2 Ignition switch
3 Engine fuse box
6 Central fuse box
100 Windscreen wiper relay
101 Rear wiper relay
102 Wash/wipe switch

103 Windscreen wiper motor
104 Washer pump
105 Rear wiper motor
106 RH washer jet heater
107 LH washer jet heater
108 Headlight washer relay
109 Headlight washer pump

110 Drivers electric window switch
111 Passenger electric window switch
112 Passenger electric window motor
113 One-touch relay
114 Drivers electric window motor

Focus 1998 on - Diagram 10

MTS
H31982

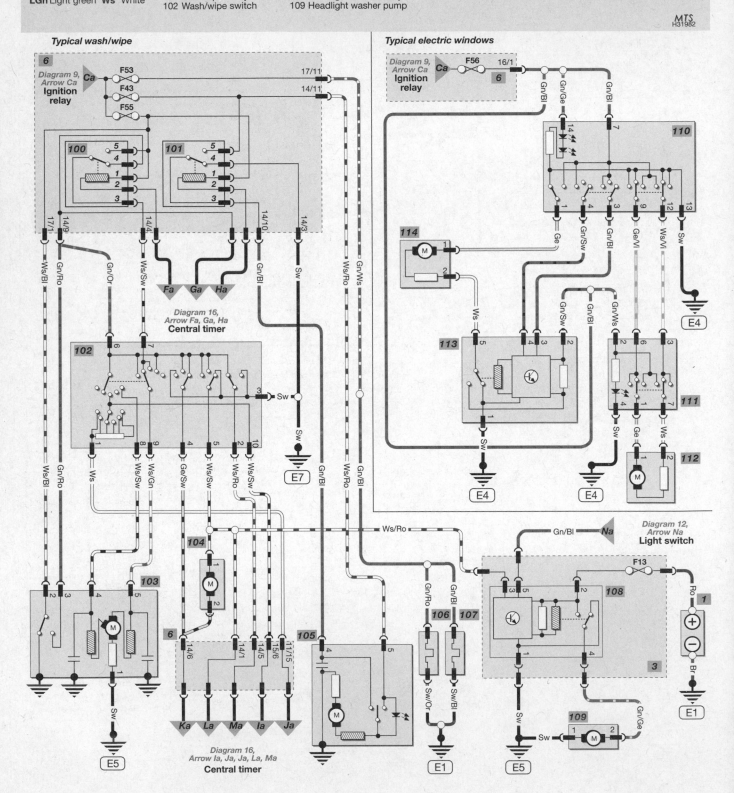

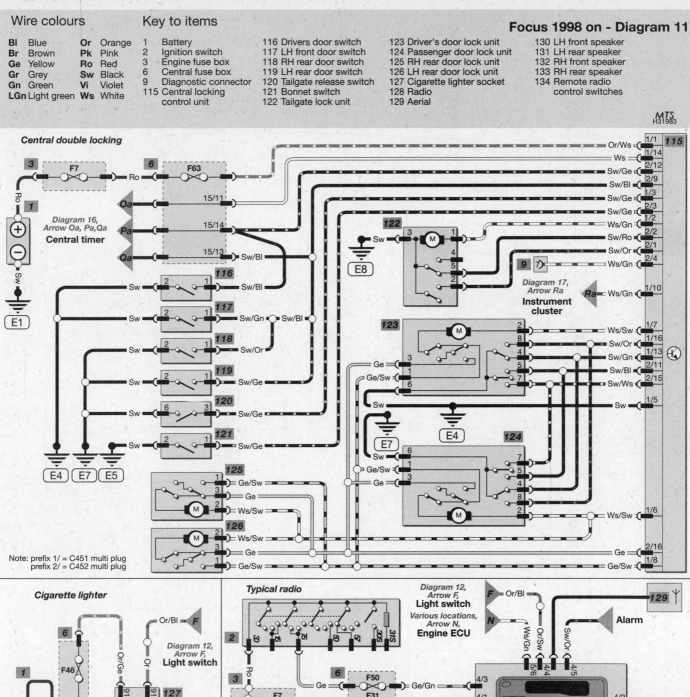

MTS
H31983

Wire colours

Bl Blue
Br Brown
Ge Yellow
Gr Grey
Gn Green
LGn Light green

Or Orange
Pk Pink
Ro Red
Sw Black
Vi Violet
Ws White

Key to items

1 Battery
2 Ignition switch
3 Engine fuse box
6 Central fuse box
9 Diagnostic connector
115 Central locking control unit

116 Drivers door switch
117 LH front door switch
118 RH rear door switch
119 LH rear door switch
120 Tailgate release switch
121 Bonnet switch
122 Tailgate lock unit

123 Driver's door lock unit
124 Passenger door lock unit
125 RH rear door lock unit
126 LH rear door lock unit
127 Cigarette lighter socket
128 Radio
129 Aerial

130 LH front speaker
131 LH rear speaker
132 RH front speaker
133 RH rear speaker
134 Remote radio control switches

Focus 1998 on - Diagram 11

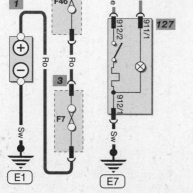

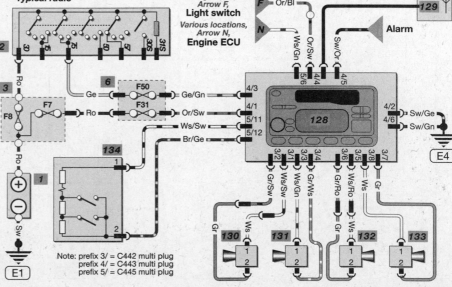

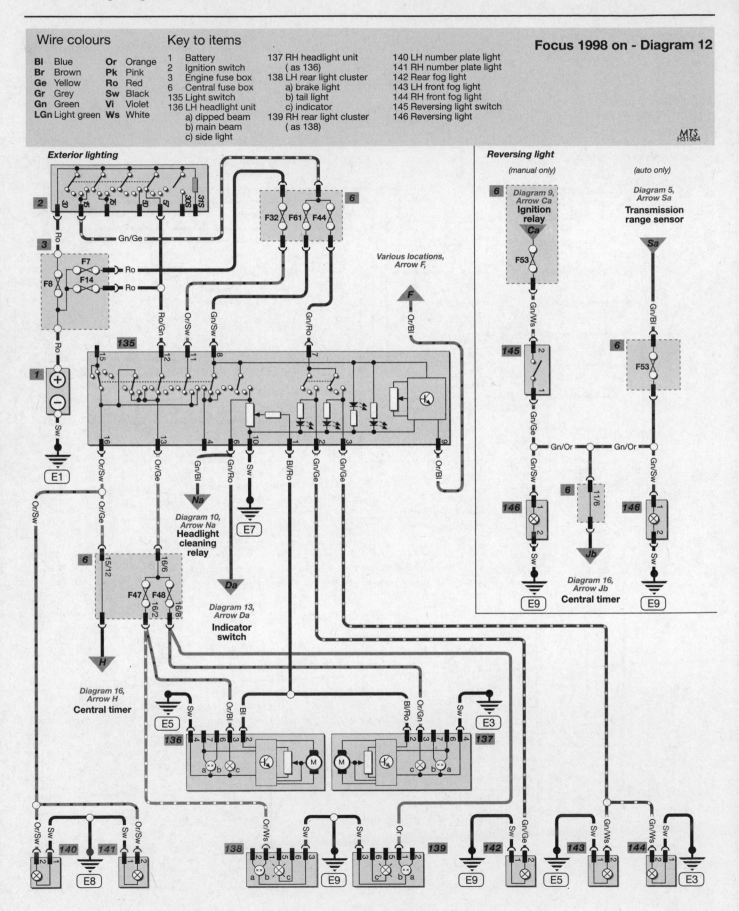

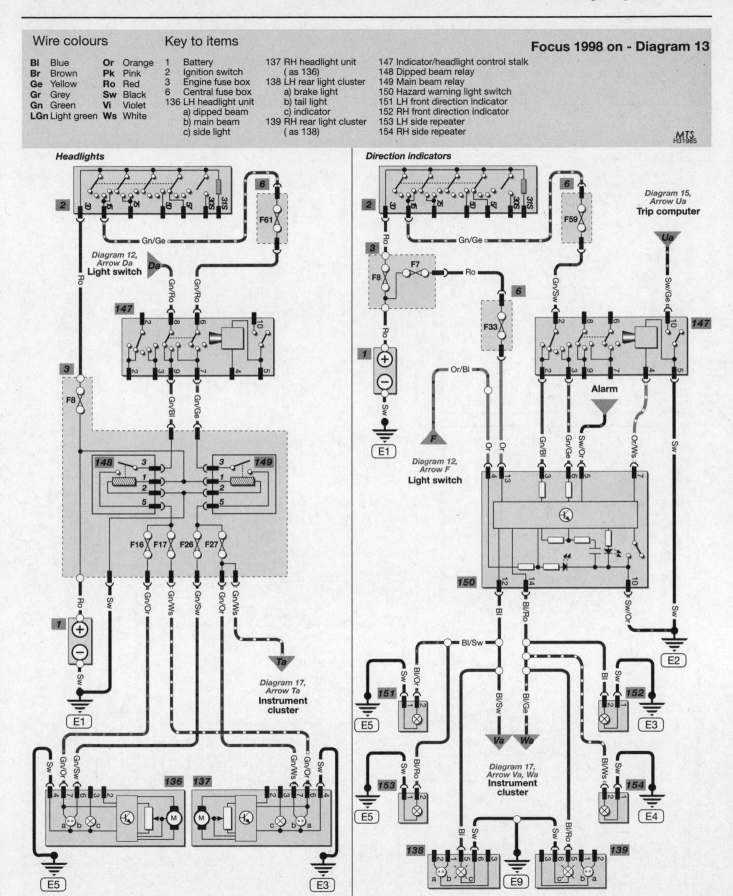

Focus 1998 on - Diagram 13

Wire colours

Bl Blue
Br Brown
Ge Yellow
Gr Grey
Gn Green
LGn Light green
Or Orange
Pk Pink
Ro Red
Sw Black
Vi Violet
Ws White

Key to items

1 Battery
2 Ignition switch
3 Engine fuse box
6 Central fuse box
136 LH headlight unit
  a) dipped beam
  b) main beam
  c) side light
137 RH headlight unit
  (as 136)
138 LH rear light cluster
  a) brake light
  b) tail light
  c) indicator
139 RH rear light cluster
  (as 138)
147 Indicator/headlight control stalk
148 Dipped beam relay
149 Main beam relay
150 Hazard warning light switch
151 LH front direction indicator
152 RH front direction indicator
153 LH side repeater
154 RH side repeater

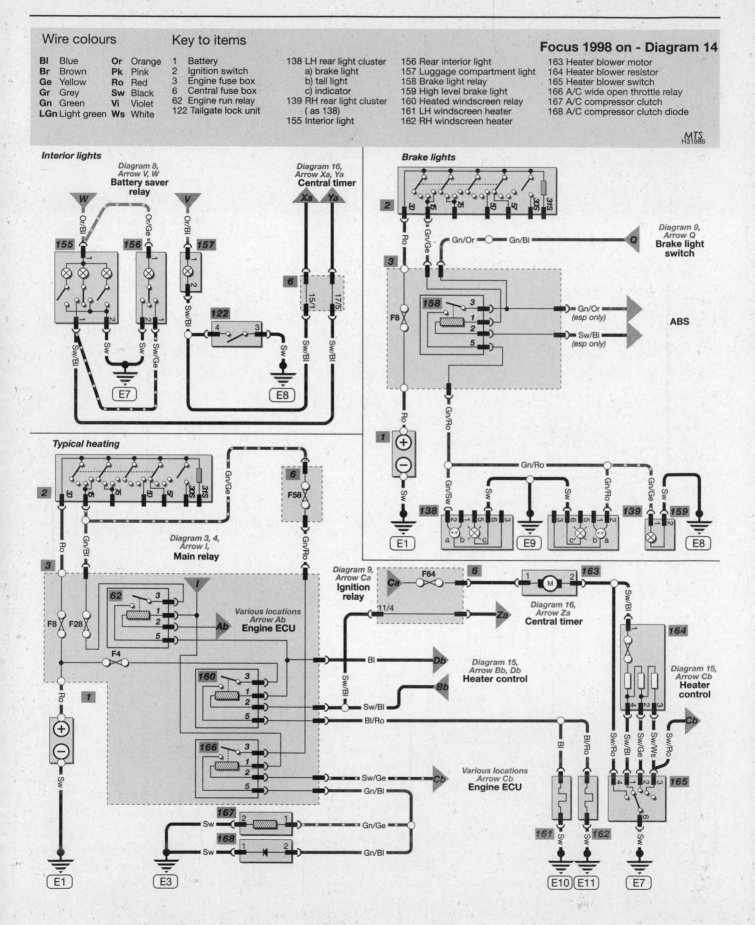

Wire colours

Bl	Blue	Or	Orange
Br	Brown	Pk	Pink
Ge	Yellow	Ro	Red
Gr	Grey	Sw	Black
Gn	Green	Vi	Violet
LGn	Light green	Ws	White

Key to items

1 Battery
2 Ignition switch
3 Engine fuse box
6 Central fuse box
62 Engine run relay
122 Tailgate lock unit
138 LH rear light cluster
  a) brake light
  b) tail light
  c) indicator
139 RH rear light cluster
  (as 138)
155 Interior light
156 Rear interior light
157 Luggage compartment light
158 Brake light relay
159 High level brake light
160 Heated windscreen relay
161 LH windscreen heater
162 RH windscreen heater
163 Heater blower motor
164 Heater blower resistor
165 Heater blower switch
166 A/C wide open throttle relay
167 A/C compressor clutch
168 A/C compressor clutch diode

Focus 1998 on - Diagram 14

MTS
H31986

Interior lights

Diagram 8, Arrow V, W **Battery saver relay**

Diagram 16, Arrow Xa, Ya **Central timer**

Brake lights

Diagram 9, Arrow Q **Brake light switch**

ABS

Typical heating

Diagram 3, 4, Arrow I, **Main relay**

Various locations Arrow Ab **Engine ECU**

Diagram 9, Arrow Ca **Ignition relay**

Diagram 16, Arrow Za **Central timer**

Diagram 15, Arrow Bb, Db **Heater control**

Diagram 15, Arrow Cb **Heater control**

Various locations Arrow Cb **Engine ECU**

Focus 1998 on - Diagram 15

Wire colours

Bl Blue
Br Brown
Ge Yellow
Gr Grey
Gn Green
LGn Light green

Or Orange
Pk Pink
Ro Red
Sw Black
Vi Violet
Ws White

Key to items

1 Battery
2 Ignition switch
3 Engine fuse box
6 Central fuse box
9 Diagnostic connector
169 Heater control unit
170 Recirculation actuator

171 De-icing switch
172 A/C compressor cycling switch
173 Dual pressure switch
174 Trip computer
175 Ice warning sensor
176 Low washer fluid sensor

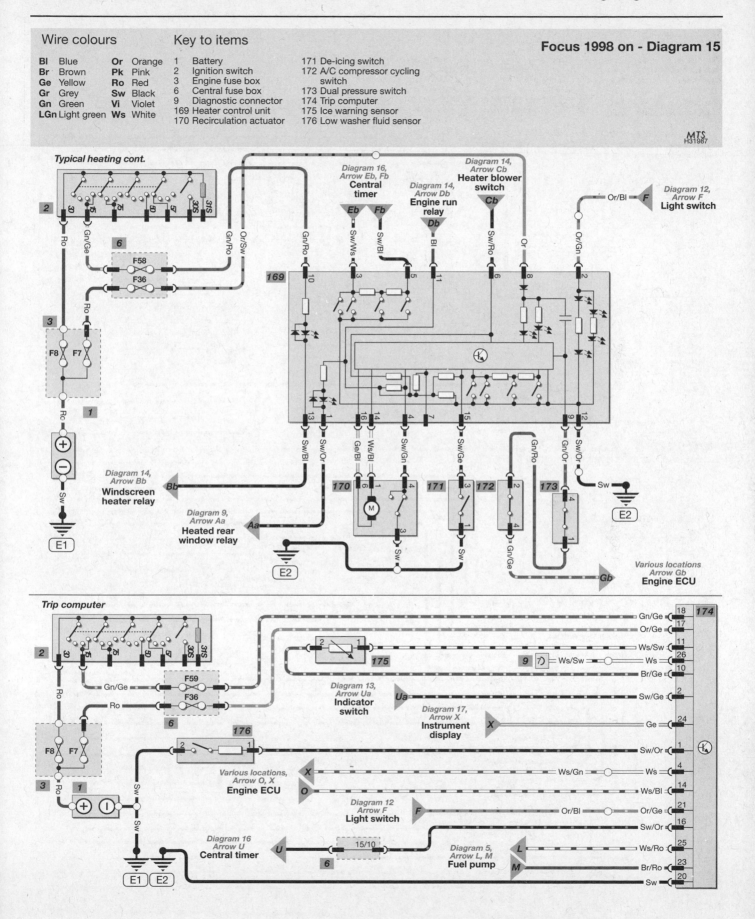

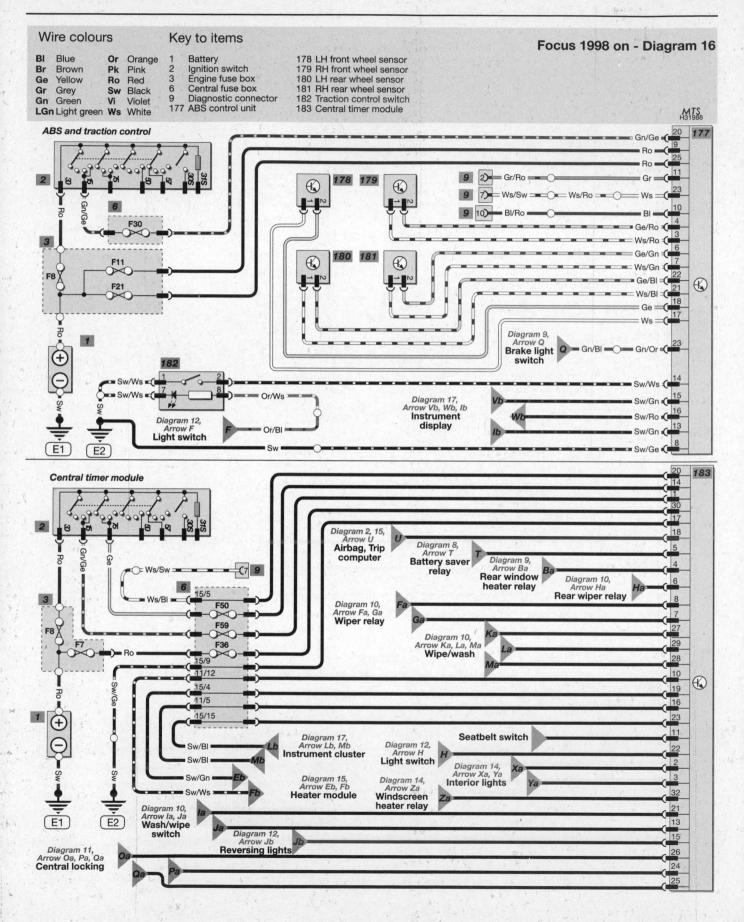

Focus 1998 on - Diagram 16

Wire colours

Bl	Blue	Or	Orange
Br	Brown	Pk	Pink
Ge	Yellow	Ro	Red
Gr	Grey	Sw	Black
Gn	Green	Vi	Violet
LGn	Light green	Ws	White

Key to items

1 Battery
2 Ignition switch
3 Engine fuse box
6 Central fuse box
9 Diagnostic connector
177 ABS control unit

178 LH front wheel sensor
179 RH front wheel sensor
180 LH rear wheel sensor
181 RH rear wheel sensor
182 Traction control switch
183 Central timer module

MTS
H31988

ABS and traction control

Central timer module

Wire colours

Bl	Blue	**Or**	Orange
Br	Brown	**Pk**	Pink
Ge	Yellow	**Ro**	Red
Gr	Grey	**Sw**	Black
Gn	Green	**Vi**	Violet
LGn	Light green	**Ws**	White

Key to items

1   Battery
2   Ignition switch
3   Engine fuse box
6   Central fuse box
184 Instrument cluster
  a) illumination
  b) catalyst warning
  c) low fuel warning

d) check engine
e) pre-glow warning
f) charge warning
g) cruise control
h) O/D off
i) ABS warning
j) coolant temp.
k) rev. counter

l) speedometer
m) fuel gauge
n) brake warning
o) low oil pressure
p) door open warning
q) traction control or
    seatbelt warning
r) passenger airbag

s) airbag warning
t) LH indicator
u) RH indicator
v) main beam warning
185 Microprocessor
186 Hand brake switch
187 Brake fluid switch
188 Oil pressure switch

Focus 1998 on - Diagram 17

MTS
H31989

Instrument display

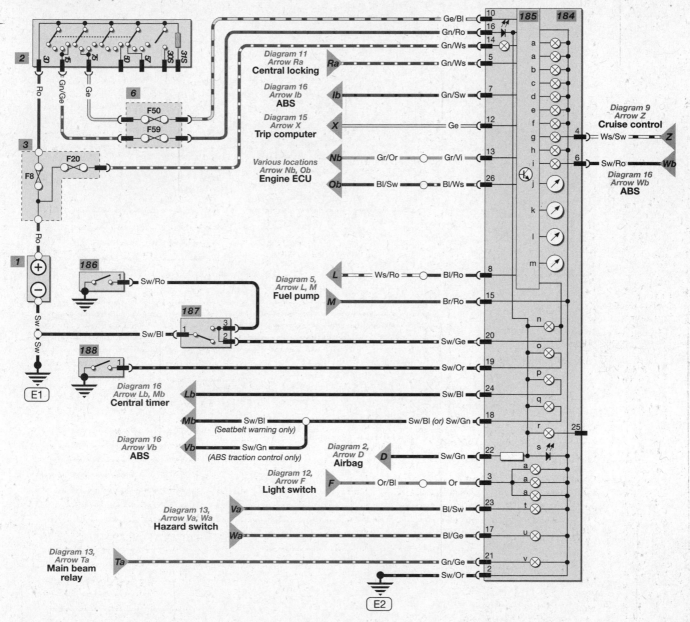

Notes

Dimensions and weights

Note: *All figures are approximate, and may vary according to model. Refer to manufacturer's data for exact figures.*

Dimensions

Overall length (depending on model):
    Hatchback . . . . 4150 to 4178 mm
    Saloon . . . . 4362 to 4369 mm
    Estate . . . . 4438 to 4465 mm
Overall width (including mirrors) . . . . 1998 mm
Overall height (typical) . . . . 1481 mm
Wheelbase . . . . 2615 mm

Weights

Kerb weight (depending on model):
    Hatchback . . . . 1125 kg (1.4 litre) to 1349 kg (diesel)
    Saloon . . . . 1166 kg (1.6 litre) to 1350 kg (diesel)
    Estate . . . . 1193 kg (1.6 litre) to 1390 kg (diesel)
Maximum roof rack load:
    Hatchback and Saloon . . . . 75 kg
    Estate . . . . 100 kg
Maximum trailer weight (braked):
    1.4 litre models . . . . 940 kg
    1.6, 1.8 and 2.0 litre petrol models . . . . 1200 kg
    Diesel models . . . . 1000 kg
Maximum trailer nose weight . . . . 50 kg

Length (distance)
Inches (in)	x 25.4	= Millimetres (mm)	x 0.0394	= Inches (in)
Feet (ft)	x 0.305	= Metres (m)	x 3.281	= Feet (ft)
Miles	x 1.609	= Kilometres (km)	x 0.621	= Miles

Volume (capacity)
Cubic inches (cu in; in³)	x 16.387	= Cubic centimetres (cc; cm³)	x 0.061	= Cubic inches (cu in; in³)
Imperial pints (Imp pt)	x 0.568	= Litres (l)	x 1.76	= Imperial pints (Imp pt)
Imperial quarts (Imp qt)	x 1.137	= Litres (l)	x 0.88	= Imperial quarts (Imp qt)
Imperial quarts (Imp qt)	x 1.201	= US quarts (US qt)	x 0.833	= Imperial quarts (Imp qt)
US quarts (US qt)	x 0.946	= Litres (l)	x 1.057	= US quarts (US qt)
Imperial gallons (Imp gal)	x 4.546	= Litres (l)	x 0.22	= Imperial gallons (Imp gal)
Imperial gallons (Imp gal)	x 1.201	= US gallons (US gal)	x 0.833	= Imperial gallons (Imp gal)
US gallons (US gal)	x 3.785	= Litres (l)	x 0.264	= US gallons (US gal)

Mass (weight)
Ounces (oz)	x 28.35	= Grams (g)	x 0.035	= Ounces (oz)
Pounds (lb)	x 0.454	= Kilograms (kg)	x 2.205	= Pounds (lb)

Force
Ounces-force (ozf; oz)	x 0.278	= Newtons (N)	x 3.6	= Ounces-force (ozf; oz)
Pounds-force (lbf; lb)	x 4.448	= Newtons (N)	x 0.225	= Pounds-force (lbf; lb)
Newtons (N)	x 0.1	= Kilograms-force (kgf; kg)	x 9.81	= Newtons (N)

Pressure
Pounds-force per square inch (psi; lbf/in²; lb/in²)	x 0.070	= Kilograms-force per square centimetre (kgf/cm²; kg/cm²)	x 14.223	= Pounds-force per square inch (psi; lbf/in²; lb/in²)
Pounds-force per square inch (psi; lbf/in²; lb/in²)	x 0.068	= Atmospheres (atm)	x 14.696	= Pounds-force per square inch (psi; lbf/in²; lb/in²)
Pounds-force per square inch (psi; lbf/in²; lb/in²)	x 0.069	= Bars	x 14.5	= Pounds-force per square inch (psi; lbf/in²; lb/in²)
Pounds-force per square inch (psi; lbf/in²; lb/in²)	x 6.895	= Kilopascals (kPa)	x 0.145	= Pounds-force per square inch (psi; lbf/in²; lb/in²)
Kilopascals (kPa)	x 0.01	= Kilograms-force per square centimetre (kgf/cm²; kg/cm²)	x 98.1	= Kilopascals (kPa)
Millibar (mbar)	x 100	= Pascals (Pa)	x 0.01	= Millibar (mbar)
Millibar (mbar)	x 0.0145	= Pounds-force per square inch (psi; lbf/in²; lb/in²)	x 68.947	= Millibar (mbar)
Millibar (mbar)	x 0.75	= Millimetres of mercury (mmHg)	x 1.333	= Millibar (mbar)
Millibar (mbar)	x 0.401	= Inches of water (inH₂O)	x 2.491	= Millibar (mbar)
Millimetres of mercury (mmHg)	x 0.535	= Inches of water (inH₂O)	x 1.868	= Millimetres of mercury (mmHg)
Inches of water (inH₂O)	x 0.036	= Pounds-force per square inch (psi; lbf/in²; lb/in²)	x 27.68	= Inches of water (inH₂O)

Torque (moment of force)
Pounds-force inches (lbf in; lb in)	x 1.152	= Kilograms-force centimetre (kgf cm; kg cm)	x 0.868	= Pounds-force inches (lbf in; lb in)
Pounds-force inches (lbf in; lb in)	x 0.113	= Newton metres (Nm)	x 8.85	= Pounds-force inches (lbf in; lb in)
Pounds-force inches (lbf in; lb in)	x 0.083	= Pounds-force feet (lbf ft; lb ft)	x 12	= Pounds-force inches (lbf in; lb in)
Pounds-force feet (lbf ft; lb ft)	x 0.138	= Kilograms-force metres (kgf m; kg m)	x 7.233	= Pounds-force feet (lbf ft; lb ft)
Pounds-force feet (lbf ft; lb ft)	x 1.356	= Newton metres (Nm)	x 0.738	= Pounds-force feet (lbf ft; lb ft)
Newton metres (Nm)	x 0.102	= Kilograms-force metres (kgf m; kg m)	x 9.804	= Newton metres (Nm)

Power
Horsepower (hp)	x 745.7	= Watts (W)	x 0.0013	= Horsepower (hp)

Velocity (speed)
Miles per hour (miles/hr; mph)	x 1.609	= Kilometres per hour (km/hr; kph)	x 0.621	= Miles per hour (miles/hr; mph)

Fuel consumption*
Miles per gallon, Imperial (mpg)	x 0.354	= Kilometres per litre (km/l)	x 2.825	= Miles per gallon, Imperial (mpg)
Miles per gallon, US (mpg)	x 0.425	= Kilometres per litre (km/l)	x 2.352	= Miles per gallon, US (mpg)

Temperature
Degrees Fahrenheit = (°C x 1.8) + 32   Degrees Celsius (Degrees Centigrade; °C) = (°F - 32) x 0.56

* It is common practice to convert from miles per gallon (mpg) to litres/100 kilometres (l/100km), where mpg x l/100 km = 282

Spare parts are available from many sources, including maker's appointed garages, accessory shops, and motor factors. To be sure of obtaining the correct parts, it may sometimes be necessary to quote the vehicle identification number. If possible, it can also be useful to take the old parts along for positive identification. Items such as starter motors and alternators may be available under a service exchange scheme – any parts returned should always be clean.

Our advice regarding spare part sources is as follows:

Officially-appointed garages

This is the best source of parts which are peculiar to your car, and are not otherwise generally available (eg, badges, interior trim, certain body panels, etc). It is also the only place at which you should buy parts if the vehicle is still under warranty.

Accessory shops

These are very good places to buy materials and components needed for the maintenance of your car (oil, air and fuel filters, spark plugs, light bulbs, drivebelts, oils and greases, brake pads, touch-up paint, etc). Parts like this sold by a reputable shop are of the same standard as those used by the car manufacturer.

Motor factors

Good factors will stock all the more important components which wear out comparatively quickly and can sometimes supply individual components needed for the overhaul of a larger assembly. They may also handle work such as cylinder block reboring, crankshaft regrinding and balancing, etc.

Tyre and exhaust specialists

These outlets may be independent or members of a local or national chain. They frequently offer competitive prices when compared with a main dealer or local garage, but it will pay to obtain several quotes before making a decision. Also ask what 'extras' may be added to the quote – for instance, fitting a new valve and balancing the wheel are both often charged on top of the price of a new tyre.

Other sources

Beware of parts of materials obtained from market stalls, car boot sales or similar outlets. Such items are not always sub-standard, but there is little chance of compensation if they do prove unsatisfactory. In the case of safety-critical components such as brake pads there is the risk not only of financial loss but also of an accident causing injury or death.

Second-hand components or assemblies obtained from a car breaker can be a good buy in some circumstances, but this sort of purchase is best made by the experienced DIY mechanic.

Vehicle identification numbers

Modifications are a continuing and unpublicised process in vehicle manufacture, quite apart from major model changes. Spare parts manuals and lists are compiled upon a numerical basis, the individual vehicle identification numbers being essential to correct identification of the component concerned.

When ordering spare parts, always give as much information as possible. Quote the vehicle type and year, vehicle identification number (VIN), and engine number, as appropriate.

The vehicle identification number (VIN) and engine number appear on a metal plate attached to the front crossmember – the VIN can be identified by having an asterisk at the beginning and end. The model plate also gives vehicle loading details, engine type, and various trim and colour codes. The VIN also appears on a plastic tag attached to the passenger side of the facia panel, visible through the windscreen, and is stamped into the bodyshell floor on the right-hand side (lift the flap provided in the carpet for access).

The engine number is stamped on the cylinder block, in the following locations, according to engine type:

a) *1.4 and 1.6 litre engines – on the front left-hand side of the engine, below the throttle housing* **(see illustration)**.
b) *1.8 and 2.0 litre petrol engines – on the front left-hand side of the engine, next to the transmission flange.*
c) *Diesel engine – on the left-hand end of the engine, above the transmission* **(see illustration)**.

The transmission identification numbers are located on a plate attached to the transmission casing, or cast into the casing itself.

Engine number location on 1.4 and 1.6 litre engines

Engine code (1) and engine number (2) locations on diesel engines

Whenever servicing, repair or overhaul work is carried out on the car or its components, observe the following procedures and instructions. This will assist in carrying out the operation efficiently and to a professional standard of workmanship.

Joint mating faces and gaskets

When separating components at their mating faces, never insert screwdrivers or similar implements into the joint between the faces in order to prise them apart. This can cause severe damage which results in oil leaks, coolant leaks, etc upon reassembly. Separation is usually achieved by tapping along the joint with a soft-faced hammer in order to break the seal. However, note that this method may not be suitable where dowels are used for component location.

Where a gasket is used between the mating faces of two components, a new one must be fitted on reassembly; fit it dry unless otherwise stated in the repair procedure. Make sure that the mating faces are clean and dry, with all traces of old gasket removed. When cleaning a joint face, use a tool which is unlikely to score or damage the face, and remove any burrs or nicks with an oilstone or fine file.

Make sure that tapped holes are cleaned with a pipe cleaner, and keep them free of jointing compound, if this is being used, unless specifically instructed otherwise.

Ensure that all orifices, channels or pipes are clear, and blow through them, preferably using compressed air.

Oil seals

Oil seals can be removed by levering them out with a wide flat-bladed screwdriver or similar implement. Alternatively, a number of self-tapping screws may be screwed into the seal, and these used as a purchase for pliers or some similar device in order to pull the seal free.

Whenever an oil seal is removed from its working location, either individually or as part of an assembly, it should be renewed.

The very fine sealing lip of the seal is easily damaged, and will not seal if the surface it contacts is not completely clean and free from scratches, nicks or grooves. If the original sealing surface of the component cannot be restored, and the manufacturer has not made provision for slight relocation of the seal relative to the sealing surface, the component should be renewed.

Protect the lips of the seal from any surface which may damage them in the course of fitting. Use tape or a conical sleeve where possible. Lubricate the seal lips with oil before fitting and, on dual-lipped seals, fill the space between the lips with grease.

Unless otherwise stated, oil seals must be fitted with their sealing lips toward the lubricant to be sealed.

Use a tubular drift or block of wood of the appropriate size to install the seal and, if the seal housing is shouldered, drive the seal down to the shoulder. If the seal housing is unshouldered, the seal should be fitted with its face flush with the housing top face (unless otherwise instructed).

Screw threads and fastenings

Seized nuts, bolts and screws are quite a common occurrence where corrosion has set in, and the use of penetrating oil or releasing fluid will often overcome this problem if the offending item is soaked for a while before attempting to release it. The use of an impact driver may also provide a means of releasing such stubborn fastening devices, when used in conjunction with the appropriate screwdriver bit or socket. If none of these methods works, it may be necessary to resort to the careful application of heat, or the use of a hacksaw or nut splitter device.

Studs are usually removed by locking two nuts together on the threaded part, and then using a spanner on the lower nut to unscrew the stud. Studs or bolts which have broken off below the surface of the component in which they are mounted can sometimes be removed using a stud extractor. Always ensure that a blind tapped hole is completely free from oil, grease, water or other fluid before installing the bolt or stud. Failure to do this could cause the housing to crack due to the hydraulic action of the bolt or stud as it is screwed in.

When tightening a castellated nut to accept a split pin, tighten the nut to the specified torque, where applicable, and then tighten further to the next split pin hole. Never slacken the nut to align the split pin hole, unless stated in the repair procedure.

When checking or retightening a nut or bolt to a specified torque setting, slacken the nut or bolt by a quarter of a turn, and then retighten to the specified setting. However, this should not be attempted where angular tightening has been used.

For some screw fastenings, notably cylinder head bolts or nuts, torque wrench settings are no longer specified for the latter stages of tightening, "angle-tightening" being called up instead. Typically, a fairly low torque wrench setting will be applied to the bolts/nuts in the correct sequence, followed by one or more stages of tightening through specified angles.

Locknuts, locktabs and washers

Any fastening which will rotate against a component or housing during tightening should always have a washer between it and the relevant component or housing.

Spring or split washers should always be renewed when they are used to lock a critical component such as a big-end bearing retaining bolt or nut. Locktabs which are folded over to retain a nut or bolt should always be renewed.

Self-locking nuts can be re-used in non-critical areas, providing resistance can be felt when the locking portion passes over the bolt or stud thread. However, it should be noted that self-locking stiffnuts tend to lose their effectiveness after long periods of use, and should then be renewed as a matter of course.

Split pins must always be replaced with new ones of the correct size for the hole.

When thread-locking compound is found on the threads of a fastener which is to be re-used, it should be cleaned off with a wire brush and solvent, and fresh compound applied on reassembly.

Special tools

Some repair procedures in this manual entail the use of special tools such as a press, two or three-legged pullers, spring compressors, etc. Wherever possible, suitable readily-available alternatives to the manufacturer's special tools are described, and are shown in use. In some instances, where no alternative is possible, it has been necessary to resort to the use of a manufacturer's tool, and this has been done for reasons of safety as well as the efficient completion of the repair operation. Unless you are highly-skilled and have a thorough understanding of the procedures described, never attempt to bypass the use of any special tool when the procedure described specifies its use. Not only is there a very great risk of personal injury, but expensive damage could be caused to the components involved.

Environmental considerations

When disposing of used engine oil, brake fluid, antifreeze, etc, give due consideration to any detrimental environmental effects. Do not, for instance, pour any of the above liquids down drains into the general sewage system, or onto the ground to soak away. Many local council refuse tips provide a facility for waste oil disposal, as do some garages. If none of these facilities are available, consult your local Environmental Health Department, or the National Rivers Authority, for further advice.

With the universal tightening-up of legislation regarding the emission of environmentally-harmful substances from motor vehicles, most vehicles have tamperproof devices fitted to the main adjustment points of the fuel system. These devices are primarily designed to prevent unqualified persons from adjusting the fuel/air mixture, with the chance of a consequent increase in toxic emissions. If such devices are found during servicing or overhaul, they should, wherever possible, be renewed or refitted in accordance with the manufacturer's requirements or current legislation.

OIL CARE · FOLLOW THE CODE

OIL BANK LINE
0800 66 33 66
www.oilbankline.org.uk

Note: It is antisocial and illegal to dump oil down the drain. To find the location of your local oil recycling bank, call this number free.

The jack supplied with the vehicle tool kit should **only** be used for changing the roadwheels in an emergency – see *Wheel changing* at the front of this book. When carrying out any other kind of work, raise the vehicle using a heavy-duty hydraulic (or 'trolley') jack, and always supplement the jack with axle stands positioned under the vehicle jacking points. If the roadwheels do not have to be removed, consider using wheel ramps – if wished, these can be placed under the wheels once the vehicle has been raised using a hydraulic jack, and the vehicle lowered onto the ramps so that it is resting on its wheels.

Only ever jack the vehicle up on a solid, level surface. If there is even a slight slope, take great care that the vehicle cannot move as the wheels are lifted off the ground. Jacking up on an uneven or gravelled surface is not recommended, as the weight of the vehicle will not be evenly distributed, and the jack may slip as the vehicle is raised.

As far as possible, do not leave the vehicle unattended once it has been raised, particularly if children are playing nearby.

Before jacking up the front of the car, ensure that the handbrake is firmly applied. When jacking up the rear of the car, place wooden chocks in front of the front wheels, and engage first gear (or P).

The jack supplied with the vehicle locates in the sill flanges, at the points marked by two indentations in the sill on each side of the car **(see illustration)**. On Hatchback models, or those with side 'skirts', a section of plastic trim must be unclipped and removed from the metal sill before fitting the jack head into place **(see illustration)**. Ensure that the jack head is correctly engaged before attempting to raise the vehicle.

When using a hydraulic jack or axle stands, the jack head or axle stand head may be placed under one of the four jacking points, or under the two support points on the front

chassis legs **(see illustration)**. When jacking or supporting under the sill, always use a block of wood (with a slot cut in its top surface, to locate in the sill flange) between the jack head or axle stand, and the sill. It is also considered good practice to use a large block of wood when supporting under other areas, to spread the load over a wider area, and reduce the risk of damage to the underside of the car (it also helps to prevent the underbody coating from being damaged by the jack or axle stand). **Do not** jack the vehicle under any other part of the sill, engine sump, floor pan, subframe, or directly under any of the steering or suspension components.

Never work under, around, or near a raised vehicle, unless it is adequately supported on stands. Do not rely on a jack alone, as even a hydraulic jack could fail under load. Makeshift methods should not be used to lift and support the car during servicing work.

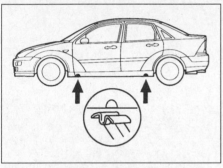

Jacking points on sill flanges (arrowed) are indicated by indentations

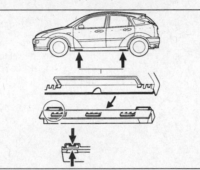

On some models, plastic covers must be unclipped for access to the sill flange jacking points

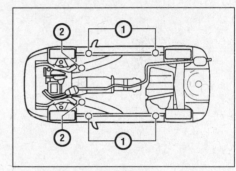

Sill jacking points (1) and chassis support points (2)

Disconnecting the battery

Several of the systems fitted to the Focus require battery power to be available at all times (permanent live). This is either to ensure their continued operation (such as the clock), or to maintain electronic memory settings which would otherwise be erased. Whenever the battery is to be disconnected therefore, first note the following points, to ensure there are no unforeseen consequences:

a) *Firstly, on any vehicle with central door locking, it is wise to remove the key from the ignition, and to keep it with you. This avoids the possibility of the key being locked inside the car, should the central locking engage when the battery is reconnected.*

b) *The radio/cassette unit fitted as standard equipment by Ford is equipped with a built-in security code, to deter thieves. If the power source to the unit is cut, the anti-theft system will activate. Even if the power source is immediately reconnected, the radio/cassette unit will not function until the correct security code has been entered. Therefore, if you do not know the correct security code for the radio/cassette unit, **do not** disconnect either of the battery terminals, or remove the radio/cassette unit*

from the vehicle. The code appears in the audio handbook supplied with the car when new; details for entering the code also appear in the audio guide. Should the code have been misplaced or forgotten, on production of the radio serial number and proof of ownership, a Ford dealer or in-car entertainment specialist may be able to help.

c) *The engine management system ECU is of the 'self-learning' type, meaning that, as it operates, it adapts to changes in operating conditions, and stores the optimum settings found (this is especially true for idle settings). When the battery is disconnected, these 'learned' settings are lost, and the ECU reverts to the base factory settings. When the engine is restarted, it may idle and run roughly until the ECU has 're-learned' the best settings. To further this 'learning' process, take the car for a road test of at least 15 minutes' duration, covering as many engine speeds and loads as possible, and concentrating on the 2000 to 4000 rpm range. On completion, let the engine idle for at least 10 minutes, turning the steering wheel occasionally and switching on high-current-draw equipment such as the heater*

fan or heated rear window.

d) *On models with electric rear windows, the windows may have to be re-programmed following disconnection of the battery. This is necessary so that the windows can 're-learn' their closed positions. A procedure for doing this is included in the vehicle handbook, under 'power windows'.*

Devices known as 'memory-savers' or 'code-savers' can be used to avoid some of the above problems. Precise details of use vary according to the device used. Typically, it is plugged into the cigar lighter socket, and is connected by its own wiring to a spare battery; the vehicle battery is then disconnected from the electrical system, leaving the memory-saver to pass sufficient current to maintain audio unit security codes and other memory values, and also to run permanently-live circuits such as the clock.

⚠ **Warning: Some of these devices allow a considerable amount of current to pass, which can mean that many of the vehicle's systems are still operational when the main battery is disconnected. If a memory-saver is used, ensure that the circuit concerned is actually 'dead' before carrying out any work on it.**

Introduction

A selection of good tools is a fundamental requirement for anyone contemplating the maintenance and repair of a motor vehicle. For the owner who does not possess any, their purchase will prove a considerable expense, offsetting some of the savings made by doing-it-yourself. However, provided that the tools purchased meet the relevant national safety standards and are of good quality, they will last for many years and prove an extremely worthwhile investment.

To help the average owner to decide which tools are needed to carry out the various tasks detailed in this manual, we have compiled three lists of tools under the following headings: *Maintenance and minor repair, Repair and overhaul*, and *Special*. Newcomers to practical mechanics should start off with the *Maintenance and minor repair* tool kit, and confine themselves to the simpler jobs around the vehicle. Then, as confidence and experience grow, more difficult tasks can be undertaken, with extra tools being purchased as, and when, they are needed. In this way, a *Maintenance and minor repair* tool kit can be built up into a *Repair and overhaul* tool kit over a considerable period of time, without any major cash outlays. The experienced do-it-yourselfer will have a tool kit good enough for most repair and overhaul procedures, and will add tools from the *Special* category when it is felt that the expense is justified by the amount of use to which these tools will be put.

Maintenance and minor repair tool kit

The tools given in this list should be considered as a minimum requirement if routine maintenance, servicing and minor repair operations are to be undertaken. We recommend the purchase of combination spanners (ring one end, open-ended the other); although more expensive than open-ended ones, they do give the advantages of both types of spanner.

☐ *Combination spanners:*
Metric - 8 to 19 mm inclusive
☐ *Adjustable spanner - 35 mm jaw (approx.)*
☐ *Spark plug spanner (with rubber insert) - petrol models*
☐ *Spark plug gap adjustment tool - petrol models*
☐ *Set of feeler gauges*
☐ *Brake bleed nipple spanner*
☐ *Screwdrivers:*
Flat blade - 100 mm long x 6 mm dia
Cross blade - 100 mm long x 6 mm dia
Torx - various sizes (not all vehicles)
☐ *Combination pliers*
☐ *Hacksaw (junior)*
☐ *Tyre pump*
☐ *Tyre pressure gauge*
☐ *Oil can*
☐ *Oil filter removal tool*
☐ *Fine emery cloth*
☐ *Wire brush (small)*
☐ *Funnel (medium size)*
☐ *Sump drain plug key (not all vehicles)*

Repair and overhaul tool kit

These tools are virtually essential for anyone undertaking any major repairs to a motor vehicle, and are additional to those given in the *Maintenance and minor repair* list. Included in this list is a comprehensive set of sockets. Although these are expensive, they will be found invaluable as they are so versatile - particularly if various drives are included in the set. We recommend the half-inch square-drive type, as this can be used with most proprietary torque wrenches.

The tools in this list will sometimes need to be supplemented by tools from the *Special* list:

☐ *Sockets (or box spanners) to cover range in previous list (including Torx sockets)*
☐ *Reversible ratchet drive (for use with sockets)*
☐ *Extension piece, 250 mm (for use with sockets)*
☐ *Universal joint (for use with sockets)*
☐ *Flexible handle or sliding T "breaker bar" (for use with sockets)*
☐ *Torque wrench (for use with sockets)*
☐ *Self-locking grips*
☐ *Ball pein hammer*
☐ *Soft-faced mallet (plastic or rubber)*
☐ *Screwdrivers:*
Flat blade - long & sturdy, short (chubby), and narrow (electrician's) types
Cross blade - long & sturdy, and short (chubby) types
☐ *Pliers:*
Long-nosed
Side cutters (electrician's)
Circlip (internal and external)
☐ *Cold chisel - 25 mm*
☐ *Scriber*
☐ *Scraper*
☐ *Centre-punch*
☐ *Pin punch*
☐ *Hacksaw*
☐ *Brake hose clamp*
☐ *Brake/clutch bleeding kit*
☐ *Selection of twist drills*
☐ *Steel rule/straight-edge*
☐ *Allen keys (inc. splined/Torx type)*
☐ *Selection of files*
☐ *Wire brush*
☐ *Axle stands*
☐ *Jack (strong trolley or hydraulic type)*
☐ *Light with extension lead*
☐ *Universal electrical multi-meter*

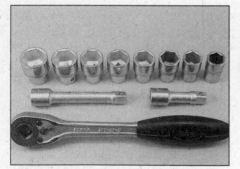

Sockets and reversible ratchet drive

Brake bleeding kit

Torx key, socket and bit

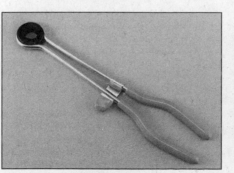

Hose clamp

Angular-tightening gauge

Special tools

The tools in this list are those which are not used regularly, are expensive to buy, or which need to be used in accordance with their manufacturers' instructions. Unless relatively difficult mechanical jobs are undertaken frequently, it will not be economic to buy many of these tools. Where this is the case, you could consider clubbing together with friends (or joining a motorists' club) to make a joint purchase, or borrowing the tools against a deposit from a local garage or tool hire specialist. It is worth noting that many of the larger DIY superstores now carry a large range of special tools for hire at modest rates.

The following list contains only those tools and instruments freely available to the public, and not those special tools produced by the vehicle manufacturer specifically for its dealer network. You will find occasional references to these manufacturers' special tools in the text of this manual. Generally, an alternative method of doing the job without the vehicle manufacturers' special tool is given. However, sometimes there is no alternative to using them. Where this is the case and the relevant tool cannot be bought or borrowed, you will have to entrust the work to a dealer.

- ☐ Angular-tightening gauge
- ☐ Valve spring compressor
- ☐ Valve grinding tool
- ☐ Piston ring compressor
- ☐ Piston ring removal/installation tool
- ☐ Cylinder bore hone
- ☐ Balljoint separator
- ☐ Coil spring compressors (where applicable)
- ☐ Two/three-legged hub and bearing puller
- ☐ Impact screwdriver
- ☐ Micrometer and/or vernier calipers
- ☐ Dial gauge
- ☐ Stroboscopic timing light
- ☐ Dwell angle meter/tachometer
- ☐ Fault code reader
- ☐ Cylinder compression gauge
- ☐ Hand-operated vacuum pump and gauge
- ☐ Clutch plate alignment set
- ☐ Brake shoe steady spring cup removal tool
- ☐ Bush and bearing removal/installation set
- ☐ Stud extractors
- ☐ Tap and die set
- ☐ Lifting tackle
- ☐ Trolley jack

Buying tools

Reputable motor accessory shops and superstores often offer excellent quality tools at discount prices, so it pays to shop around.

Remember, you don't have to buy the most expensive items on the shelf, but it is always advisable to steer clear of the very cheap tools. Beware of 'bargains' offered on market stalls or at car boot sales. There are plenty of good tools around at reasonable prices, but always aim to purchase items which meet the relevant national safety standards. If in doubt, ask the proprietor or manager of the shop for advice before making a purchase.

Care and maintenance of tools

Having purchased a reasonable tool kit, it is necessary to keep the tools in a clean and serviceable condition. After use, always wipe off any dirt, grease and metal particles using a clean, dry cloth, before putting the tools away. Never leave them lying around after they have been used. A simple tool rack on the garage or workshop wall for items such as screwdrivers and pliers is a good idea. Store all normal spanners and sockets in a metal box. Any measuring instruments, gauges, meters, etc, must be carefully stored where they cannot be damaged or become rusty.

Take a little care when tools are used. Hammer heads inevitably become marked, and screwdrivers lose the keen edge on their blades from time to time. A little timely attention with emery cloth or a file will soon restore items like this to a good finish.

Working facilities

Not to be forgotten when discussing tools is the workshop itself. If anything more than routine maintenance is to be carried out, a suitable working area becomes essential.

It is appreciated that many an owner-mechanic is forced by circumstances to remove an engine or similar item without the benefit of a garage or workshop. Having done this, any repairs should always be done under the cover of a roof.

Wherever possible, any dismantling should be done on a clean, flat workbench or table at a suitable working height.

Any workbench needs a vice; one with a jaw opening of 100 mm is suitable for most jobs. As mentioned previously, some clean dry storage space is also required for tools, as well as for any lubricants, cleaning fluids, touch-up paints etc, which become necessary.

Another item which may be required, and which has a much more general usage, is an electric drill with a chuck capacity of at least 8 mm. This, together with a good range of twist drills, is virtually essential for fitting accessories.

Last, but not least, always keep a supply of old newspapers and clean, lint-free rags available, and try to keep any working area as clean as possible.

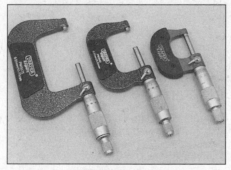
Micrometers

Dial test indicator ("dial gauge")

Strap wrench

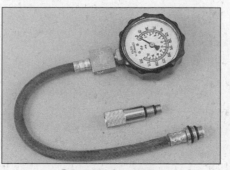
Compression tester

Fault code reader

This is a guide to getting your vehicle through the MOT test. Obviously it will not be possible to examine the vehicle to the same standard as the professional MOT tester. However, working through the following checks will enable you to identify any problem areas before submitting the vehicle for the test.

Where a testable component is in borderline condition, the tester has discretion in deciding whether to pass or fail it. The basis of such discretion is whether the tester would be happy for a close relative or friend to use the vehicle with the component in that condition. If the vehicle presented is clean and evidently well cared for, the tester may be more inclined to pass a borderline component than if the vehicle is scruffy and apparently neglected.

It has only been possible to summarise the test requirements here, based on the regulations in force at the time of printing. Test standards are becoming increasingly stringent, although there are some exemptions for older vehicles.

An assistant will be needed to help carry out some of these checks.

The checks have been sub-divided into four categories, as follows:

1 Checks carried out **FROM THE DRIVER'S SEAT**

2 Checks carried out **WITH THE VEHICLE ON THE GROUND**

3 Checks carried out **WITH THE VEHICLE RAISED AND THE WHEELS FREE TO TURN**

4 Checks carried out on **YOUR VEHICLE'S EXHAUST EMISSION SYSTEM**

---

1 Checks carried out **FROM THE DRIVER'S SEAT**

Handbrake

☐ Test the operation of the handbrake. Excessive travel (too many clicks) indicates incorrect brake or cable adjustment.

☐ Check that the handbrake cannot be released by tapping the lever sideways. Check the security of the lever mountings.

Footbrake

☐ Depress the brake pedal and check that it does not creep down to the floor, indicating a master cylinder fault. Release the pedal, wait a few seconds, then depress it again. If the pedal travels nearly to the floor before firm resistance is felt, brake adjustment or repair is necessary. If the pedal feels spongy, there is air in the hydraulic system which must be removed by bleeding.

☐ Check that the brake pedal is secure and in good condition. Check also for signs of fluid leaks on the pedal, floor or carpets, which would indicate failed seals in the brake master cylinder.

☐ Check the servo unit (when applicable) by operating the brake pedal several times, then keeping the pedal depressed and starting the engine. As the engine starts, the pedal will move down slightly. If not, the vacuum hose or the servo itself may be faulty.

Steering wheel and column

☐ Examine the steering wheel for fractures or looseness of the hub, spokes or rim.

☐ Move the steering wheel from side to side and then up and down. Check that the steering wheel is not loose on the column, indicating wear or a loose retaining nut. Continue moving the steering wheel as before, but also turn it slightly from left to right.

☐ Check that the steering wheel is not loose on the column, and that there is no abnormal

movement of the steering wheel, indicating wear in the column support bearings or couplings.

Windscreen, mirrors and sunvisor

☐ The windscreen must be free of cracks or other significant damage within the driver's field of view. (Small stone chips are acceptable.) Rear view mirrors must be secure, intact, and capable of being adjusted.

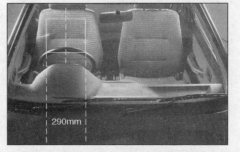

☐ The driver's sunvisor must be capable of being stored in the "up" position.

Seat belts and seats

Note: *The following checks are applicable to all seat belts, front and rear.*

☐ Examine the webbing of all the belts (including rear belts if fitted) for cuts, serious fraying or deterioration. Fasten and unfasten each belt to check the buckles. If applicable, check the retracting mechanism. Check the security of all seat belt mountings accessible from inside the vehicle.

☐ Seat belts with pre-tensioners, once activated, have a "flag" or similar showing on the seat belt stalk. This, in itself, is not a reason for test failure.

☐ The front seats themselves must be securely attached and the backrests must lock in the upright position.

Doors

☐ Both front doors must be able to be opened and closed from outside and inside, and must latch securely when closed.

2 Checks carried out WITH THE VEHICLE ON THE GROUND

Vehicle identification

☐ Number plates must be in good condition, secure and legible, with letters and numbers correctly spaced – spacing at (A) should be at least twice that at (B).

☐ The VIN plate and/or homologation plate must be legible.

Electrical equipment

☐ Switch on the ignition and check the operation of the horn.

☐ Check the windscreen washers and wipers, examining the wiper blades; renew damaged or perished blades. Also check the operation of the stop-lights.

☐ Check the operation of the sidelights and number plate lights. The lenses and reflectors must be secure, clean and undamaged.

☐ Check the operation and alignment of the headlights. The headlight reflectors must not be tarnished and the lenses must be undamaged.

☐ Switch on the ignition and check the operation of the direction indicators (including the instrument panel tell-tale) and the hazard warning lights. Operation of the sidelights and stop-lights must not affect the indicators - if it does, the cause is usually a bad earth at the rear light cluster.

☐ Check the operation of the rear foglight(s), including the warning light on the instrument panel or in the switch.

☐ The ABS warning light must illuminate in accordance with the manufacturers' design. For most vehicles, the ABS warning light should illuminate when the ignition is switched on, and (if the system is operating properly) extinguish after a few seconds. Refer to the owner's handbook.

Footbrake

☐ Examine the master cylinder, brake pipes and servo unit for leaks, loose mountings, corrosion or other damage.

☐ The fluid reservoir must be secure and the fluid level must be between the upper (A) and lower (B) markings.

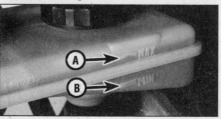

☐ Inspect both front brake flexible hoses for cracks or deterioration of the rubber. Turn the steering from lock to lock, and ensure that the hoses do not contact the wheel, tyre, or any part of the steering or suspension mechanism. With the brake pedal firmly depressed, check the hoses for bulges or leaks under pressure.

Steering and suspension

☐ Have your assistant turn the steering wheel from side to side slightly, up to the point where the steering gear just begins to transmit this movement to the roadwheels. Check for excessive free play between the steering wheel and the steering gear, indicating wear or insecurity of the steering column joints, the column-to-steering gear coupling, or the steering gear itself.

☐ Have your assistant turn the steering wheel more vigorously in each direction, so that the roadwheels just begin to turn. As this is done, examine all the steering joints, linkages, fittings and attachments. Renew any component that shows signs of wear or damage. On vehicles with power steering, check the security and condition of the steering pump, drivebelt and hoses.

☐ Check that the vehicle is standing level, and at approximately the correct ride height.

Shock absorbers

☐ Depress each corner of the vehicle in turn, then release it. The vehicle should rise and then settle in its normal position. If the vehicle continues to rise and fall, the shock absorber is defective. A shock absorber which has seized will also cause the vehicle to fail.

Exhaust system

☐ Start the engine. With your assistant holding a rag over the tailpipe, check the entire system for leaks. Repair or renew leaking sections.

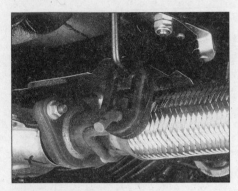

3 Checks carried out **WITH THE VEHICLE RAISED AND THE WHEELS FREE TO TURN**

Jack up the front and rear of the vehicle, and securely support it on axle stands. Position the stands clear of the suspension assemblies. Ensure that the wheels are clear of the ground and that the steering can be turned from lock to lock.

Steering mechanism

☐ Have your assistant turn the steering from lock to lock. Check that the steering turns smoothly, and that no part of the steering mechanism, including a wheel or tyre, fouls any brake hose or pipe or any part of the body structure.

☐ Examine the steering rack rubber gaiters for damage or insecurity of the retaining clips. If power steering is fitted, check for signs of damage or leakage of the fluid hoses, pipes or connections. Also check for excessive stiffness or binding of the steering, a missing split pin or locking device, or severe corrosion of the body structure within 30 cm of any steering component attachment point.

Front and rear suspension and wheel bearings

☐ Starting at the front right-hand side, grasp the roadwheel at the 3 o'clock and 9 o'clock positions and rock gently but firmly. Check for free play or insecurity at the wheel bearings, suspension balljoints, or suspension mountings, pivots and attachments.

☐ Now grasp the wheel at the 12 o'clock and 6 o'clock positions and repeat the previous inspection. Spin the wheel, and check for roughness or tightness of the front wheel bearing.

☐ If excess free play is suspected at a component pivot point, this can be confirmed by using a large screwdriver or similar tool and levering between the mounting and the component attachment. This will confirm whether the wear is in the pivot bush, its retaining bolt, or in the mounting itself (the bolt holes can often become elongated).

☐ Carry out all the above checks at the other front wheel, and then at both rear wheels.

Springs and shock absorbers

☐ Examine the suspension struts (when applicable) for serious fluid leakage, corrosion, or damage to the casing. Also check the security of the mounting points.

☐ If coil springs are fitted, check that the spring ends locate in their seats, and that the spring is not corroded, cracked or broken.

☐ If leaf springs are fitted, check that all leaves are intact, that the axle is securely attached to each spring, and that there is no deterioration of the spring eye mountings, bushes, and shackles.

☐ The same general checks apply to vehicles fitted with other suspension types, such as torsion bars, hydraulic displacer units, etc. Ensure that all mountings and attachments are secure, that there are no signs of excessive wear, corrosion or damage, and (on hydraulic types) that there are no fluid leaks or damaged pipes.

☐ Inspect the shock absorbers for signs of serious fluid leakage. Check for wear of the mounting bushes or attachments, or damage to the body of the unit.

Driveshafts (fwd vehicles only)

☐ Rotate each front wheel in turn and inspect the constant velocity joint gaiters for splits or damage. Also check that each driveshaft is straight and undamaged.

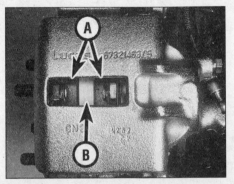

Braking system

☐ If possible without dismantling, check brake pad wear and disc condition. Ensure that the friction lining material has not worn excessively, (A) and that the discs are not fractured, pitted, scored or badly worn (B).

☐ Examine all the rigid brake pipes underneath the vehicle, and the flexible hose(s) at the rear. Look for corrosion, chafing or insecurity of the pipes, and for signs of bulging under pressure, chafing, splits or deterioration of the flexible hoses.

☐ Look for signs of fluid leaks at the brake calipers or on the brake backplates. Repair or renew leaking components.

☐ Slowly spin each wheel, while your assistant depresses and releases the footbrake. Ensure that each brake is operating and does not bind when the pedal is released.

□ Examine the handbrake mechanism, checking for frayed or broken cables, excessive corrosion, or wear or insecurity of the linkage. Check that the mechanism works on each relevant wheel, and releases fully, without binding.

□ It is not possible to test brake efficiency without special equipment, but a road test can be carried out later to check that the vehicle pulls up in a straight line.

Fuel and exhaust systems

□ Inspect the fuel tank (including the filler cap), fuel pipes, hoses and unions. All components must be secure and free from leaks.

□ Examine the exhaust system over its entire length, checking for any damaged, broken or missing mountings, security of the retaining clamps and rust or corrosion.

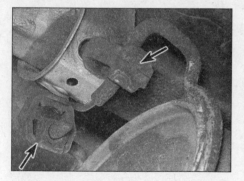

Wheels and tyres

□ Examine the sidewalls and tread area of each tyre in turn. Check for cuts, tears, lumps, bulges, separation of the tread, and exposure of the ply or cord due to wear or damage. Check that the tyre bead is correctly seated on the wheel rim, that the valve is sound and properly seated, and that the wheel is not distorted or damaged.

□ Check that the tyres are of the correct size for the vehicle, that they are of the same size

and type on each axle, and that the pressures are correct.

□ Check the tyre tread depth. The legal minimum at the time of writing is 1.6 mm over at least three-quarters of the tread width. Abnormal tread wear may indicate incorrect front wheel alignment.

Body corrosion

□ Check the condition of the entire vehicle structure for signs of corrosion in load-bearing areas. (These include chassis box sections, side sills, cross-members, pillars, and all suspension, steering, braking system and seat belt mountings and anchorages.) Any corrosion which has seriously reduced the thickness of a load-bearing area is likely to cause the vehicle to fail. In this case professional repairs are likely to be needed.

□ Damage or corrosion which causes sharp or otherwise dangerous edges to be exposed will also cause the vehicle to fail.

4 Checks carried out on YOUR VEHICLE'S EXHAUST EMISSION SYSTEM

Petrol models

□ The engine should be warmed up, and running well (ignition system in good order, air filter element clean, etc).

□ Before testing, run the engine at around 2500 rpm for 20 seconds. Let the engine drop to idle, and watch for smoke from the exhaust. If the idle speed is too high, or if dense blue or black smoke emerges for more than 5 seconds, the vehicle will fail. Typically, blue smoke signifies oil burning (engine wear); black smoke means unburnt fuel (dirty air cleaner element, or other fuel system fault).

□ An exhaust gas analyser for measuring carbon monoxide (CO) and hydrocarbons (HC) is now needed. If one cannot be hired or borrowed, have a local garage perform the check.

CO emissions (mixture)

□ The MOT tester has access to the CO limits for all vehicles. The CO level is measured at idle speed, and at 'fast idle' (2500 to 3000 rpm). The following limits are given as a general guide:

At idle speed – Less than 0.5% CO
At 'fast idle' – Less than 0.3% CO
Lambda reading – 0.97 to 1.03

□ If the CO level is too high, this may point to poor maintenance, a fuel injection system problem, faulty lambda (oxygen) sensor or catalytic converter. Try an injector cleaning treatment, and check the vehicle's ECU for fault codes.

HC emissions

□ The MOT tester has access to HC limits for all vehicles. The HC level is measured at 'fast idle' (2500 to 3000 rpm). The following limits are given as a general guide:

At 'fast idle' – Less then 200 ppm

□ Excessive HC emissions are typically caused by oil being burnt (worn engine), or by a blocked crankcase ventilation system ('breather'). If the engine oil is old and thin, an oil change may help. If the engine is running badly, check the vehicle's ECU for fault codes.

Diesel models

□ The only emission test for diesel engines is measuring exhaust smoke density, using a calibrated smoke meter. The test involves accelerating the engine at least 3 times to its maximum unloaded speed.

Note: *On engines with a timing belt, it is VITAL that the belt is in good condition before the test is carried out.*

□ With the engine warmed up, it is first purged by running at around 2500 rpm for 20 seconds. A governor check is then carried out, by slowly accelerating the engine to its maximum speed. After this, the smoke meter is connected, and the engine is accelerated quickly to maximum speed three times. If the smoke density is less than the limits given below, the vehicle will pass:

Non-turbo vehicles: 2.5m-1
Turbocharged vehicles: 3.0m-1

□ If excess smoke is produced, try fitting a new air cleaner element, or using an injector cleaning treatment. If the engine is running badly, where applicable, check the vehicle's ECU for fault codes. Also check the vehicle's EGR system, where applicable. At high mileages, the injectors may require professional attention.

Engine

- ☐ Engine fails to rotate when attempting to start
- ☐ Engine rotates, but will not start
- ☐ Engine difficult to start when cold
- ☐ Engine difficult to start when hot
- ☐ Starter motor noisy or excessively-rough in engagement
- ☐ Engine starts, but stops immediately
- ☐ Engine idles erratically
- ☐ Engine misfires at idle speed
- ☐ Engine misfires throughout the driving speed range
- ☐ Engine hesitates on acceleration
- ☐ Engine stalls
- ☐ Engine lacks power
- ☐ Engine backfires
- ☐ Oil pressure warning light illuminated with engine running
- ☐ Engine runs-on after switching off
- ☐ Engine noises

Cooling system

- ☐ Overheating
- ☐ Overcooling
- ☐ External coolant leakage
- ☐ Internal coolant leakage
- ☐ Corrosion

Fuel and exhaust systems

- ☐ Excessive fuel consumption
- ☐ Fuel leakage and/or fuel odour
- ☐ Excessive noise or fumes from exhaust system

Clutch

- ☐ Pedal travels to floor – no pressure or very little resistance
- ☐ Clutch fails to disengage (unable to select gears)
- ☐ Clutch slips (engine speed increases, with no increase in vehicle speed)
- ☐ Judder as clutch is engaged
- ☐ Noise when depressing or releasing clutch pedal

Manual transmission

- ☐ Noisy in neutral with engine running
- ☐ Noisy in one particular gear
- ☐ Difficulty engaging gears
- ☐ Jumps out of gear
- ☐ Vibration
- ☐ Lubricant leaks

Automatic transmission

- ☐ Fluid leakage
- ☐ Transmission fluid brown, or has burned smell
- ☐ General gear selection problems
- ☐ Transmission will not downshift (kickdown) with accelerator pedal fully depressed
- ☐ Engine will not start in any gear, or starts in gears other than Park or Neutral
- ☐ Transmission slips, shifts roughly, is noisy, or has no drive in forward or reverse gears

Driveshafts

- ☐ Vibration when accelerating or decelerating
- ☐ Clicking or knocking noise on turns (at slow speed on full-lock)

Braking system

- ☐ Vehicle pulls to one side under braking
- ☐ Noise (grinding or high-pitched squeal) when brakes applied
- ☐ Excessive brake pedal travel
- ☐ Brake pedal feels spongy when depressed
- ☐ Excessive brake pedal effort required to stop vehicle
- ☐ Judder felt through brake pedal or steering wheel when braking
- ☐ Brakes binding
- ☐ Rear wheels locking under normal braking

Suspension and steering

- ☐ Vehicle pulls to one side
- ☐ Wheel wobble and vibration
- ☐ Excessive pitching and/or rolling around corners, or during braking
- ☐ Wandering or general instability
- ☐ Excessively-stiff steering
- ☐ Excessive play in steering
- ☐ Lack of power assistance
- ☐ Tyre wear excessive

Electrical system

- ☐ Battery will not hold a charge for more than a few days
- ☐ Ignition/no-charge warning light remains illuminated with engine running
- ☐ Ignition/no-charge warning light fails to come on
- ☐ Lights inoperative
- ☐ Instrument readings inaccurate or erratic
- ☐ Horn inoperative, or unsatisfactory in operation
- ☐ Windscreen wipers inoperative, or unsatisfactory in operation
- ☐ Windscreen washers inoperative, or unsatisfactory in operation
- ☐ Electric windows inoperative, or unsatisfactory in operation
- ☐ Central locking system inoperative, or unsatisfactory in operation

Introduction

The vehicle owner who does his or her own maintenance according to the recommended service schedules should not have to use this section of the manual very often. Modern component reliability is such that, provided those items subject to wear or deterioration are inspected or renewed at the specified intervals, sudden failure is comparatively rare. Faults do not usually just happen as a result of sudden failure, but develop over a period of time. Major mechanical failures in particular are usually preceded by characteristic symptoms over hundreds or even thousands of miles. Those components which do

occasionally fail without warning are often small and easily carried in the vehicle.

With any fault finding, the first step is to decide where to begin investigations. Sometimes this is obvious, but on other occasions, a little detective work will be necessary. The owner who makes half a dozen haphazard adjustments or replacements may be successful in curing a fault (or its symptoms), but will be none the wiser if the fault recurs, and ultimately may have spent more time and money than was necessary. A calm and logical approach will be found to be more satisfactory in the long run. Always take into account any

warning signs or abnormalities that may have been noticed in the period preceding the fault – power loss, high or low gauge readings, unusual smells, etc – and remember that failure of components such as fuses or spark plugs may only be pointers to some underlying fault.

The pages which follow provide an easy-reference guide to the more common problems which may occur during the operation of the vehicle. These problems and their possible causes are grouped under headings denoting various components or systems, such as Engine, Cooling system, etc. The Chapter and/or Section which deals with the problem is also shown in brackets. Whatever the fault, certain basic principles apply. These are as follows:

Verify the fault. This is simply a matter of being sure that you know what the symptoms are before starting work. This is particularly important if you are investigating a fault for someone else, who may not have described it very accurately.

Don't overlook the obvious. For example, if the vehicle won't start, is there fuel in the tank? (Don't take anyone else's word on this particular point, and don't trust the fuel gauge either). If an electrical fault is indicated, look for loose or broken wires before digging out the test gear.

Cure the disease, not the symptom. Substituting a flat battery with a fully-charged one will get you off the hard shoulder, but if the underlying cause is not attended to, the new battery will go the same way. Similarly, changing oil-fouled spark plugs for a new set will get you moving again, but remember that the reason for the fouling (if it wasn't simply an incorrect grade of plug) will have to be established and corrected.

Don't take anything for granted. Particularly, don't forget that a 'new' component may itself be defective (especially if it's been rattling around in the boot for months), and don't leave components out of a fault diagnosis sequence just because they are new or recently-fitted. When you do finally diagnose a difficult fault, you'll probably realise that all the evidence was there from the start.

Consider what work, if any, has recently been carried out. Many faults arise through careless or hurried work. For instance, if any work has been performed under the bonnet, could some of the wiring have been dislodged or incorrectly routed, or a hose trapped? Have all the fasteners been properly tightened? Were new, genuine parts and new gaskets used? There is often a certain amount of detective work to be done in this case, as an apparently-unrelated task can have far-reaching consequences.

Engine

Engine fails to rotate when attempting to start

- ☐ Battery terminal connections loose or corroded (see *Weekly checks*)
- ☐ Battery discharged or faulty (Chapter 5A)
- ☐ Broken, loose or disconnected wiring in the starting circuit (Chapter 5A)
- ☐ Defective starter solenoid or ignition switch (Chapter 5A or 12)
- ☐ Defective starter motor (Chapter 5A)
- ☐ Starter pinion or flywheel ring gear teeth loose or broken (Chapter 2A, 2B, 2C or 5A)
- ☐ Engine earth strap broken or disconnected (Chapter 5A)
- ☐ Engine suffering 'hydraulic lock' (eg, from water ingested after traversing flooded roads, or from a serious internal coolant leak) – consult a Ford dealer for advice
- ☐ Automatic transmission not in position P or N (Chapter 7B)

Engine rotates, but will not start

- ☐ Fuel cut-off switch energised (Chapter 4A)
- ☐ Fuel tank empty
- ☐ Battery discharged (engine rotates slowly) (Chapter 5A)
- ☐ Battery terminal connections loose or corroded (see *Weekly checks*)
- ☐ Ignition components damp or damaged – petrol models (Chapter 1A or 5B)
- ☐ Immobiliser fault, or 'uncoded' ignition key being used (Chapter 12 or *Roadside repairs*)
- ☐ Crankshaft sensor fault (Chapter 4A or 4B)
- ☐ Broken, loose or disconnected wiring in the ignition circuit – petrol models (Chapter 1A or 5B)
- ☐ Worn, faulty or incorrectly-gapped spark plugs – petrol models (Chapter 1A)
- ☐ Preheating system faulty – diesel models (Chapter 4B)
- ☐ Fuel injection system fault (Chapter 4A or 4B)
- ☐ Air in fuel system – diesel models (Chapter 4B)
- ☐ Major mechanical failure (eg, timing belt snapped) (Chapter 2A, 2B or 2C)

Engine difficult to start when cold

- ☐ Battery discharged (Chapter 5A)
- ☐ Battery terminal connections loose or corroded (see *Weekly checks*)
- ☐ Worn, faulty or incorrectly-gapped spark plugs – petrol models (Chapter 1A)
- ☐ Other ignition system fault – petrol models (Chapter 1A or 5B)
- ☐ Preheating system faulty – diesel models (Chapter 4B)
- ☐ Fuel injection system fault (Chapter 4A or 4B)
- ☐ Wrong grade of engine oil used (*Weekly checks*, Chapter 1A or 1B)
- ☐ Low cylinder compression (Chapter 2A, 2B or 2C)

Engine difficult to start when hot

- ☐ Air filter element dirty or clogged (Chapter 1A or 1B)
- ☐ Fuel injection system fault (Chapter 4A or 4B)
- ☐ Low cylinder compression (Chapter 2A, 2B or 2C)

Starter motor noisy or excessively-rough in engagement

- ☐ Starter pinion or flywheel ring gear teeth loose or broken (Chapter 2A, 2B, 2C or 5A)
- ☐ Starter motor mounting bolts loose or missing (Chapter 5A)
- ☐ Starter motor internal components worn or damaged (Chapter 5A)

Engine starts, but stops immediately

- ☐ Loose or faulty electrical connections in the ignition circuit – petrol models (Chapter 1A or 5B)
- ☐ Vacuum leak at the throttle body or inlet manifold – petrol models (Chapter 4A)
- ☐ Blocked injectors/fuel injection system fault (Chapter 4A or 4B)
- ☐ Air in fuel, possibly due to loose fuel line connection – diesel models (Chapter 4B)

Engine idles erratically

- ☐ Air filter element clogged (Chapter 1A or 1B)
- ☐ Vacuum leak at the throttle body, inlet manifold or associated hoses – petrol models (Chapter 4A)
- ☐ Worn, faulty or incorrectly-gapped spark plugs – petrol models (Chapter 1A)
- ☐ Valve clearances incorrect (Chapter 2A, 2B or 2C)
- ☐ Uneven or low cylinder compression (Chapter 2A, 2B or 2C)
- ☐ Camshaft lobes worn (Chapter 2A, 2B or 2C)
- ☐ Timing belt incorrectly fitted (Chapter 2A, 2B or 2C)
- ☐ Blocked injectors/fuel injection system fault (Chapter 4A or 4B)
- ☐ Air in fuel, possibly due to loose fuel line connection – diesel models (Chapter 4B)

Engine misfires at idle speed

- ☐ Worn, faulty or incorrectly-gapped spark plugs – petrol models (Chapter 1A)
- ☐ Faulty spark plug HT leads – petrol models (Chapter 1A)
- ☐ Vacuum leak at the throttle body, inlet manifold or associated hoses – petrol models (Chapter 4A)
- ☐ Blocked injectors/fuel injection system fault (Chapter 4A or 4B)
- ☐ Faulty injector(s) – diesel models (Chapter 4B)
- ☐ Uneven or low cylinder compression (Chapter 2A, 2B or 2C)
- ☐ Disconnected, leaking, or perished crankcase ventilation hoses (Chapter 4C)

Engine (continued)

Engine misfires throughout the driving speed range

- ☐ Fuel filter choked (Chapter 1A or 1B)
- ☐ Fuel pump faulty, or delivery pressure low – petrol models (Chapter 4A)
- ☐ Fuel tank vent blocked, or fuel pipes restricted (Chapter 4A or 4B)
- ☐ Vacuum leak at the throttle body, inlet manifold or associated hoses – petrol models (Chapter 4A)
- ☐ Worn, faulty or incorrectly-gapped spark plugs – petrol models (Chapter 1A)
- ☐ Faulty spark plug HT leads (where fitted) – petrol models (Chapter 1A)
- ☐ Faulty injector(s) – diesel models (Chapter 4B)
- ☐ Faulty ignition coil – petrol models (Chapter 5A)
- ☐ Uneven or low cylinder compression (Chapter 2A, 2B or 2C)
- ☐ Blocked injector/fuel injection system fault (Chapter 4A or 4B)
- ☐ Blocked catalytic converter (Chapter 4A or 4B)
- ☐ Engine overheating – petrol models (Chapter 3)
- ☐ Fuel tank level low – diesel models (Chapter 4B)

Engine hesitates on acceleration

- ☐ Worn, faulty or incorrectly-gapped spark plugs – petrol models (Chapter 1A)
- ☐ Vacuum leak at the throttle body, inlet manifold or associated hoses – petrol models (Chapter 4A)
- ☐ Blocked injectors/fuel injection system fault (Chapter 4A or 4B)
- ☐ Faulty injector(s) – diesel models (Chapter 4B)
- ☐ Faulty clutch pedal switch (Chapter 4A or 4B)

Engine stalls

- ☐ Vacuum leak at the throttle body, inlet manifold or associated hoses – petrol models (Chapter 4A)
- ☐ Fuel filter choked (Chapter 1A or 1B)
- ☐ Fuel pump faulty, or delivery pressure low – petrol models (Chapter 4A)
- ☐ Fuel tank vent blocked, or fuel pipes restricted (Chapter 4A or 4B)
- ☐ Blocked injectors/fuel injection system fault (Chapter 4A or 4B)
- ☐ Faulty injector(s) – diesel models (Chapter 4B)

Engine lacks power

- ☐ Air filter element blocked (Chapter 1A or 1B)
- ☐ Fuel filter choked (Chapter 1A or 1B)
- ☐ Fuel pipes blocked or restricted (Chapter 4A or 4B)
- ☐ Valve clearances incorrect (Chapter 2A, 2B or 2C)
- ☐ Worn, faulty or incorrectly-gapped spark plugs – petrol models (Chapter 1A)
- ☐ Engine overheating – petrol models (Chapter 4A)
- ☐ Fuel tank level low – diesel models (Chapter 4B)
- ☐ Accelerator cable problem – petrol models (Chapter 4A)
- ☐ Accelerator position sensor faulty – diesel models (Chapter 4B)
- ☐ Vacuum leak at the throttle body, inlet manifold or associated hoses – petrol models (Chapter 4A)
- ☐ Blocked injectors/fuel injection system fault (Chapter 4A or 4B)
- ☐ Faulty injector(s) – diesel models (Chapter 4B)
- ☐ Timing belt incorrectly fitted (Chapter 2A, 2B or 2C)
- ☐ Fuel pump faulty, or delivery pressure low – petrol models (Chapter 4A)
- ☐ Uneven or low cylinder compression (Chapter 2A, 2B or 2C)
- ☐ Blocked catalytic converter (Chapter 4A or 4B)
- ☐ Injection pump timing incorrect – diesel models (Chapter 4B)
- ☐ Brakes binding (Chapter 1A, 1B or 9)
- ☐ Clutch slipping (Chapter 6)

Engine backfires

- ☐ Timing belt incorrectly fitted (Chapter 2A, 2B or 2C)
- ☐ Vacuum leak at the throttle body, inlet manifold or associated hoses – petrol models (Chapter 4A)
- ☐ Blocked injectors/fuel injection system fault (Chapter 4A or 4B)
- ☐ Blocked catalytic converter (Chapter 4A or 4B)
- ☐ Spark plug HT leads incorrectly fitted – petrol models (Chapter 1A or 5B)
- ☐ Ignition coil unit faulty – petrol models (Chapter 5B)

Oil pressure warning light illuminated with engine running

- ☐ Low oil level, or incorrect oil grade (see Weekly checks)
- ☐ Faulty oil pressure sensor, or wiring damaged (Chapter 5A)
- ☐ Worn engine bearings and/or oil pump (Chapter 2A, 2B or 2C)
- ☐ High engine operating temperature (Chapter 3)
- ☐ Oil pump pressure relief valve defective (Chapter 2A, 2B or 2C)
- ☐ Oil pump pick-up strainer clogged (Chapter 2A, 2B or 2C)

Engine runs-on after switching off

- ☐ Excessive carbon build-up in engine (Chapter 2A, 2B or 2C)
- ☐ High engine operating temperature (Chapter 3)
- ☐ Fuel injection system fault (Chapter 4A or 4B)

Engine noises

Pre-ignition (pinking) or knocking during acceleration or under load

- ☐ Ignition timing incorrect/ignition system fault – petrol models (Chapter 1A or 5B)
- ☐ Incorrect grade of spark plug – petrol models (Chapter 1A)
- ☐ Incorrect grade of fuel (Chapter 4)
- ☐ Knock sensor faulty – some petrol models (Chapter 4A)
- ☐ Vacuum leak at the throttle body, inlet manifold or associated hoses – petrol models (Chapter 4A)
- ☐ Excessive carbon build-up in engine (Chapter 2A, 2B or 2C)
- ☐ Blocked injector/fuel injection system fault (Chapter 4A or 4B)
- ☐ Faulty injector(s) – diesel models (Chapter 4B)

Whistling or wheezing noises

- ☐ Leaking inlet manifold or throttle body gasket – petrol models (Chapter 4A)
- ☐ Leaking exhaust manifold gasket or pipe-to-manifold joint (Chapter 4A or 4B)
- ☐ Leaking vacuum hose (Chapter 4A, 4B, 5B or 9)
- ☐ Blowing cylinder head gasket (Chapter 2A, 2B or 2C)
- ☐ Partially blocked or leaking crankcase ventilation system (Chapter 4C)

Tapping or rattling noises

- ☐ Valve clearances incorrect (Chapter 2A, 2B or 2C)
- ☐ Worn valve gear or camshaft (Chapter 2A, 2B or 2C)
- ☐ Ancillary component fault (coolant pump, alternator, etc) (Chapter 3, 5A, etc)

Knocking or thumping noises

- ☐ Worn big-end bearings (regular heavy knocking, perhaps less under load) (Chapter 2D)
- ☐ Worn main bearings (rumbling and knocking, perhaps worsening under load) (Chapter 2D)
- ☐ Piston slap – most noticeable when cold, caused by piston/bore wear (Chapter 2D)
- ☐ Ancillary component fault (coolant pump, alternator, etc) (Chapter 3, 5A, etc)
- ☐ Engine mountings worn or defective (Chapter 2A, 2B or 2C)
- ☐ Front suspension or steering components worn (Chapter 10)

Cooling system

Overheating

- ☐ Insufficient coolant in system (see *Weekly checks*)
- ☐ Thermostat faulty (Chapter 3)
- ☐ Radiator core blocked, or grille restricted (Chapter 3)
- ☐ Cooling fan faulty, or resistor pack fault on models with twin fans (Chapter 3)
- ☐ Inaccurate cylinder head temperature sender (Chapter 3, 4A or 4B)
- ☐ Airlock in cooling system (Chapter 3)
- ☐ Expansion tank pressure cap faulty (Chapter 3)
- ☐ Engine management system fault (Chapter 4A or 4B)

Overcooling

- ☐ Thermostat faulty (Chapter 3)
- ☐ Inaccurate cylinder head temperature sender (Chapter 3, 4A or 4B)
- ☐ Cooling fan faulty (Chapter 3)
- ☐ Engine management system fault (Chapter 4A or 4B)

External coolant leakage

- ☐ Deteriorated or damaged hoses or hose clips (Chapter 1A or 1B)
- ☐ Radiator core or heater matrix leaking (Chapter 3)
- ☐ Expansion tank pressure cap faulty (Chapter 1A or 1B)
- ☐ Coolant pump internal seal leaking (Chapter 3)
- ☐ Coolant pump gasket leaking (Chapter 3)
- ☐ Boiling due to overheating (Chapter 3)
- ☐ Cylinder block core plug leaking (Chapter 2D)

Internal coolant leakage

- ☐ Leaking cylinder head gasket (Chapter 2A, 2B or 2C)
- ☐ Cracked cylinder head or cylinder block (Chapter 2)

Corrosion

- ☐ Infrequent draining and flushing (Chapter 1A or 1B)
- ☐ Incorrect coolant mixture or inappropriate coolant type (see *Weekly checks*)

Fuel and exhaust systems

Excessive fuel consumption

- ☐ Air filter element dirty or clogged (Chapter 1A or 1B)
- ☐ Fuel injection system fault (Chapter 4A or 4B)
- ☐ Engine management system fault (Chapter 4A or 4B)
- ☐ Crankcase ventilation system blocked (Chapter 4C)
- ☐ Tyres under-inflated (see *Weekly checks*)
- ☐ Brakes binding (Chapter 1A, 1B or 9)
- ☐ Fuel leak, causing apparent high consumption (Chapter 1A, 1B, 4A or 4B)

Fuel leakage and/or fuel odour

- ☐ Damaged or corroded fuel tank, pipes or connections (Chapter 4A or 4B)
- ☐ Evaporative emissions system fault – petrol models (Chapter 4C)

Excessive noise or fumes from exhaust system

- ☐ Leaking exhaust system or manifold joints (Chapter 1A, 1B, 4A or 4B)
- ☐ Leaking, corroded or damaged silencers or pipe (Chapter 1A, 1B, 4A or 4B)
- ☐ Broken mountings causing body or suspension contact (Chapter 1A or 1B)

Clutch

Pedal travels to floor – no pressure or very little resistance

- ☐ Air in hydraulic system/faulty master or slave cylinder (Chapter 6)
- ☐ Faulty hydraulic release system (Chapter 6)
- ☐ Clutch pedal return spring detached or broken (Chapter 6)
- ☐ Broken clutch release bearing or fork (Chapter 6)
- ☐ Broken diaphragm spring in clutch pressure plate (Chapter 6)

Clutch fails to disengage (unable to select gears)

- ☐ Air in hydraulic system/faulty master or slave cylinder (Chapter 6)
- ☐ Faulty hydraulic release system (Chapter 6)
- ☐ Clutch disc sticking on transmission input shaft splines (Chapter 6)
- ☐ Clutch disc sticking to flywheel or pressure plate (Chapter 6)
- ☐ Faulty pressure plate assembly (Chapter 6)
- ☐ Clutch release mechanism worn or incorrectly assembled (Chapter 6)

Clutch slips (engine speed increases, with no increase in vehicle speed)

- ☐ Faulty hydraulic release system (Chapter 6)
- ☐ Clutch disc linings excessively worn (Chapter 6)
- ☐ Clutch disc linings contaminated with oil or grease (Chapter 6)
- ☐ Faulty pressure plate or weak diaphragm spring (Chapter 6)

Judder as clutch is engaged

- ☐ Clutch disc linings contaminated with oil or grease (Chapter 6)
- ☐ Clutch disc linings excessively worn (Chapter 6)
- ☐ Faulty or distorted pressure plate or diaphragm spring (Chapter 6).
- ☐ Worn or loose engine or transmission mountings (Chapter 2A, 2B or 2C)
- ☐ Clutch disc hub or transmission input shaft splines worn (Chapter 6)

Noise when depressing or releasing clutch pedal

- ☐ Worn clutch release bearing (Chapter 6)
- ☐ Worn or dry clutch pedal bushes (Chapter 6)
- ☐ Worn or dry clutch master cylinder piston (Chapter 6)
- ☐ Faulty pressure plate assembly (Chapter 6)
- ☐ Pressure plate diaphragm spring broken (Chapter 6)
- ☐ Broken clutch disc cushioning springs (Chapter 6)

Manual transmission

Noisy in neutral with engine running

- ☐ Lack of oil (Chapter 1A or 1B)
- ☐ Input shaft bearings worn (noise apparent with clutch pedal released, but not when depressed) (Chapter 7A)*
- ☐ Clutch release bearing worn (noise apparent with clutch pedal depressed, possibly less when released) (Chapter 6)

Noisy in one particular gear

- ☐ Worn, damaged or chipped gear teeth (Chapter 7A)*

Difficulty engaging gears

- ☐ Clutch fault (Chapter 6)
- ☐ Worn, damaged, or poorly-adjusted gearchange cables (Chapter 7A)
- ☐ Lack of oil (Chapter 1A or 1B)
- ☐ Worn synchroniser units (Chapter 7A)*

Jumps out of gear

- ☐ Worn, damaged, or poorly-adjusted gearchange cables (Chapter 7A)
- ☐ Worn synchroniser units (Chapter 7A)*
- ☐ Worn selector forks (Chapter 7A)*

Vibration

- ☐ Lack of oil (Chapter 1A or 1B)
- ☐ Worn bearings (Chapter 7A)*

Lubricant leaks

- ☐ Leaking driveshaft or selector shaft oil seal (Chapter 7A)
- ☐ Leaking housing joint (Chapter 7A)*
- ☐ Leaking input shaft oil seal (Chapter 7A)*

*Although the corrective action necessary to remedy the symptoms described is beyond the scope of the home mechanic, the above information should be helpful in isolating the cause of the condition, so that the owner can communicate clearly with a professional mechanic.

Automatic transmission

Note: *Due to the complexity of the automatic transmission, it is difficult for the home mechanic to properly diagnose and service this unit. For problems other than the following, the vehicle should be taken to a dealer service department or automatic transmission specialist. Do not be too hasty in removing the transmission if a fault is suspected, as most of the testing is carried out with the unit still fitted. Remember that, besides the sensors specific to the transmission, many of the engine management system sensors described in Chapter 4A are essential to the correct operation of the transmission.*

Fluid leakage

☐ Automatic transmission fluid is usually dark red in colour. Fluid leaks should not be confused with engine oil, which can easily be blown onto the transmission by airflow.

☐ To determine the source of a leak, first remove all built-up dirt and grime from the transmission housing and surrounding areas using a degreasing agent, or by steam-cleaning. Drive the vehicle at low speed, so airflow will not blow the leak far from its source. Raise and support the vehicle, and determine where the leak is coming from. The following are common areas of leakage:
a) *Fluid pan*
b) *Dipstick tube (Chapter 1A)*
c) *Transmission-to-fluid cooler unions (Chapter 7B)*

Transmission fluid brown, or has burned smell

☐ Transmission fluid level low (Chapter 1A)

General gear selection problems

☐ Chapter 7B deals with checking the selector cable on automatic transmissions. The following are common problems which may be caused by a faulty cable or sensor:
a) *Engine starting in gears other than Park or Neutral.*
b) *Indicator panel indicating a gear other than the one actually being used.*
c) *Vehicle moves when in Park or Neutral.*
d) *Poor gear shift quality or erratic gear changes.*

Transmission will not downshift (kickdown) with accelerator pedal fully depressed

☐ Low transmission fluid level (Chapter 1A)
☐ Engine management system fault (Chapter 4A)
☐ Faulty transmission sensor or wiring (Chapter 7B)
☐ Incorrect selector cable adjustment (Chapter 7B)

Engine will not start in any gear, or starts in gears other than Park or Neutral

☐ Faulty transmission sensor or wiring (Chapter 7B)
☐ Engine management system fault (Chapter 4A)
☐ Incorrect selector cable adjustment (Chapter 7B)

Transmission slips, shifts roughly, is noisy, or has no drive in forward or reverse gears

☐ Transmission fluid level low (Chapter 1A)
☐ Faulty transmission sensor or wiring (Chapter 7B)
☐ Engine management system fault (Chapter 4A)

Note: *There are many probable causes for the above problems, but diagnosing and correcting them is considered beyond the scope of this manual. Having checked the fluid level and all the wiring as far as possible, a dealer or transmission specialist should be consulted if the problem persists.*

Driveshafts

Vibration when accelerating or decelerating

☐ Worn inner constant velocity joint (Chapter 8)
☐ Bent or distorted driveshaft (Chapter 8)
☐ Worn intermediate bearing (Chapter 8)

Clicking or knocking noise on turns (at slow speed on full-lock)

☐ Worn outer constant velocity joint (Chapter 8)
☐ Lack of constant velocity joint lubricant, possibly due to damaged gaiter (Chapter 8)
☐ Worn intermediate bearing (Chapter 8)

Braking system

Note: *Before assuming that a brake problem exists, make sure that the tyres are in good condition and correctly inflated, that the front wheel alignment is correct, and that the vehicle is not loaded with weight in an unequal manner. Apart from checking the condition of all pipe and hose connections, any faults occurring on the anti-lock braking system should be referred to a Ford dealer for diagnosis.*

Vehicle pulls to one side under braking

☐ Worn, defective, damaged or contaminated brake pads/shoes on one side (Chapter 1A, 1B or 9)
☐ Seized or partially-seized brake caliper piston/wheel cylinder (Chapter 1A, 1B or 9)
☐ A mixture of brake pad/shoe lining materials fitted between sides (Chapter 1A, 1B or 9)
☐ Brake caliper/backplate mounting bolts loose (Chapter 9)
☐ Worn or damaged steering or suspension components (Chapter 1A, 1B or 10)

Noise (grinding or high-pitched squeal) when brakes applied

☐ Brake pad/shoe friction lining material worn down to metal backing (Chapter 1A, 1B or 9)
☐ Excessive corrosion of brake disc/drum (may be apparent after the vehicle has been standing for some time (Chapter 1A, 1B or 9)
☐ Foreign object (stone chipping, etc) trapped between brake disc and shield (Chapter 1A, 1B or 9)

Excessive brake pedal travel

☐ Faulty master cylinder (Chapter 9)
☐ Air in hydraulic system (Chapter 1A, 1B, 6 or 9)
☐ Faulty vacuum servo unit (Chapter 9)

Brake pedal feels spongy when depressed

☐ Air in hydraulic system (Chapter 1A, 1B, 6 or 9)
☐ Deteriorated flexible rubber brake hoses (Chapter 1A, 1B or 9)
☐ Master cylinder mounting nuts loose (Chapter 9)
☐ Faulty master cylinder (Chapter 9)

Excessive brake pedal effort required to stop vehicle

☐ Faulty vacuum servo unit (Chapter 9)
☐ Faulty vacuum pump – diesel models (Chapter 9)
☐ Disconnected, damaged or insecure brake servo vacuum hose (Chapter 9)
☐ Primary or secondary hydraulic circuit failure (Chapter 9)
☐ Seized brake caliper/wheel cylinder piston (Chapter 9)
☐ Brake pads/shoes incorrectly fitted (Chapter 9)
☐ Incorrect grade of brake pads/shoes fitted (Chapter 9)
☐ Brake pad/shoe linings contaminated (Chapter 1A, 1B or 9)

Judder felt through brake pedal or steering wheel when braking

Note: *Under heavy braking on models equipped with ABS, vibration may be felt through the brake pedal. This is a normal feature of ABS operation, and does not constitute a fault*

☐ Excessive run-out or distortion of discs/drums (Chapter 1A, 1B or 9)
☐ Brake pad/shoe linings worn (Chapter 1A, 1B or 9)
☐ Brake caliper/backplate mounting bolts loose (Chapter 9)
☐ Wear in suspension or steering components or mountings (Chapter 1A, 1B or 10)
☐ Front wheels out of balance (see *Weekly checks*)

Brakes binding

☐ Seized brake caliper/wheel cylinder piston (Chapter 9)
☐ Incorrectly-adjusted handbrake mechanism (Chapter 9)
☐ Faulty master cylinder (Chapter 9)

Rear wheels locking under normal braking

☐ Rear brake pad/shoe linings contaminated or damaged (Chapter 1 or 9)
☐ Rear brake discs/drums warped (Chapter 1A, 1B or 9)
☐ Rear brake load sensing proportioning valve faulty – Estate models (Chapter 9)

Suspension and steering

Note: *Before diagnosing suspension or steering faults, be sure that the trouble is not due to incorrect tyre pressures, mixtures of tyre types, or binding brakes.*

Vehicle pulls to one side

- ☐ Defective tyre (see *Weekly checks*)
- ☐ Excessive wear in suspension or steering components (Chapter 1A, 1B or 10)
- ☐ Incorrect front wheel alignment (Chapter 10)
- ☐ Accident damage to steering or suspension components (Chapter 1A or 1B)

Wheel wobble and vibration

- ☐ Front wheels out of balance (vibration felt mainly through the steering wheel) (see *Weekly checks*)
- ☐ Rear wheels out of balance (vibration felt throughout the vehicle) (see *Weekly checks*)
- ☐ Roadwheels damaged or distorted (see *Weekly checks*)
- ☐ Faulty or damaged tyre (see *Weekly checks*)
- ☐ Worn steering or suspension joints, bushes or components (Chapter 1A, 1B or 10)
- ☐ Wheel nuts loose (Chapter 1A or 1B)

Excessive pitching and/or rolling around corners, or during braking

- ☐ Defective shock absorbers (Chapter 1A, 1B or 10)
- ☐ Broken or weak spring and/or suspension component (Chapter 1A, 1B or 10)
- ☐ Worn or damaged anti-roll bar or mountings (Chapter 1A, 1B or 10)

Wandering or general instability

- ☐ Incorrect front wheel alignment (Chapter 10)
- ☐ Worn steering or suspension joints, bushes or components (Chapter 1A, 1B or 10)
- ☐ Roadwheels out of balance (see *Weekly checks*)
- ☐ Faulty or damaged tyre (see *Weekly checks*)
- ☐ Wheel nuts loose (Chapter 1A or 1B)
- ☐ Defective shock absorbers (Chapter 1A, 1B or 10)

Excessively-stiff steering

- ☐ Seized steering linkage balljoint or suspension balljoint (Chapter 1A, 1B or 10)
- ☐ Broken or incorrectly-adjusted auxiliary drivebelt (Chapter 1A or 1B)
- ☐ Incorrect front wheel alignment (Chapter 10)
- ☐ Steering rack damaged (Chapter 10)

Excessive play in steering

- ☐ Worn steering column/intermediate shaft joints (Chapter 10)
- ☐ Worn track rod balljoints (Chapter 1A, 1B or 10)
- ☐ Worn steering rack (Chapter 10)
- ☐ Worn steering or suspension joints, bushes or components (Chapter 1A, 1B or 10)

Lack of power assistance

- ☐ Broken or incorrectly-adjusted auxiliary drivebelt (Chapter 1A or 1B)
- ☐ Incorrect power steering fluid level (see *Weekly checks*)
- ☐ Restriction in power steering fluid hoses (Chapter 1A or 1B)
- ☐ Faulty power steering pump (Chapter 10)
- ☐ Faulty steering rack (Chapter 10)

Tyre wear excessive

Tyres worn on inside or outside edges

- ☐ Tyres under-inflated (wear on both edges) (see *Weekly checks*)
- ☐ Incorrect camber or castor angles (wear on one edge only) (Chapter 10)
- ☐ Worn steering or suspension joints, bushes or components (Chapter 1A, 1B or 10)
- ☐ Excessively-hard cornering or braking
- ☐ Accident damage

Tyre treads exhibit feathered edges

- ☐ Incorrect toe-setting (Chapter 10)

Tyres worn in centre of tread

- ☐ Tyres over-inflated (see *Weekly checks*)

Tyres worn on inside and outside edges

- ☐ Tyres under-inflated (see *Weekly checks*)

Tyres worn unevenly

- ☐ Tyres/wheels out of balance (see *Weekly checks*)
- ☐ Excessive wheel or tyre run-out
- ☐ Worn shock absorbers (Chapter 1A, 1B or 10)
- ☐ Faulty tyre (see *Weekly checks*)

Electrical system

Note: *For problems associated with the starting system, refer to the faults listed under 'Engine' earlier in this Section.*

Battery will not hold a charge for more than a few days

- ☐ Battery defective internally (Chapter 5A)
- ☐ Battery terminal connections loose or corroded (see *Weekly checks*)
- ☐ Auxiliary drivebelt worn or incorrectly adjusted (Chapter 1A or 1B)
- ☐ Alternator not charging at correct output (Chapter 5A)
- ☐ Alternator or voltage regulator faulty (Chapter 5A)
- ☐ Short-circuit causing continual battery drain (Chapter 5A or 12)

Ignition/no-charge warning light remains illuminated with engine running

- ☐ Auxiliary drivebelt broken, worn, or incorrectly adjusted (Chapter 1A or 1B)
- ☐ Internal fault in alternator or voltage regulator (Chapter 5A)
- ☐ Broken, disconnected, or loose wiring in charging circuit (Chapter 5A or 12)

Ignition/no-charge warning light fails to come on

- ☐ Warning light bulb blown (Chapter 12)
- ☐ Broken, disconnected, or loose wiring in warning light circuit (Chapter 5A or 12)
- ☐ Alternator faulty (Chapter 5A)

Electrical system (continued)

Lights inoperative

- [ ] Bulb blown (Chapter 12)
- [ ] Corrosion of bulb or bulbholder contacts (Chapter 12)
- [ ] Blown fuse (Chapter 12)
- [ ] Faulty relay (Chapter 12)
- [ ] Broken, loose, or disconnected wiring (Chapter 12)
- [ ] Faulty switch (Chapter 12)

Instrument readings inaccurate or erratic

Instrument readings increase with engine speed

- [ ] Faulty instrument panel voltage regulator (Chapter 12)

Fuel or temperature gauges give no reading

- [ ] Faulty gauge sender unit (Chapter 3, 4A or 4B)
- [ ] Wiring open-circuit (Chapter 12)
- [ ] Faulty gauge (Chapter 12)

Fuel or temperature gauges give continuous maximum reading

- [ ] Faulty gauge sender unit (Chapter 3, 4A or 4B)
- [ ] Wiring short-circuit (Chapter 12)
- [ ] Faulty gauge (Chapter 12)

Horn inoperative, or unsatisfactory in operation

Horn operates all the time

- [ ] Horn push either earthed or stuck down (Chapter 12)
- [ ] Horn cable-to-horn push earthed (Chapter 12)

Horn fails to operate

- [ ] Blown fuse (Chapter 12)
- [ ] Cable or connections loose, broken or disconnected (Chapter 12)
- [ ] Faulty horn (Chapter 12)

Horn emits intermittent or unsatisfactory sound

- [ ] Cable connections loose (Chapter 12)
- [ ] Horn mountings loose (Chapter 12)
- [ ] Faulty horn (Chapter 12)

Windscreen wipers inoperative, or unsatisfactory in operation

Wipers fail to operate, or operate very slowly

- [ ] Wiper blades stuck to screen, or linkage seized or binding (Chapter 12)
- [ ] Blown fuse (Chapter 12)
- [ ] Battery discharged (Chapter 5A)
- [ ] Cable or connections loose, broken or disconnected (Chapter 12)
- [ ] Faulty relay (Chapter 12)
- [ ] Faulty wiper motor (Chapter 12)

Wiper blades sweep over too large or too small an area of the glass

- [ ] Wiper blades incorrectly fitted, or wrong size used (see *Weekly checks*)
- [ ] Wiper arms incorrectly positioned on spindles (Chapter 12)
- [ ] Excessive wear of wiper linkage (Chapter 12)
- [ ] Wiper motor or linkage mountings loose or insecure (Chapter 12)

Wiper blades fail to clean the glass effectively

- [ ] Wiper blade rubbers dirty, worn or perished (see *Weekly checks*)
- [ ] Wiper blades incorrectly fitted, or wrong size used (see *Weekly checks*)
- [ ] Wiper arm tension springs broken, or arm pivots seized (Chapter 12)
- [ ] Insufficient windscreen washer additive to adequately remove road film (see *Weekly checks*)

Windscreen washers inoperative, or unsatisfactory in operation

One or more washer jets inoperative

- [ ] Blocked washer jet
- [ ] Disconnected, kinked or restricted fluid hose (Chapter 12)
- [ ] Insufficient fluid in washer reservoir (see *Weekly checks*)

Washer pump fails to operate

- [ ] Broken or disconnected wiring or connections (Chapter 12)
- [ ] Blown fuse (Chapter 12)
- [ ] Faulty washer switch (Chapter 12)
- [ ] Faulty washer pump (Chapter 12)

Washer pump runs for some time before fluid is emitted from jets

- [ ] Faulty one-way valve in fluid supply hose (Chapter 12)

Electric windows inoperative, or unsatisfactory in operation

Window glass will only move in one direction

- [ ] Faulty switch (Chapter 12)

Window glass slow to move

- [ ] Battery discharged (Chapter 5A)
- [ ] Regulator seized or damaged, or in need of lubrication (Chapter 11)
- [ ] Door internal components or trim fouling regulator (Chapter 11)
- [ ] Faulty motor (Chapter 11)

Window glass fails to move

- [ ] Blown fuse (Chapter 12)
- [ ] Faulty relay (Chapter 12)
- [ ] Broken or disconnected wiring or connections (Chapter 12)
- [ ] Faulty motor (Chapter 11)

Central locking system inoperative, or unsatisfactory in operation

Complete system failure

- [ ] Remote handset battery discharged, where applicable
- [ ] Blown fuse (Chapter 12)
- [ ] Faulty relay (Chapter 12)
- [ ] Broken or disconnected wiring or connections (Chapter 12)
- [ ] Faulty motor (Chapter 11)

Latch locks but will not unlock, or unlocks but will not lock

- [ ] Remote handset battery discharged, where applicable
- [ ] Faulty master switch (Chapter 12)
- [ ] Broken or disconnected latch operating rods or levers (Chapter 11)
- [ ] Faulty relay (Chapter 12)
- [ ] Faulty motor (Chapter 11)

One solenoid/motor fails to operate

- [ ] Broken or disconnected wiring or connections (Chapter 12)
- [ ] Faulty operating assembly (Chapter 11)
- [ ] Broken, binding or disconnected latch operating rods or levers (Chapter 11)
- [ ] Fault in door latch (Chapter 11)

A

ABS (Anti-lock brake system) A system, usually electronically controlled, that senses incipient wheel lockup during braking and relieves hydraulic pressure at wheels that are about to skid.

Air bag An inflatable bag hidden in the steering wheel (driver's side) or the dash or glovebox (passenger side). In a head-on collision, the bags inflate, preventing the driver and front passenger from being thrown forward into the steering wheel or windscreen.

Air cleaner A metal or plastic housing, containing a filter element, which removes dust and dirt from the air being drawn into the engine.

Air filter element The actual filter in an air cleaner system, usually manufactured from pleated paper and requiring renewal at regular intervals.

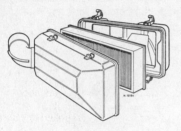

Air filter

Allen key A hexagonal wrench which fits into a recessed hexagonal hole.

Alligator clip A long-nosed spring-loaded metal clip with meshing teeth. Used to make temporary electrical connections.

Alternator A component in the electrical system which converts mechanical energy from a drivebelt into electrical energy to charge the battery and to operate the starting system, ignition system and electrical accessories.

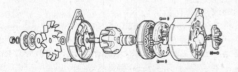

Alternator (exploded view)

Ampere (amp) A unit of measurement for the flow of electric current. One amp is the amount of current produced by one volt acting through a resistance of one ohm.

Anaerobic sealer A substance used to prevent bolts and screws from loosening. Anaerobic means that it does not require oxygen for activation. The Loctite brand is widely used.

Antifreeze A substance (usually ethylene glycol) mixed with water, and added to a vehicle's cooling system, to prevent freezing of the coolant in winter. Antifreeze also contains chemicals to inhibit corrosion and the formation of rust and other deposits that

would tend to clog the radiator and coolant passages and reduce cooling efficiency.

Anti-seize compound A coating that reduces the risk of seizing on fasteners that are subjected to high temperatures, such as exhaust manifold bolts and nuts.

Anti-seize compound

Asbestos A natural fibrous mineral with great heat resistance, commonly used in the composition of brake friction materials. Asbestos is a health hazard and the dust created by brake systems should never be inhaled or ingested.

Axle A shaft on which a wheel revolves, or which revolves with a wheel. Also, a solid beam that connects the two wheels at one end of the vehicle. An axle which also transmits power to the wheels is known as a live axle.

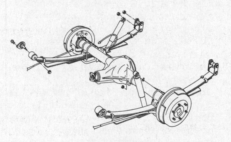

Axle assembly

Axleshaft A single rotating shaft, on either side of the differential, which delivers power from the final drive assembly to the drive wheels. Also called a driveshaft or a halfshaft.

B

Ball bearing An anti-friction bearing consisting of a hardened inner and outer race with hardened steel balls between two races.

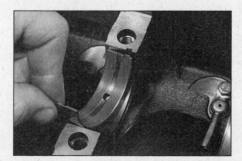

Bearing

Bearing The curved surface on a shaft or in a bore, or the part assembled into either, that permits relative motion between them with minimum wear and friction.

Big-end bearing The bearing in the end of the connecting rod that's attached to the crankshaft.

Bleed nipple A valve on a brake wheel cylinder, caliper or other hydraulic component that is opened to purge the hydraulic system of air. Also called a bleed screw.

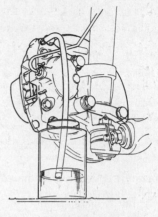

Brake bleeding

Brake bleeding Procedure for removing air from lines of a hydraulic brake system.

Brake disc The component of a disc brake that rotates with the wheels.

Brake drum The component of a drum brake that rotates with the wheels.

Brake linings The friction material which contacts the brake disc or drum to retard the vehicle's speed. The linings are bonded or riveted to the brake pads or shoes.

Brake pads The replaceable friction pads that pinch the brake disc when the brakes are applied. Brake pads consist of a friction material bonded or riveted to a rigid backing plate.

Brake shoe The crescent-shaped carrier to which the brake linings are mounted and which forces the lining against the rotating drum during braking.

Braking systems For more information on braking systems, consult the *Haynes Automotive Brake Manual*.

Breaker bar A long socket wrench handle providing greater leverage.

Bulkhead The insulated partition between the engine and the passenger compartment.

C

Caliper The non-rotating part of a disc-brake assembly that straddles the disc and carries the brake pads. The caliper also contains the hydraulic components that cause the pads to pinch the disc when the brakes are applied. A caliper is also a measuring tool that can be set to measure inside or outside dimensions of an object.

Camshaft A rotating shaft on which a series of cam lobes operate the valve mechanisms. The camshaft may be driven by gears, by sprockets and chain or by sprockets and a belt.

Canister A container in an evaporative emission control system; contains activated charcoal granules to trap vapours from the fuel system.

Canister

Carburettor A device which mixes fuel with air in the proper proportions to provide a desired power output from a spark ignition internal combustion engine.

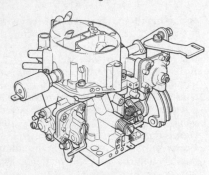

Carburettor

Castellated Resembling the parapets along the top of a castle wall. For example, a castellated balljoint stud nut.

Castellated nut

Castor In wheel alignment, the backward or forward tilt of the steering axis. Castor is positive when the steering axis is inclined rearward at the top.

Catalytic converter A silencer-like device in the exhaust system which converts certain pollutants in the exhaust gases into less harmful substances.

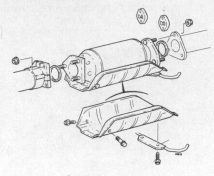

Catalytic converter

Circlip A ring-shaped clip used to prevent endwise movement of cylindrical parts and shafts. An internal circlip is installed in a groove in a housing; an external circlip fits into a groove on the outside of a cylindrical piece such as a shaft.

Clearance The amount of space between two parts. For example, between a piston and a cylinder, between a bearing and a journal, etc.

Coil spring A spiral of elastic steel found in various sizes throughout a vehicle, for example as a springing medium in the suspension and in the valve train.

Compression Reduction in volume, and increase in pressure and temperature, of a gas, caused by squeezing it into a smaller space.

Compression ratio The relationship between cylinder volume when the piston is at top dead centre and cylinder volume when the piston is at bottom dead centre.

Constant velocity (CV) joint A type of universal joint that cancels out vibrations caused by driving power being transmitted through an angle.

Core plug A disc or cup-shaped metal device inserted in a hole in a casting through which core was removed when the casting was formed. Also known as a freeze plug or expansion plug.

Crankcase The lower part of the engine block in which the crankshaft rotates.

Crankshaft The main rotating member, or shaft, running the length of the crankcase, with offset "throws" to which the connecting rods are attached.

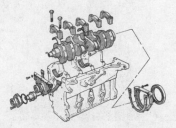

Crankshaft assembly

Crocodile clip See Alligator clip

D

Diagnostic code Code numbers obtained by accessing the diagnostic mode of an engine management computer. This code can be used to determine the area in the system where a malfunction may be located.

Disc brake A brake design incorporating a rotating disc onto which brake pads are squeezed. The resulting friction converts the energy of a moving vehicle into heat.

Double-overhead cam (DOHC) An engine that uses two overhead camshafts, usually one for the intake valves and one for the exhaust valves.

Drivebelt(s) The belt(s) used to drive accessories such as the alternator, water pump, power steering pump, air conditioning compressor, etc. off the crankshaft pulley.

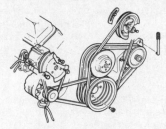

Accessory drivebelts

Driveshaft Any shaft used to transmit motion. Commonly used when referring to the axleshafts on a front wheel drive vehicle.

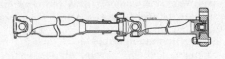

Driveshaft

Drum brake A type of brake using a drum-shaped metal cylinder attached to the inner surface of the wheel. When the brake pedal is pressed, curved brake shoes with friction linings press against the inside of the drum to slow or stop the vehicle.

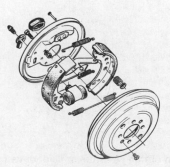

Drum brake assembly

E

EGR valve A valve used to introduce exhaust gases into the intake air stream.

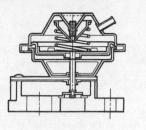

EGR valve

Electronic control unit (ECU) A computer which controls (for instance) ignition and fuel injection systems, or an anti-lock braking system. For more information refer to the *Haynes Automotive Electrical and Electronic Systems Manual.*

Electronic Fuel Injection (EFI) A computer controlled fuel system that distributes fuel through an injector located in each intake port of the engine.

Emergency brake A braking system, independent of the main hydraulic system, that can be used to slow or stop the vehicle if the primary brakes fail, or to hold the vehicle stationary even though the brake pedal isn't depressed. It usually consists of a hand lever that actuates either front or rear brakes mechanically through a series of cables and linkages. Also known as a handbrake or parking brake.

Endfloat The amount of lengthwise movement between two parts. As applied to a crankshaft, the distance that the crankshaft can move forward and back in the cylinder block.

Engine management system (EMS) A computer controlled system which manages the fuel injection and the ignition systems in an integrated fashion.

Exhaust manifold A part with several passages through which exhaust gases leave the engine combustion chambers and enter the exhaust pipe.

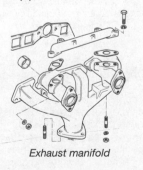

Exhaust manifold

F

Fan clutch A viscous (fluid) drive coupling device which permits variable engine fan speeds in relation to engine speeds.

Feeler blade A thin strip or blade of hardened steel, ground to an exact thickness, used to check or measure clearances between parts.

Feeler blade

Firing order The order in which the engine cylinders fire, or deliver their power strokes, beginning with the number one cylinder.

Flywheel A heavy spinning wheel in which energy is absorbed and stored by means of momentum. On cars, the flywheel is attached to the crankshaft to smooth out firing impulses.

Free play The amount of travel before any action takes place. The "looseness" in a linkage, or an assembly of parts, between the initial application of force and actual movement. For example, the distance the brake pedal moves before the pistons in the master cylinder are actuated.

Fuse An electrical device which protects a circuit against accidental overload. The typical fuse contains a soft piece of metal which is calibrated to melt at a predetermined current flow (expressed as amps) and break the circuit.

Fusible link A circuit protection device consisting of a conductor surrounded by heat-resistant insulation. The conductor is smaller than the wire it protects, so it acts as the weakest link in the circuit. Unlike a blown fuse, a failed fusible link must frequently be cut from the wire for replacement.

G

Gap The distance the spark must travel in jumping from the centre electrode to the side

Adjusting spark plug gap

electrode in a spark plug. Also refers to the spacing between the points in a contact breaker assembly in a conventional points-type ignition, or to the distance between the reluctor or rotor and the pickup coil in an electronic ignition.

Gasket Any thin, soft material - usually cork, cardboard, asbestos or soft metal - installed between two metal surfaces to ensure a good seal. For instance, the cylinder head gasket seals the joint between the block and the cylinder head.

Gasket

Gauge An instrument panel display used to monitor engine conditions. A gauge with a movable pointer on a dial or a fixed scale is an analogue gauge. A gauge with a numerical readout is called a digital gauge.

H

Halfshaft A rotating shaft that transmits power from the final drive unit to a drive wheel, usually when referring to a live rear axle.

Harmonic balancer A device designed to reduce torsion or twisting vibration in the crankshaft. May be incorporated in the crankshaft pulley. Also known as a vibration damper.

Hone An abrasive tool for correcting small irregularities or differences in diameter in an engine cylinder, brake cylinder, etc.

Hydraulic tappet A tappet that utilises hydraulic pressure from the engine's lubrication system to maintain zero clearance (constant contact with both camshaft and valve stem). Automatically adjusts to variation in valve stem length. Hydraulic tappets also reduce valve noise.

I

Ignition timing The moment at which the spark plug fires, usually expressed in the number of crankshaft degrees before the piston reaches the top of its stroke.

Inlet manifold A tube or housing with passages through which flows the air-fuel mixture (carburettor vehicles and vehicles with throttle body injection) or air only (port fuel-injected vehicles) to the port openings in the cylinder head.

J

Jump start Starting the engine of a vehicle with a discharged or weak battery by attaching jump leads from the weak battery to a charged or helper battery.

L

Load Sensing Proportioning Valve (LSPV) A brake hydraulic system control valve that works like a proportioning valve, but also takes into consideration the amount of weight carried by the rear axle.

Locknut A nut used to lock an adjustment nut, or other threaded component, in place. For example, a locknut is employed to keep the adjusting nut on the rocker arm in position.

Lockwasher A form of washer designed to prevent an attaching nut from working loose.

M

MacPherson strut A type of front suspension system devised by Earle MacPherson at Ford of England. In its original form, a simple lateral link with the anti-roll bar creates the lower control arm. A long strut - an integral coil spring and shock absorber - is mounted between the body and the steering knuckle. Many modern so-called MacPherson strut systems use a conventional lower A-arm and don't rely on the anti-roll bar for location.

Multimeter An electrical test instrument with the capability to measure voltage, current and resistance.

N

NOx Oxides of Nitrogen. A common toxic pollutant emitted by petrol and diesel engines at higher temperatures.

O

Ohm The unit of electrical resistance. One volt applied to a resistance of one ohm will produce a current of one amp.

Ohmmeter An instrument for measuring electrical resistance.

O-ring A type of sealing ring made of a special rubber-like material; in use, the O-ring is compressed into a groove to provide the sealing action.

O-ring

Overhead cam (ohc) engine An engine with the camshaft(s) located on top of the cylinder head(s).

Overhead valve (ohv) engine An engine with the valves located in the cylinder head, but with the camshaft located in the engine block.

Oxygen sensor A device installed in the engine exhaust manifold, which senses the oxygen content in the exhaust and converts this information into an electric current. Also called a Lambda sensor.

P

Phillips screw A type of screw head having a cross instead of a slot for a corresponding type of screwdriver.

Plastigage A thin strip of plastic thread, available in different sizes, used for measuring clearances. For example, a strip of Plastigage is laid across a bearing journal. The parts are assembled and dismantled; the width of the crushed strip indicates the clearance between journal and bearing.

Plastigage

Propeller shaft The long hollow tube with universal joints at both ends that carries power from the transmission to the differential on front-engined rear wheel drive vehicles.

Proportioning valve A hydraulic control valve which limits the amount of pressure to the rear brakes during panic stops to prevent wheel lock-up.

R

Rack-and-pinion steering A steering system with a pinion gear on the end of the steering shaft that mates with a rack (think of a geared wheel opened up and laid flat). When the steering wheel is turned, the pinion turns, moving the rack to the left or right. This movement is transmitted through the track rods to the steering arms at the wheels.

Radiator A liquid-to-air heat transfer device designed to reduce the temperature of the coolant in an internal combustion engine cooling system.

Refrigerant Any substance used as a heat transfer agent in an air-conditioning system. R-12 has been the principle refrigerant for many years; recently, however, manufacturers have begun using R-134a, a non-CFC substance that is considered less harmful to the ozone in the upper atmosphere.

Rocker arm A lever arm that rocks on a shaft or pivots on a stud. In an overhead valve engine, the rocker arm converts the upward movement of the pushrod into a downward movement to open a valve.

Rotor In a distributor, the rotating device inside the cap that connects the centre electrode and the outer terminals as it turns, distributing the high voltage from the coil secondary winding to the proper spark plug. Also, that part of an alternator which rotates inside the stator. Also, the rotating assembly of a turbocharger, including the compressor wheel, shaft and turbine wheel.

Runout The amount of wobble (in-and-out movement) of a gear or wheel as it's rotated. The amount a shaft rotates "out-of-true." The out-of-round condition of a rotating part.

S

Sealant A liquid or paste used to prevent leakage at a joint. Sometimes used in conjunction with a gasket.

Sealed beam lamp An older headlight design which integrates the reflector, lens and filaments into a hermetically-sealed one-piece unit. When a filament burns out or the lens cracks, the entire unit is simply replaced.

Serpentine drivebelt A single, long, wide accessory drivebelt that's used on some newer vehicles to drive all the accessories, instead of a series of smaller, shorter belts. Serpentine drivebelts are usually tensioned by an automatic tensioner.

Serpentine drivebelt

Shim Thin spacer, commonly used to adjust the clearance or relative positions between two parts. For example, shims inserted into or under bucket tappets control valve clearances. Clearance is adjusted by changing the thickness of the shim.

Slide hammer A special puller that screws into or hooks onto a component such as a shaft or bearing; a heavy sliding handle on the shaft bottoms against the end of the shaft to knock the component free.

Sprocket A tooth or projection on the periphery of a wheel, shaped to engage with a chain or drivebelt. Commonly used to refer to the sprocket wheel itself.

Starter inhibitor switch On vehicles with an automatic transmission, a switch that prevents starting if the vehicle is not in Neutral or Park.

Strut See MacPherson strut.

T

Tappet A cylindrical component which transmits motion from the cam to the valve stem, either directly or via a pushrod and rocker arm. Also called a cam follower.

Thermostat A heat-controlled valve that regulates the flow of coolant between the cylinder block and the radiator, so maintaining optimum engine operating temperature. A thermostat is also used in some air cleaners in which the temperature is regulated.

Thrust bearing The bearing in the clutch assembly that is moved in to the release levers by clutch pedal action to disengage the clutch. Also referred to as a release bearing.

Timing belt A toothed belt which drives the camshaft. Serious engine damage may result if it breaks in service.

Timing chain A chain which drives the camshaft.

Toe-in The amount the front wheels are closer together at the front than at the rear. On rear wheel drive vehicles, a slight amount of toe-in is usually specified to keep the front wheels running parallel on the road by offsetting other forces that tend to spread the wheels apart.

Toe-out The amount the front wheels are closer together at the rear than at the front. On front wheel drive vehicles, a slight amount of toe-out is usually specified.

Tools For full information on choosing and using tools, refer to the *Haynes Automotive Tools Manual.*

Tracer A stripe of a second colour applied to a wire insulator to distinguish that wire from another one with the same colour insulator.

Tune-up A process of accurate and careful adjustments and parts replacement to obtain the best possible engine performance.

Turbocharger A centrifugal device, driven by exhaust gases, that pressurises the intake air. Normally used to increase the power output from a given engine displacement, but can also be used primarily to reduce exhaust emissions (as on VW's "Umwelt" Diesel engine).

U

Universal joint or U-joint A double-pivoted connection for transmitting power from a driving to a driven shaft through an angle. A U-joint consists of two Y-shaped yokes and a cross-shaped member called the spider.

V

Valve A device through which the flow of liquid, gas, vacuum, or loose material in bulk may be started, stopped, or regulated by a movable part that opens, shuts, or partially obstructs one or more ports or passageways. A valve is also the movable part of such a device.

Valve clearance The clearance between the valve tip (the end of the valve stem) and the rocker arm or tappet. The valve clearance is measured when the valve is closed.

Vernier caliper A precision measuring instrument that measures inside and outside dimensions. Not quite as accurate as a micrometer, but more convenient.

Viscosity The thickness of a liquid or its resistance to flow.

Volt A unit for expressing electrical "pressure" in a circuit. One volt that will produce a current of one ampere through a resistance of one ohm.

W

Welding Various processes used to join metal items by heating the areas to be joined to a molten state and fusing them together. For more information refer to the *Haynes Automotive Welding Manual.*

Wiring diagram A drawing portraying the components and wires in a vehicle's electrical system, using standardised symbols. For more information refer to the *Haynes Automotive Electrical and Electronic Systems Manual.*

Note: *References throughout this index are in the form* **"Chapter number • Page number"**

Haynes Manuals – The Complete UK Car List

Title	Book No.
ALFA ROMEO Alfasud/Sprint (74 - 88) up to F *	0292
Alfa Romeo Alfetta (73 - 87) up to E *	0531
AUDI 80, 90 & Coupe Petrol (79 - Nov 88) up to F	0605
Audi 80, 90 & Coupe Petrol (Oct 86 - 90) D to H	1491
Audi 100 & 200 Petrol (Oct 82 - 90) up to H	0907
Audi 100 & A6 Petrol & Diesel (May 91 - May 97) H to P	3504
Audi A3 Petrol & Diesel (96 - May 03) P to 03	4253
Audi A4 Petrol & Diesel (95 - 00) M to X	3575
Audi A4 Petrol & Diesel (01 - 04) X to 54	4609
AUSTIN A35 & A40 (56 - 67) up to F *	0118
Austin/MG/Rover Maestro 1.3 & 1.6 Petrol (83 - 95) up to M	0922
Austin/MG Metro (80 - May 90) up to G	0718
Austin/Rover Montego 1.3 & 1.6 Petrol (84 - 94) A to L	1066
Austin/MG/Rover Montego 2.0 Petrol (84 - 95) A to M	1067
Mini (59 - 69) up to H *	0527
Mini (69 - 01) up to X	0646
Austin/Rover 2.0 litre Diesel Engine (86 - 93) C to L	1857
Austin Healey 100/6 & 3000 (56 - 68) up to G *	0049
BEDFORD CF Petrol (69 - 87) up to E	0163
Bedford/Vauxhall Rascal & Suzuki Supercarry (86 - Oct 94) C to M	3015
BMW 316, 320 & 320i (4-cyl) (75 - Feb 83) up to Y *	0276
BMW 320, 320i, 323i & 325i (6-cyl) (Oct 77 - Sept 87) up to E	0815
BMW 3- & 5-Series Petrol (81 - 91) up to J	1948
BMW 3-Series Petrol (Apr 91 - 99) H to V	3210
BMW 3-Series Petrol (Sept 98 - 03) S to 53	4067
BMW 520i & 525e (Oct 81 - June 88) up to E	1560
BMW 525, 528 & 528i (73 - Sept 81) up to X *	0632
BMW 5-Series 6-cyl Petrol (April 96 - Aug 03) N to 03	4151
BMW 1500, 1502, 1600, 1602, 2000 & 2002 (59 - 77) up to S *	0240
CHRYSLER PT Cruiser Petrol (00 - 03) W to 53	4058
CITROËN 2CV, Ami & Dyane (67 - 90) up to H	0196
Citroën AX Petrol & Diesel (87 - 97) D to P	3014
Citroën Berlingo & Peugeot Partner Petrol & Diesel (96 - 05) P to 55	4281
Citroën BX Petrol (83 - 94) A to L	0908
Citroën C15 Van Petrol & Diesel (89 - Oct 98) F to S	3509
Citroën C3 Petrol & Diesel (02 - 05) 51 to 05	4197
Citroën CX Petrol (75 - 88) up to F	0528
Citroën Saxo Petrol & Diesel (96 - 04) N to 54	3506
Citroën Visa Petrol (79 - 88) up to F	0620
Citroën Xantia Petrol & Diesel (93 - 01) K to Y	3082
Citroën XM Petrol & Diesel (89 - 00) G to X	3451
Citroën Xsara Petrol & Diesel (97 - Sept 00) R to W	3751
Citroën Xsara Picasso Petrol & Diesel (00 - 02) W to 52	3944
Citroën ZX Diesel (91 - 98) J to S	1922
Citroën ZX Petrol (91 - 98) H to S	1881
Citroën 1.7 & 1.9 litre Diesel Engine (84 - 96) A to N	1379
FIAT 126 (73 - 87) up to E *	0305
Fiat 500 (57 - 73) up to M *	0090
Fiat Bravo & Brava Petrol (95 - 00) N to W	3572
Fiat Cinquecento (93 - 98) K to R	3501
Fiat Panda (81 - 95) up to M	0793
Fiat Punto Petrol & Diesel (94 - Oct 99) L to V	3251
Fiat Punto Petrol (Oct 99 - July 03) V to 03	4066
Fiat Regata Petrol (84 - 88) A to F	1167
Fiat Tipo Petrol (88 - 91) E to J	1625
Fiat Uno Petrol (83 - 95) up to M	0923
Fiat X1/9 (74 - 89) up to G *	0273
FORD Anglia (59 - 68) up to G *	0001
Ford Capri II (& III) 1.6 & 2.0 (74 - 87) up to E *	0283
Ford Capri II (& III) 2.8 & 3.0 V6 (74 - 87) up to E	1309

Title	Book No.
Ford Cortina Mk I & Corsair 1500 ('62 - '66) up to D*	0214
Ford Cortina Mk III 1300 & 1600 (70 - 76) up to P *	0070
Ford Escort Mk I 1100 & 1300 (68 - 74) up to N *	0171
Ford Escort Mk I Mexico, RS 1600 & RS 2000 (70 - 74) up to N *	0139
Ford Escort Mk II Mexico, RS 1800 & RS 2000 (75 - 80) up to W *	0735
Ford Escort (75 - Aug 80) up to V *	0280
Ford Escort Petrol (Sept 80 - Sept 90) up to H	0686
Ford Escort & Orion Petrol (Sept 90 - 00) H to X	1737
Ford Escort & Orion Diesel (Sept 90 - 00) H to X	4081
Ford Fiesta (76 - Aug 83) up to Y	0334
Ford Fiesta Petrol (Aug 83 - Feb 89) A to F	1030
Ford Fiesta Petrol (Feb 89 - Oct 95) F to N	1595
Ford Fiesta Petrol & Diesel (Oct 95 - Mar 02) N to 02	3397
Ford Fiesta Petrol & Diesel (Apr 02 - 05) 02 to 54	4170
Ford Focus Petrol & Diesel (98 - 01) S to Y	3759
Ford Focus Petrol & Diesel (Oct 01 - 05) 51 to 05	4167
Ford Galaxy Petrol & Diesel (95 - Aug 00) M to W	3984
Ford Granada Petrol (Sept 77 - Feb 85) up to B *	0481
Ford Granada & Scorpio Petrol (Mar 85 - 94) B to M	1245
Ford Ka (96 - 02) P to 52	3570
Ford Mondeo Petrol (93 - Sept 00) K to X	1923
Ford Mondeo Petrol & Diesel (Oct 00 - Jul 03) X to 03	3990
Ford Mondeo Petrol & Diesel (July 03 - 07) 03 to 56	4619
Ford Mondeo Diesel (93 - 96) L to N	3465
Ford Orion Petrol (83 - Sept 90) up to H	1009
Ford Sierra 4-cyl Petrol (82 - 93) up to K	0903
Ford Sierra V6 Petrol (82 - 91) up to J	0904
Ford Transit Petrol (Mk 2) (78 - Jan 86) up to C	0719
Ford Transit Petrol (Mk 3) (Feb 86 - 89) C to G	1468
Ford Transit Diesel (Feb 86 - 99) C to T	3019
Ford 1.6 & 1.8 litre Diesel Engine (84 - 96) A to N	1172
Ford 2.1, 2.3 & 2.5 litre Diesel Engine (77 - 90) up to H	1606
FREIGHT ROVER Sherpa Petrol (74 - 87) up to E	0463
HILLMAN Avenger (70 - 82) up to Y	0037
Hillman Imp (63 - 76) up to R *	0022
HONDA Civic (Feb 84 - Oct 87) A to E	1226
Honda Civic (Nov 91 - 96) J to N	3199
Honda Civic Petrol (Mar 95 - 00) M to X	4050
Honda Civic Petrol & Diesel (01 - 05) X to 55	4611
Honda Jazz (01 - Feb 08) 51 - 57	4735
HYUNDAI Pony (85 - 94) C to M	3398
JAGUAR E Type (61 - 72) up to L *	0140
Jaguar MkI & II, 240 & 340 (55 - 69) up to H *	0098
Jaguar XJ6, XJ & Sovereign; Daimler Sovereign (68 - Oct 86) up to D	0242
Jaguar XJ6 & Sovereign (Oct 86 - Sept 94) D to M	3261
Jaguar XJ12, XJS & Sovereign; Daimler Double Six (72 - 88) up to F	0478
JEEP Cherokee Petrol (93 - 96) K to N	1943
LADA 1200, 1300, 1500 & 1600 (74 - 91) up to J	0413
Lada Samara (87 - 91) D to J	1610
LAND ROVER 90, 110 & Defender Diesel (83 - 07) up to 56	3017
Land Rover Discovery Petrol & Diesel (89 - 98) G to S	3016
Land Rover Discovery Diesel (Nov 98 - Jul 04) S to 04	4606
Land Rover Freelander Petrol & Diesel (97 - Sept 03) R to 53	3929
Land Rover Freelander Petrol & Diesel (Oct 03 - Oct 06) 53 to 56	4623
Land Rover Series IIA & III Diesel (58 - 85) up to C	0529
Land Rover Series II, IIA & III 4-cyl Petrol (58 - 85) up to C	0314

Title	Book No.
MAZDA 323 (Mar 81 - Oct 89) up to G	1608
Mazda 323 (Oct 89 - 98) G to R	3455
Mazda 626 (May 83 - Sept 87) up to E	0929
Mazda B1600, B1800 & B2000 Pick-up Petrol (72 - 88) up to F	0267
Mazda RX-7 (79 - 85) up to C *	0460
MERCEDES-BENZ 190, 190E & 190D Petrol & Diesel (83 - 93) A to L	3450
Mercedes-Benz 200D, 240D, 240TD, 300D & 300TD 123 Series Diesel (Oct 76 - 85)	1114
Mercedes-Benz 250 & 280 (68 - 72) up to L *	0346
Mercedes-Benz 250 & 280 123 Series Petrol (Oct 76 - 84) up to B *	0677
Mercedes-Benz 124 Series Petrol & Diesel (85 - Aug 93) C to K	3253
Mercedes-Benz C-Class Petrol & Diesel (93 - Aug 00) L to W	3511
MGA (55 - 62) *	0475
MGB (62 - 80) up to W	0111
MG Midget & Austin-Healey Sprite (58 - 80) up to W *	0265
MINI Petrol (July 01 - 05) Y to 05	4273
MITSUBISHI Shogun & L200 Pick-Ups Petrol (83 - 94) up to M	1944
MORRIS Ital 1.3 (80 - 84) up to B	0705
Morris Minor 1000 (56 - 71) up to K	0024
NISSAN Almera Petrol (95 - Feb 00) N to V	4053
Nissan Almera & Tino Petrol (Feb 00 - 07) V to 56	4612
Nissan Bluebird (May 84 - Mar 86) A to C	1223
Nissan Bluebird Petrol (Mar 86 - 90) C to H	1473
Nissan Cherry (Sept 82 - 86) up to D	1031
Nissan Micra (83 - Jan 93) up to K	0931
Nissan Micra (93 - 02) K to 52	3254
Nissan Primera Petrol (90 - Aug 99) H to T	1851
Nissan Stanza (82 - 86) up to D	0824
Nissan Sunny Petrol (May 82 - Oct 86) up to D	0895
Nissan Sunny Petrol (Oct 86 - Mar 91) D to H	1378
Nissan Sunny Petrol (Apr 91 - 95) H to N	3219
OPEL Ascona & Manta (B Series) (Sept 75 - 88) up to F *	0316
Opel Ascona Petrol (81 - 88)	3215
Opel Astra Petrol (Oct 91 - Feb 98)	3156
Opel Corsa Petrol (83 - Mar 93)	3160
Opel Corsa Petrol (Mar 93 - 97)	3159
Opel Kadett Petrol (Nov 79 - Oct 84) up to B	0634
Opel Kadett Petrol (Oct 84 - Oct 91)	3196
Opel Omega & Senator Petrol (Nov 86 - 94)	3157
Opel Rekord Petrol (Feb 78 - Oct 86) up to D	0543
Opel Vectra Petrol (Oct 88 - Oct 95)	3158
PEUGEOT 106 Petrol & Diesel (91 - 04) J to 53	1882
Peugeot 205 Petrol (83 - 97) A to P	0932
Peugeot 206 Petrol & Diesel (98 - 01) S to X	3757
Peugeot 206 Petrol & Diesel (02 - 06) 51 to 06	4613
Peugeot 306 Petrol & Diesel (93 - 02) K to 02	3073
Peugeot 307 Petrol & Diesel (01 - 04) Y to 54	4147
Peugeot 309 Petrol (86 - 93) C to K	1266
Peugeot 405 Petrol (88 - 97) E to P	1559
Peugeot 405 Diesel (88 - 97) E to P	3198
Peugeot 406 Petrol & Diesel (96 - Mar 99) N to T	3394
Peugeot 406 Petrol & Diesel (Mar 99 - 02) T to 52	3982
Peugeot 505 Petrol (79 - 89) up to G	0762
Peugeot 1.7/1.8 & 1.9 litre Diesel Engine (82 - 96) up to N	0950
Peugeot 2.0, 2.1, 2.3 & 2.5 litre Diesel Engines (74 - 90) up to H	1607
PORSCHE 911 (65 - 85) up to C	0264

Title	Book No.
Porsche 924 & 924 Turbo (76 - 85) up to C	0397
PROTON (89 - 97) F to P	3255
RANGE ROVER V8 Petrol (70 - Oct 92) up to K	0606
RELIANT Robin & Kitten (73 - 83) up to A *	0436
RENAULT 4 (61 - 86) up to D *	0072
Renault 5 Petrol (Feb 85 - 96) B to N	1219
Renault 9 & 11 Petrol (82 - 89) up to F	0822
Renault 18 Petrol (79 - 86) up to D	0598
Renault 19 Petrol (89 - 96) F to N	1646
Renault 19 Diesel (89 - 96) F to N	1946
Renault 21 Petrol (86 - 94) C to M	1397
Renault 25 Petrol & Diesel (84 - 92) B to K	1228
Renault Clio Petrol (91 - May 98) H to R	1853
Renault Clio Diesel (91 - June 96) H to N	3031
Renault Clio Petrol & Diesel (May 98 - May 01) R to Y	3906
Renault Clio Petrol & Diesel (June '01 - '05) Y to 55	4168
Renault Espace Petrol & Diesel (85 - 96) C to N	3197
Renault Laguna Petrol & Diesel (94 - 00) L to W	3252
Renault Laguna Petrol & Diesel (Feb 01 - Feb 05) X to 54	4283
Renault Mégane & Scénic Petrol & Diesel (96 - 99) N to T	3395
Renault Mégane & Scénic Petrol & Diesel (Apr 99 - 02) T to 52	3916
Renault Megane Petrol & Diesel (Oct 02 - 05) 52 to 55	4284
Renault Scenic Petrol & Diesel (Sept 03 - 06) 53 to 06	4297
ROVER 213 & 216 (84 - 89) A to G	1116
Rover 214 & 414 Petrol (89 - 96) G to N	1689
Rover 216 & 416 Petrol (89 - 96) G to N	1830
Rover 211, 214, 216, 218 & 220 Petrol & Diesel (Dec 95 - 99) N to V	3399
Rover 25 & MG ZR Petrol & Diesel (Oct 99 - 04) V to 54	4145
Rover 414, 416 & 420 Petrol & Diesel (May 95 - 98) M to R	3453
Rover 45 / MG ZS Petrol & Diesel (99 - 05) V to 55	4384
Rover 618, 620 & 623 Petrol (93 - 97) K to P	3257
Rover 75 / MG ZT Petrol & Diesel (99 - 06) S to 06	4292
Rover 820, 825 & 827 Petrol (86 - 95) D to N	1380
Rover 3500 (76 - 87) up to E *	0365
Rover Metro, 111 & 114 Petrol (May 90 - 98) G to S	1711
SAAB 95 & 96 (66 - 76) up to R *	0198
Saab 90, 99 & 900 (79 - Oct 93) up to L	0765
Saab 900 (Oct 93 - 98) L to R	3512
Saab 9000 (4-cyl) (85 - 98) C to S	1686
Saab 9-3 Petrol & Diesel (98 - Aug 02) R to 02	4614
Saab 9-5 4-cyl Petrol (97 - 04) R to 54	4156
SEAT Ibiza & Cordoba Petrol & Diesel (Oct 93 - Oct 99) L to V	3571
Seat Ibiza & Malaga Petrol (85 - 92) B to K	1609
SKODA Estelle (77 - 89) up to G	0604
Skoda Fabia Petrol & Diesel (00 - 06) W to 06	4376
Skoda Favorit (89 - 96) F to N	1801
Skoda Felicia Petrol & Diesel (95 - 01) M to X	3505
Skoda Octavia Petrol & Diesel (98 - Apr 04) R to 04	4285
SUBARU 1600 & 1800 (Nov 79 - 90) up to H *	0995
SUNBEAM Alpine, Rapier & H120 (67 - 74) up to N *	0051
SUZUKI SJ Series, Samurai & Vitara (4-cyl) Petrol (82 - 97) up to P	1942
Suzuki Supercarry & Bedford/Vauxhall Rascal (86 - Oct 94) C to M	3015
TALBOT Alpine, Solara, Minx & Rapier (75 - 86) up to D	0337

Title	Book No.
Talbot Horizon Petrol (78 - 86) up to D	0473
Talbot Samba (82 - 86) up to D	0823
TOYOTA Avensis Petrol (98 - Jan 03) R to 52	4264
Toyota Carina E Petrol (May 92 - 97) J to P	3256
Toyota Corolla (80 - 85) up to C	0683
Toyota Corolla (Sept 83 - Sept 87) A to E	1024
Toyota Corolla (Sept 87 - Aug 92) E to K	1683
Toyota Corolla Petrol (Aug 92 - 97) K to P	3259
Toyota Corolla Petrol (July 97 - Feb 02) P to 51	4286
Toyota Hi-Ace & Hi-Lux Petrol (69 - Oct 83) up to A	0304
Toyota Yaris Petrol (99 - 05) T to 05	4265
TRIUMPH GT6 & Vitesse (62 - 74) up to N *	0112
Triumph Herald (59 - 71) up to K *	0010
Triumph Spitfire (62 - 81) up to X	0113
Triumph Stag (70 - 78) up to T *	0441
Triumph TR2, TR3, TR3A, TR4 & TR4A (52 - 67) up to F *	0028
Triumph TR5 & 6 (67 - 75) up to P *	0031
Triumph TR7 (75 - 82) up to Y *	0322
VAUXHALL Astra Petrol (80 - Oct 84) up to B	0635
Vauxhall Astra & Belmont Petrol (Oct 84 - Oct 91) B to J	1136
Vauxhall Astra Petrol (Oct 91 - Feb 98) J to R	1832
Vauxhall/Opel Astra & Zafira Petrol (Feb 98 - Apr 04) R to 04	3758
Vauxhall/Opel Astra & Zafira Diesel (Feb 98 - Apr 04) R to 04	3797
Vauxhall/Opel Astra Petrol (04 - 07) 04 - 07	4732
Vauxhall/Opel Astra Diesel (04 - 07) 04 - 07	4733
Vauxhall/Opel Calibra (90 - 98) G to S	3502
Vauxhall Carlton Petrol (Oct 78 - Oct 86) up to D	0480
Vauxhall Carlton & Senator Petrol (Nov 86 - 94) D to L	1469
Vauxhall Cavalier Petrol (81 - Oct 88) up to F	0812
Vauxhall Cavalier Petrol (Oct 88 - 95) F to N	1570
Vauxhall Chevette (75 - 84) up to B	0285
Vauxhall/Opel Corsa Diesel (Mar 93 - Oct 00) K to X	4087
Vauxhall Corsa Petrol (Mar 93 - 97) K to R	1985
Vauxhall/Opel Corsa Petrol (Apr 97 - Oct 00) P to X	3921
Vauxhall/Opel Corsa Petrol & Diesel (Oct 00 - Sept 03) X to 53	4079
Vauxhall/Opel Corsa Petrol & Diesel (Oct 03 - Aug 06) 53 to 06	4617
Vauxhall/Opel Frontera Petrol & Diesel (91 - Sept 98) J to S	3454
Vauxhall Nova Petrol (83 - 93) up to K	0909
Vauxhall/Opel Omega Petrol (94 - 99) L to T	3510
Vauxhall/Opel Vectra Petrol & Diesel (95 - Feb 99) N to S	3396
Vauxhall/Opel Vectra Petrol & Diesel (Mar 99 - May 02) T to 02	3930
Vauxhall/Opel Vectra Petrol & Diesel (June 02 - Sept 05) 02 to 55	4618
Vauxhall/Opel 1.5, 1.6 & 1.7 litre Diesel Engine (82 - 96) up to N	1222
VW 411 & 412 (68 - 75) up to P *	0091
VW Beetle 1200 (54 - 77) up to S	0036
VW Beetle 1300 & 1500 (65 - 75) up to P	0039
VW 1302 & 1302S (70 - 72) up to L *	0110
VW Beetle 1303, 1303S & GT (72 - 75) up to P	0159
VW Beetle Petrol & Diesel (Apr 99 - 01) T to 51	3798
VW Golf & Jetta Mk 1 Petrol 1.1 & 1.3 (74 - 84) up to A	0716
VW Golf, Jetta & Scirocco Mk 1 Petrol 1.5, 1.6 & 1.8 (74 - 84) up to A	0726

Title	Book No.
VW Golf & Jetta Mk 1 Diesel (78 - 84) up to A	0451
VW Golf & Jetta Mk 2 Petrol (Mar 84 - Feb 92) A to J	1081
VW Golf & Vento Petrol & Diesel (Feb 92 - Mar 98) J to R	3097
VW Golf & Bora Petrol & Diesel (April 98 - 00) R to X	3727
VW Golf & Bora 4-cyl Petrol & Diesel (01 - 03) X to 53	4169
VW Golf & Jetta Petrol & Diesel (04 - 07) 53 to 07	4610
VW LT Petrol Vans & Light Trucks (76 - 87) up to E	0637
VW Passat & Santana Petrol (Sept 81 - May 88) up to E	0814
VW Passat 4-cyl Petrol & Diesel (May 88 - 96) E to P	3498
VW Passat 4-cyl Petrol & Diesel (Dec 96 - Nov 00) P to X	3917
VW Passat Petrol & Diesel (Dec 00 - May 05) X to 05	4279
VW Polo & Derby (76 - Jan 82) up to X	0335
VW Polo (82 - Oct 90) up to H	0813
VW Polo Petrol (Nov 90 - Aug 94) H to L	3245
VW Polo Hatchback Petrol & Diesel (94 - 99) M to S	3500
VW Polo Hatchback Petrol (00 - Jan 02) V to 51	4150
VW Polo Petrol & Diesel (02 - May 05) 51 to 05	4608
VW Scirocco (82 - 90) up to H *	1224
VW Transporter 1600 (68 - 79) up to V	0082
VW Transporter 1700, 1800 & 2000 (72 - 79) up to V *	0226
VW Transporter (air-cooled) Petrol (79 - 82) up to Y *	0638
VW Transporter (water-cooled) Petrol (82 - 90) up to H	3452
VW Type 3 (63 - 73) up to M *	0084
VOLVO 120 & 130 Series (& P1800) (61 - 73) up to M *	0203
Volvo 142, 144 & 145 (66 - 74) up to N *	0129
Volvo 240 Series Petrol (74 - 93) up to K	0270
Volvo 262, 264 & 260/265 (75 - 85) up to C *	0400
Volvo 340, 343, 345 & 360 (76 - 91) up to J	0715
Volvo 440, 460 & 480 Petrol (87 - 97) D to P	1691
Volvo 740 & 760 Petrol (82 - 91) up to J	1258
Volvo 850 Petrol (92 - 96) J to P	3260
Volvo 940 petrol (90 - 98) H to R	3249
Volvo S40 & V40 Petrol (96 - Mar 04) N to 04	3569
Volvo S40 & V50 Petrol & Diesel (Mar 04 - Jun 07) 04 to 07	4731
Volvo S70, V70 & C70 Petrol (96 - 99) P to V	3573
Volvo V70 / S80 Petrol & Diesel (98 - 05) S to 55	4263

AUTOMOTIVE TECHBOOKS

Title	Book No.
Automotive Electrical and Electronic Systems Manual	3049
Automotive Gearbox Overhaul Manual	3473
Automotive Service Summaries Manual	3475
Automotive Timing Belts Manual – Austin/Rover	3549
Automotive Timing Belts Manual – Ford	3474
Automotive Timing Belts Manual – Peugeot/Citroën	3568
Automotive Timing Belts Manual – Vauxhall/Opel	3577

DIY MANUAL SERIES

Title	Book No.
The Haynes Air Conditioning Manual	4192
The Haynes Car Electrical Systems Manual	4251
The Haynes Manual on Bodywork	4198
The Haynes Manual on Brakes	4178
The Haynes Manual on Carburettors	4177
The Haynes Manual on Diesel Engines	4174
The Haynes Manual on Engine Management	4199
The Haynes Manual on Fault Codes	4175
The Haynes Manual on Practical Electrical Systems	4267
The Haynes Manual on Small Engines	4250
The Haynes Manual on Welding	4176

* Classic reprint

Preserving Our Motoring Heritage

< The Model J Duesenberg
Derham Tourster.
Only eight of these
magnificent cars were
ever built – this is the
only example to be found
outside the United States
of America

Almost every car you've ever loved, loathed or desired is gathered under one roof at the Haynes Motor Museum. Over 300 immaculately presented cars and motorbikes represent every aspect of our motoring heritage, from elegant reminders of bygone days, such as the superb Model J Duesenberg to curiosities like the bug-eyed BMW Isetta. There are also many old friends and flames. Perhaps you remember the 1959 Ford Popular that you did your courting in? The magnificent 'Red Collection' is a spectacle of classic sports cars including AC, Alfa Romeo, Austin Healey, Ferrari, Lamborghini, Maserati, MG, Riley, Porsche and Triumph.

A Perfect Day Out

Each and every vehicle at the Haynes Motor Museum has played its part in the history and culture of Motoring. Today, they make a wonderful spectacle and a great day out for all the family. Bring the kids, bring Mum and Dad, but above all bring your camera to capture those golden memories for ever. You will also find an impressive array of motoring memorabilia, a comfortable 70 seat video cinema and one of the most extensive transport book shops in Britain. The Pit Stop Cafe serves everything from a cup of tea to wholesome, home-made meals or, if you prefer, you can enjoy the large picnic area nestled in the beautiful rural surroundings of Somerset.

John Haynes O.B.E.,
Founder and
Chairman of the
museum at the wheel
of a Haynes Light 12. >

< Graham Hill's Lola
Cosworth Formula 1
car next to a 1934
Riley Sports.

The Museum is situated on the A359 Yeovil to Frome road at Sparkford, just off the A303 in Somerset. It is about 40 miles south of Bristol, and 25 minutes drive from the M5 intersection at Taunton.
Open 9.30am - 5.30pm (10.00am - 4.00pm Winter) 7 days a week, *except Christmas Day, Boxing Day and New Years Day*
Special rates available for schools, coach parties and outings Charitable Trust No. 292048